Using Quicken® 5

Stephen Nelson

Using Quicken® 5

Library of Congress Catalog No.: 91-67195

ISBN 0-88022-888-1

94 93 92 4 3 2

Interpretation of the printing code: the rightmost double-digit number is the year of the book's printing; the rightmost single-digit number, the number of the book's printing. For example, a printing code of 91-1 shows that the first printing of the book occurred in 1991.

Screens reproduced in this book were created by using Collage Plus from Inner Media, Inc., Hollis, NH.

Publisher: Lloyd J. Short

Associate Publisher: Karen A. Bluestein

Acquisitions Manager: Rick Ranucci

Product Development Manager: Thomas H. Bennett

Managing Editor: Paul Boger

Book Designer: Scott Cook

Production Team: Jeff Baker, Scott Boucher, Brad Chinn, Brook Farling, Sandy Grieshop, Audra Hershman, Betty Kish, Phil Kitchel, Bob LaRoche, Laurie Lee, Anne Owen, Juli Pavey, Howard Peirce, Joe Ramon, Tad Ringo, Linda Seifert, John Sleeva, Mary Beth Wakefield

Product Director
Shelley O'Hara

Production Editor
H. Leigh Davis

Editors
Jo Anna Arnott
Fran Blauw
Donald R. Eamon

Technical Editor
Cory D. Garnaas

Composed in Garamond and MCP Digital
by Que Corporation

About the Author

Stephen Nelson

Stephen Nelson, a certified public accountant, provides financial consulting and computer-based financial modeling services to a variety of firms and investors—principally in the areas of real estate and manufacturing.

Nelson's experience includes a stint as the treasurer and controller of Caddex Corpration, a venture capital-funded start-up software development company and a pioneer in the electronic publishing field. Prior to that, he was a senior consultant with Arthur Andersen & Co., where he provided financial and systems consulting services to clients in a variety of industries.

Nelson has written more than 70 articles on personal finance for national publications, including *Lotus Magazine*, *Macworld*, *PC Magazine*, *Home Office Computing*, and *INC Magazine*. He is the author of Que's *Using DacEasy*, 2nd Edition; *Using Harvard Project Manager*; *Using TimeLine*; *Using Prodigy*; *Using Pacioli 2000*; and *Using Quicken 3 for the Mac*.

Nelson holds a bachelor of science degree in accounting from Central Washington University and a master of business administration degree with a finance emphasis from the University of Washington.

Trademark Acknowledgments

Que Corporation has made every effort to supply trademark information about company names, products, and services mentioned in this book. Trademarks indicated below were derived from various sources. Que Corporation cannot attest to the accuracy of this information.

DacEasy is a registered trademark of DacEasy, Inc., an Insilco company.

dBASE is a registered trademark of Ashton-Tate Corporation.

Hewlett-Packard is a registered trademark and LaserJet is a trademark of Hewlett-Packard Co.

IBM is a registered trademark of International Business Machines Corporation.

Lotus, 1-2-3, and Magellan are registered trademarks of Lotus Development Corporation.

Mace Utilities is a registered trademark of Paul Mace Software, Inc.

MS-DOS is a registered trademark of Microsoft Corporation.

The Norton Utilities is a registered trademark of Peter Norton Computing, Inc.

PC Tools Deluxe is a registered trademark of Central Point Software, Inc.

Peachtree is a registered trademark of Peachtree Software, Inc.

Quicken is a registered trademark and Billminder is a trademark of Intuit.

TurboTax is a registered trademark of ChipSoft, Inc.

Trademarks of other products mentioned in this book are held by the companies producing them.

ACKNOWLEDGMENTS

I would like to thank Mari Latterell, product manager at Intuit, for her helpful comments and suggestions.

Contents at a Glance

III Supercharging Quicken

IV Putting Quicken To Work

V Protecting Yourself from Embezzlement, Forgery, and Other Disasters

Introduction

In college, one of my better accounting professors spent most of his lecture one fall day describing how John D. Rockefeller Sr. made his fortune. According to the professor, Rockefeller made his fortune by being a good accountant. The professor's point wasn't that Rockefeller's entry into the oil business didn't amount to perfect timing. He didn't minimize Standard Oil's strategy of vertical integration; it owned the oil fields, the refineries, and even the gas stations. He also didn't discount the effectiveness of Rockefeller's aggressive business tactics. All these, the professor admitted, were important—perhaps even essential. What was more important, the professor said, was that Rockefeller knew better than any of his competitors how much it cost to get the oil, refine the oil, and sell the oil. As a result, he always knew whether he was making money or losing money. And he used this information as a foundation for making his business decisions. In the end, of course, Rockefeller became a billionaire.

Your financial goals—business or personal—are probably more modest than Rockefeller's were. Your reasons for wanting to use Quicken, however, probably resemble Rockefeller's reasons for desiring good, relevant accounting: You want to make better personal or business decisions. That's what this book is really about: making better financial decisions by using financial information—financial information that Quicken can help you collect, store, and use.

If you are considering the installation of a personal or small-business accounting package like Quicken, if you have decided to install Quicken and want a little extra help, or if you already have begun using Quicken and want a reference source that goes beyond the information provided in the user's manual, *Using Quicken 5* will help. In this text is a wealth of information about Quicken Version 5.0 and about managing your personal or small-business finances.

After you read this Introduction, you will know what Quicken Version 5.0 is and whether the program suits your needs. This Introduction also identifies the contents of each chapter.

What Is Quicken?

Quicken is a computer-based bookkeeping system you can use to manage your personal or business finances. Used in the simplest way, Quicken maintains your check register for you by deducting payments and adding deposits to your checking account balance. Quicken eliminates the possibility of you overdrawing your account because of an arithmetic error.

The real value of Quicken, however, stems from several other features the program provides. First, Quicken enables you to use your computer and printer to generate checks, which is a real time-saver if you find yourself writing many checks at home every month. Second, Quicken enables you to use the information stored in your check register to report on your income and outgo, track tax deductions, and compare your actual income and expenses to what you originally budgeted. Third, Quicken can be used to perform bookkeeping for most personal and business assets and liabilities, including personal investments, business receivables, personal credit lines and mortgages, and business payables. With these extra features, individuals can track and manage their finances closely, and many small businesses can use Quicken as a full-fledged accounting package. (Quicken enables you to generate personal and business income statements, balance sheets, and cash-flow statements.)

When To Use Quicken

Answering the question "When should I use Quicken?" depends on whether you are using the program for personal or small-business purposes. If you are considering Quicken for personal use, four factors indicate that Quicken represents a good investment of your time and money:

- When check writing and checking-account record keeping take more time than you want to spend. Quicken does most of the work related to keeping your check book: recording transactions, writing checks, reconciling account balances, and maintaining the check register. Because Quicken does the work for you, the program saves you a tremendous amount of time.
- When you need to track your tax deductions carefully. Quicken tracks the amounts you spend on tax-deductible items. At the end of the year, totaling your charitable contribution deductions is as simple as printing a report.
- When you want to budget income and expense amounts and compare what you earn and spend with what you budgeted. Budgets, contrary to their reputation, are not equivalent to financial handcuffs that prevent you from enjoying life. Budgets are tools that enable you to identify your financial priorities. They help you monitor your progress in organizing your financial life so that you meet your financial objectives. Quicken makes budgeting easy.
- When you want to monitor and track personal assets, such as investments, and personal liabilities, such as your mortgages and credit card debt.

If you are considering Quicken for business, three factors indicate that Quicken represents a good investment of your time and money and a reasonable accounting alternative:

- You do not need or want to use a small-business accounting package that requires double-entry bookkeeping. Packages such as DacEasy, Peachtree, and others require that you use double-entry bookkeeping. Although this procedure is a powerful and valuable tool, if you are not familiar with double-entry bookkeeping, you probably can spend your time better in ways other than learning accounting methods. Quicken provides a single-entry, easy-to-use accounting system.
- You do not need a fancy billing and accounts receivable system. Quicken enables you to perform record keeping for accounts receivable. If you have fewer than two dozen transactions a month, Quicken provides a satisfactory solution. If your transaction volume exceeds this amount, however, you may want to consider a full-fledged accounts receivable package that prepares invoices, calculates finance charges, and easily handles high volumes of customer invoices and payments.

- You do not need an automated inventory record-keeping system. Although Quicken enables you to track other assets, such as inventory, the program does not enable you to track the number of units of these other assets—only the dollars. With inventory, however, you not only need to know the dollar value of inventory, you need to know the number of units of inventory. Suppose that you sell snow skis. You need to know the number of pairs of skis you have as well as the dollar value of your ski inventory.

What This Book Contains

Using Quicken 5 is divided into 5 parts and 21 chapters. If you read the book from cover to cover, you may notice a little repetition in some places; repetition is inevitable because the book also serves as a reference.

Part I, "Getting Started Using Quicken," includes three chapters that, as the title implies, help you get started.

Chapter 1, "Preparing To Use Quicken," guides you through the steps you need to take before you start using Quicken, including ordering any preprinted forms you will need, deciding which Quicken options to use, learning to use the system, choosing a starting date, and installing the software. Chapter 1 describes each of these steps in detail.

Chapter 2, "Getting Around in Quicken," gives you a quick introduction to the mechanics of actually working with the program. You learn how to start the program, select menu options, tap Quicken's on-line help feature, and use the built-in calculator. If you already have started using Quicken, you may want to skim this material.

Chapter 3, "Describing Your Accounts," walks you through the steps to set up your second and subsequent bank accounts. The chapter also describes a few basic concepts you need to know from the start if you will be using Quicken for more than just a single bank account. If you plan to use Quicken for personal and business purposes, take a few minutes to read through this chapter.

Part II, "Learning the Basics," gives you all the information you need to use Quicken's basic functions.

Chapter 4, "Using the Register," explains the steps for using Quicken's fundamental feature: its register. The chapter doesn't assume that you know anything about Quicken. Rather, you read a complete explanation of what the register is, what information it contains, and how you use it. If you're a new user of Quicken or think you can use a little help with the basics, start with this chapter after you have completed Part I.

Chapter 5, "Making the Register Easier To Use," describes some of the special menu options, which, although not essential, can make the Quicken register easier to use. When you're comfortable with the information covered in Chapter 4, spend some time in Chapter 5. Your time investment should pay rich dividends.

Chapter 6, "Writing and Printing Checks," describes one of Quicken's core features—the capability to print checks. The chapter includes instructions for completing the Write Checks screen, where you provide the information Quicken needs to print a check, and gives instructions for recording, reviewing, editing, and printing checks. Not everyone wants or needs to use Quicken to print checks, but if you do, Chapter 6 is the place to start after you understand the Quicken register.

Chapter 7, "Making Check Writing Easier," describes how to use the special menu options available on the Write Checks screen to speed up the check-writing process. The chapter includes information on the Edit Find, Quick Entry, and Activities function key options. Although this information in Chapter 7 is not essential to writing checks, it will make writing and printing checks even faster.

Chapter 8, "Reconciling Your Bank Account," discusses one of the important steps you can take to protect your cash and the accuracy and reliability of your financial records. This chapter first reviews the reconciliation process in general terms and then describes the steps for reconciling your accounts in Quicken, correcting and catching errors, and printing and using the reconciliation reports that Quicken creates.

Chapter 9, "Caring for Quicken Files," describes how to take care of the files that Quicken uses to store your financial records. Chapter 9 describes how to back up and restore your Quicken files, how to make copies of the files, and how to purge from the files old information you no longer need.

Part III, "Supercharging Quicken," moves beyond the simple applications covered in Part II and helps you get more from Quicken.

Chapter 10, "Organizing Your Finances Better," discusses one of Quicken's optional and most powerful features—the capability to categorize and classify your spending. The categories make it easy to determine tax deductions, the amounts spent for various items, and the types of money that go into your bank accounts. The classes also enable you to look at specific groups of categories, such as personal expenses or business expenses. Chapter 10 defines Quicken's categories and classes, describes why and when you should use them, shows the predefined categories provided within Quicken, and explains how to use these categories. The chapter also outlines the steps for adding, deleting, and modifying your own categories and classes.

Chapter 11, "Fine-Tuning Quicken," describes the two ways you can customize, or fine-tune, Quicken's operation. One way is to use the commands under the Main Menu option **Set Preferences**. The other way is to start Quicken with parameters. This chapter describes both approaches.

Chapter 12, "Tracking Your Net Worth, Other Assets, and Liabilities," describes some of the special features that Quicken Version 5.0 provides for personal use. You can track cash and other assets, such as real estate, as well as liabilities, such as credit cards and a mortgage. Chapter 12 also describes how to use the loan calculator, which is new to Quicken 5.0.

Chapter 13, "Monitoring Your Investments," describes the new investment register feature that Quicken Version 5.0 provides for investors. If you want to monitor your investments better, read through Chapter 13 to see the tools and options that Quicken 5.0 provides specifically for managing investments.

Chapter 14, "Tapping the Power of Quicken's Reports," shows you how to sort, extract, and summarize the information contained in the Quicken registers by using the Reports menu options. Quicken's reports enable you to gain better control over and insight into your income, expenses, and cash flow.

Chapter 15, "Paying Bills Electronically," describes how you can use Quicken to pay your bills electronically by using the CheckFree service. Electronic payment isn't for everybody, but if you're a Quicken user, you should at least know what's involved and whether it makes sense for you. Chapter 15 gives you this information.

Part IV, "Putting Quicken To Work," moves away from the mechanics of using Quicken's features and talks about how to incorporate Quicken as a financial-management tool.

Chapter 16, "Using Quicken To Budget," discusses one of Quicken's most significant benefits—budgeting and monitoring your success in following a budget. This chapter reviews the steps for budgeting, describes how Quicken helps with budgeting, and provides some tips on how to budget more successfully. If you are not comfortable with the budgeting process, Chapter 16 should give you enough information to get started. If you find budgeting an unpleasant exercise, the chapter also provides some tips on making budgeting a more positive experience.

Chapter 17, "Using Quicken for Home Accounting," discusses how Quicken should be used by individuals for personal financial record keeping. Using any software, and particularly an accounting program, is more than mechanics. This chapter answers questions about where Quicken fits in for home users, how Quicken changes the way you keep your personal financial records, and when Quicken options should be used.

Chapter 18, "Using Quicken in Your Business," covers some of the special techniques and procedures for using Quicken in business accounting. This chapter begins by discussing the overall approach to using Quicken in a business. Next, the following six basic accounting tasks are detailed: invoicing customers, tracking receivables, tracking inventory, accounting for fixed assets, preparing payroll, and job costing.

Chapter 19, "Using Quicken To Prepare for Income Taxes," is a short chapter, but an important one. This chapter tells you how to make sure that the financial records you create with Quicken provide the information you will need to prepare your federal and state income tax returns. The chapter also briefly discusses the general mechanics of passing data between Quicken and an income tax preparation package, such as Turbotax.

Part V, "Protecting Yourself from Embezzlement, Forgery, and Other Disasters," covers material that usually isn't addressed in computer tutorials—which is unfortunate, because this is critical information that you should have.

Chapter 20, "Preventing Forgery and Embezzlement," describes the steps you can take to protect your Quicken system and the money it counts. The first part of the chapter outlines procedures for protecting yourself from check forgery and embezzlement. The second part of the chapter outlines the ways you can minimize intentional and unintentional human errors with Quicken.

Chapter 21, "Preventing System Disasters," also covers some unpleasant topics. The chapter talks about hardware malfunctions, disk failures, computer viruses, and various other software problems. Given the importance of what you're trying to do with Quicken—manage your money better—it seems only reasonable to take a few pages to describe some of the technical problems you may encounter and what you can do to address them.

Using Quicken 5 also provides four appendixes.

Appendix A, "Tips for Specific Business Situations," provides a laundry list of accounting tips for different kinds of business people, including lawyers, consultants, other professionals, restaurant managers and owners, retailers and wholesalers, and even nonprofit organizations. If you're planning to use Quicken for a business, consider skimming through Appendix A.

Appendix B, "Using This Book with Version 4.0," outlines the differences between Version 4.0 of Quicken and the current version, Version 5.0. With this appendix, you should be able to use this book for either version of Quicken.

Appendix C, "Planning for Your Retirement," although not directly related to the operation of Quicken, offers helpful information for everyone. Too often, people fail to plan for retirement until it is too late. Read this appendix to learn how to make the most of your life in retirement.

Appendix D, "Using the QuickPay Payroll Utility," briefly describes the QuickPay payroll utility, how the utility works, and when it is an appropriate business solution. If you're preparing payroll by using Quicken, review this Appendix to learn whether you should acquire the QuickPay program.

Part I

Getting Started Using Quicken

Includes

1

Preparing To Use Quicken

Preparing to use Quicken is not difficult. But if you are new to computers or to the language and mechanics of installing software on a computer, receiving a little hand-holding and emotional support is nice. This chapter walks you through the steps for preparing to use Quicken. Don't worry if you don't know enough about computers, Quicken, or computer-based accounting systems. Simply follow the instructions and steps described in this chapter. In a few pages, you will know which supplies you need to begin using Quicken and when you should begin using Quicken. After reading this chapter, you will have installed Quicken.

Ordering Check Forms

You don't need to print your checks with Quicken to benefit from using the product, but Quicken's check-writing feature is a time-saver. The time savings, however, do not come cheaply. You spend between $30 and $50 for 250 computer check forms. In most cases, then, you spend more for check forms over the course of a year than you originally spent for Quicken. Obviously, you want to make sure that you make the right decision about ordering check forms. Two situations merit the expense of the check forms: if you write many, many checks at home or business—say, more than two dozen checks each month; or if you plan to use Quicken for a business and want the professional appearance of computer-printed checks.

You still will use manual checks—checks you write by hand—even if you choose to use Quicken check forms. Home users, for example, will need manual checks for trips to the store. And business owners will need manual checks for unexpected deliveries that require immediate cash payments.

If you decide to use Quicken to print checks, you must order check forms for every bank account for which you want to print checks by using your computer. The cheapest and easiest source of check forms is Intuit, the manufacturer of Quicken.

Complete and mail the order form included in the Quicken package; Intuit prints check forms with your name and address at the top of the form and the bank and account information at the bottom of the form. Do not worry about the bank accepting your new checks.

When deciding where to start numbering your computer check forms, consider two things: First, you will want to start the computer-printed check form numbers far enough away from your manual check numbers so that they do not overlap or duplicate and cause confusion in your record keeping and reconciliations; second, you may want to start numbering your computer-printed check forms with a number that shows you at a glance whether you wrote a check by using Quicken or manually.

When you select check forms, you make a series of choices related to color, style, or lettering, and decide whether the check form is multipart or has voucher stubs. Table 1.1. summarizes your options.

Table 1.1
Summary of Quicken Check Form Options

Name	*Colors*	*Form Size (inches)*	*Number of Parts*	*Comments*
Prestige Antique	Tan	3.5 x 8.5	1	Antique refers to parchment background; printed three to a sheet.

Name	*Colors*	*Form Size (inches)*	*Number of Parts*	*Comments*
Prestige Standard	Gray	3.5 x 8.5	1 or 2	You can choose blue, green, or maroon accent strip; printed three to a sheet.
Prestige Payroll/ Voucher	Gray	7.0 x 8.5	1 or 2	You can choose blue, green, or maroon accent strip; larger form size due to voucher stub.
Standard	Blue or Green	3.5 x 8.5	1, 2, or 3	Printed three to a sheet.
Voucher/ Payroll	Blue or Gray	7.0 x 8.5	1, 2, or 3	Larger form size due to voucher stub.
Laser	Blue or Green	3.5 x 8.5	1	8.5 x 10.5 sheets—each with 3 check forms—fit into printer paper tray.
Laser Voucher/ Payroll	Blue or Green	3.5 x 8.5	1 or 2	8.5 x 11 sheets—each with 1 check form—fit into printer paper tray.
Wallet-size Computer	Blue or Green	2 5/6 x 6	1 or 2	Has a 2 1/2-inch check stub so that overall form width is 8 1/2-inches.

You are on your own when you select the color, size, and the style of lettering you want. This discussion, however, provides a couple of hints about the number of parts your check form should have and whether or not your check form should have a voucher stub or remittance advice.

The number of parts in a check form refers to the number of printed copies. A one-part form means that only the actual check form that you sign is printed. A two-part form means that a copy of the check is printed at the same time as the original. With a three-part form, you get two copies in addition to the original.

Multipart forms probably are not necessary for most home uses. In a business, however, the second and third parts can be attached to paid invoices as a fast and convenient way of keeping track of which checks paid which invoices. An extra copy of the check form may be valuable to keep in your check register until the canceled check comes back from the bank. You then have all your checks in one place. The third copy also can be placed in a numerical sequence file to help you identify the payee more quickly than if you had only the check number.

One precaution to consider if you use multipart forms is that the forms may wear out your impact printer's head (the points that hit the printer ribbon and cause characters to be printed). Check your printer's multipart form rating by referring to your printer manual. Verify that your printer is rated for at least the number of parts you want to print.

The *voucher stub*, also called the *remittance advice*, is the blank piece of paper about the same size as the check form and is attached to the check form. Voucher stubs provide extra space for you to describe or document the reason for the check. You also can use this area to show any calculations involved in arriving at the total check amount. You may, for example, use the voucher stub space to describe how an employee's payroll amount was calculated or to define the invoices for which that check was issued. As with multipart forms, voucher stubs probably make more sense for business use rather than home use.

If you are not sure which check forms to choose, try Quicken's starter kit. The starter kit costs about $35 at this writing, includes 250 checks, and gives you a chance to experiment with preprinted check forms.

Choosing a Conversion Date

Choosing the conversion date is another critical decision you must make before you can enjoy the many advantages of an automated accounting system. The conversion date is the day on which you plan to stop using your old manual system and begin using your new Quicken system. The less you expect from Quicken, the less important the conversion date is.

If you intend to use Quicken to organize your income tax deductions, calculate business profits, or to plan budgets, consider the issue of a clean accounting cutoff point for the date you begin record keeping with Quicken. From the conversion date forward, Quicken provides your accounting information. Before the conversion date, your old accounting system must provide your accounting information. Pick a natural cutoff date that makes switching from one system to another easy. The best time to begin using any accounting package is usually at the beginning of the year. All the income and expense transactions for the new year are recorded in the same place. Picking a good cutoff date may seem trivial, but having your tax deductions for one year recorded and summarized in one place is handy.

If you cannot start using Quicken at the beginning of the year, the next best time is at the beginning of the month. If you start at the beginning of a month, you must combine your old accounting or record-keeping information with Quicken's information to get totals for the year. When calculating tax deductions, for example, you need to add the amounts Quicken shows to whatever your old system shows. Your old system may not be anything fancy—perhaps a shoe box full of receipts.

You should watch for a few things when choosing an accounting cutoff date. You may put the same income or expense transaction in both systems and, therefore, count the transaction twice when you add the two systems together to get the annual totals. You may neglect to record a transaction because you think that you recorded the transaction in the other system. In either case, your records are wrong. To begin using Quicken at the beginning of the month, spend some time summarizing your accounting information from the old system. Make sure that you do not include the same transaction (income received or an expense paid) twice. This repetition can occur if you pay the expense once using the old system and then again using Quicken.

For the same reasons, the worst time to begin using Quicken is in the middle of a month. With no natural cutoff point, you are likely to count some transactions on both systems and forget to record others in either system.

If you don't use Quicken to summarize income and expense transactions or monitor how well you are sticking to a budget, and all you really want is a tool to maintain your checkbook and produce checks, the conversion date isn't as important.

Installing the Software

To use Quicken, your computer must meet the following minimum hardware requirements:

- IBM personal computer or compatible
- 384K of memory for Version 5 (448K for DOS 3.0 and later); 320K of memory for Version 4 (Use CHKDSK, the DOS command, to determine the amount of memory available on your computer.)
- Two floppy disk drives, one of which is a high-density 1.2 or 1.44-megabyte drive; or one floppy disk drive and a hard disk
- MS-DOS or PC DOS Version 2.0 or higher (Use VER, the DOS command, to determine the DOS version installed on your computer.)
- Any printer (except one that uses thermal paper)
- An 80-column color or monochrome monitor

The steps for installing the Quicken system vary depending on whether your computer uses only floppy disks or has a floppy and a hard disk drive. Refer to the appropriate section that follows to install Quicken on your system.

Installing on a Hard Disk System

If you haven't been using Version 4 of Quicken, you should know a few things about the Quicken hard disk installation program, INSTALL, before you use the program. INSTALL creates a directory named QUICKEN5 on your hard disk, in which the program files are stored. Your data files also are stored in the QUICKEN5 directory, unless you change the system settings (described in Chapter 11). In case you are not familiar with the terms, *program files* refers to the files that contain the actual Quicken software instructions, and *data files* refers to the files that contain your financial information.

INSTALL also creates a batch file named Q.BAT so that all you have to do is press Q at the C> prompt to run QUICKEN. If you already have a Q.BAT file—if you have been using Quicken Version 4, for example—INSTALL renames the old file Q2.BAT.

INSTALL also verifies that the CONFIG.SYS file's BUFFERS statement equals or exceeds 10 and that the FILES statement equals or exceeds 10. INSTALL resets these statements because Quicken runs with several files open and performs many reads from the hard disk. For more information on the CONFIG.SYS file and the BUFFERS and FILES statements, see your DOS manual. If you do not have a CONFIG.SYS file, INSTALL creates one with the appropriate BUFFERS and FILES statements. If the CONFIG.SYS file you currently have does not have these statements, INSTALL adds them. If the statements exist but are set to less than 10, INSTALL increases the statement settings to 10. INSTALL does not cause any problems by changing your computer's CONFIG.SYS file.

To install Quicken on a hard disk system, perform the following steps:

1. Turn on your computer and monitor. Make sure that the correct system date and time are set. (Type *date* or *time* at the C> prompt.) DATE is the DOS command for setting the system date. TIME is the DOS command for setting the system time. Refer to your DOS user's manual if you need help using the DATE or TIME commands.

2. Place the Quicken help disk in drive A. (If you have a 3 1/2-inch disk, the help and program portions of Quicken are on the disk.) Type *a:install* and press Enter.

   The introductory install screen, shown in figure 1.1, appears.

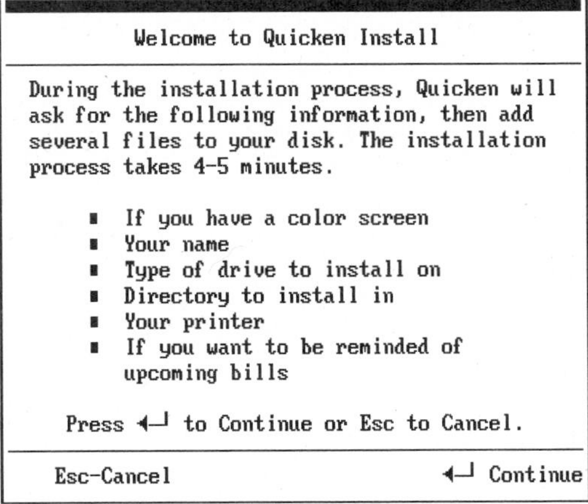

Fig. 1.1. *The Welcome to Quicken Install screen.*

3. Press Enter. Quicken displays the Screen Color screen shown in figure 1.2.

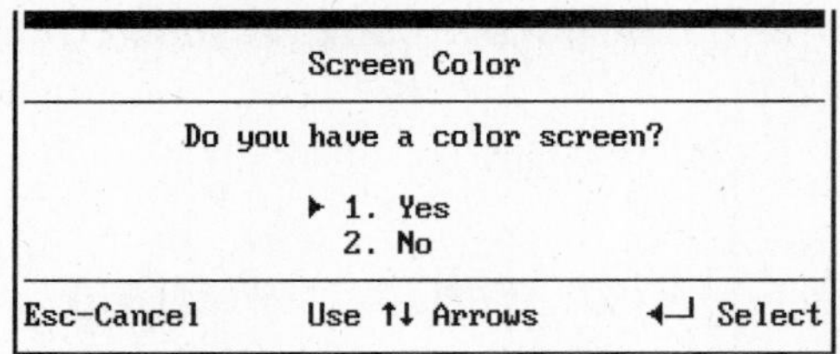

Fig. 1.2. The Screen Color screen.

4. Select the appropriate number to identify your screen type. Quicken next displays the Enter Your Name screen, shown in figure 1.3.

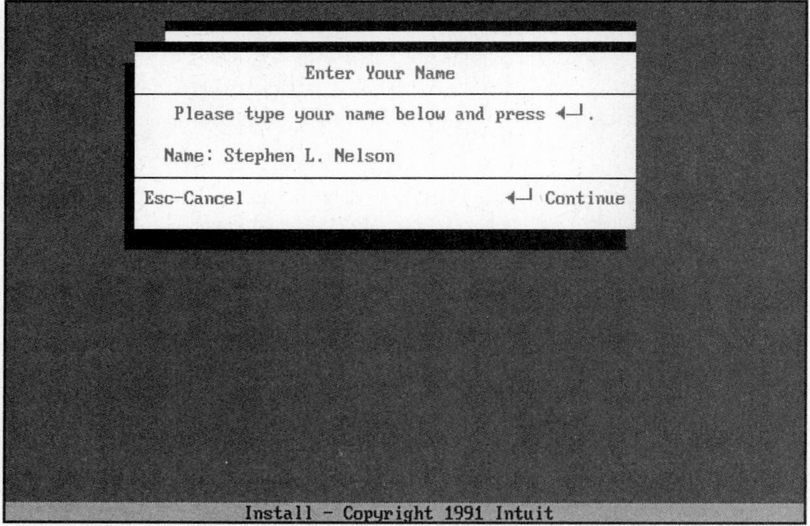

Fig. 1.3. The Enter Your Name screen.

5. Type your name. Then, press Enter.
6. Quicken displays the screen you use to specify on which disk you want to install Quicken, as shown in figure 1.4.

If you have two floppy drives, the screen shown in figure 1.4 includes both floppy drives.

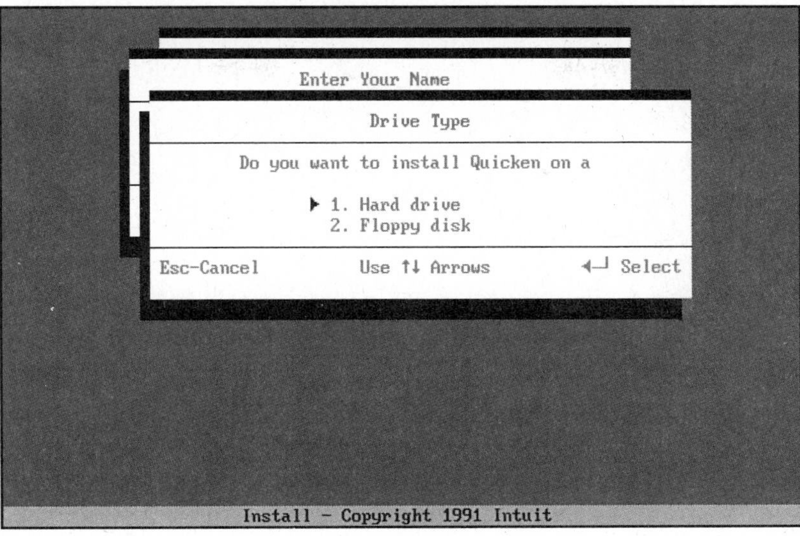

Fig. 1.4. *The Drive Type screen.*

7. Select the appropriate number to designate a hard disk installation, and press Enter to continue. Quicken displays the specify directory location screen shown in figure 1.5. The default directory that Quicken creates and installs itself into is \QUICKEN5.

   If you previously used Version 4 of Quicken and stored the program and data files in \QUICKEN4, installing Quicken Version 5 in the \QUICKEN4 directory will not damage the Quicken Version 4 data files. If you want to use some other directory, you specify it here by typing the default directory. When the correct directory is displayed, press Enter.

8. Quicken displays the Choose a Printer list (see fig. 1.6). Use the Choose a Printer screen to identify your printer. To choose a printer from the list, highlight your choice by using the up- and down-arrow keys. If you cannot find your printer, select another printer that your printer emulates.

   You should be able to find which printers your printer emulates by checking the printer user's manual. If you cannot find your printer on the list and also cannot find a printer your printer emulates, select the **<Other Dot-Matrix>** or **<Other Laser>** options. After you select the printer, press Enter.

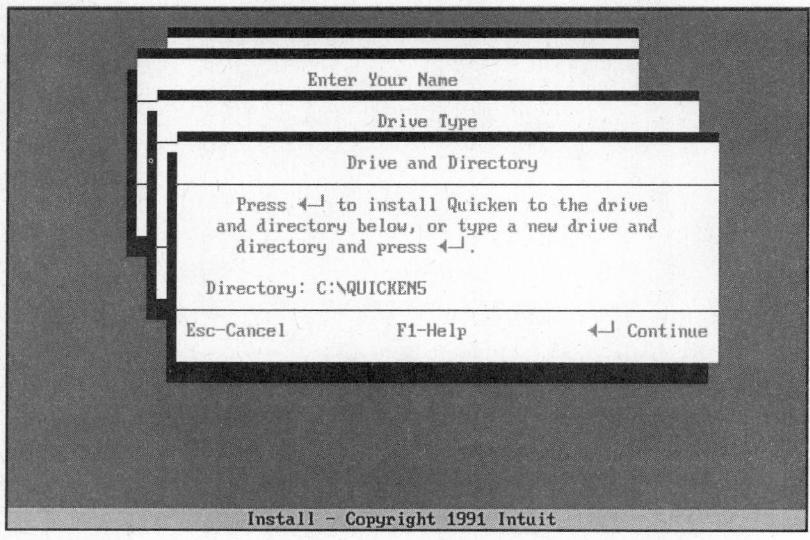

Fig. 1.5. The Drive and Directory screen.

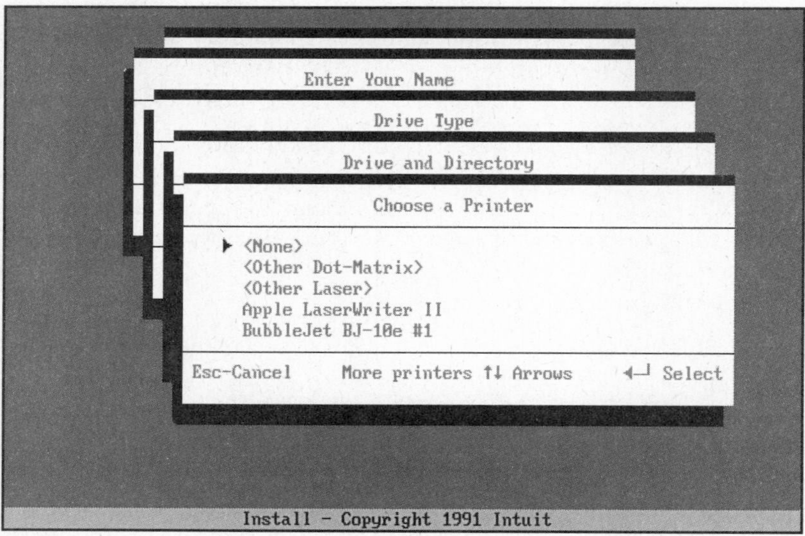

Fig. 1.6. The Choose a Printer screen.

9. Quicken asks whether you want the Billminder option installed, as shown in figure 1.7. Press Enter to answer yes or press 2 and press

Enter to answer no. The Billminder reminds you of bills you should pay. When you turn on your computer or when you enter Quicken, you are reminded that bills must be paid. This handy feature can save you the price of Quicken and this book many times over by eliminating or minimizing late-payment fees.

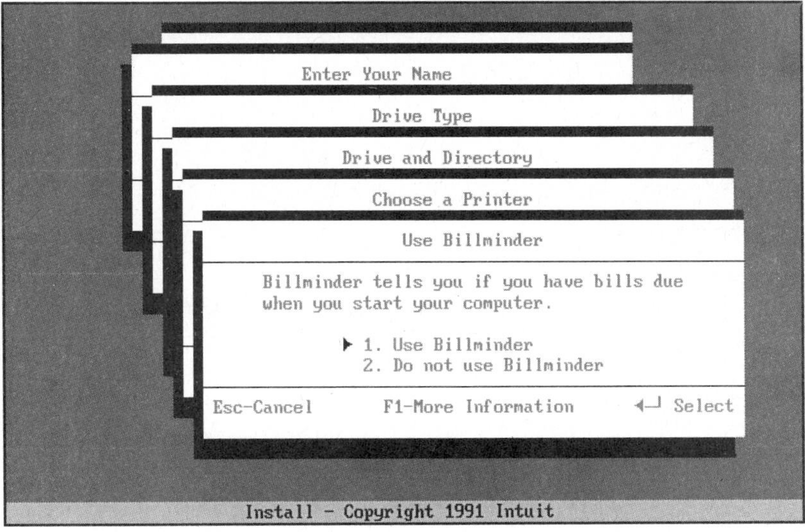

Fig. 1.7. *The Use Billminder screen.*

10. Quicken displays the Confirm Settings screen with all your installation settings listed (see fig. 1.8). To accept the settings, press Enter. If one of the settings is incorrect, press Esc one or more times to return to that setting's screen. Then, make the necessary changes.

Quicken starts the file-copying part of the installation. As Quicken installs the program, you'll see a message on the screen that says, `Installing Quicken`. If necessary, Quicken also prompts you to insert the program disk in drive A.

Quicken tells you when the installation is complete by displaying a screen with the message, `Installation of Quicken is complete`. To return to the C> prompt, press Enter.

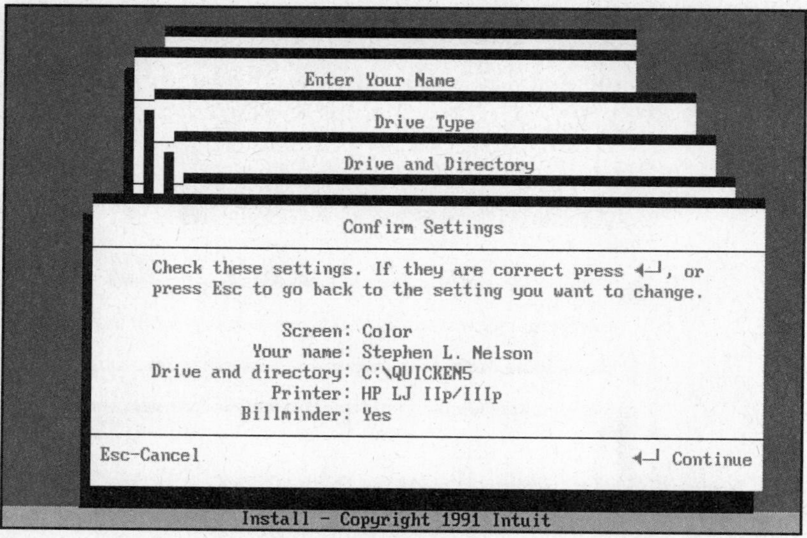

Fig. 1.8. *The Confirm Settings screen.*

Installing on a Dual Floppy Disk System

To install Quicken on a dual floppy disk system, perform the following steps:

1. Place your DOS disk in drive A and turn on your computer and monitor. Make sure that your system has the correct date and time set. (Type *date* at the A> prompt.) Format two blank floppy disks.

   One of the disks should be a high-density floppy disk. (Refer to your DOS manual for information on the FORMAT command if you are not sure of how to format disks.) Label the high-density disk *Quicken program copy*; label the other disk *Quicken data disk*.

2. Insert the *Quicken program copy* disk in your computer's high-density floppy drive. If both drives are high density, you can use either drive.

If you're using a 5 1/4-inch drive, the formatted disk must be empty of all files including the system files that make a disk bootable. If you're not sure how to make an unbootable disk, refer to your DOS user's manual.

3. Place the Quicken 5 1/4-inch *Install Disk 1* or the 3 1/2-inch *Install Disk* in the other drive.
4. Change the drive so that the drive with the Quicken *Install Disk* is active. For example, to make the B drive active, type *b:*. Or, to make the A drive active, type *a:*.
5. Type *install* at the DOS prompt. Quicken displays the Welcome to Quicken Install screen (see fig. 1.1).
6. Repeat steps 3 through 10 of the hard disk installation process.

In step 7, you specify a floppy disk rather than a hard disk as the program's location, and Quicken asks to which floppy drive the program files should be copied. Because you're working with floppy disks, you will see one or two additional messages prompting you for more information concerning floppy drives.

Starting Quicken 5.0 the First Time

To start Quicken, press the letter Q at the DOS prompt. The first time you start Quicken, the program displays the Welcome to Quicken 5.0 screen shown in figure 1.9. As figure 1.9 indicates, Quicken gives you the following three choices as to how you want to start Quicken:

- Read the brief 10-minute overview.
- Take the manual-based 60-minute tour.
- Create your own Quicken data file.

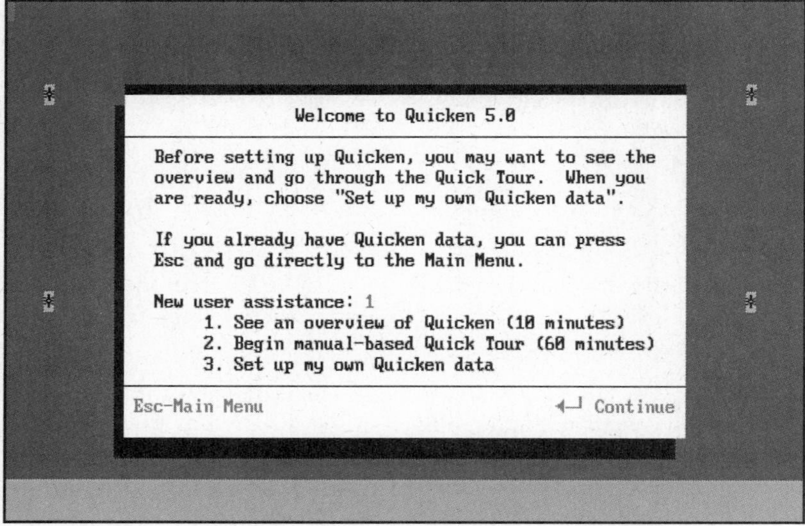

Fig. 1.9. The Welcome to Quicken 5.0 screen.

You select one of these three first-time set-up options by typing the number in front of the option. For example, to select the **See an overview** option, press 1 and press Enter. If you don't want any of the three options, press Esc to display the Quicken Main Menu (see fig. 1.10).

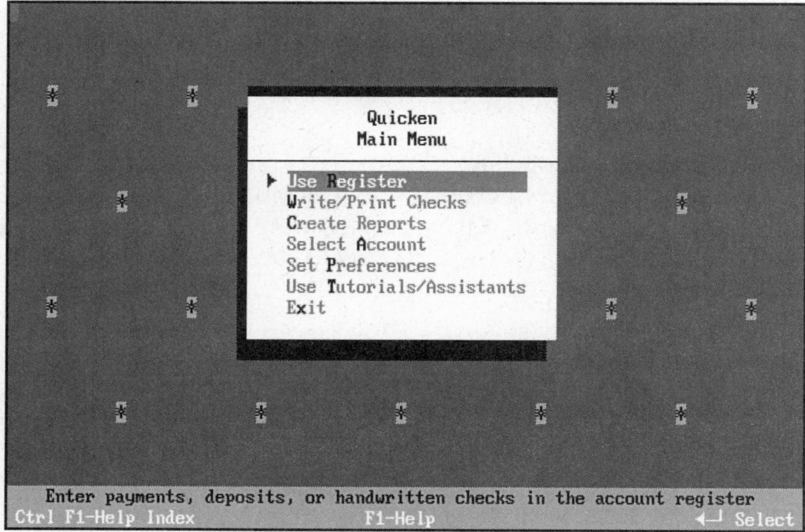

Fig. 1.10. The Quicken Main Menu.

The overview simply explains what Quicken is and shows you how it works. If you're a new user of Quicken, take the time to watch the overview, which is a series of sample Quicken screens with explanations. If you want to stop the overview after it starts, press Esc and Enter. Quicken displays its Main Menu. Quicken also displays its Main Menu after you complete the overview.

The manual-based quick tour, in combination with the Quick Tour chapter in the Quicken user's manual, guides you through several sample Quicken procedures. With this book in hand, you shouldn't need to take the manual-based quick tour. If you do take the tour, however, you ultimately end up at the Quicken Main Menu (see fig. 1.10).

The **Set up my own Quicken data** option explains the way Quicken organizes your financial records, accounts, and categories. Creating your own Quicken data tests you on your newly gained knowledge. This option also walks you through the steps for setting up the file you will use for keeping your financial records with Quicken.

Describing any of these three options here would be like describing how to use an on-line tutorial that describes how to use Quicken. Providing a tutorial on a tutorial is one tutorial too many. You should experiment with these tools, however. New users of Quicken will find the tools particularly helpful.

Setting Up Your Financial Records

You may already have set up your financial records as part of selecting the third option from the Welcome to Quicken screen. If you have, you can skip this entire chapter section. If you haven't, however, you'll need to set up the file, accounts, and categories you'll use to store and organize your financial records.

If you're a new user of Quicken, you can do this one of two ways: by using the File Assistant or by using the **Select/Set Up** command. And if you're a current user of a previous version of Quicken, you can do this by converting your old Quicken data files. The paragraphs that follow describe the steps for performing each of these tasks.

Setup for New Quicken Users

If you're a new user of Quicken, you have two methods at your disposal for creating the data file you use to store your financial records: the File Assistant and the **Select/Set Up File** command.

To set up a new file using the File Assistant, follow these steps:

1. From the Quicken Main Menu (see fig. 1.10), select the **Use Tutorials/Assistants** command by pressing the letter T. Quicken next displays the Tutorials and Assistants menu (see fig. 1.11).

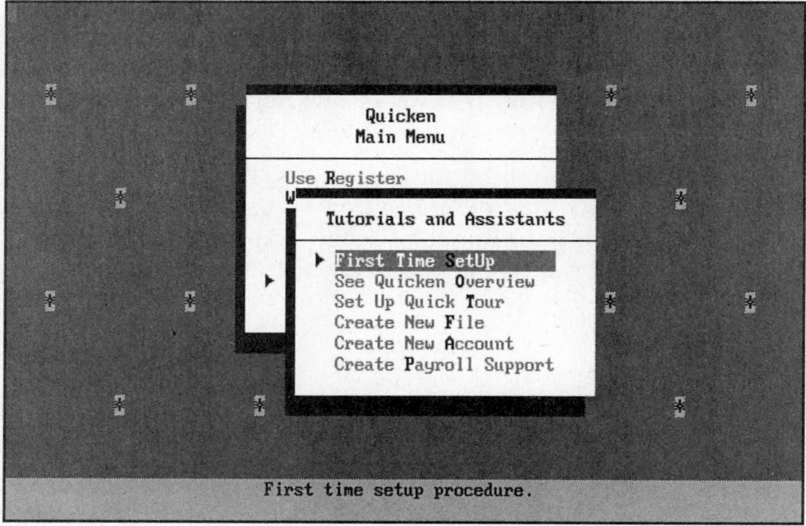

***Fig. 1.11.** The Tutorials and Assistants menu.*

2. Select the **Create New File** command from the Tutorials and Assistants menu by pressing the letter F. Quicken next displays the Create New File Assistant screen (see fig. 1.12).

The Tutorials and Assistant menu also gives you access to the first-time setup options described earlier in the chapter. To display the Welcome to Quicken 5.0 screen (see fig. 1.9), select the **First Time Setup** command by pressing the letter S. To start the 10-minute overview without displaying the Welcome to Quicken 5.0 screen, select the **See Quicken Overview** command by pressing the letter O. To start the manual-based Quick Tour without displaying the Welcome to Quicken 5.0 screen, select the **Set Up Quick Tour** command by pressing the letter T.

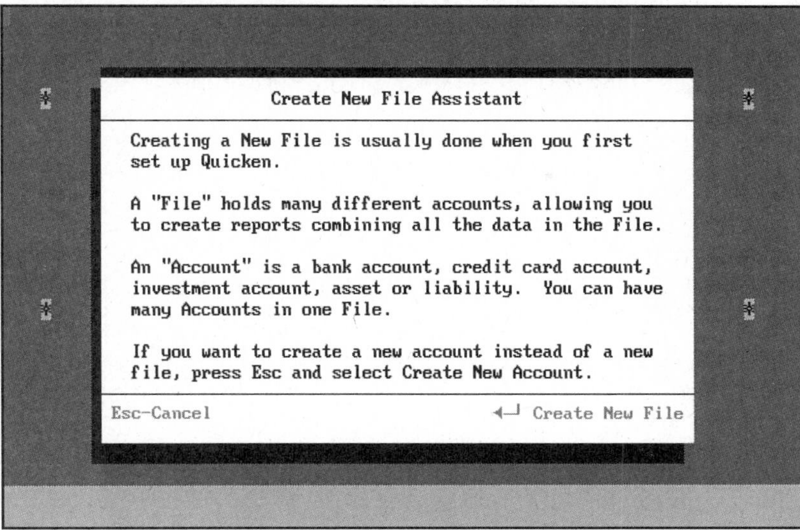

Fig. 1.12. The Create New File Assistant screen.

3. Press Enter to continue past the Create New File Assistant screen. Quicken displays the Set Up a File screen (see figure 1.13).

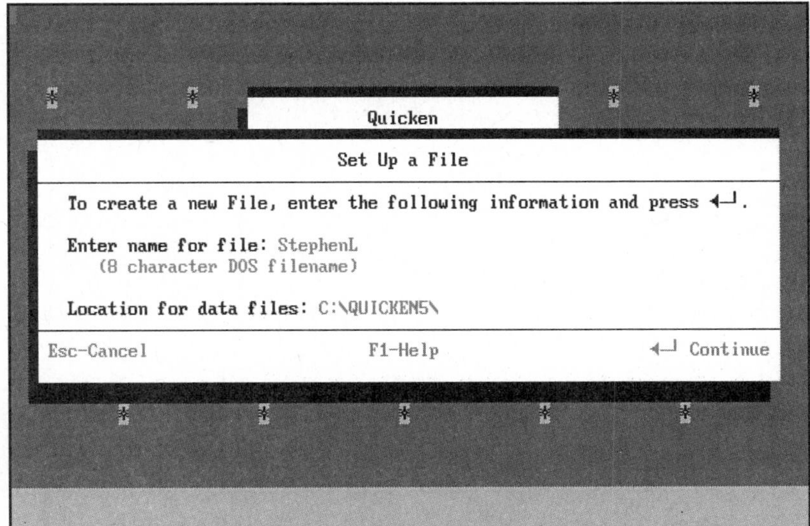

Fig. 1.13. The Set Up a File screen.

4. Quicken creates an eight-character name for the DOS file it will use to store your financial records based on the user name you gave during the installation. For example, as shown in figure 1.13, I entered my name as *Stephen L. Nelson*. So, Quicken created a default file named `StephenL`. You can use some other filename here by typing the characters. Whatever you enter here, however, must be a valid DOS filename. If you are unsure of DOS file-naming conventions, see your DOS users manual.

5. When the file name is correct, press Enter to move the cursor to the `Location for data files` field.

6. By default, Quicken stores the file in the Quicken program directory—probably QUICKEN5. You can specify another directory in which the new file should be located. Do this by typing the complete path name of the desired directory. If you're unsure of how to specify path names, see your DOS users manual.

If you're a new computer user, don't worry about specifying some other file name or directory. The defaults work just fine.

7. When the new file location is correctly specified, press Enter. Quicken displays the Select Standard Categories screen (see fig. 1.14).

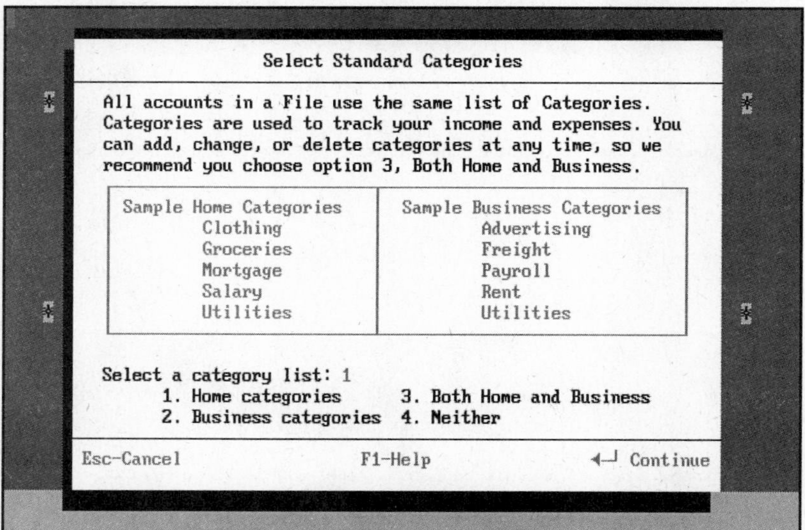

Fig. 1.14. The Select Standard Categories screen.

At this point, you need to decide whether you want to use the standard categories predefined by Quicken or your own categories. If you want to use Quicken's categories, you can direct Quicken to use one or both of the predefined category lists.

1. Press 1 if you want to use Quicken's home categories. Press 2 if you want to use Quicken's business categories. If you want to use both, press 3. If you want to use neither, press 4.

   A category describes and summarizes common business and personal income and expenses, such as salary, insurance, utilities, and so on. (Chapter 10 describes Quicken's categories in more detail.)

2. After you complete the Select Standard Categories screen, press Enter, and the Set Up an Account screen appears (see fig. 1.15). This screen provides two fields that you need to fill in with information: an account name and an account type.

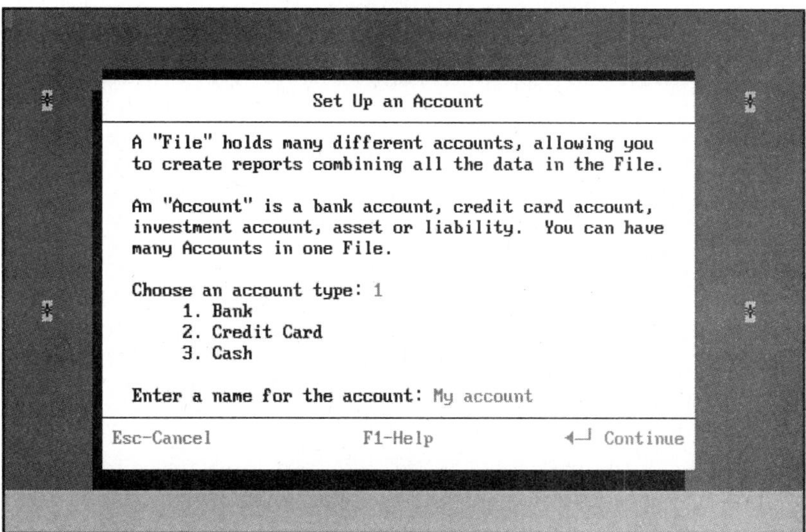

Fig. 1.15. *The Set Up an Account screen.*

3. In the Account Type field, indicate whether the account is an asset or a liability and what kind of asset or liability. If you are setting up a bank account, the account type should be 1. Press Enter to move to the Name field.

4. Enter a description of the account using the Name field. The Name field can be up to 15 characters long and can use any characters

except [,], /, and : . You also can include spaces. Press Enter to move to the `Balance` field.

In describing your bank account, you may want to abbreviate the bank name and then use the last four digits to distinguish between various accounts at the same bank. For example, Standard Bank of Washington, account 9173526471, would become StdWash 6471. Standard Bank of Oregon, account 7386427389, would become StdOre 7389. Standard Bank of Washington, account 9173533721, would become StdWash 3721. This procedure enables you to separate the different accounts for the same banks.

5. Quicken displays the Account Balance and Date screen (see fig. 1.16.)

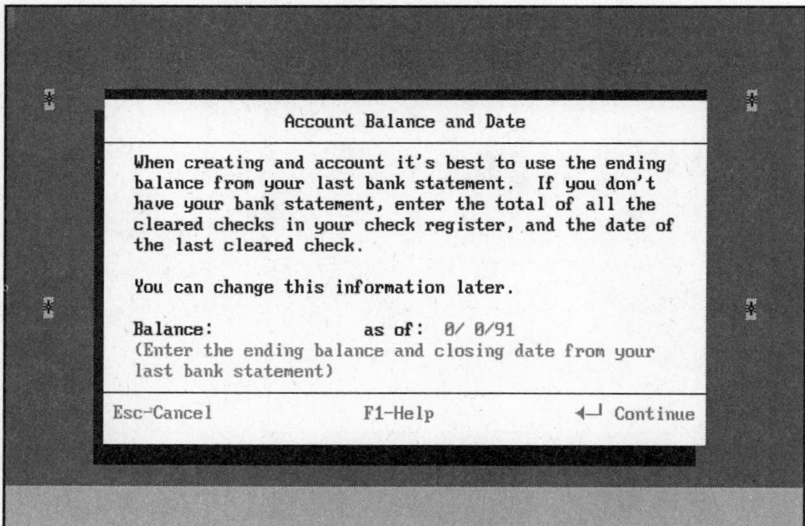

Fig. 1.16. The Account Balance and Date screen.

6. Enter the starting account balance. For a bank account, this amount should be the current account balance according to your records. You must enter a balance, even if it is 0.

7. Enter the date. The `as of` date should be the date on which the balance you entered is correct.

8. When you finish entering information for the Set Up New Account screen, press Enter.

9. Quicken displays the File Assistant screen shown in figure 1.17. The File Assistant screen identifies the filename and location, the standard categories you selected, the account type, the account name, the account balance, and the as of date. If any of the information is incorrect, press the Tab key to move the cursor to the field. Then, replace the incorrect information by typing the correct entry.

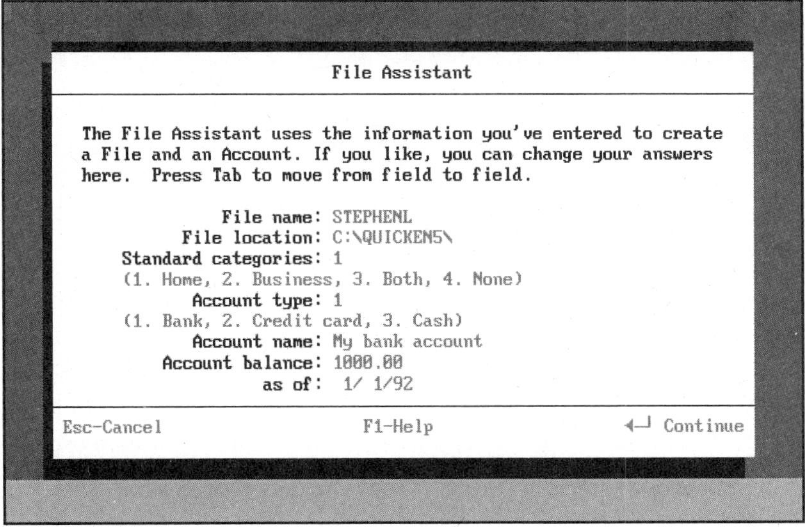

Fig. 1.17. The File Assistant screen.

10. When the information shown on the File Assistant screen is completely correct, press the Enter key or the Tab key as many times as necessary to move the cursor to the last field on the screen. Then, press Enter. Quicken displays the File Assistant Note screen, shown in figure 1.18.

11. At this point, you haven't actually created a file. Rather, you've collected the information necessary for creating a file. To direct the File Assistant to create the file, press Enter. Quicken's File Assistant then executes the Quicken commands necessary to create a file according to the information it's collected. As the File Assistant does this, it explains each step as it goes along. When the File Assistant finishes creating a new file, it returns you to the Quicken Main Menu.

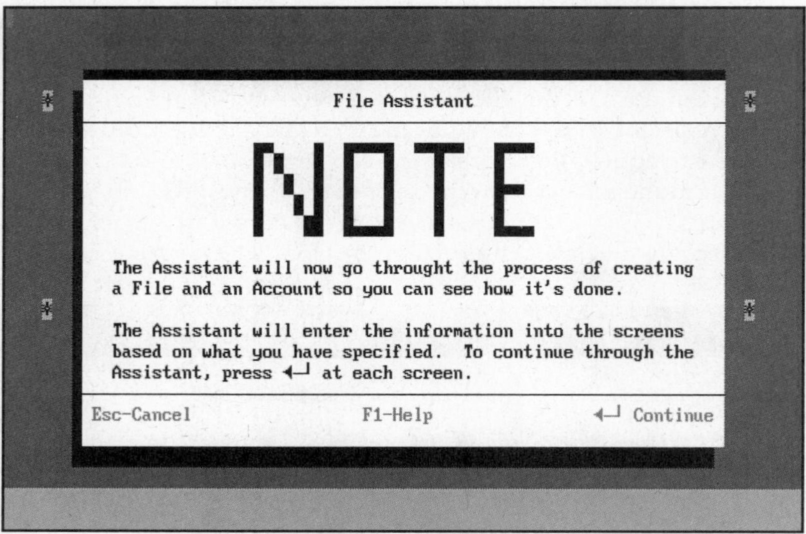

Fig. 1.18. *The File Assistant Note screen.*

After you create a file by using the File Assistant, you may not need as much hand-holding and explanation the next time you set up a file. When that's the case, you can use the **Select/Set Up** command. To set up new file using the **Select/Set Up File** command, follow these steps:

1. From the Quicken Main Menu (see fig. 1.10), select the **Set Preferences** command by pressing the letter P. Quicken next displays the Set Preferences menu (see fig. 1.19).

2. Select the **File Activities** command from the Set Preferences menu by pressing the letter F. Quicken displays the File Activities menu (see fig. 1.20).

3. Select the **Select/Set Up File** command by typing the letter S. Quicken displays the Select/Set Up File screen (see fig. 1.21).

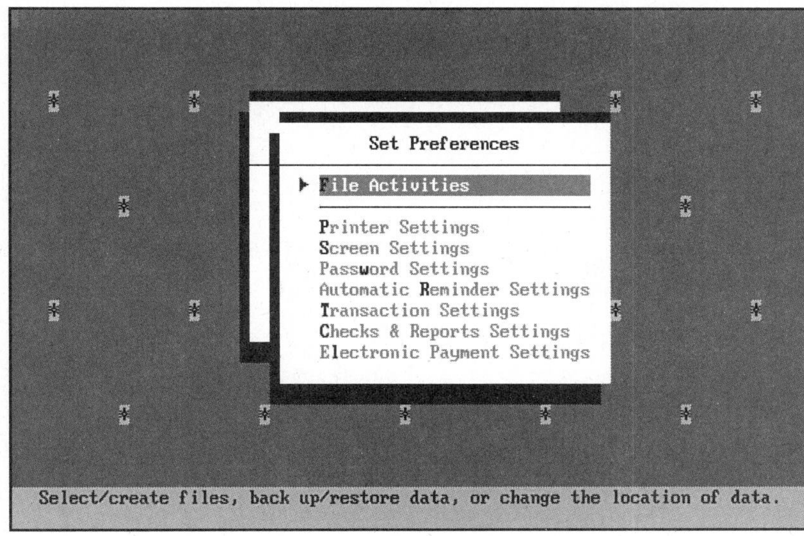

Fig. 1.19. The Set Preferences menu.

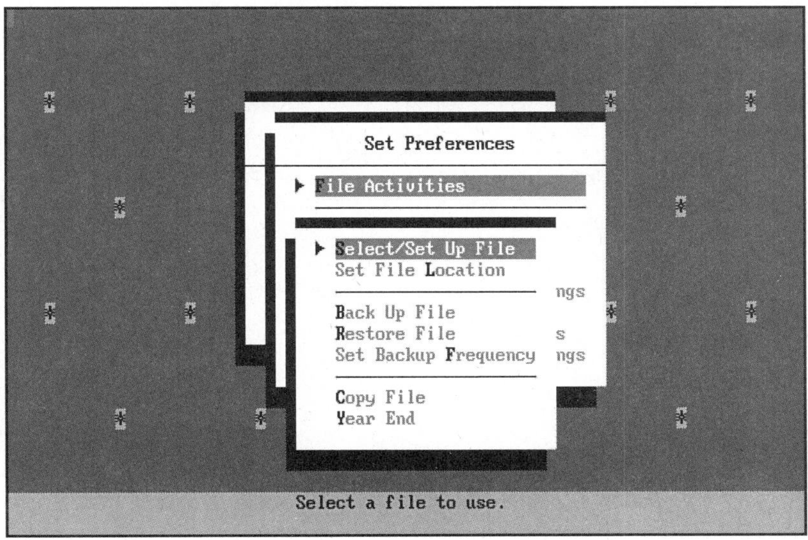

Fig. 1.20. The File Activities menu.

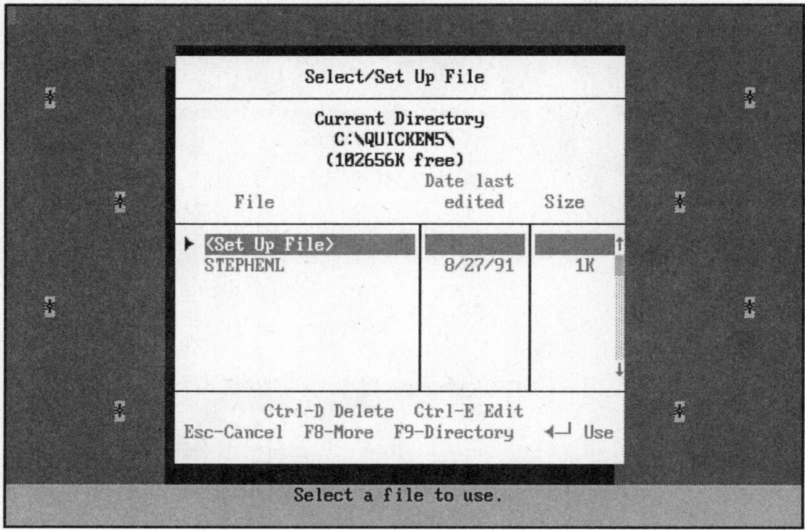

Fig. 1.21. *The Select/Set Up File screen.*

4. Use the up- and down-arrow keys to highlight the `<Set Up File>` item on the screen. Then, press Enter. Quicken displays the Set Up File screen shown in figure 1.22.

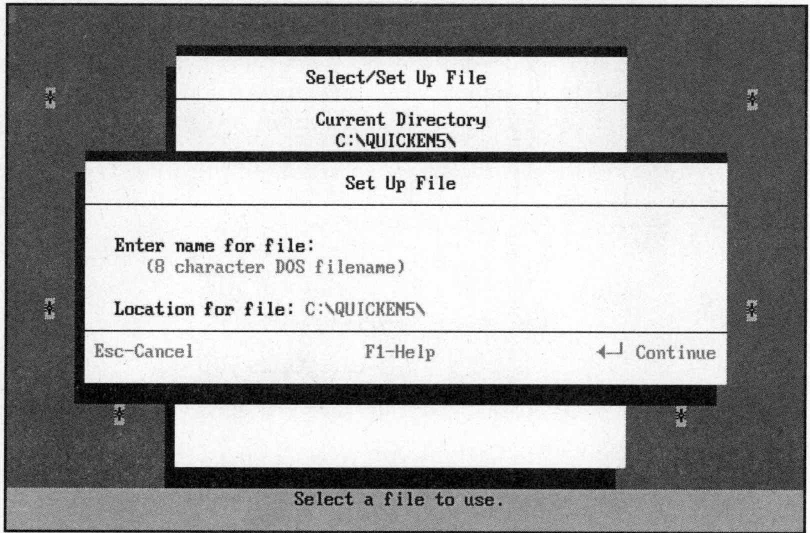

Fig. 1.22. *The Set Up File screen.*

5. Enter the name you want DOS to use for your financial records file. Whatever you enter must be a valid, DOS filename. Refer to your DOS users manual if you have questions about DOS file-naming conventions.

6. When the filename is correct, press Enter or Tab to move the cursor to the `Location for File` field. By default, Quicken stores data files in the Quicken program directory. If you want the file stored in a different directory, enter that directory's pathname.

7. When the file location is correct, press Enter. Quicken displays the Default Categories screen (see figure 1.23).

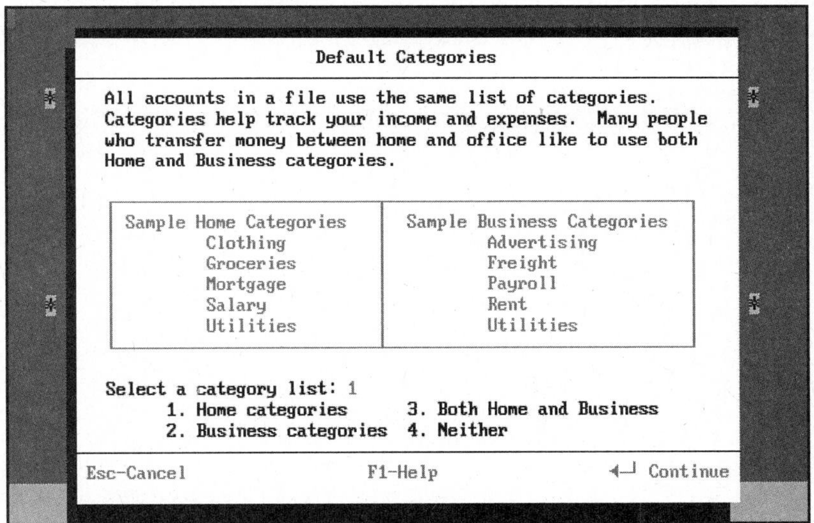

Fig. 1.23. The Default Categories screen.

8. Press 1 if you want to use Quicken's home categories. Press 2 if you want to use Quicken's business categories. If you want to use both, press 3. If you want to use neither, press 4.

9. When you've identified the default categories you want, press Enter. Quicken redisplays the Select/Set Up File screen (see fig. 1.21).

10. Use the arrow keys to highlight the new file. Then, press Enter. Quicken displays the Select Account to Use screen (see fig. 1.24).

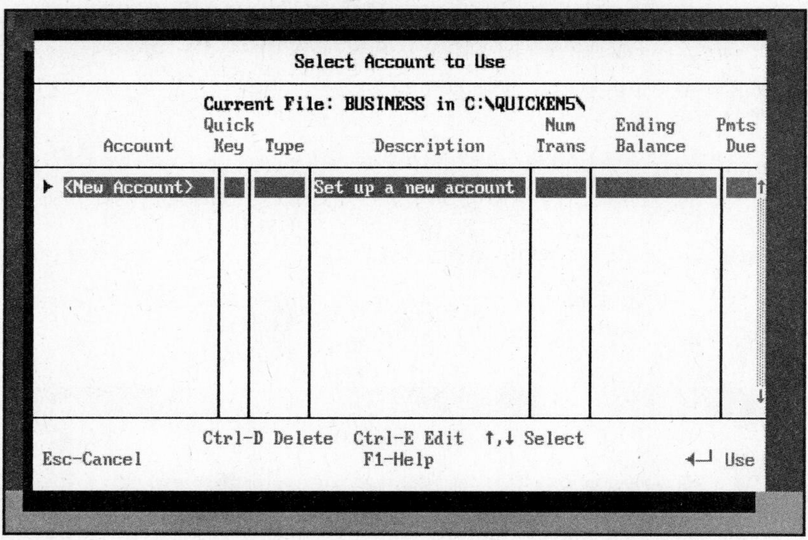

Fig. 1.24. The Select Account to Use screen.

11. Press Enter to select the `<New Account>` item. Quicken displays the Set Up New Account screen (see fig. 1.25).

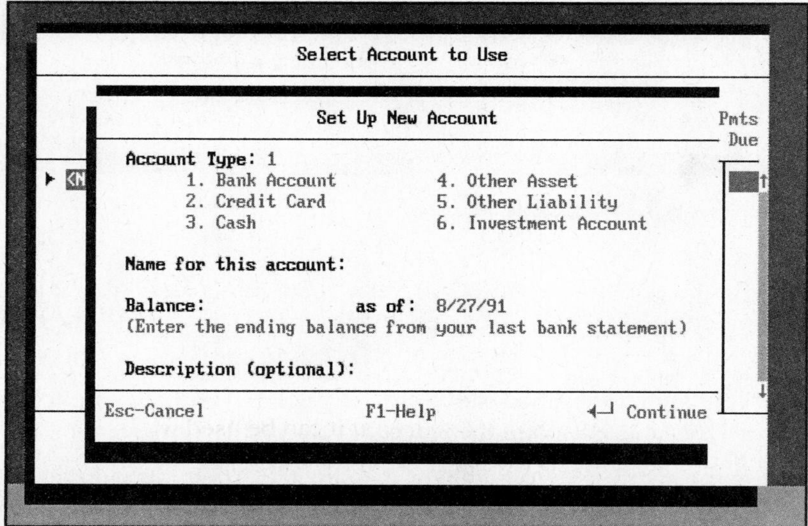

Fig. 1.25. The Set Up New Account screen.

12. In the `Account Type` field, indicate whether the account is an asset or a liability and what kind of asset or liability. If you are setting up a bank account, the account type should be 1. Press Enter to move to the `Name` field.
13. Enter a description of the account in the `Name` field. The `Name` field can be up to 15 characters long and can use any characters except [,], /, and : . You also can include spaces. Press Enter to move to the `Balance` field.
14. Enter the starting account balance. For a bank account, this amount should be the current account balance according to your records. You must enter a balance, even if it is 0.
15. Enter the date. The as of date should be the date on which the balance you entered is correct.
16. (Optional) Fill in the `Description` field to provide an additional 21 characters of account description.
17. When you finish entering information for the Set Up New Account screen, press Enter. Quicken redisplays the Select Account to Use screen.
18. Press Esc to return to the Quicken Main Menu.

Setup for Current Quicken Users

If you've already been using Quicken 3.0 or 4.0, you can update your existing data and use it as the basis for creating your Quicken 5.0 financial records file.

You also can update your Quicken 1.0 or 2.0 data, but to do so you'll need a special file conversion utility from Intuit. Contact Intuit's customer service department and request the Quicken 2.0 Copy and Update Utility.

To update a Quicken 3.0 or 4.0 file so that it can be used with Quicken 5.0, follow these steps:

1. Make a backup copy of the Quicken 3.0 or 4.0 account group file by using whatever backup method you're already familiar with: the Quicken backup command, the DOS Copy or Backup command, or a third-party backup utility.

2. Select the **Set Preferences** command from the Quicken Main Menu by pressing the letter P (see fig. 1.10). Quicken displays the Set Preferences menu (see fig. 1.19).

3. Select the **File Activities** command by pressing the letter F. Quicken displays the File Activities menu (see fig. 1.20).

4. Select the **Select/Set Up File** command by pressing the letter S. Quicken displays the Select/Set Up File screen (see fig. 1.21).

5. If the Quicken 3.0 or 4.0 file isn't shown on the Select/Set Up File screen, press the F9 Function key. Quicken displays the Set File Location box (see fig. 1.26).

   Enter the path for the Quicken 3.0 or 4.0 file. For example, if the Quicken 3.0 file you want to convert to a Quicken 5.0 file is stored in the QUICKEN3 subdirectory of the ACCOUNTS directory on the C hard drive, enter *c:\accounts\quicken3*. Press Enter. Quicken redisplays the Select/Set Up File box and lists the Quicken files in the newly specified directory.

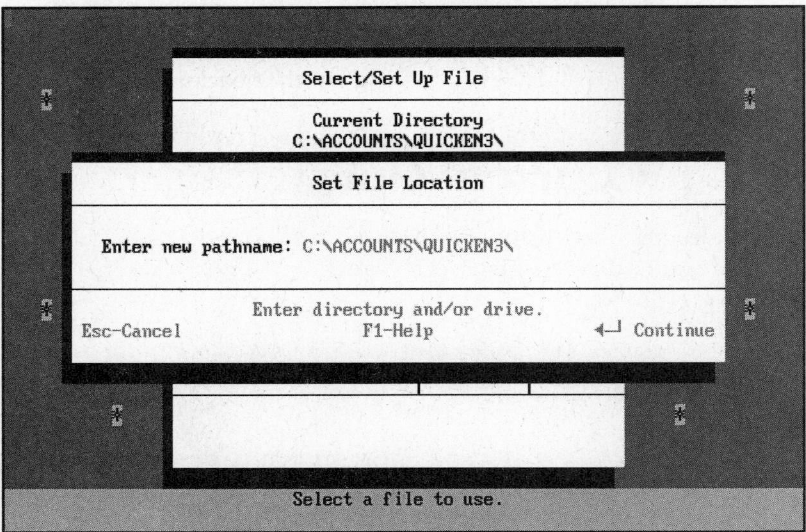

***Fig. 1.26.** The Set File Location box.*

6. Use the up- and down-arrow keys to highlight the Quicken 3.0 or 4.0 file that you want to convert to a Quicken 5.0 file. Then, press Enter. Quicken displays the message box shown in figure 1.27.

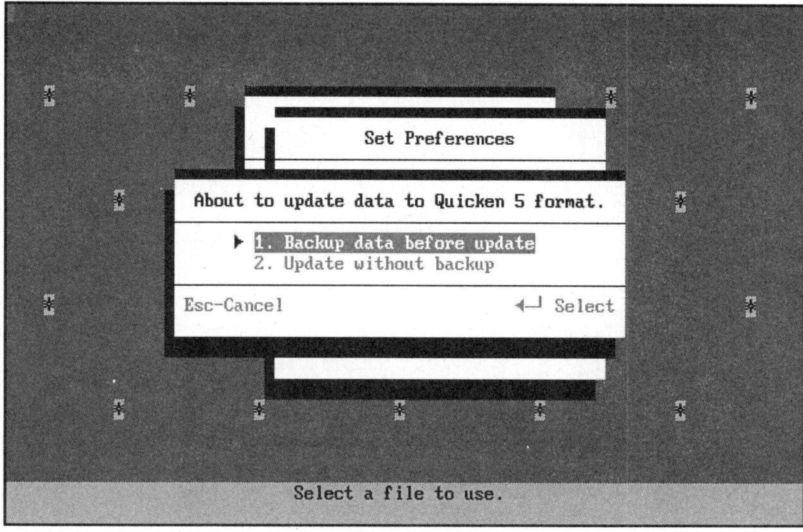

Fig. 1.27. *The* `About to update data` *message box.*

7. Because you already backed up data in step 1, press the number 2 to update the data without making another backup copy.

8. Quicken next displays the Select/Set Up File screen (see fig. 1.21). Use the up- and down-arrow keys to highlight the account you want. Then, press Enter. Quicken displays the Register screen for the selected account.

Configuring Your Printer

You should configure your computer before going any further. If you identified your printer during the installation, the only task you need to complete as part of configuring your printer is describing how your computer and printer are connected.

To describe how your printer and computer connect, follow these three steps:

1. Select the **Set Preferences** command from the Main Menu by pressing the letter P (see fig. 1.10). Quicken displays the Set Preferences menu (see fig. 1.19).

2. Select the **Printer Settings** command from the Set Preferences menu by pressing the letter P. Quicken displays the Printer Settings submenu (see fig. 1.28).

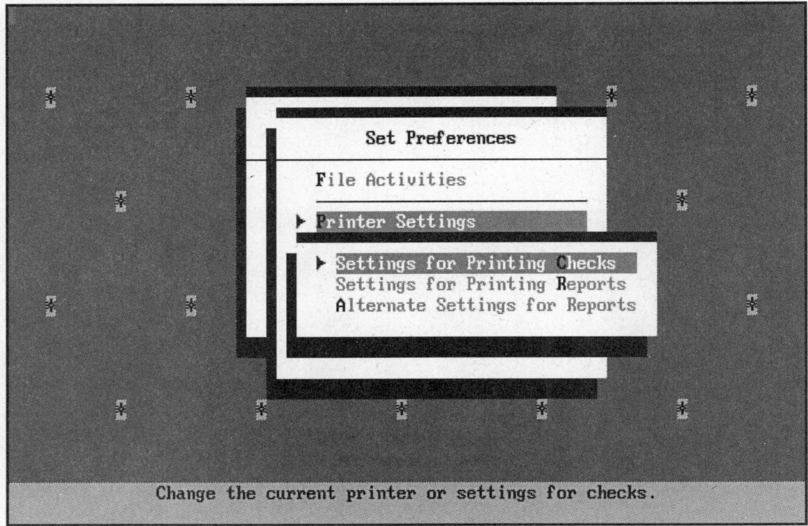

Fig. 1.28. *The Printer Settings submenu.*

3. Quicken enables you to maintain three sets of printer configuration settings: one setting for printing checks, a primary setting for printing reports, and an alternate setting for printing reports.

   Use the arrow keys to highlight the printer configuration setting your want to modify. Then, press Enter. Quicken displays the Printer Settings screen with the Select Printer box and Print Styles box overlaid on the screen (see fig. 1.29).

Each printer configuration setting identifies the printer, describes the printer-to-computer connection, and controls how the printer operates.

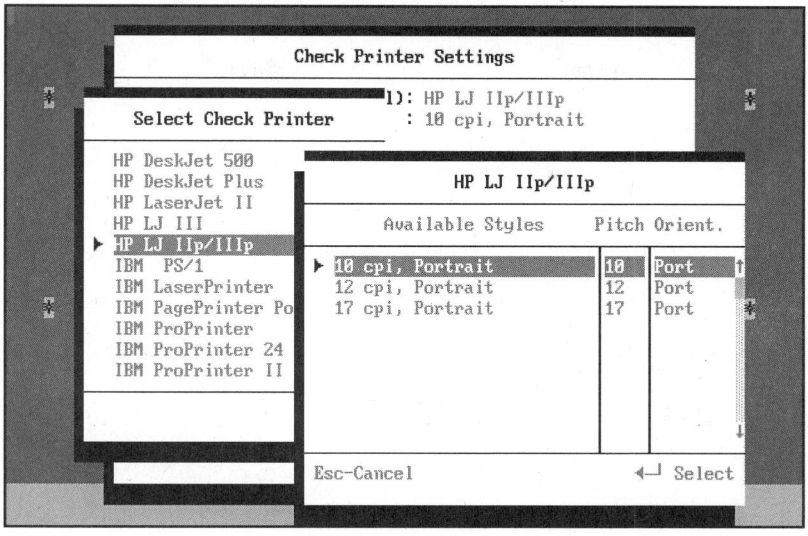

Fig. 1.29. *The Printer Settings screen with the Select Printer and Print Styles boxes overlaid.*

4. Press Esc twice to remove the Select Printer and Print Styles boxes. With these two boxes removed, the full Printer Settings screen shows, as seen in figure 1.30.

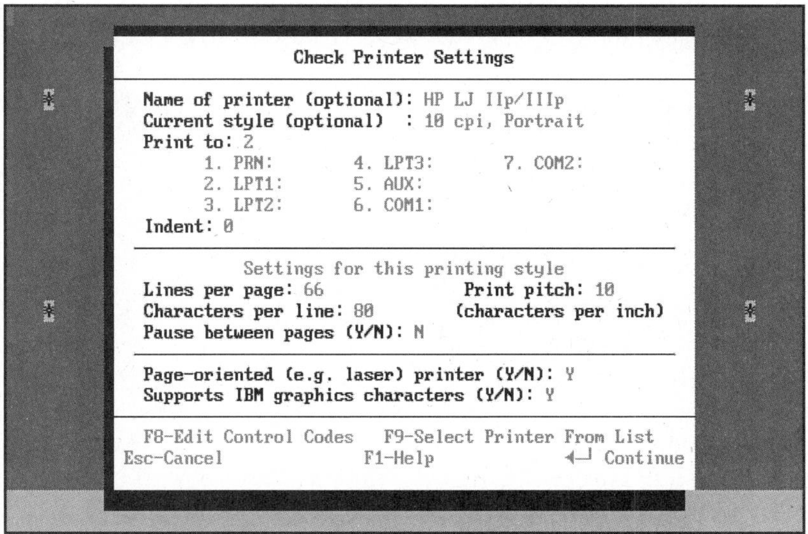

Fig. 1.30. *The Check Printer Settings screen.*

5. Press the Tab or Enter key twice to move the cursor to the `Print to` field. The `Print to` field tells Quicken which communications port should be used to send checks and reports to the printer. The PRN, LPT1, LPT2 and LPT3 options refer to parallel ports. The AUX, COM1, and COM2 options refer to serial ports.

6. Press the number that identifies the correct communications port. For example, press 1 to select PRN. If you aren't sure which port your printer uses, follow the printer cable to the back of your computer. The socket into which the printer cable plugs may be labeled.

If you have a choice about how your printer and computer should communicate, choose a parallel port. Parallel connections enable the printer and computer to talk to each other at the same time—in parallel, which usually results in faster communication.

When you choose a serial port, the computer can send information to the printer only when the printer is not sending information back to the computer and vice versa. With a serial port, your computer and printer take turns communicating with each other.

7. Save the printer settings by pressing Enter when the cursor is positioned on the `Supports IBM Graphics Characters` field. Or, press Ctrl-Enter or F10 when the cursor is positioned on the Printer settings option on the Change Settings menu. Quicken redisplays the Change Settings menu. Press Esc to return to the Main Menu. From the Main Menu, press E to exit.

If you selected the undefined printer steps, you must follow these additional steps before saving the printer setting:

1. (Optional) Type the name of the printer in the `Name of Printer` field.

2. (Optional) Press Enter or Tab to move the cursor to the `Print to` field. Type the number that identifies the communications port that connects the printer and the computer.

3. (Optional) Press Enter or Tab to move the cursor to the `Indent` field. Use the `Indent` field to tell Quicken how many characters to move in from the left margin of the form or paper to begin printing. Each time Quicken begins printing a line, the program moves that many characters to the right. Enter a number from 0 to 80, but

be careful that you do not enter a number so large that Quicken does not have room to print. For laser printers, you can use an indent setting equal to 0. For impact printers, start with an indent setting equal to 0, but you may need to increase this setting if Quicken starts printing too far on the left side of your paper. If Quicken prints off the page on the right side of the paper, reduce your indent setting.

4. (Optional) Press Enter or Tab to move to the `Lines Per Page` field. Use the Lines Per Page setting to tell Quicken how many lines you want printed on a page. Quicken assumes that 6 lines equal an inch. If you are using 11-inch paper, therefore, set this value to 66. If you are using 14-inch paper, set this value to 84.

   To tell whether the lines per page setting is correct, compare where Quicken starts printing on successive pages. If the printing doesn't start at the same distance from the top of the page, you need to adjust the lines per page setting. The setting is too high if Quicken starts printing lower on the second page than on the first. Your setting is too low if Quicken starts printing higher on the second page than on the first.

5. (Optional) Press Enter or Tab to move to the `Print Pitch` field. Use the print pitch setting to tell Quicken how many characters your printer prints in an inch. Typical pitch, or characters per inch, settings are 10, 12, and 15. Check your printer manual to determine your printer's pitch. You also can use a ruler to measure the number of characters, including blank spaces, printed in one inch on a sample of the printer's output.

6. (Optional) Press Enter or Tab to move to the `Characters Per Line` field. Use the `Characters Per Line` field setting to tell Quicken how many characters fit on a line. This setting usually equals 80 if your pitch setting is 10. The characters per line usually equal 96 if your pitch setting is 12.

7. (Optional) Press Enter or Tab to move the cursor to the `Pause Between Pages` field. Use this field to tell Quicken whether to stop after printing a full page so that you can insert a new piece of paper or adjust the printer. Press Y for yes or N for no.

8. (Optional) Press Enter or Tab to move to the `Page-oriented Printer` field. Printers that use individual sheets of paper are, from Quicken's perspective, page-oriented. Use the `Page-oriented Printer` field to tell Quicken whether your printer uses individual sheets of paper. Press Y for yes or N for no.

9. (Optional) Press Enter or Tab to move to the `Supports IBM Graphics Characters` field. Use this field to tell Quicken whether your printer supports the extended IBM character set. If available on your printer, Quicken uses IBM graphics characters in the extended character set in headings on your reports. Press Y for yes or N for no.

10. (Optional) Press F8 to access the Printer Control Codes screen (see fig. 1.31). You use the Printer Control Codes screen to enter the special sequences of letters, numbers, and other keyboard characters that cause your printer to perform in a specific manner or print in a certain style, such as condensed print.

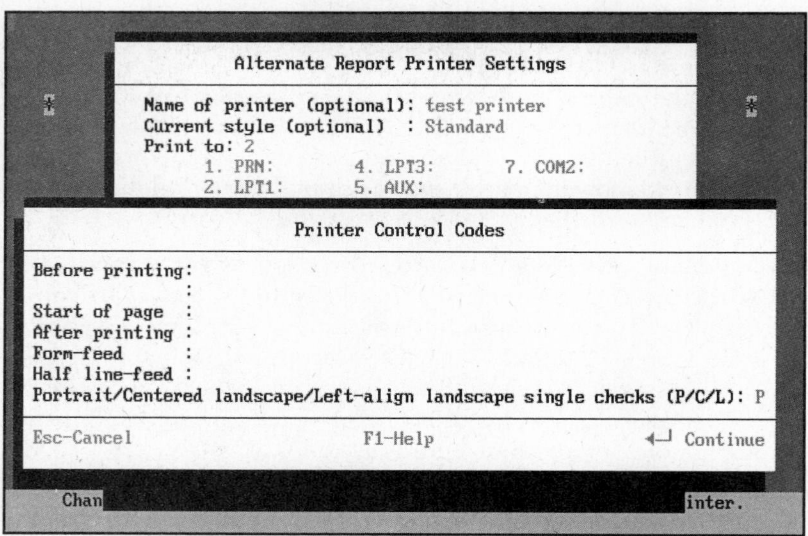

Fig. 1.31. The Printer Control Codes screen.

To determine which printer control codes are appropriate for your printer, look them up in your printer manual. Type the control code that Quicken should initially send your printer in the `Before Printing` field. Press Enter or Tab to move the cursor to the `Start of Page` field and type the control code that Quicken should send your printer as it starts a new page. Press Enter or Tab to move the cursor to the `After Printing` field and type the control code that

Quicken should send your printer when finished printing. Press Enter or Tab to move the cursor to the `Form-feed` field and type the control code that Quicken should send to cause your printer to advance to the top of the next page. Press Enter or Tab to move the cursor to the `Half Line-feed` field and type the control code that Quicken should send to cause your printer to advance one line.

The last field on the Printer Control Codes screen tells Quicken how you'll feed single check forms through a printer. Press P if you'll feed the check form through the printer in normal portrait fashion. Press C if you'll feed the check form through the printer in centered landscape fashion. Press L if you'll feed the check form through the printer in left-aligned fashion.

11. Save the printer settings by pressing Enter when the cursor is positioned on the `Supports IBM Graphics Characters` field. Or, press Ctrl-Enter or F10 when the cursor is positioned on any other screen in the system. Quicken redisplays the Change Settings menu. Press Esc to return to the Main Menu. From the Main Menu, Press E to exit.

If you connect a new printer after the initial installation, you need to identify the new printer. To identify a new printer, follow these steps:

1. Select the **Set Preferences** command from the menu by pressing the letter P (see fig. 1.10). Quicken displays the Set Preferences menu (see fig. 1.19).
2. Select the **Printer Settings** command from the Set Preferences menu by pressing the letter P. Quicken displays the Printer Settings submenu (see fig. 1.29).
3. Quicken enables you to maintain three sets of printer configuration settings: one setting for printing checks, a primary setting for printing reports, and an alternate setting for printing reports. Use the arrow keys to highlight the printer configuration setting you want to modify. Then, press Enter.

   Quicken displays the Printer Settings screen with the Select Printer box and Print Styles box overlaid on the screen (see fig. 1.29).
4. Press Esc once so that just the Select Printer box is displayed (see fig. 1.32).

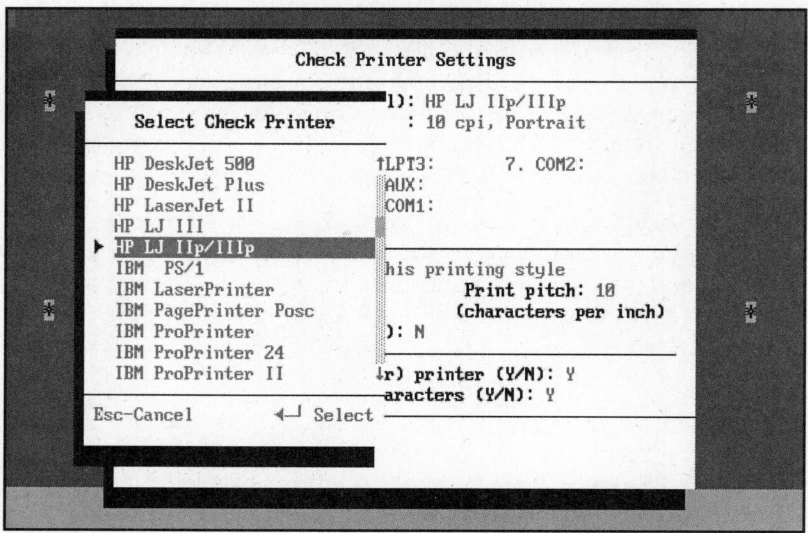

Fig. 1.32. The Check Printer Settings screen with the Select Check Printer box displayed.

5. Use the up- and down-arrow keys to highlight your printer. Then, press Enter. Quicken displays the Print Style box shown in figure 1.29.

6. Use the up- and down-arrow keys to highlight the print size and page orientation you want. Then, press Enter. Quicken displays the Print Settings screen without the Select Printer and Print Style boxes.

7. Save the printer settings by pressing Enter when the cursor is positioned on the `Supports IBM Graphics Characters` field. Or, press Ctrl-Enter or F10 when the cursor is positioned on the Printer settings option on the Change Settings menu. Quicken redisplays the Change Settings menu. Press Esc to return to the Main Menu. From the Main Menu, press E to exit.

Chapter Summary

This chapter described the steps you take to prepare to use Quicken: ordering check forms, choosing the conversion date, and installing the software. Now that you have Quicken installed, you are ready to begin using the system. Before you start entering actual checks and deposits, writing checks, or reconciling accounts, take a few minutes to peruse the contents of the next chapter. Chapter 2 covers the basics of using the Quicken program and should make getting the most from Quicken that much easier.

2

Getting Around in Quicken

Quicken is not difficult to use, especially when you begin by learning the helpful operations described in this chapter. You will learn about accessing Quicken's help screens, selecting menu options, using the Quicken screens to collect financial information for storage, and using Quicken's calculator.

Using Help

Think of Quicken's Help feature as a user's manual stored in your computer's memory. You can access this manual from anywhere in Quicken by pressing F1. Quicken's Help feature is context-sensitive; that is, it provides the manual and opens it to the correct page. If you select **Help** from Quicken's Main Menu, for example, you receive information about the Main Menu options (see fig. 2.1).

Often, the information provided by the Help key (F1) requires more than one screen. Use the PgDn and PgUp keys to see the next or preceding pages of information. Usually, a Help screen, such as the Main Menu, references other Help topics, too. Quicken identifies these other Help topics by displaying the topic name in black letters rather than blue letters. Figure 2.1, for example, references **Using Help**, **Use Register**, **Write/Print Checks**, and so forth. To see the Help screens for a referenced topic, press Tab until the topic is highlighted. Then, press Enter. After you read the Help information, press Esc to return to the program. Quicken returns to where you were when you pressed the Help key.

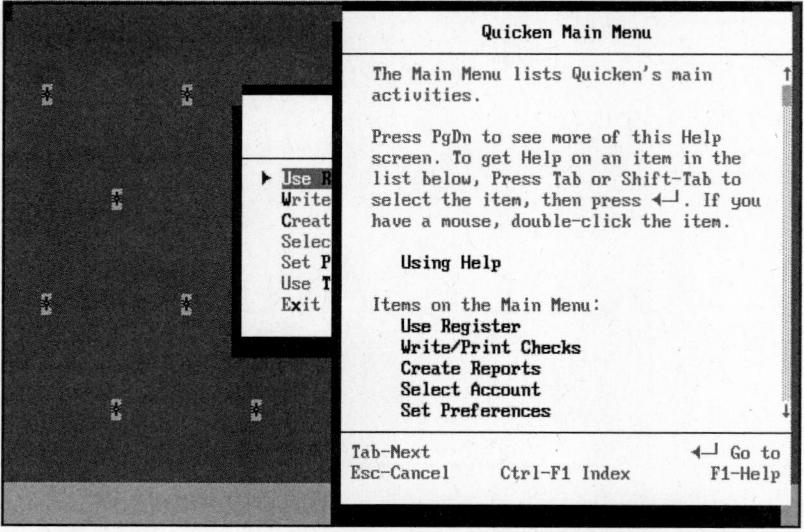

Fig. 2.1. Help for Quicken's Main Menu.

If you press F1 twice, you access the Help Table of Contents screen, which organizes topics into related groups (see fig. 2.2). If you press Ctrl-F1, you access the Help Index screen, which lists all the topics for which you can get Help (see fig. 2.3). To select a topic, press Tab until the topic is highlighted. Then, press Enter. To leave any of the Help screens, press Esc.

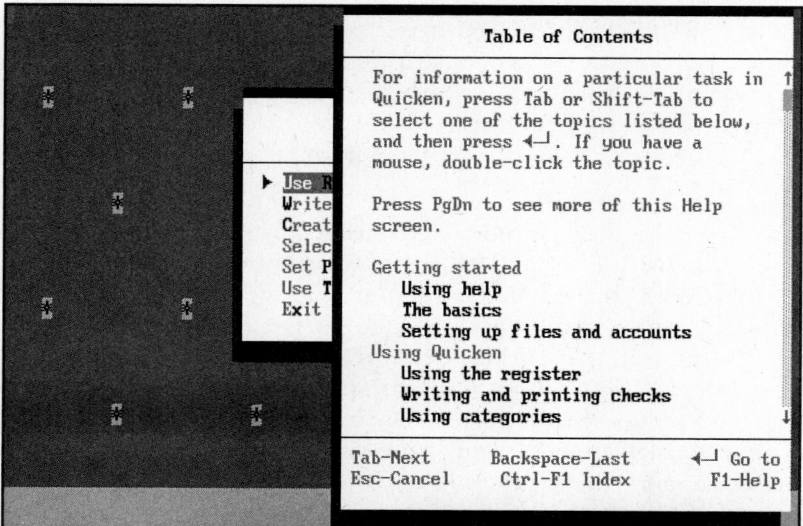

Fig. 2.2. The Help Table of Contents screen.

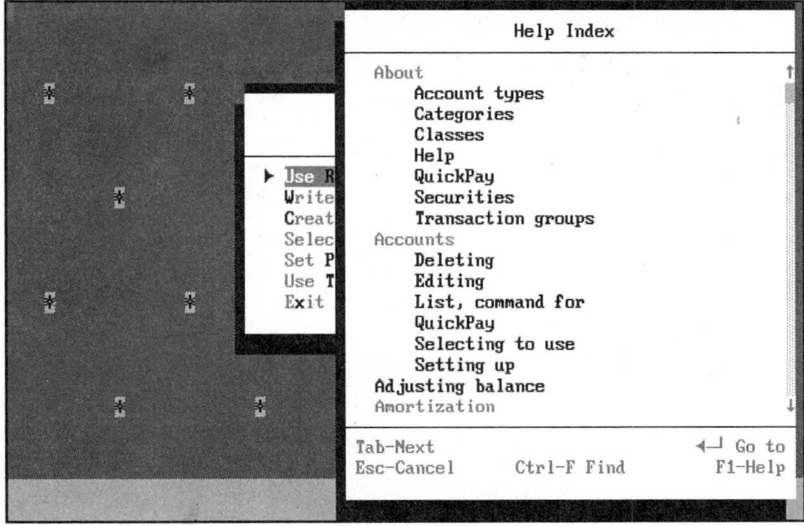

Fig. 2.3. The Help Index screen.

Using and Selecting Menu Options

Quicken provides the following three ways to select menu options:

- Typing or clicking the mouse on the option letter
- Highlighting the option and pressing Enter
- Using the shortcut keys

The first way to select an option from a menu is to type or click the left mouse button on the letter that identifies that option. If you want to select the **Write/Print Checks** option from the Main Menu, for example, you can press W. Quicken will display the Write Checks screen (see fig. 2.4). To exit the screen and return to the Main Menu, press Esc. Or, click the right mouse button.

The second way to select menu options is to use the cursor-movement keys to highlight the appropriate selection. If you press the up- and down-arrow keys, the highlighted option moves up and down. When the option you want to select is highlighted, press Enter.

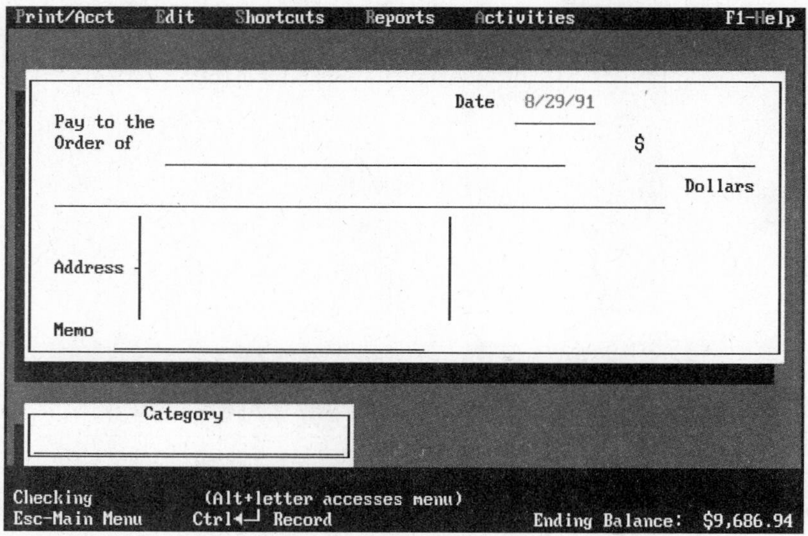

Fig. 2.4. The Write Checks screen.

At the top of the data-entry screens, such as the Write Check screen (see fig. 2.4), Quicken provides other menus. The Write Checks, screen, for example, has a Print/Acct menu, an Edit menu, a Shortcuts menu, a Reports menu, and an Activities menu. The selection techniques described earlier also apply to these menus. First, however, you need to activate the menus and display the menu you want. To do this, press the Alt key and the first letter of the menu name. To select the Edit menu, for example, press Alt and the letter E (see fig. 2.5).

The third way to select menu options is to use one of the shortcut key combinations. Not every menu option has a shortcut key, but most of the options you use regularly do. To execute a shortcut, hold down the Ctrl key and press the appropriate letter key. For example, one way to delete a check or deposit in the register is to select the **Delete Transaction** option from the Edit menu (see fig. 2.5), and confirm that you want to delete a transaction by pressing Enter. You also can press the Ctrl and D keys to accomplish the same thing. Quicken shows you the shortcut keys (for example, Ctrl-D) to the right of the options (see fig. 2.5). Chapter 5 describes the **Delete Transaction** option in detail.

After you activate one of the menus, you can use the left- and right-arrow keys to display the other menus. If the Edit menu is displayed, for example, pressing the right-arrow key displays the Shortcuts menu (see fig. 2.6).

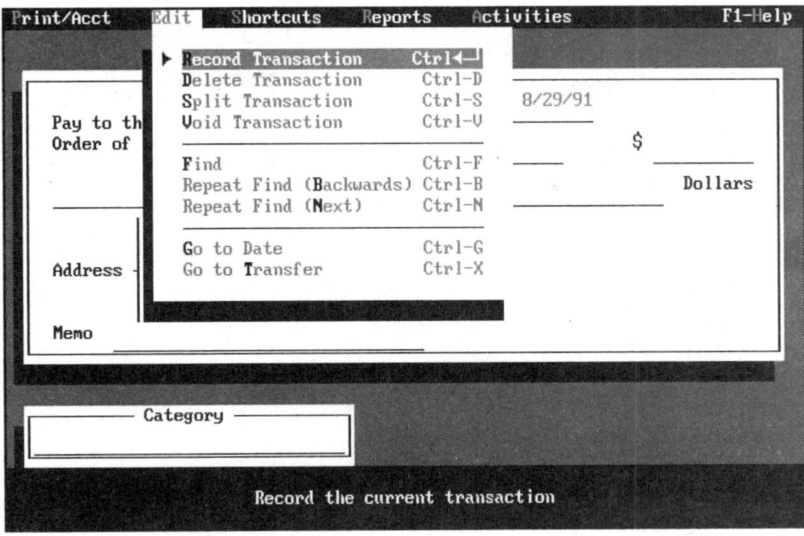

Fig. 2.5. The Edit menu.

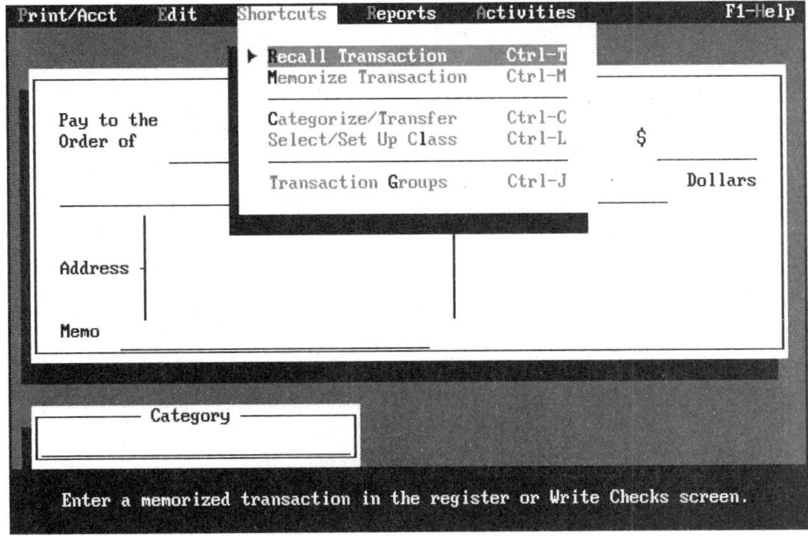

Fig. 2.6. The Shortcuts menu.

Shortcut keys are described more in the chapters discussing the associated menu options. For now, remember that shortcut keys are another way to execute menu options and that they save time.

Collecting Data On-Screen

Collecting data on-screen involves moving between fields, entering and editing fields, and saving your work. Quicken provides you with a variety of ways to accomplish these tasks, explained in the following sections. To follow this information on your computer, move to the Write Checks screen by selecting the **Write/Print Checks** option from Quicken's Main Menu.

Moving between Fields

Quicken provides a variety of ways to move between fields. You can move from field to field by pressing Enter. You can move to the next field by pressing Tab and to the preceding field by pressing Shift-Tab. You can move between fields by using the arrow keys. Pressing Ctrl-← moves the cursor to the beginning of the preceding field, and pressing Ctrl-→ moves the cursor to the beginning of the next field. You can move to any field by pointing to the field and clicking the left mouse button. Finally, you also can use the Home and End keys to move to the first and last fields on the screen. If the cursor is at the start of the field, pressing Home moves the cursor to the first field on the screen; if the cursor is at the end of the field, pressing End moves the cursor to the last field. Table 2.1 summarizes the cursor-movement keys.

If you followed the earlier discussion and moved to the Write Checks screen and you want to practice using the cursor-movement keys, try each of the keys or key combinations listed in table 2.1.

Trying the keys really does make them easier to understand.

Table 2.1
Cursor-Movement Keys for Moving between Fields

Key	*New Cursor Placement*
Enter	The next field
Tab	The next field

Key	*New Cursor Placement*
Shift-Tab	The preceding field
Arrow Keys	The next or preceding field, according to the arrow
Ctrl-←	The beginning of the preceding field
Ctrl-→	The beginning of the next field
Home	The first field on the screen (from start of a field)
End	The last field on the screen (from end of a field)

Entering and Editing Data On-Screen

Entering or editing a field of data is as easy as moving between fields. To enter data into a field, type the appropriate characters. Whether Quicken accepts only numeric or alphabetic and numeric data depends on the field you are entering. Refer to the chapter pertaining to the screen you are using for more information.

Usually, you should type dollar amounts as numeric data by using the number keys on your keyboard. Do not enter the dollar symbol or any commas because Quicken adds these symbols for you. If an amount represents a negative number, however, precede the number with a minus sign, as in –1.47. Quicken assumes that the number is an even dollar amount unless you use a decimal when entering the number. For example, entering *1245* displays as `$1,245.00`, and entering *12.45* displays as `$12.45`.

If you make an error while entering an amount, use the arrow keys to position the cursor on the numbers you want to change. You also can click the characters you want to change with the left mouse button. You also can use Home and End to move the cursor within a field. Press Home to move the cursor to the start of a field, and press End to move the cursor to the end of a field. To delete numbers, use the Backspace or Del key. The Backspace key removes the number preceding the cursor location; the Del key removes the number at the cursor location. To delete the entire field, press Ctrl-Backspace.

Most of the remaining data stored in the system (data other than dollar amounts) can be alphabetic, numeric, or both. Where alphabetic characters are allowed, you can use upper- or lowercase characters. Try typing the name of someone to whom you frequently write checks, such as the bank. You can use spaces, capital letters, numbers, and whatever else you want or need.

You can edit or change an entry in a text field by retyping the field's contents or by using the arrow keys or by clicking the mouse to position the cursor on the characters you want to change. To delete characters, use the Backspace or Del key. To add characters to existing text, press the Ins key and type the needed characters. To add characters to the end of the text, position the cursor at the end of the text by using the right-arrow key, and type the remaining characters. Again, if you just want to clear the field so that you can start over, press Ctrl-Backspace.

For date fields, Quicken provides a special editing capability. By pressing the + key, you can add one day to the date; by pressing the – key, you can subtract one day. Try this feature by entering *1/1/91* in the Date field. Pressing + changes the date to `1/2/91`, and pressing – changes the date to `12/31/90`. If the date is only the month and year—as in a few places in the Quicken system—you can move the date ahead one month by pressing the + key and back one month by pressing the – key.

Several date-editing tools exist. By pressing the letter T, you enter the current system date. By pressing the letter M, you enter the first date of the current month. By pressing the letter H, you enter the last date of the current month. By pressing the letter Y, you enter the first date of the year. Finally, by pressing the letter R, you enter the last date of the year.

Saving Your Work

When you finish entering data on-screen and want to save the data, you have four ways to save your work:

- Press F10
- Press Enter from the last field on-screen
- Press Ctrl-Enter
- Click on the phrase Ctrl-Enter with the left mouse button

If you are recording a check, Quicken displays a blank Write Checks screen so that you can enter another check. If you are recording a transaction in the register, Quicken displays the next empty row in the register so that you can record another transaction.

Using the Calculator

One of Quicken's tools (beginning with Version 3) is the on-line calculator that you can use by pressing the shortcut key combination Ctrl-O. Figure 2.7 shows the Calculator screen.

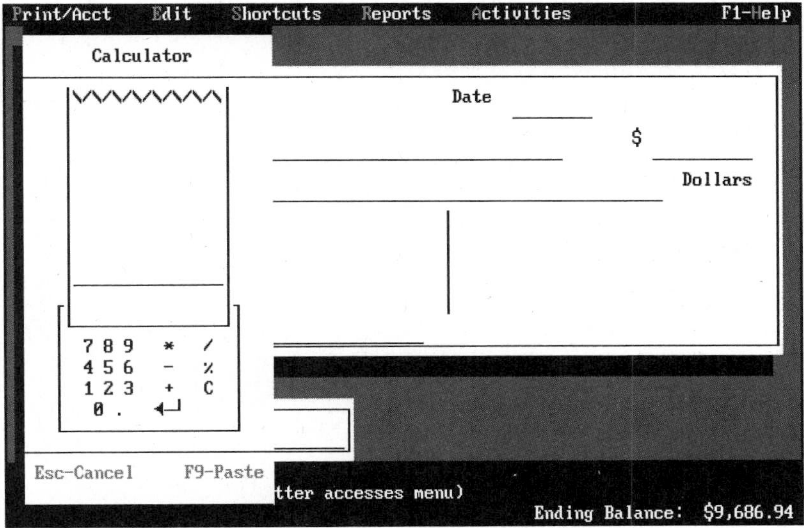

Fig. 2.7. The calculator screen before you begin entering numbers.

Quicken verifies that Num Lock (number lock—a key on the keypad) is on so that you can use the numeric keypad to enter numbers. If the Num Lock key is off, Quicken temporarily toggles the key on while you are using the calculator.

Use the on-line calculator as you do a regular calculator. For example, to add three invoices for $12.87, $232.01, and $49.07, and subtract a $50 credit memo, you press the following keys:

12.87 + 232.01 + 49.07 – 50

Press Enter or the equal sign. Quicken performs the math and displays the results as shown in figure 2.8. The calculator tape shows the numbers and the math operators. To clear the on-line calculator, press C.

If you do not clear the calculator tape, Quicken saves the numbers and the math operators and they will reappear the next time you access the calculator.

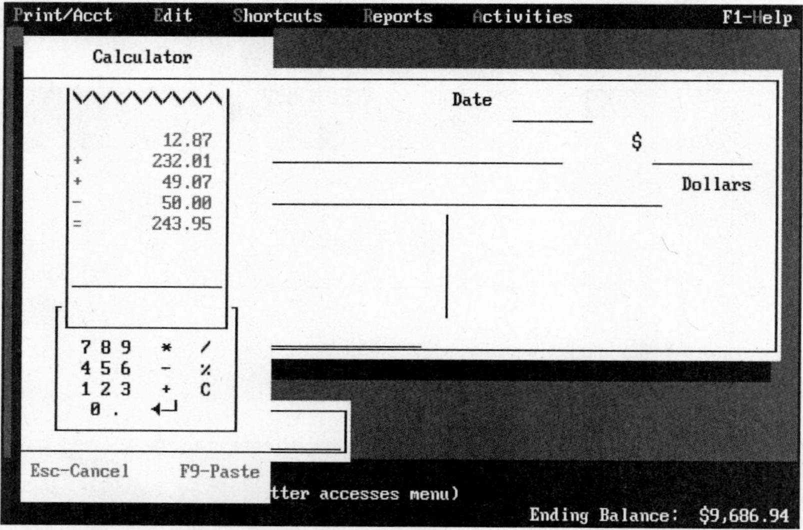

Fig. 2.8. The Calculator tape shows the numbers and the math operators.

To multiply numbers, use the asterisk. For example, to multiply $232.01 by .25, press the following keys:

*232.01 * .25*

Press Enter or the equal sign.

To divide numbers, use the slash. For example, to divide $527.32 by 2, you press the following keys:

527.32 / 2

Press Enter or the equal sign.

If you want to add or subtract a percentage, the on-line calculator also provides a percent key. For example, to add 25% to 200, press *200 + 25%* and then Enter. Quicken calculates and displays the result shown in figure 2.9.

Press Esc to exit the on-line calculator. If you are calculating an amount to enter as a value in a screen field, you also can press F9, and Quicken enters the calculation result into the field where the cursor was located when you pressed Ctrl-O.

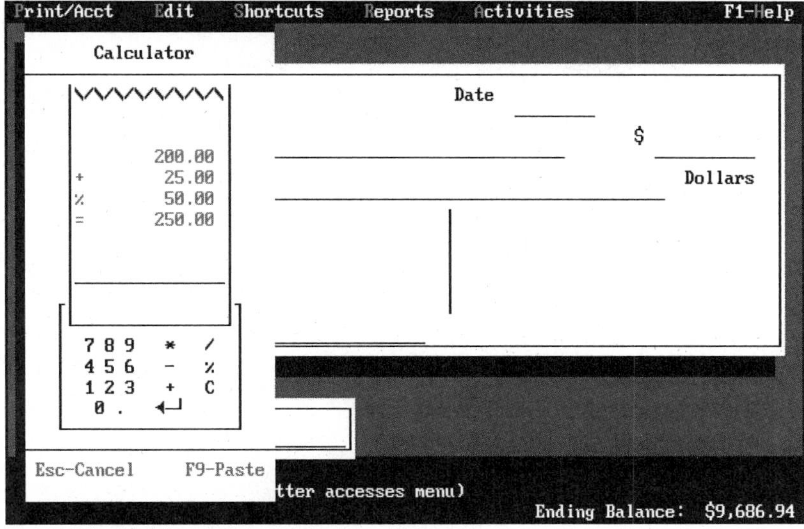

Fig. 2.9. Using the percent key with the Quicken calculator.

Learning To Use Quicken

Using Quicken is usually easy, but you may sometimes be perplexed and find yourself scratching your head. To minimize the hassles and headaches of learning a new program, consider several additional resources.

For a sturdy foundation, read the Quicken user's manual and this book—or at least the chapters that apply to those parts of the program you will use.

Talk to other Quicken users who might be working through problems similar to yours and finding helpful solutions. Formal and informal users' groups are excellent support systems. The store that sold you Quicken, the store or computer consultant who helps you with your hardware and software, or the CPA who prepares your annual financial statements or tax return may be able to direct you to Quicken users' groups.

Spend some time experimenting with the software. Try different transactions, explore the menus and screens, and pore over the reports. Experimenting increases your confidence in the system, gives you experience in working with live business or family data, and most importantly, confirms which options accomplish which tasks.

Chapter Summary

This chapter described the basics of getting around in Quicken: using Help, selecting menu options, collecting data on-screen, and using the calculator. The chapter also provided some tips for learning to use Quicken.

If you need to define more than one bank account to use with Quicken, you need to read Chapter 3. If you don't need to define more than one bank account, you are ready to learn the basics of using Quicken—such as writing and printing checks, using Quicken's register, reconciling your bank account, and caring for Quicken's files—which are covered beginning with Chapter 4.

3

Describing Your Accounts

If you followed the steps outlined in Chapter 1, you already have defined one bank account as part of installing Quicken, but you may want to define other bank accounts. You may, for example, have more than one checking account, a savings account or two, and even certificates of deposit for which you will keep records with Quicken. If you want to use Quicken to track more than one account, you need to describe these accounts to Quicken. You then can use Quicken to record changes in the accounts and track transfers between accounts.

Working with Accounts

The next few paragraphs cover the basics of working with the Quicken accounts. These basics include how to add another account, how to edit and delete accounts, and how to tell Quicken which account you want. You also receive some tips on creating accounts—information that should make working with multiple accounts easier.

Adding Another Account

You need to describe, or identify, accounts for each bank account you want to track with Quicken. You defined only one account as part of installing the software, but you can have as many as 255 accounts in a file, and you can have multiple files. (Files are discussed in more detail later in the chapter.)

This chapter explains how to add another account by using the **Select Account** command. You also can use the **Create New Account** command on the Tutorials and Assistants menu, however.

To set up another bank account, choose the **Select Account** option from Quicken's Main Menu (see fig. 3.1). Quicken displays the Select Account to Use screen shown in figure 3.2. The Select Account to Use screen will show the bank account you defined as part of installing the Quicken program.

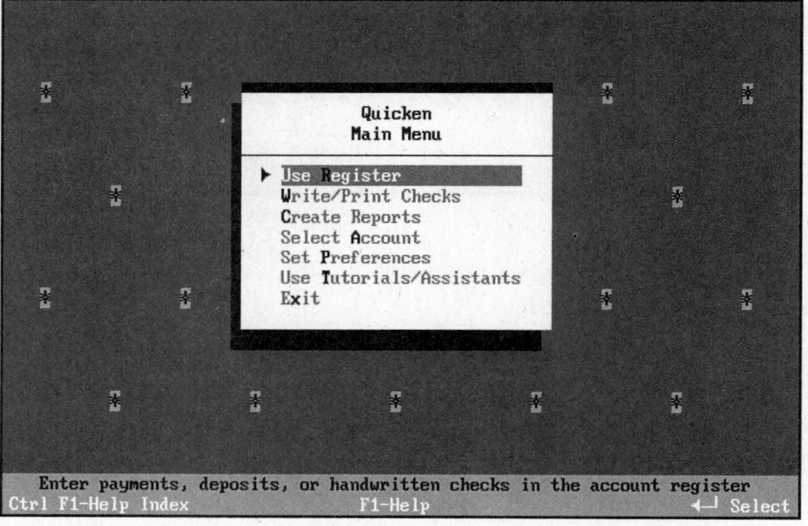

***Fig. 3.1.** Selecting from Quicken's Main Menu.*

To add another account, follow these steps:

1. Using the arrow keys, select the `New Account` entry on the Select Account to Use screen.

2. Press Enter. The Set Up New Account screen appears as shown in figure 3.3.

3. With the cursor on the `Account Type` field, press 1 to choose `Bank Account`. (Chapter 12 describes setting up credit card, cash, other asset, and other liability accounts. Chapter 13 describes setting up investment accounts.)

4. Move the cursor to the `Name` field. Type a name or short description of the bank account in the `Name` field. Use characters, letters, spaces, and any symbols except brackets ([]), a slash (/), or a colon (:).

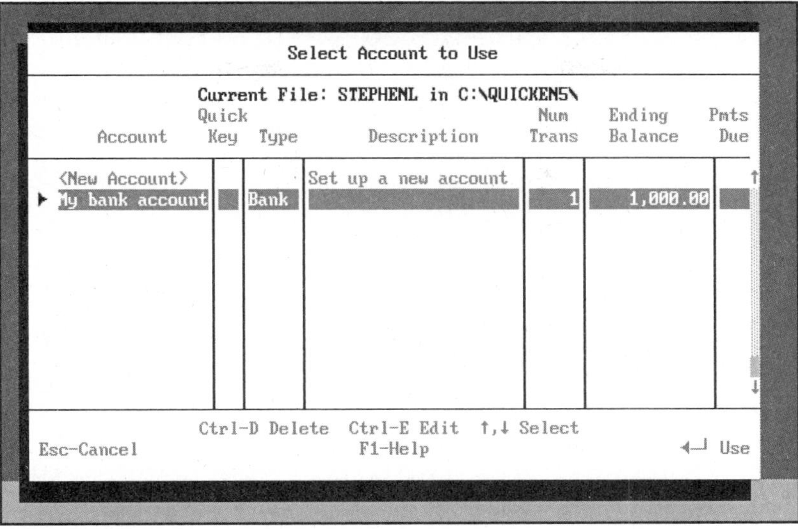

Fig. 3.2. The Select Account to Use screen.

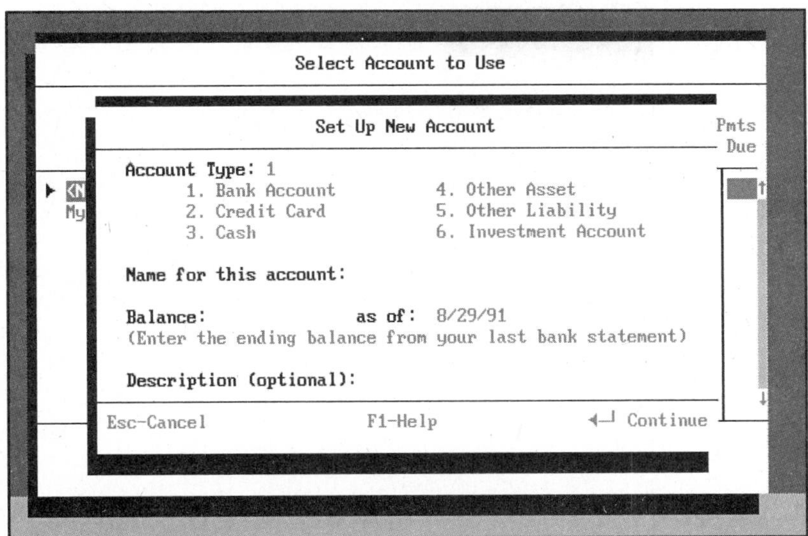

Fig. 3.3. The Set Up New Account screen.

Remember that you have only 15 spaces for the account name. Use an abbreviation of the bank's name; Big National could become Big Natl, for example. This leaves room for the last four digits of the account number. You then can distinguish accounts easily, as shown by the following example:

BigNatl-1234 for a checking account
BigNatl-3272 for a savings account
BigNatl-7113 for CDs

5. Move the cursor to the `Balance` field. Type the bank account balance as of the conversion date. Do not use commas or dollar signs when you enter the balance.

6. Move the cursor to the `as of` date field. Type the date of the balance amount using the MM/DD/YY format. Remember that you can use the + and – keys to move the date ahead and back one day.

7. (Optional) Move the cursor to the `Description` field. Type a further description of the account, such as the account number.

8. Press Enter to save your changes and return to the Select Account to Use screen. To add more accounts, repeat steps 1 through 8.

When you first set up accounts for Quicken, creating accounts can get out of hand. You might, for example, define Quicken accounts for every checking account you have regardless of whether the account is active. You also might define Quicken accounts for each of your savings accounts, credit unions, money market accounts, and perhaps even accounts for certificates of deposit. Rather than indiscriminately defining accounts for every bank account you have, consider a few ideas and rules for determining which of your bank accounts also should be Quicken accounts:

- If you want to write checks on the account by using Quicken, you must define a Quicken account.

- If you want to use Quicken's reconciliation feature to explain differences between your records and the bank's, credit union's, or brokerage house's statement, you must define a Quicken account.

- If you have transactions in an account that you want to include in Quicken's tax deduction summaries or profit and loss statements, you must define a Quicken account. For example, you might have charitable contributions or mortgage interest transactions.

Other factors can indicate that you probably do not need to define a bank, credit union, or brokerage house account as a Quicken account:

- If you do not have any deposits into or withdrawals from the account other than interest income or bank service fees, your monthly statement will suffice for your financial records.
- If you have only a handful of transactions a month—fewer than a dozen—and none represents an account transfer from or to an account for which you will use Quicken, you probably do not need to track the account in Quicken. This choice, however, is a matter of personal preference.
- If you otherwise would not track an account, you probably should not bother to put the account into Quicken—even if you have the best of intentions about becoming more diligent in your record keeping.

Editing Existing Accounts

You also can use the Select Account to Use screen to edit the names and descriptions of existing accounts. You might do this, for example, if you originally described the account incorrectly. Or, you may want to edit an account name and description if you have transferred the account in total to a new account number or even a new bank. Maybe you moved from Denver to San Francisco and are still using the same bank, but a different branch. Quicken does not, however, enable you to change the account type, balance, or "as of" date after you add the account. If these dates are wrong, you need to delete and then re-create the account. To edit an account, follow these steps:

1. With the arrow keys, mark the account you want to edit on the Select Account to Use screen.
2. Press Ctrl-E. The Edit Account screen appears, filled with the current information for the account.
3. (Optional) Edit the bank account name in the `Name` field.
4. (Optional) Move the cursor to the `Description` field. Edit the bank account description in the `Description` field.
5. (Optional) If you want to assign a quick key you can use to easily move to another account, move the cursor to the `Quick Key Assignment` field. Enter a number. In the future, you can press the Ctrl key and this number to quickly select an account.

The Edit Account screen also enables you to attach a tax schedule and tax schedule line number to an account. If you do this, transfers to and from an account are summarized so you can more easily complete a particular line of a particular tax schedule. Refer to Chapters 10 and 19 for more information on collecting income tax return data by using Quicken.

6. Press Enter to save your changes and return to the Select Account to Use screen.

To edit additional accounts, repeat steps 1 through 5.

Deleting Existing Accounts

You also can use the Select Account to Use screen to delete accounts you no longer use. Perhaps you closed an account or maybe you decided an account isn't worth tracking with Quicken. To delete an account, follow these steps:

1. With the arrow keys, mark the account you want to delete on the Select Account to Use screen.

2. Press Ctrl-D. The `Deleting Account` message box appears (see fig. 3.4), providing the name of the account to be deleted and alerting you to the permanence of the deletion.

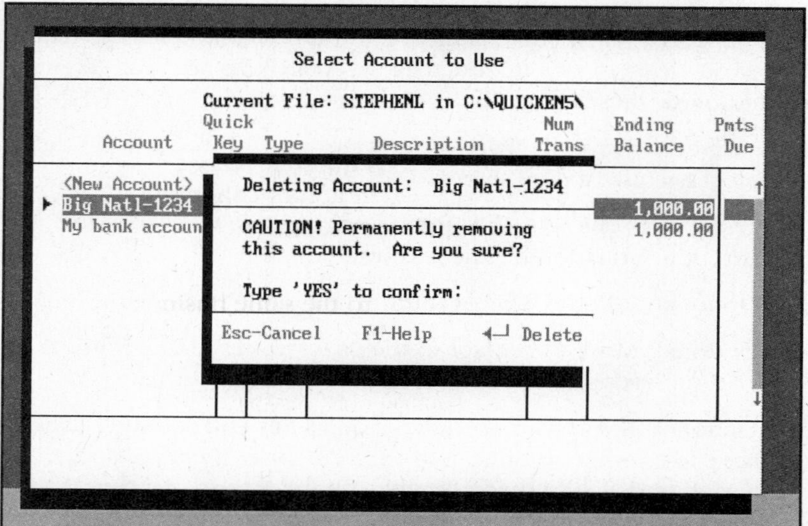

Fig. 3.4. The `Deleting Account` *message box.*

3. Type *yes* to delete the selected account. If you do not want to delete the account, press Esc.

When you delete an account, you delete the account description and any transactions you have recorded in the account. Be sure you really want to delete the account before taking the steps to do so.

Selecting an Account

When you start working with multiple accounts, you need to tell Quicken which account you want to use. Suppose that you decide to use Quicken to track a savings and a checking account. Whenever you enter a savings account deposit, you need to make sure that you record the deposit for the savings account and not the checking account. Similarly, if you withdraw money from the checking account, you need to make sure the withdrawal is correctly recorded there and not in the savings account. To record accounts correctly, you use the Select Account to Use screen. Use the arrow keys to mark the account you want, and then press Enter.

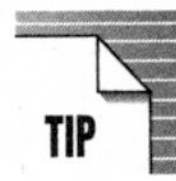

> Entering all transactions for an account at one time is more efficient. Consider collecting several transactions for an account and then recording them at one time.

Working with Files

When you begin defining multiple accounts, you also run head on into the issue of files. Quicken stores accounts you define in files, and it enables you to have more than one file. The obvious question, then, when you begin defining new accounts is to which file an account should be added. You usually will find these decisions fairly easy to make.

The general rule is that you store related accounts together in their own file. Accounts are related when they pertain to the same business or the same household. If you use Quicken for home accounting and for a commercial printing business, you use two files—one for home and one for business. If you use Quicken for three businesses—a consulting practice, a small publishing business, and restaurant—you use three files—one for each of the three businesses.

Adding New Files

As part of installing Quicken, you automatically create at least one file by using the **Create New File** command on the Tutorials and Assistants menu or the **Select/Set File** command on the File Activities submenu. Chapter 1, "Preparing To Use Quicken," explains how you use both these commands. You may, however, need to add new files even after the installation. Accordingly, if you have questions about adding files with the **Create New File** command or the **Select/Set Up File** command, refer to Chapter 1.

Editing File Names

You also can use the **Select/Set Up** command to edit the names of existing files. You may want to edit a file name, for example, if you named the file incorrectly. If you name files based on the business name, changing the name of the business also may mean you want to change the name of the file. Suppose that the account group for the business Acme Manufacturing is ACME_MFG. If the business name changes to Acme, Incorporated, you can change the account group name to ACME_INC. To edit an account group's name, follow these steps:

1. Select the **Set Preferences** command from the Quicken Main Menu (see fig. 3.1). Quicken displays the Set Preferences menu (see fig. 3.5).

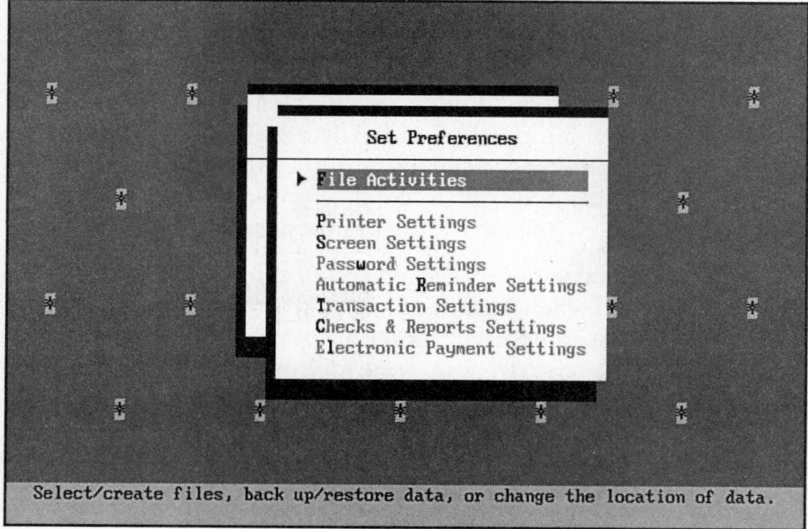

Fig. 3.5. The Set Preferences menu.

2. Select the **File Activities** command from the Set Preferences menu. Quicken displays the File Activities menu (see fig. 3.6).

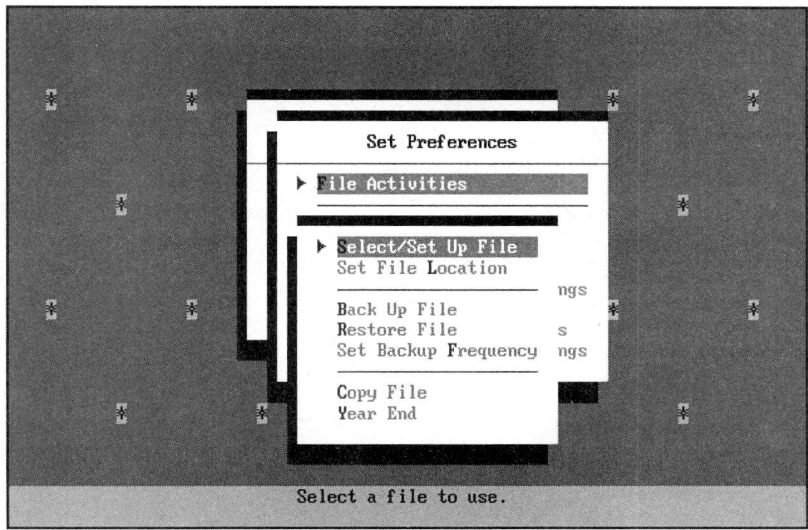

Fig. 3.6. The File Activities menu.

3. Select the **Select/Set Up File** command from the File Activities menu. Quicken displays the Select/Set Up File screen (see fig. 3.7).

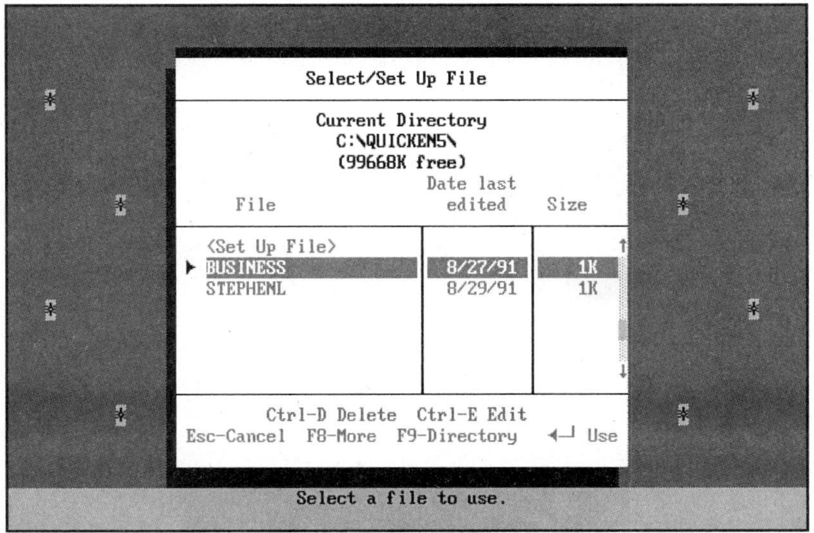

Fig. 3.7. The Select/Set Up File screen.

4. (Optional) To edit an account group in some directory other than C:/QUICKEN5/, press F9. Quicken displays the Set File Location screen (see fig. 3.8) for specifying another location for Quicken's account groups. Press Enter.

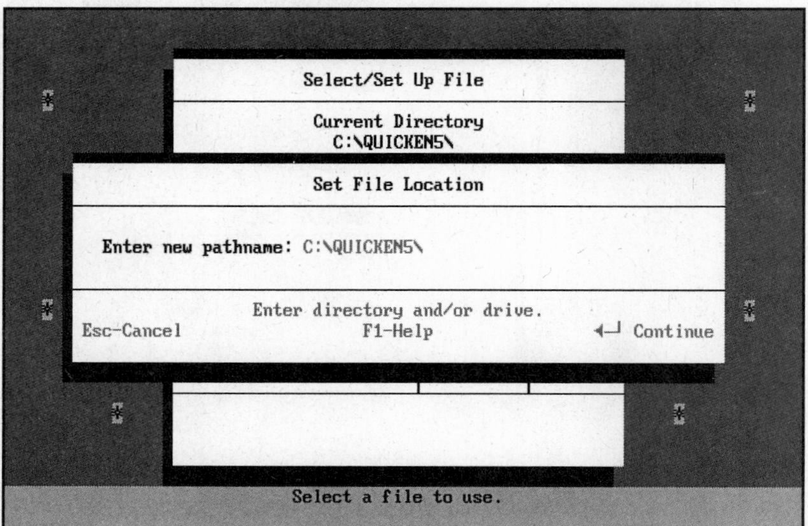

Fig. 3.8. The Set File Location screen.

5. Select the account group you want to edit from the Select/Set Up File screen by using the arrow keys.
6. Press Ctrl-E. The Rename A File screen appears (see fig. 3.9).
7. Edit the file name in the `Name` field. Be sure to enter a valid DOS file name.
8. Press Enter to save your changes and return to the Select/Set Up File screen. To edit additional files, repeat steps 1 through 5.

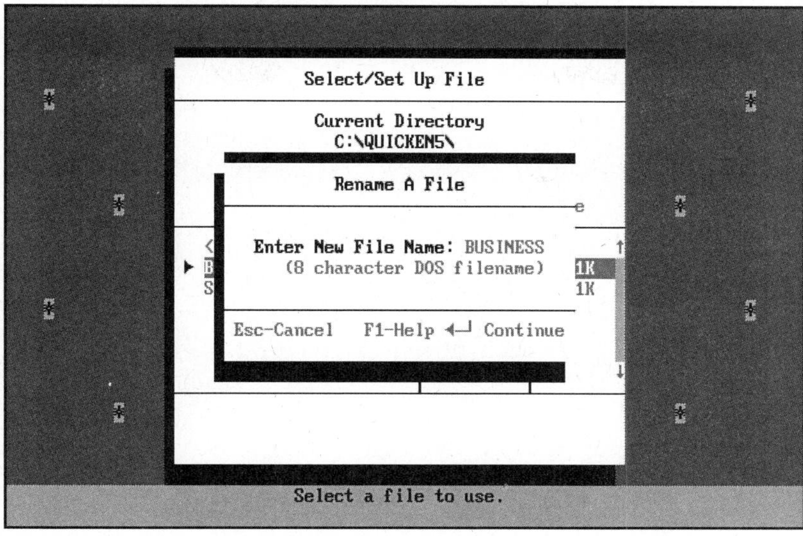

Fig. 3.9. The Rename A File screen.

Deleting Files

You also can use the **Select/Set Up File** command and screen to delete files. Generally, you should never delete a file, because when you do, you are essentially deleting all the accounts in the file. If you no longer are tracking any of the accounts in the file, you can delete the group. This may be the case if you set up a special account for learning to use Quicken and you no longer use the account. You also no longer need the file used for a business if you sell the business. To delete a file, display the Select/Set Up File screen and follow these steps:

1. (Optional) If you want to delete an account group in some directory other than C:QUICKEN5/, press F9. Quicken displays the Set File Location screen (see fig. 3.8), which you can use to specify some other directory as the location in which to look for Quicken files. Press Enter.

2. Select the file you want to delete from the Select/Set Up File screen by using the arrow keys.

3. Press Ctrl-D. Quicken displays the `Deleting File` message box (see fig. 3.10). The message box gives the name of the file that Quicken is about to delete and asks you to confirm the deletion.

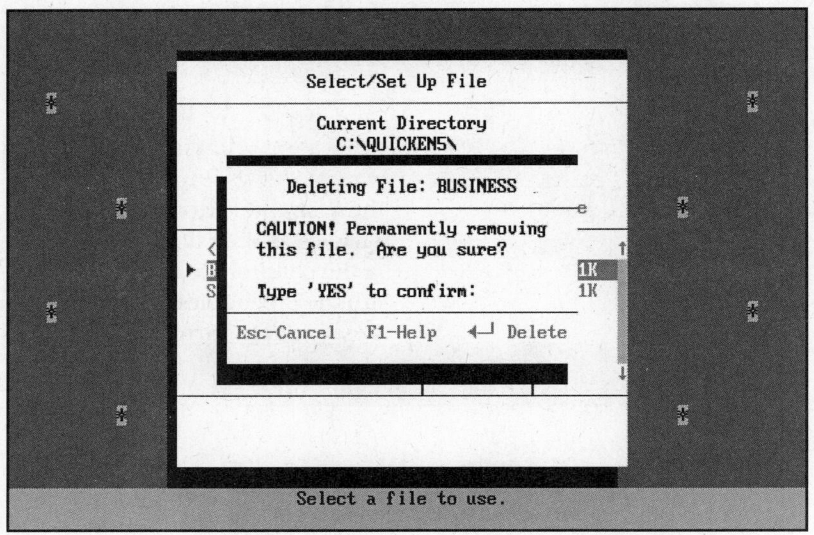

***Fig. 3.10.** The* `Deleting File` *message box.*

4. Type *yes* to delete the file. If you do not want to delete the file, press Esc.

5. Press Enter to complete the deletion and return to the Select/Set Up File screen. To delete additional files, repeat steps 1 through 5.

Selecting a File

When you work with more than one file, you need to tell Quicken with which file you want to work. To do this, use the Select/Set Up File screen. Use the arrow keys to mark the file you want, and then press Enter.

Chapter Summary

This chapter described how you add, edit, and delete bank account descriptions. You also learned about files. With the information in the first three chapters, you should be ready to use Quicken. In essence, these first three chapters covered the details of getting started with Quicken—the things you need to do before you actually start working with the program.

The next section of the book describes the basics of using Quicken and covers such tasks as recording financial transactions with Quicken, printing registers, writing checks, and so on. These chapters don't cover as much about business and personal accounting topics as they do about using the Quicken system. When you finish reading the chapters in Part II, "Learning the Basics," you will be well acquainted with the mechanics of actually using the Quicken program. That knowledge is essential to turning Quicken into a tool you can use for business or personal financial management.

Part II

Learning the Basics

Includes

Using the Register

Making the Register Easier To Use

Writing and Printing Checks

Making Check Writing Easier

Reconciling Your Bank Account

Caring for Quicken Files

4

Using the Register

Your checkbook, or check register, is your most fundamental financial tool. You probably agree that your check register largely summarizes your financial life. Money flows into the account in the form of wages for a household or sales collections for a business. Money flows out of the account to pay expenses.

Moving your check register to Quicken provides two major benefits. First, Quicken does the arithmetic of deducting withdrawals and adding deposits—a trivial contribution until you remember the last time an error in your arithmetic caused you to bounce a check. Second, Quicken records each of your checking account transactions in the check register so that you can use Quicken's Reports feature to summarize and extract information from the register—information that helps you plan and control your finances more effectively.

Quicken's register is the program's major component. Every other program feature—writing checks, reconciling accounts, and printing reports—depends on the register. Every user works with Quicken's register directly by entering transactions into the register and indirectly by using the information stored in the register. In fact, any of the financial transactions you record can be entered directly into the Quicken register.

If you want to use Quicken to write checks, the Write/Print Checks screen and option probably provide a more convenient format for collecting the information Quicken prints on the face of the check.

This chapter describes the basics of using Quicken's register, including the following:

- Understanding the Register screen
- Recording transactions in the register
- Reviewing and editing register transactions
- Printing the register

Chapter 5, "Making the Register Easier To Use," describes three additional sets of menu options—Edit, Shortcuts, and Activities—to make using the check register even easier. Chapter 12, "Tracking Your Net Worth, Other Assets, and Liabilities," describes how you can use the register to track assets besides cash and even to track liabilities like credit cards and bank loans. Chapter 13, "Monitoring Your Investments," describes a special set of tools that the newest version of Quicken provides for managing your investments.

Understanding the Register Screen

You select the **Register** option on Quicken's Main Menu to access the Register screen. You use the Register screen, shown in figure 4.1, to record most of the checking account transactions—manual checks, deposits, interest, bank fees, and so on—that affect your checking account.

The only transaction you do not usually record with the **Register** option is a check you record and print with the **Write/Print Checks** option (see Chapters 6 and 7). After collecting the information, Quicken records the transaction in the register and updates the account balance. The steps you take to record a transaction on the Register screen are described in the next section.

The Register screen can be broken down into three parts: the menu bar at the top of the screen, the actual check register, and the information bar at the bottom of the screen.

The menu bar shows the menus you can use on the Register screen to access commands: Print/Acct, Edit, Shortcuts, Reports, and Activities.

The second part of the Register screen is the actual check register you use to record account transactions. Take a minute to review the register—it probably resembles the register you now use to record checks manually. (The fields are described later in the chapter.)

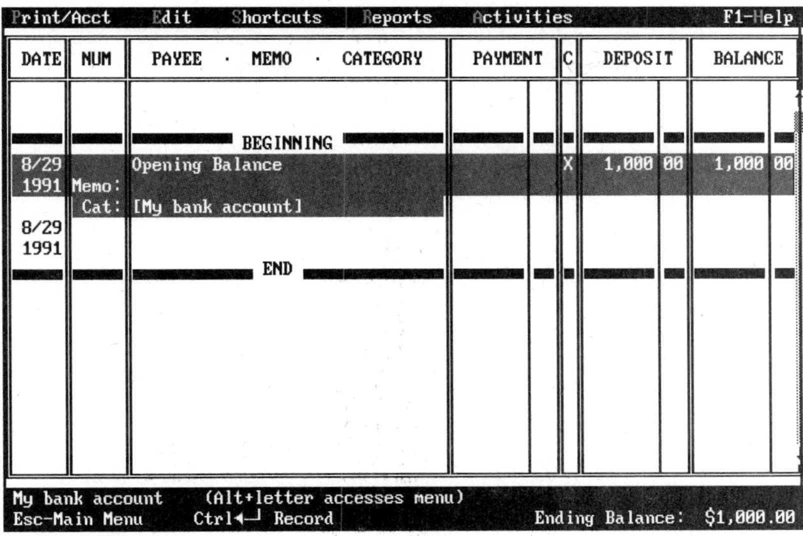

Fig. 4.1. The Register screen.

The third part of the Register screen is the information bar at the bottom. This bar shows the bank account name (checking), information on what the Esc and Enter keys do, and the balance in the account.

Before you start recording transactions in a register, you can use this information to make sure that you have selected the correct account and to gauge the effect of the transactions you want to record.

Recording a Check in the Register

Recording a check in the Quicken register closely parallels recording a check by hand in a paper checkbook register. The Register screen, however, makes the whole process easier. You can record any check in the register, including checks you want to print. Typically, however, you record checks you have written previously by hand directly into the register. You record checks you want to print using the Write/Print Checks screen and option, which are described in Chapter 6.

To record a check, take the following steps:

1. Select **Use Register** from Quicken's Main Menu if the register is not displayed already. Quicken displays the Register screen (see fig. 4.1). If you are working with more than one account, you may need to select the account first (see Chapter 3).

2. Enter the check date in the `Date` field. Enter the check date in the MM/DD/YY format.

   The first time you use Quicken, the program fills the `Date` field with the system date. After you record your first transaction by using the Register screen, Quicken fills the `Date` field with the last date you used. To edit the date, you have two choices. First, you can move to the month, day, or year you want to change and type over what already is showing on-screen. Second, you can use the special date entry keys, such as + and – keys, and the T, M, H, W, and R keys. (For more information on how these keys work, refer to Chapter 2.)

Businesses and individuals often receive discounts for paying bills early. Consider early payment in setting the check date. Not taking early payment discounts is an extremely expensive way to borrow money from the vendor. Suppose that a vendor normally requires payment within 30 days but allows a 2 percent discount for payments received within 10 days. If you pay within 30 rather than 10 days, you essentially pay the vendor a 2 percent interest charge for paying 20 days later. Because one year contains roughly 18 20-day periods, the 2 percent for 20 days equals approximately 36 percent annually.

Although you may need to "borrow" this money, you probably can find a much cheaper lender. As a rule of thumb, if a vendor gives you a 1 percent discount for paying 20 days early, you are borrowing the vendor's money at about an 18 percent annual interest rate if you do not pay early. A 3 percent discount works out to a whopping 54 percent a year.

3. Press Enter or Tab and Quicken moves the cursor to the `Num` field. Enter the number of the check in the `Num` field. You also can use the + and – keys to change the check number one number at a time. Checks you recorded on the Write/Print Checks screen but have not printed show asterisks as check numbers.

If you want to enter a check you later want to print, you can enter the check number as asterisks. The Write/Print Checks screen and option, however, provide a more convenient method of writing and printing checks. Refer to Chapter 6 for detailed information on Quicken's Write/Print Checks feature.

4. Press Enter or Tab to move the cursor to the `Payee` field. Enter the name of the person or business the check pays. You have space for up to 31 characters.

5. Press Enter or Tab to move the cursor to the `Payment` field. Enter the check amount, using up to 10 numbers for the amount. You can enter a check as large as $9,999,999.99. The decimal point counts as one of the 10 characters but the commas do not.

6. Press Enter or Tab to reach the cleared (`C`) field, which shows whether a transaction has been recorded by the bank. Use this field as part of reconciling, or explaining the difference between your check register account balance and the balance the bank shows on your monthly statement. To mark a transaction as cleared, enter an asterisk (*), the only character Quicken accepts here, in the `C` field. During reconciliation, Quicken changes the asterisk to an X (see Chapter 8).

7. (Optional) Press Enter or Tab twice to move the cursor through the `Deposit` field and to the `Memo` field. Use the `Memo` field to describe the reasons for a transaction. You can use up to 31 characters to describe a transaction. If you are making several payments a month to the bank, the `Memo` field enables you to specify the house payment, the school loan, the hot tub, the boat, and so on.

8. (Optional) Press Enter or Tab to move the cursor to the `Category` field. You use the `Category` field to describe the category into which a transaction falls, such as utilities expense, interest expense, or entertainment. Use Ctrl-C to access the existing categories provided by Quicken or those you have added previously (see fig. 4.2). Now, use the arrow keys to mark the category into which the check falls and press Enter or double-click the mouse on the category.

   You also can use the `Category` field to describe the class into which a transaction falls. (Categories and classes are described in Chapter 10.) Figure 4.3 shows a check to the Seattle Power Company. The category is Utilities.

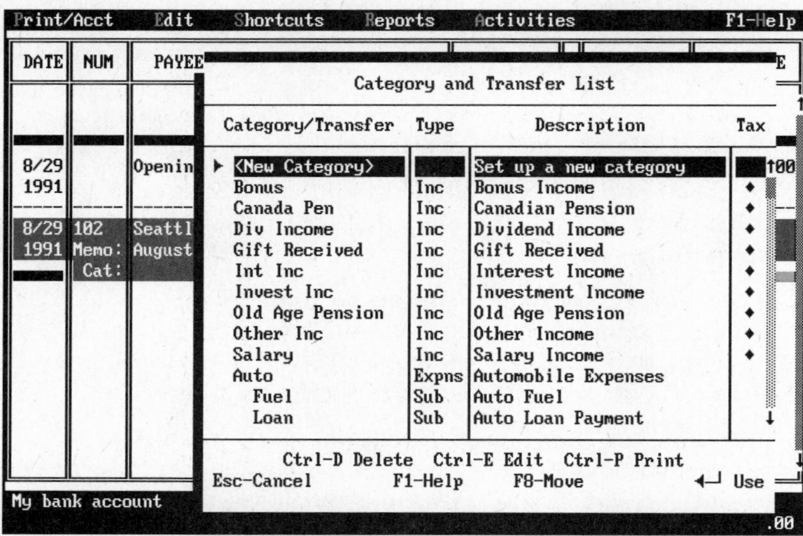

Fig. 4.2. Press Ctrl-C to see a list of defined categories.

```
Print/Acct   Edit   Shortcuts   Reports   Activities                F1-Help
DATE  NUM   PAYEE · MEMO · CATEGORY    PAYMENT  C  DEPOSIT    BALANCE

                  BEGINNING
8/29        Opening Balance                     X  1,000 00   1,000 00
1991                  [My bank accou→
8/29  102   Seattle Power Company       75 39
1991  Memo: August
       Cat: Utilities

My bank account    (Alt+letter accesses menu)
Esc-Main Menu      Ctrl←┘ Record              Ending Balance:  $1,000.00
```

Fig. 4.3. A sample check entered in the register.

TIP

Quicken provides a feature known as auto-completion, which you can use when you know a few of the category names. If you type enough of a category name to uniquely identify that name and press Enter, Quicken types the rest of the category name for you.

Suppose that you have a category named Utilities and it is the only category name that starts with the letter U. If you enter U in the `Category` field and press Enter, Quicken types the remaining letters of the word—tilities. The only trick to the auto-completion feature is that you need to type enough of the category name to uniquely identify it. You also can use the auto-completion feature to enter the account number for a field.

9. Record the transaction by pressing Enter when the cursor is on the last field, `Category`, or record the transaction while the cursor is on any screen field by pressing Ctrl-Enter or F10 or by clicking on the words Ctrl-Enter at the bottom of the screen, in the information bar. The transaction is recorded.

If you press Enter when the cursor is on the last field—`Category`—Quicken displays a prompt that asks you to confirm that you want to record the transaction. If you select `Record Transaction`, the transaction is recorded.

When you record a transaction, a flashing message in the lower left-hand corner of the screen says `RECORDING`. (If your computer is very fast, you can hardly read the message.) When Quicken finishes recording the transaction, your computer beeps and an empty row is added to the bottom of the register, with the cursor positioned at the empty `Date` field. Because Quicken arranges checking account transactions by date, it rearranges transactions if you enter them in an order other than the order of their dates.

Quicken also calculates the new `Balance` field when you record a transaction (see fig. 4.4). If the balance is too large for a positive or negative number to display, Quicken displays asterisks in the `Balance` field. Quicken uses negative numbers to indicate you have overdrawn your account. If you have a color monitor, Quicken displays negative amounts in a different color.

```
Print/Acct   Edit   Shortcuts   Reports   Activities                    F1-Help

DATE  NUM   PAYEE  ·  MEMO  ·  CATEGORY    PAYMENT   C   DEPOSIT    BALANCE

                      BEGINNING
8/29        Opening Balance                          X   1,000 00   1,000 00
1991                      [My bank accou→
8/29  102   Seattle Power Company           75 39                     924 61
1991        August          Utilities
8/29
1991  Memo:
      Cat:

My bank account     (Alt+letter accesses menu)
Esc-Main Menu     Ctrl◄┘ Record                  Ending Balance:  $924.61
```

***Fig. 4.4.** The register showing the new balance after a check is recorded.*

Recording a Deposit in the Register

As you might expect, recording a deposit in the Quicken register is like recording a deposit in your checkbook's paper register.(You should not have to record the starting balance with a deposit transaction because it should have been recorded when you initially described the account.)

To record a deposit or starting balance, follow these steps:

1. Select **Use Register** from Quicken's Main Menu if the register is not displayed already. Quicken displays the Register screen. If you are working with more than one account, you may need to select the account first (see Chapter 3).

2. Enter the deposit date in the `Date` field in MM/DD/YY format. Remember that you can use the + and – keys to change the date one day at a time.

3. (Optional) Press Enter or Tab to move cursor to the `Num` field. Enter the receipt number of the deposit in the `Num` field. Remember that

you also can use the + and – keys to change the Num one number at a time.

4. Press Enter or Tab to move the cursor to the Payee field. Enter a description of the deposit transaction. You have space for up to 31 characters. For example, a business recording a deposit from a customer might describe the deposit by using the customer name, such as Acme Manufacturing. A home user recording a payroll deposit might describe the deposit as payroll check. Interest might be described as October interest income.

5. Press Enter or Tab three times to move the cursor through the Payment and C fields to the Deposit field. As with the Payment field, Quicken enables you to enter only numbers, with amounts under $9,999,999.99.

6. (Optional) Press Enter or Tab to move the cursor to the Memo field. Use the Memo field to describe the reasons for a transaction. You can use up to 31 characters to describe a transaction. A business, for example, may note the invoice a customer's deposit paid. A home user may indicate the payroll period covered by a payroll check.

7. (Optional) Press Enter or Tab to move the cursor to the Category field for describing the deposit's category, such as gross sales, wages, or interest income. Use Ctrl-C to access the existing categories provided by Quicken or those you have previously added. Use the arrow keys to mark the category into which the check falls, and then press Enter.

   You also can use the Category field to describe the income category into which a transaction falls. (Categories and classes are described further in Chapter 10.) Figure 4.5 shows a deposit for recording interest income.

8. Record the transaction by pressing Enter when the cursor is on the last field, Category, or record the transaction while the cursor is in any field by pressing Ctrl-Enter or F10 or by clicking with the mouse on the words Ctrl-Enter at the bottom of the screen in the information bar.

If you press Enter when the cursor is on the last field—Category—Quicken displays a prompt on-screen that asks you to confirm that you want to record the transaction. If you select Record Transaction, the transaction is recorded.

```
Print/Acct   Edit   Shortcuts   Reports   Activities                F1-Help
DATE  NUM   PAYEE · MEMO · CATEGORY       PAYMENT  C  DEPOSIT     BALANCE
                   BEGINNING
8/29        Opening Balance                       X  1,000 00    1,000 00
1991                      [My bank accou→
8/29  102   Seattle Power Company           75 39                  924 61
1991        August          Utilities
8/29        Big National Bank                          5 75        930 36
1991  Memo: August interest income
      Cat:  Int Inc
8/31
1991
                   END
My bank account    (Alt+letter accesses menu)
Esc-Main Menu      Ctrl←┘ Record                 Ending Balance:  $930.36
```

Fig. 4.5. A sample deposit recorded in the register.

Recording Other Withdrawals

The steps for recording other withdrawals—such as automated teller machine transactions, wire transfers, and automatic payments—parallel the steps for recording a check. You enter the date, number, payee, the payment amount, and, optionally, a memo description and a category. Record the withdrawal by pressing Enter when the cursor is in the `Category` field, by pressing Ctrl-Enter or F10 when the cursor is in any other field, or by clicking on Ctrl-Enter at the bottom of the screen in the information bar.

Consider the monthly service fees a bank charges when choosing a bank and in keeping minimum balances. Most banks charge monthly service fees of about $5. Some banks waive the $5 fee if you keep a balance of $200 at all times in your account. The $5 a month translates into $60 a year. Because $60 in fee savings equals $60 in interest, the interest rate the bank pays people who keep their minimum balance at $200 is $60/$200 or 30 percent. The return is even better than that for most people because the interest income gets taxed, but the fee savings do not. Probably no other $200 investment in the world is risk-free and pays 30 percent interest.

Recording Transfers between Accounts

You can use the Category field to record transfers from one account to another. Suppose, for example, that you are recording a check drawn on your checking account for deposit to your credit union account with the Acme Credit Union. The check is not an expense, so it should not be categorized as utilities, medical, insurance, or something else. It is a transfer of funds from one account to another. You can identify such transfers by entering the account name in brackets, as shown in figure 4.6.

```
Print/Acct   Edit   Shortcuts   Reports   Activities                 F1-Help

DATE | NUM  | PAYEE  ·  MEMO  ·  CATEGORY | PAYMENT |C| DEPOSIT | BALANCE

                      BEGINNING
8/29 |      |Opening Balance              |         |X| 1,000 00| 1,000 00
1991 |      |             [My bank accou→ |         | |         |
8/29 |102   |Seattle Power Company        |   75 39 | |         |   924 61
1991 |      |August         Utilities     |         | |         |
8/29 |      |Big National Bank            |         | |     5 75|   930 36
1991 |      |August interest→Int Inc      |         | |         |
8/29 |      |Deposit to savings           |  250 00 | |         |   680 36
1991 |Memo: |                             |         | |         |
     | Cat: |[Acme]                       |         | |         |
8/29 |      |                             |         | |         |
1991 |      |                             |         | |         |
                         END

My bank account      (Alt+letter accesses menu)
Esc-Main Menu     Ctrl◄┘ Record                 Ending Balance:  $680.36
```

Fig. 4.6. *The Category field completed to record a transfer between accounts.*

Be sure that the account has been set up first before you try to transfer to or from the account. Quicken enables you to add categories, but not accounts, during the use of the register.

When you press Ctrl-C, Quicken not only lists categories, but also accounts. Accordingly, you also can use the Ctrl-C technique to see accounts for transfers. The accounts are located at the end of the category list and you can access them more quickly by pressing the End key to reach the end of the list. When you have located the proper account, press Enter and Quicken inserts the account name in the Description field in the register.

If you record a transfer, Quicken records the transfer in the registers for both accounts. In the transaction shown in figure 4.6, a payment of $250 is recorded for the checking account and, at the same time, a deposit of $250 is recorded for the credit union savings account. Figure 4.7 shows the register for the credit union savings account with the $250 deposit. You can toggle between the two registers by pressing Ctrl-X.

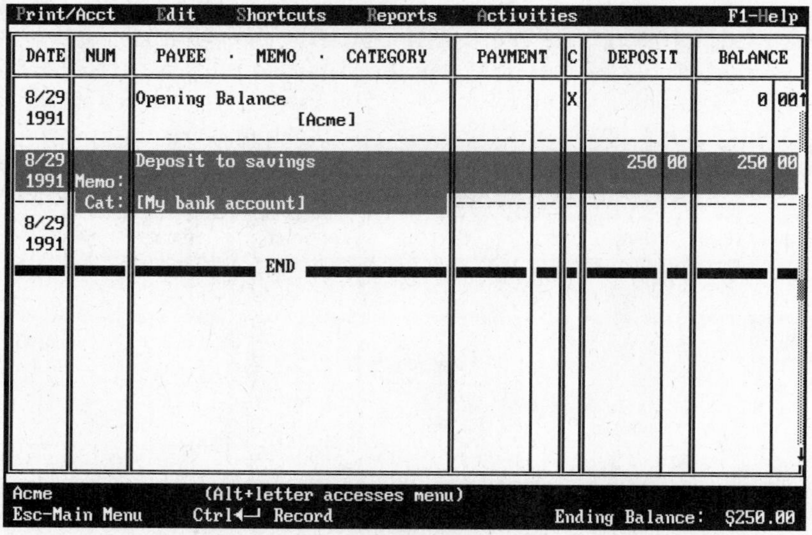

```
Print/Acct   Edit   Shortcuts   Reports   Activities                F1-Help
DATE  NUM   PAYEE  ·  MEMO  ·  CATEGORY   PAYMENT  C  DEPOSIT   BALANCE
8/29        Opening Balance                        X                0 00
1991                       [Acme]
8/29        Deposit to savings                        250 00     250 00
1991 Memo:
      Cat: [My bank account]
8/29
1991                   END
Acme              (Alt+letter accesses menu)
Esc-Main Menu     Ctrl←┘ Record                 Ending Balance:  $250.00
```

Fig. 4.7. The other part of the transfer transaction.

Reviewing and Editing Register Transactions

You can review and edit transactions by using the Use Register option from the Main Menu at any time. You may want to review a transaction to make sure that you recorded the transaction correctly. You also may want to review a transaction to see whether you received a deposit and to see whether you remembered to pay a particular bill.

You can move from transaction to transaction in the register screen in two ways—you can use the navigation keys, or you can use the mouse. To use the keyboard, you use the following keys:

Up- and down-arrow keys	*Move from row to row*
PgUp	*Move up a page*
PgDn	*Move down a page*
Home	*Move to first transaction in register*
End	*Move to last transaction in register*

To use the mouse to see other register transactions, you use the scroll bar. The scroll bar is the vertical bar along the right edge of the register with arrows at both ends. Using the scroll bar gives you three additional ways to move the viewed portion of the register. To move to the previous page of register transactions, for example, you can click on the up arrow at the top of the scroll bar. To move the next page of register transactions, you can click on the down arrow at the bottom of the scroll bar.

You can move the viewed portion of the register by dragging the scroll bar marker. The scroll bar marker is the dark square on the scroll bar that shows you approximately which portion of the register is currently displayed. To drag the scroll bar marker, click the marker, continue holding down the mouse button, and drag the scroll bar marker up or down. You also can move to the previous or next page of register transactions by clicking the scroll bar. Click the scroll bar above the scroll bar marker to see the previous page of transactions. Click the scroll bar below the marker to see the following page of transactions.

To edit a transaction, move to the transaction you want to change, edit the fields that you want to change, and rerecord the transaction by pressing Ctrl-Enter or F10, by pressing Enter while the cursor is on the `Category` field, or by clicking on Ctrl-Enter at the bottom of the screen in the informational bar.

Using Postdated Transactions

Postdated transactions are checks and deposits dated in the future. Traditionally, people use postdated checks as a way to delay a payment. The payee cannot or should not cash the check before the future date. With Quicken, you can use postdated transactions to delay checks being cashed. Perhaps more importantly, you can forecast your cash flows and balances by entering those checks and deposits that you know are in the future.

The steps for entering postdated transactions mirror those for entering regular transactions. The only difference, of course, is that the check or deposit date is in the future. When you enter postdated transactions, Quicken calculates two account balances: the current balance, which is the account balance for the current date, and the ending balance, which is the account balance after the last postdated transaction. Quicken determines the current date by looking at the system date.

Figure 4.8 shows the Big National register with a postdated transaction. The ending balance, $180.36, incorporates all the transactions for the account, including postdated transactions. The current balance, $680.36, is the account balance at the current date.

Quicken also identifies postdated transactions by drawing a double-dashed line between the regular and the postdated transactions. In figure 4.8, for example, see the double-dashed line between the last two transactions shown on-screen.

Print/Acct Edit Shortcuts Reports Activities F1-Help

DATE	NUM	PAYEE · MEMO · CATEGORY	PAYMENT	C	DEPOSIT	BALANCE
		BEGINNING				
8/29 1991		Opening Balance [My bank accou→		X	1,000 00	1,000 00
8/29 1991	102	Seattle Power Company August Utilities	75 39			924 61
8/29 1991		Big National Bank August interest→Int Inc			5 75	930 36
8/29 1991		Deposit to savings [Acme]	250 00			680 36
8/31 1991	103 Memo: Cat:	Puget Sound Mortgage September payment Housing	500 00			180 36

My bank account (Alt+letter accesses menu) Current Balance: $680.36
Esc-Main Menu Ctrl↵ Record Ending Balance: $180.36

Fig. 4.8. The register showing a postdated transaction, the current balance, and the ending balance.

Printing a Register

You will want to print a paper register each time you enter a group of check and deposit transactions. A printed copy of the register enables you to review checking account transactions without turning on your computer. It also can provide a way to recover your financial records if no backup files exist. (Chapter 9 describes the steps for backing up your Quicken data files.)

The Print/Acct menu, which you use to print the register, has six options (see fig. 4.9). This chapter discusses only the second option: **Print Register**. The **Select/Set Up Account** option is the same as the Main Menu option **Select Account**, described in Chapter 3. **Change Printer Styles** is the same as the **Printer Settings** option on the Set Preferences menu, described in Chapter 1. **Back Up File**, **Export**, and **Import** are described in Chapter 9.

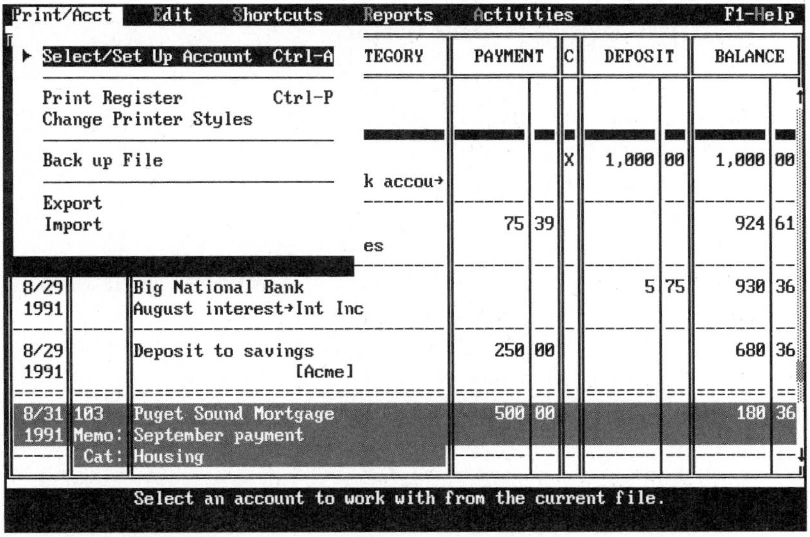

Fig. 4.9. *The Print/Acct menu.*

To print a register, take the following steps:

1. Select the Print/Acct menu by pressing Alt-P. Next, select the **Print Register** option (see fig. 4.9) or press Ctrl-P. Quicken displays the Print Register screen (see fig. 4.10).

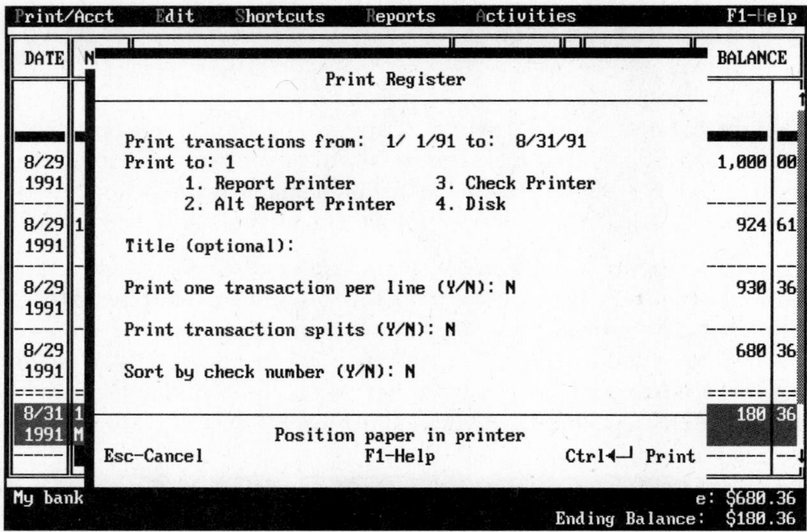

Fig. 4.10. *The Print Register screen.*

2. Verify that your printer is set to use regular paper—and not check forms.

3. Enter the date of the first check or deposit transaction you want printed on the register. If you are printing only the transactions for the day's batch of transactions, enter the `Print transactions from` date as the current date. If you are printing a copy of the month's transactions, enter the `Print transactions from` date as the first day of the month. (Remember that the + and – keys change the date one day at a time, that the T letter key sets the date to the current system date, and that the M and H letter keys set the date to the first day and last day of the month.)

4. Press Enter or Tab to move the cursor to the `to` date field. Enter the date of the last check or deposit transaction. If you are printing only the transactions for the day's batch of transactions, enter the `to` date as the current date. If you are printing a copy of the month's transactions, enter the `to` date as the last day of the month.

5. Press Enter or Tab to move the cursor to the `Print to` field. Use the `Print to` field to specify which printer will print the register. Quicken lists up to three printers you might have defined as part of the installation process, and it lists a fourth option, `Disk`. To specify the `Print to` setting, type the number that corresponds to the printer you want to use.

6. (Optional) Press Tab or Enter to move the cursor to the `Title` field. Enter a special title or description you want Quicken to print on the top of each page of the register. You might, for example, enter *August Check Register* for August's register.

7. (Optional) Press Enter or Tab to move the cursor to the `Print one transaction per line` field. Press Y if you want Quicken to print the register in a compact form using only one line per transaction and using abbreviations for many of the fields.

8. (Optional) Press Enter or Tab to move the cursor to the `Print transaction splits` field. If you split transactions—you used more than one category for the transaction—you can cause Quicken to print each of those categories by pressing Y in this field (see Chapter 5.)

9. (Optional) Press Enter or Tab to move the cursor to the `Sort by check number` field. Usually, Quicken arranges the check and deposit transactions by date. You can, however, press Y to arrange transactions by the check numbers. If a check deposit does not have a number or has the same number as another transaction, Quicken uses the date as a secondary sorting tool.

10. (Optional) If you select 4 at the `Print to` field, you can create an ASCII file on disk. Quicken displays the Print To Disk box, which collects the file name you want to use for the ASCII file, the number of lines per page, and the page width. Enter the name you want Quicken to use for the ASCII file in the File field. If you want to use a data directory different from the Quicken data directory, QUICKEN5, you also can specify a path name. (See your DOS user's manual for information on path names.) Set the number of register lines Quicken prints between page breaks in the `Lines per page` field. If you are using 11-inch paper, the page length is usually 66 lines. Set the number of characters, including blanks, that Quicken prints on a line in the `Width` field. If you are using 8 1/2-inch paper, the characters per line figure usually is 80. Figure 4.11 shows a completed Print To Disk box.

11. When the Print Register screen is complete and you are ready to print, press Ctrl-Enter.

Quicken generates a copy of the register like that shown in figure 4.12 or figure 4.13. Figure 4.12 shows the register when the `Print one transaction per line` field is set to the N default. Figure 4.13 shows the same register when the field is set to Y.

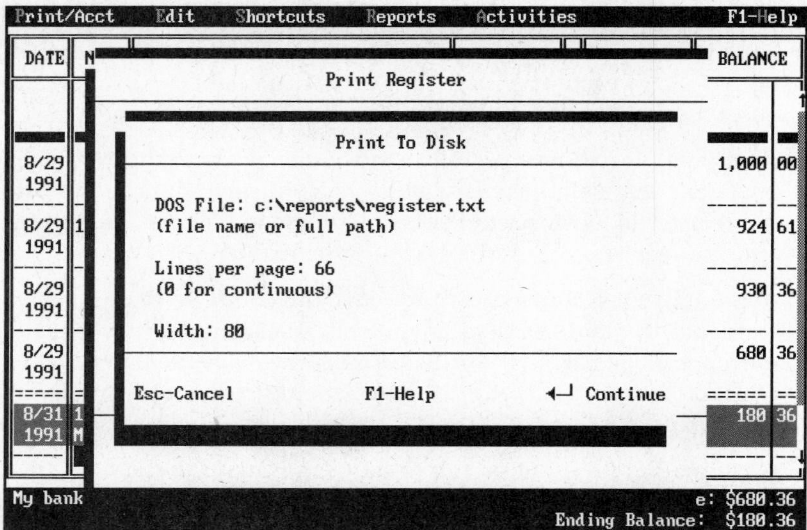

Fig. 4.11. The Print To Disk box.

```
                                  Check Register
My bank account                                                            Page 1
8/29/91

           Date  Num           Transaction            Payment  C  Deposit   Balance
           ----- ----- ------------------------------ --------- - --------- ---------

           8/29        Opening Balance                          X  1,000.00  1,000.00
           1991 memo:
                 cat: [My bank account]

           8/29 102    Seattle Power Company              75.39                 924.61
           1991 memo: August
                 cat: Utilities

           8/29        Big National Bank                              5.75      930.36
           1991 memo: August interest income
                 cat: Int Inc

           8/29        Deposit to savings                250.00                 680.36
           1991 memo:
                 cat: [Acme]

           8/31 103    Puget Sound Mortgage              500.00                 180.36
           1991 memo: September payment
                 cat: Housing
```

Fig. 4.12. The register with transactions printed on several lines.

Check Register

My bank account Page 1
8/29/91

Date	Num	Payee	Memo	Category	Amount	C	Balance
8/29/91		Opening Balance		[My bank account]	1,000.00	X	1,000.00
8/29/91	102	Seattle Power Company	August	Utilities	-75.39		924.61
8/29/91		Big National Bank	August interest income	Int Inc	5.75		930.36
8/29/91		Deposit to savings		[Acme]	-250.00		680.36
8/31/91	103	Puget Sound Mortgage	September payment	Housing	-500.00		180.36

***Fig. 4.13.** The register with one transaction printed on each line.*

At the end of each month, print a copy of the register for the transactions you entered in that month. Store the register with the bank statement for the month. That way, if you ever have questions about a previous month—or the bad luck to lose your Quicken data file—you can reconstruct transactions from previous months. You can discard the now redundant individual registers that show each of the groups of transactions for the month. You don't need these with a copy of the entire month.

Chapter Summary

This chapter introduced you to Quicken's register—the central repository of all your checking account information. The basics include knowing the components of the check register screen; using the register to record checks, deposits, and other checking account transactions; reviewing and editing register transactions; and printing the register.

The next chapter describes three additional sets of tools to facilitate your use of the register: the Edit menu, the Shortcuts menu, and the Activities menu.

5

Making the Register Easier To Use

Chapter 5 can make working with registers more efficient by describing sets of options on the Edit, Shortcuts, and Activities menus. Among other functions, these menus can help you search through your register for specific transactions or save and reuse information you record repeatedly in your check register. The Edit menu provides options that make it easier for you to add, modify, and remove transactions. The Shortcuts menu offers features that speed up the process of recording transactions. The Activities menu options, although not directly related to the register, make working with the Quicken program easier.

Using the Edit Menu Tools

The Edit menu, shown in figure 5.1, provides you with 10 options. As noted earlier, the Edit menu essentially provides features that make it easier for you to record transactions in the register. The actions that many of the menu options produce probably are already well known to you by now; for that reason, many of the following descriptions are brief.

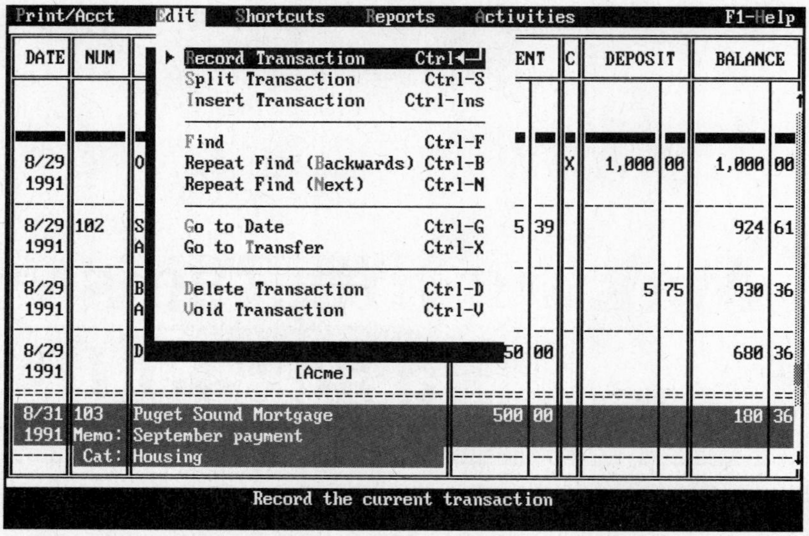

Fig. 5.1. The Edit menu.

Recording, Inserting, Deleting, and Voiding Transactions

The Edit menu lists four basic options: **Record Transaction**, **Insert Transaction**, **Delete Transaction**, and **Void Transaction**. None of these four options is difficult to use, so you will not need a step-by-step discussion. Rather, each can be described in a few sentences.

- **Record Transaction** (Ctrl-Enter) is the same as pressing Ctrl-Enter or F10. Selecting **Record Transaction** from the Edit menu records the transaction in the register and your disk.

- **Insert Transaction** (Ctrl-Ins) inserts an empty row above the currently highlighted transaction. You can use this empty row to record another transaction. Usually, transactions are recorded in the empty row at the end of the register.

- **Delete Transaction** (Ctrl-D) removes the selected transaction from the register and your disk. You also can use **Delete Transaction** to erase the Register screen's fields if you have not yet recorded the transaction. After you select **Delete Transaction**, Quicken asks you to confirm the deletion by displaying the message shown in figure 5.2. To delete the transaction, select the first option. If you change your mind, select the second option or press Esc.

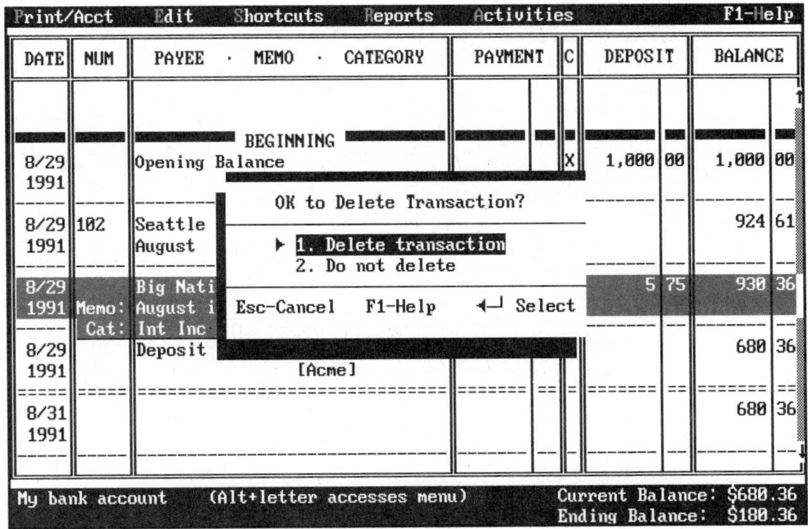

Fig. 5.2. The `OK to Delete Transaction` *message.*

- **Void Transaction** (Ctrl-V) is the fourth option on the Edit menu. After you select **Void Transaction**, Quicken asks you to confirm the voiding of the transaction by displaying the message shown in figure 5.3. To void the transaction, select the first option. If you select **Void Transaction**, Quicken inserts the word `VOID` before the payee name, changes the payment or deposit amounts to zero, and sets the cleared flag to `X` to indicate that the transaction isn't outstanding. Figure 5.4 shows the now voided check to Puget Sound Mortgage.

If you void a previously recorded transaction, Quicken doesn't update the balance until you record the voided transaction.

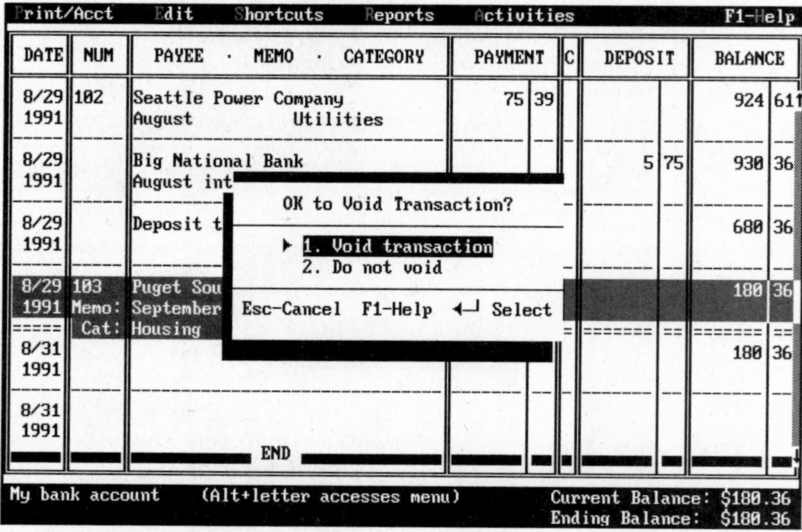

Fig. 5.3. The `OK to Void Transaction` *message.*

```
Print/Acct   Edit   Shortcuts   Reports   Activities                F1-Help
DATE | NUM   | PAYEE · MEMO · CATEGORY     | PAYMENT |C| DEPOSIT | BALANCE
8/29 | 102   | Seattle Power Company       |  75 39  | |         |  924 61
1991 |       | August       Utilities      |         | |         |
8/29 |       | Big National Bank           |         | |   5 75  |  930 36
1991 |       | August interest→Int Inc     |         | |         |
8/29 |       | Deposit to savings          | 250 00  | |         |  680 36
1991 |       |             [Acme]          |         | |         |
8/29 | 103   | VOID:Puget Sound Mortgage   |         |X|         |  180 36
1991 | Memo: | September payment           |         | |         |
     | Cat:  | Housing                     |         | |         |
8/31 |       |                             |         | |         |  180 36
1991 |       |                             |         | |         |
8/31 |       |                             |         | |         |
1991 |       |                             |         | |         |
                              END
My bank account    (Alt+letter accesses menu)    Current Balance: $180.36
Esc-Main Menu      Ctrl← Record                  Ending Balance:  $180.36
```

Fig. 5.4. A void check.

If you void a transaction that is part of a transfer from one account to another, voiding any part of the transaction also voids the other parts of the transaction—those recorded in the other registers.

Void Transaction enables you to keep track of voided transactions in your check register alongside actual transactions. You should keep an audit trail, or record, of voided and stop-payment checks. Use **Void Transaction** to perform this sort of record keeping. Chapter 19 treats audit trails.

Splitting Transactions

The regular register screen provides one field for recording the category into which a check fits. A check written to the power company, for example, might belong in the "Utilities" category and a payroll deposit might be "Wages." But some transactions fit in more than one category. A check written to the bank to pay a mortgage payment, for example, might actually pay principal, interest, insurance, and property taxes. So occasionally, you need to be able to break down a transaction into multiple categories. Selecting **Split Transaction** (Ctrl-S) from the Edit menu provides additional `Category` fields so that you can use more than one category for a transaction or further describe a transaction. To split a transaction, follow these steps:

1. Press Alt-E to display the Edit menu and select **Split Transaction**, or press Ctrl-S. Selecting this option accesses the Split Transaction screen, shown in figure 5.5.

2. Enter the category name in the `Category` field. The `Category` field on the Split Transaction screen is used like the `Category` field on the Register screen. You also can use the field to record transfers. Thirty lines are available on the Split Transaction screen for descriptions or for categories.

Remember that Quicken provides defined home and business categories. The home category list has descriptions for most general household expenses, and the business category list has general business income and expense categories. Press Ctrl-C to view and select from a list of the defined categories.

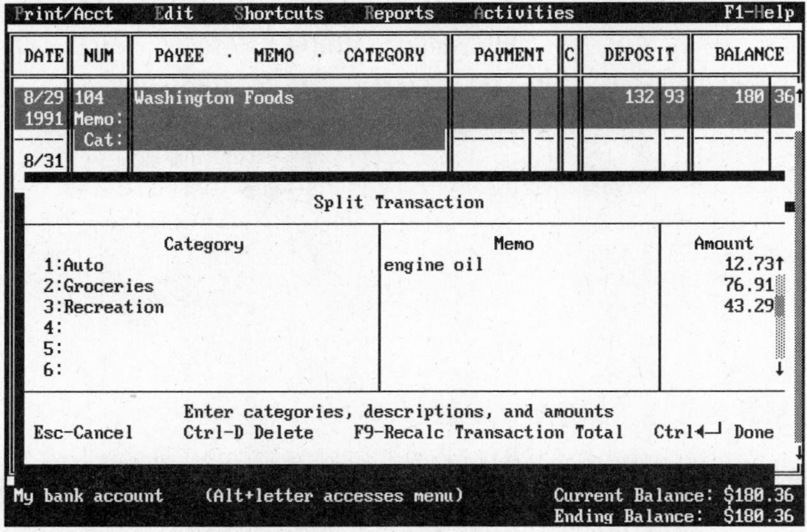

Fig. 5.5. *The Split Transaction screen.*

3. (Optional) Press Enter or Tab to move the cursor to the `Description` field. Type a description of the category or the amount. The `Description` field provides a 27-character space for further description of a transaction or an explanation of your category choice.

4. Press Enter or Tab to move the cursor to the `Amount` field. You use the `Amount` field in two ways, depending on whether you select **Split Transaction** before or after you enter the payment or deposit amount on the Register screen.

   If you select **Split Transaction** before you enter a figure in the `Amount` field, Quicken adds each of the amounts you enter in the `Amount` fields on the Split Transaction screen. Quicken then takes the total of these amounts and puts that total in the `Payment` or the `Deposit` field on the Register screen. If the total of the split transaction amounts is negative, Quicken places the amount in the `Payment` field; if the total is positive, Quicken places the amount in the `Deposit` field.

   If you select **Split Transaction** after you enter the payment or deposit amount on the Register screen, Quicken pulls the amount entered onto the Split Transaction screen into the first `Amount` field. When you enter the register amount as a payment, Quicken pulls the amount onto the Split Transaction screen as a negative number; when you enter the amount as a deposit, Quicken pulls the amount onto the screen as a positive number. If you then enter a number in the first `Amount` field on the Split Transaction screen, Quicken calculates the difference between the Register screen amount and the amount you have entered and places this difference in the second `Amount` field on the Split Transaction screen.

Usually, you want to enter dollar amounts in the Split Transaction screen's `Amount` fields. You also can enter percentages. Quicken then uses these percentages to calculate the Split amount. (If you enter a check for $150 and 30 percent of this should be entered in the first `Split Transaction Amount` field, you can just enter 30% in the field. When you press Tab or Enter to move to the next field, Quicken calculates the number that equals 30 percent of $150 and enters this value in the field.)

5. Press Enter or Tab to move to the next line of the Split Transaction screen. Repeat steps 2, 3, and 4 for each category and amount combination you want to record. You can record up to 30 category and amount combinations.

   If you use all 30 of the `Split Transaction Amount` fields, the sum of the split transaction amounts may not equal the register amount. In this case, you must adjust manually the Register screen amount or one of the Split Transaction screen amounts. You also can press F9 to total the `Amount` fields on the Split Transaction screen and to insert that total into the `Amount` field on the Register screen.

6. Press Ctrl-Enter or F10 to leave the Split Transaction screen and return to the register.

7. After making your changes on the Split Transaction screen, press Ctrl-Enter or F10 to record the transaction. Quicken indicates a transaction is split by displaying the word `SPLIT` below the transaction number (see fig. 5.6).

   If you split transactions, you may want to see the extra category names, descriptions, and amounts on the printed version of the register. When you select **Print Register** from the Acct/Print menu, the Print Register field includes a Print Split Transactions setting switch. Use this switch to tell Quicken whether you want the additional categories and amounts of a split transaction printed on the register. (See Chapter 4, "Using the Register," for more information on printing the register.)

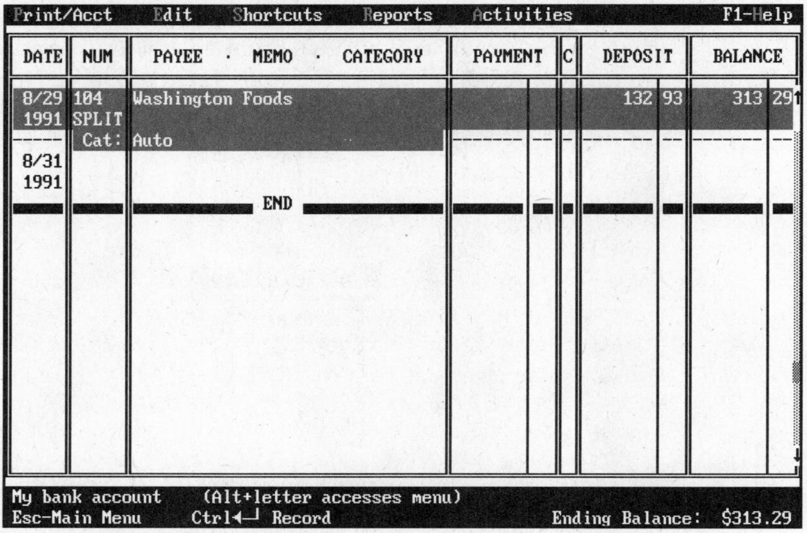

Fig. 5.6. Quicken identifies split transactions with the word SPLIT *under the Num field.*

Locating Transactions

You may write only a handful of checks and make only one or two deposits in a month. Even with such low volumes, however, you will soon have several dozen transactions in a register. As you write more checks and make additional deposits, searching through your register for specific transactions becomes more and more difficult. You may eventually want to know whether you recorded a deposit or paid a bill, or when you last paid a vendor. Quicken provides three Edit menu options for locating specific transactions: **Find**, **Repeat Find** (backwards), and **Repeat Find** (next).

You can search through the register for transactions using any of the fields you store for transactions. For example, you can look for transactions where the payee is "Stouffer's Office Supplies," where the category is "utilities," or where the amount is "$54.91."

Using the Find Option

To search through the transactions you recorded in the register, follow these steps:

1. Press Alt-E to display the Edit menu, and then select the **Find** option or press Ctrl-F. Quicken displays the Transaction to Find screen shown in figure 5.7.

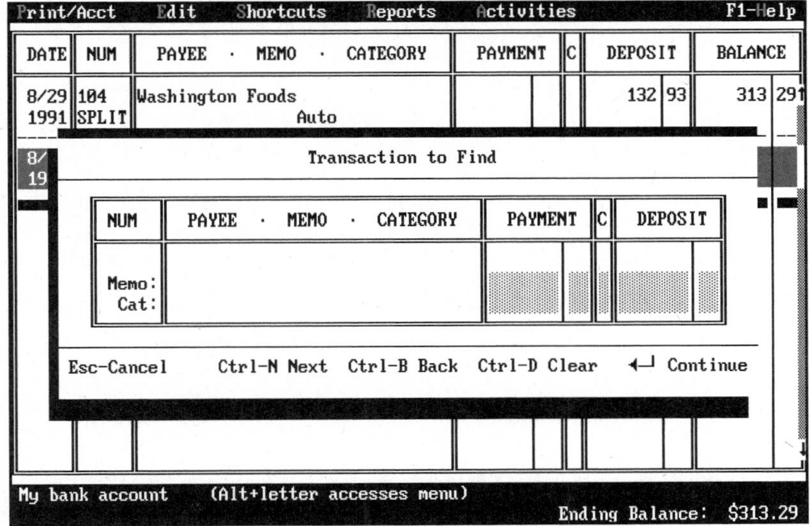

Fig. 5.7. *The Transaction to Find screen.*

2. (Optional) To search through the register for checks or deposits with a specific entry in the `Num` field, enter what the transaction you want to find shows in its `Num` field.

3. (Optional) To search through the register for checks or deposits with a specific entry in the `Payee` field, enter the appropriate entry in the `Transaction to Find Payee` field.

4. (Optional) To search through the register for a transaction equal to a specific amount, enter the amount in either the `Payment` or the `Deposit` field. The amount you look for is called a *search argument*.

If you enter an amount in the Payment field on the Transaction to Find screen, Quicken searches through the checks in the register for that amount. If you enter an amount in the Deposit field, Quicken searches for that amount among the deposits in the register. If Quicken finds a transaction that matches your search argument, the transaction is highlighted on the Register screen.

5. (Optional) To search through the register for checks or deposits with a specific entry in the C field, enter what the transaction you want to find shows in its C field (X or *). You may want to perform this search to find cleared or outstanding transactions.
6. (Optional) To search through the register for checks or deposits with a specific entry in the Memo field, enter what the transaction you want to find shows in its Memo field.
7. (Optional) To search through the register for checks or deposits with a specific entry in the Category field, enter the information the desired transaction shows in this transaction's Category field.
8. When you finish entering the search argument or arguments, press Ctrl-Enter or F10, or press Enter when the cursor is on the Category field.

   Quicken asks which direction you want to search by displaying the screen shown in figure 5.8. **Find backwards** (Ctrl-B) looks through transactions with dates earlier than the transaction currently selected on the Register screen. **Find next** (Ctrl-N) looks through transactions with dates later than the date of the transaction currently selected on the Register screen.
9. Select **Find backwards** or **Find next**.

Quicken searches for an exact match to what you type. If you enter an asterisk in the C field, for example, Quicken searches for those transactions that you marked as cleared with an asterisk. If you enter *Walt Lumens* in the Payee field, Quicken searches for transactions with the Payee description field exactly equal to Walt Lumens. Quicken does not recognize case; WALT LUMENS, walt lumens, and wALT lUMENS are all exact matches from Quicken's perspective. If the Payee field is Walter Lumens, W. Lumens, or Mr. Walt Lumens, however, Quicken does not find the transaction.

If Quicken does not find a transaction that matches your search argument, the program displays the message No matching transactions were found, as shown in figure 5.9.

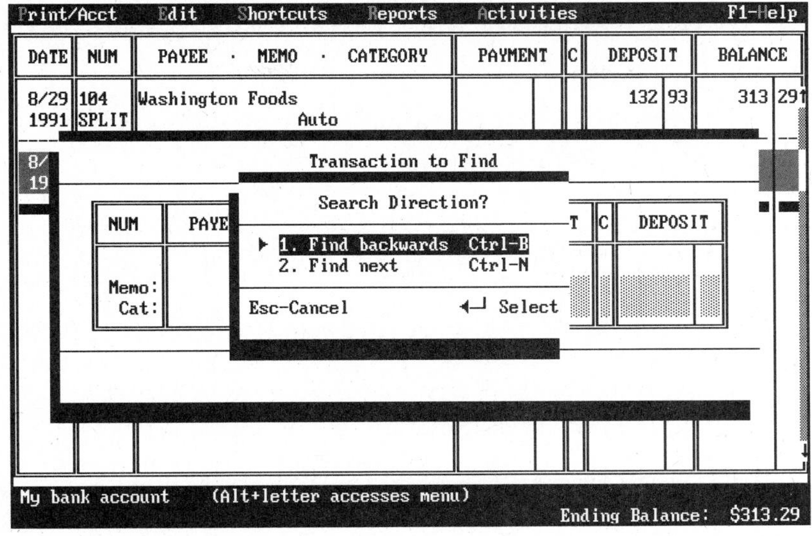

Fig. 5.8. The Search Direction screen.

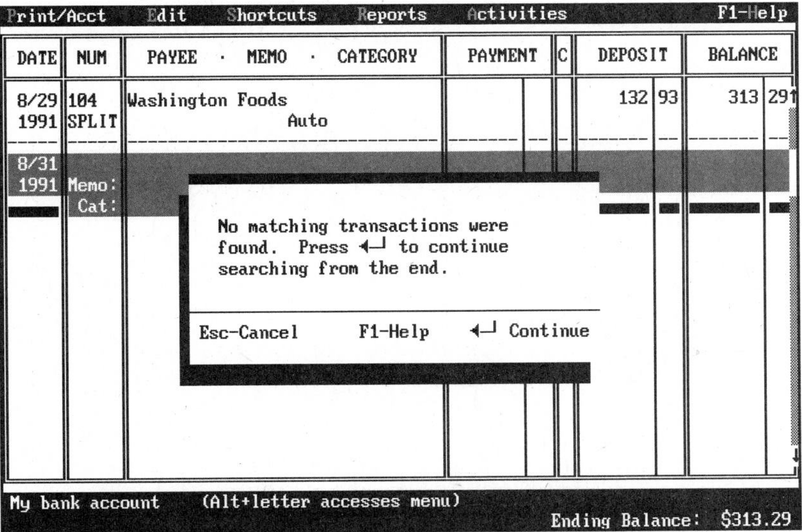

Fig. 5.9. The No matching transactions were found *message.*

Using Key-Word Matches

Key-word matches enable you to search a field that includes or excludes certain letters, characters, or series of characters. Key-word matches use three characters: the period (.), question mark (?), and tilde (~). Periods are wild card indicators that can represent any character, a group of characters, or even no characters. The question mark represents any character. The tilde identifies a word, character, or characters you want to exclude from your search. Table 5.1 summarizes what various search arguments do and do not find.

Table 5.1
Summary of Search Arguments Using Special Characters*

Argument	*What It Finds*	*What It Does Not Find*
..interest	interest car loan interest mortgage interest	car loan interest expense mortgage expense war loan
interest..	interest interest expense	car loan car loan interest mortgage expense mortgage interest war loan
..interest..	interest car loan interest interest expense mortgage interest	car loan mortgage expense war loan
~..interest	car loan interest expense mortgage expense war loan	interest car loan interest mortgage interest
~interest..	car loan car loan interest mortgage expense mortgage interest war loan	interest interest expense
~..interest..	car loan mortgage expense war loan	car loan interest interest interest expense mortgage interest

Argument	What It Finds	What It Does Not Find
?ar loan	car loan war loan	car loan interest interest interest expense mortgage expense mortgage interest
~?ar loan	interest car loan interest interest expense mortgage expense mortgage interest	car loan war loan

For a sample list of memo descriptions containing the following: car loan, car loan interest, interest, interest expense, mortgage expense, mortgage interest, and war loan.

Combining Exact and Key-Word Matches

You can search with more than one exact match or key-word argument. Figure 5.10 shows the Transaction to Find screen set to search for transactions with the phrase "big national bank" in the `Payee` field and an asterisk in the cleared field.

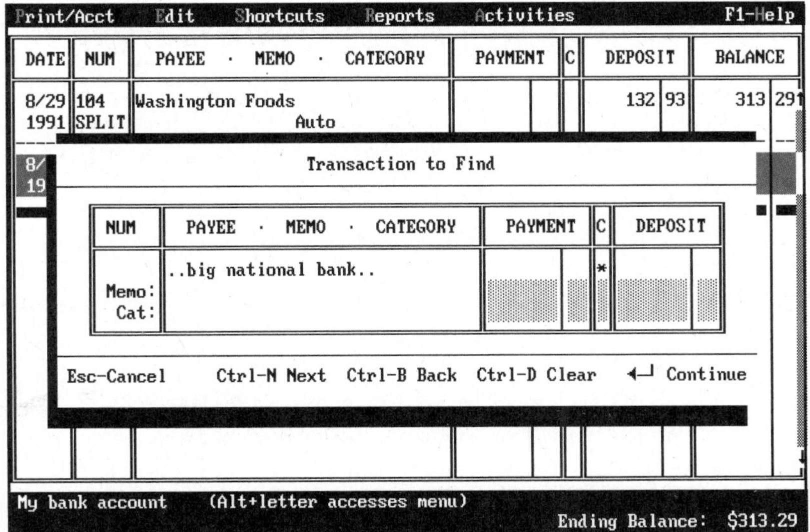

Fig. 5.10. *Searching for transactions that include the phrase* `big national bank` *in the* `Payee` *field.*

If you use more than one match test, the Find operation locates any transactions that meet all match tests. With the Transaction to Find screen shown in figure 5.10, for example, Find does not locate transactions with the phrase "big national bank" used in the `Payee` field unless the asterisk character also is used in the `C` field. Find also does not locate transactions with the asterisk character used in the `C` field unless the phrase "big national bank" also is used in the `Payee` field.

Repeating a Find Request

When Quicken executes a Find operation, it selects the first transaction that meets the search argument or arguments you entered. If you were precise in specifying the exact match or key word match, the first transaction Quicken finds may be the one you want. That transaction also could be similar to the one you want, but not an exact match, so Quicken gives you two additional Find options: **Repeat Find backwards** (Ctrl-B) and **Repeat Find next** (Ctrl-N). **Repeat Find backwards** (Ctrl-B) executes the find operation already specified on the Transaction to Find screen, and it looks through checks and deposits before the selected transaction. Similarly, **Repeat Find next** (Ctrl-N) executes the find operation already specified on the Transaction to Find screen, but it looks through checks and deposits after the selected transaction.

Using the Go to Date Option

You may have wondered about the absence of a date field on the Transaction to Find screen. You use the **Go to Date** option (Ctrl-G) on the Edit menu to look for a transaction or account balance for a specific date. Specify the date you want to use as the basis for your search on the Go to Date screen, shown in figure 5.11.

Quicken initially displays the current system date as the Go to Date. You can change the date by typing the date you want over the default date. (You also can use the + and – special date entry keys to enter the date. If you don't remember how to use these keys, refer to Chapter 2.)

After you set the date you want, Quicken finds and displays the first transaction with the date you entered. If no transaction has the date you entered, the transaction with the date closest to the date you entered is displayed.

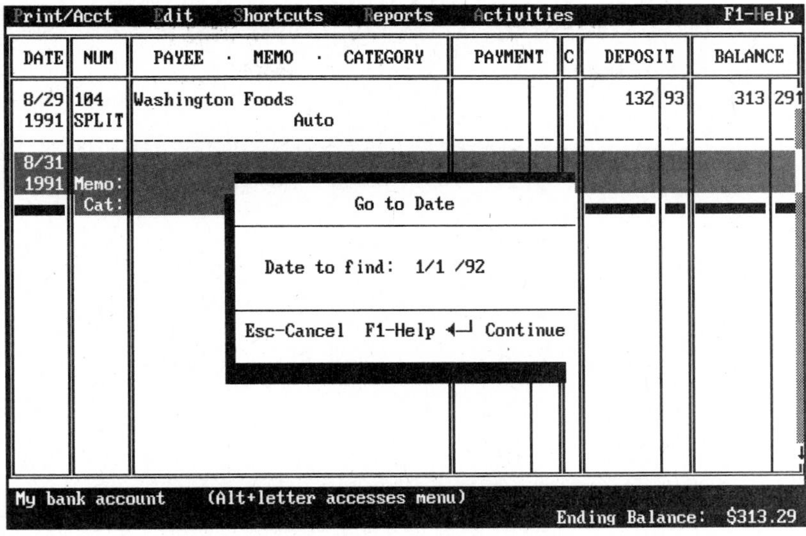

Fig. 5.11. The Go to Date screen.

Because Quicken arranges transactions in the register by date, you do not need to specify a search direction for the **Go to Date** option. By comparing the date on the currently selected transaction to the Go to Date, Quicken determines which direction it needs to search. If the Go to Date is earlier than the date on the selected transaction, Quicken looks through the previous transactions; if the Go to Date is later than the date on the selected transaction, Quicken searches succeeding transactions.

Using the Go to Transfer Option

If the currently selected transaction is a transfer, you can use the **Go to Transfer** option on the Edit menu to display the register with the corresponding transaction. For example, figure 5.12 shows that the deposit to savings check is selected. By looking at the `Category` field, which displays `[Acme]`, you can see that this is a transfer transaction. The name of the account to which the transfer is taking place is shown in the `Category` field with brackets around the name.

Print/Acct Edit Shortcuts Reports Activities F1-Help

DATE	NUM	PAYEE · MEMO · CATEGORY	PAYMENT		C	DEPOSIT		BALANCE	
8/29 1991		Opening Balance [My bank accou→			X	1,000	00	1,000	00
8/29 1991	102	Seattle Power Company August Utilities	75	39				924	61
8/29 1991		Big National Bank August interest→Int Inc				5	75	930	36
8/29 1991	Memo: Cat:	Deposit to savings [Acme]	250	00				680	36
8/29 1991	103	Puget Sound Mortgage September payme→Housing	500	00				180	36
8/29 1991	104 SPLIT	Washington Foods Auto				132	93	313	29

My bank account (Alt+letter accesses menu)
Esc-Main Menu Ctrl←┘ Record Ending Balance: $313.29

Fig. 5.12. *The deposit to savings check is part of a transfer.*

If you select **Go to Transfer** (Ctrl-X) from the Edit menu, Quicken displays the account register with the corresponding transaction selected. Figure 5.13 shows the corresponding transaction in the savings register. In the first account, Big National, the transaction is a payment because it reduces that account balance. In the second account, Acme, the transaction is listed as a deposit.

If you use the **Go to Transfer** option on a split transaction, Quicken asks you to identify the category to which you want to go. With a split transaction, you can make transfers to more than one account. If you try to change a split transaction from one of the other registers, Quicken tells you that the transaction was created through a transfer, and you must return to the original transaction to make changes.

Using the Shortcuts Menu Tools

Quicken already may be fast enough for you. After all, it does not take that much time to type in the half dozen fields you enter to record a check or a deposit. But you can streamline your record keeping further with several of the options on the Shortcuts menu (see fig. 5.14). You can use the **Recall Transaction** and **Memorize Transaction** options to store and then reuse recurring transactions. With the **Transaction Groups** option, you can store and then reuse whole sets of transactions. (Normal **Categorize/Transfer** and **Select/Set Up Class** options are covered in Chapter 10.)

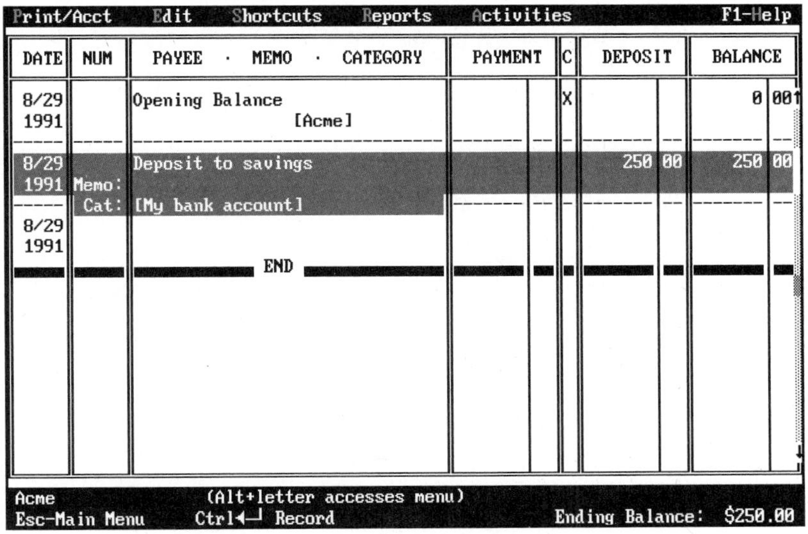

```
Print/Acct   Edit   Shortcuts   Reports   Activities                F1-Help
DATE  NUM   PAYEE · MEMO · CATEGORY       PAYMENT   C   DEPOSIT   BALANCE
8/29        Opening Balance                         X                0 00
1991                  [Acme]
8/29        Deposit to savings                          250 00     250 00
1991  Memo:
      Cat:  [My bank account]
8/29
1991
                        END
Acme              (Alt+letter accesses menu)
Esc-Main Menu     Ctrl◄┘ Record                Ending Balance:  $250.00
```

Fig. 5.13. *The corresponding transfer transaction.*

Memorizing Transactions

Many of the checks you write and the deposits you make are often similar or identical to previous checks and deposits. A household, for example, may record the mortgage check, the car loan check, the utility bill check, and the payroll deposit each month. A business may write checks for the monthly rent, payroll, and expenses like supplies or insurance.

Because so many register transactions are largely the same every month, Quicken gives you the capability to store transaction information in a memorized transactions list. Rather than entering the information over and over, you can reuse transaction information. To memorize a transaction, follow these steps:

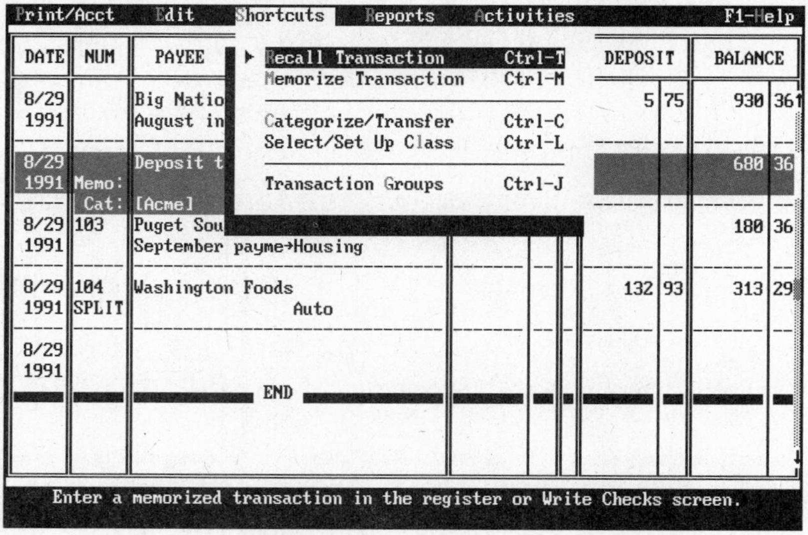

```
Print/Acct   Edit   Shortcuts   Reports   Activities                F1-Help
DATE  NUM   PAYEE        ▸ Recall Transaction        Ctrl-T   DEPOSIT    BALANCE
8/29        Big Natio      Memorize Transaction      Ctrl-M      5 75     930 36
1991        August in      Categorize/Transfer       Ctrl-C
8/29        Deposit t      Select/Set Up Class       Ctrl-L               680 36
1991  Memo:                Transaction Groups        Ctrl-J
      Cat:  [Acme]
8/29  103   Puget Sou                                                     180 36
1991        September payme→Housing
8/29  104   Washington Foods                                 132 93       313 29
1991  SPLIT                  Auto
8/29
1991
                             END
Enter a memorized transaction in the register or Write Checks screen.
```

Fig. 5.14. The Shortcuts menu.

1. Select the register transaction you want to memorize, such as the one shown in figure 5.15.

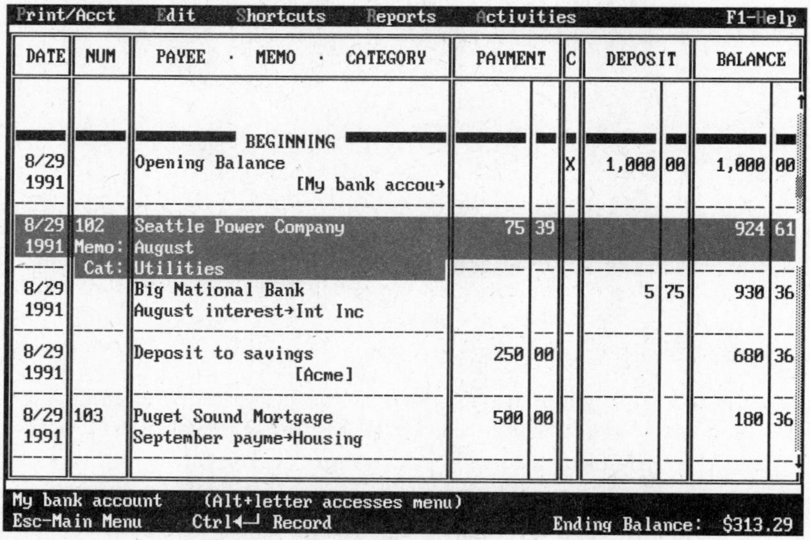

```
Print/Acct   Edit   Shortcuts   Reports   Activities                F1-Help
DATE  NUM   PAYEE · MEMO · CATEGORY    PAYMENT  C  DEPOSIT     BALANCE
                     BEGINNING
8/29        Opening Balance                     X  1,000 00   1,000 00
1991                 [My bank accou→
8/29  102   Seattle Power Company       75 39                   924 61
1991  Memo: August
      Cat:  Utilities
8/29        Big National Bank                          5 75     930 36
1991        August interest→Int Inc
8/29        Deposit to savings         250 00                   680 36
1991                 [Acme]
8/29  103   Puget Sound Mortgage       500 00                   180 36
1991        September payme→Housing
My bank account    (Alt+letter accesses menu)
Esc-Main Menu      Ctrl◄┘ Record                  Ending Balance:  $313.29
```

Fig. 5.15. You may decide to memorize a monthly loan payment.

2. Press Alt-S to display the Shortcuts menu and then select the **Memorize Transaction** option or press Ctrl-M. Quicken highlights the selected transaction and alerts you that the marked information is about to be memorized (see fig. 5.16). The marked information includes the payee, payment or deposit amounts, cleared memo, and category; the `Date` and `Cleared` fields are not marked.

```
Print/Acct   Edit   Shortcuts   Reports   Activities                F1-Help
DATE  NUM    PAYEE  ·  MEMO  ·  CATEGORY    PAYMENT   C  DEPOSIT    BALANCE

                     BEGINNING
8/29        Opening Balance                           X  1,000 00   1,000 00
1991                        [My bank accou→
8/29  102   Seattle Power Company            75 39                    924 61
1991  Memo: August
      Cat:  Utilities
8/29        Big National Bank
1991        August interest→Int Inc
                                      The highlighted information
8/29        Deposit to savings        is about to be memorized.
1991                        [Acme]
8/29  103   Puget Sound Mortgage      Esc-Cancel          ←┘ Memorize
1991        September payme→Housing
My bank account    (Alt+letter accesses menu)
                                                  Ending Balance:  $313.29
```

Fig. 5.16. *The memorization message.*

If you memorize a split transaction, Quicken displays a message box action amount. To answer the message, press A if you want the actual amounts memorized or P if you want Quicken to memorize the percentages that the amounts represent.

3. To finish the memorize operation, press Enter. Quicken saves a copy of the transaction in the memorized transaction list. The copy is named after what is in the `Payee` field.

Recalling a Transaction

The **Recall Transaction** option works in conjunction with the **Memorize Transaction** option just described. Selecting **Recall Transaction** (Ctrl-T) enables you to fill a row in the register with memorized transactions. Suppose that Quicken memorizes the payment shown in figure 5.15. When you need to record the payment the following month, select **Recall Transaction** from the Shortcuts menu. The Memorized Transactions List is displayed, as shown in figure 5.17. Only the utilities payment is shown, because this transaction is the only one that has been memorized.

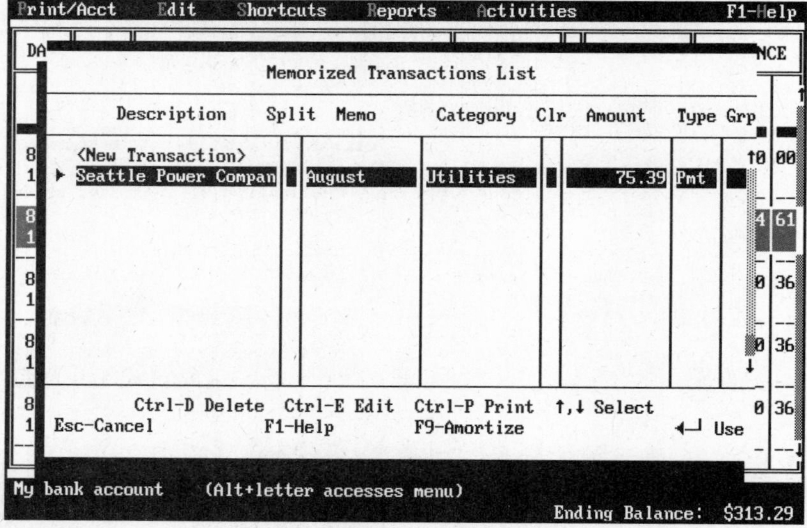

Fig. 5.17. The Memorized Transactions List screen.

Figure 5.17 shows the information saved as part of the Memorize Transaction operation. Eight fields are shown on-screen, all of which may have been filled to record a register transaction.

The payee name is in the `Description` column; the memo is in the `Memo` column; the category name is in the `Category` column; and the check amount is in the `Amount` column. If you split a check transaction, an `S` appears in the `Split` column. Quicken also places the abbreviation `Pmt` in the `Type` field to identify the transaction as a payment, `Dep` in the `Type` field to identify the transaction as a deposit, or `Check` in the `Type` field to identify the transaction as a check. The `Clr` column shows whether you have marked the transaction as cleared (see Chapter 8). The Grp column identifies whether the memorized transaction is part of a group of transactions (described later in the chapter).

To use, or recall, a memorized transaction, take the following steps:

1. Press Alt-S to display the Shortcuts menu, and then select the **Recall Transaction** option or press Ctrl-T. Quicken displays the Memorized Transaction List (see fig. 5.17).
2. Move the selection triangle to the left of the Description field to the transaction you want to use.
3. Press Enter, and Quicken fills the next empty row in the register with the information from the memorized transaction.
4. Edit the information from the memorized transaction so that it correctly reflects the transaction you want to record. For a check, you probably will want to enter a check number. For both checks and deposits, you often will want to edit the Amount and Memo fields. The current date is automatically entered in the register. (You cannot postdate a memorized transaction.)
5. To record the check, press Ctrl-Enter. Quicken records the transaction in the register.

The Memorized Transactions List screen hints at another way to memorize transactions. If you select the New Transaction item on the list and press Enter, Quicken displays a pop-up box on-screen that collects each of the memorized fields. You enter the necessary fields and press Enter. Quicken then adds a memorized transaction to the list.

Deleting Memorized Transactions

You also use the **Recall Transaction** option to delete memorized transactions from the Memorized Transactions List. You might want to delete a memorized transaction, for example, with the final payment on a house or car loan. To delete a memorized transaction, follow these steps:

1. Press Alt-S to display the Shortcuts menu, and then select the **Recall Transaction** option or press Ctrl-T. Quicken displays the Memorized Transactions List.

2. Highlight the transaction you want to delete.

3. When the transaction you want to delete is marked, press Ctrl-D. Quicken alerts you that it is about to delete a memorized transaction, as shown in figure 5.18. To delete the transaction, press Enter; otherwise, press Esc.

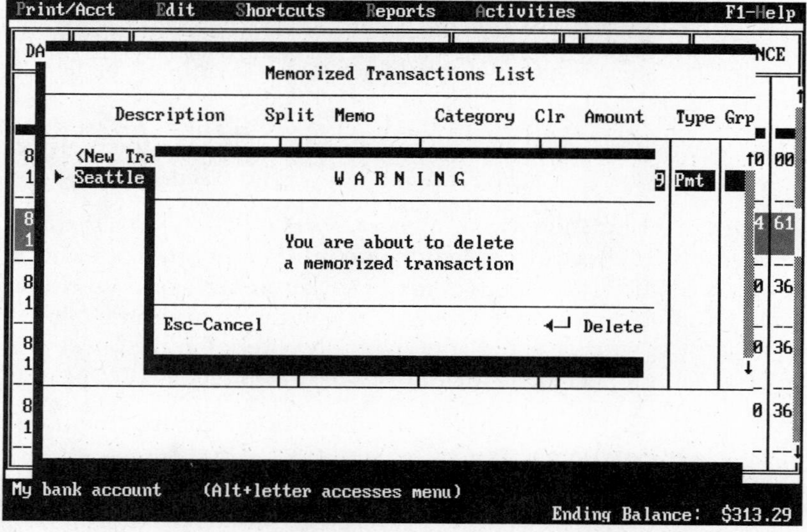

***Fig. 5.18.** The* `You are about to delete a memorized transaction` *message.*

Editing Memorized Transactions

You also can edit memorized transactions by using the **Recall Transaction** option. You may want to do this if the amount of a memorized transaction changed. To edit a memorized transaction, follow these steps:

1. Press Alt-S to display the Shortcuts menu, and then select the **Recall Transaction** option or press Ctrl-T. Quicken displays the Memorized Transactions List.

2. Highlight the transaction you want to edit and press Ctrl-E. Quicken displays the Edit/Setup Memorized Transaction box (see fig. 5.19).

3. Change the fields as necessary and then press Enter or F10.

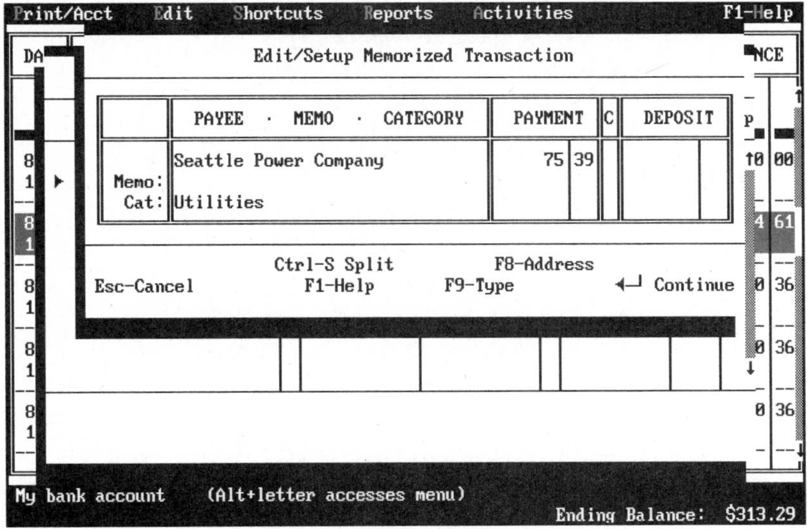

Fig. 5.19. The Edit/Setup Memorized Transaction box.

Listing Memorized Transactions

Quicken also enables you to print a list of the transactions you have memorized. Most of the time, you will not need this feature. As long as Quicken is running, the memorized transactions list is at your finger tips if you press Ctrl-T. One example of when you might want a printed list is for an annual review of transactions. If you decide that you want a printed copy of the list, follow these steps:

1. Press Alt-S to display the Shortcuts menu, and then select the **Recall Transaction** option or press Ctrl-T. Quicken displays the Memorized Transactions List.

2. Press Ctrl-P. Quicken displays the Print Memorized Transactions List screen, which you use to specify settings for printing the list. (This screen is like the Print Register screen.)

3. Indicate printer settings, and Quicken then prints the Memorized Transactions list (see fig. 5.20).

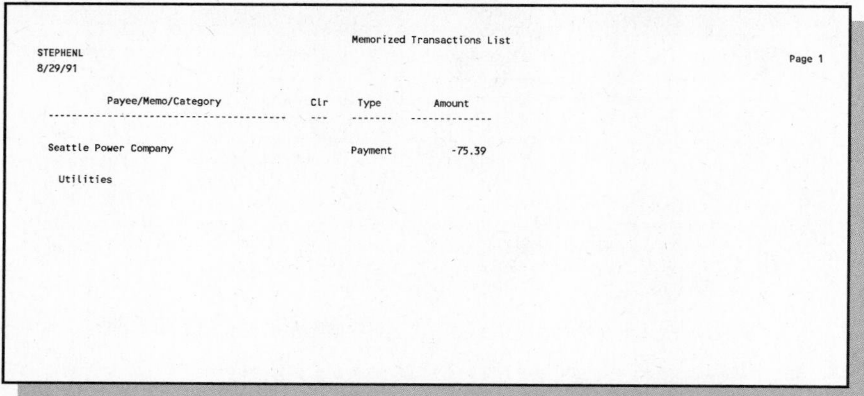

Memorized Transactions List

STEPHENL
8/29/91

Page 1

Payee/Memo/Category	Clr	Type	Amount
Seattle Power Company		Payment	-75.39
Utilities			

Fig. 5.20. A printed Memorized Transactions List.

Consider each of the transactions you now regularly record as candidates for the Memorized Transactions List: rent, house payment, utility payment, school loans, payroll deposits, bank service fees, and so on. The easiest time to memorize transactions is when you initially record a transaction, so every time you enter a transaction, ask yourself whether the transaction is one you will enter repeatedly. You also can memorize split transactions.

Using the Categorize/Transfer Option

With the **Categorize/Transfer** option (Ctrl-C), you can create or retrieve a category. Creating a new category is described in Chapter 10, but Quicken provides predefined home and business categories that you can retrieve.

To find and use a predefined category, take the following steps:

1. Press Alt-S to display the Shortcuts menu, and then select the **Categorize/Transfer** option or press Ctrl-C. Quicken displays the Category and Transfer List screen with predefined categories and any accounts you may have created (see fig. 5.21).

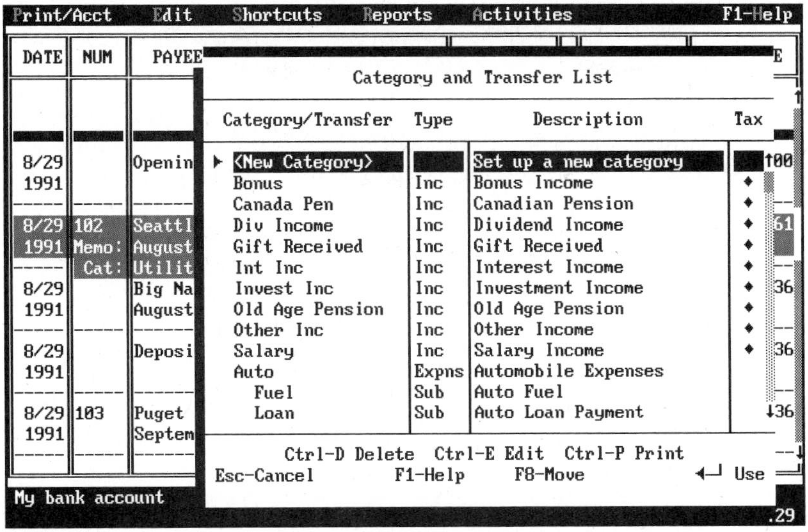

```
Print/Acct   Edit   Shortcuts   Reports   Activities                F1-Help
DATE  NUM   PAYEE
                    Category and Transfer List

                    Category/Transfer  Type   Description            Tax
8/29        Openin  ▸ <New Category>          Set up a new category
1991                  Bonus            Inc    Bonus Income            ♦
                      Canada Pen       Inc    Canadian Pension        ♦
8/29  102   Seattl    Div Income       Inc    Dividend Income         ♦
1991  Memo: August    Gift Received    Inc    Gift Received           ♦
      Cat:  Utilit    Int Inc          Inc    Interest Income         ♦
8/29        Big Na    Invest Inc       Inc    Investment Income       ♦
1991        August    Old Age Pension  Inc    Old Age Pension         ♦
                      Other Inc        Inc    Other Income            ♦
8/29        Deposi    Salary           Inc    Salary Income           ♦
1991                  Auto             Expns  Automobile Expenses
                        Fuel           Sub    Auto Fuel
8/29  103   Puget       Loan           Sub    Auto Loan Payment
1991        Septem
                       Ctrl-D Delete  Ctrl-E Edit  Ctrl-P Print
                    Esc-Cancel       F1-Help     F8-Move        ◄┘ Use
My bank account
```

Fig. 5.21. *The Category and Transfer List screen.*

2. Select the category or account you want to use and press Enter or double-click on the category with the mouse. Quicken retrieves the category or account name from the list and puts it in the `Category` field.

   You also can use the PgUp, PgDn, Home, and End keys to move quickly through long lists of categories. Pressing PgUp displays the preceding page of categories in the list; pressing PgDn displays the next page of categories in the list; pressing Home displays the first page of categories, and pressing End displays the last page of categories. The Category and Transfer List screen also provides a scroll bar that mouse users can take advantage of for moving up and down the list. (Refer to the preceding chapter's discussion of using the register's scroll bar if you don't know how scroll bars function.)

Setting Up a Transaction Group

Frequently, you might encounter a set of consistent monthly transactions. A household might have the monthly bills: a mortgage, the utility bill, and the car payment. A business might have employee payroll checks. Instead of memorizing and recalling individual transactions, you can set up a group of memorized transactions. Transaction groups enable you to recall several memorized transactions at the same time.

To create a transaction group, follow these steps:

1. Following the steps described earlier in this chapter, memorize each of the transactions you want to include in a transaction group.
2. Press Alt-S to display the Shortcuts menu, and then select the **Transaction Groups** option or press Ctrl-J. Quicken displays the Select Transaction Group to Execute screen, as shown in figure 5.22.

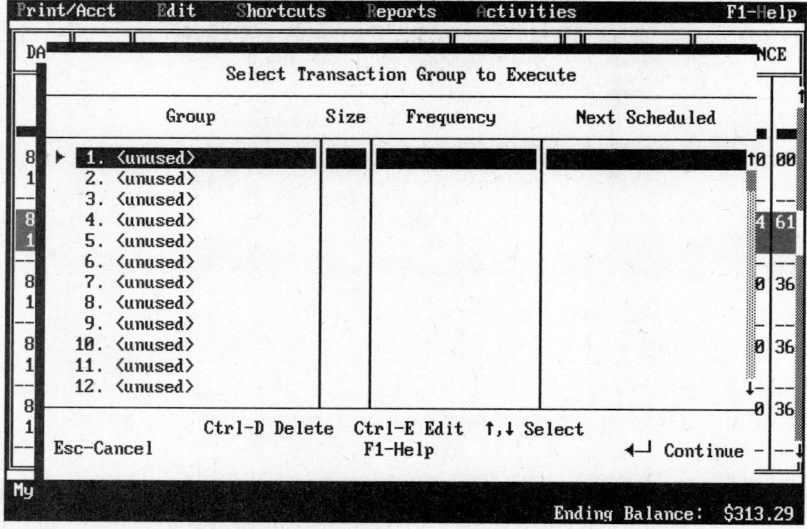

Fig. 5.22. The Select Transaction Group to Execute screen.

3. Use the up- and down-arrow keys to mark the first unused transaction group, and then press Enter. Quicken displays the Describe Group screen (see fig. 5.23). If you are defining your first transaction, you will mark group 1 and press Enter. If a transaction group already exists, choose an empty group.
4. Give a name or description to the group. You can use a maximum of 20 characters to describe the group.
5. Press Enter or Tab to move the cursor to the `Account to load before executing` field. Enter the account name for which the transactions should be recorded. This action causes the appropriate account to be selected before you recall the transactions in a group. If you only work with one account, you do not need to fill in this field.

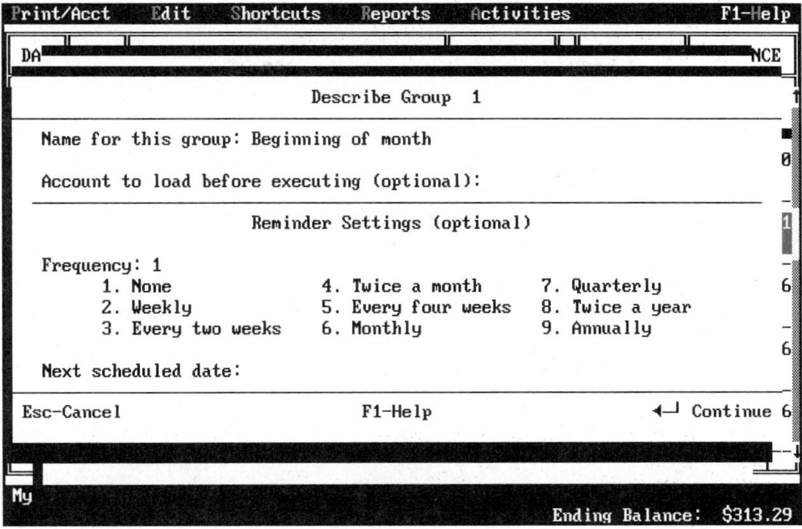

Fig. 5.23. The Describe Group screen.

6. Press Enter or Tab to move the cursor to the `Frequency` field. Set the frequency using one of the nine settings shown in figure 5.23: None, Weekly, Every two weeks, Twice a month, Every four weeks, Monthly, Quarterly, Twice a year, or Annually. Select the frequency you want by typing the number that corresponds to the desired frequency.

7. If you set the frequency to something other than None, you also must set the next scheduled date. Press Enter or Tab to move the cursor to the `Next scheduled date` field. Enter the date in the MM/DD/YY format. You can use the standard Quicken + and – keys to change this date to the one desired.

8. Press Enter, and Quicken displays the Assign Transactions to Group screen (see fig. 5.24). The Assign Transactions to Group screen lists all the possible memorized transactions.

9. Use the arrow keys to mark memorized transactions that should be part of the transaction group. When a transaction that should be included is marked, press the space bar to assign the transaction to the group. The last column on the Assign Transactions to Group screen, `Grp`, displays the group number. To unassign a transaction, press space bar again. Figure 5.24 shows the utilities payment memorized transactions selected for transaction group 1.

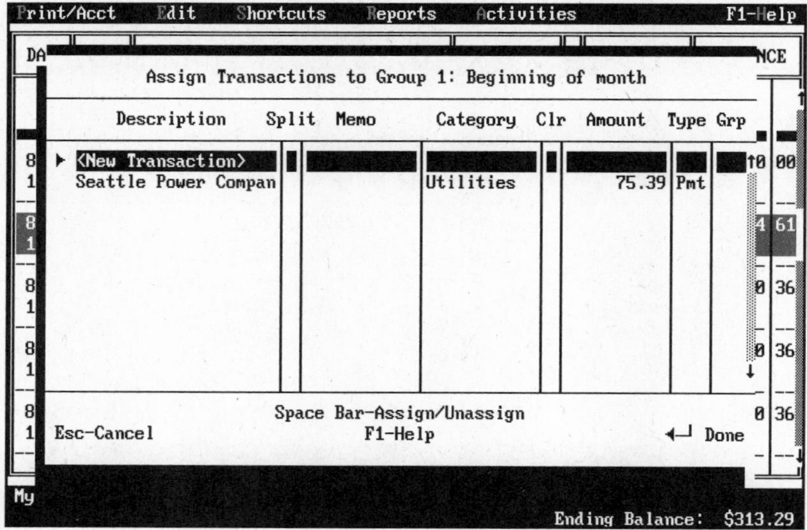

Fig. 5.24. The Assign Transactions to Group screen.

The space bar is a toggle switch that alternately assigns and unassigns the transaction that is highlighted or marked.

10. After the transactions that should be assigned to a group are all marked, press Enter to save your work.

Quicken again displays the Select Transaction Group to Execute screen. The newly defined transaction group appears (see fig. 5.25).

Executing a Transaction Group

To create a set of register transactions using a transaction group, follow these steps:

1. Press Alt-S to display the Shortcuts menu and select the **Transaction Groups** option or press Ctrl-J. Quicken displays the Select Transaction Group to Execute screen (see fig. 5.22).

2. Move the selection triangle to the left of the `Description` field for the transaction group you want to use.

3. Press Enter, and Quicken prompts you for the Transaction Group Date, as shown in figure 5.26.

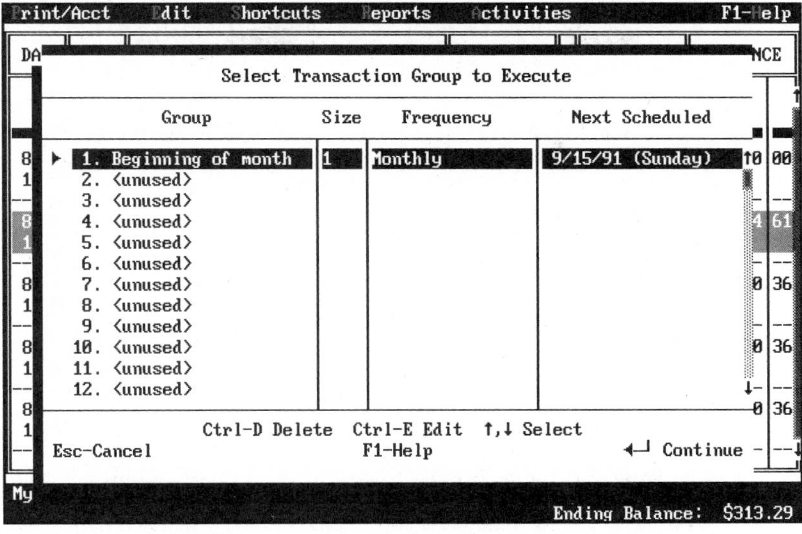

Fig. 5.25. A newly defined transaction group appearing on the Select Transaction Group to Execute screen.

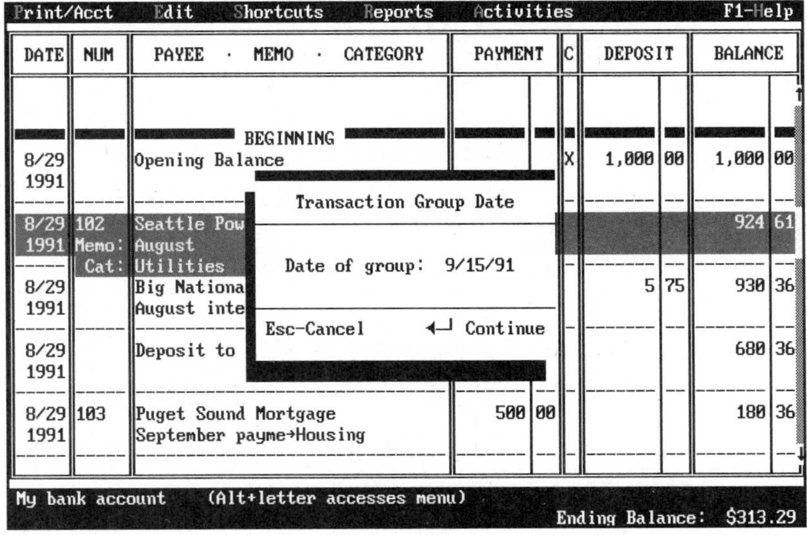

Fig. 5.26. The Transaction Group Date screen.

4. Enter the date you want checks and deposits in the transaction group to show when they are recorded in the register.

5. Press Enter when the `Transaction Group Date` field is correct. Quicken records the memorized transactions in the register, saves the transactions, and displays the message shown in figure 5.27.

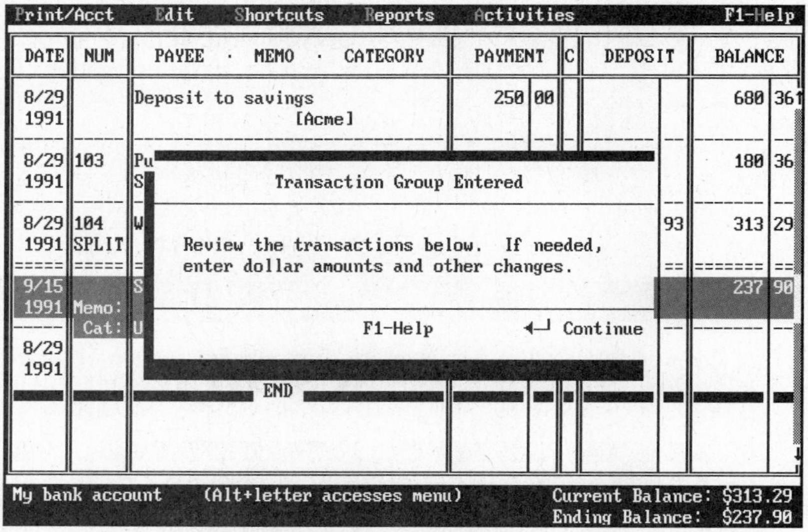

```
Print/Acct   Edit   Shortcuts   Reports   Activities                F1-Help
DATE  NUM    PAYEE · MEMO · CATEGORY   PAYMENT  C  DEPOSIT   BALANCE
8/29         Deposit to savings         250 00                680 36
1991                 [Acme]
8/29  103    Pu                                               180 36
1991         S        Transaction Group Entered
8/29  104    W                                          93    313 29
1991  SPLIT     Review the transactions below.  If needed,
                enter dollar amounts and other changes.
9/15         S                                                237 90
1991  Memo:
       Cat:  U       F1-Help            Continue
8/29
1991
                     END
My bank account   (Alt+letter accesses menu)    Current Balance: $313.29
                                                Ending Balance:  $237.90
```

Fig. 5.27. The `Transaction Group Entered` *message.*

6. As necessary, edit the information for each of the memorized transactions added as part of the transaction group, and then record the transaction.

The execute transaction group operation also moves the next scheduled date for the transaction group forward, using whatever interval you specified.

Changing and Deleting Transaction Groups

If you want to change or modify a transaction group, you again use the **Transaction Groups** option on the Shortcuts menu and select the previously set-up transaction group. Access the Describe Group and Assign

Transactions screens, as shown in figures 5.23 and 5.24. Make the required changes on the appropriate screen and press Enter to continue to the next screen.

Because transaction groups segregate your checks into groups you pay together at one time, changes in payment due dates mean that you need to change the transaction group. For example, if you refinance your mortgage, the due date might change from the fifth to the fifteenth. If you have separate transaction groups for checks you write at the beginning of the month and those you write during the middle of the month, you may need to change your transaction groups.

If you want to delete a transaction group, you also select the **Transaction Groups** option from the Shortcuts menu. Use the arrow keys to mark the group you want to delete and press Ctrl-D. Quicken displays a message alerting you that it is about to delete the marked transaction group. To remove the transaction group, press Enter.

Using the Activities Menu

The register Activities menu has several options, as shown in figure 5.28. The **Write Checks** option (Ctrl-W) accesses the Write Checks screen, as does the **Write/Print Checks** option on Quicken's Main Menu. You use the **Write Checks** option so that Quicken prints checks for you. The **Write/Print Checks** option is described in Chapters 6 and 7. The **Reconcile** option accesses the Reconciliation screen and options (see Chapter 8). The **Set Up Budgets** option, which accesses the Set Up Budgets spreadsheet, is described in Chapter 16. The **Loan Calculator**—which relates to loan payments, interest, and balance calculations—is described in Chapter 12.

The **Order Supplies** option displays the Print Supply Order Form screen, shown in figure 5.29, which you print and then use as a three-page order form for purchasing supplies. These forms can be used to order check forms and envelopes from Intuit (the manufacturer of Quicken). Although the actual order form is not shown here, the form is similar to the order form that Intuit provides in the Quicken package.

The fourth Activities menu option, **Loan Calculator** (Ctrl-O), accesses the on-line, 10-key calculator. Figure 5.30 shows the calculator, which is described in Chapter 2.The **Use DOS** option brings up DOS and displays the DOS prompt, as in figure 5.31.

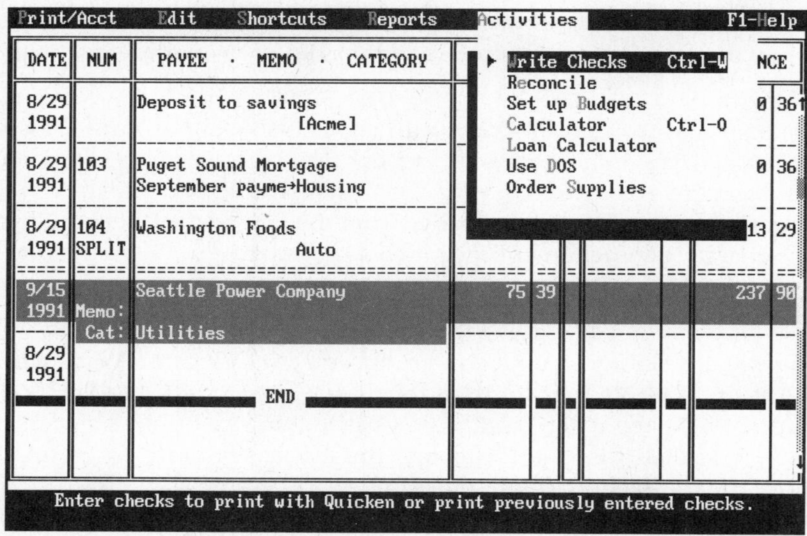

Fig. 5.28. The Activities menu.

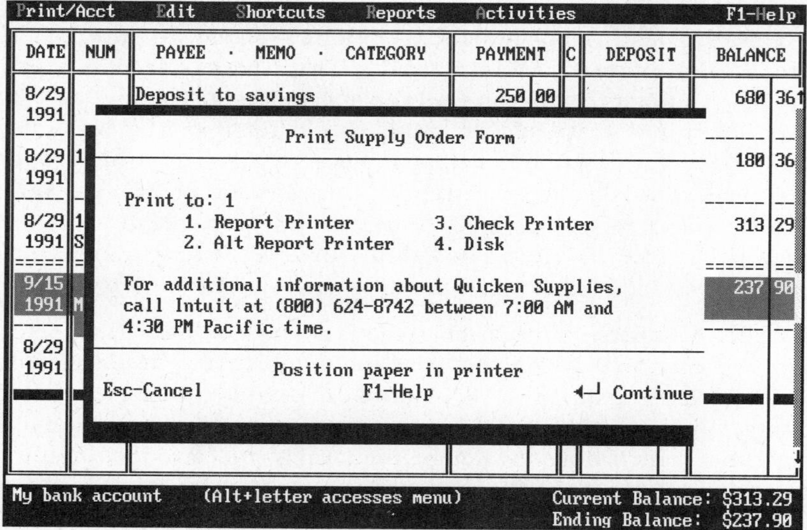

Fig. 5.29. The Print Supply Order Form screen.

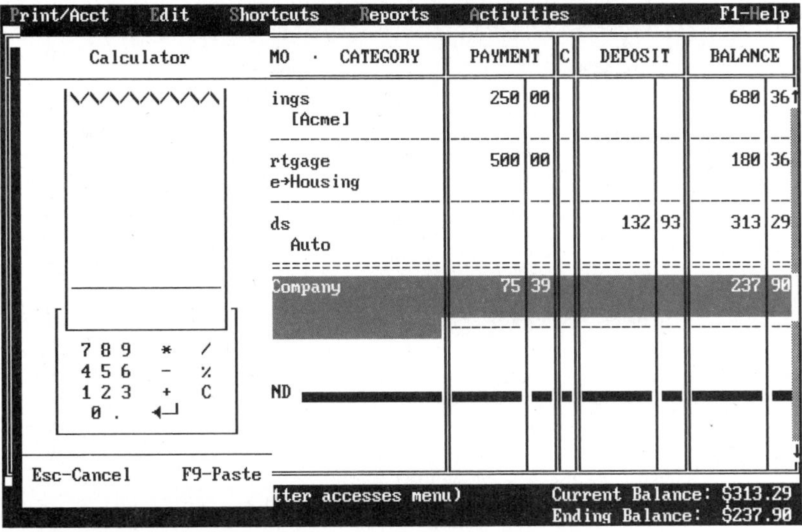

Fig. 5.30. The calculator available from the Activities menu.

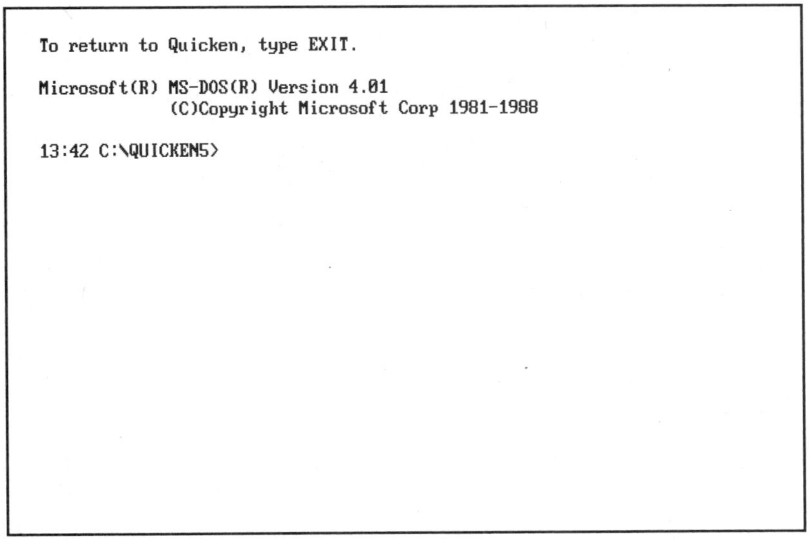

```
To return to Quicken, type EXIT.

Microsoft(R) MS-DOS(R) Version 4.01
             (C)Copyright Microsoft Corp 1981-1988

13:42 C:\QUICKEN5>
```

Fig. 5.31. The DOS prompt screen after executing the Use DOS option.

This feature is handy when you want to execute DOS commands before leaving Quicken. For example, you may want to format a disk to make a backup copy of a bank account.

Chapter Summary

This chapter described the three register menus not covered in the preceding chapter. The Edit menu provides tools you can use to make easier recording, editing, and deleting of individual transactions. The Shortcuts menu provides tools for memorizing and reusing transactions you record repeatedly. The Activities menu provides a grab bag of options—some of which are only introduced here and are described in more detail in subsequent chapters of this book.

6

Writing and Printing Checks

With Quicken's check-printing feature, you can write checks and pay bills faster and more efficiently than you ever thought possible. You can pay bills faster because Quicken provides a collection of shortcuts and time-saving techniques that automate and speed up check writing and bill paying. You can pay bills more efficiently because Quicken helps you keep track of the bills coming due and provides categories with which you can classify the ways you are spending your money.

As noted in Chapter 4, you don't actually ever have to use the **Write/Print Checks** option that Quicken includes on the Main Menu. If you do want to print checks, the Write/Print Checks screen has some advantages. First, the screen enables you to include the address of the person to whom you will be writing the check—something the register does not enable you to do. Second, you use a screen that resembles the actual check form, which often makes entering the data easier. Also, using the Write/Print Checks screen and option doesn't require additional work because Quicken records the information you collect directly into the Quicken register.

This chapter describes the basics of using the **Write/Print Checks** option on the Main Menu. Included in this chapter are discussions of the following topics:

- Understanding the Write Checks screen
- Writing a check
- Reviewing and editing checks
- Printing and reprinting checks

Understanding the Write Checks Screen

You use the Write Checks screen, shown in figure 6.1, to collect the information you use to print check forms. After collecting the information, Quicken records the check in the check register. You then can print the check. To access the Write Checks screen, select the **Write/Print Checks** option from Quicken's Main Menu.

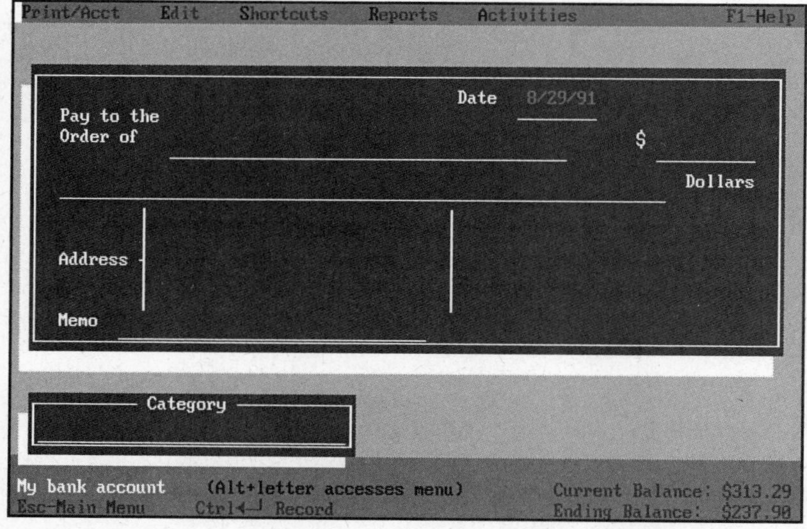

Fig. 6.1. *The Write Checks screen.*

The Write Checks screen can be broken down into three parts: the menu bar at the top of the screen, the check form, and the information bar at the bottom of the screen.

The menu bar shows the menus you use from the Write Checks screen to access commands. These menus should look familiar if you have worked with the Register screen: Print/Acct, Edit, Shortcuts, Reports, and Activities.

The second part of the screen is the actual check form you complete to have your checks printed. The steps for completing the form are described in the following section, "Writing a Check."

The third part of the Write Checks screen is the information bar at the bottom of the screen. This bar shows several pieces of information, including the account you currently are using, descriptions of what the Esc and Enter keys do, and the current and ending balance in the account.

Writing a Check

The mechanics of writing a check with Quicken closely resemble those for manually writing a check. The only real difference is that Quicken's Write Checks screen makes the process easier. With Quicken, writing a check means you simply complete the Write Checks screen. You fill in as many as seven fields: `Date`, `Payee`, `Amount`, `Address`, `Message`, `Memo`, and `Category`. After you write the check, you're ready to record and print the check.

To write a check, you take the following steps:

1. Select the **Write/Print Checks** option from Quicken's Main Menu, or, if you're already on the Register screen, press Alt-A to display the Activities menu and select the **Write Checks** option. Quicken displays the Write Checks screen shown in figure 6.1.

2. Enter the date of the check in the `Date` field. Write the date in the MM/DD/YY format (such as 12/11/92). The first time you use Quicken, the program fills the `Date` field with the system date (the current date according to your computer's internal memory). After you write your first check using the Write Checks screen, Quicken fills the `Date` field with the last date used. To edit the date, you have two choices. First, you can move the cursor to the part of the date—month, day, or year—you want to change and type over data already on-screen. Second, you can use the special date editing keys, which are explained in detail in Chapter 2.

As mentioned in Chapter 4, businesses and individuals often receive discounts for paying bills early, so consider early payment in setting the check date. In effect, not taking early payment discounts is an extremely expensive way to borrow money from the vendor. Suppose that a vendor normally requires payment within 30 days but gives a two percent discount for payments received within 10 days. If you pay within 30 rather than 10 days, you pay the vendor a two percent interest charge for paying 20 days later. Because one year contains roughly 18 20-day periods, the two percent for 20 days equals approximately 36 percent annually.

Although you may need to borrow this money, you probably can find a much cheaper lender. As a rule of thumb, if a vendor gives you a one percent discount for paying 20 days early, you are borrowing money from him at about an 18 percent annual interest rate if you do not pay early. A three percent discount works out to a whopping 54 percent per year.

3. Press Enter or Tab to move the cursor to the `Pay to the Order of` field. This field is where you enter the name of the person or business, called the *payee*, that the check pays. Type in the field the name you want to appear on the check.

   Because you have space for up to 40 characters, you should not have any problem fitting in the payee's name. In fact, you should have room to enter "and" and "or" payees. (An "and" payee, for example, is *Vader Ryderwood and Russell Dardenelle*. Both Vader and Russell must endorse such a check to cash it. An "or" payee is entered as *Vader Ryderwood or Russell Dardenelle* and requires Vader or Russell to endorse the check to cash it.)

4. Press Enter or Tab to move the cursor to the `Amount` field. The `Amount` field shows the amount of the check. You can use up to 10 characters to enter the amount. Quicken enables you to enter only numbers, commas, and periods in the `Amount` field. Quicken enters commas if you do not and if room is available for them. The largest value you can enter in the `Amount` field is 9999999.99. Because this number is difficult to read without commas (the number is $9,999,999.99), you probably will want to use commas. If you use some of the 10 characters for commas, the largest value you can enter is 999,999.99. When you complete the `Amount` field and press Enter, Quicken writes out the amount on the next line of the check—just as you do when writing a check manually. To save space, Quicken may abbreviate hundred as Hndrd, thousand as Thsnd, and million as Mill.

5. (Optional) Press Enter or Tab to move the cursor to the next field, the first line of the address block. The optional `Address` field provides five 30-character lines. If you use envelopes with windows and enter the payee's address in this field, the address shows in the envelope window. You save time that otherwise is spent addressing envelopes.

   Assuming that you are using the `Address` field, you need to type the payee's name on the first line. Quicken provides a shortcut for you. If you type ' (apostrophe) or " (quotation marks), Quicken copies the name from the `Pay to the Order of` field. (Because the `Pay to the Order of` field has space for 40 characters and the address lines have only 30 characters, this shortcut may cut off up to the last 10 characters of the payee's name.)

6. (Optional) If you set the extra message line switch to yes, press Enter or Tab to move the cursor to the `Msg` field. The extra message switch is on the Set Preferences menu under the **Checks and Reports** option and is described in Chapter 11. This field gives you

another 24 characters for additional information you want printed on the check, such as an account number for a credit card or a loan number for a mortgage. Because this information does not show through an envelope window, do not use the line for address information.

7. (Optional) Press Enter or Tab to move the cursor to the second line of the address block. Enter the street address or post office box.
8. (Optional) Press Enter or Tab to move the cursor to the third line of the address block. Enter the city, state, and ZIP code.
9. (Optional) Press Enter or Tab to move the cursor to the other address lines—there are six altogether—and enter any additional address information.
10. (Optional) Press Enter or Tab to move the cursor to the `Memo` field. You can use this field as you use the extra message line to further describe the reasons for a check, such as *May rent*, or you can use the line to tell the payee your account number or loan number.
11. (Optional) Press Enter or Tab to move the cursor to the `Category` field. You use the `Category` field to describe the category into which a check falls, such as utilities expense, interest expense, or entertainment. You also can use the `Category` field to describe the class into which a check falls. (Categories and classes are described in Chapter 10, "Organizing Your Finances Better.") Quicken provides a listing of the most typical categories for home or business use to enable you to quickly categorize your most frequent transactions. You access the defined list by pressing Ctrl-C. To use the `Category` field to describe a category, enter the name you used to define the category.

Quicken 5 provides a feature called auto-completion, which you can use after you have learned a few of the category names. If you type enough letters of a category name to uniquely identify the category and then press Enter, Quicken types the rest of the category name for you. Suppose, for example, that you have a category named "Entertainment," and that it is the only category name that starts with the three letters, ent. If you type *ent* and press Enter, Quicken types the remaining letters of the word for you—*ertainment*. You also can use the auto-completion feature in other situations, most of which apply to the investment monitoring features and are described in Chapter 13. You also can use the auto-completion feature to enter an account name in the `Category` field when transferring money to another account.

12. To record the check, press Enter when the cursor is on the `Category` field. Alternatively, you can press F10 or Ctrl-Enter when the cursor is on any of the fields. Figure 6.2 shows a completed Write Checks screen.

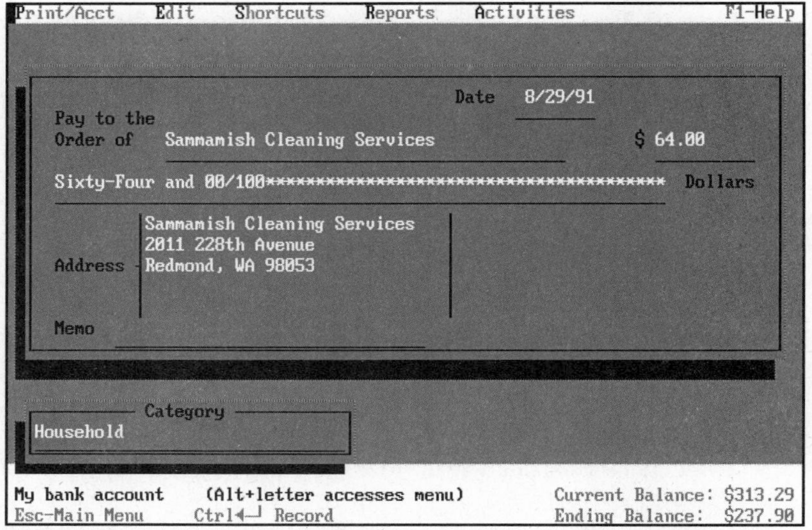

Fig. 6.2. A completed Write Checks screen.

13. After you press Ctrl-Enter or F10, Quicken displays the prompt shown in figure 6.3 and asks you to confirm that you want to record the check. If you select **Record transaction**, the check is recorded.

Whichever method you choose to record a check, you briefly see a flashing message in the lower left corner of the screen that says `RECORDING`. (If you use a very fast computer, you may not be able to read the message because it appears and disappears so quickly.) After Quicken finishes recording the check, your computer beeps, and the recorded check scrolls off the screen. A new, blank check form that was hidden by the preceding check is left on-screen—ready to be filled.

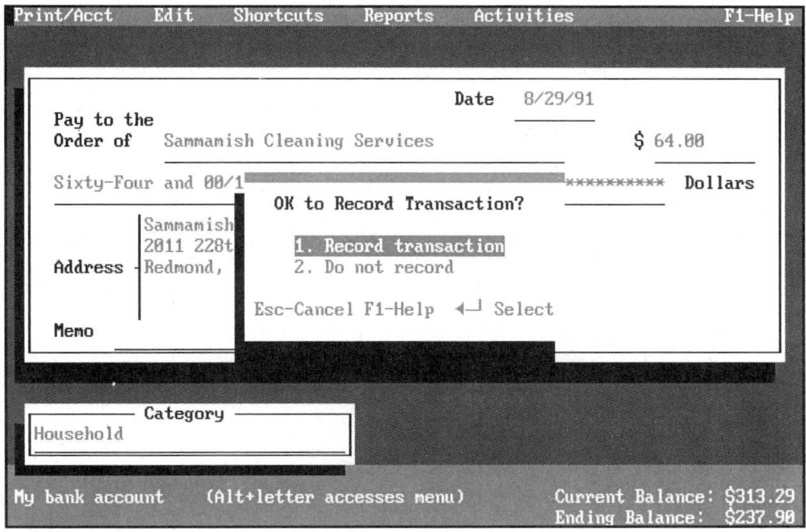

Fig. 6.3. *The OK to Record Transaction query.*

Reviewing and Editing Checks

You can return to, review, and edit the checks you create with the **Write/Print Checks** option until you print them. For example, you can correct errors and change check amounts for new bills. Suppose that you write a check to pay several bills from the same person or business—perhaps the bank with whom you have your mortgage, your car loan, and a personal line of credit. If you receive another bill from the bank, you may need to change the check amount.

You can use the PgUp, PgDn, Home, and End keys on the Write Checks screen to move through the checks you have created but not yet printed:

PgUp	Displays the preceding check
PgDn	Displays the next check
Home	Displays the first check
End	Displays the last check

Quicken arranges by date the checks you have created with the Write Checks screen but have not printed. Those checks with the earliest dates are listed first, followed chronologically by later checks. Checks with the same date are arranged in the order you entered them. To edit a check you already have recorded, press PgUp or PgDn to move to the check you want to change and then edit the appropriate fields.

If you decide you don't want to print a check, you simply delete it. To delete the check, press Ctrl-D while the check is displayed. You also can select **Delete Transaction** from the Edit menu on the Write Checks screen. Chapter 7 describes the Edit menu options.

Postdating Checks

Chapter 4, "Using the Register," talks about using postdated transactions. All the same reasons described there also apply to postdated checks. But when writing checks with Quicken, postdating takes on an added feature. Quicken can review postdated checks for those that you should print. To do this, Quicken uses a built-in program called the Billminder. Billminder looks for postdated checks it thinks you should print. The process works slightly differently depending on whether you're using Quicken on a hard disk system or on a floppy disk system. On a hard disk system, you are reminded of postdated checks and of transactions groups every time you turn on your computer. Quicken uses a pop-up message box (see fig. 6.4).

On both hard disk and floppy disk systems, you are reminded of postdated checks and of transaction groups every time you start Quicken. On a floppy disk system, Quicken displays a message at the bottom of the Main Menu like that shown in figure 6.5.

If you enter postdated checks, Quicken adds the current account balance to the information bar at the bottom of the Write Checks screen. The current balance is the checking account balance—not including postdated checks (see fig. 6.3).

Printing Checks

The Print/Acct menu, which you use to print the register, has six options (see fig. 6.6). This chapter describes only the second option—**Print Checks**— which you use to print checks created with the **Write/Print Checks** option. (If you already have worked with the Quicken register, you will notice that the Write Checks Print/Acct menu closely resembles the register's Print/Acct menu.)

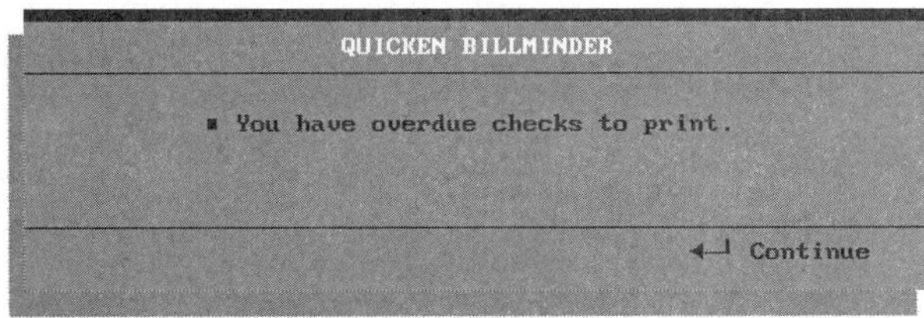

Fig. 6.4. The pop-up Billminder message box.

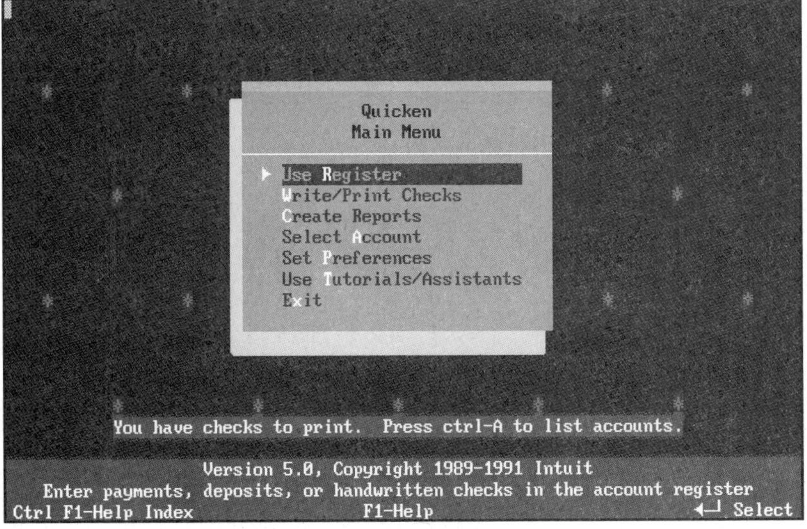

Fig. 6.5. The Billminder feature also displays a reminder message at the bottom of the Main Menu.

Refer to other chapters of *Using Quicken 5 for DOS* for information on the other five options. **Change Printer Styles** is the same as the **Printer Settings** option on the Set Preferences menu and is described in Chapter 1, "Preparing To Use Quicken." The **Select/Set Up Account** option is the same as the **Select Account** Main Menu option and is described in Chapter 3. The **Back Up File**, **Export**, and **Import** options are described in Chapter 9, "Caring for Quicken Files."

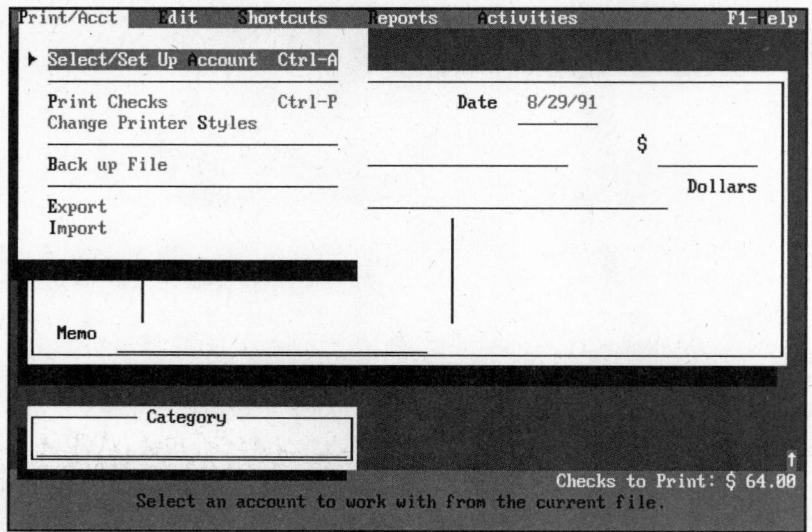

Fig. 6.6. The Print/Acct menu.

To print checks, follow these steps:

1. Load the check forms into your printer in the same way that you load regular paper.

   If you are using an impact printer, insert the continuous form checks into the printer as you would insert continuous form paper. If you are using a laser printer, place the check form sheets in the printer paper tray, as you would regular sheets of paper. (You use continuous form checks for impact printers and check form sheets for laser printers.)

2. Press Alt-P to display the Print/Acct menu, and then select the **Print Checks** option.

   Quicken displays the Print Checks screen, shown in figure 6.7. The Print Checks screen displays two messages that give you information about the checks ready to be printed and provides three fields for you to use to control the printing of your checks. The two messages tell you how many checks you have to print, and, if relevant, how many checks are postdated. Figure 6.7 shows that you have one check to print.

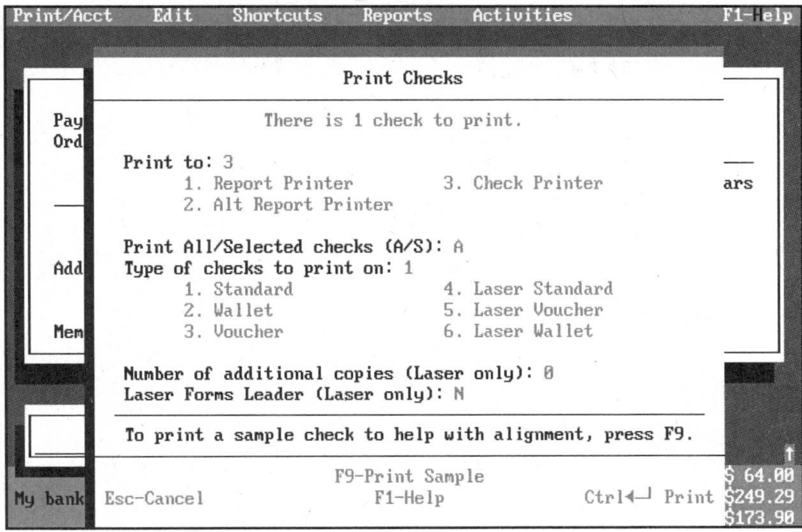

Fig. 6.7. The Print Checks screen.

3. With the cursor positioned on the `Print to` field, select the printer you want to use by pressing 1, 2, or 3. If you described your printer when installing Quicken, you should see your printer name here. If you don't see it, refer to the Chapter 1 section called "Configuring Your Printer."

4. Press Enter or Tab to move the cursor to the `Print All/Selected checks` field. To print all the checks entered on the Write Checks screen, leave this field set to A for All. To print only some of the checks, press S.

5. Press Enter or Tab to move the cursor to the `Print checks dated through` field. The `Print checks dated through` field accepts a date through which you want Quicken to print postdated checks.

   Suppose that today is 5/10/92 and that the checks waiting to be printed are dated 5/10/92, 5/11/92, and 5/12/92. If you set the date of this field to 5/11/92, Quicken prints the checks dated 5/10/92 and 5/11/92. Quicken does not, however, print the check dated 5/12/92.

6. (Optional) Use F9 to print a sample check. Pressing F9 prints one check form with the fields filled. Sample checks are essential for vertically and horizontally aligning checks if you are using an impact printer. (If you use a laser printer, you do not need to use this feature.) Figure 6.8 shows the sample check printed by Quicken.

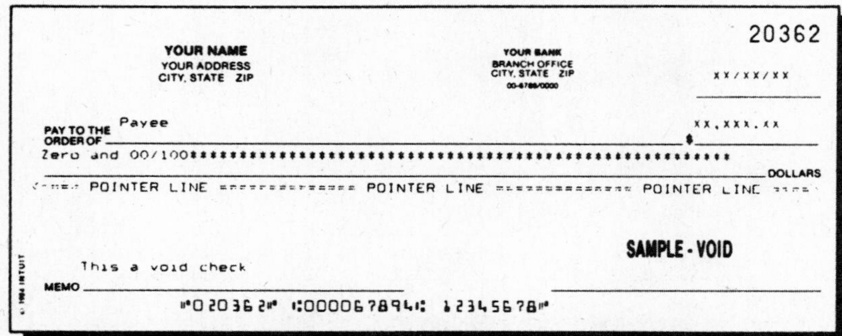

Fig. 6.8. A sample check.

The `Date` field is filled as XX/XX/XX. The `Pay to the Order of` field is filled with Payee. The `Amount` fields are filled with XX,XXX.XX and Zero and 00/100***. The `Memo` field is filled with the phrase `This is a void check.`

Quicken also prints a pointer line, as shown in figure 6.8. The pointer line enables you to tell Quicken how the check form is aligned vertically. Quicken uses this information to align the check forms vertically.

For impact printers, if you elect to use the sample check feature, Quicken displays the Type Position Number screen, which you can use to align the check form vertically. To use this alignment capability, enter the number from the check form's pin-feed strips that the pointer line points to. (Pin-feed strips are the strips of holes on the sides of the check forms. Your printer uses these holes to move the check forms through the printer.) Only even numbers show on the pin-feed strips. The odd numbers are identified by hash marks. (The pin-feed strips aren't shown in figure 6.8, so you should look at the actual check form in your computer.)

To align the check horizontally, manually adjust the check form in the printer to the right or left. You may decide, for example, that the fields shown in figure 6.8 are a little too far, perhaps an eighth of an inch, to the left. In that case, you manually move the check forms over to the left an eighth of an inch. Quicken prints the next check with its check form spaces filled an eighth of an inch to the right compared to the preceding check form.

7. Press Enter or Tab to move the cursor to the `Type of checks to print on` field. Then, specify the kind of check form:

1	Designates regular checks
2	Designates wallet checks
3	Designates voucher checks
4	Designates laser checks
5	Designates laser voucher checks
6	Designates laser wallet checks

   If you are using multiple part laser check forms, you need to specify the number of additional copies that should be printed.

   If you are using regular checks, such as those shown in figure 6.8, press 1. (Chapter 1, "Preparing To Use Quicken," describes in more detail Quicken's various check form options.)

8. (Optional) If you answered the `Print All/Selected checks` field with an `S`, Quicken then displays the Select Checks to Print screen (see fig. 6.9), from which you can select the checks you want to print. To select a check you want printed, use the arrow keys to move the selection triangle. When the selection triangle is next to the check you want to print, press the space bar to select the check. To deselect a check previously marked for printing, move the selection triangle to that check and press the space bar again.

   If you selected the checks to print, press Enter, F10, or Ctrl-Enter to leave the Select Checks to Print screen. Quicken then asks for the next check number.

9. Quicken uses the Enter Check Number screen to ask you for the number of the next check to print (see fig. 6.10). Quicken displays the number of the next check. If the number Quicken displays is the same as the number that appears in the upper left corner of the next check form, press Enter to print the check. If the number Quicken displays is not correct, type the correct check number. You also can use the + and – keys to change the number.

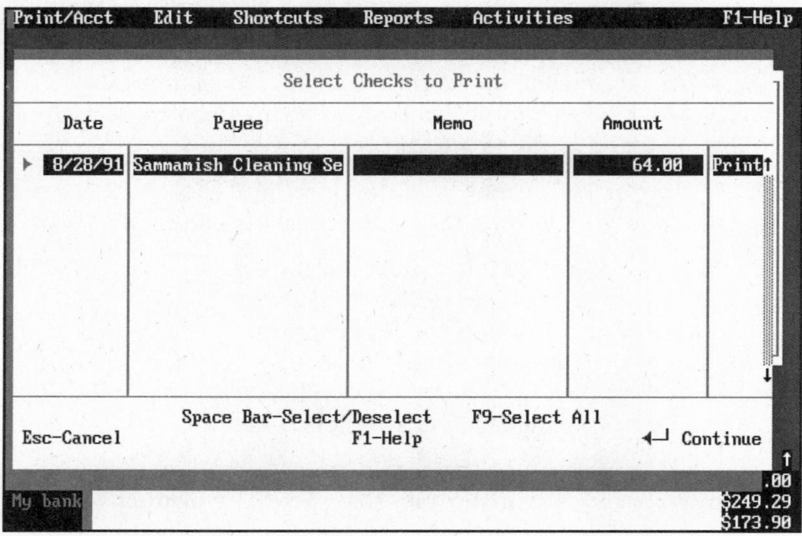

Fig. 6.9. The Select Checks to Print screen.

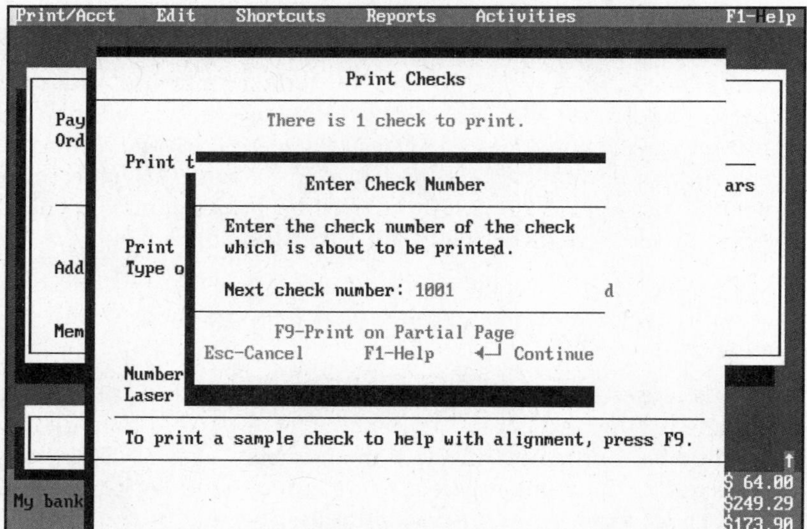

Fig. 6.10. The Enter Check Number screen.

10. Press Enter to print the checks. Figure 6.11 shows a sample check to Big National Bank printed with the vertical and horizontal alignment correct. After Quicken finishes printing the checks, the program asks you if the checks printed correctly. Figure 6.12 shows the screen that Quicken uses to ask the question. If each of your checks printed correctly, press Enter.

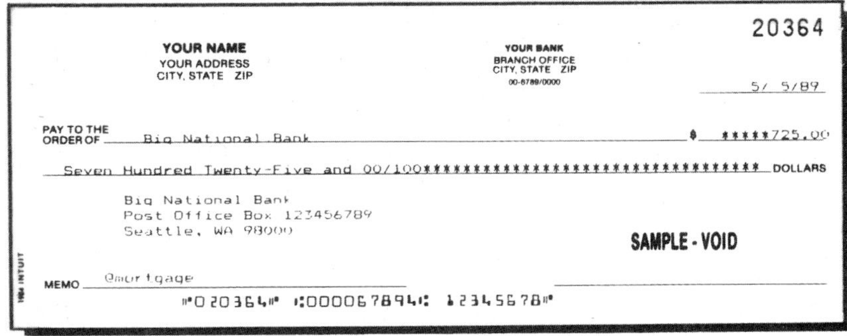

Fig. 6.11. A sample check made payable to Big National Bank.

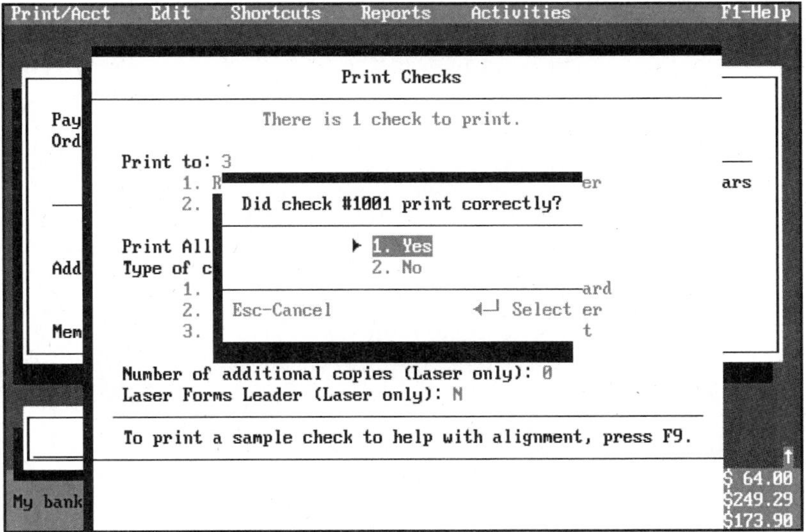

Fig. 6.12. Quicken asks whether the check printed correctly.

If one or more of your checks printed incorrectly—perhaps the alignment was not right or the check forms jammed in the printer halfway through printing—answer No. Quicken asks for the number of the first check that printed incorrectly. Quicken then returns to the Print Checks screen, and you repeat each of the Print Checks steps to reprint the checks that printed incorrectly. Quicken allows only the check numbers printed to be entered.

Write *VOID* in large letters across the face of checks that Quicken incorrectly prints. This precaution prevents you and anyone else from later signing and cashing the checks.

Reprinting a Check

If you decide later, even after leaving the Print Checks screen, that you want to reprint a check, you can do so. Suppose that the original check somehow gets lost or destroyed. You still have to pay the person, so you need to reprint the check. Rather than reenter all the same information a second time, you can reprint the original information. (If you lose a check, consider placing a stop-payment order with your bank.)

When you describe checks you want to print using the Write Checks screen, Quicken actually records the checks in the register. Because Quicken hasn't assigned check numbers, however, the check number field shows asterisks. These asterisks indicate that the check is one that you have set up to print using the Write Checks screen (see fig. 6.13). When Quicken prints the checks, it replaces the asterisks with the actual check number.

By itself, this bit of information isn't all that exciting, but it does enable you to trick Quicken into reprinting a check. All you need do is change a check's number to asterisks. Quicken then assumes that the check is one you want to print and that you created it on the Write Checks screen. To print the check after you have changed the number to asterisks, you follow the steps described earlier for printing a check.

Print/Acct Edit Shortcuts Reports Activities F1-Help

DATE	NUM	PAYEE · MEMO · CATEGORY	PAYMENT		C	DEPOSIT		BALANCE	
8/29 1991		Deposit to savings [Acme]	250	00				680	36
8/29 1991	103	Puget Sound Mortgage September payme→Housing	500	00				180	36
8/29 1991	104 SPLIT	Washington Foods Auto				132	93	313	29
8/30 1991	***** Memo: Cat:	Sammamish Cleaning Services Household	64	00				249	29
9/15 1991		Seattle Power Company Utilities	75	39				173	90
8/29 1991		END							

My bank account (Alt+letter accesses menu) Current Balance: $313.29
Esc-Main Menu Ctrl◂┘ Record Ending Balance: $173.90

Fig. 6.13. *Quicken stores checks to be printed in the register and identifies them by setting the check numbers to asterisks.*

Chapter Summary

This chapter described the basics of using another of Quicken's major time-saving features—the Write/Print Checks tool. These basics include the components of the Write Checks screen; how to use the write checks screen to record and postdate checks; and how to review, edit, and print checks. The next chapter describes the three sets of tools you can use to make using the **Write Checks** option even easier to use.

Making Check Writing Easier

The basic features of the **Write/Print Checks** option described in Chapter 6 make writing and printing checks with Quicken fast and easy. You can write checks faster and more easily if you use three other Write Checks menu's options:

Edit

Shortcuts

Activities

This chapter describes how you can use these three options. If you previously worked with the Register screen's Edit, Shortcuts, and Activities menus, you will recognize that the corresponding Write Checks menus work similarly. In fact, the only real difference between working with these options in the Register screen or working with the same options in the Write/Print Checks screen is that the screens are different. So, if you already are familiar with these menus, you may want to skim this chapter. (The one Write Checks menu option not yet discussed, **Reports**, accesses the same menu as the **Reports** option on the Main Menu and is described in Chapter 13.)

Using the Edit Menu Tools

The Edit menu shown in figure 7.1 provides you with nine options. Each Edit menu option is described in the following sections. Essentially, all nine options enable you to modify the unprinted checks.

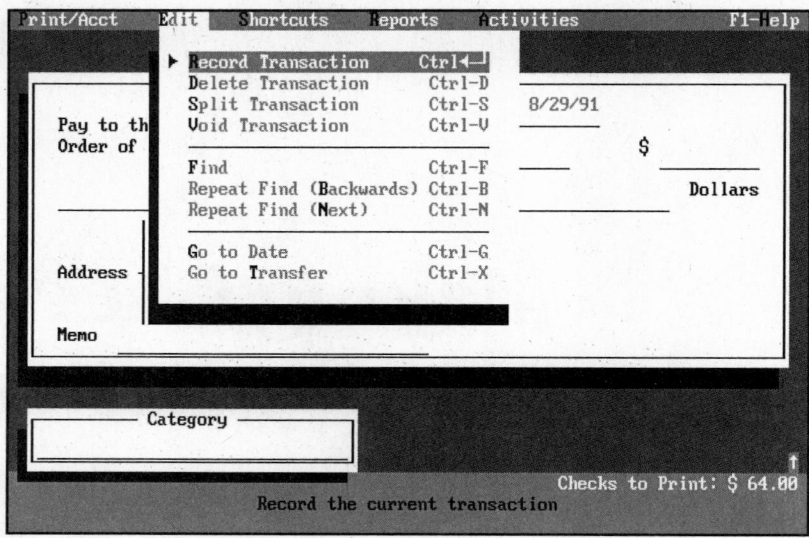

Fig. 7.1. The Edit menu provides you with nine options.

Recording and Deleting Checks

The **Record Transaction** option records (saves) checks in the register and on a hard or a floppy disk. You also can record checks by pressing Ctrl-Enter or F10.

The **Delete Transaction** option removes the check displayed on the Write Checks screen from the register and from a hard or a floppy disk. If you haven't yet recorded the check, you can use the **Delete Transaction** option to erase information in the Write Checks screen's fields. When you select **Delete Transaction** (or press Ctrl-D), Quicken asks you to confirm that you want to delete the transaction (see fig. 7.2).

To delete the check, select the first option, **Delete transaction**. If you change your mind, select **Do not delete** or press Esc.

Using Split Transactions

The Write Checks screen provides a field for recording the category into which a check fits. A check written to the power company may be described as belonging in the Utilities category. A check written to pay for office supplies may belong in the Supplies category. Many transactions, however, fit in more than one category. When you need to break down a check into more than one category, use the **Split Transaction** option from the Edit menu. The **Split Transaction** option provides additional category fields and more space to describe and document a check.

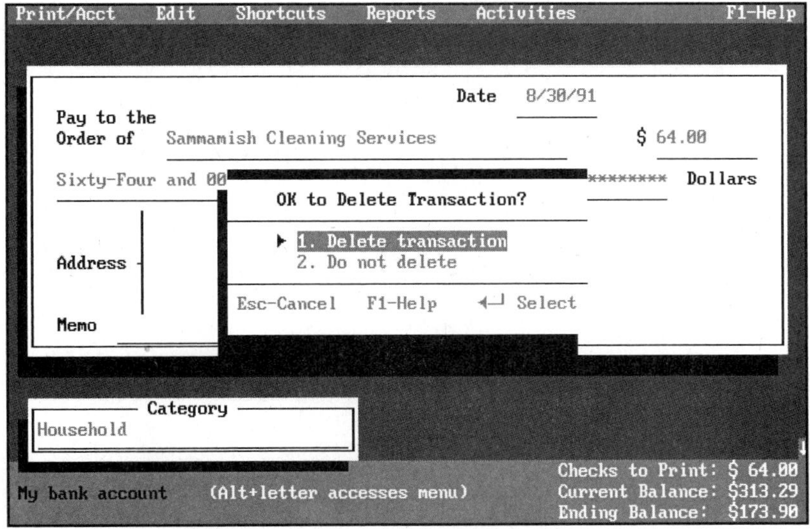

***Fig. 7.2.** The* `OK to Delete Transaction` *query.*

To split a transaction, use the following procedure:

1. Press Alt-E to display the Edit menu and select **Split Transaction** (or press Ctrl-S). The Split Transaction screen appears (see fig. 7.3).

2. Enter the category name in the `Category` field. You can use the `Category` field on the Split Transaction screen in the same way as the `Category` field on the Write Checks screen. You also can use the `Category` field to record transfers. Up to 30 lines are available on the Split Transaction screen for descriptions or categories.

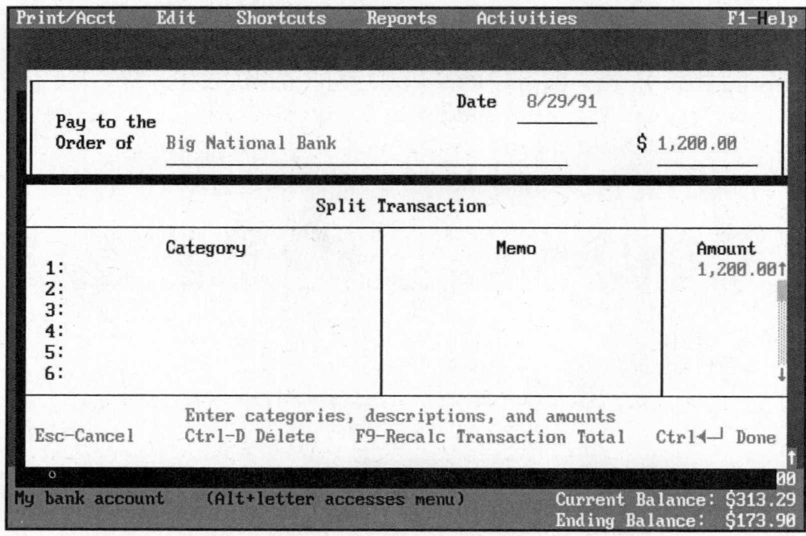

Fig. 7.3. The Split Transaction screen.

Quicken provides defined home and business categories. The home category list provides descriptions for most general household expenses, and the business category list includes general business income and expense categories. To access these categories, press Ctrl-C from the Write/Print Checks or the Register screen.

3. (Optional) To move the cursor to the `Description` field, press Enter or Tab. Type a description of the category or the amount. The `Description` field provides a 27-character space you can use to describe a transaction, to explain why you selected a category, or to detail how you calculated the check amount.

4. Press Enter or Tab to move the cursor to the `Amount` field. You can use the `Amount` field in two ways, depending on whether you select **Split Transaction** before or after you enter the amount on the Write Checks screen.

   If you select **Split Transaction** before you make an entry in the `Amount` field on the Write Checks screen, Quicken adds together each of the amounts you enter in the `Amount` field on the Split Transaction screen. Quicken then puts this total in the `Amount` field on the Write Checks screen.

If you select **Split Transaction** after entering an amount on the Write Checks screen, Quicken shows this amount in the first `Amount` field on the Split Transaction screen. If you then enter a number in the first `Amount` field on the Split Transaction screen, Quicken calculates the difference between the Write Checks screen amount and the new amount you entered and then places this difference in the second `Amount` field on the Split Transaction screen.

As previously noted in Chapter 5, you also can enter percents in the Split Transaction screen's Amount fields. If you enter a check for $1,200 and 25 percent of this amount is to be entered in the first Split Transaction field, move the cursor to the field, type *25%*, and press Enter. When you press Tab or Enter to move to the next field, Quicken calculates the number that equals 25 percent of 1,200 and enters this value in the field.

5. Press Enter or Tab to move to the next line of the Split Transaction screen. Repeat steps 2, 3, and 4 for each category and amount combination you want to record. You can record up to 30 category and amount combinations. Figure 7.4 shows a completed Split Transaction screen.

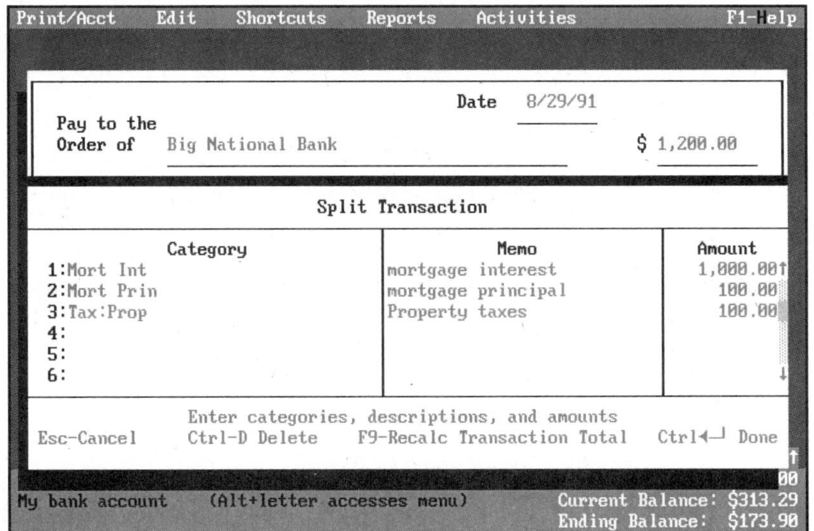

Fig. 7.4. A completed Split Transaction screen.

If you use all 30 split transaction `Amount` fields, Quicken has nowhere to make the Write Checks screen amount equal to the total Split Transaction amount. You must adjust manually the Write Checks screen amount or one of the Split Transaction screen amounts. You also can press F9 to total the `Amount` fields on the Split Transaction screen and to insert this total into the `Amount` field on the Write Checks screen.

6. To leave the Split Transaction screen and return to the Write Checks screen, Press Ctrl-Enter or F10.

7. After making all desired changes on the Split Transaction screen, record the transaction. Quicken indicates a split transaction by displaying the word `SPLIT` on-screen below the `Category` field (see fig. 7.5).

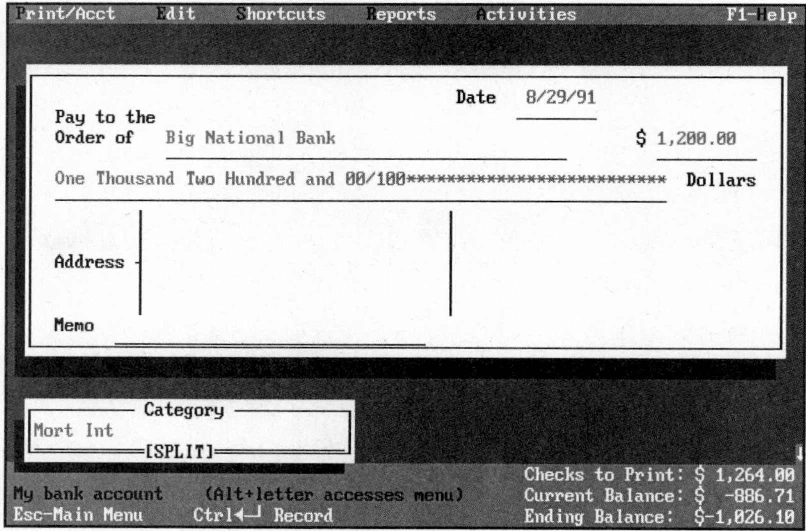

Fig. 7.5. Quicken identifies a split transaction with the word `[SPLIT]` *below the Category field on the Write Checks screen.*

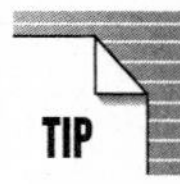

If you use check forms with vouchers and enter individual invoices and invoice amounts on the Split Transaction screen, Quicken prints this information on the voucher. Vendors then can record your payments correctly, and you no longer have to spend time trying to explain which invoice a check pays. Remember that room is available on the voucher only for the first 15 lines of the Split Transaction screen. If you use all 30 lines of the Split Transaction screen, only half of the split transaction detail appears.

Voiding Checks

Just as you can void transactions in the register, you also can void unprinted checks. You may void a check that, after entering, you decide not to pay but for which you still want to keep records. Voiding a check means you keep a record that reports you wrote—but didn't actually send—a check. To void unprinted checks, follow this procedure:

1. With the check you want to void displayed, select the **Void Transaction** option from the Edit menu (or press Ctrl-V). The register appears with the to-be-voided transaction highlighted and the `OK to Void Transaction?` message displayed.
2. To complete the voiding process, press Ctrl-Enter.
3. Press Ctrl-W to return to the Write Checks screen.

Using the Find Options

The Edit menu provides three Find options: **Find**, **Repeat Find (backwards)**, and **Repeat Find (next)**. These Find options enable you to search rapidly through checks you previously created (but have not yet printed) with the Write Checks screen.

Finding Exact Matches

One way to search through unprinted checks is to use an exact match. An exact match means that you look for a check that has a payee, the amount, the category, or another piece of check information exactly equal to what you want. The amount you are looking for is known as a *search argument*.

To search through checks you created but didn't print, follow these steps:

1. Press Alt-E to display the Edit menu and select the **Find** option (or press Ctrl-F). The Transaction to Find screen shown in figure 7.6 appears.

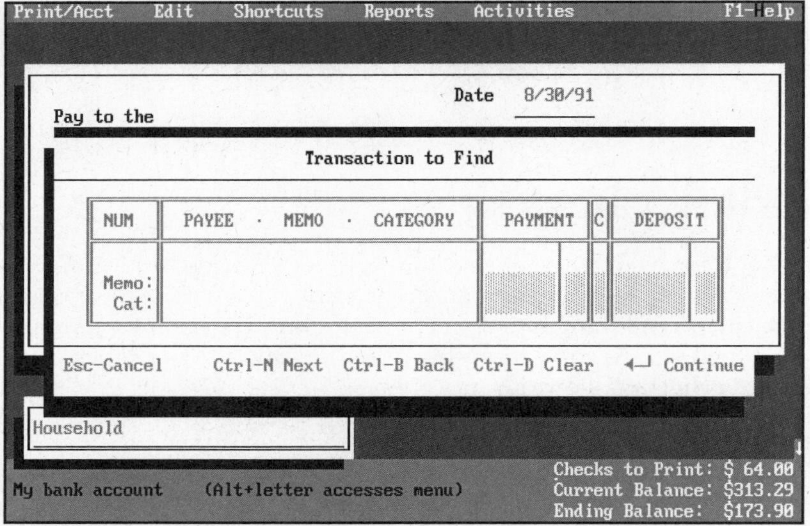

Fig. 7.6. The Transaction to Find screen.

2. Perform one or more of the following searches:

   To search through the register for checks with a specific entry in the `Payee` field, enter the payee entry of the check you are seeking in the `Payee` field.

   To search for checks equal to a specific amount, enter the amount in the `Payment` field. Quicken searches through the unprinted checks for the amount you entered. The amount you are looking for is the search argument.

   To search for unprinted checks with a specific `Memo` field entry, enter the memo entry of the check you are seeking in the `Memo` field.

   To search for unprinted checks with a specific `Category` field entry, enter the category entry of the check you are seeking in the `Category` field.

Do not enter an amount in the `Num`, `C`, or `Deposit` fields. Although the `Num`, `C`, and `Deposit` fields appear on the Transaction to Find screen, these amounts do not appear on the Write Checks screen. Therefore, you cannot use the `Num`, `C`, or `Deposit` fields to find checks created with the Write Checks screen.

3. After you enter the search arguments, press Ctrl-Enter or F10. Alternatively, press Enter when the cursor is on the category field.

   Quicken asks in which direction you want to search by displaying the screen shown in figure 7.7. You have two options: **Find backwards** and **Find next**. **Find backwards** (Ctrl-B) searches through transactions dated earlier than the transaction currently selected on the Register screen. **Find next** (Ctrl-N) searches through transactions dated later than the transaction currently selected on the Register screen.

4. Select **Find backwards** or **Find next**.

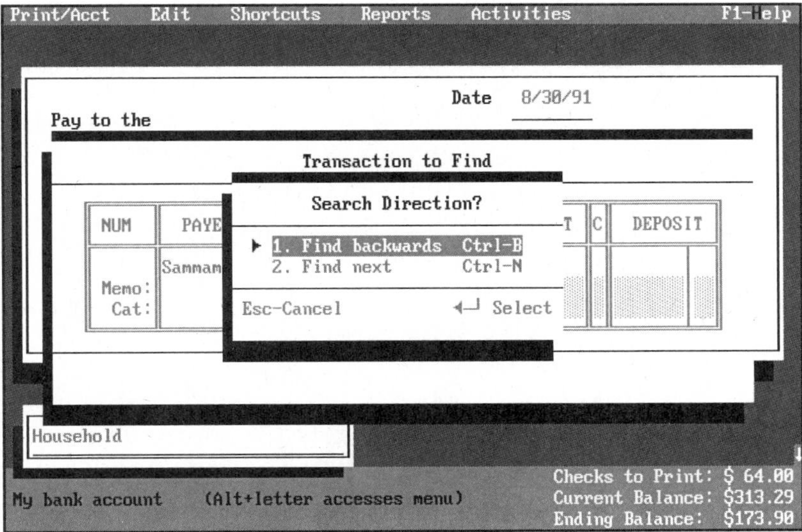

Fig. *7.7. Quicken asks whether you want to search through checks dated before or after the currently selected transaction.*

Quicken searches for the exact words you type. For example, if you enter 75 in the `Payment` field, Quicken searches for checks equal to $75.00. If you type *mortgage* in the Memo field, Quicken looks for checks with *mortgage* in this field. Because Quicken's search isn't case sensitive, *Mortgage*, *MORTGAGE*, and *mortgage* are all exact matches from Quicken's perspective. If the Memo field reads *May mortgage*, however, Quicken does not find the check.

If Quicken finds a check that matches the search argument, Quicken displays the check on the Write Checks screen. If Quicken does not find a check that matches the search argument, the program displays the message No matching transactions were found (see fig. 7.8).

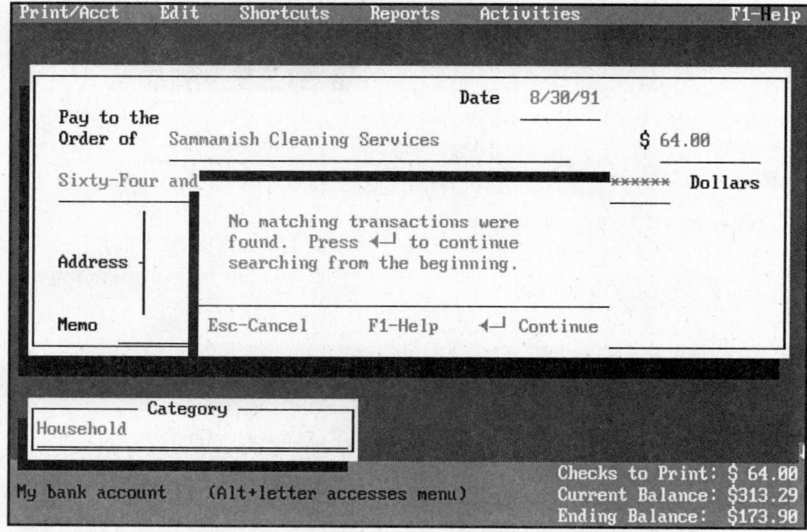

Fig. 7.8. *The* No matching transactions were found *message.*

Finding Key-Word Matches

Key-word matches enable you to search based on a field that includes or excludes certain letters, characters, or series of characters. Key-word matches use three special characters: periods, question marks, and tildes. Periods act as wild-card indicators that can represent any character, group of characters, or even no character. The question mark can represent any one character. The tilde character identifies a word, character, or group of characters to exclude from the search.

Combining Exact Matches and Key-Word Matches

You can search by using more than one exact match or key-word search argument. Figure 7.9, for example, shows the Transaction to Find screen filled to search for checks using *big national* in the `Payee` field and *mortgage* in the `Memo` field. The same techniques that work for searching through the register also work for searching through unprinted checks. For more information about key-word matches, refer to "Using Key-Word Matches" in Chapter 5.

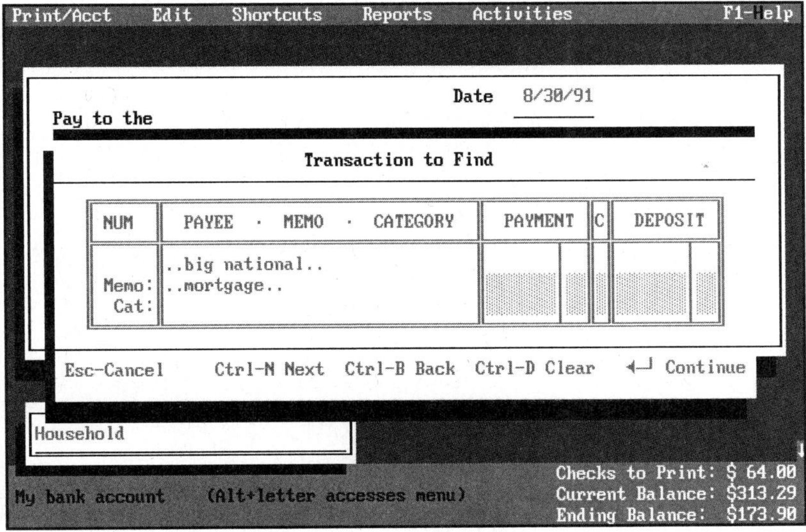

***Fig. 7.9.** Using key-word matches on the Transaction to Find screen.*

If you use more than one match test, Quicken locates only the checks that meet all the tests. Given the Transaction to Find screen shown in figure 7.9, Quicken does not locate checks with the phrase *big national* in the `Payee` field unless the word *mortgage* is in the `Memo` field and vice versa.

Repeating a Search

When executing a Find operation, Quicken selects the first check that matches the search arguments you entered. If you were precise in specifying the exact match or key-word match, the first check Quicken finds may be the one you want. Because the first check Quicken finds often is not be the one you want, however, Quicken gives you two other Find options: **Repeat Find (backwards)** and **Repeat Find (next)**. **Repeat Find (backwards)** executes the find operation already specified on the Transaction to Find screen—**Repeat Find (backwards)** searches through checks dated earlier than the currently displayed check. Similarly, **Repeat Find (next)** executes the find operation already specified on the Transaction to Find screen. **Repeat Find (next)** searches through checks dated later than the currently displayed check.

Using the Go to Date Option

To search for a specific day's transactions, use the **Go to Date** option or press Ctrl-G. With the check you want to void displayed, specify the date you want to use as the basis for a search on the Go to Date screen, shown in figure 7.10.

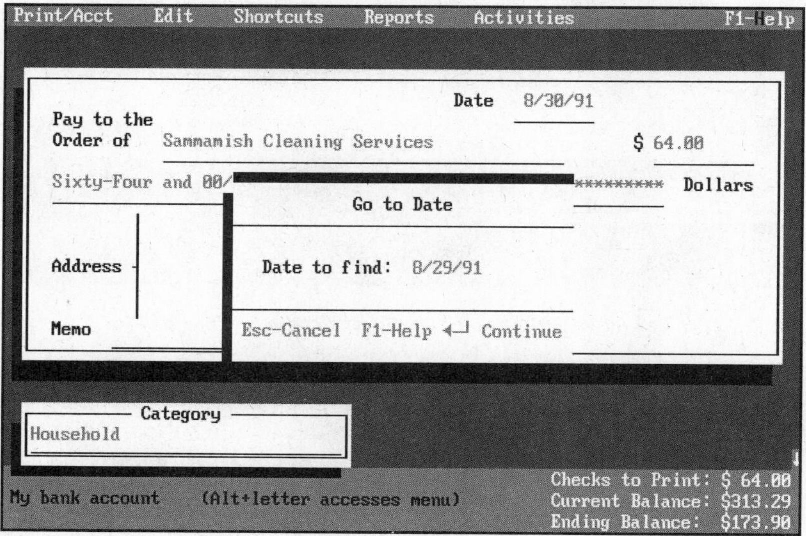

***Fig. 7.10.** Quicken can search through checks by using a date.*

Initially, Quicken displays the current system date on the Go to Date screen. To specify a date for the search, type the date you want over the default date.

You also can use the + and – keys to move the date forward or backward one day at a time.

After you specify a date and press Enter, Quicken finds and displays the first check with the date you entered. If no check with the entered date is found, Quicken displays the check with the date closest to the entered date.

Because Quicken arranges all checks by the check date, you do not need to specify a search direction when using the **Go to Date** option. By comparing the date on the currently displayed check to the date you enter, Quicken determines the direction to search. If the date for which you want to search falls before the date on the current check, Quicken looks through the previous checks. If the date you want to search for falls after the date on the current check, Quicken looks through checks dated after the current check.

Using the Go to Transfer Option

You can select the **Go to Transfer** option (Ctrl-X) to go to the transfer transaction related to the currently displayed check. If you entered the transfer account in the Category field, recorded the check, and then executed the **Go to Transfer** option, Quicken displays the Account register that shows the corresponding transaction. Pressing Ctrl-X again returns you to the original check register.

Usually, you enter an account here because you're transferring money from a checking account to another bank account by writing a check. To review account transfers, see Chapters 4 and 5.

Using the Shortcuts Menu Tools

To speed the check-writing process, Quicken's Shortcuts menu provides several options (see fig. 7.11).

The following paragraphs describe how to use the **Recall Transaction** and **Memorize Transaction** options to store and reuse recurring transactions, how to use the **Categorize/Transfer** option, and how to use the **Transaction Groups** option to store and reuse whole sets of transactions. The **Select/Set Up Class** option is discussed in Chapter 10.

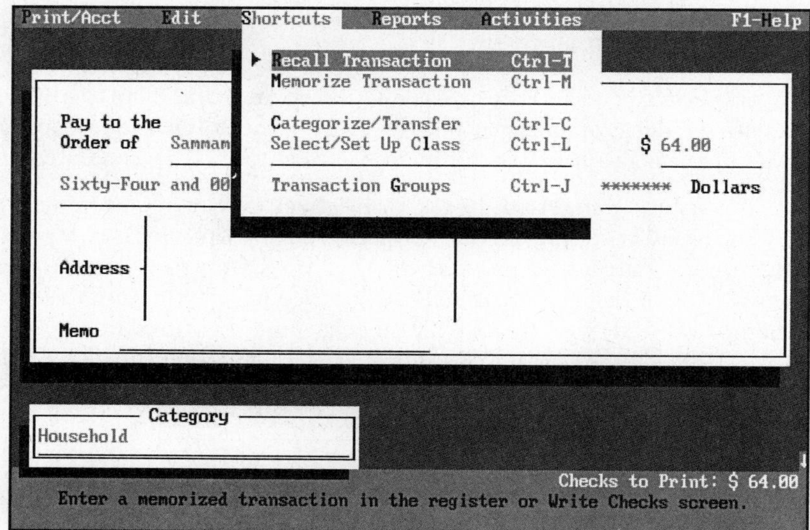

Fig. 7.11. The Shortcuts menu provides tools for speeding up check writing.

Memorizing Transactions

Many checks you write probably are similar from week to week and month to month. For a household, you may write a mortgage check, a car loan check, a utility bill check, and so on. For a business, you may write weekly payroll checks to employees and monthly checks to major vendors. Because checks often are similar, Quicken enables you to store check information in a special list known as the Memorized Transactions List. Instead of reentering the same information, you can reuse transaction information. The **Memorize Transaction** option is valuable if you address checks, because you do not have to reenter the payee's address every time you write a check.

If you have read Chapter 5, you already know about using memorized transactions in the register. **Memorize Transaction** works similarly on the Write Checks screen. Therefore, if you feel well versed in the mechanics of memorized transactions, skip or skim the next few paragraphs. The only substantive difference between memorized transactions for the register and memorized transactions for unprinted checks is that if you memorize an unprinted check, Quicken memorizes the address information. (Address information doesn't appear in the register.)

To memorize a transaction, follow these steps:

1. Display the check you want to memorize on the Write Checks screen (see fig. 7.12).
2. Press Alt-S to display the Shortcuts menu, and then select the **Memorize Transaction** option or press Ctrl-M. Quicken alerts you that the marked information is about to be memorized (see fig. 7.13).
3. To complete the memorization process, press Enter. Quicken saves a copy of the transaction in the Memorized Transactions List.

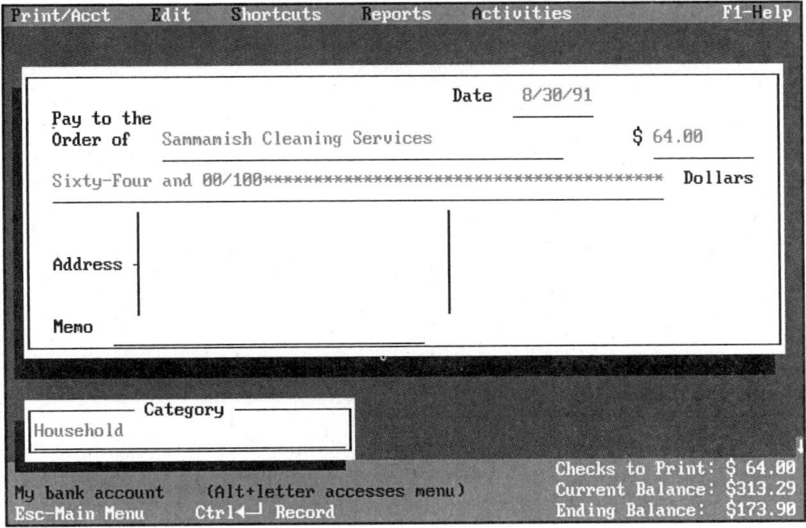

Fig. 7.12. *You may decide to memorize a monthly housecleaning or janitorial check.*

Recalling a Transaction

Selecting **Recall Transaction** (Ctrl-T) enables you to complete the Write Checks screen by using information from memorized transactions. Suppose that you use the **Memorize Transaction** option to memorize the monthly cleaning payment shown in figure 7.12. When you need to pay Sammamish Cleaning Services again, select **Recall Transaction** from the Shortcuts menu or press Ctrl-T. Either approach displays the Memorized

Transactions List shown in figure 7.14. The Memorized Transactions List screen shows all memorized transactions. You want to recall, however, only those transactions that show Chk in the Type column. Chk indicates the transaction was memorized from the Write Checks screen. Chk transactions include information that appears only on the Write Checks screen, such as the address data and the extra message line.

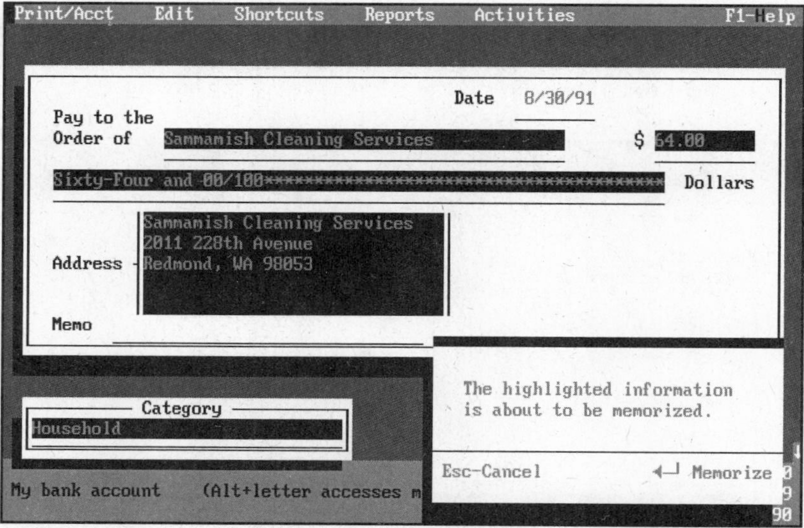

Fig. 7.13. Quicken tells you that the marked information is about to be memorized.

Figure 7.14 shows some of the information saved as part of the **Memorize Transaction** operation. The address information and message also are saved, but the address and message do not show on the Memorized Transactions List.

If you memorize a split check transaction, Quicken displays a message box that asks if you want to memorize the split amounts as amounts or as percentages of the check amount. To answer the message, enter *A* if you want the actual amounts memorized or *P* to memorize the percentages that the amounts represent. This feature is handy if a memorized check amount varies, but the split is always based on the same percentages.

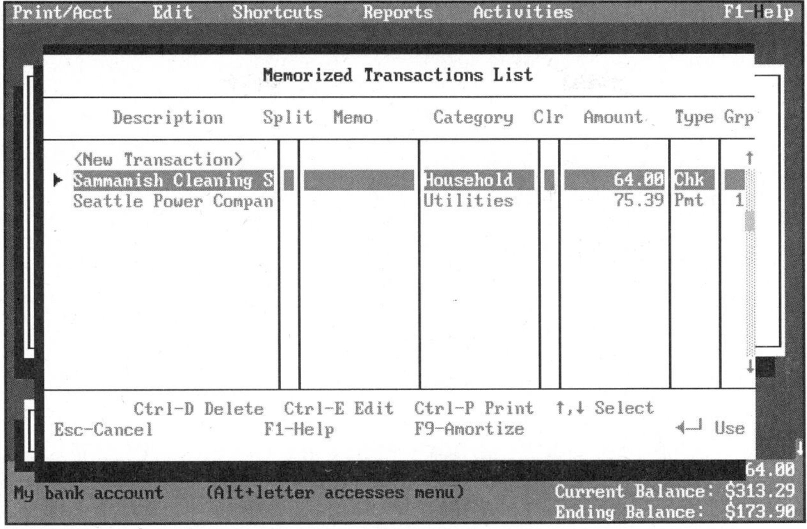

Fig. 7.14. *The Memorized Transactions List.*

The payee name is in the `Description` field, the memo is in the `Memo` field, the category name is in the `Category` field, and the check amount is in the `Amount` field. If you split a check transaction, an `S` appears in the `Split` field. Quicken also places the abbreviation `Chk` in the `Type` field to identify the transaction as a check. The `Grp` field indicates whether the memorized transaction is part of a group of transactions. Transaction groups are described later in the chapter.

To use (or recall) a memorized transaction, take the following steps:

1. If you have not done so already, press Alt-S to display the Shortcuts menu and select the **Recall Transaction** option, or press Ctrl-T. Quicken displays the Memorized Transactions List (see fig. 7.14).

2. Use the up- and down-arrow keys to move the selection triangle to the left of the `Description` field of the check you want to write.

3. Press Enter. Quicken uses the memorized transaction to fill the Write Checks screen.

4. Edit the information from the memorized transaction so that the information correctly reflects the check you want to write.

5. To record the check, press Ctrl-Enter. Quicken records the check transaction in the register.

Editing Memorized Transactions

Over time, the check information you memorize may need to be updated. Updating check information, however, doesn't present a problem. To edit a memorized transaction, follow these steps:

1. Press Alt-S to display the Shortcuts menu and select the **Recall Transaction** option (or press Ctrl-T). Quicken displays the Memorized Transactions List.

2. Highlight the transaction you want to edit and press Ctrl-E. Quicken displays the Edit/Setup Memorized Transactions box (see fig. 7.15).

3. Change the fields as necessary and then press Ctrl-Enter or F10.

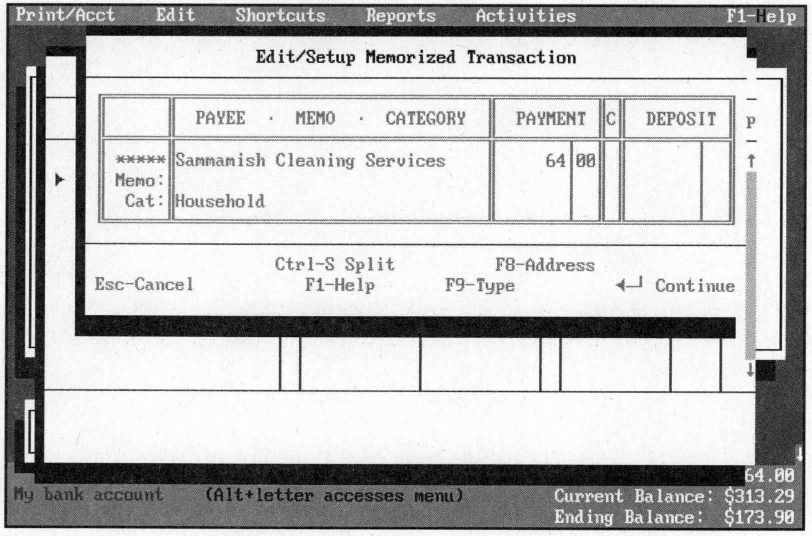

***Fig. 7.15.** The Edit/Setup Memorized Transaction box.*

Deleting Memorized Transactions

At some point, the original reasons you had for memorizing a transaction may no longer apply. Eventually, you may pay off the mortgage or a car loan, children may outgrow the need for day care, or you may choose to stop spending money on an item, such as club dues or cable television.

You can use the **Recall Transaction** option to delete memorized transactions from the Memorized Transactions List.

To delete a transaction from the list, follow these steps:

1. Press Alt-S to display the Shortcuts menu and select the **Recall Transaction** option (or press Ctrl-T). Quicken displays the Memorized Transactions List (see fig. 7.14).
2. Use the up- and down-arrow keys to highlight the transaction you want to delete.
3. After you highlight the transaction to delete, press Ctrl-D. Quicken alerts you that you are about to delete a memorized transaction (see fig. 7.16).
4. To delete the memorized transaction, press Enter. If you decide not to delete the memorized transaction, press Esc.

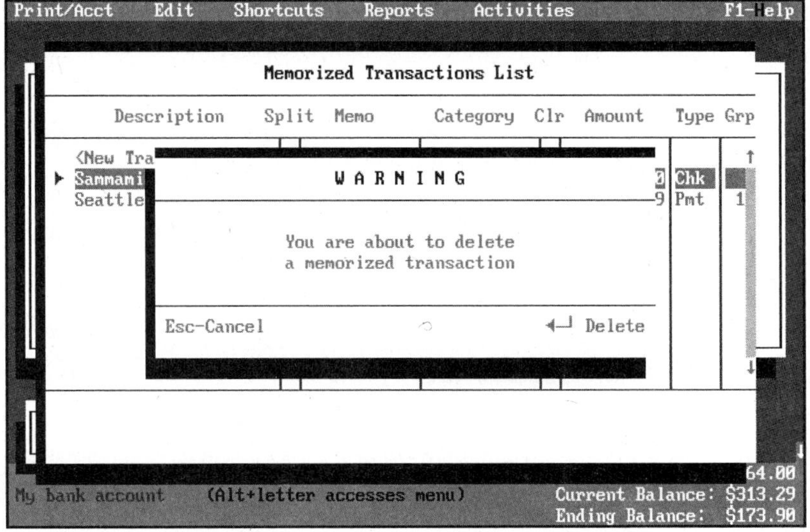

Fig. 7.16. *The* You are about to delete a memorized transaction *message.*

Printing Memorized Transactions

Quicken enables you to print lists of memorized transactions. Assuming that you entered payee addresses, a printed list of memorized transactions can act as a directory of the people and businesses to whom you write checks.

To print a list of memorized transactions, follow these steps:

1. Press Alt-S to display the Shortcuts menu and then select the **Recall Transaction** option (or press Ctrl-T). The Memorized Transactions List screen appears (see fig. 7.14).
2. Press Ctrl-P. Quicken displays the Print Memorized Transactions List screen, which is similar to the Print Checks screen described in Chapter 6. Specify the printer setting you want to use to print the report.
3. Indicate the printer you want to use and press Enter. Quicken prints the list (see fig. 7.17).

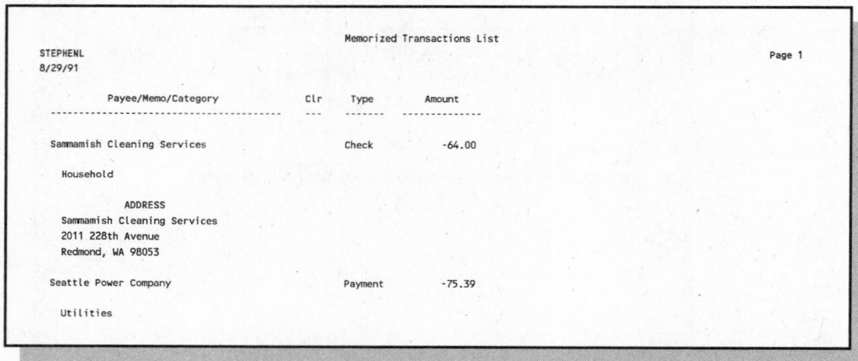

```
                         Memorized Transactions List
STEPHENL                                                          Page 1
8/29/91

      Payee/Memo/Category          Clr    Type       Amount
------------------------------     ---   -------  -------------

Sammamish Cleaning Services              Check         -64.00

  Household

        ADDRESS
  Sammamish Cleaning Services
  2011 228th Avenue
  Redmond, WA 98053

Seattle Power Company                    Payment       -75.39

  Utilities
```

***Fig. 7.17.** The printed Memorized Transactions List.*

Consider as candidates for the Memorized Transactions List each check you regularly write using Quicken: rent, house payment, utility payment, school loans, and so on. Using the **Memorized Transaction** option saves you time you otherwise spend typing, finding addresses, and describing checks.

Using the Categorize/Transfer Option

With the **Categorize/Transfer** option (Ctrl-C), you can create or retrieve a category. Remember that Quicken provides predefined home and business categories. (Creating new categories is discussed in Chapter 10.)

To find and use a predefined category, follow this process:

1. Press Alt-S to display the Shortcuts menu and select the **Categorize/Transfer** option (or press Ctrl-C). The Category and Transfer List screen appears, which lists each of the predefined categories and all accounts you have created (see fig. 7.18). The accounts are listed at the end of the Category and Transfer List.

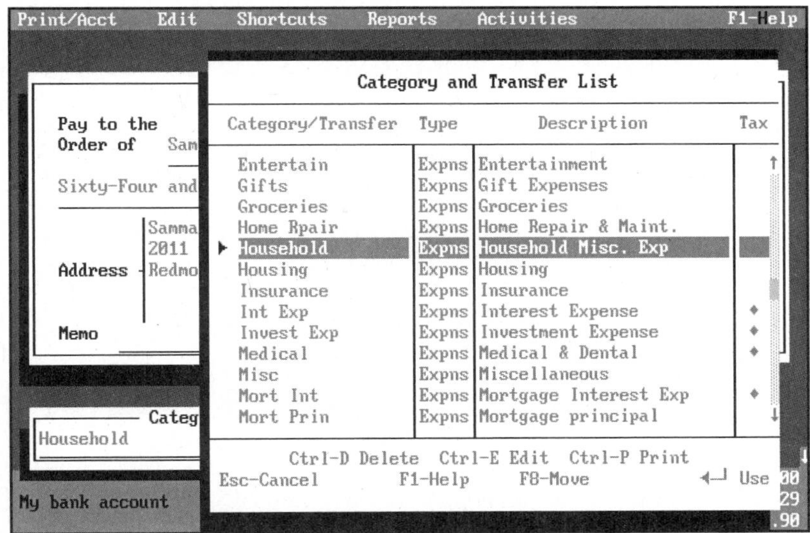

Fig. 7.18. The Category and Transfer List screen.

2. Use the up- and down-arrow keys to select the category or account you want to use and then press Enter, or by using the mouse, double-click on the category. Quicken retrieves the category or account name from the list and puts the name in the `Category` field. The Category and Transfer List screen also provides a scroll bar, which mouse users can manipulate to move up and down the list. If you don't know how scroll bars work, refer to Chapter 4 for a discussion of moving the register with a scroll bar.

You also can use the PgUp, PgDn, Home, and End keys to move quickly through long lists of categories. Pressing PgUp displays the preceding page of categories in the list; pressing PgDn displays the following page of categories in the list; pressing Home displays the first page of categories; and pressing End displays the last page of categories.

Setting Up a Transaction Group

The capability of recalling a single memorized check saves time, but Quicken provides you with another option: you can recall sets of memorized transactions, or *transaction groups*. Transaction groups enable you to recall several memorized checks at the same time. Rather than repeatedly using **Recall Transaction** to retrieve checks from the Memorized Transactions List, you can recall an entire group of checks in one step.

The first step to using a transaction group is creating a transaction group. To create a transaction group, follow these steps:

1. Follow the steps described in a previous section, "Memorizing Transactions," to memorize the transactions you want to include in a transaction group.

2. Press Alt-S to display the Shortcuts menu and then select the **Transaction Groups** option (or press Ctrl-J). Quicken displays the Select Transaction Group to Execute screen, as shown in figure 7.19.

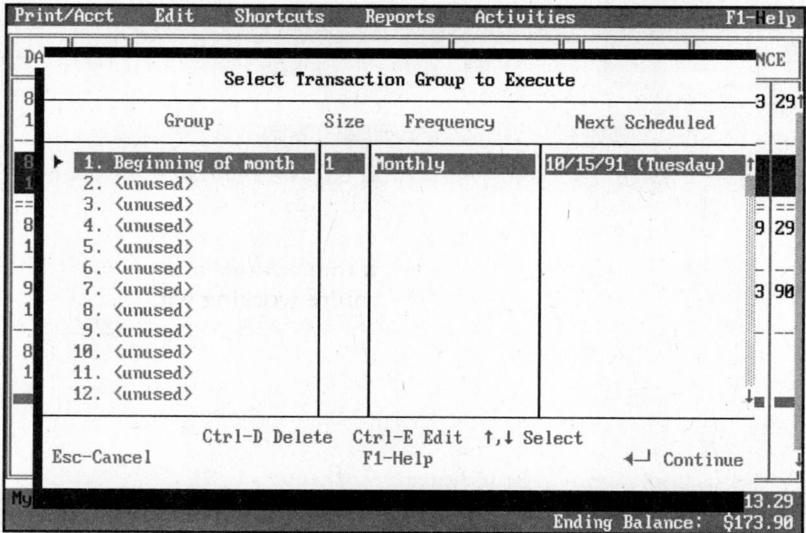

Fig. 7.19. The Select Transaction Group to Execute screen.

3. Use the up- and down-arrow keys to mark the first unused transaction group and then press Enter. The Describe Group screen appears (see fig. 7.20). If you are defining the first transaction group, mark Group 1 and press Enter. If you previously have defined a transaction group, use Group 2. (Group 1 was used for figures in Chapter 5, so Group 2 is used here.) Quicken provides 12 empty transaction groups.

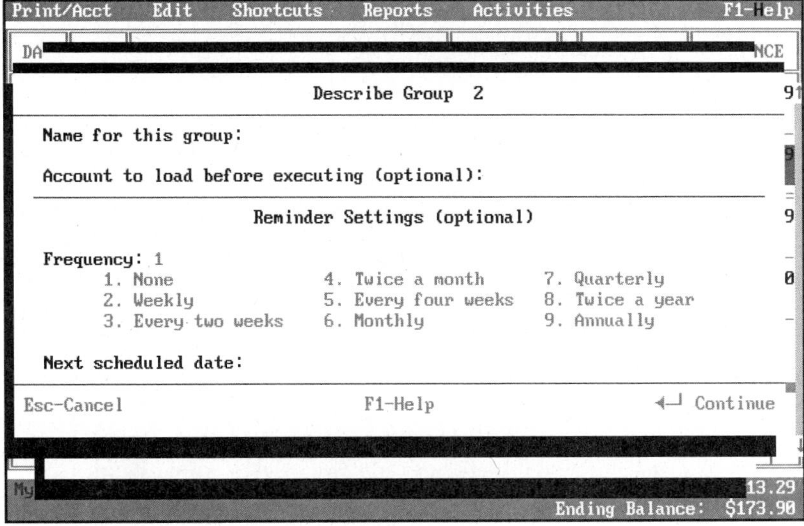

Fig. 7.20. *The Describe Group screen.*

4. Enter a name or description for the transaction group. You can use up to 20 characters to describe the group.

5. To move the cursor to the `Account to load before executing` field, press Enter or Tab. Enter the account on which the checks are going to be written. This step causes the appropriate account to be selected before you recall the check transactions in a group. You don't need this field, obviously, if you're working with only one account.

6. To move the cursor to the `Frequency` field, press Enter or Tab. Set the frequency by using one of the nine settings shown in figure 7.20: `None`, `Weekly`, `Every two weeks`, `Twice a month`, `Every four weeks`, `Monthly`, `Quarterly`, `Twice a year`, or `Annually`. Select the desired frequency by typing the number that corresponds with the desired frequency.

7. If you set the frequency to any setting other than `None`, you also must set the next scheduled date.

The next scheduled date is the date for which Billminder reminds you of the transaction group.) Press Enter or Tab to move the cursor to the `Next scheduled date` field. Enter the date in the MM/DD/YY format.

8. Press Enter. Quicken displays the Assign Transactions to Group screen (see fig. 7.21). The Assign Transactions to Group screen lists all memorized transactions.

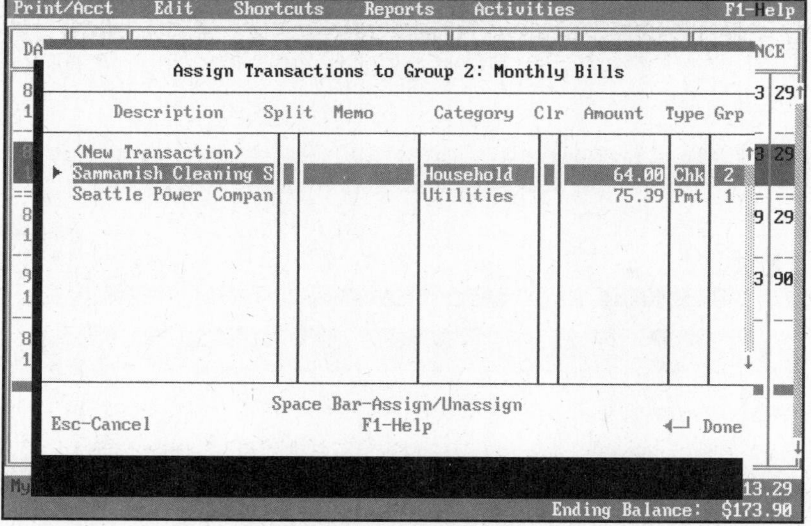

Fig. 7.21. The Assign Transactions to Group screen.

9. Use the arrow keys to mark memorized transactions that you want to include as part of the transaction group. When a transaction is marked, press the space bar to assign the transaction to the group. After a transaction is assigned to a group, the `Grp` field on the Assign Transactions screen displays the group number. To *unassign* a transaction, press the space bar again while the transaction is highlighted. Figure 7.21 shows memorized transactions selected for Group 2.

10. After you mark all the memorized transactions that you want to include as part of the transaction group, press Enter to save the work. Quicken displays the Select Transaction Group to Execute screen with the newly defined transaction group listed (see fig. 7.22).

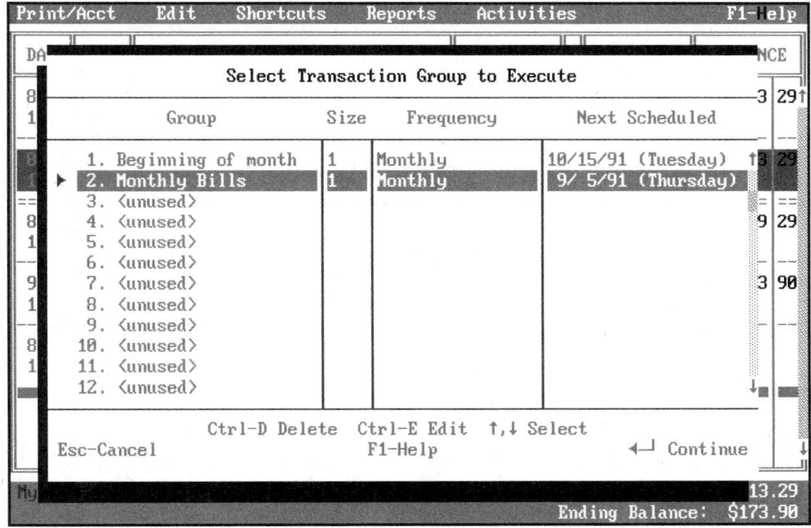

Fig. 7.22. *The newly defined transaction group appears on the Select Transaction Group to Execute screen.*

Executing a Transaction Group

After you create a transaction group of memorized check transactions, you can use the transaction group to recall simultaneously the entire set of memorized checks.

To write a series of checks using a transaction group, follow these steps:

1. Press Alt-S to display the Shortcuts menu and select the **Transaction Groups** option. Quicken displays the Select Transaction Group to Execute screen (see fig. 7.19).

2. Use the up- and down-arrow keys to move the selection triangle to the left of the `Description` field of the transaction group you want to use.

3. Press Enter. Quicken prompts you for the Transaction Group Date, as shown in figure 7.23. Quicken switches to the register when displaying the Transaction Group Date screen.

```
Print/Acct   Edit   Shortcuts   Reports   Activities                 F1-Help

DATE  NUM    PAYEE · MEMO · CATEGORY       PAYMENT  C  DEPOSIT   BALANCE

8/29  104    Washington Foods                           132 93    313 29
1991  SPLIT              Auto
8/29         VOID:Big National Bank                 X             313 29
1991  SPLIT
      Cat:   Mort Int      Transaction Group Date
8/30  *****  Sammamish C                                          249 29
1991
                           Date of group:  9/ 5/91
9/15         Seattle Pow                                          173 90
1991
                           Esc-Cancel       ↵ Continue
8/29
1991
                           END

My bank account   (Alt+letter accesses menu)   Current Balance: $313.29
                                               Ending Balance:  $173.90
```

Fig. 7.23. The Transaction Group Date screen.

4. Enter the date you want shown on checks in the transaction group. Remember that you can use the + and – keys to change the date one day at a time.

5. Press Enter when the Transaction Group Date screen shows the correct date. Quicken writes each check and displays the Transaction Group Entered screen. Quicken also moves forward the next scheduled date for the transaction group, using the frequency you specified.

The next scheduled date is the date for which Billminder reminds you of the transaction group.

6. Edit the information on each of the checks as necessary. To use the Write Checks screen to edit, press Ctrl-W.

Changing and Deleting Transaction Groups

Because transaction groups segregate checks into groups you pay together at one time, changes in payment due dates mean that you need to change the transaction group. For example, if you refinance a mortgage, the due date may change from the fifth to the fifteenth of the month. If you have separate transaction groups for checks you write at the beginning of the month and checks you write in the middle of the month, you may need to change your transaction groups.

To modify a transaction group, use the **Transaction Groups** option on the Shortcuts menu and select a transaction group. Access the Describe Group and Assign Transactions to Group screens shown in figures 7.20 and 7.21. Make the required changes on the appropriate screen and press Enter to continue to the next screen.

To delete a transaction group, select the **Transaction Groups** option from the Shortcuts menu. Use the arrow keys to mark the group you want to delete and then press Ctrl-D. Quicken displays a message alerting you that the marked transaction group is about to be deleted. To delete the transaction group, press Enter. Press Esc if you decide not to delete the transaction group.

Using the Activities Menu

The Write Checks Activities menu provides access to other Quicken tools you may need when writing checks. The Write Checks Activities menu has five options (see fig. 7.24).

Choosing **Register** accesses the Register screen and menu options, just as the **Register** option on Quicken's Main Menu does. The register is described in Chapters 4 and 5.

Selecting **Reconcile** accesses the Reconciliation screen and options, just as the **Reconcile** option on Quicken's Main Menu does. Reconciling is described in Chapter 8.

Choosing **Set Up Budgets** accesses the Quicken budgeting spreadsheet. Chapter 16 describes how to use Quicken's budgeting features.

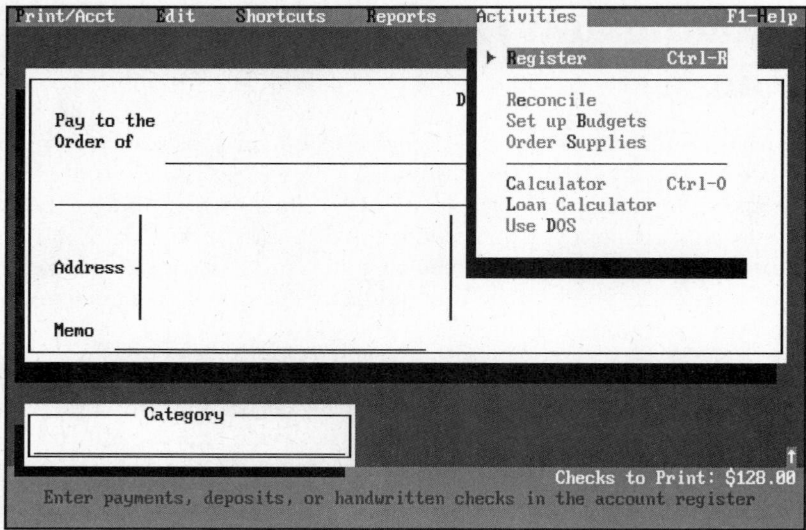

***Fig. 7.24.** The Write Checks Activities menu.*

Selecting **Order Supplies** accesses the Print Supply Order Form screen, shown in figure 7.25. You print this three-page order form to purchase supplies, such as check forms and envelopes, from Intuit, the manufacturer of Quicken. The supply order form is similar to the order form that Intuit provides in the Quicken package.

Choosing **Calculator** accesses the on-line, 10-key calculator that Quicken provides (see fig. 7.26). Chapter 2 describes the on-line calculator in detail.

Choosing **Loan Calculator** accesses the on-line loan payment calculator. Refer to Chapter 12 for information on how to use this handy tool.

Selecting **Use DOS** calls up DOS and displays the DOS prompt in figure 7.27.

The **Use DOS** feature is handy when you want to execute DOS commands before leaving Quicken. For example, you may want to format a disk to make a backup copy of an account. To return to Quicken from DOS, type *exit* at the C> prompt.

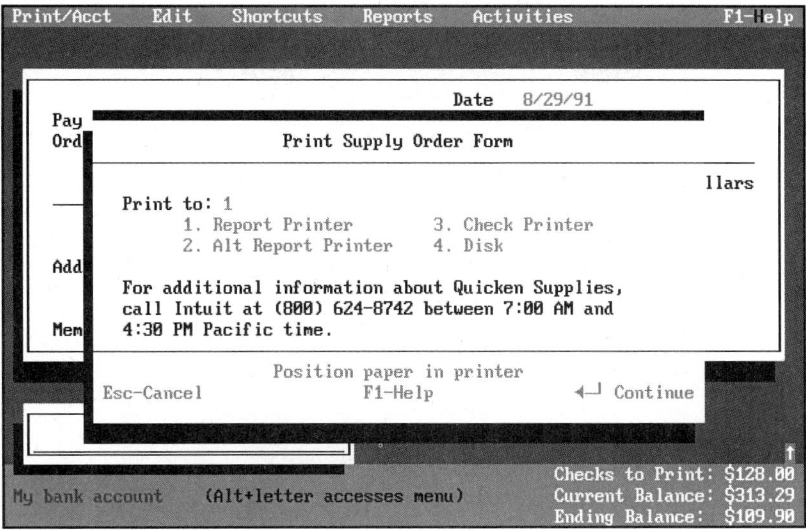

Fig. 7.25. The Print Supply Order Form screen.

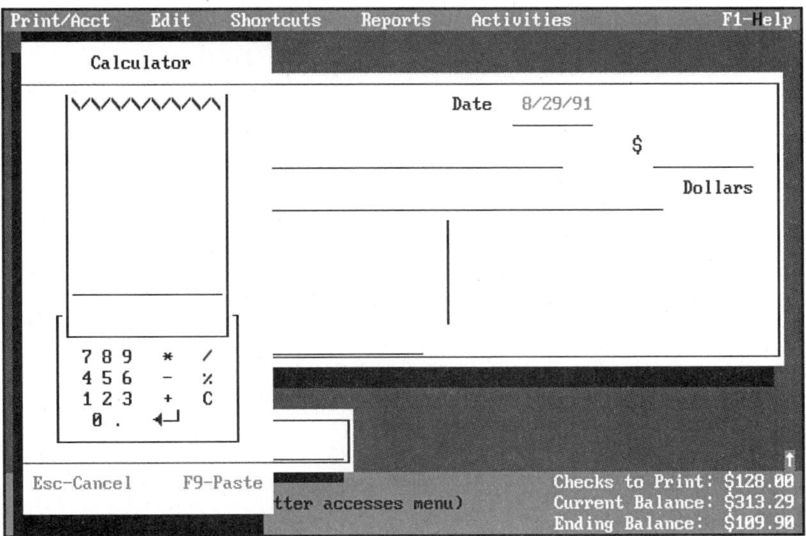

Fig. 7.26. The on-line calculator.

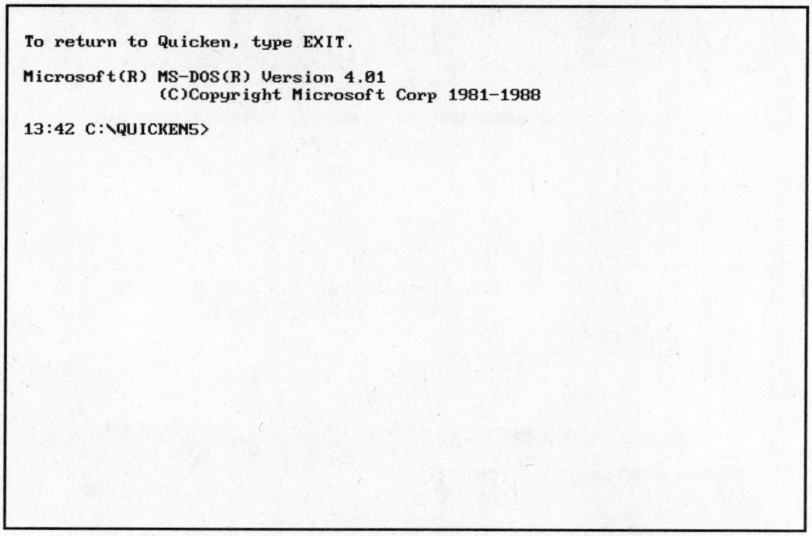

```
To return to Quicken, type EXIT.

Microsoft(R) MS-DOS(R) Version 4.01
             (C)Copyright Microsoft Corp 1981-1988

13:42 C:\QUICKEN5>
```

***Fig.** 7.27. The DOS prompt after executing the Use DOS option.*

Chapter Summary

This chapter described the details of using the three sets of Write Checks menu options not covered in the preceding chapter: the Edit, Shortcuts, and Activities menus. The options on these three menus make using the Write Checks screen even easier and faster. The Edit menu options make recording, editing, and deleting checks easier; the Shortcuts menu options speed the process of using Quicken to print checks; and the Activities menu options access other Quicken and system features you may need while writing and printing checks.

8

Reconciling Your Bank Account

Regularly reconciling your bank account is one of the most important steps you can take to protect your cash and the accuracy and reliability of your financial records, but most people probably don't reconcile—except out of a sense of guilt or frustration. The work is tedious and usually aggravating as you search, often futilely, for the transaction that explains the difference between the bank's records and your personal records. Fortunately, Quicken provides a fast and easy method of reconciliation. This chapter describes the steps for reconciling accounts in Quicken, printing and using reconciliation reports, and correcting and catching reconciliation errors.

Reviewing the Reconciliation Process

Reconciling a bank account is not difficult. You probably already understand the mechanics of the reconciliation process. For those readers who are a bit rusty with the process, however, the next few paragraphs briefly describe how reconciliation works.

To reconcile a bank account, you perform three basic steps:

1. Review the bank statement for new transactions and errors. You want to verify that you have recorded each transaction correctly.

2. Find the transactions not recorded by the bank, or cleared, and total these transactions.

3. Verify that the difference between the check register balance and the bank balance equals the total of the cleared transactions. If the totals don't agree, you need to repeat steps 1 and 2.

If you still find the process confusing, examine your monthly bank statement. The back of your current bank statement probably explains the whole process step-by-step.

Reviewing the Bank Statement

The first step in reconciling an account is to review the bank statement. First find any new transactions that the bank recorded and that you now need to record. These transactions may include bank service fees, overdraft charges, and interest income. You need to record these transactions in the register before you proceed with the reconciliation.

For each transaction, confirm that the checking account transaction recorded in the register and on the bank statement are the same amount. If you find a transaction not recorded in both places for the same amount, review the discrepancy and identify the incorrect transaction.

Carefully review each canceled check for authenticity. If a check forger successfully draws a check on your account, you can discover the forgery by reviewing canceled checks. As Chapter 19 explains, you need to find forgeries if you hope to recover the money.

Checking Cleared Transactions

The second step in checking account reconciliation is to calculate the total dollar value of those transactions that have not cleared the bank. By adding up all checks that have not cleared (usually known as *outstanding checks*) and also all deposits (usually known as *deposits in transit*), you calculate an amount that represents the logical difference between the bank's records and your records.

Usually, the mechanics of this step work in the following way: you look through the bank statement to identify checks and deposits that have cleared and then mark cleared transactions in the register. After you mark all the cleared transactions in the register, adding up all the transactions that haven't cleared is a simple matter.

Verifying that Balances Correspond

The final step is a quick one: you verify that the difference between the check register balance and the bank statement balance is the total of the transactions that haven't cleared. If you have correctly performed steps 1 and 2 in the reconciliation process, the two amounts should differ by the total of all transactions not yet cleared. If the two amounts don't differ by precisely this amount, you must repeat steps 1 and 2 until you locate and correct the error.

Using Quicken To Reconcile Your Account

Quicken makes reconciling a bank account easier by automating the steps and doing the arithmetic. To reconcile an account, follow these steps:

1. Select **Reconcile** from the Activities menu on the Write Checks or Register screen. Quicken then displays the screen shown in figure 8.1.

2. In the `Bank Statement Opening Balance` field, type the bank statement balance shown at the start of the period the statement covers if the balance differs from the one shown. This number appears on the bank statement.

3. Press Enter or Tab to move the cursor to the `Bank Statement Ending Balance` field and type the bank statement balance shown at the end of the period the bank statement covers. This number appears on your bank statement.

4. Press Enter or Tab to move the cursor to the `Service Charge` field. If you have not recorded monthly service fees, record these fees now by entering the appropriate amount in the `Service Charge` field.

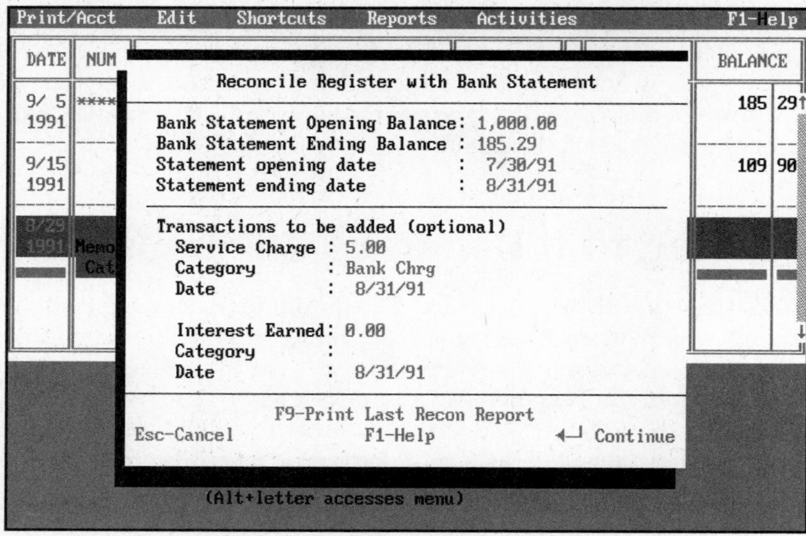

Fig. 8.1. *The Reconcile Register with Bank Statement screen.*

5. (Optional) Press Enter or Tab to move the cursor to the `Service Charge Category` field. If you entered an amount in the Service Charge field and want to assign the charge to a category, enter the appropriate category name in the `Service Charge Category` field. (Remember that you can access the Category and Transfer List screen by pressing Ctrl-C.)

6. Press Enter or Tab to move the cursor to the `Interest Earned` field. If you have not recorded monthly interest income on the account, record the interest earned now by entering the appropriate amount in the `Interest Earned` field.

7. (Optional) Press Enter or Tab to move the cursor to the `Interest Earned Category` field. If you entered an amount in the `Interest Earned` field and want to assign the income to a category, enter the appropriate category name here.

8. Press Enter to access the Transaction List screen, which shows each checking account transaction (see fig. 8.2).

9. Mark checks and deposits that have cleared (were recorded by) the bank. To mark an item as cleared, use the up- and down-arrow keys to move the selection triangle to the left of the transaction you want to mark. When the triangle is in place, press the space bar. Quicken enters an asterisk in the cleared column.

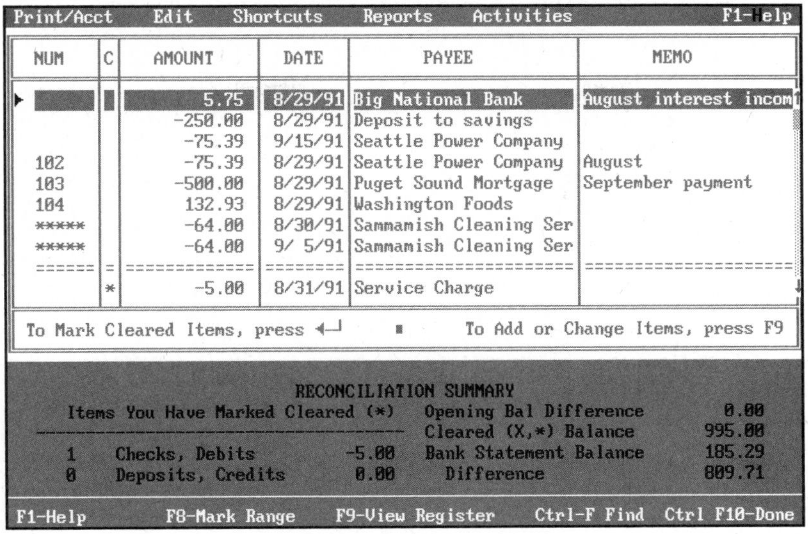

```
Print/Acct    Edit    Shortcuts    Reports    Activities                F1-Help

 NUM    C    AMOUNT       DATE         PAYEE                   MEMO

              5.75      8/29/91  Big National Bank      August interest incom
           -250.00      8/29/91  Deposit to savings
            -75.39      9/15/91  Seattle Power Company
 102        -75.39      8/29/91  Seattle Power Company  August
 103       -500.00      8/29/91  Puget Sound Mortgage   September payment
 104        132.93      8/29/91  Washington Foods
 *****      -64.00      8/30/91  Sammamish Cleaning Ser
 *****      -64.00      9/ 5/91  Sammamish Cleaning Ser
 ====== = ============= ======== ====================== =====================
        *    -5.00      8/31/91  Service Charge

 To Mark Cleared Items, press ←┘      ▪      To Add or Change Items, press F9

                         RECONCILIATION SUMMARY
   Items You Have Marked Cleared (*)   Opening Bal Difference         0.00
   ----------------------------------  Cleared (X,*) Balance        995.00
   1    Checks, Debits        -5.00    Bank Statement Balance       185.29
   0    Deposits, Credits      0.00      Difference                 809.71

F1-Help       F8-Mark Range    F9-View Register    Ctrl-F Find  Ctrl F10-Done
```

Fig. 8.2. *Checking account transactions shown in a list.*

To mark a range of transactions as cleared, press F8. The Mark Range of Check Numbers as Cleared screen appears (see fig. 8.3). You use this screen to specify that all transactions with check numbers within the indicated range should be marked as cleared. As you mark transactions, the Transactions List screen includes the number and dollar amount of the check and deposit transactions you marked as cleared, the cleared transaction total, the ending balance, and the difference between the two. You are finished with the reconciliation when the difference equals zero.

10. (Optional) To correct transactions you entered incorrectly in the register, press F9 to redisplay the same information in an abbreviated form of the standard register. Edit the transactions in the register in the usual manner. To change the displayed screen back to the abbreviated transaction list, press F9 again. (Chapter 5 describes how to use the Quicken register.)

    Figure 8.4 shows sample transactions as they appear in the register.

11. When the difference between the cleared balance and the bank statement balance is zero, press Ctrl-End to indicate that you are finished with the reconciliation. When you press Ctrl-End, Quicken changes each asterisk in the C field to an X, and asks whether you want to print a reconciliation report (see fig. 8.5).

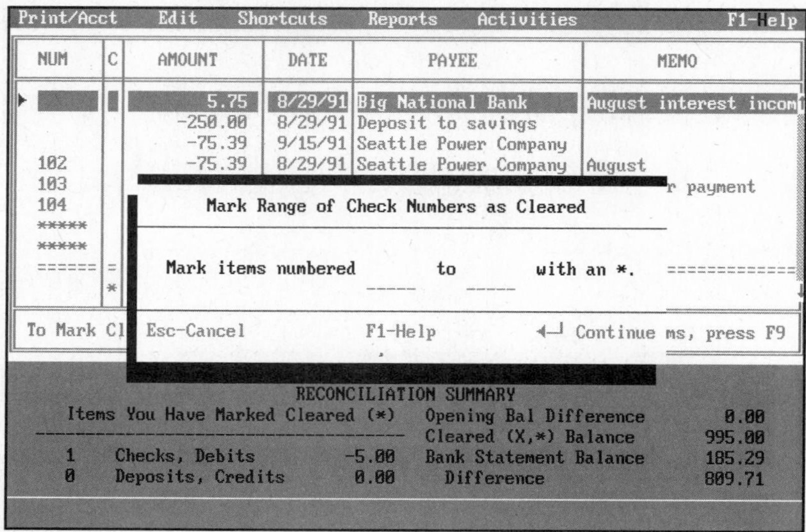

Fig. 8.3. The Mark Range of Check Numbers as Cleared screen.

Print/Acct Edit Shortcuts Reports Activities F1-Help

DATE	NUM	PAYEE · MEMO · CATEGORY	PAYMENT	C	DEPOSIT	BALANCE
8/29 1991	Memo: Cat:	Big National Bank August interest income Int Inc			5 75	930 36
8/29 1991		Deposit to savings [Acme]	250 00			
8/29 1991	103	Puget Sound Mortgage September payme Housing	500 00			
8/29 1991	104	Washington Foods Auto			132 93	

Fig. 8.4. Checking account transactions shown in the register.

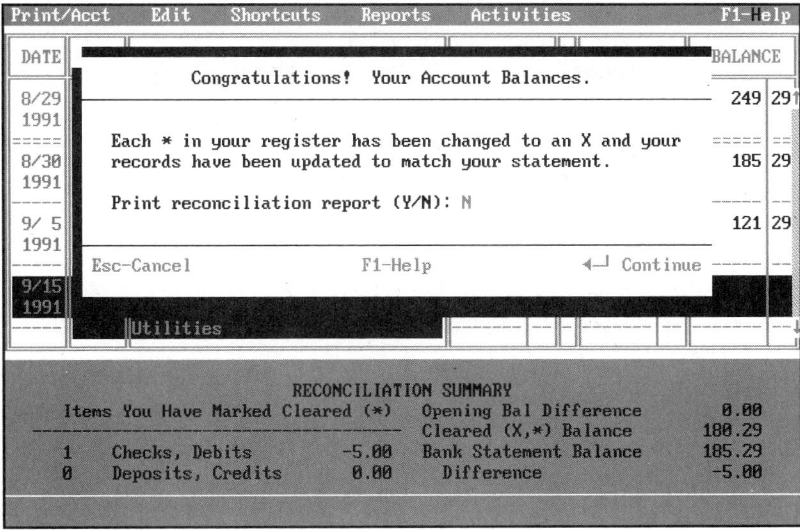

Fig. 8.5. *Quicken congratulates you when your account balances.*

If you understand double-entry bookkeeping, you probably recognize that Quicken uses the labels Debit and Credit incorrectly from your perspective. Do not be confused by this usage. The screen uses the terms from the bank's perspective to further help people who do not understand double-entry bookkeeping.

Printing Reconciliation Reports

Many people like to keep printed records of their reconciliations. Printed copies of the reconciliation report show how you reconciled your records with the bank, indicate all checks and deposits still outstanding, and show all transactions that cleared the bank in a given month—information that may be helpful if you subsequently discover that the bank made an error or that you made a reconciliation error.

To print a reconciliation report, follow these steps:

1. Press Y (from the screen shown in figure 8.5) to print a reconciliation report. The Print Reconciliation Report screen shown in figure 8.6 appears.

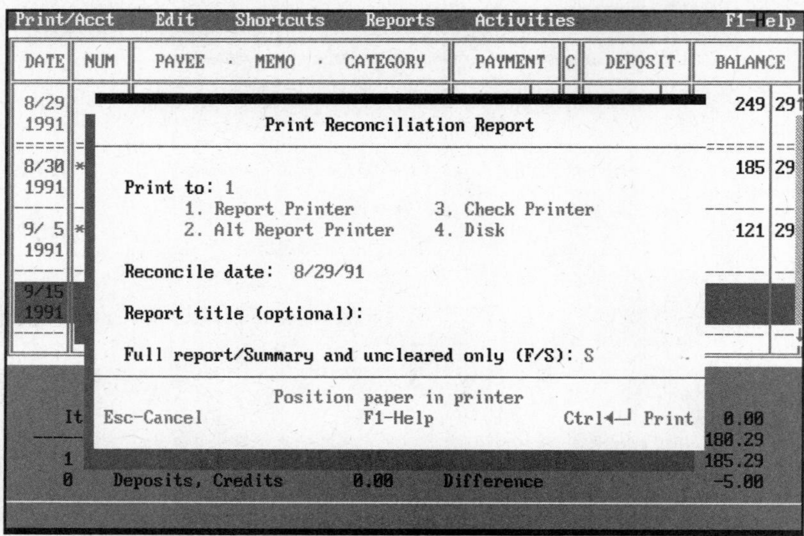

Fig. 8.6. *The Print Reconciliation Report screen.*

2. Complete the `Print to` field by pressing 1 for printer 1, 2 for printer 2, 3 for printer 3, or 4 for disk. (If you used printer names on the Printer Settings screen, you see those printer names on the Print Reconciliation Report screen.)

   If you choose to print to disk an ASCII file, select `Disk` on the Print Reconciliation Report screen. Quicken then requests three additional pieces of information: the file name, the number of lines per page, and the width (see fig. 8.7). In the File field, enter the name you want Quicken to use for the created ASCII file. To use a data directory other than QUICKEN5, enter the drive and directory you chose, such as C:\QUICKEN3\PRNT_TXT. Next, enter the number of lines per page, usually 66. Finally, enter the width of the page (80) or if you are using a condensed mode, you may enter a larger number, such as 132.

3. To move the cursor to the `Reconcile date` field, press Enter or Tab and then enter the date you performed the reconciliation.

4. Press Enter or Tab to move the cursor to the `Report title` field, and then enter a report title for the reconciliation report. You may want to use the month and year to distinguish one report from another.

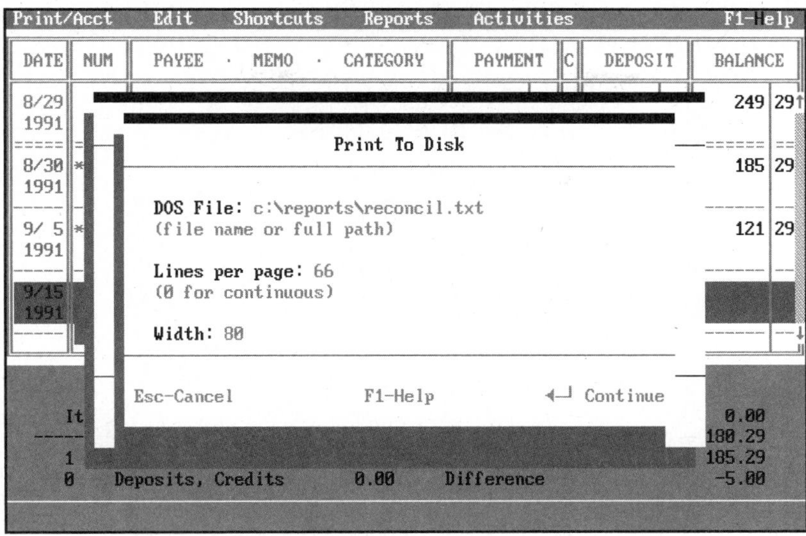

Fig. 8.7. The Print To Disk screen.

5. Press Enter or Tab to move the cursor to the `Full report/Summary and uncleared only` field. This field enables you to choose how much detail shows on the reconciliation report. The default is `Summary`, because `Full` includes all the detail on every transaction you mark as cleared. Answer the `Full report/Summary and uncleared only` field by pressing F for `Full` or S for `Summary`.

6. Verify that the printer is turned on and loaded with paper. Press Enter to print the reconciliation report. Quicken warns you if the printer is not ready.

Reviewing the Reconciliation Report

The printed reconciliation report includes three distinct components: the Reconciliation Summary, the Cleared Transaction Detail, and the Uncleared Transaction Detail. (If you select `Summary`, only the first and third parts of the reconciliation report print.)

The Reconciliation Summary report, shown in figure 8.8, essentially restates the Reconciliation Summary shown at the bottom of the abbreviated check register screen. The Reconciliation Summary has two sections:

Bank Statement—Cleared Transactions

Your Records—Uncleared Transactions

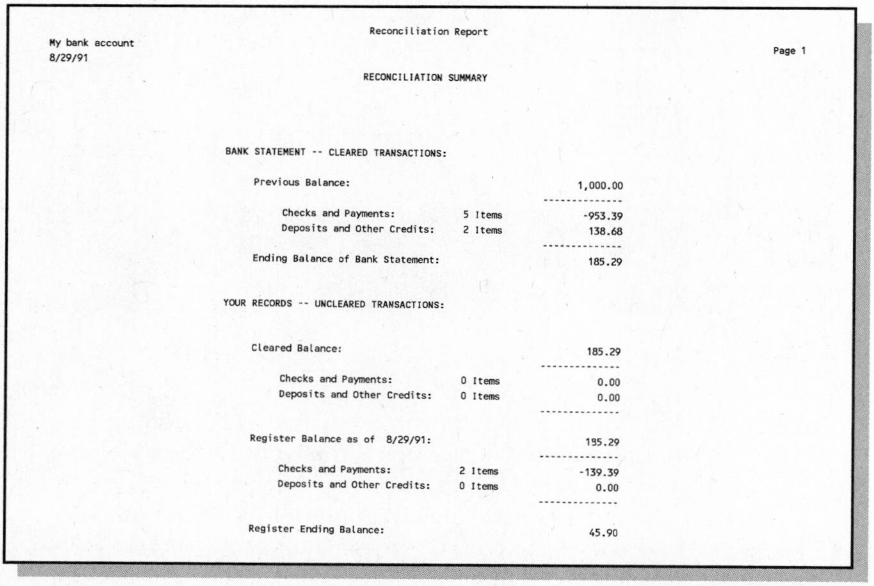

```
                              Reconciliation Report
My bank account
8/29/91                                                                    Page 1

                              RECONCILIATION SUMMARY


     BANK STATEMENT -- CLEARED TRANSACTIONS:

        Previous Balance:                                   1,000.00
                                                       -------------
           Checks and Payments:           5 Items            -953.39
           Deposits and Other Credits:    2 Items             138.68
                                                       -------------
        Ending Balance of Bank Statement:                     185.29

     YOUR RECORDS -- UNCLEARED TRANSACTIONS:

        Cleared Balance:                                      185.29
                                                       -------------
           Checks and Payments:           0 Items               0.00
           Deposits and Other Credits:    0 Items               0.00
                                                       -------------

        Register Balance as of  8/29/91:                      185.29
                                                       -------------
           Checks and Payments:           2 Items            -139.39
           Deposits and Other Credits:    0 Items               0.00
                                                       -------------

        Register Ending Balance:                               45.90
```

Fig. 8.8. *The printed Reconciliation Summary report.*

The first section calculates the ending balance according to the bank statement by subtracting the cleared checks and adding the cleared deposits from the beginning bank balance. The second section calculates the ending register balance by subtracting the outstanding checks and adding the deposits in transit from the ending bank balance.

The Reconciliation Summary report isn't a report you read—rather the report documents how you reconciled the account. For this reason, you don't actually need to spend time reviewing this report—unless, for some reason, you need to go back later and explain to the bank what the balance should be or go back and see which transactions were outstanding when you reconciled.

The Cleared Transaction Detail report, shown in figure 8.9, shows each of the cleared checks and payment transactions and each of the cleared deposits and other credit transactions you marked with an asterisk as part of the most recent reconciliation. The report does not include transactions you marked as cleared in some prior reconciliation.

Reconciliation Report

My bank account
8/29/91

Page 2

CLEARED TRANSACTION DETAIL

Date	Num	Payee	Memo	Category	Clr	Amount
Cleared Checks and Payments						
8/29/91	102	Seattle Power Co	August	Utilities	x	-75.39
8/29/91		Deposit to savin		[Acme]	x	-250.00
8/29/91	103	Puget Sound Mort	September payme	Housing	x	-559.00
8/29/91		Service Charge		Bank Chrg	x	-5.00
8/30/91	*****	Sammamish Cleani		Household	x	-64.00
Total Cleared Checks and Payments				5 Items		-953.39
Cleared Deposits and Other Credits						
8/29/91		Big National Ban	August interest	Int Inc	x	5.75
8/29/91	104	Washington Foods		Auto	x	132.93
Total Cleared Deposits and Other Credits				2 Items		138.68
Total Cleared Transactions				7 Items		-814.71

Fig. 8.9. *The Cleared Transaction Detail report.*

The Cleared Transaction Detail report includes most of the information related to a transaction, including the transaction date, the check or transaction number, the payee name or transaction description, any memo description, and the amount. Checks and payments are displayed as negative amounts because these amounts decrease the account balance. Deposits are displayed as positive amounts because these amounts increase the account balance. Because of space constraints, some `Payee`, `Memo`, and `Category` field entries are truncated on the right. The total amount and number of cleared transactions on the Cleared Transaction Detail report support the data shown in the first section of the Reconciliation Summary.

The Uncleared Transaction Detail report, shown in figures 8.10 and 8.11, is identical to the Cleared Transaction Detail report except that the still uncleared transactions for your checking account are summarized. The report is broken down into transactions dated prior to the reconciliation date and transactions dated subsequent to the reconciliation date.

```
                              Reconciliation Report
My bank account                                                                   Page 3
8/29/91
                        UNCLEARED TRANSACTION DETAIL UP TO  8/29/91

            Date     Num         Payee           Memo          Category   Clr    Amount
          -------- ----- --------------- -------------- -------------- --- -----------

          Uncleared Checks and Payments

                                                                              -----------
          Total Uncleared Checks and Payments              0 Items                   0.00

          Uncleared Deposits and Other Credits

                                                                              -----------
          Total Uncleared Deposits and Other Credits       0 Items                   0.00

                                                                              ===========
          Total Uncleared Transactions                     0 Items                   0.00
```

Fig. 8.10. Uncleared transactions dated prior to the reconciliation date.

```
                              Reconciliation Report
My bank account                                                                   Page 4
8/29/91
                        UNCLEARED TRANSACTION DETAIL AFTER  8/29/91

            Date     Num         Payee           Memo          Category   Clr    Amount
          -------- ----- --------------- -------------- -------------- --- -----------

          Uncleared Checks and Payments

          9/ 5/91  ***** Sammamish Cleani                  Household               -64.00
          9/15/91        Seattle Power Co                  Utilities               -75.39
                                                                              -----------
          Total Uncleared Checks and Payments              2 Items                -139.39

          Uncleared Deposits and Other Credits

                                                                              -----------
          Total Uncleared Deposits and Other Credits       0 Items                   0.00

                                                                              ===========
          Total Uncleared Transactions                     2 Items                -139.39
```

Fig. 8.11. Uncleared transactions dated subsequent to the reconciliation date.

Like the Cleared Transaction Detail report, the Uncleared Transaction Detail report includes most of the information related to a transaction, including the transaction date, the check or transaction number, the payee name or transaction description, any memo description, and the amount. Checks and payments are shown as negative amounts because they decrease the account balance. Deposits are shown as positive amounts because they increase the account balance. The total amount and total number of cleared transactions on the Uncleared Transaction Detail report support the data shown in the second section of the Reconciliation Summary.

Creating Balance Adjustment Transactions

If you cannot reconcile an account, that is, if the difference amount shown on the Reconciliation Summary equals any number other than zero, as a last resort you may want to make a balance adjustment. A balance adjustment means that Quicken creates a transaction that forces the difference amount to equal zero. You can make a balance adjustment by pressing Esc on the Register screen before you have reduced the difference between the cleared balance and the bank statement balance to zero. Quicken then displays the Reconciliation is Not Complete screen, shown in figure 8.12.

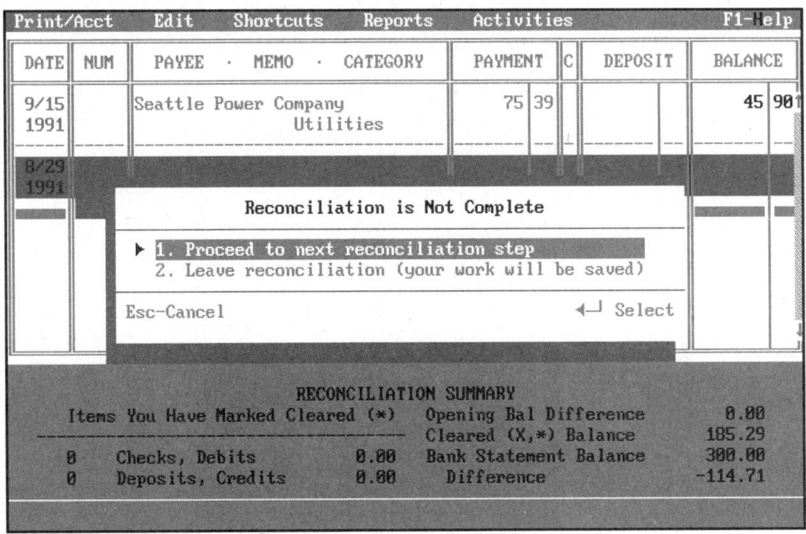

Fig. 8.12. The Reconciliation is Not Complete screen.

The Reconciliation is Not Complete screen identifies two alternatives: `Proceed to next reconciliation step`, and `Leave reconciliation (your work will be saved)`. If you select the second alternative, Quicken returns to the Main Menu.

If you select the first alternative, Quicken displays the screen shown in figure 8.13. This screen informs you of the magnitude of the problem and possible causes. If you still want to create an adjustment transaction, follow these steps:

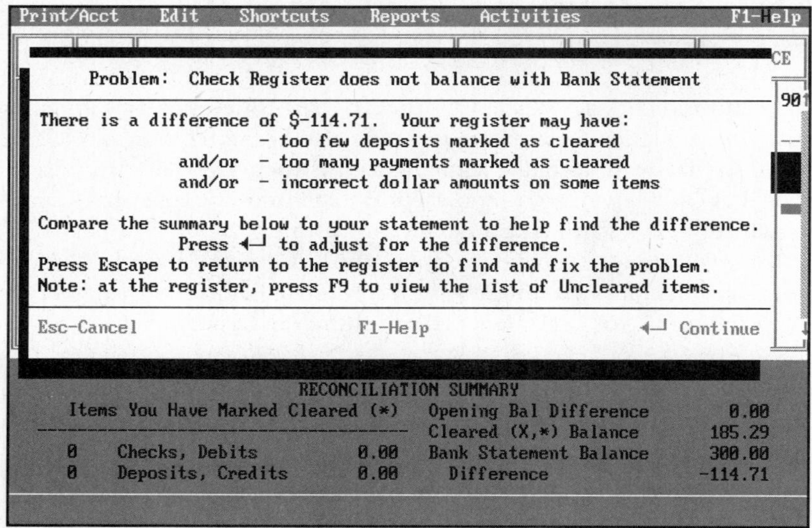

Fig. 8.13. *The Check Register does not balance with Bank Statement screen.*

1. Press Enter to continue. Quicken alerts you that the difference still exists by displaying the Check Register does not balance with Bank Statement screen (see fig. 8.13).

2. Press Enter to continue. The Adding Balance Adjustment Entry screen appears (see fig. 8.14). This screen alerts you that the adjustment is about to be made and suggests that you may want to reconsider the decision.

3. To make the adjustment, press Y for Yes. If you do not want to make the adjustment, press N for No. To leave this screen and return to the Abbreviated Register screen, press Esc.

4. (Optional) To categorize an adjustment transaction (press Ctrl-C to see a Category and Transfer List screen), enter a category name in the optional `Category` field.

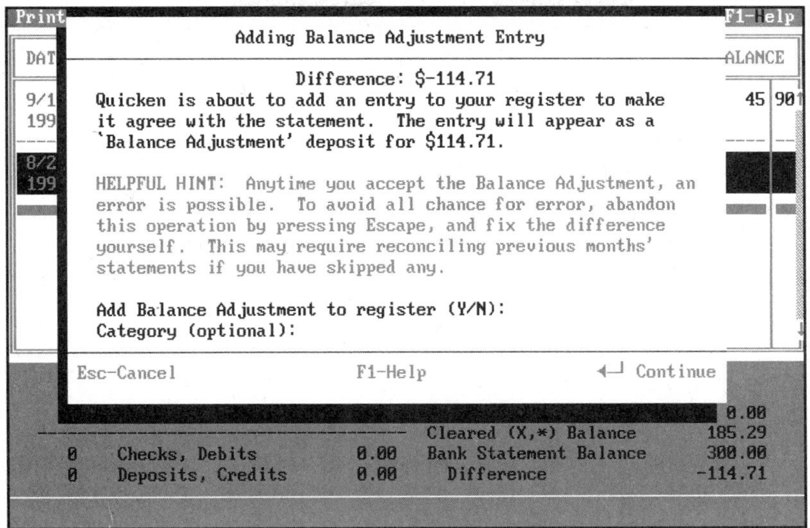

Fig. 8.14. The Adding Balance Adjustment Entry screen.

Quicken next tells you that the register has been adjusted to agree with the bank statement balance and displays a screen you can use to print the reconciliation report, as shown in figure 8.15. To print a reconciliation report, press Y for Yes. The Print Reconciliation Report screen appears, which you use as described previously in this chapter to print the reconciliation report. Figure 8.16 shows a sample adjustment transaction.

Although Quicken provides the adjustment feature, you probably should not use the feature because this feature camouflages errors in the register. As a result, you never really can be sure where the error occurs. The difference amount equals a number other than zero because you are missing one or more transactions in the register or because you incorrectly marked a transaction as cleared, or perhaps you transposed some numbers (such as typing $87.00 as $78.00). The difference also may occur because someone has forged checks or embezzled from your account. If you cannot reconcile the account, make sure that the previous month's reconciliation resulted in a difference equal to zero. If the previous month's reconciliation shows a difference other than zero, you must reconcile that month, and perhaps the months prior to that one, before you can get the current month's difference to be displayed as zero.

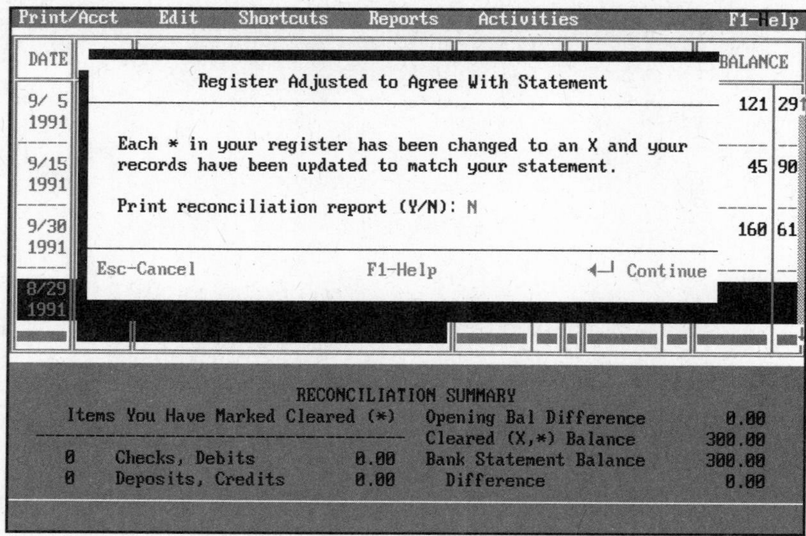

Fig. 8.15. The Register Adjusted to Agree With Statement screen.

```
Print/Acct   Edit   Shortcuts   Reports   Activities                    F1-Help
DATE   NUM    PAYEE · MEMO · CATEGORY       PAYMENT   C   DEPOSIT    BALANCE
8/29          Service Charge                   5 00   X               249 29
1991                   Bank Chrg
8/30   *****  Sammamish Cleaning Services     64 00   X               185 29
1991                   Household
9/ 5   *****  Sammamish Cleaning Services     64 00                   121 29
1991                   Household
9/15          Seattle Power Company           75 39                    45 90
1991                   Utilities
9/30          Balance Adjustment                      X    114 71
1991
8/29
1991
                            END
My bank account    (Alt+letter accesses menu)     Current Balance: $249.29
Esc-Main Menu      Ctrl◄┘ Record                  Ending Balance:  $160.61
```

Fig. 8.16. A sample adjustment transaction created by Quicken.

Catching Common Errors

You easily can make several errors when recording transactions in a checking account; these errors may make reconciling an account difficult or even impossible. At times, a general search for errors may not be as helpful as looking for certain kinds of errors; the next few paragraphs identify—and explain tricks for catching—some of the more common errors.

Transposing Numbers

Transposing numbers is a frequent error in recording any financial transaction. People accidentally transpose two of the numbers in an amount. If the difference is divisible by 9, a transposition error is likely. For example, you may write a check for $32.67 and record the check as $23.67 or $32.76. This error appears obvious, but is surprisingly easy to make and often difficult to catch. When you review each transaction, you see all the correct numbers; however, the numbers are arranged in a slightly different order.

When searching for transposed numbers you can focus on the decimal places of the transaction where the transposition error may have occurred. Table 8.1 summarizes by amounts where the transposition error may have occurred.

Table 8.1
Possible Locations of Transposition Errors

Error Amount	*Decimal Places of Transposition*
$.09 to $.72	In cents. For example, $.12 versus. $.21 or $1.19 versus. $1.91.
$.90 to $7.20	Between the dollar decimal position immediately to left of decimal place and the cents decimal position to right of decimal place. For example, $32.56 versus $35.26 or $2,004.56 versus $2,005.46.
$9.00 to $72.00	Between the two positions immediately to the left of decimal place. For example, $1,423 versus $1,432 or $281 versus $218.
$90 to $720	Between second and third positions immediately to the left of decimal place. For example, $1,297 versus $1,927 or $1,124 versus $1,214.

Forgetting To Record Transactions

The most common mistake is forgetting to record transactions. In a personal checking account, these omissions often include decreases in the account—for example, automated teller machine withdrawals—and increases in the account, such as interest income. In a business checking account, manual checks seem to be a common culprit; you tear out a blank check for a purchasing trip and subsequently forget to record the check.

If the amounts differ because of one transaction, identifying the missing transaction can be as easy as finding a transaction on the bank statement that equals the difference. Also, check the sequence of checks to see whether any are missing.

Entering Payments as Deposits or Deposits as Payments

Another error is to enter a payment transaction as a deposit transaction or a deposit transaction as a payment transaction. This error, until found, can be particularly frustrating. If you look at the register, you see that every transaction is recorded, and every number is correct.

An easy way to find such an error is to divide the error by half and see whether the result equals some transaction amount. If the result does match a transaction amount, you may have incorrectly recorded the transaction. Suppose that you currently have a difference of $1,234.56 between the register and the bank statement balances. If you divide $1,234.56 by 2, you get an amount of $617.28. If you see a $617.28 transaction in the register, verify that you recorded this transaction in the correct column. If you recorded a $617.28 payment as a deposit or if you recorded a $617.28 deposit as a payment, the difference will equal twice the transaction amount, or $1,234.56.

Offsetting Errors

You may have more than one error in your account, and these errors may partially offset each other. Suppose that you forgot to record an automated teller machine withdrawal of $40 and then made a transposition error in which you recorded a deposit as $216 instead of the correct amount of $261.

The difference equals $5, which is the combined effect of both transactions and is calculated as the following:

– 40 + (261 – 216) = $5

Although the difference seems small, you actually have two large errors in the account.

With offsetting errors, remember that when you find one of the errors, you may feel that you are moving further away from the goal of a zero difference. Do not get discouraged if one minute you are $5 away from completing the reconciliation, and the next minute, you are $50 away from completing the reconciliation. Clearly, you are making progress if you find errors—even if the difference grows larger.

Chapter Summary

This chapter described how to reconcile your account with Quicken. You learned about the Reconciliation screen, menu options, and reports that you can use to simplify the process of reconciling your bank accounts. The **Reconcile** option helps you turn what once was an unpleasant financial chore into a quick and easy task.

9

Caring for Quicken Files

Quicken stores in files the financial information you enter into the register. This chapter—the last in the "Learning the Basics" section—covers how to care for Quicken files. This chapter reviews the kinds of files Quicken creates, how to back up and restore files, how to shrink files to get rid of outdated information, and how to export and import file data.

Reviewing the Quicken Files

To operate Quicken, you do not need to know the function of each of the program's files. Occasionally, however, this knowledge is helpful. If a file becomes damaged or corrupted, knowing whether the file is important to your use of Quicken is valuable. If you use one of the popular hard disk management programs, knowing which files are which is helpful if you want to compress or encrypt certain files. You may want to compress files so that they occupy less space on the hard disk. To ensure the confidentiality of financial records, you may want to encrypt the files to prevent others from reading the data.

When you install Quicken, the following series of program files is copied to the hard disk or to the program floppy disk:

Q.EXE, Q.OVL	The actual Quicken program files
Q.HLP	On-line help file accessed with F1
BILLMIND.EXE	Program to look for checks, groups due

QCHECKS.DOC	Blank supply order form
PRINTER2.DAT	Printer driver file
HOME.QIF	Defined home category list
BUSINESS.QIF	Defined business category list
TAX.SCD	Tax form schedule information

Quicken also creates the following files:

Q.CFG	Configuration and set up information
Q.BAT	A batch file that starts Quicken
Q3.DIR	List of account descriptions and check due dates

For each account group you set up, Quicken creates four more files by combining the file name with four different file extensions. Assuming that you use a file named STEVENL, Quicken creates the following files:

STEPHENL.QDT	Data file
STEPHENL.QNX	Data file index (used to sort transactions)
STEPHENL.QMT	Memorized transaction list for file (stores memorized transactions)
STEPHENL.QDI	Dictionary file for file (stores addresses of unprinted checks and split transaction descriptions)

Quicken also stores the data files for the manual-based quick tour in the Quicken directory. These data files use the file name SAMPLE and the four data file extensions QDT, QNX, QMT, and QDI.

Backing Up and Restoring Files

Backing up means that you are making a second copy of your Quicken data files (including Q3.DIR). Back up your files because, if your original Quicken data files are damaged, you can use the backup copies to restore the damaged files to their original condition. You can back up and restore by using DOS file commands or one of the popular hard disk management programs. For the sake of convenience, you may find the Quicken back up and restore options easier to use. This section discusses these back up and restore options.

Backing Up Files

You need to make two important decisions about backing up files. First, you must decide how often you need to back up. Although opinions on the subject vary, a good habit to form is to back up your data files after completing any session in which you enter or change accounting data. When you finish entering the first set of account transactions, for example, back up all the data files.

Most people back up their account records daily, weekly, or monthly. After you spend time working with Quicken and become familiar with account group restoration procedures, you can estimate more accurately how often you need to back up account groups. If you discover that backing up the files requires as much effort as re-creating six months of record keeping, you may decide to back up Quicken data files only at six-month intervals.

Second, you need to decide how many old backup copies to keep. Usually, two or three copies are adequate. (This rule of thumb is called the grandfather, father, and son scheme.) Suppose that you back up the account groups every day. On Thursday, a co-worker accidentally deletes the group. If you keep two old backup copies besides the most recent backup copy, you have backups from Wednesday, Tuesday, and Monday. If the Wednesday copy is damaged (an unlikely but possible situation), you still have the Tuesday and Monday copies. The more recent a backup copy, the easier data is to recover, but using an old backup copy still is easier than reentering all the data from the original documents.

Store these account group backup copies in a safe place. Do not keep all backup copies in the same location. If you experience a fire or if someone burglarizes your business or house, you may lose all the copies—no matter how many backups you keep. Store at least one copy at an off-site location. If you use Quicken at home, you can keep a backup copy in your desk at work; if you use Quicken for business, keep a backup copy at home.

To back up your Quicken files, follow these steps:

1. Select the **Set Preferences** option from Quicken's Main Menu. The Set Preferences menu shown in figure 9.1 appears.

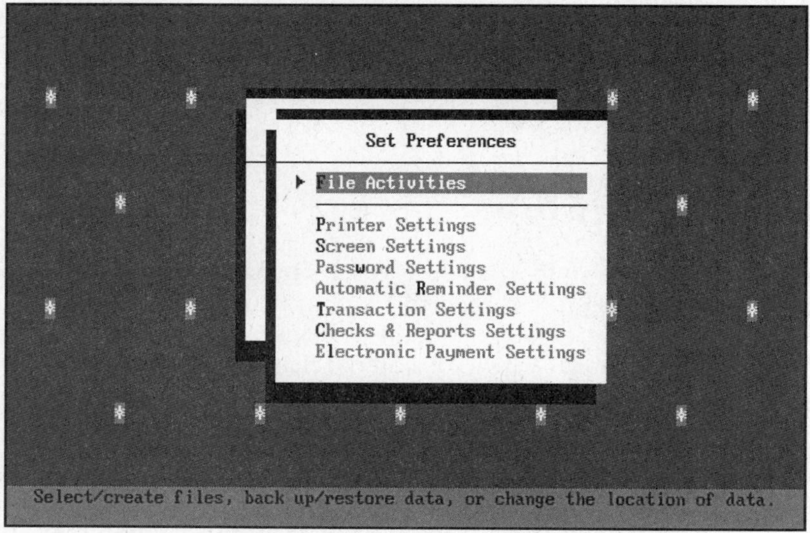

Fig. 9.1. *The Set Preferences menu.*

2. Select the **File Activities** option from the Set Preferences menu. The File Activities menu shown in figure 9.2 appears.

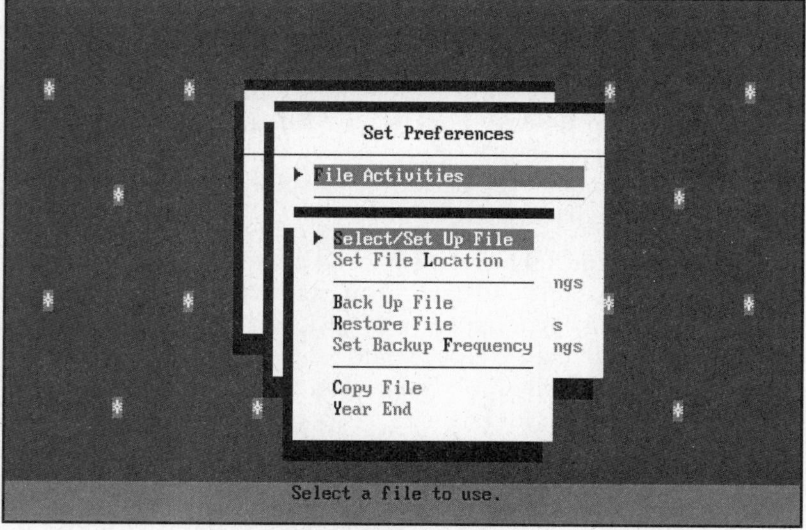

Fig. 9.2. *The File Activities menu.*

3. Select **Back Up File** from the File Activities menu. Quicken prompts you to select the appropriate disk drive (see fig. 9.3). After you select the backup disk and press Enter, the Select File to Back Up screen shown in figure 9.4 appears. This screen is similar to the Select/Set Up File screen—only the title is different.

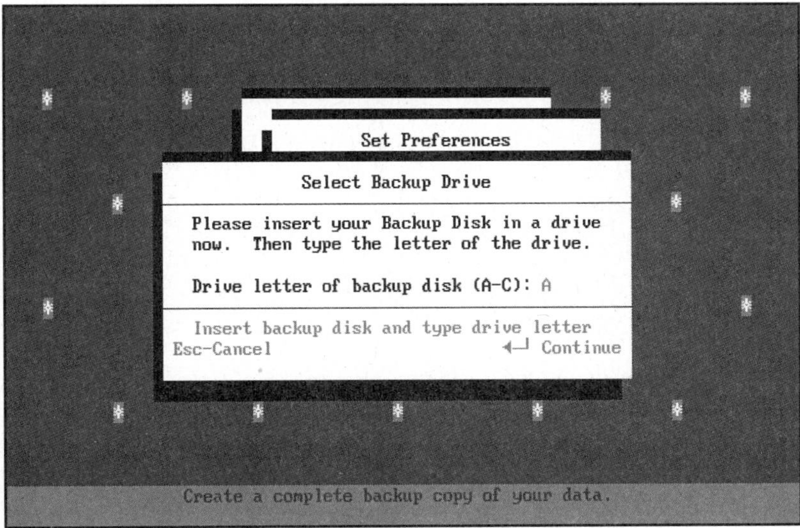

Fig. 9.3. *The* `Select Backup Drive` *message.*

4. Use the up- and down-arrow keys to move the selection triangle to the left of the file you want to back up and press Enter.

   The message `Backing Up` then appears as Quicken copies the selected file to the backup disk. When Quicken finishes backing up, the message `File backed up successfully` appears, as shown in figure 9.5.

5. Remove the backup disk from the disk drive and store the disk in a safe place.

If the file you are trying to back up does not fit on the disk, an error message alerts you that the disk is full, and you should press Esc to cancel. The warning message `Account not backed up` appears. If the disk is full, press Esc, insert a different backup disk, and repeat steps 1-4.

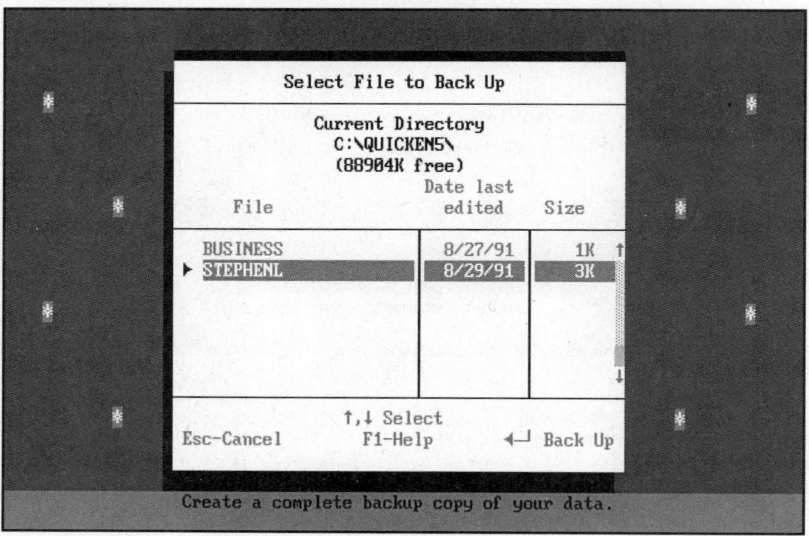

Fig. 9.4. The Select File to Back Up screen.

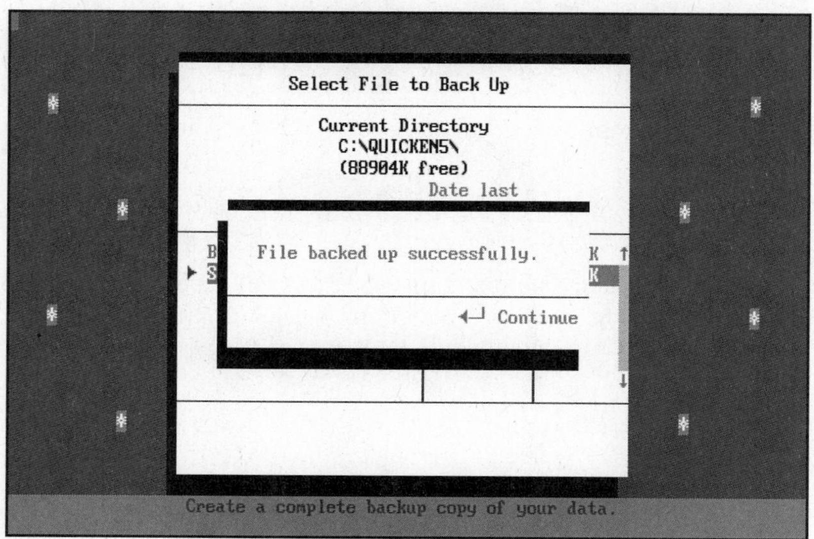

Fig. 9.5. The `File backed up successfully` *message.*

Restoring Backed-Up Files

Eventually, someone or something may accidentally delete or destroy an account group. Your computer can malfunction; a co-worker may spill the contents of the pencil sharpener or a cup of coffee on the floppy disk that contains the Quicken data files. But if you have backed up the files recently, and if you were diligent about printing copies of the register, you should not have any serious problems. You can restore your Quicken files by using the backup copies.

To retrieve the data you copied with the **Back Up File** option, follow this procedure:

1. From Quicken's Main Menu, select the **Set Preferences** option. The Set Preferences menu appears (see fig. 9.1).
2. From the Set Preferences menu, select the **File Activities** option. Quicken displays the File Activities menu (see fig. 9.2).
3. Select the **Restore File** option. Quicken prompts you to identify the backup disk drive and to insert the backup disk in drive A (see fig. 9.6). After you insert the backup disk and press Enter, Quicken displays the Select File to Restore screen (see fig. 9.7).
4. Use the up- and down-arrow keys to move the selection triangle to the left of the file you want to restore and then press Enter.

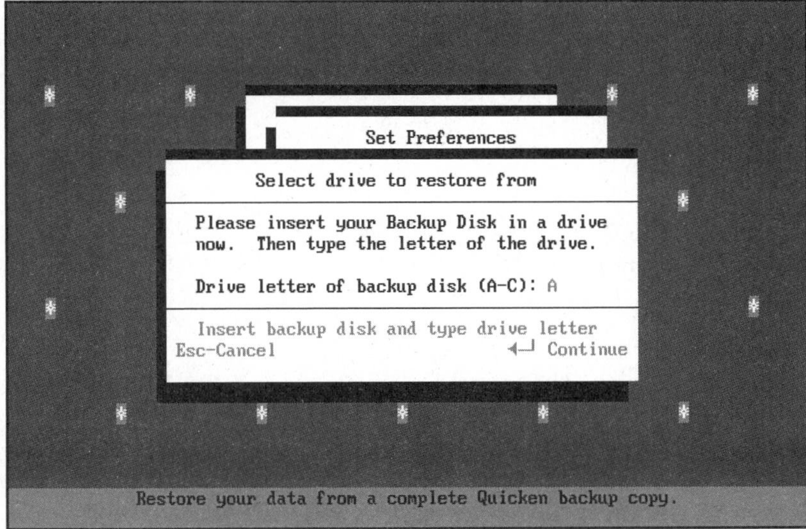

Fig. 9.6. The Select Drive to Restore From screen.

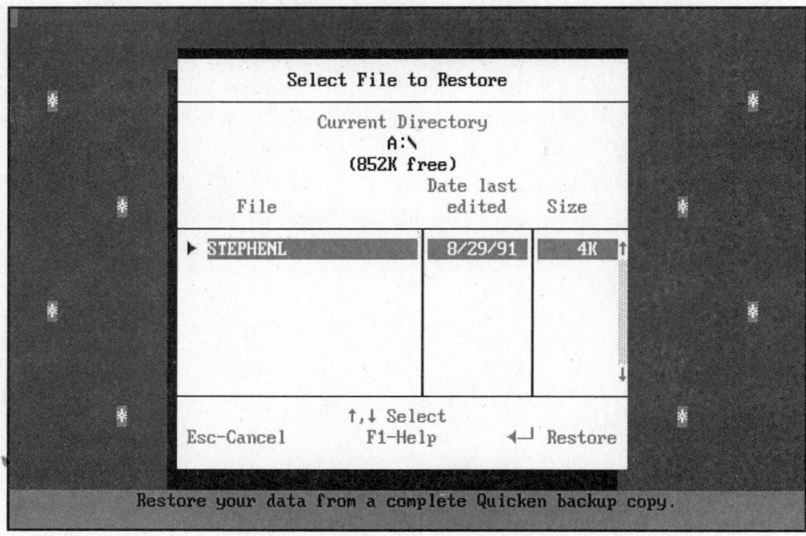

Fig. 9.7. The Select File to Restore screen.

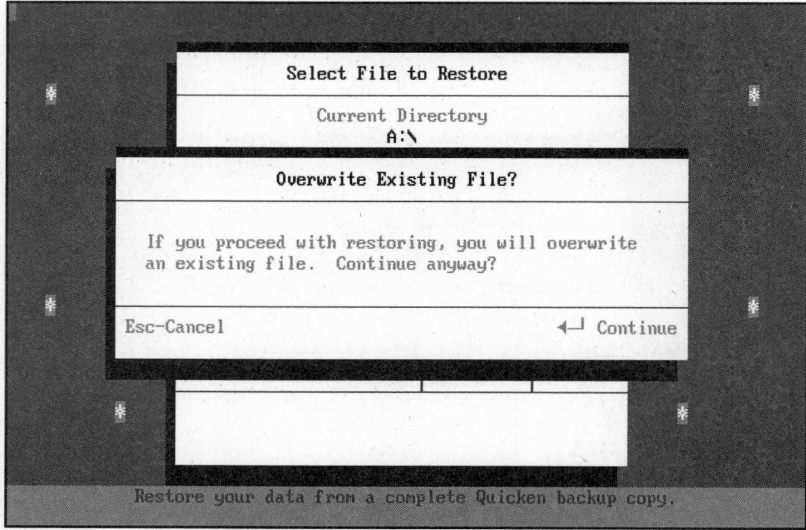

Fig. 9.8. The `Overwrite Existing File` *message.*

Quicken alerts you that the restoration operation will overwrite the existing file (see fig. 9.8). To continue with the restoration, press Enter.

When the file is restored, Quicken displays the `File restored successfully` message shown in figure 9.9.

You cannot restore the currently selected file. If you try to restore the currently selected file, the message shown in figure 9.10 alerts you to this error. If you originally set up only one file, you need to set up a second, dummy file that you can select as the current file before you use the restore option.

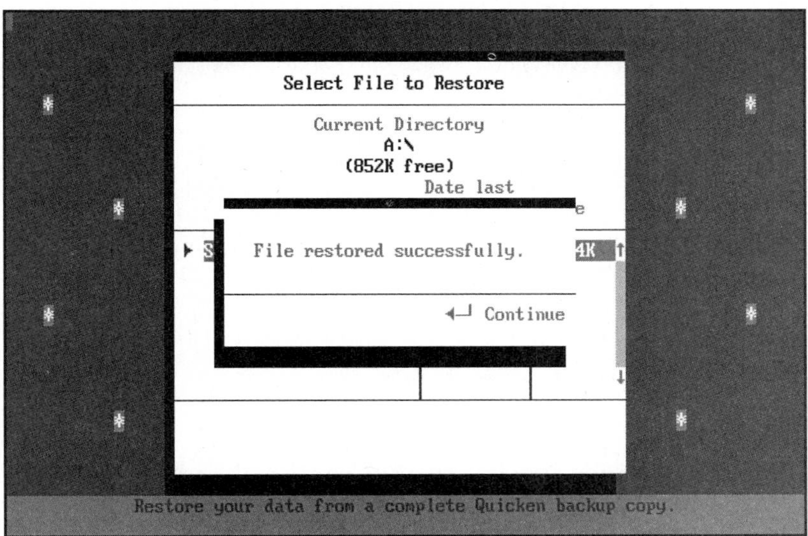

Fig. 9.9. *The* `File restored successfully` *message.*

Remember that in Quicken you can work with several accounts. Chapter 3 lists the steps for setting up accounts. Refer to Chapter 3 if you have questions about this procedure.

5. Using the most recent copy of the register, reenter each transaction that you entered between the time you backed up and the time you lost the data. You need to reenter transactions for each account.

6. Back up these files in the event another accident causes you to lose the Quicken files again.

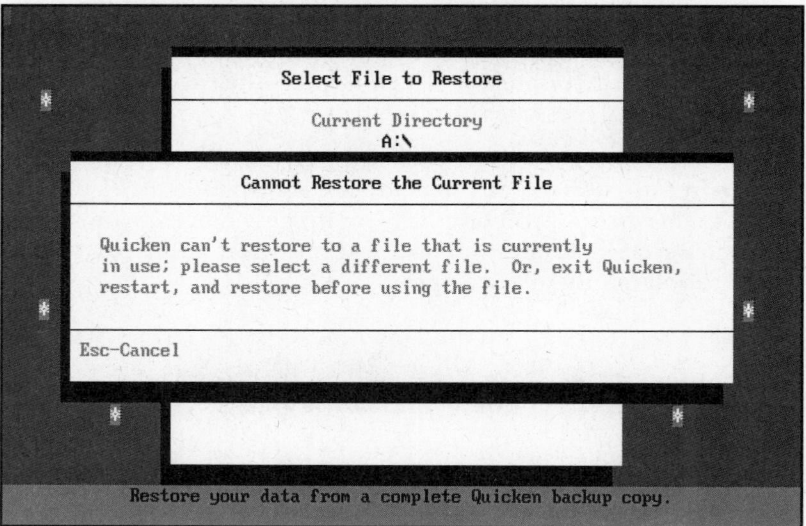

Fig. 9.10. *The* Cannot Restore the Current File *message.*

Using the Backup Reminder

Without regular backups, you may lose financial records. Obviously, backing up your files is important. Because backing up is this important, Quicken provides a backup reminder feature that you can set so that Quicken periodically reminds you to back up a specified file.

To use the backup reminder feature, first select the file for which you want to be reminded to back up when the file isn't the current file—you need to take this step because backup reminders attach to specific files—and then follow these steps:

1. From Quicken's Main Menu, select the **Set Preferences** option. The Set Preferences menu appears (see fig. 9.1).

2. From the Set Preferences menu, select the **File Activities** menu. The File Activities menu appears (see fig. 9.2).

3. Select the **Set Backup Frequency** option. The Backup Frequency Reminder box appears (see fig. 9.11).

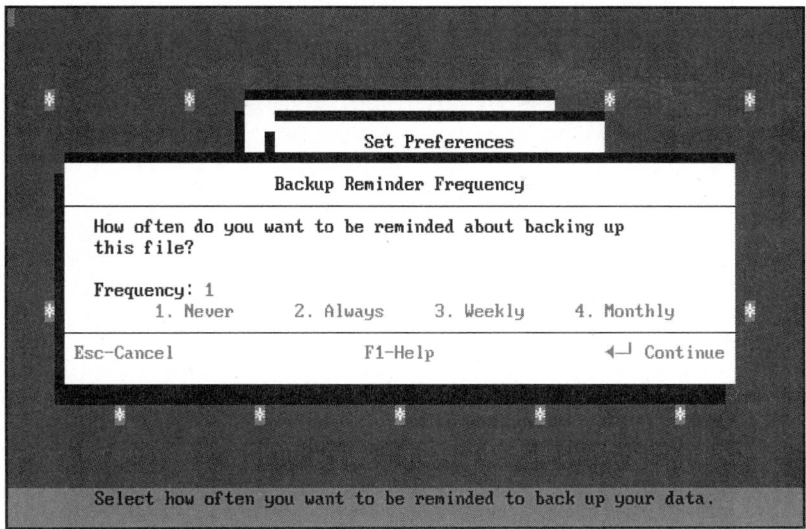

Fig. 9.11. *The Backup Reminder Frequency box.*

4. Indicate how often you want to be reminded to back up the current file. Type 1 if you never want to be reminded to back up. Type 2 to be reminded every time you exit the Quicken program. Type 3 to be reminded once a week. Type 4 to be reminded once a month.

   After you set a backup frequency reminder, Quicken monitors backups you make of a particular file. If the time arrives for you to again backup a file, Quicken displays a message upon exiting the program that tells you to backup a particular file.

Remember that the backup reminders attach to specific files. Accordingly, if you decide to use this handy feature, you probably want to set backup frequencies for each file so that you don't forget a file.

If disaster befalls data files that you did not back up, you must reenter each register transaction. Up-to-date printed copies of each register can show what you need to reenter. If you don't have up-to-date copies of each of the registers, you need to reenter each transaction, using the original source documents—checks, deposits receipts, and so on. Of course, you don't ever want to reenter data from original documents, so regularly back up the files and store the backup disks in a safe place.

Shrinking Files

Theoretically, Quicken enables you to store up to 65,353 transactions in an account group's registers. Practically, these limitations are much lower. Floppy disk users may be limited by the Quicken data disks: a 360K, 5 1/4-inch floppy disk has space for about 3,000 transactions, and a 720K, 3 1/2-inch disk has space for about 6,000 transactions. If you use a hard disk, you may not be limited by disk space, but you probably do not want to work with thousands or tens of thousands of transactions in registers.

Quicken provides a twofold solution for dealing with the problem of ever-growing data files: Quicken enables you to create archive copies of files and to create fresh copies of files that include only transactions that fall after a certain date. In effect, this twofold solution means that you can break down large files into smaller, more manageable files.

When To Shrink Files

For most users, the most convenient time to shrink the files is after completing the annual income tax return and after any year-end reporting. At this time, all transactions from the prior year should have cleared the bank, and you have printed all necessary Quicken reports. Now, an archive copy of the files can provide a permanent copy of the data you used to prepare the year's financial reports. A fresh copy of the file also enables you to start a new year without a load of old, unnecessary data.

How To Shrink Files

To shrink files, use the **Year End** option on the File Activities menu (see fig. 9.2). Because you can shrink only the currently selected account, you need to use the **Select/Set Up File** option to select an account to shrink. If you do not select an account before using the **Year End** option, Quicken warns you before shrinking the files.

When you are ready to shrink files, follow these steps:

1. From Quicken's Main Menu, select the **Change Setting** option. The Set Preferences menu appears.

2. From the Set Preferences menu, select the **File Activities** option. Quicken displays the File Activities menu.

3. From the File Activities menu, select the **Year End** option. The Year End screen appears (see fig. 9.12).

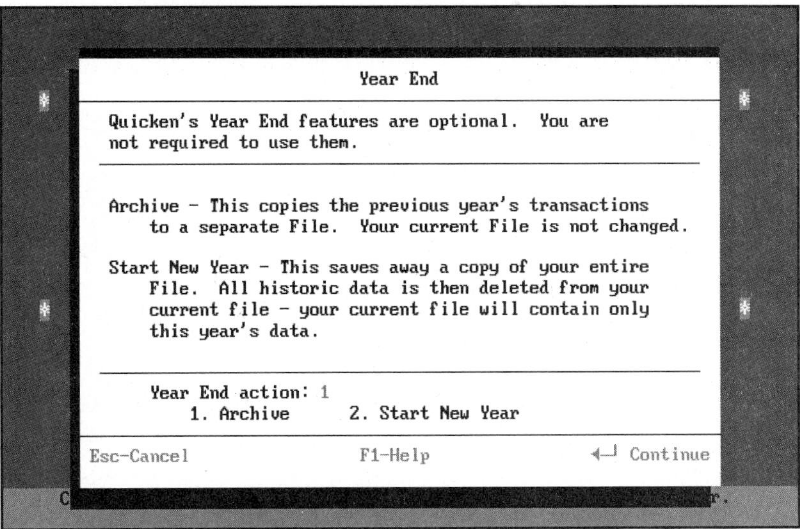

Fig. 9.12. The Year End screen.

4. Identify the year-end action you want to take. Type a *1* to create a year-end archive copy of the current file. Type a *2* to create a fresh copy of the file that includes only transactions from the current year.

If you type a 2 to create a fresh file copy, Quicken may include some transactions from previous years, such as investment transactions and any uncleared transactions. You need to keep these transactions in a working copy of a file because the investment transactions are needed for investment record-keeping and the uncleared transactions are needed for bank reconciliations.

If you create a separate set of Quicken data files for each year, consider including the year number in the account group name. You can name the data files from 1989 as QDATA89, the data files from 1990 as QDATA90, the data files from 1991 as QDATA91, and so on. Including the year number in account group names enables you to easily determine which year's records are contained in a particular data file.

5. If you select the **Archive** option in step 4, the Archive File screen shown in figure 9.13 appears. By default, Quicken names the archive file with the current file name and the previous year, locates the file in the Quicken program directory, and includes transactions only through the end of the previous year. If any of these default settings are incorrect, move the cursor to the incorrect field, and then make the necessary corrections. When the screen is complete, press Enter when the cursor is on the last field or press Ctrl-Enter or F10. Quicken creates the archive file copy and then displays an on-screen message that asks if you want to work with the archive file or the current file. Using the arrow keys, indicate the file.

6. If you select the **Start New Year** option in step 4, the Start New Year screen appears (see fig. 9.14). Enter the file name you want Quicken to use for the new file in the `Copy all transactions to file` field. Indicate the date that, if a transaction date falls after, controls the transactions that get copied to the new file in the `Include transactions with dates after` field. Optionally, specify the location for the new file in the `Location of New File` field. When the screen is complete, press Enter when the cursor is on the last field or press Ctrl-Enter or F10. Quicken creates the new file copy and then displays a message that asks if you want to work with the archive file or the current file. (The archive copy is the file upon which the new file is based. The current file is the new file.) Using the arrow keys, indicate the file.

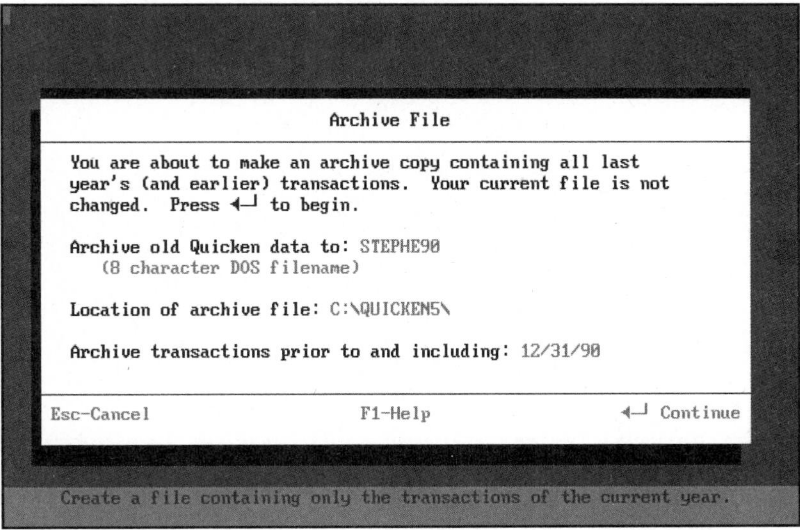

Fig. 9.13. *The Archive File screen.*

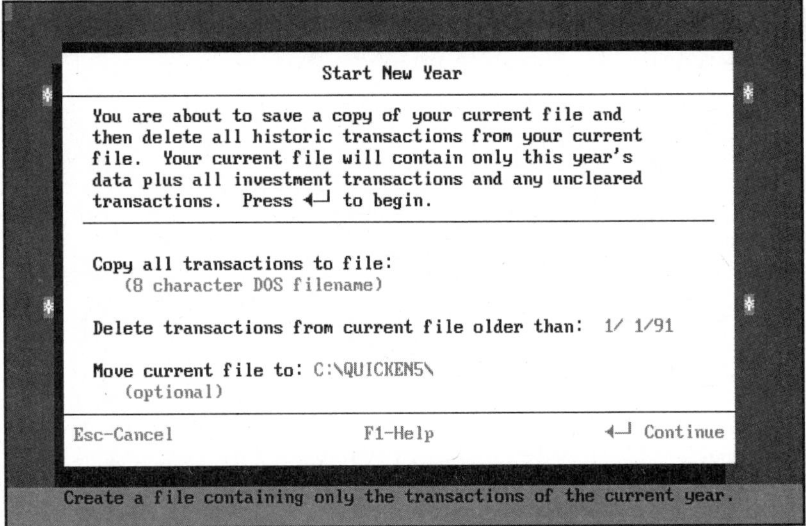

Fig. 9.14. *The Start New Year screen.*

The previous version of Quicken provided another file shrinking tool, the **Copy File** option. This option still appears on the File Activities menu, although there's no longer much reason to use this feature. If you do want to use the **Copy File** option, display the File Activities menu just as if you were going to select the **Year End** option. Then, rather than selecting the **Year End** command, select the **Copy File** command. Quicken displays the Copy File screen, shown in figure 9.15. Enter the name you want to use for the file, the location, and the range of dates that, if a transaction falls between, should be included in the new file. You also need to indicate whether to include or exclude uncleared transactions.

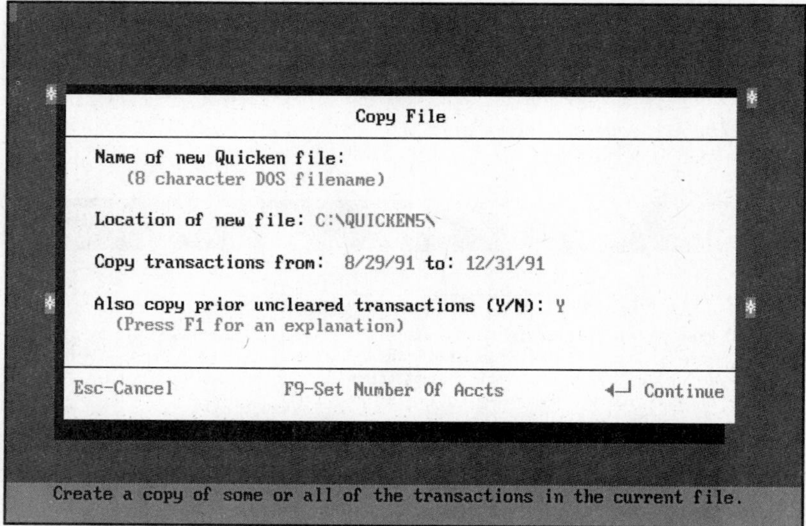

Fig. 9.15. The Copy File screen.

Locating Files

If you accept the program defaults, Quicken stores data files in C:\QUICKEN5 for hard disk users and drive B for floppy disk users. You have the option, however, of having Quicken locate the files somewhere besides the default location when you specify where the files for an account group are to be located when you set up or shrink an account group.

If you locate Quicken files in a place other than the default directory, you need to tell Quicken where these files are. To inform Quicken of the location of the files, use the **Set File Location** option on the File Activities menu.

To use the **Set File Location** option, follow these steps:

1. Select the **Set Preferences** option from Quicken's Main Menu. The Set Preferences menu appears.
2. Select the **File Activities** option from the Set Preferences menu. The File Activities menu appears.
3. Select the **Set File Location** option on the File Activities menu. Quicken displays the Set File Location screen shown in figure 9.16.

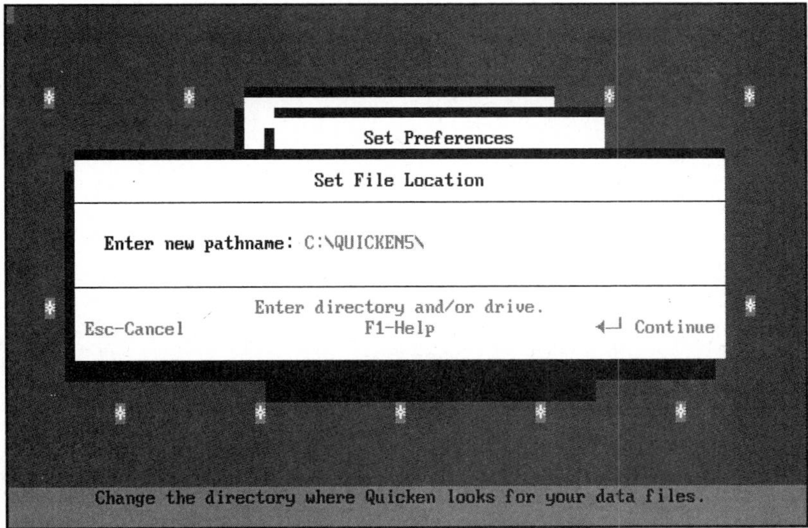

Fig. 9.16. *The Set File Location screen.*

4. Enter the drive and directory where the Quicken data files are located.

   The drive and directory you enter must be a valid DOS path name. The drive letter must be valid and followed by a colon. Directories and subdirectories must exist. (The hard disk installation program creates the directory QUICKEN5.) If you use a directory and subdirectory together, the combination must constitute a valid path name. The subdirectory specified must be in the directory specified. (For more information on directories, subdirectories, and path names, see the DOS user's manual.)

5. Press Enter to save the changes.

Exporting and Importing Files

Exporting is the process by which a software program makes a copy of a file in a format that another program can read. You may want to export the information stored in the Quicken register so that you can retrieve and use the information in a database program, such as dBASE, or in a spreadsheet program, such as 1-2-3.

Importing is the process by which information created by one software program is retrieved by a second software program. You may want to import into Quicken the information created by an accounting program, such as DacEasy, so that you can use Quicken's reports to summarize the information.

Exporting and importing represent two sides of the same coin: exporting creates a file by using the information stored in the Quicken register, and importing retrieves information from another file into the Quicken register. Although most Quicken users never need to export or import files, Quicken provides the tools to do both. The **Export** and **Import** options appear on the Write Checks and Register versions of the Print/Acct menus.

Exporting Files

The **Export** option enables you to create an ASCII text file from register transactions. You then can use the ASCII file in another software program. Most word processing, spreadsheet, and database applications commonly enable you to import ASCII text files from Quicken.

To execute an export operation, take the following steps:

1. While on the Write Checks or the Register screen, press Alt-P to display the Print/Acct menu (see fig. 9.17).
2. Select **Export** from the Print/Acct menu. Quicken displays the Export Transactions to QIF File screen shown in figure 9.18.
3. In the `DOS File` field, enter the DOS file name to use for the new ASCII file. You also can include a path name.
4. (Optional) To limit exported transactions to within a certain range of dates, fill in the `Export transactions from` and `to` date fields. You can use the + and - keys to change the date one day at a time.

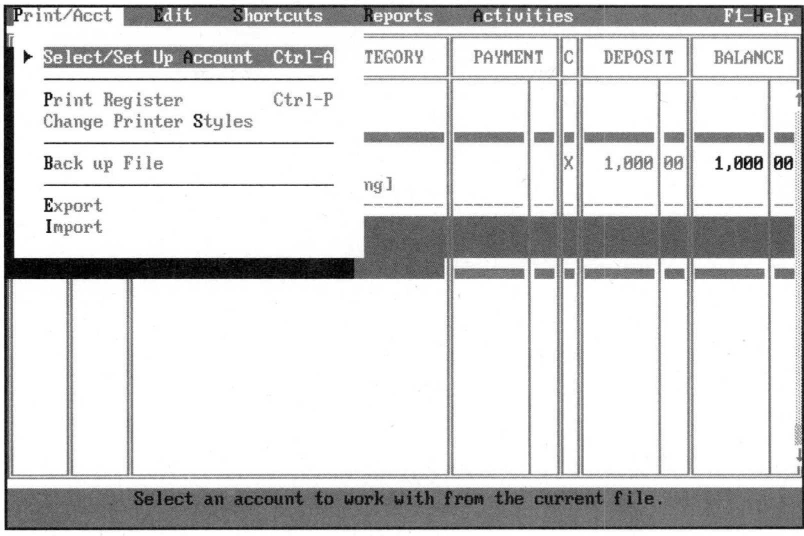

Fig. 9.17. The Print/Acct menu.

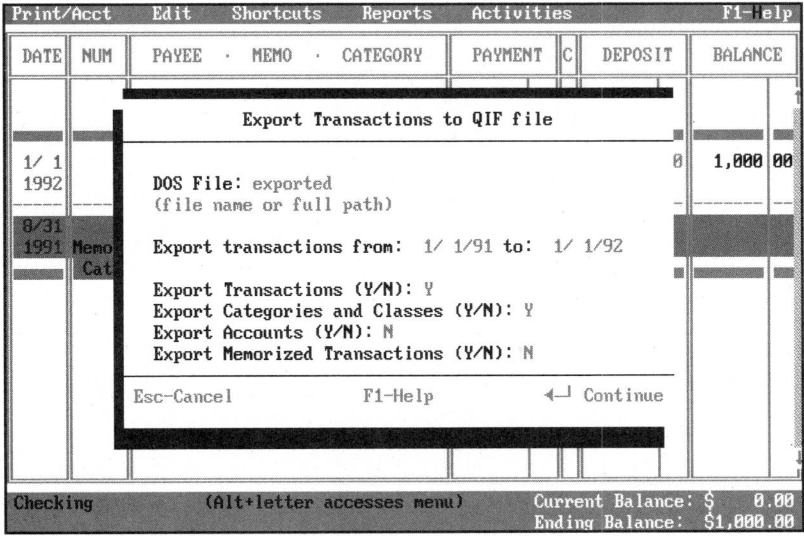

Fig. 9.18. The Export Transactions to QIF File screen.

5. (Optional) Quicken enables you to export transactions, categories, and classes. To change the default settings, move the cursor to the Yes/No answer field on the Export Transactions to QIF file screen. Then, type Y for yes or N for no.

6. To start the export operation, press Enter when the cursor is on the `Export transaction to` date field. Alternatively, press Ctrl-Enter or F10 when the cursor is on one of the other screen fields.

Quicken creates an ASCII file that contains the exported transactions. At the beginning of the file, Quicken prints a line to identify the type of account from which transactions were exported. This information begins with an exclamation point and the word `type` and is followed by the actual type name. Transactions exported from a bank account, for example, show `Bank` as the first line.

The following is the actual ASCII information that Quicken uses to record each transaction in the register.

```
D7/24/89
T–1,000.00
        CX
        N*****
PBig National Bank
L[Savings]
^
```

The first line begins with `D` and shows the transaction date. The second line begins with `T` and shows the transaction amount as –1000.00. (The amount is negative because the transaction is a payment.) The third line begins with a `C` and shows the cleared status. The fourth line shows the transaction number set to asterisks because the check has not yet been printed. The fifth line begins with `P` and shows the payee. The sixth line begins with `L` and shows the `Category` field entry. If you split a transaction, Quicken creates several `L` lines. The last line shows only a caret (`^`), which designates the end of a transaction.

Other kinds of exported data—categories, classes, accounts, and memorized transactions—work in a similar way. Each kind of data starts with a header to identify the exported data: *!Type:Cat* for categories, *!Type:Class* for classes, *!Account* for accounts, and *!Type:Memorized* for memorized transactions. Then, each field in the data type that describes an item starts with a code. Suppose that you want to export the class name *West* and the description *Western*. The ASCII file looks like the following:

```
!Type:Class
N West
D Western
^
```

The codes for category, account, and memorized transactions are not mentioned here. You can easily obtain this information from the Quicken user's manual.

The **Export** option does not produce the same ASCII file as the **Print to Disk** option described in Chapters 4 and 6. **Export** creates an ASCII file with each transaction field on a separate line. You may use this option if you are trying to import the Quicken data into another software program—such as an accounting program—that uses the information. The Print Register's **Print to Disk** setting creates an ASCII text file that looks like a printed check register. You may use this option to create a list of certain Quicken transactions that you can retrieve by a word processing program, edit with the word processor, and then print or use in a document.

Importing Files

The **Import** option retrieves files stored in the Quicken QIF format. This format is the same one Quicken uses when exporting data (see preceding section). The steps for importing parallel those for exporting data.

To import files, take the following steps:

1. While on the Write Checks or Register screen, press Alt-P to display the Print/Acct menu (see fig. 9.17).
2. Select **Import** from the Print/Acct menu. The Import from QIF File or CheckFree screen appears, as shown in figure 9.19.
3. Enter the DOS file name of the file you want Quicken to import. You also can include a path name.
4. To move the cursor to the `Import Transactions` field, press Enter or Tab. To import transactions, press Y for yes and then press Enter.

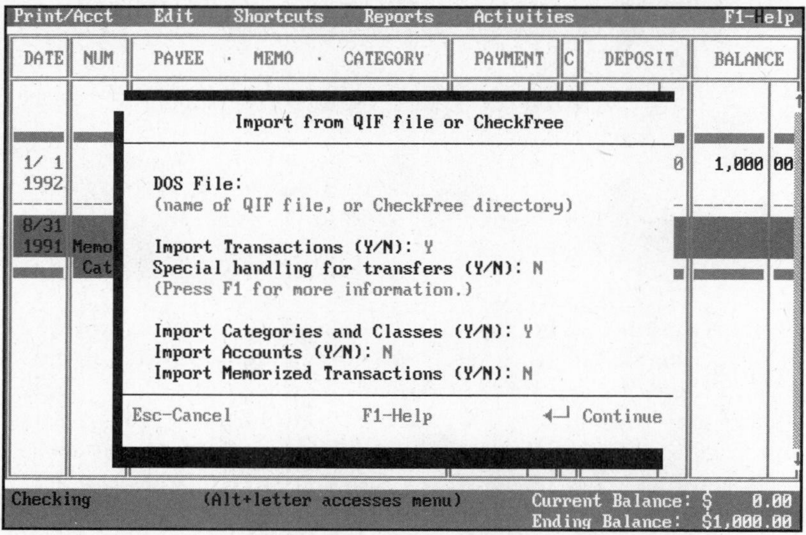

Fig. 9.19. *The Import from QIF File or CheckFree screen.*

5. (Optional) To move the cursor to the `Special handling for transfers` field, press Enter or Tab. To import transactions with account transfers included in the `Category` field, press N for no and then press Enter.

6. (Optional) To move the cursor to the `Import Categories and Classes` field, press Enter or Tab. To import categories and classes, press Y for yes and then press Enter.

7. (Optional) To move the cursor to the `Import Accounts` field, press Enter or Tab. To import accounts, press Y for yes and press Enter.

8. (Optional) To move the cursor to the `Import Memorized Transactions` field, press Enter or Tab. To import memorized transactions, press Y for yes and then press Enter.

9. To import the file, press Enter when the cursor is on the `Import Memorized Transactions` field. Alternatively, press Ctrl-Enter or F10 when the cursor is on one of the other screen fields. Quicken imports the file and records the transaction in the register.

10. If the imported file does not contain categories, you may be prompted to add categories.

11. Upon completion, Quicken tells you that the import was successful.

Chapter Summary

This chapter described the steps and the logic for taking care of Quicken data files. The chapter identified the Quicken files and explained how to back up and restore files, how to shrink files, and how to tell Quicken where the files are located. The chapter also described how to export information from Quicken and how to import information from another program into a Quicken register.

This chapter completes "Learning the Basics." You now are ready for the next three sections of *Using Quicken 5 for DOS*: "Supercharging Quicken," "Putting Quicken To Work," and "Protecting Yourself from Forgery, Embezzlement, and Other Disasters."

Part III

Supercharging Quicken

Includes

Organizing Your Finances Better

Fine-Tuning Quicken

Tracking Your Net Worth, Other Assets, and Liabilities

Monitoring Your Investments

Tapping the Power of Quicken's Reports

Paying Bills Electronically

10

Organizing Your Finances Better

Many of the previous chapters of this book mention Quicken's categories. *Categories* enable you to summarize the information in a check register, track tax deductions, and monitor the money flowing into and out of a checking account. The previous discussions of Quicken's categories, however, were rather superficial. In fact, so far this book has only touched on the power of categories.

This chapter, however, goes into depth on the subject of categories and how you can use categories to organize finances better. This chapter describes—and tells you why and when to use—categories, and shows the predefined categories Quicken provides for business and personal use. This chapter also describes the steps for adding, deleting, and editing categories you create. Finally, this chapter covers a related tool, Quicken's *classes*.

Working with Categories

To review briefly, categories enable you to group the payments that flow from an account and the deposits that flow into an account. The deposits into an account may stem from two sources: earned wages from a full-time job and profits from a part-time business. Payments can stem from four expenditures: rent, food, transportation, and, perhaps, part-time business expenses. By grouping each payment from and each deposit into an account, Quicken easily adds up the totals for each kind of payment and deposit. You then can see exactly how much each category contributes to the cash flow. You may find, for example, that cash flows into and from your account are like the cash flows summarized in table 10.1.

Table 10.1
Personal Cash Flows

Deposits		
	Wages from job	$15,400
	Business profits	4,300
Total Deposits		19,700
Withdrawals		
	Housing	6,000
	Food	3,000
	Transportation	3,000
	Business Expenses	500
Total Withdrawals		12,500
Cash Flows		7,200

The information shown in table 10.1 is valuable because categorizing your income and outgo is the first step in beginning to manage personal or business finances. Categories enable you to do the following:

- Track and tally income tax deductions for individual retirement accounts, mortgage interest deductions, or charitable contributions
- Break down checking account deposits and payments into groups of similar transactions so that you can summarize personal income and outgo
- Budget income and outgo and compare budgeted amounts with actual amounts

If you want to use Quicken for a business, the predefined categories enable you to prepare most of the reports you need for managing business finances. These reports include the following:

- A report that resembles and performs most of the arithmetic required to complete the federal income tax form Schedule C. The Schedule C form reports the profits or losses from a business or profession.

- Income and cash-flow statements on a monthly and annual basis that enable you to understand cash flows and measure business profits or losses
- Employee payroll checks and reports

If any of the reports listed look like benefits you want to enjoy as part of using Quicken, you want to use Quicken's categories. How involved or complicated the use of these categories becomes depends on your goals.

Building a List of Categories

The information needs you are tracking determine the various categories you want to use to group similar payments or deposits. Three basic rules apply when building a list of categories.

The first rule: if you want to use categories for tallying and tracking income tax deductions, you need a category for each deduction. If you use the individual retirement account deduction, the mortgage interest deduction, and the state and local taxes deduction, you need categories for each of these deductions. The following list shows the itemized deductions you may want to track to more easily prepare a personal income tax return. The list is based on the federal income tax form, Schedule A.

Sample personal tax deduction categories

Medical and dental*
Medical and dental—other*
State and local income taxes
Real estate taxes
Other taxes, including personal property taxes
Deductible home mortgage interest paid to financial institutions
Deductible home mortgage interest paid to individuals
Deductible points
Deductible investment interest
Deductible personal interest (being phased out)
Contributions by cash or check
Contributions other than by cash or check
Casualty or theft losses†
Moving expenses†
Unreimbursed employee expenses
Union dues, tax preparation fees, investment publications, and fees

Individual retirement account
Other miscellaneous expenses

**The first medical expense category includes prescription medicines and drugs, insulin, doctors, dentists, nurses, hospitals, and medical insurance premiums. The second includes items like hearing aids, dentures, eyeglasses, transportation, and lodging.*

†This itemized deduction must be supported by an additional tax form. Therefore, you also want to consider setting up the individual amounts that need to be reported on that form as categories.

The following list shows the income and deduction categories you may want to use to prepare a business income tax return. This list is based on the Schedule C federal income tax form.

Income categories

Gross receipts or sales
Sales returns and allowances
Cost of goods sold*
Rental/interest
Other income

Deduction categories

Advertising
Bad debts from sales or services
Bank service charges
Car and truck expenses
Commissions
Depletion
Depreciation†
Dues and publications
Employee benefit programs
Freight
Insurance
Interest—mortgage
Interest—other
Laundry and cleaning
Legal and professional services
Office expense
Pension and profit-sharing plans
Rent on business property

Repairs
Supplies
Taxes (payroll and business)
Travel
Meals and entertainment
Utilities and telephone
Wages
Wages—job credit
Other deductions

**The cost of goods sold must be calculated or verified by using part III of Schedule C.*

†This deduction amount must be supported by an additional tax form; consider setting up as categories the individual amounts reported on the second form.

The second rule: if you want to use categories to summarize cash inflows and outflows, you need a category for each income or expense account you want to use in the summaries. To account for your work expenses and a spouse's work expenses, you need categories for both sets of expenses.

The third rule: if you want to use categories to budget—so that at a later date, you can compare what you budgeted and what you actually spent—you need a category for each comparison you want to make. To budget entertainment expenses and clothing expenses, you need categories for both.

By applying these three rules, you can build a list of the categories you want to use. As an aid in creating the list, figure 10.1 shows the category list that Quicken provides for personal accounts. Figure 10.2 shows the category list Quicken provides for business accounts.

Consider these lists as starting points. The predefined personal, or home, category list provides a long list of income and spending categories that you may find useful for personal accounting. Depending on the situation, some categories you don't need may be provided, and other categories you do need may be missing. Similarly, the predefined business list provides income and spending categories you may find useful in business accounting. If you apply the rules described previously for devising categories, you may have no problem when using the predefined lists as starting points for constructing a category list that works well for you.

Category and Transfer List

STEPHENL
8/31/91

Page 1

Category	Description	Tax Rel	Type	Budget Amount
Bonus	Bonus Income	*	Inc	
Canada Pen	Canadian Pension	*	Inc	
Div Income	Dividend Income	*	Inc	
Gift Received	Gift Received	*	Inc	
Int Inc	Interest Income	*	Inc	
Invest Inc	Investment Income	*	Inc	
Old Age Pension	Old Age Pension	*	Inc	
Other Inc	Other Income	*	Inc	
Salary	Salary Income	*	Inc	
Auto	Automobile Expenses		Expns	
Fuel	Auto Fuel		Sub	
Loan	Auto Loan Payment		Sub	
Service	Auto Service		Sub	
Bank Chrg	Bank Charge		Expns	
Charity	Charitable Donations	*	Expns	
Childcare	Childcare Expense		Expns	
Christmas	Christmas Expenses		Expns	
Clothing	Clothing		Expns	
Dining	Dining Out		Expns	
Dues	Dues		Expns	
Education	Education		Expns	
Entertain	Entertainment		Expns	
Gifts	Gift Expenses		Expns	
Groceries	Groceries		Expns	
Home Rpair	Home Repair & Maint.		Expns	
Household	Household Misc. Exp		Expns	
Housing	Housing		Expns	
Insurance	Insurance		Expns	
Int Exp	Interest Expense	*	Expns	
Invest Exp	Investment Expense	*	Expns	
Medical	Medical & Dental	*	Expns	
Misc	Miscellaneous		Expns	
Mort Int	Mortgage Interest Exp	*	Expns	
Mort Prin	Mortgage principal		Expns	
Other Exp	Other Expenses	*	Expns	
Recreation	Recreation Expense		Expns	
RRSP	Reg Retirement Sav Plan		Expns	
Subscriptions	Subscriptions		Expns	
Supplies	Supplies	*	Expns	
Tax	Taxes	*	Expns	
Fed	Federal Tax	*	Sub	
FICA	Social Security Tax	*	Sub	
Other	Misc. Taxes	*	Sub	
Prop	Property Tax	*	Sub	
State	State Tax	*	Sub	
Telephone	Telephone Expense		Expns	
UIC	Unemploy. Ins. Commission	*	Expns	
Utilities	Water, Gas, Electric		Expns	
Gas & Electric	Gas and Electricity		Sub	
Water	Water		Sub	

Fig. 10.1. *The category list that Quicken provides for personal or household use.*

After you complete the list, review the categories for any redundancies produced by two of the rules calling for the same category. For personal use of Quicken, for example, you can add a category to budget for monthly individual retirement account (IRA) payments. You also can add a category to tally IRA payments because these payments represent potential tax deductions. Because both categories are the same, cross one category off the list.

Category and Transfer List

BUSINESS
8/31/91

Page 1

Category	Description	Tax Rel	Type	Budget Amount
Gr Sales	Gross Sales	*	Inc	
Other Inc	Other Income	*	Inc	
Rent Income	Rent Income	*	Inc	
Ads	Advertising		Expns	
Car	Car & Truck	*	Expns	
Commission	Commissions	*	Expns	
Freight	Freight	*	Expns	
Int Paid	Interest Paid	*	Expns	
L&P Fees	Legal & Prof. Fees	*	Expns	
Late Fees	Late Payment Fees	*	Expns	
Rent Paid	Rent Paid	*	Expns	
Repairs	Repairs	*	Expns	
Returns	Returns & Allowances	*	Expns	
Tax	Taxes	*	Expns	
Travel	Travel Expenses	*	Expns	
Wages	Wages & Job Credits	*	Expns	
Checking	Seafirst Checking		Bank	

***Fig. 10.2.** The category list that Quicken provides for business use.*

Sometimes, however, overlapping or redundant categories are not as easy to spot. A tax deduction you need to calculate may be only a small part of a budgeting category, or a budgeting amount you need to calculate may be only a portion of a tax-deduction category. You need to use categories smaller than the tax-deduction amount or the budgeting amount so that you can add up the individual categories that make up a tax deduction, accounting amount, or budgeted amount.

Categories act as building blocks you use to calculate the amounts you really want to know. For example, you can use the following categories to calculate the tax-deduction amounts and the budgeted amounts shown in table 10.2:

Mortgage interest
Mortgage principal
Mortgage late-payment fees
Credit card late-payment fees
Property taxes

Table 10.2
Personal Budget and Tax Amounts

Amounts	*Categories Used*
Late fees (a budgeted amount)	Mortgage late-payment fees Credit card late-payment fees
Housing (a budgeted amount)	Mortgage principal Mortgage interest Property taxes
Mortgage interest (deduction)	Mortgage interest Mortgage late-payment fees
Property taxes (deduction)	Property taxes

Using Subcategories

If you decide to use categories as building blocks to calculate other budgeted or tax-deduction amounts, you need to know about subcategories. Taking the first row of the data from table 10.2, suppose that you create two building block categories to track late-payment fees on a mortgage and credit cards—LMortgage and LCredit. (The L stands for late.) If you also set up a category for late fees, LateFees, you can assign mortgage late-payment fees to the category and subcategory combination LateFees and LMortgage. You also can assign credit card late-payment fees to the category and subcategory combination LateFees and LCredit.

To record the subcategories, enter the primary income or expense category first, a colon, and then the subcategory. If you calculate further categorized LateFees by the two kinds of late fees you may pay—LMortgage and LCredit—you record late fees on a mortgage by entering *LateFees:LMortgage*. You record late fees on a credit card by entering *LateFees:LCredit*. Figure 10.3 shows the Category field on the Register screen filled with both a category and a subcategory.

On the reports, the totals for LMortgage, LCredit, and LateFees appear. Figure 10.4 shows an example of a report that illustrates the effect of subcategories.

```
Print/Acct   Edit   Shortcuts   Reports   Activities                    F1-Help

DATE   NUM    PAYEE · MEMO · CATEGORY           PAYMENT   C   DEPOSIT   BALANCE

8/29          Service Charge                      5 00   X              249 29
1991                      Bank Chrg

8/30   *****  Sammamish Cleaning Services        64 00   X              185 29
1991                      Household

9/ 5   *****  Sammamish Cleaning Services        64 00                  121 29
1991                      Household

9/15          Seattle Power Company              75 39                   45 90
1991                      Utilities

8/31          Big National Bank                  28 70
1991   Memo:  August
        Cat:  LateFees:LMortgage

My bank account      (Alt+letter accesses menu)      Current Balance: $185.29
Esc-Main Menu        Ctrl←┘ Record                   Ending Balance:  $ 45.90
```

Fig. 10.3. Separate categories and subcategories with a colon.

Showing Subcategories on a Report
8/ 1/91 Through 8/31/91

STEPHENL-Bank,Cash,CC Accounts | Page 1
8/31/91

Category Description		8/ 1/91- 8/31/91
INFLOWS		
Interest Income		5.75
TOTAL INFLOWS		5.75
OUTFLOWS		
Automobile Expenses		-12.73
Bank Charge		5.00
Groceries		-76.91
Household Misc. Exp		64.00
Housing		559.00
Late Fees:		
Late Credit Cards	35.00	
Late Mortgage Payment	28.70	
Total Late Fees		63.70
Mortgage Interest Exp		0.00
Mortgage principal		0.00
Recreation Expense		-43.29
Taxes:		
Property Tax	0.00	
Total Taxes		0.00
Water, Gas, Electric		75.39
TOTAL OUTFLOWS		634.16
OVERALL TOTAL		-628.41

Fig. 10.4. Using subcategories gives you the capability of showing greater detail.

Setting Up Categories

When you create files, you can use the defined home or business categories on the Default Categories screen as the foundation of the category list (see fig. 10.5).

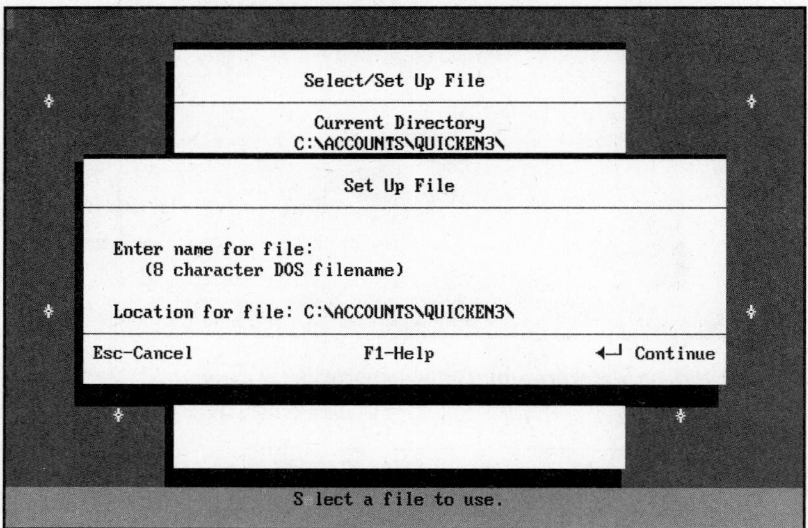

Fig. 10.5. *Setting up categories.*

If you specify that the home categories are used, you already have set up all the categories shown in figure 10.1. If you specify that the business categories are used, you already have set up all the categories shown in figure 10.2. Even if you elect to use one of the sample category lists, however, you may need to modify the category list.

To help you identify tax-deductible expenses, review last year's tax return. On Form 1040 (Federal Individual Tax Return), Schedule A lists deductible itemized expenses, including medical bills, personal interest, contributions, moving expenses, investments, and so on. Call a CPA if you have specific questions when trying to identify a potential tax-deductible expense.

Adding Categories

You can add categories in two ways. Both methods are described here, and you can pick the method you find most convenient. To add categories by using the Shortcuts menu option, **Categorize/Transfer**, follow these steps:

1. Press Alt-S to access the Shortcuts menu from the Write/Print Checks or Register screens, which you access from the Main Menu.
2. Select **Categorize/Transfer** or use the shortcut key combination Ctrl-C. After you select **Categorize/Transfer**, the Category and Transfer List screen appears, as shown in figure 10.6.

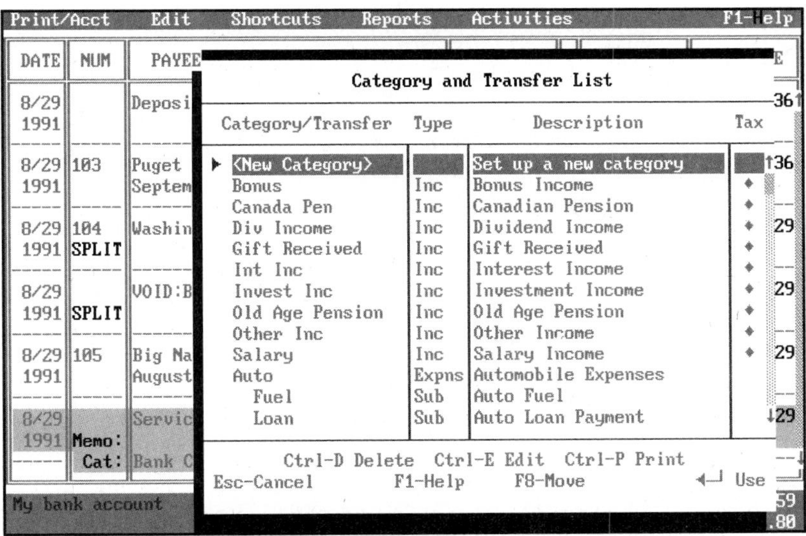

***Fig. 10.6.** The Category and Transfer List screen.*

3. Select the first item on the list, `New Category`. You can use the Home key to move to the first item on the list. Quicken then displays the Set Up Category screen, shown in figure 10.7.

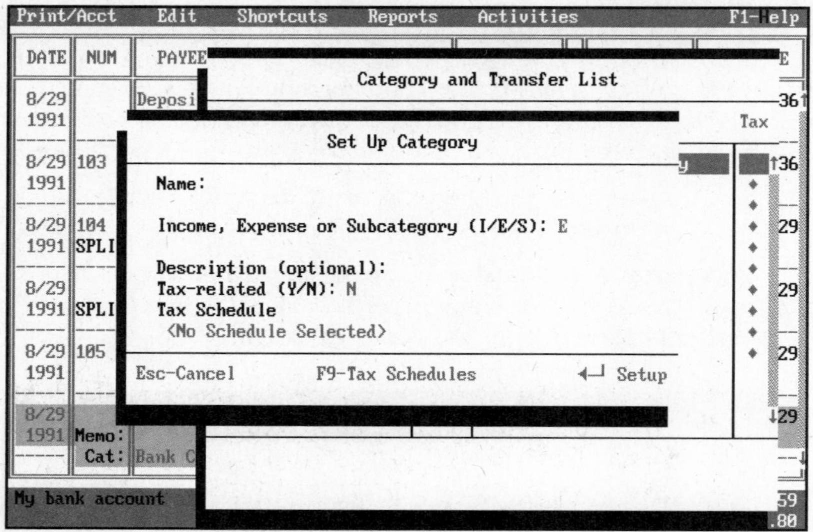

Fig. 10.7. The Set Up Category screen.

4. Type the category name you want to use in the `Name` field.

5. Press Enter or Tab to move the cursor to the `Income, Expense,` or `Subcategory` field. Type an *I* if the category is for income, an *E* if the category is for expenses, and an *S* if the category is a subcategory. (You do not need to tell Quicken whether a subcategory is an income or expense figure because the program knows this by looking at the subcategory's category.)

6. (Optional) Press Enter or Tab to move the cursor to the `Description` field. You can use up to 25 characters to describe the category.

7. (Optional) Press Enter or Tab to move the cursor to the `Tax-related` field. The `Tax-related` field determines whether or not the tax reports include the category. You use this field to mark those categories for which you need totals to prepare personal income tax returns.

8. (Optional) If you are setting up a category to report a specific kind of taxable income or tax deduction, press F9. The Tax Schedule box appears, listing two dozen common tax schedules (see fig. 10.8). Using the arrow keys, highlight the schedule's lines. This list depends on the schedule. Use the arrow keys to highlight the specific

lines on which the category is reported and then press Enter. A Schedule Copy Number box appears (see fig. 10.9). Enter the schedule copy number on which this category is reported and then press Enter. (Usually, this value is 1 because most people file only a single copy of each schedule.) Quicken returns you to the Set Up Category screen.

9. To save the category, press Enter when the cursor is on the Tax-related field. Alternatively, press Ctrl-Enter or F10 when the cursor is on any of the screen fields.

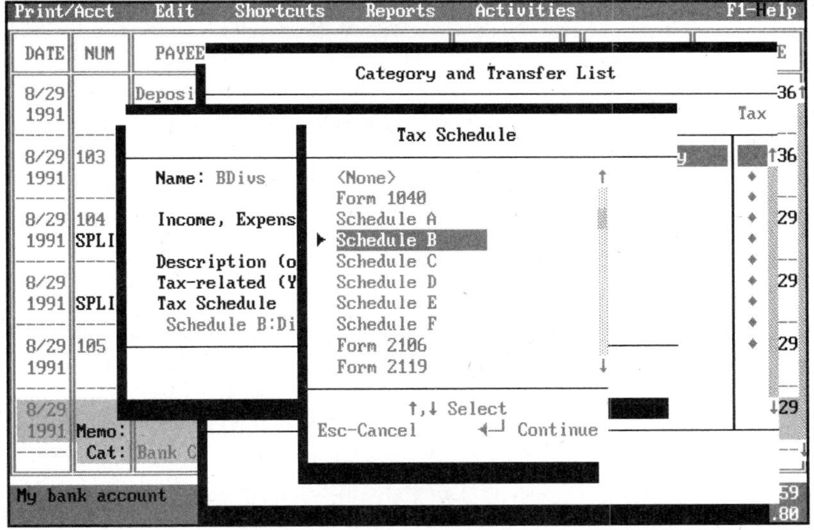

Fig. 10.8. The Tax Schedule box.

You can shortcut the entire process of adding a category. To use the shortcut, follow these steps:

1. Move the cursor to the `Category` field on the Write/Print Checks screen, the Register screen, or the Split Transactions screen, which you access by pressing Ctrl-S from the Write/Print Checks or Register screens.

2. Type the new category name you want to add. If the category doesn't already exist, the Category Not Found message box appears (see fig. 10.10).

Print/Acct Edit Shortcuts Reports Activities F1-Help
DATE NUM PAYEE
Category and Transfer List
Tax Schedule
Name: BD
Income,
Descrip
Tax-rel
Tax Sch
Schedu
Schedule Copy Number
Copy: 1
Esc-Cancel F1-Help ◄┘ Continue
Tax
8/29 1991 Deposi
8/29 1991 103
8/29 1991 104 SPLI
8/29 1991 SPLI
8/29 1991 105
8/29 1991 Memo: Cat: Bank C
My bank account

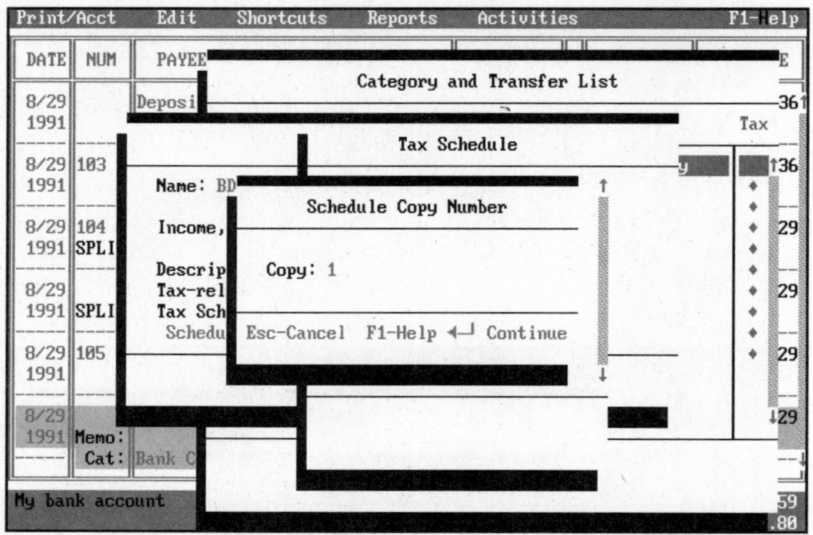

Fig. 10.9. The Schedule Copy Number box.

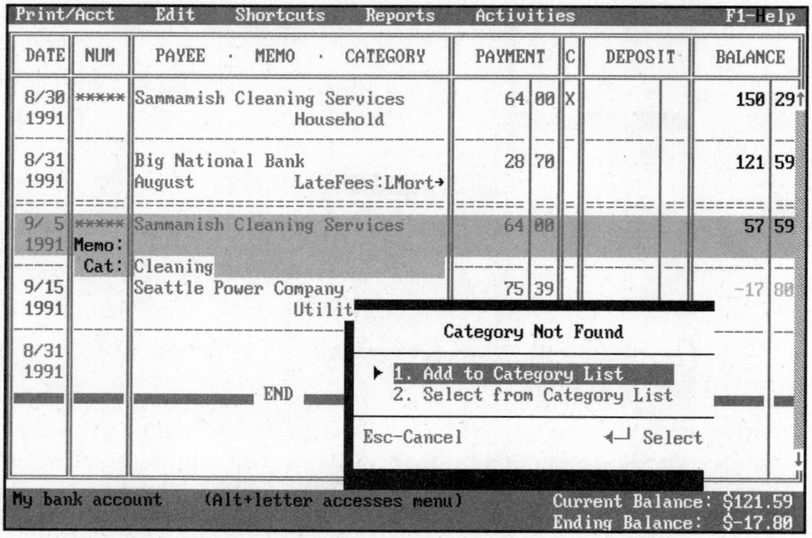

Print/Acct Edit Shortcuts Reports Activities F1-Help
DATE NUM PAYEE · MEMO · CATEGORY PAYMENT C DEPOSIT BALANCE
8/30 1991 ***** Sammamish Cleaning Services Household 64 00 X 150 29
8/31 1991 Big National Bank August LateFees:LMort→ 28 70 121 59
9/ 5 1991 ***** Sammamish Cleaning Services Memo: Cat: Cleaning 64 00 57 59
9/15 1991 Seattle Power Company Utilit 75 39 -17 80
8/31 1991
END
Category Not Found
1. Add to Category List
2. Select from Category List
Esc-Cancel ◄┘ Select
My bank account (Alt+letter accesses menu)
Current Balance: $121.59
Ending Balance: $-17.80

Fig. 10.10. The Category Not Found box.

3. To add a category, choose `Add to Category List`. The Set Up New Category box appears, which you complete as discussed in steps 4 through 9 of the preceding stepped procedure described to add categories.

If you choose the `Select from Category List` option, Quicken displays the Category List screen and marks the category that comes closest to the name you entered.

Generally, you have plenty of room for as many categories as you need. The precise maximum number, however, depends on the computer's available memory, the length of the category names and descriptions, and the other information stored in memory. You usually have room for about 150 categories with 384K of memory and more than 1,000 categories with 512K of memory.

Deleting Categories

You also may want to delete categories—either because you don't use a particular category or because you added the category incorrectly. Deleting categories is even easier than adding categories. To delete categories, follow these steps:

1. Press Alt-S to access the Shortcuts menu from the Write/Print Checks or Register screens.
2. Select **Categorize/Transfer** from the Shortcuts menu, or use the shortcut key combination Ctrl-C. After you select **Categorize/Transfer**, the Category and Transfer List screen appears.
3. Select the item on the list that you want to delete. Use the arrow keys to move down the list of categories one item at a time, or use PgUp and PgDn to move up and down the list one screen at a time. Pressing Home moves you to the beginning of the list, and pressing End moves you to the end of the list; or use the mouse on the scroll bar.
4. When the item you want to delete is marked, press Ctrl-D. The warning screen shown in figure 10.11 appears.

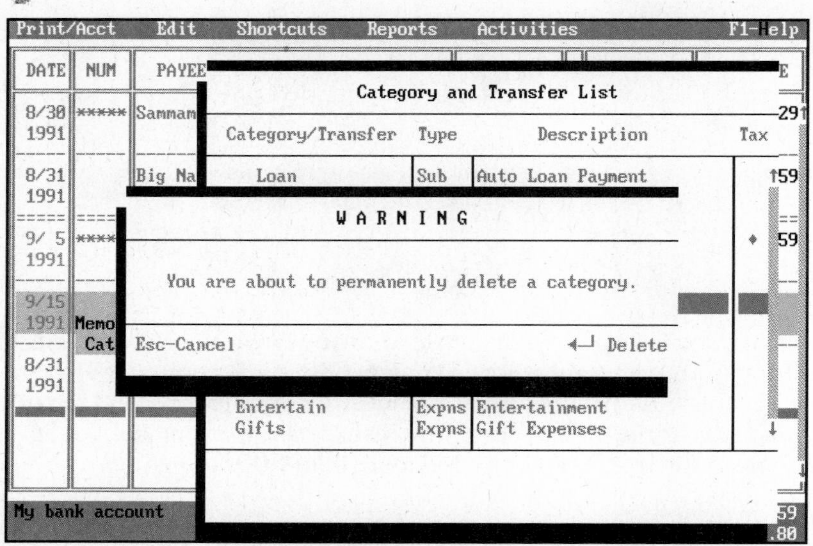

Fig. 10.11. Quicken warns you that a category is about to be permanently deleted.

5. To remove the category from the category list, press Enter. If you don't want to remove the category, press Esc.

After you delete a category, you cannot use the category unless you add the category again. If you already used the deleted category to describe transactions, you need to return to the register and change the invalid category to current, valid categories. (Chapters 4 and 5 describe how to use the register.)

Editing Categories

You also can edit a category. Suppose that you run a business and use Quicken to account for, among other things, the wages you pay. Further, suppose that the Wages category was always used for employees working in Washington state. If you create a new category named OR_WAGES to account for the wages you pay to employees working in Oregon, you may want to change the name of the Wages category to WA_WAGES to reflect the change in the significance of the account.

The steps for editing a category roughly parallel the steps for adding one. To edit a category, follow these steps:

1. Press Alt-S to access the Shortcuts menu from the Write/Print Checks or Register screens.
2. Select **Categorize/Transfer** from the Shortcuts menu, or use the shortcut key combination Ctrl-C. After you select **Categorize/ Transfer**, the Category and Transfer List screen appears, as shown in figure 10.6.
3. Select the item on the list that you want to edit. Use the arrow keys to move down the list of categories one item at a time. Use PgUp and PgDn to move up and down the list one screen at a time. Pressing Home moves the cursor to the first item on the list; pressing End moves the cursor to the last item on the list or use the mouse on the scroll bar.
4. When the item you want to edit is marked, press Ctrl-E. The Edit Category screen appears, as shown in figure 10.12.

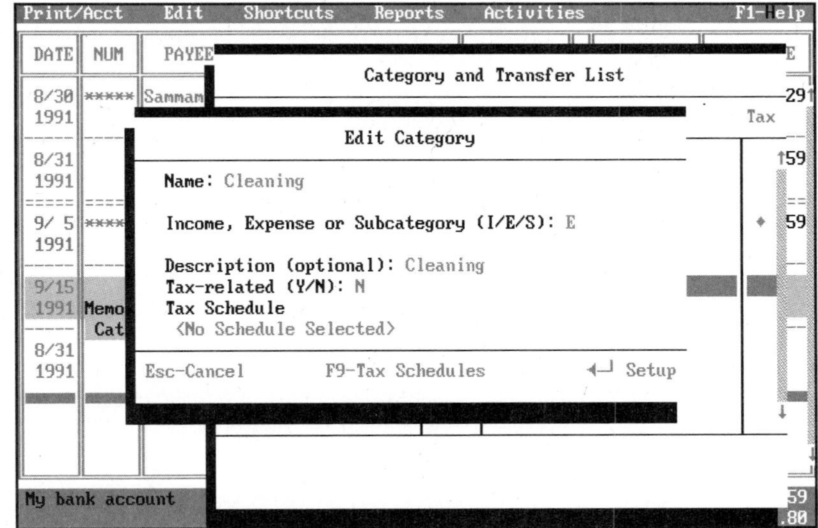

Fig. 10.12. *The Edit Category screen.*

5. (Optional) Retype or edit the category name you want to use in the Name field.
6. (Optional) Press Enter or Tab to move the cursor to the Income, Expense, or Subcategory field. If necessary, change the Income, Expense, or Subcategory field by typing an *I* for income, an *E* for expenses, or an *S* for subcategory.

7. (Optional) Press Enter or Tab to move the cursor to the `Description` field. If necessary, retype or edit the existing description.

8. (Optional) Press Enter or Tab to move the cursor to the `Tax-related` field. If necessary, change the `Tax-related` field.

9. (Optional) Press F9 to display the Tax Schedule box (see fig. 10.8). Use the arrow keys to identify the appropriate schedule. Press Enter to display the Tax Line box (not shown). Use the arrow keys to identify the appropriate line of the schedule. Press Enter to display the Schedule Copy Number box (see fig. 10.9). Type the schedule number and press Enter. Quicken again displays the Edit Category screen.

10. To save the changes to the category, press Enter when the cursor is on the `Tax-related` field, or press Ctrl-Enter or F10 when the cursor is on any of the screen fields.

Printing a Category and Transfer List

When you select **Categorize/Transfer** from the Shortcuts menu, a list of categories and accounts appears. Occasionally, you may want a printed copy of this list. You also may want to review the list with a tax advisor at her office to verify you are tracking all tax deduction categories, or you may want to keep a paper copy of the list as an aid to entering transactions. To print a copy of the category and transfer list, follow these steps:

1. Press Alt-S to access the Shortcuts menu from the Write/Print Checks or Register screens.

2. Select **Categorize/Transfer** or use the shortcut combination, Ctrl-C. After you select **Categorize/Transfer**, the Category and Transfer List screen appears (see fig. 10.6).

3. Press Ctrl-P. The Print Category and Transfer List box appears. This screen, which resembles the Print Register screen, provides fields that you use to select the printer settings you want to use.

4. Indicate the printer settings you want to use—press 1 for the first setting, 2 for the second setting, and so on. Next, press F10 or Ctrl-Enter. Quicken prints a copy of the Category and Transfer List (see Figs. 10.1 and 10.2).

For help in completing the Print Category and Transfer List screen, refer to the discussion in Chapter 4 on printing a register. The Print Register screen, which you use to print a register, works the same way as the Print Category and Transfer List screen.

Working with Classes

Categories and subcategories group revenues and expenses by the type of transaction. For example, income transactions may be categorized as gross sales, other income, and so on. Expense transactions may be categorized as car and truck expenses, supply expenses, utilities, and so on. But you may want to slice the data in other ways. You also may want to see income or expenses by job or project, by salesman or product line, and by geographic location or functional company areas.

Classes add a second dimension to the income and expense summaries that categories provide. Nonbusiness use of Quicken probably does not require this second dimension. Business owners, however, can find Quicken's classes a powerful way to view financial data from a second perspective.

Besides using two categories—Product and Service—to track income, you can use classes to determine which salespeople actually are booking the orders. With three salespeople, use these three classes: Joe, Bill, and Sue. Besides seeing the sales of company products and company services, you also can see things like the sales Bill made, the product sales Joe made, and the service sales Sue made. In effect, you have two different perspectives on this income—the kind of income, which shows either as a product or service, and salespeople, which shows as Joe, Bill, or Sue (see table 10.3).

Table 10.3
Two Perspectives on Income

Kind of income	*Salespeople booking orders*		
	Joe	*Bill*	*Sue*
Product	Joe's product sales	Bill's product sales	Sue's product sales
Service	Joe's service sales	Bill's service sales	Sue's service sales

Defining a Class

The first step in using classes is to define the classes you want to use. The classes you choose depend on how you need or want to view the financial data you collected with Quicken. Unfortunately, giving specific advice on picking appropriate classes is difficult. Classes usually are specific to the particular personal or business finances. You can, however, follow one rough rule of thumb: look at the kinds of questions you currently ask but cannot answer by using categories alone. A real estate investor may want to use classes that correspond to individual properties. A law firm may want to use classes that represent each of the partners. Other businesses have still different views of financial data. After you define the classes you want to use, you are ready to add the classes in Quicken. You can add as many classes as you want.

To add classes, follow these steps:

1. Press Alt-S to access the Shortcuts menu from the Write/Print Checks or Register screens.
2. Choose the **Select/Set Up Class** option from the Shortcuts menu. The Class List screen shown in figure 10.13 appears.

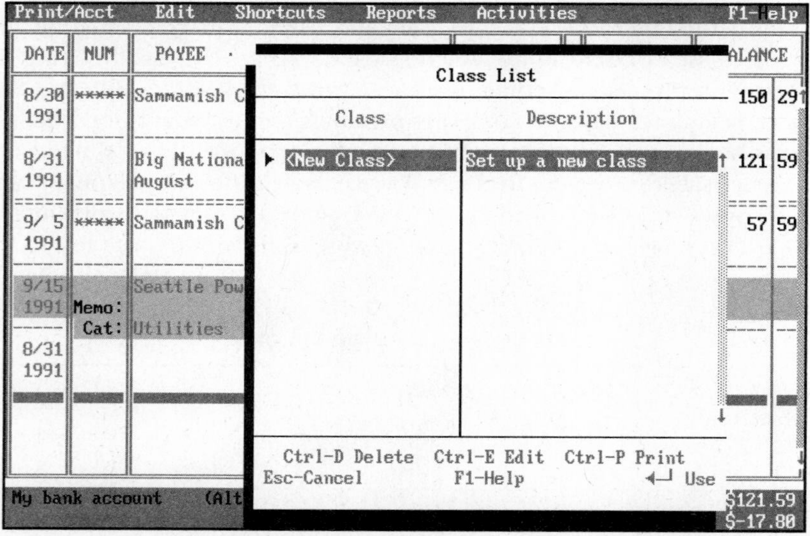

Fig. 10.13. The Class List screen.

3. Mark the `New Class` item on the list and press Enter. The Set Up Class screen appears (see fig. 10.14).

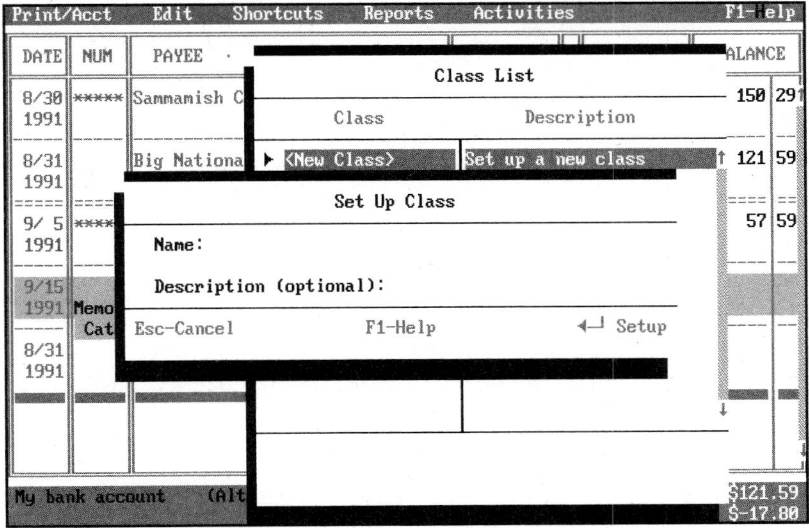

Fig. 10.14. The Set Up Class screen.

4. Type the name you want to use for the class.
5. (Optional) Press Enter or Tab to move the cursor to the `Description` field. Type a description for the class.
6. To save the class, press Enter when the cursor is on the `Description` field, or press Ctrl-Enter or F10 when the cursor is on the `Name` or `Description` field.

Editing and Deleting Classes

If you start defining classes, you also need to know how to edit and delete these classes. The classification scheme you use undoubtedly can change over time. Suppose that you are a real estate investor and you use classes to track properties. You probably buy and sell properties over a period of time. Alternatively, if you are a bookkeeper for a law firm, the lawyers working at the firm probably change over a period of time. Both of these examples indicate a need for editing classes. The steps for editing and deleting are simple and familiar if you previously edited or deleted categories.

To edit a class, follow these steps:

1. Press Alt-S to access the Shortcuts menu from the Write/Print Checks or Register screens.
2. Choose **Select/Set Up Class** from the Shortcuts menu. The Class List screen appears (see fig. 10.13).
3. Use the up- and down-arrow keys to move to the class you want to edit.
4. Press Ctrl-E after selecting, from the Class List, the class you want to delete. Quicken displays the Edit Class box, as shown in figure 10.15.
5. (Optional) If necessary or desired, retype or edit the class name.
6. (Optional) Press Enter or Tab to move to the `Description` field. If necessary or desired, retype or edit the class description.
7. To save the changes to the class, press Enter when the cursor is on the `Description` field, or press Ctrl-Enter or F10 when the cursor is on the `Name` or `Description` field.

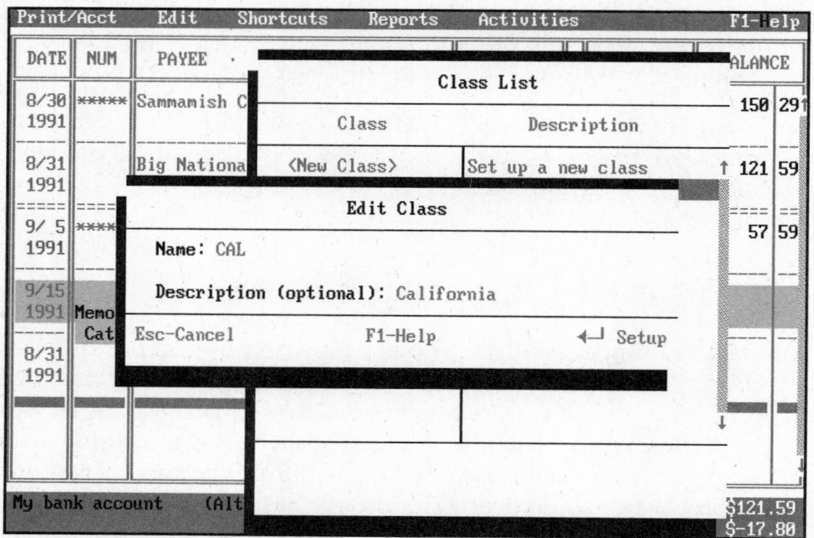

Fig. 10.15. The Edit Class screen.

To delete a class, follow these steps:

1. Press Alt-S to access the Shortcuts menu from the Write/Print Checks or Register screens.
2. Choose **Select/Set Up Class** from the Shortcuts menu. The Class List screen shown in figure 10.13 appears.
3. Use the up- and down-arrow keys to move to the class you want to delete.
4. After the class you want to delete is selected on the Class List, press Ctrl-D. Quicken warns you, as shown in figure 10.16, that a class is about to be deleted.
5. Press Enter to complete the deletion or press Esc to cancel the deletion.

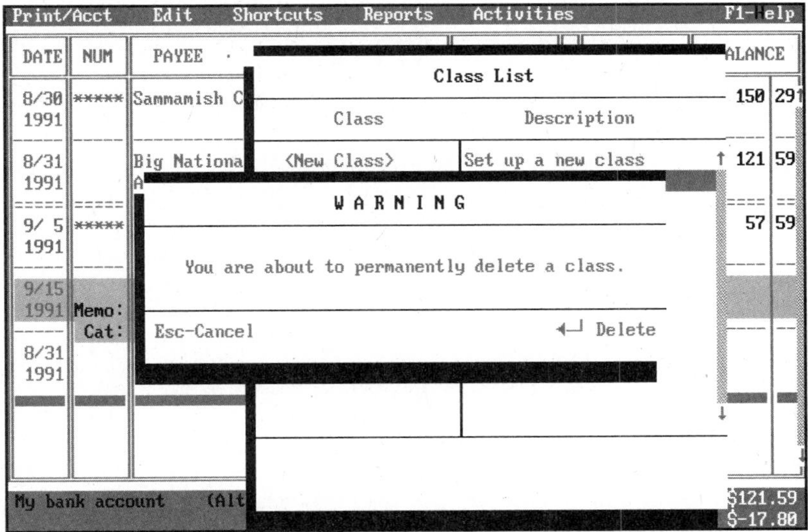

Fig. 10.16. Quicken warns that you are about to delete a class.

Using Subclasses

If you use classes to add another dimension to the reporting and recording process, you also may want to use subclasses. Subclasses are classes within classes. If you use a geographical scheme to create classes, the classes may be states. Within each state, you may choose to use subclasses corresponding to portions of the state. For example, Washington, a class, may have the subclasses Eastern Washington and Western Washington. California, another class, may have the subclasses Northern California (excluding the Bay Area), Bay Area, Southern California (excluding Los Angeles County), and Los Angeles County. You enter, edit, and delete subclasses by following the same procedures described previously for classes.

Subclasses are helpful for sales taxes based on a state, county, or city with different tax rates for each jurisdiction, or if you must report sales within each jurisdiction.

Recording Classes and Subclasses

You use the `Category` field on the Write Checks, Register, or Split Transaction screens to record classes. To record a class, enter a slash followed by the class name in the `Category` field after any category or subcategory names. For example, if you want to record the income category, SALES, and the California class, CAL, for a transaction, type *SALES/CAL* in the `Category` field on the data screen. The same auto-completion feature described previously in the book also applies to classes. If you type enough of a class for Quicken to identify the class, Quicken completes the entry for you.

If you use subclasses, enter the primary class, a colon, and then the subclass. For example, if the class CAL has the subclass NORTH, you can record sales for Northern California by typing *SALES/CAL:NORTH* in the `Category` field.

If you have more then one subclass—classes within classes within classes—you also separate the additional subclasses with colons.

The Quicken user's manual describes a whole series of ways you can use classes. For the most part, the ideas are good. Some accounting problems exist with many of the manual's suggestions. From the start, think about these problems so that you don't go to a great deal of work and then find out you wasted time. The basic problem with classes is that they don't give you a way to budget. You cannot, for example, budget by classes. This may not seem too important to you right now, but before you begin to use classes, review Chapter 16. Business users will probably also benefit by reading Chapter 18.

Chapter Summary

Quicken's categories and classes give you a means to organize finances better. This chapter described how you can modify Quicken's defined categories and how you use subcategories. This chapter also defined classes; described when to use the class features; and detailed the steps for adding, editing, and deleting classes.

11

Fine-Tuning Quicken

Quicken works fine if you install the program as described in Chapter 1. But you can do a few things to fine-tune Quicken. First, the Set Preferences menu provides several options that enable you to control how Quicken works. Second, Version 5.0 of Quicken enables you to start the program with parameters that control how Quicken runs. This chapter covers both topics.

Using the Set Preferences Menu

Four of the options on the Set Preferences menu (see fig. 11.1) give you varying degrees of control over how the Quicken program operates. These four options are **Screen Settings**, **Automatic Reminder Settings**, **Transaction Settings**, and **Checks & Reports Settings**. (Other chapters cover the remaining Set Preferences options: Chapter 1 describes the **Printer Settings** option, Chapter 9 describes the **File Activities** option, Chapter 15 describes the **Electronic Payment** option, and Chapter 20 describes the **Password Settings** option.)

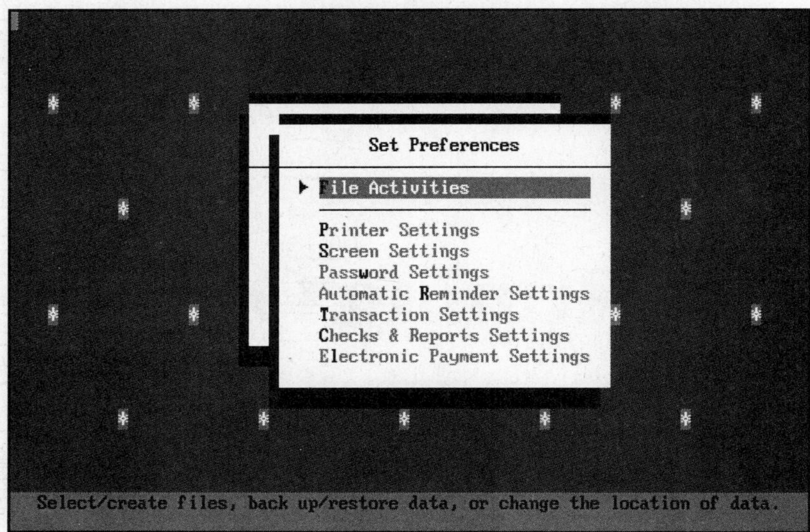

Fig. 11.1. *The Set Preferences menu.*

Changing Screen Colors

Quicken gives you control over the colors the program uses on menus and screens. If your monitor is monochrome, you can choose between monochrome and shades of gray. If your monitor is color, you can choose a navy and azure combination, white and navy, or red and gray. You cannot hurt anything by experimenting with the various color combinations.

To change the color settings that Quicken uses, follow these steps:

1. Select the **Set Preferences** option from Quicken's Main Menu.
2. Select the **Screen Settings** option from the Set Preferences menu. Quicken displays the Screen Settings menu (see fig. 11.2).
3. Select the **Screen Colors** option from the Screen Settings menu. Quicken displays the Change Color Scheme screen, as shown in figure 11.3.

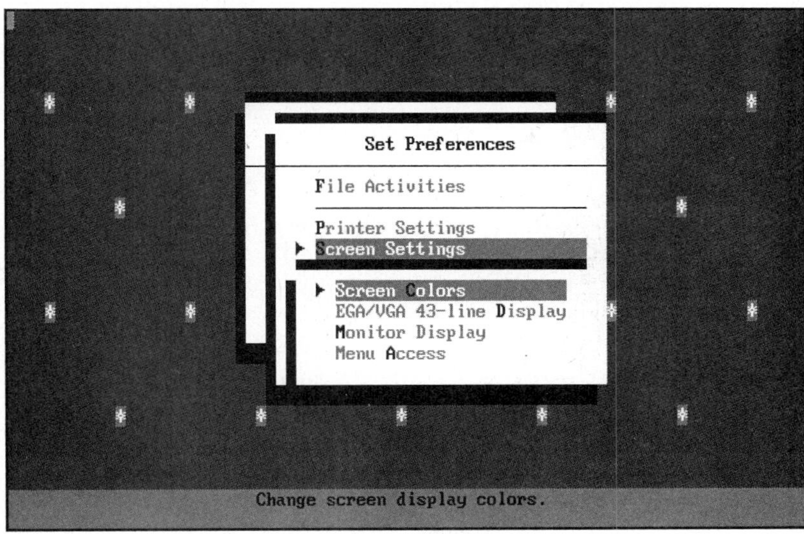

Fig. 11.2. The Screen Settings menu.

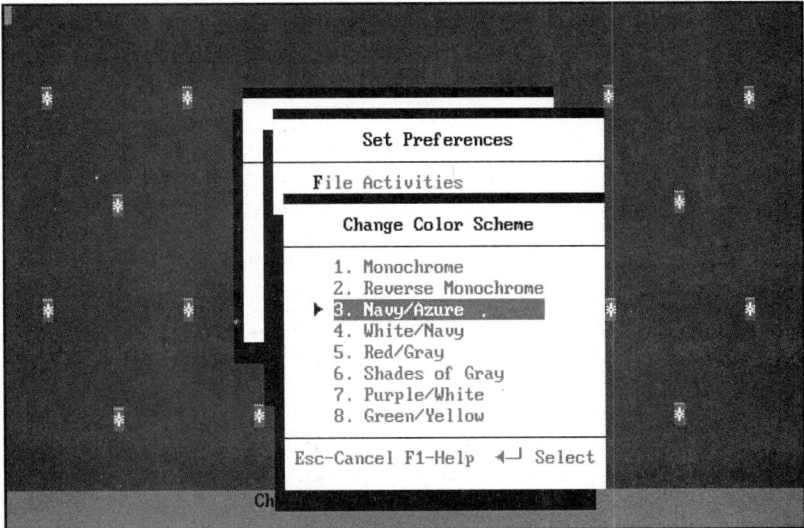

Fig. 11.3. The Change Color Scheme screen.

4. Use the arrow keys to move the cursor to the color combination you want to use and press Enter. Alternatively, press the number of the color scheme you want to use: 1 for Monochrome, 2 for Reverse Monochrome, 3 for Navy/Azure, 4 for White/Navy, and so on.

The default color option for a monochrome monitor is Monochrome, but you also should try Shades of Gray to see which works best for you. If you have a monochrome monitor and the screen display is unclear or portions of the screen don't show, you probably have the monitor type defined as color. The default color scheme for a color monitor is Navy/Azure, but you should try each of the other color schemes to see which works best. If you are color-blind, for example, one of the other color schemes may be easier to see.

Changing the Display

If your computer uses an Enhanced Graphics Adapter (EGA) or video graphics adapter (VGA) monitor and card, you can set the 43 line register/reports field to `Y` for Yes, which doubles—from 6 to 12—the number of lines Quicken displays in the register. If you have an EGA monitor, try this option. Having more register information on-screen is helpful. If the compressed version of the register strains your eyes, set the toggle back to `N`.

All the figures in this book use the standard, uncompressed versions of the register and report screens.

To change the display that Quicken uses, follow these steps:

1. Select the **Set Preferences** option from Quicken's Main Menu.
2. Select the **Screen Settings** option from the Set Preferences menu.
3. Select the **EGA/VGA 43-Line Display** option from the Screen Settings menu (see fig 11.2). Quicken displays the Display Mode screen (see fig. 11.4).
4. Press 2, and then press Enter.

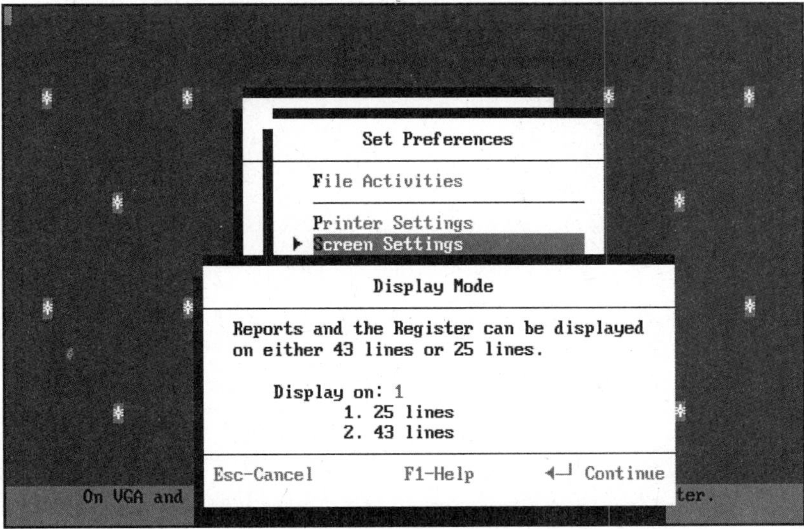

Fig. 11.4. The Display Mode screen.

Changing Screen Update Speed

The **Monitor Display** option on the Set Preferences menu enables you to choose between slow and fast for the screen update speed. Quicken initially assumes that you want the fast option. If Quicken ascertains that your monitor update speed should be fast, the program does not enable you to change the setting to slow. If Quicken determines that your monitor may not be able to handle the fast speed, it enables you to change the speed to slow.

If your monitor cannot handle the fast speed setting, you may see little flecks and patches—sometimes called snow—on-screen. If you notice snow on your monitor, set the monitor speed to slow.

To set the monitor speed to slow, follow these steps:

1. Select the **Set Preferences** option from Quicken's Main Menu.
2. Select the **Screen Settings** option from the Set Preferences menu.
3. Select **Monitor Display** from the Screen Settings menu. Quicken displays the Monitor Display screen.

4. Press the number of the speed setting: 1 for Slow and 2 for Fast.
5. When the speed setting you want to use is indicated, press Enter.

Changing Menu Access

Before Version 5.0, Quicken used the function keys rather than Alt-letter key combinations to display menus that appear on the Write Checks and Register screens. If you are a former Version 3.0 or 4.0 user and want to continue using the function keys, Quicken Version 5.0 enables you to do so.

To access menus with function keys, follow these steps:

1. Select the **Set Preferences** option from Quicken's Main Menu.
2. Select the **Screen Settings** option from the Set Preferences menu.
3. Select the **Menu Access** option from the Screen Settings menu. Quicken displays the Menu Access screen (see fig. 11.5).

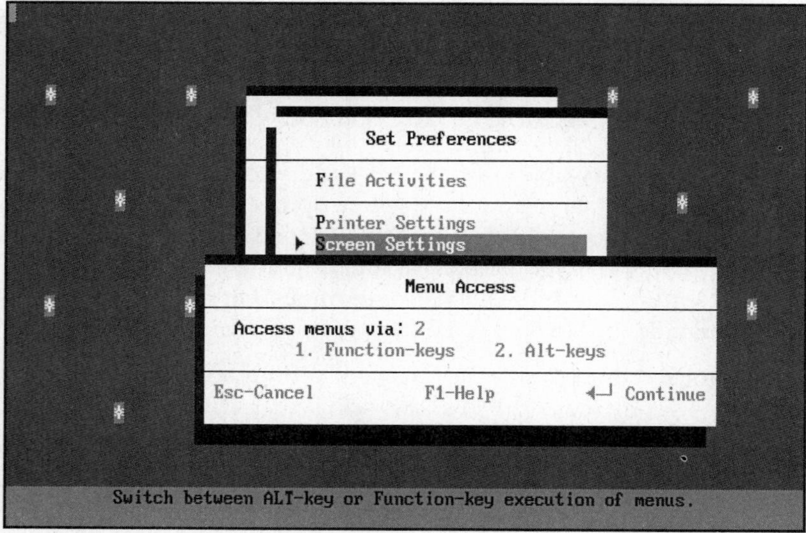

Fig. 11.5. *The Menu Access screen.*

4. Press 1, and then press Enter.

   The change in menu access will not take effect until the next time you start the Quicken program.

Controlling Billminder

The **Automatic Reminder Settings** option on the Set Preferences menu (see fig. 11.2) enables you to turn the Billminder program off and on and enables you to control how many days in advance the Billminder program reminds you of postdated checks, scheduled transaction groups, and investment reminders.

To use the **Automatic Reminder Settings** option, follow these steps:

1. Select the **Set Preferences** option from Quicken's Main Menu.
2. Select the **Automatic Reminder Settings** option from the Set Preferences menu. Quicken displays the Automatic Reminder Settings screen (see fig. 11.6).

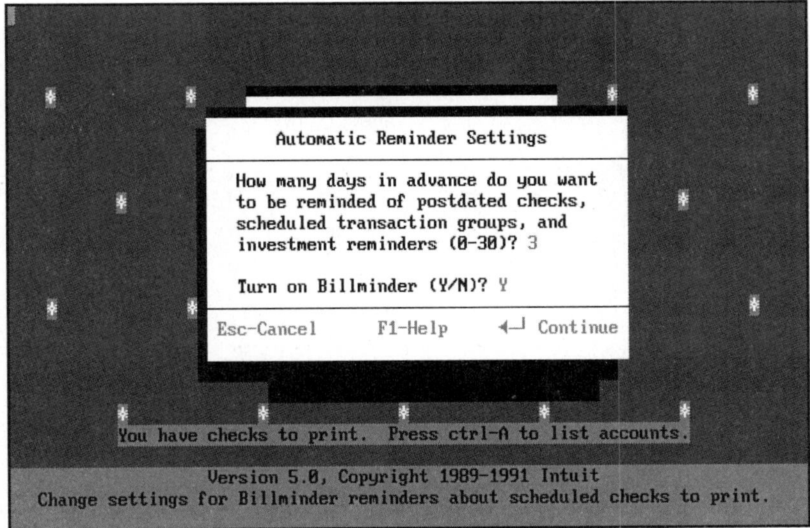

Fig. 11.6. *The Automatic Reminder Settings screen.*

3. Enter the number of days in advance that you want to be reminded of postdated checks, scheduled transactions, and investment reminders.
4. Press Enter or Tab to move the cursor to the `Turn on Billminder` field. Then type *Y* if you want the Billminder turned on; type *N* if you don't. Press Enter when the Automatic Reminder Settings screen is complete.

Quicken reminds hard disk users differently from floppy disk users. Because of this difference, the rules for specifying the Days in Advance setting also differ. Hard disk users are reminded of postdated checks and scheduled transaction groups every time they turn on the computer. If you are a hard disk user, therefore, you should set the days in advance to one less than the number of days between times you turn on your computer. If, for example, you use your computer every other day, the difference in days between use is two. One number less than two is one. Therefore, you should set the days in advance as one. Whenever you turn on your computer, you are reminded of the bills that should be paid that day and the bills that can be paid the next day. But the bills that can be paid the next day need to be paid today because you will not use your computer tomorrow.

Floppy disk users follow a slightly different procedure. Floppy disk users are reminded of postdated checks and scheduled transaction groups on the Quicken Main Menu. Quicken reminds floppy disk users, therefore, only when the Quicken program is started. If you are a floppy disk user, set the Days in advance field to one day less than the number of days between times you use Quicken. If you use Quicken on a weekly basis—for example, every Saturday morning—set the `Days in Advance` field to 6. You are reminded every Saturday morning of the bills to be paid for the next six days.

Fine-Tuning Transaction Settings

The Transactions Settings screen, shown in figure 11.7, enables you to work with seven other settings. You can use these settings to fine-tune Quicken so that the program processes transactions in the way you find most helpful. The settings on this screen are described in the following sections.

If you want to change any of these settings, first perform these steps:

1. Select the **Set Preferences** option from Quicken's Main Menu.
2. Select the **Transaction Settings** option from the Set Preferences menu. Quicken displays the Transaction Settings screen as shown in figure 11.7.

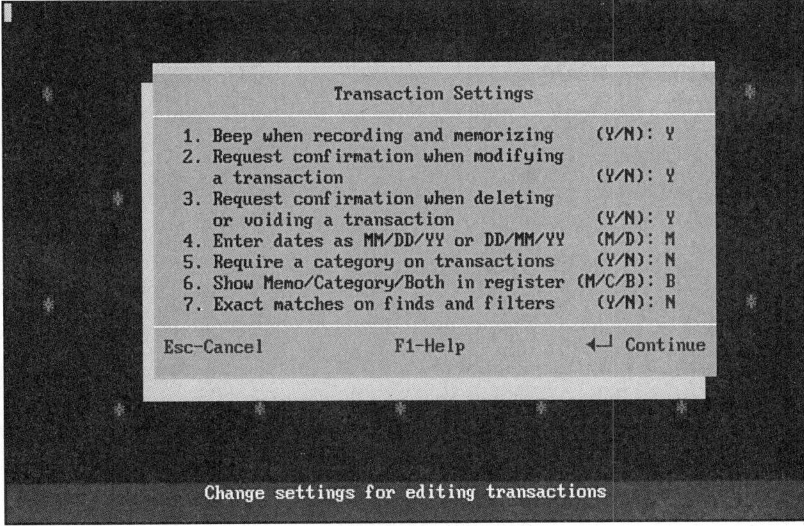

Fig. 11.7. *The Transaction Settings screen.*

3. (Optional) Use the arrow keys or the Tab key to move the cursor to the `Beep when recording and memorizing` setting. Press N if you want to turn off the beep that Quicken makes when the program records and memorizes transactions; leave the setting at Y if you want to keep the beep. (You may want to consider this option if you enter many transactions. You also use this setting to turn on the beep if you previously have turned the beep off.)

4. (Optional) Use the arrow keys or the Tab key to move the cursor to the `Request confirmation when modifying a transaction` setting. To turn off the confirmation messages, press N. The Request confirmation when modifying a transaction setting turns on and off the pop-up confirmation messages that display to give you a second chance before recording a modified transaction.

5. (Optional). Use the arrow keys or the Tab key to move the cursor to the `Request confirmation when deleting or voiding a transaction` setting. To turn off the confirmation message, press N.

6. (Optional) Use the arrow keys or the Tab key to move the cursor to the `Date format` setting. If you want dates to appear in month/day/year format—June 1, 1991 appears as 6/1/91, for example—press M for month first. If you want the dates to appear in day/month/year—June 1, 1991 appears as 1/6/91—press D for day first.

7. (Optional) Use the arrow keys or the Tab key to move the cursor to the `Require` category on transactions setting. If you want Quicken to display a reminder message that asks you to confirm transactions you enter without a valid category, press Y. You do not have to use categories if this switch is set to Y, but you have to confirm that you do not want to use a category. If you plan to use categories, you should set this switch to Y for Yes. (Chapter 10 describes the categories feature in detail.)
8. (Optional) Use the arrow keys or the Tab key to move the cursor to the `Show Memo/Category/Both` setting. This setting determines which information appears on the memo line of the check register when the transaction isn't selected. Press M to designate that only the memo should appear; press C to designate that only the category should appear; press B to designate that both the memo and category should appear. Because you do not have enough room to fully display both the `Memo` and `Category` fields, if you select B, Quicken abbreviates the two fields.
9. (Optional). Press Enter or Tab to move the cursor to the `Exact matches on finds and filters` setting. If you want Quicken to search only for exactly what you specify as a search argument when using the Find command or to include items on a report that exactly match a filter, press Y. (Report filters are described in Chapter 14.)
10. When the Transaction Settings screen is complete, press Enter when the cursor is on the screen's last field. Or, press F10 or Ctrl-Enter when the cursor is on one of the other fields. Quicken returns you to the Set Preferences menu.

Fine-Tuning Check and Report Printing

The Checks and Reports Settings screen, shown in figure 11.8, enables you to control many aspects of check and report printing.

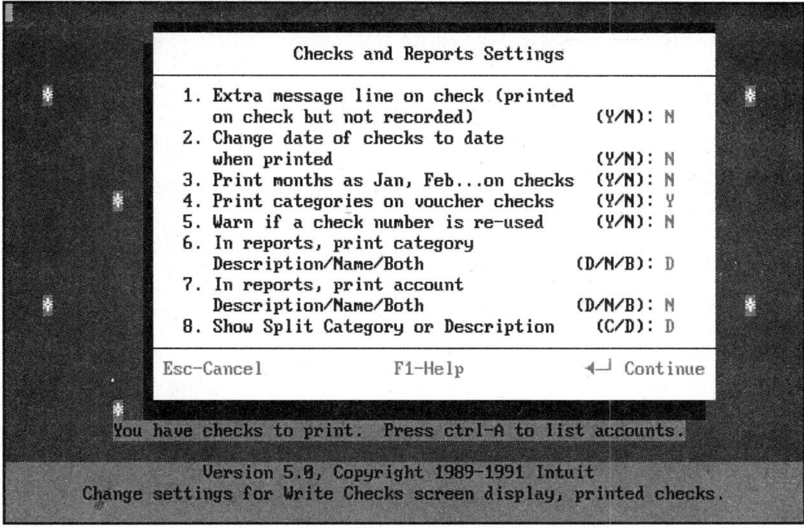

Fig. 11.8. *The Checks and Reports Settings screen.*

1. Select the **Set Preferences** option from Quicken's Main Menu.

2. Select the **Checks & Reports** Settings option from the Set Preferences menu. Quicken displays the Checks and Reports Settings screen.

3. (Optional) Use the arrow keys or the Tab key to move the cursor to the `Extra message line on check` setting. To see and use the extra message line that appears to the right of the address box on your checks, press Y. To remove the extra message line, press N.

4. (Optional). Use the arrow keys or the Tab key to move the cursor to the `Change date of checks date when printed` setting. If you want Quicken to print the current system date as the check date when printing checks, press Y. When the check date you enter differs from the check printing date, the check's date will be changed.

5. (Optional). If you want Quicken to print the three-character abbreviation for the month on checks, move the cursor to the `Print Months as Jan, Feb...on Checks` setting. Then press Y.

6. (Optional) Use the arrow keys or the Tab key to move the cursor to the `Print categories on voucher checks` setting. If you want

what you enter in the `Category` field or the `Split Transaction screen` fields to appear on the voucher portion of checks, set this setting to yes by pressing Y.

You do not need the `Category` field information printed on the voucher stub unless someone you pay a check needs to know which income and expense categories a check affects. If you decide not to use the `Category` fields to record categories, and instead use the fields for information such as the invoices a check pays, you can have this information printed on the check stub. This field does not apply unless your checks have voucher stubs.

7. (Optional) Use the arrow keys or the Tab key to move the cursor to the `Warn if a check number is re-used` setting. If you want Quicken to display a message in a pop-up box when you use a check number you have used previously, set this field to Y for Yes.

8. (Optional) Use the arrow keys or the Tab key to move the cursor to the `In reports use category Description/Name/Both` setting. This field determines whether the category name, category description, or both appear on reports. You have three choices: pressing D designates that only the description appears; pressing N designates that only the name appears; pressing B designates that both the name and description appear. D is the default setting and the one you probably want to use.

9. (Optional). Use the arrow keys or the Tab key to move the cursor to `In reports, print account Description/Name/Both`. Press D if you want the account description to appear on reports. Press N if you want the account name to appear. Press B if you want both pieces of information to appear.

10. (Optional). Use the arrow keys or the Tab key to move the cursor to the `Show Split Category or Description` setting. If you want Quicken to display just the category name rather than the category description for split transactions, press C.

11. When the Checks and Reports Settings screen correctly reflects the settings you want, press Enter when the cursor is on the last field. Alternatively, you can press F10 or Ctrl-Enter when the cursor is on one of the other fields. Quicken returns you to the Set Preferences menu.

Starting Quicken with Parameters

Quicken enables you to start the program with parameters. (Parameters are codes you type following the "q" you type to start the program.) These parameters enable you to select an account as part of starting Quicken. These parameters also enable you to select the menu access method as part of starting Quicken. Although the parameters may sound complicated, they really are not difficult. The following sections describe how to use the parameters that Quicken provides.

Selecting an Account

To start Quicken, type the letter *q* at the DOS prompt. You can specify which account should be selected by following the letter "q" with the name of the account. For example, to start Quicken and simultaneously select the account named "checking," type the following at the DOS prompt:

Q CHECKING

If an account isn't in the current group, you also can identify the file as a second parameter. If, for example, you want to select the account "checking" in the account group "QDATA," type the following at the DOS prompt:

Q CHECKING QDATA

Leave a space between the letter "q" and the word "checking" and between the words "checking" and "QData".

Selecting an account when you start Quicken isn't difficult and can be quite handy. You do need to remember one trick, however. If the account is two words, you need to enclose the account in quotation marks so that Quicken doesn't think one part of the name is the file name. For example, in the case of an account named "Big National" in the QDATA file, you enter the parameter in the applicable one of the two following forms:

Q "BIG NATIONAL"
Q "BIG NATIONAL" QDATA

You also can specify the path of the file—something you need to do when the file is not in the Quicken program directory.

Selecting Menu Access

You also can start Quicken with a parameter that selects the menu access method. As noted earlier in the chapter, in previous versions of Quicken, you used function keys to access the menus; in the current version, you use Alt-letter key combinations. One way to control menu access is by using the **Menu Access** option on the Screen Settings menu (see fig. 11.2). You also can control menu access by using the /f and /i command parameters. For example, type *q /f* to start Quicken with function key access to windows.

Using Versions 4.0 and 3.0 Key Definitions

Quicken 5.0 and 4.0 use slightly different key definitions of the Home and End keys than earlier versions of Quicken. Table 11.1 summarizes the different definitions.

Table 11.1
Key Definitions

Key(s)	*Versions 4.0 and 5.0*	*Versions 3.0 and earlier*
Home	First character in field	First transaction in register
End	Last character in field	Last transaction in register
Home Home	First field on-screen	Not used
End End	Last field on-screen	Not used
Ctrl-Home	First transaction in register	Same as Home
Ctrl-End	Last transaction in register	Same as End

Although Version 5.0 key definitions are more consistent with the standard uses of the two keys, you may want to use Version 3.0 key definitions and the /a parameter. To use the Version 3.0 key definitions for the Home and End keys, for example, type the following at the DOS prompt:

q /a

Leave a space between the letter "q" and the character sequence "/a."

After you start Quicken using the /a parameter, Quicken continues to use the Version 3.0 key definitions until you tell Quicken to stop. To tell Quicken to stop using the Version 3.0 key definitions and return to the Version 5.0 definitions, use the /s parameter. For example, type the following at the DOS prompt:

q /s

One other command-line parameter exists. However, it's unlikely that you will every need to use it. The /e parameter tells Quicken not to use your computer's expanded memory. Normally, Quicken will use your computer's expanded memory for overlays and reports. However, if you're having problems with your expanded memory, you could use this command-line parameter until you get the problems fixed.

Chapter Summary

You can fine-tune Quicken's operation in two ways: with the Set Preferences menu options and with parameters you include when you start Quicken. This chapter described both methods. Understanding how you can fine-tune Quicken and having the steps for doing so laid out enable you to get Quicken to work just the way you want.

12

Tracking Your Net Worth, Other Assets, and Liabilities

Quicken was designed originally as a checking account record-keeping tool. The newest releases of Quicken, Versions 3.0, 4.0, and 5.0, however, can do much more than just keep track of your checking account. Using Quicken's familiar check-register format, you can maintain financial records for any asset or liability.

Assets refer to things that you own and that have lasting value. For individuals, assets include items such as a house, cars, furniture, and investments. For businesses, assets include the money customers owe, the inventory held for resale, and any fixtures or equipment used in the business. Liabilities refer to money you owe others. For individuals, liabilities include mortgages, car loans, credit card debts, and income taxes. For businesses, liabilities include amounts owed suppliers, wages payable to employees, and loans from banks and leasing companies.

The benefits of using Quicken to track your assets (other than bank accounts) and to track your liabilities essentially match the benefits associated with tracking bank accounts. By carefully tracking other assets, you know what those assets currently are worth and why they have changed in value. By carefully tracking your liabilities, you maintain firm control over your debts, ensure your ability to continue regular payments, and keep records of why the dollar amounts of your debts have changed. By carefully tracking your assets and liabilities, you can use Quicken to generate reports that calculate your personal or business financial net worth. (The only real drawback, or cost, of tracking your other assets and liabilities is the additional effort required on your part. In many cases, however, the benefits discussed earlier more than merit the cost.)

This chapter describes in general terms how to use Quicken to perform record keeping for other assets and liabilities. Then it delivers information on why and how you can use Quicken to generate balance sheets. (If you become enthused about the record-keeping possibility of Quicken, you also will want to read Chapter 13, Chapter 17, and Chapter 18.)

Setting Up Accounts for Other Assets and Liabilities

You need to set up a Quicken account for each asset or liability for which you want to keep records with Quicken. You can track any asset or liability you want. No real limit or restriction exists on what you can or cannot do, except that within a file, you can have only up to 255 accounts. The only thing you need to remember is that the accounts you want to appear together on a balance sheet must be set up in the same file. Typically, that means all your business accounts need to be in one file and all your personal accounts need to be in another file. After you define the files, you take the following steps to set up accounts:

1. Choose the **Select Account** option on Quicken's Main Menu. Quicken displays the Select Account to Use screen shown in figure 12.1.

2. To add a new account, select `New Account` from the list. Quicken then displays the Set Up New Account screen shown in figure 12.2.

3. With the cursor at the `Account Type` field, enter the account type. Quicken provides four asset account types to choose from: Bank Account, Cash, Other Asset, and Investment Account. If the asset is a bank account, set the account type to 1. If the asset is cash in your wallet or in the petty cash box, set the account type to 3. If the account is an investment, set the account type to 6. (Refer to Chapter 13 for the specifics of defining an investment account.) For any other asset—accounts receivable, real estate, and so on—enter the account type as 4. Quicken also provides two liability account types: Credit Card and Other Liability. If the liability is the balance on your Visa or MasterCard account, set the account type to 2; otherwise, set the account type to 5.

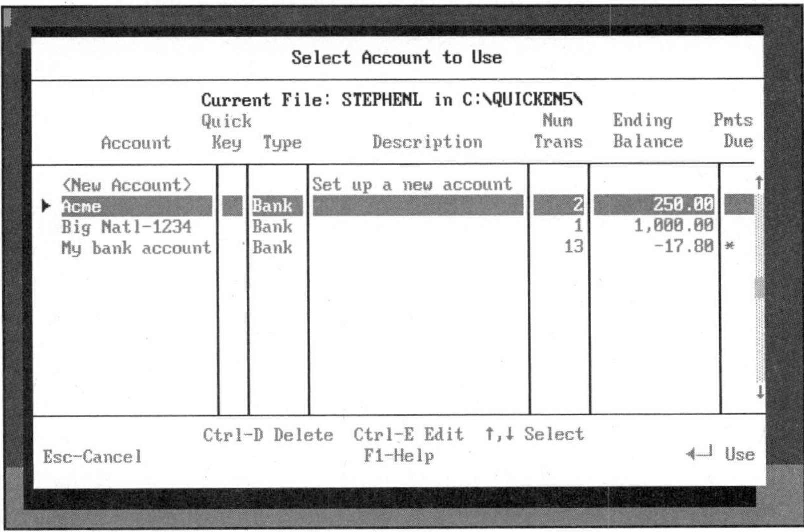

Fig. 12.1. The Select Account to Use screen.

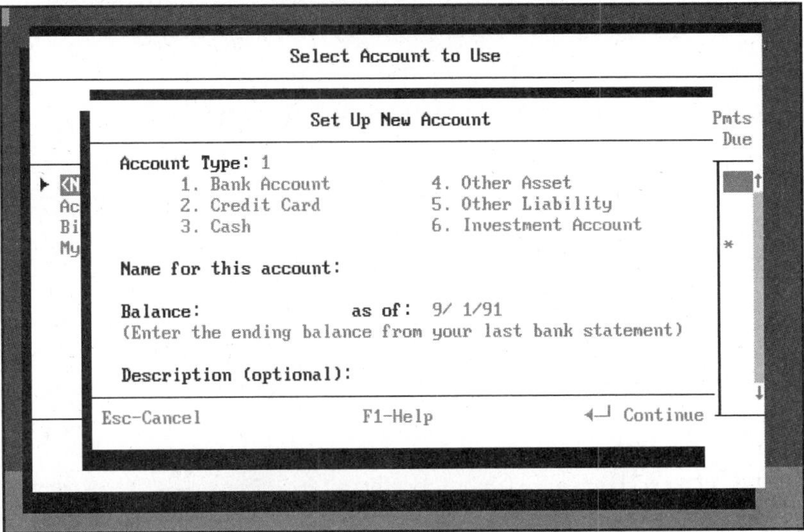

Fig. 12.2. The Set Up New Account screen.

4. Press Enter or Tab to move the cursor to the Name field. Enter a description of the account. The Name field can be up to 15 characters long and can use any character except [,], /, and :. You can include spaces.

5. Press Enter or Tab to move to the `Balance` field. If you want to set up an opening balance for an asset or liability, enter this amount here. Assets can, for example, be listed at their original cost or their current fair market value. Liabilities can be listed at the current balances.

Be sure to make a note in your records as to the basis of your assets—for example, original cost, fair market value, and so on.

6. Press Enter or Tab to move the cursor to the `As of date` field. Enter the date on which the balance you entered is correct.

7. (Optional) Press Enter or Tab to move the cursor to the `Description` field. Fill in the `Description` field to provide an additional 21 characters of account description.

8. If you enter your credit cards, Quicken asks for the credit limit on your cards (see fig. 12.3).

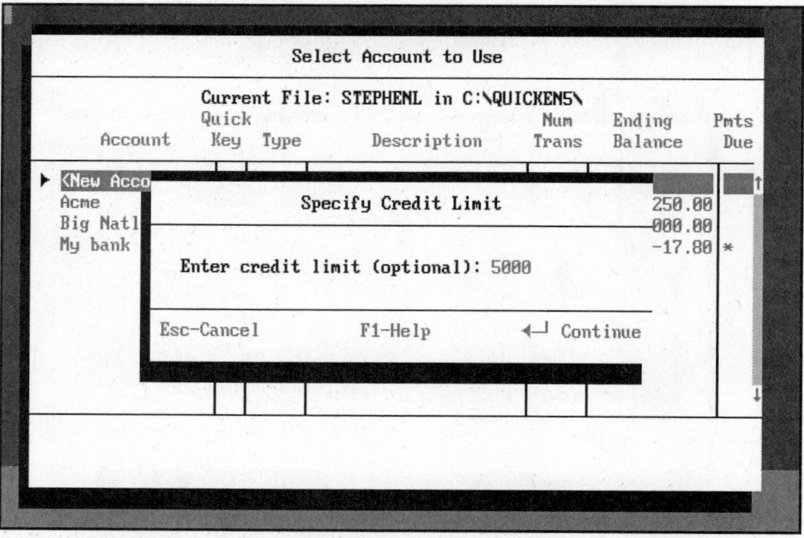

Fig. 12.3. The Specify Credit Limit screen.

9. When you finish entering information for the new asset or liability account, press Enter.

Keeping Financial Records

After you initially set up an account—whether an asset or a liability—you maintain the account in one of two ways.

First, you can select the account using the **Select Account** option, and then you can use the Register option to enter transactions that increase or decrease the account, just as you do for a checking account. (To select an account, choose **Select Account** from Quicken's Main Menu. Quicken displays the Select Account to Use screen shown in figure 12.1. Use the arrow keys to mark the account you want, and then press Enter.)

Figure 12.4 shows how a register of a major real estate asset—a personal residence—may look. The Other Assets register looks almost identical to the regular Bank Account register and works the same way. Transaction amounts that decrease the asset account balance are recorded in the `Decrease` field of the register. (On the bank account version of the Register screen, this field is labeled `Payment`.) Transaction amounts that increase the asset account are recorded in the `Increase` field of the register. (On the bank account version of the check register, this field is labeled `Deposit`). The total Real Estate account balance shows at the bottom right corner of the screen. If you have postdated transactions—those with dates in the future—the current balance also shows.

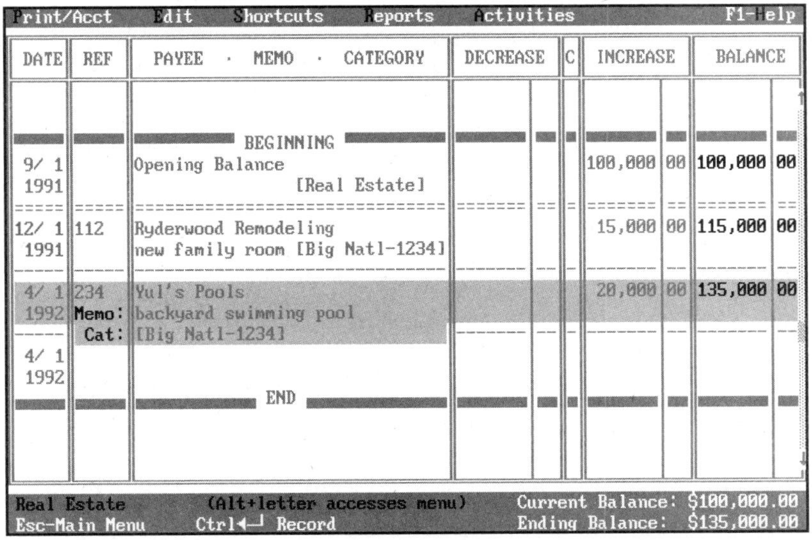

```
Print/Acct   Edit   Shortcuts   Reports   Activities                 F1-Help

DATE  REF    PAYEE  ·  MEMO  ·  CATEGORY    DECREASE  C  INCREASE    BALANCE

                    BEGINNING
9/ 1        Opening Balance                            100,000 00  100,000 00
1991                       [Real Estate]
12/ 1 112   Ryderwood Remodeling                        15,000 00  115,000 00
1991        new family room [Big Natl-1234]
4/ 1  234   Yul's Pools                                 20,000 00  135,000 00
1992  Memo: backyard swimming pool
       Cat: [Big Natl-1234]
4/ 1
1992
                       END

Real Estate        (Alt+letter accesses menu)    Current Balance: $100,000.00
Esc-Main Menu      Ctrl←┘ Record                 Ending Balance:  $135,000.00
```

***Fig. 12.4.** A sample register used to record the value of a personal residence.*

In the example shown in figure 12.4, the opening balance of $100,000 shows what you may have paid originally for your home. The two subsequent transactions shown—one for the addition of a new family room and the other for a new backyard swimming pool—show the events that changed the value of your home. By keeping these records, you may be able to keep better track of the value of your home and the reasons for any change in your home's value.

When working with the Other Assets register, you can access the same menu options as when you are working with the Bank Account register, except that **Update Account Balances** replaces **Reconcile**. (See "Updating Account Balances" later in this chapter.)

Figure 12.5 shows a register that you can use to track what you owe on a loan such as a business credit line or a home mortgage. The Other Liability register also mirrors the check register in appearance and operation. Transaction amounts that increase the amount owed are recorded in the `Increase` field of the register. (On the bank account version of the Register screen, this field is labeled `Payment`.) Transaction amounts that decrease the amount owed are recorded in the `Decrease` field of the register. (On the bank account version of the register, this field is labeled `Deposit`.) The total liability balance shows at the bottom right corner of the screen. If you have postdated transactions, the current balance also shows. You do not use the `C` field when tracking a liability account.

```
Print/Acct   Edit   Shortcuts   Reports   Activities                F1-Help
DATE  REF   PAYEE · MEMO · CATEGORY      INCREASE  C  DECREASE   BALANCE
                    BEGINNING
9/ 1        Opening Balance              90,000 00               90,000 00
1991                  [Mortgage]
10/ 1 124   Big National                               100 00
1991 Memo:  October payment
      Cat:  [Big Natl-1234]
10/ 1
1991
                    END
Mortgage         (Alt+letter accesses menu)    Current Balance: $90,000.00
Esc-Main Menu    Ctrl◄┘ Record                 Ending Balance:  $89,900.00
```

Fig. 12.5. The register used to track the balances on a loan.

In the example shown in figure 12.5, the opening balance of $90,000 shows what you may have borrowed originally on a mortgage. The subsequent transaction shown—the October mortgage payment—shows the reduction in the outstanding loan balance stemming from the principal portion of the October loan payment.

When working with the Other Liability register, the menu options you can use are the same as when working with the Bank Account register, except that the **Update Account Balances** option replaces the **Reconcile** option.

Only the principal reductions are recorded in the register for a loan or mortgage. The interest portion is reported as interest expense.

Entering transactions directly into a register is one way to maintain correct account balances for another asset or liability account. You can, however, choose a second way to maintain correct account balances for other assets and liabilities. Quicken enables you to use an account name in the `Category` field on the Write/Print Checks and Register screens. Quicken then uses the information from the checking account transaction to record the appropriate transaction in one of the other asset or liability accounts. If you are writing a check to the bank that holds your mortgage and enter the account name mortgage in the `Category` field to show the principal portion of the payment, Quicken records a decrease in the mortgage liability account equal to the principal portion of the payment you are making from your checking account. Figure 12.6 shows a $1,000 check being written to Big National Bank for a mortgage payment. The principal amount of this payment that is applied to the current mortgage balance is $100. When you record the check, a $100 decrease in your Mortgage account also is recorded.

A convenient way to jump between different parts of the same transfer transaction is to use the Edit menu option **Go to Transfer**. You can use the shortcut key combination, Ctrl-X.

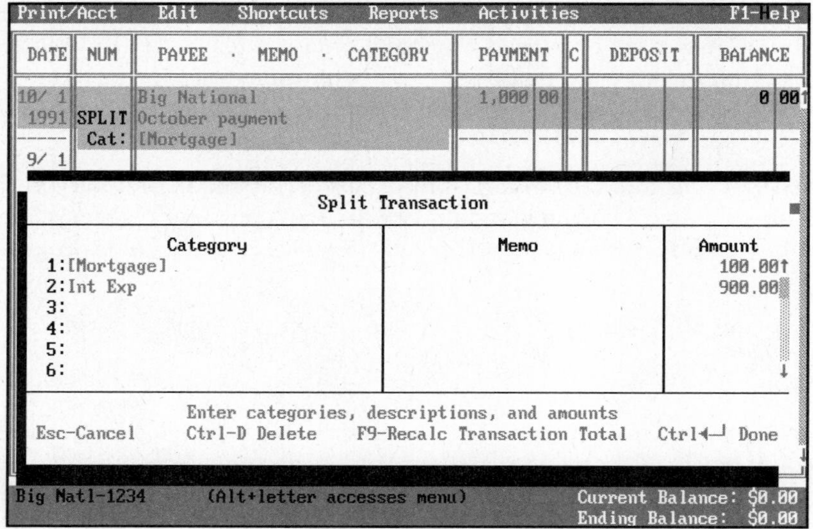

Fig. 12.6. *A $1,000 check being written to the mortgage company.*

Using the Loan Calculator

Version 5.0 of Quicken provides a new tool for loan payment and balance record-keeping, a loan calculator. You can use this calculator two ways. One way to use the loan calculator is to calculate loan payments. The other way is to use the loan calculator to calculate the interest and principal portions of memorized payments.

Calculating Loan Payments

Probably the simplest use of the loan calculator is using it to calculate loan payments. If you know the loan amount, annual interest rate, years the loan will be outstanding, and the number of payments made in a year, Quicken speedily calculates the payment amount. What's more, the loan calculator will produce a payment, or amortization, schedule. A payment, or amortization, schedule shows the portion of your payments that goes to paying interest and the portion that goes to reducing the principal you owe.

To calculate loan payments and produce a payment schedule, follow these steps:

1. From the Register or Write Checks screens, select the Activities menu (see fig. 12.7).

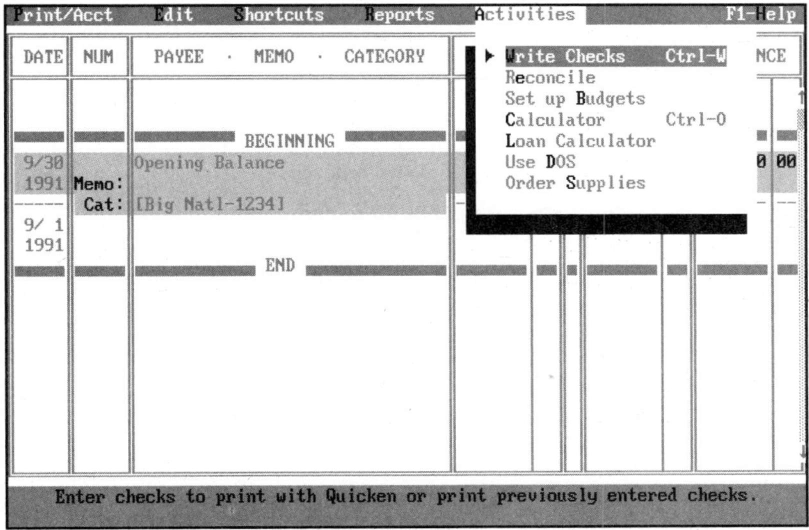

Fig. 12.7. The Activities menu.

2. Select the **Loan Calculator** option from the Activities menu. Quicken displays the loan calculator box (see fig. 12.8).

3. With the cursor at the `Principal` field, enter the loan balance amount.

4. Press Enter or Tab to move the cursor to the `Annual interest rate` field. Then, enter the annual interest rate. For example, if the annual loan interest rate is 12.5 percent, enter 12.5.

Don't mistake the annual percentage rate (APR) for the annual interest rate. The APR includes all the costs of obtaining credit and includes not only interest charges but only loan fees and other borrowing costs. The APR, which is required by truth-in-lending laws, provides a way to compare the overall cost of obtaining a loan. However, it shouldn't be used to calculate the loan payment.

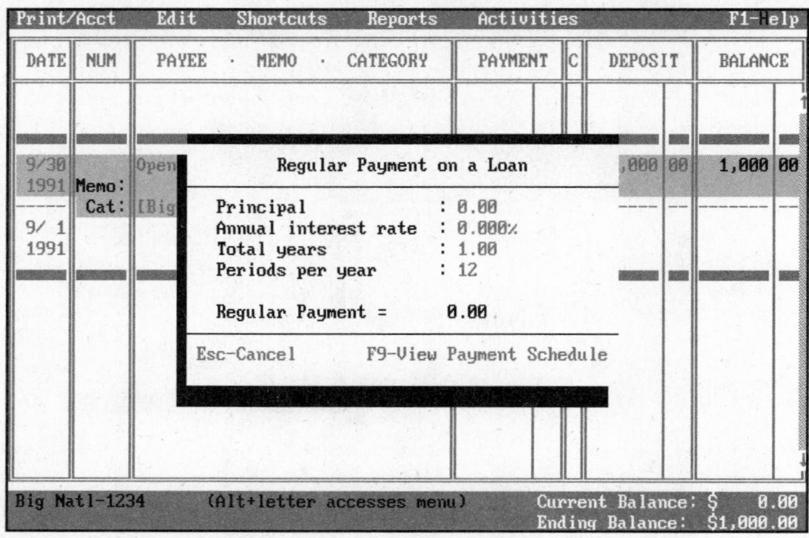

***Fig. 12.8.** The loan calculator box.*

5. Press Enter or Tab to move the cursor to the `Total years` field. Enter the number of years over which you will make payments. For example, if a loan is a 5-year car loan, enter *5*. If a loan is a 30-year mortgage, enter *30*.

6. Press Enter or Tab to move the cursor to the `Periods per year` field. Enter the number of payments you will make each year. Typically, because you will make monthly payments, this input will be *12*.

7. Press Enter when the four input fields are calculated. Quicken calculates the loan payment amount in the `Regular payment` field. Figure 12.9 shows the monthly payment on a $12,000 loan with 12.5 percent interest and 4 years of monthly payments to be $318.96.

8. (Optional) To see a payment schedule for the loan, press F9. Quicken displays the Approximate Payment Schedule box shown in figure 12.10. It shows the approximate interest and principal portions of each loan payment as well as the loan balance after the payment. To move up and down in the payment schedule, use the PgUp and PgDn keys. Or, use the mouse on the scroll bar. You can also use the Home and End keys: Home displays the first page of the payment schedule, and End displays the last page of the payment schedule.

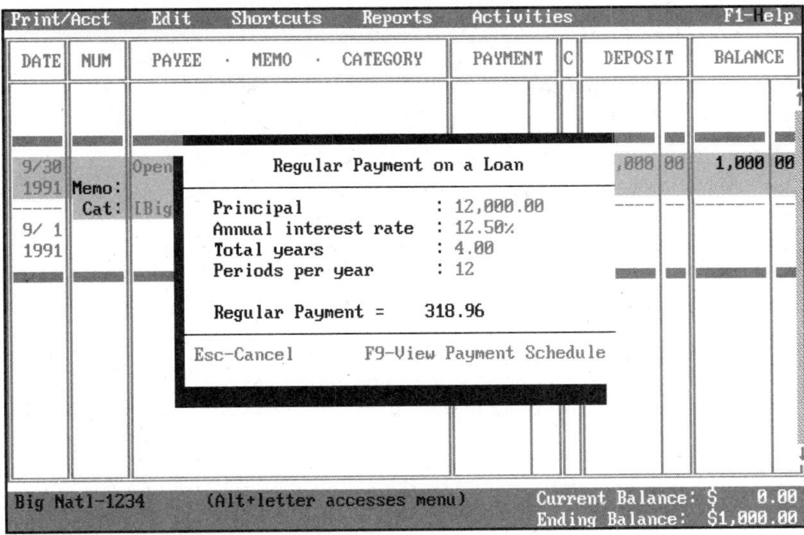

Fig. 12.9. The loan calculator showing the monthly payment on a 4-year, 12.5 percent, $12,000 loan.

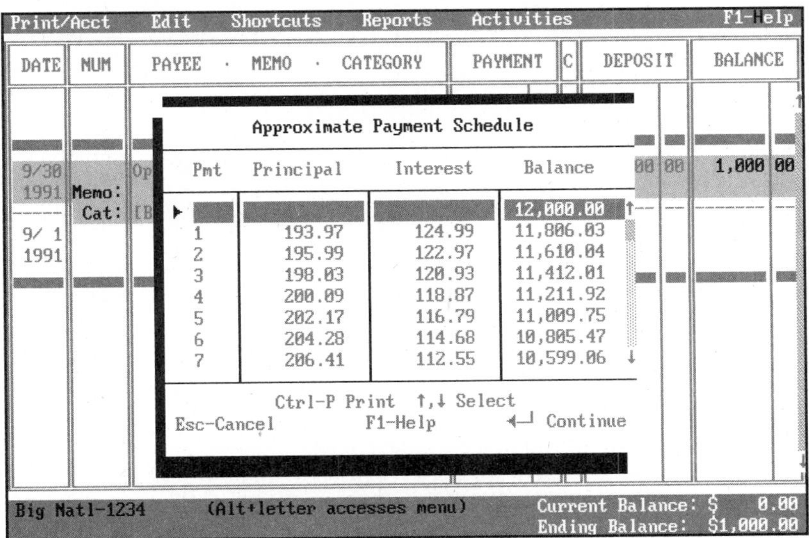

Fig. 12.10. The Approximate Payment Schedule box.

9. (Optional) To print a copy of the payment schedule, press Ctrl-P. Quicken displays the Print Payment Schedule screen, which is similar to the Print Checks screen described in Chapter 6. Indicate the printer you want to use. Then, press Enter and Quicken prints the schedule.

Quicken calculates an arrangement known as a "payment in arrears" or an "ordinary annuity". This means the payment is made at the end of the payment period. This is the usual case. With some loans, however, payments are made at the beginning of the period. This arrangement is known as a "payment in advance" or an "annuity due." To convert a "payment in arrears" payment to a "payment in advance" payment, divide the payment amount that Quicken calculates by the factor:

(1+(annual interest rate/periods in a year))

So, to convert the $318.96 payment in arrears to a payment in advance, you make the following calculation:

$318.96/(1+(.125/12))

which produces the calculation result $315.67.

Memorizing Transactions

The Loan Calculator can also be used with memorized payments. In effect, using the payment schedule information, you can memorize not only the loan payment amount, but also the loan interest expense and loan principal reduction associated with each payment.

To use the payment schedule information with a memorized loan payment, follow these steps:

1. From either the Register or Write Checks screen, press Alt-S to display the Shortcuts menu (see fig. 12.11).
2. Select the **Recall Transaction** option to display the Memorized Transactions List (see fig. 12.12).

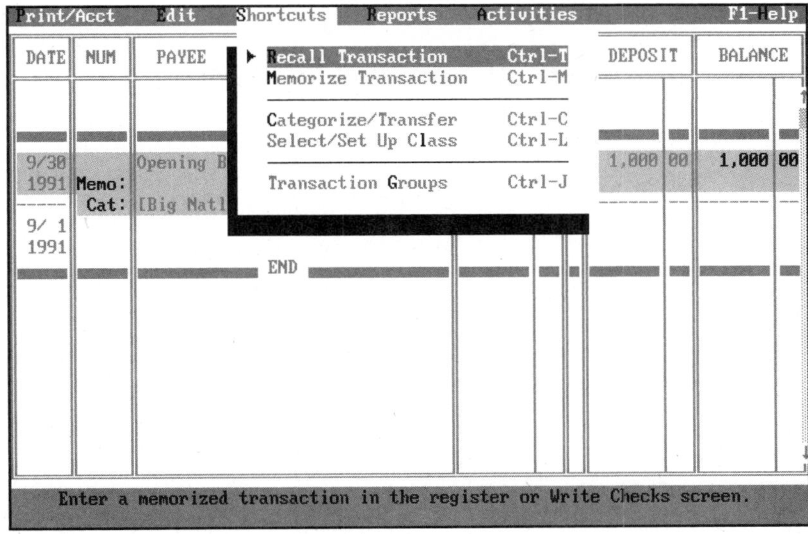

Fig. 12.11. The Shortcuts menu.

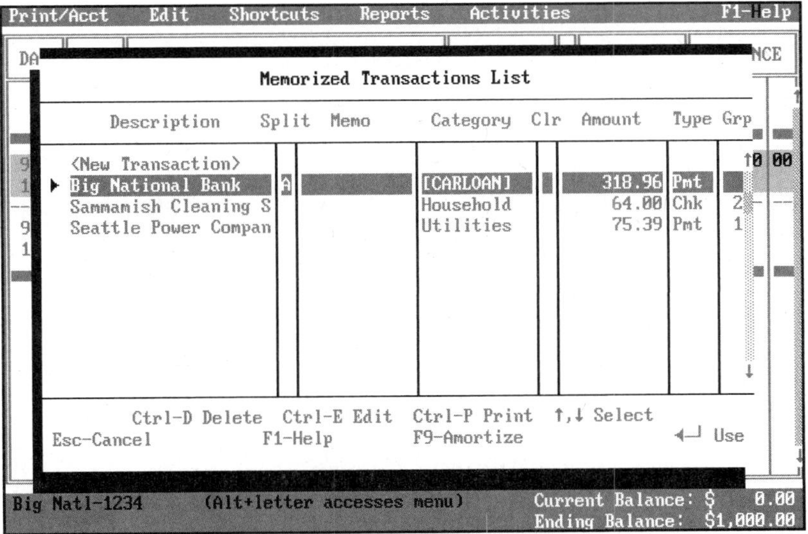

Fig. 12.12. The Memorized Transactions List.

3. Using with the arrow keys or the mouse, highlight the memorized loan payment transaction to which you want to attach a payment schedule. (If you haven't already set up the memorized loan payment, you need to do so following the steps described in either Chapter 5 or 7. Remember too that loan payment transactions should be split between a category for recording interest expense and an other liability account for tracking the loan balance.)

4. Press F9. Quicken displays the Set Amortization Information screen (see fig. 12.13).

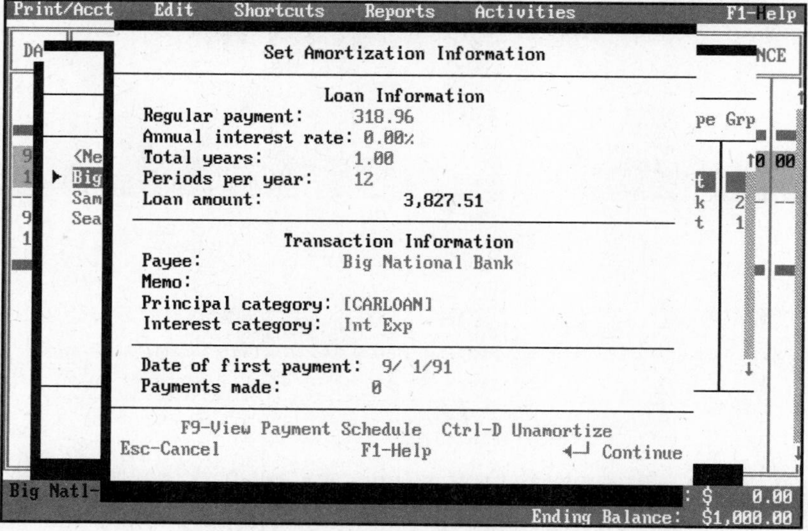

Fig. 12.13. The Set Amortization Information screen.

5. With the cursor at the `Regular payment` field, enter the usual loan payment amount.

6. Press Enter or Tab to move the cursor to the `Annual interest rate` field. Then, enter the annual interest rate.

7. Press Enter or Tab to move the cursor to the `Total years` field. Enter the number of years over which you will make payments.

8. Press Enter or Tab to move the cursor to the `Periods per year` field. Enter the number of payments you will make each year. As noted earlier, this input will typically be 12.

9. When all four input fields are entered, Quicken calculates the loan balance and displays this amount in the `Loan balance` field. For example, figure 12.14 shows the monthly payment on a $12,000 loan with 12.5 percent interest and 4 years of monthly payments to be $318.96. (There may be a slight rounding error of a penny or two.)

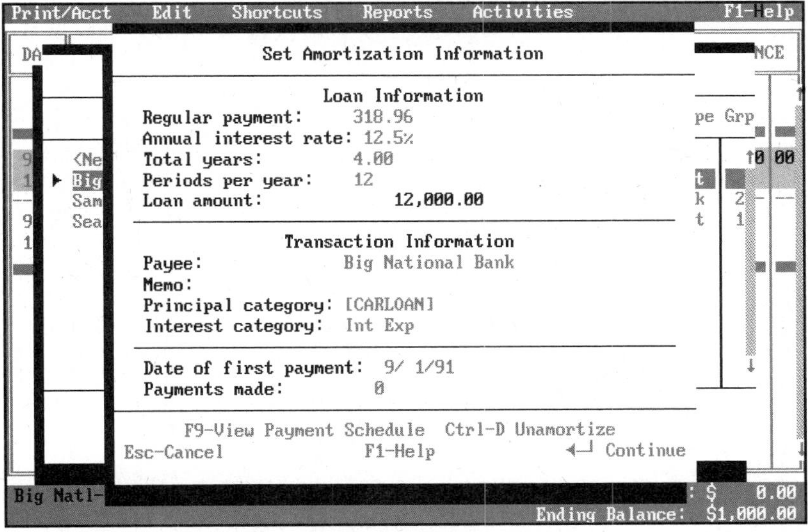

***Fig. 12.14.** The Loan balance given a $318.96 monthly payment on a 4-year, 12.5 percent loan.*

10. (Optional) Press F9 to display a payment schedule like that shown in figure 12.10.

11. Press Enter or Tab to move the cursor the `Date of first payment` field. Then, enter the date you made or will make the first loan payment.

12. Press Enter or Tab to move the cursor to the `Number of payments made` field. Then, enter the number of payments you have previously made. (This will be zero if you have not previously made payments.)

13. With the cursor at the `Number of payments made` field, press Enter to return to the Memorized Transactions List screen.

At this point, you are finished. Whenever you want to record the loan payment, you just recall the memorized loan payment. Quicken keeps track of which payment is being made—the first payment, the second payment, the third payment and so forth—and then uses the payment schedule information to split the payment amount between the interest expense and the loan principal reduction. After you have recalled a memorized loan payment as many times as you indicated there were payments left, Quicken removes the loan payment from the memorized transactions list.

When Quicken prepares the approximate payment schedule, it makes certain assumptions of necessity. For example, it assumes that you always make the payment on the same day of the month. It assumes that each month has the same number of days. And, it assumes that interest on your loan is calculated, or compounded, only at the time each payment is made. Obviously, however, these simplifying assumptions will not always match reality. You may not always remember to pay a loan the same say each month—or the mail may be delayed. Not every month has the same number of days. And your bank may have some special way of calculating interest. The end result of these discrepancies is that the split between interest and principal will be slightly incorrect—perhaps by a few pennies or perhaps by a few dollars. To deal with this problem, you need to update the loan account balance at the end of each year. You can use the **Update Account Balances** option on the Activities menu for this. The category to which the discrepancies should be assigned will, of course, be interest expense.

Reviewing Tips for Working with Other Assets and Liabilities

The register basically works the same, regardless of the account type. A few tips and techniques, however, can help you when using Quicken to account for other assets and liabilities. These tips and techniques include dealing with the nuances and subtleties of the cash and credit card account type, using the **Update Account Balances** option for cash accounts and the **Reconcile/Pay Credit Card Bill** option accessed from the Credit Card register.

Dealing with Cash Accounts

The cash account option works well when you want to keep complete, detailed records of all your miscellaneous cash outlays that are paid out of pocket and not with a check—such as $5 for stamps, $12 for lunch, $7.50 for parking, and so on. Often, you do not need this level of control or detail. When you do want to keep detailed records, the cash account type provides just the tool to get the job done. Quicken warns you, however, that you cannot use the **Write/Print Checks** option with this type of account.

> For businesses, the cash account type is a convenient way to keep track of petty-cash expenditures and reimbursements. Even very large businesses can benefit by using Quicken for petty-cash accounting.

Figure 12.15 shows the Cash account register screen. Notice that this screen is almost identical to the Bank Account Register screen. Money flowing in and out of the account is recorded in the `Spend` and `Receive` fields. On the Bank Account Register screen, money flowing out of the account is recorded in the `Payment` field and money flowing into the account is recorded in the `Deposit` field. On the Other Assets and Other Liability account register screens, money flowing into and out of the account is recorded in the `Increase` and `Decrease` fields.

```
Print/Acct   Edit   Shortcuts   Reports   Activities                F1-Help

DATE  REF   PAYEE  ·  MEMO  ·  CATEGORY    SPEND        RECEIVE    BALANCE

                    BEGINNING
9/ 1        Opening Balance                                100 00     100 00
1991                        [Petty Cash]
9/ 3        Apex Parking                     6 50                      93 50
1991        parking          Auto
9/12        Postmaster                      25 00                      68 50
1991  Memo: stamps
       Cat: Supplies
9/12
1991
                    END

Petty Cash          (Alt+letter accesses menu)     Current Balance: $100.00
Esc-Main Menu       Ctrl◄┘ Record                  Ending Balance:  $ 68.50
```

Fig. 12.15. *The Cash account register screen.*

As with the Other Assets and Other Liability account registers, the C field usually is not used. You can use this column, however, to match receipts against entries to indicate that you have backup records.

Updating Account Balances

On the Activities menu for cash accounts, other assets, and other liabilities accounts, **Update Account Balances** replaces **Reconcile**. (On the credit card account Activities menu, **Pay Credit Card Bill** replaces **Reconcile**. This option is described later in the chapter.) Figure 12.16 shows the cash account Activities menu.

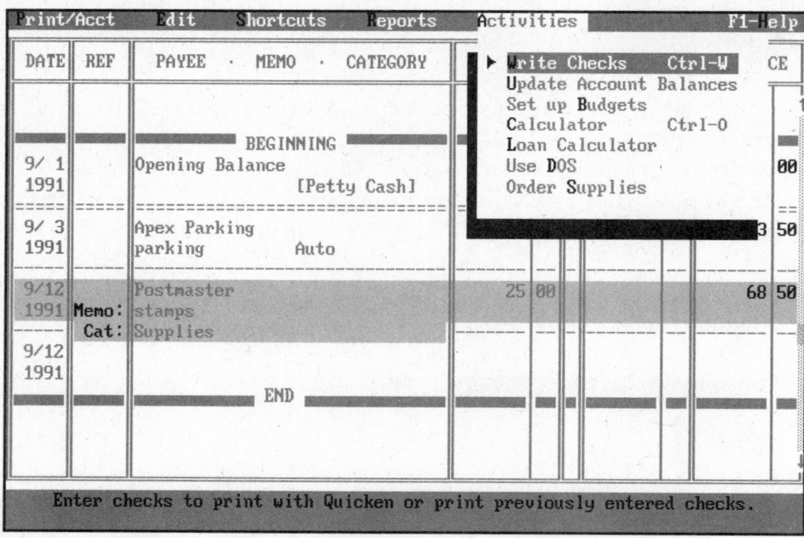

Fig. 12.16. The cash account Activities menu.

Selecting **Update Account Balances** provides a screen you use to reconcile, or adjust, an account. Suppose that the register you use to keep track of your petty cash or pocket cash shows $68.50 as the on-hand cash balance, but the actual balance is $61.88. You can use the Update Account Balance screen to record an adjustment, as shown in figure 12.17.

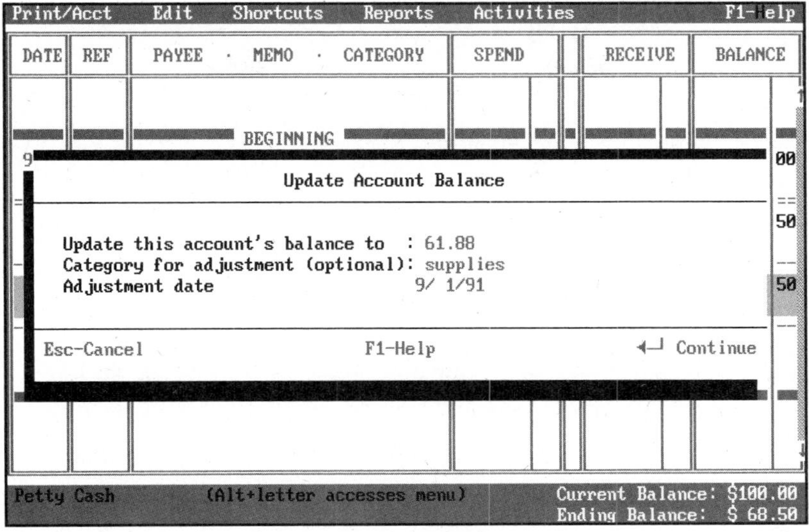

Fig. 12.17. *The Update Account Balance screen.*

To adjust an account's balance, follow these steps:

1. Select the **Use Register** option from the Main Menu.
2. Press Alt-A to display the Activities menu.
3. Choose **Update Account Balance** from the Activities menu. Quicken displays the Update Account Balance screen (see fig. 12.17).
4. Enter the amount to which the account balance should be adjusted in the `Update this account's balance to` field.
5. (Optional) Press Enter or Tab to move the cursor to the `Category for adjustment` field. Enter the category that explains the difference between the old and new account balances, and then press Enter to have Quicken create the adjustment transaction. Remember that you can press Ctrl-C to see the Category and Transfer List screen. Figure 12.18 shows the adjustment transaction created by the **Update Account Balance** transaction so that the account balance shows as $61.88.

```
Print/Acct   Edit   Shortcuts   Reports   Activities                  F1-Help
DATE   REF   PAYEE · MEMO · CATEGORY    SPEND       RECEIVE     BALANCE

              BEGINNING
9/ 1         Opening Balance                          100 00      100 00
1991                   [Petty Cash]
====  =====  ========================  ======  ==  ======  ==  ======  ==
9/ 3         Apex Parking               6 50                       93 50
1991         parking          Auto
9/12         Postmaster                25 00                       68 50
1991         stamps           Supplies
9/12         Balance Adjustment         6 62                       61 88
1991   Memo:
        Cat: Supplies
9/12
1991
              END
Petty Cash         (Alt+letter accesses menu)     Current Balance: $100.00
Esc-Main Menu      Ctrl← Record                   Ending Balance:  $ 61.88
```

Fig. 12.18. *The transaction recorded by the Update Account Balance screen.*

You often really don't know which category explains the difference between the old and new account balances. The reason is that the difference is explained by transactions that you either forgot to record or recorded incorrectly. In effect, what you are trying to do here is record or correct, using the Update Account Balance screen, erroneous or missing transactions. In a pinch, if you cannot figure out which category you should use, use the one that you use most frequently with this register. A warning needs to be issued, however. You cannot guess or estimate tax deduction amounts. You therefore really shouldn't use this tip to increase tax deductions. The Internal Revenue Service may disallow deductions that cannot be supported with evidence as to the type and amount.

Dealing with Credit Card Accounts

The credit card account type is helpful if you want to keep track of the details of your credit card spending and pay off your account balance over time instead of on a monthly basis.

If you always pay your credit card in full every month, you do not need to use the credit card account type, unless you want to track exactly where and when charges are made. The reason you don't need to use the credit card account type is that you usually can record the details of your credit card spending when you record the check payment to the credit card company. What is more, because the credit card balance always is reduced to zero every month, you do not need to keep track of the balance. The steps involved in using the Credit Card account register to perform record keeping for your credit cards parallel the steps for using any other register. First, you set up the account and record the beginning balance. (Because you are working with a liability, the beginning balance is what you owe.) Second, you use the register to record credit card spending. As noted earlier in the chapter, you also are asked for the credit limit on the credit card so Quicken can track your available credit.

The check you write actually is recorded as a reduction in the amount owed on your credit card. You already have recorded the credit card spending by recording transactions in the Credit Card register.

As with the other asset and liability registers, some minor differences exist between the Bank Account Register screen and menu options and the Credit Card Register screen and menu options. The `CHARGE` field in the Credit Card register is where you record each use of your credit card. The `PAYMENT` field is where you record payments made to the credit card company. If you fill in the `Credit Limit` field when you set up the credit card account, Quicken shows the credit remaining in the lower right corner of the screen above the `Ending Balance` field. Figure 12.19 shows the Credit Card Register screen.

Paying Credit Card Bills

The credit card Activities menu differs slightly from the standard Quicken Activities menu, replacing the **Reconcile** option with **Reconcile/Pay Credit Card Bill**, as shown in figure 12.20.

If you select **Reconcile/Pay Credit Card Bill**, Quicken displays the Credit Card Statement Information screen shown in figure 12.21.

```
Print/Acct   Edit   Shortcuts   Reports   Activities              F1-Help
DATE  REF  PAYEE  ·  MEMO  ·  CATEGORY     CHARGE   C  PAYMENT   BALANCE
                       BEGINNING
9/ 1       Opening Balance                 456 78  X              456 78
1991                       [visa]
9/15       Azteca Restaurant                23 94                 480 72
1991       lunch           Entertain
9/19       Milt's Truck Farm                14 63                 495 35
1991       gas for station→Auto:Fuel
9/19
1991  Memo:
       Cat:
visa            (Alt+letter accesses menu)    Credit Remaining:$4,504.65
Esc-Main Menu     Ctrl←┘ Record               Ending Balance:  $   495.35
```

Fig. 12.19. The Credit Card Register screen.

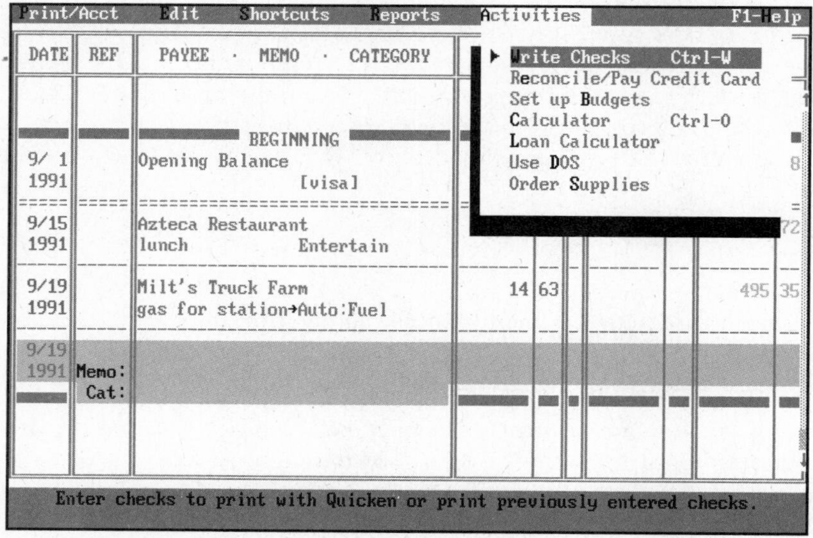

Fig. 12.20. The credit card version of the Activities menu.

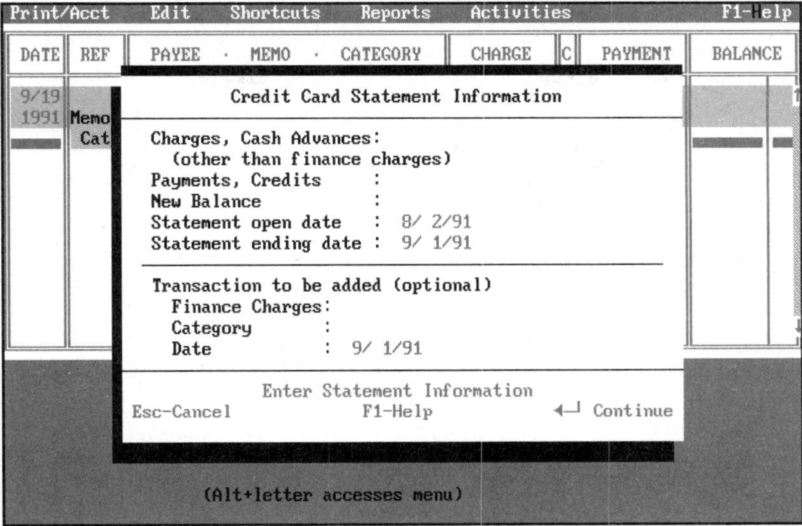

Fig. 12.21. *The Credit Card Statement Information screen.*

Selecting **Reconcile/Pay Credit Card Bill** enables you to reconcile your credit card register balance with the monthly credit card statement, record finance charges, and record a handwritten check or set up a check to be printed by Quicken.

You fill in several fields to begin this process, but the process parallels the one you use for reconciling your bank account, which is described in Chapter 8. In fact, the Credit Card Statement Information screen closely resembles the one used to start the bank account reconciliation process.

To use the **Pay Credit Card Bill** option, select the **Use Register** option from the Main Menu and follow these steps:

1. With the register for a credit card displayed, press Alt-A to access the Activities menu.

2. Select the **Reconcile/Pay Credit Card Bill** option from the Activities menu. Quicken displays the Credit Card Statement Information screen shown in figure 12.21.

3. Enter the credit card charges and cash advances as a positive number in the `Charges, Cash Advances` field.

4. Enter the total payments made in the `Payments, Credits` field also as a positive amount. If your statement shows credit slip transactions (because a store issued you a refund), also include these transactions in the `Payments, Credits` field.

5. Enter the ending credit card balance from your statement in the `New Balance` field. (Assuming that you owe money to the credit card company, the number you enter is a positive one.)

6. Enter the first day covered by the credit card statement in the `Statement opening date` field. Then, enter the last day covered by the credit card statement in the `Statement ending date` field.

7. Enter the monthly interest charges as a positive number in the `Finance Charges` field and enter the category to which you want finance charges assigned. (Quicken uses this information to record a transaction for the monthly interest you are charged on the credit card.)

8. After you complete the Credit Card Statement Information screen, press Enter. Quicken displays the credit card transactions list shown in figure 12.22. This screen and the abbreviated Register screen, accessed by pressing F9, work like the reconciliation screens described in Chapter 8.

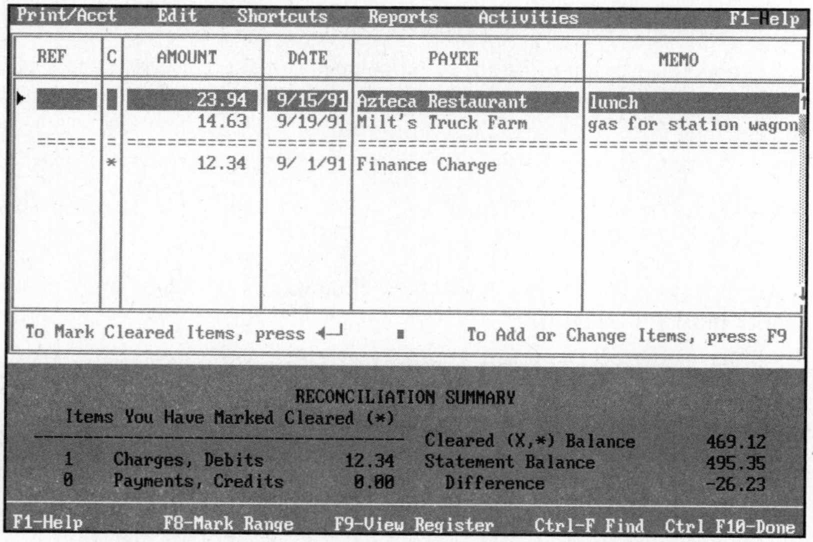

```
Print/Acct   Edit   Shortcuts   Reports   Activities                F1-Help

 REF   C    AMOUNT      DATE            PAYEE                    MEMO

▸             23.94    9/15/91  Azteca Restaurant       lunch
              14.63    9/19/91  Milt's Truck Farm       gas for station wagon
======  =  ==========  ========  ====================  ====================
       *      12.34    9/ 1/91  Finance Charge

 To Mark Cleared Items, press ←┘      ▪      To Add or Change Items, press F9

                        RECONCILIATION SUMMARY
   Items You Have Marked Cleared (*)
  -----------------------------------    Cleared (X,*) Balance        469.12
   1    Charges, Debits         12.34    Statement Balance            495.35
   0    Payments, Credits        0.00      Difference                 -26.23

F1-Help      F8-Mark Range    F9-View Register    Ctrl-F Find   Ctrl F10-Done
```

Fig. 12.22. The credit card transactions list screen.

9. Mark credit card transactions as cleared by pressing the space bar when the transaction is highlighted. A cleared credit card transaction is one that appears on the credit card statement. After you mark all the cleared credit card transactions, the cleared balance amount should equal the statement balance amount. If the two amounts do not equal each other, you missed recording a transaction or marking a transaction as cleared. (Chapter 8 gives tips on finding and correcting reconciliation errors for a bank account. These tips also apply to reconciling a credit card statement.)

10. When you finish the reconciliation process—the difference amount shows as zero—press Ctrl-F10. Quicken next displays the Make Credit Card Payment screen, shown in figure 12.23.

    If the reconciliation is not complete, Quicken displays a screen asking you to proceed or leave the reconciliation. At this time, Quicken displays an Adjusting Register To Agree with Statement screen. To accept Quicken's adjustments, press Enter; to cancel, press Esc.

    If you press Ctrl-F10 before reconciling the balance to zero, Quicken makes the necessary adjustments to reconcile the balance (refer to Chapter 8).

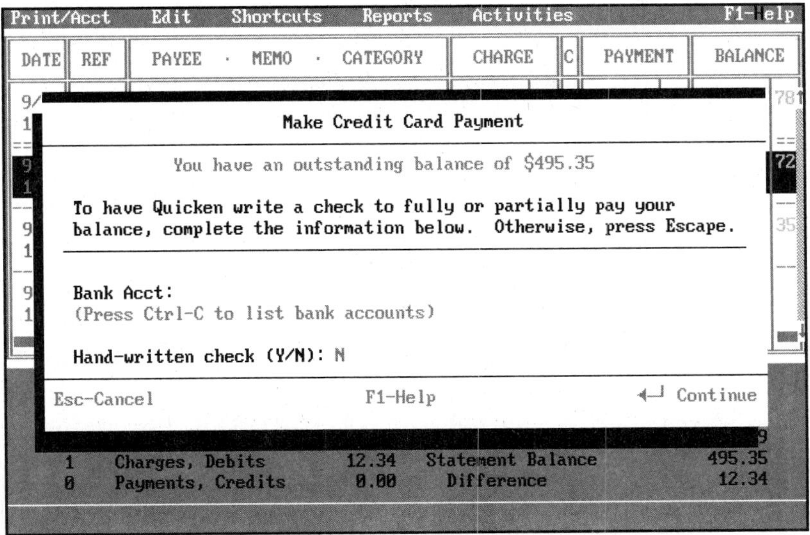

Fig. 12.23. The Make Credit Card Payment screen.

11. If you don't want to pay your credit card bill, press Esc from the Make Credit Card Payment screen. If you do want to pay your credit card bill, complete steps 12 and 13.

12. With the cursor positioned on the `Bank account` field, enter the name of the bank account on which you will write the check to pay the credit card bill. (Pressing Ctrl-C accesses the Category and Transfer List screen. At the end of the Category and Transfer List screen, Quicken shows account names.)

13. Move the cursor to the `Hand-written check` field. Set the `Hand-written check` field to N if you want Quicken to move you to the Write Checks screen so that you can print a check to the credit card company on the specified bank account. Set the `Hand-written check` field to Y if you want Quicken to move to the Register screen for the specified bank account so that you can record the check you wrote to the credit card company. In either case, Quicken enters the payment amount as the entire credit card balance. If you want to pay less than that amount, change the amount in the `Payment amount` field.

Measuring Your Net Worth

A balance sheet is one of the traditional tools individuals and businesses can use to measure net worth. A balance sheet lists the assets you own and the liabilities you owe. The difference between assets and liabilities is called *owner's equity* or *net worth*. Notice that a balance sheet is quite different from reports like income statements and cash-flow reports, which summarize what has happened over a period of time. A balance sheet provides a snapshot of your personal or business finances at a particular point in time.

> Before you produce a balance sheet, make sure that all your assets and liability accounts are in the same file.

Creating a balance sheet with Quicken is a two-step process. The first step is to set up an account for each of your assets, along with a beginning balance amount that equals the assets' cost or value. Assets generally are items you have paid for and that have lasting value. Personal assets include items like cash in your wallet, the surrender value of a life insurance policy, any investments, a home, and durable personal items like your car and furniture. Business assets usually include cash, accounts receivable, inventory, and other property and equipment.

The second step in creating a balance sheet is to set up an account for each of your liabilities, along with the balances owed. Liabilities are amounts you currently owe other people, banks, or businesses. Personal liabilities include items like credit card balances, income taxes owed, car loans, and a mortgage. Business liabilities usually include items like accounts payable, wages and salaries owed employees, income and payroll taxes, and bank credit lines and loans.

Determine the cost or market value of all your assets and liabilities as of the same date. The cost or market value information needs to be accurate or your net worth calculation will not be accurate. Use only one method for valuing your assets or liabilities, such as historical cost or fair market value. Mixing the different methods does not yield beneficial results. You also should note on your opening balances whether you used historical cost or fair market value. If you do use fair market value, document where the fair market value estimate came from.

After you enter the costs or market values of all your assets and liabilities, Quicken calculates your net worth by subtracting your liabilities from your assets. Hopefully, the difference is a positive one. For businesses and individuals, you want the net worth amount to grow larger over time, because this amount acts as a financial cushion.

Figure 12.24 shows an example of a personal balance sheet, or net worth statement, created by Quicken. At the top of the page, Quicken lists each of the asset accounts along with their balances on the `As of` date. Below that, Quicken lists each of the liability accounts along with their balances on total—which is the same thing as net worth. In figure 12.24, the net worth amount is $11,137.94.

A business balance sheet looks the same, although the assets and liabilities listed probably are different. Chapter 14 describes how to print a business balance sheet and each of Quicken's other reports.

```
                         Personal Net Worth
                           As of 1/10/91
PERSONAL-All Accounts                                                    Page 1
1/10/91
                                                  1/10/91
                   Acct                           Balance
          -------------------------------------  -----------
          ASSETS
            Cash and Bank Accounts
              Cash-Checking # 1987461               1,000.00
              Petty Cash-Business Petty Cash          161.88
                                                  -----------
            Total Cash and Bank Accounts            1,161.88

            Other Assets
              Real Estate-personal residence      100,000.00
                                                  -----------
            Total Other Assets                    100,000.00

                                                  -----------
          TOTAL ASSETS                            101,161.88

          LIABILITIES
            Credit Cards
              Credit Card                              23.94
                                                  -----------
            Total Credit Cards                         23.94

            Other Liabilities
              Mortgage-Home mortgage               90,000.00
                                                  -----------
            Total Other Liabilities                90,000.00

                                                  -----------
          TOTAL LIABILITIES                        90,023.94

                                                  -----------
          OVERALL TOTAL                            11,137.94
                                                  ===========
```

Fig. 12.24. An example of a personal balance sheet.

Chapter Summary

With the enhancements provided in Versions 4.0 and 5.0, you easily can use Quicken for almost all of your personal or small-business accounting needs. This chapter described how to use Quicken to perform record keeping for assets like real estate or accounts receivable and for liabilities like credit card debts and loans. If you are interested, yet need a little more help, refer to Chapters 13, 17, and 18. Chapter 13 describes the features Version 5.0 provides to help you monitor your investments. Chapter 17 describes using Quicken as a home accounting package. Chapter 18 describes using Quicken as business accounting package.

13

Monitoring Your Investments

Quicken 5.0 provides features that enable you to monitor and report on your investments. Quicken provides a register specifically for investments, several menu options that make monitoring and managing your investments easier, and a series of investment reports. Together, these tools enable you to monitor investment transactions, measure performance, track market values, and create reports for income tax planning and preparation.

This chapter describes how to prepare to monitor your investments with Quicken and how to track mutual funds and other investments using the Quicken investment register. To save you from reviewing material you already know, the chapter does not explain the parts of the investment register that also are part of the regular Quicken register. If you are not well acquainted with the basics of Quicken, refer to the second section of this book, "Learning the Basics."

Preparing To Monitor Investments

To monitor investments with Quicken, you need to set up an investment account. Quicken provides two investment account categories: the *mutual fund account* and the *investment and cash account*. The mutual fund account is a simplified investment account that you use for a single mutual fund. The investment and cash account is a more powerful investment account that you use for other investments and investment groups.

The basic difference between the two accounts is difficult to grasp. If you learn the difference now, however, you will find it much easier to decide when to set up mutual fund accounts and when to set up investment and cash accounts.

The mutual fund account keeps track of the market value and the number of shares you hold of a single investment. The investment and cash account keeps track of the market value of multiple securities, the shares, and the cash balance. (The cash balance usually would represent the money with which you buy additional stocks, bonds, and so forth.)

Given these distinctions, the easiest approach is to set up a mutual fund account for each mutual fund investment you hold, set up an investment and cash account for each brokerage account you hold, and set up an investment and cash account for any collection of individual investments that you want to track and manage together in one register. As you work with the Quicken investment options, you will be able to fine-tune these suggestions.

To set up either type of investment account, follow these steps:

1. Choose the **Select Account** option from Quicken's Main Menu. Quicken displays the Select Account to Use screen shown in figure 13.1.

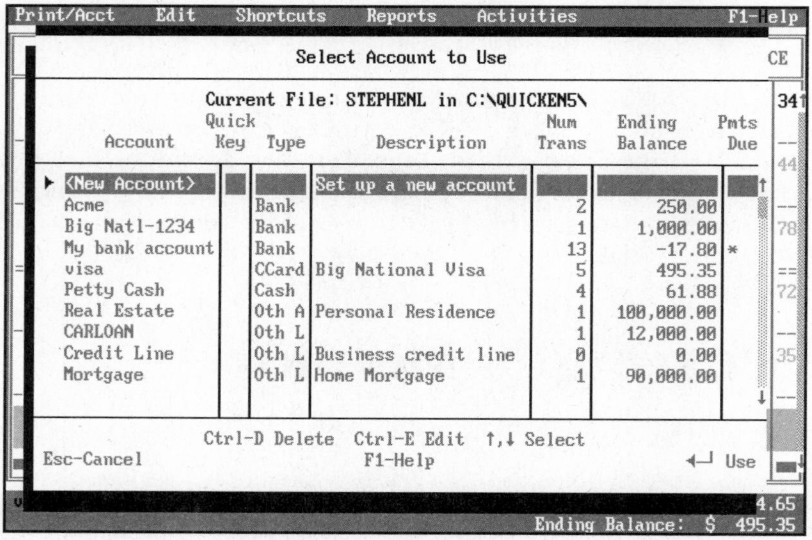

Print/Acct Edit Shortcuts Reports Activities F1-Help

Select Account to Use

Current File: STEPHENL in C:\QUICKEN5\

Account	Quick Key	Type	Description	Num Trans	Ending Balance	Pmts Due
<New Account>			Set up a new account			
Acme		Bank		2	250.00	
Big Natl-1234		Bank		1	1,000.00	
My bank account		Bank		13	-17.80	*
visa		CCard	Big National Visa	5	495.35	
Petty Cash		Cash		4	61.88	
Real Estate		Oth A	Personal Residence	1	100,000.00	
CARLOAN		Oth L		1	12,000.00	
Credit Line		Oth L	Business credit line	0	0.00	
Mortgage		Oth L	Home Mortgage	1	90,000.00	

Ctrl-D Delete Ctrl-E Edit ↑,↓ Select

Esc-Cancel F1-Help ↵ Use

Ending Balance: $ 495.35

Fig. 13.1. *The Select Account to Use screen.*

2. Select the **New Account** option from the list. Quicken displays the Set Up New Account screen shown in figure 13.2.

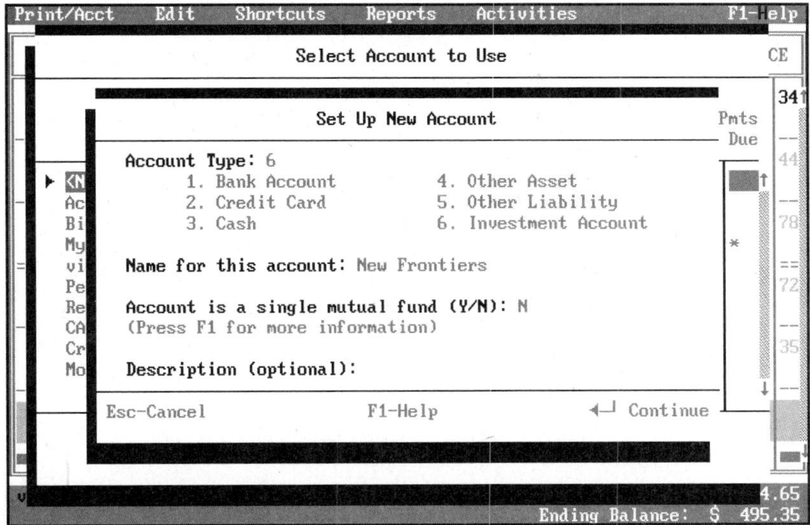

Fig. 13.2. The Set up New Account screen.

3. Press 6 in the `Account Type` field to indicate that this is an investment account.

4. Press Enter or Tab to move the cursor to the `Name for this account` field and enter a description of the account. The account name can be up to 15 characters long and can contain any characters except [,], /, and :. You can include spaces in the account name.

5. Press Enter or Tab to move the cursor to the `Account is a single mutual fund` field. If you want to set up a mutual fund account, set this field to Y for yes. If you want to set up an investment and cash account, press N for no.

6. Press Enter or Tab to move the cursor to the `Description` field. The `Description` field provides 21 spaces for additional investment description.

7. When you finish entering information for the new account, press Enter.

If you are creating a mutual fund account and have set the `Account is a single mutual fund` field to Y, Quicken displays the Set Up Mutual Fund Security screen (see fig. 13.3). The account description appears in the `Name` field.

If you set the `Account is a single mutual fund` field to N, you do not need to complete steps 8, 9, and 10.

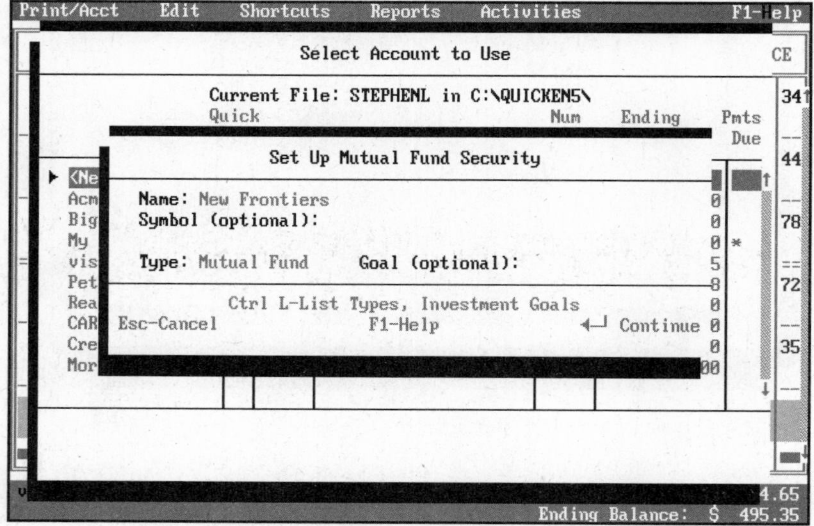

Fig. 13.3. The Set Up Mutual Fund Security screen.

8. (Optional) Enter the mutual fund symbol in the `Symbol` field if you plan to import price data from another file.

   The symbol that you enter in the `Symbol` field should be whatever you use to identify the mutual fund in the other file. For more information on this process, refer to "Updating Your Investment Records for Market Values" elsewhere in this chapter.

9. In the `Type` field, specify the type of mutual fund: Bond, CD, Mutual Fund, or Stock. Press Ctrl-L to see an on-screen list of the valid types, and select an item from the list (see fig. 13.4).

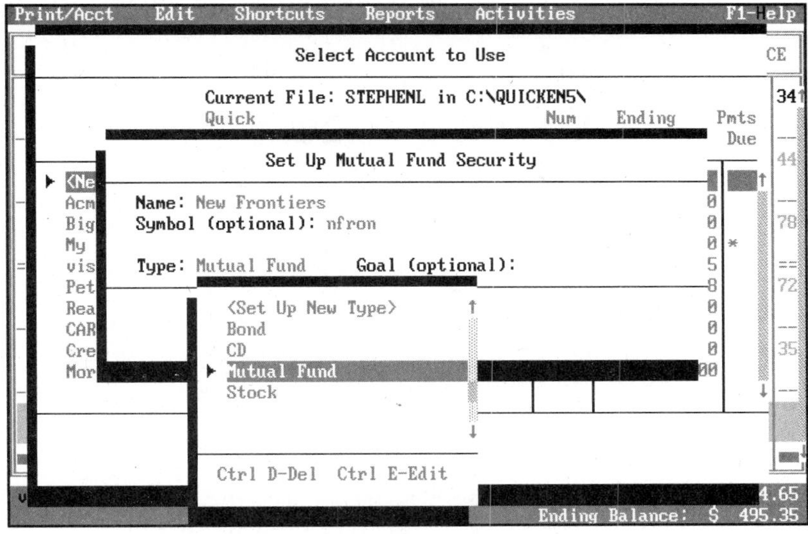

Fig. 13.4. The Investment Types List screen.

10. (Optional). Specify an investment goal: College Fund, Growth, High-Risk Income, and Low-Risk Income. To see an on-screen list of valid goals, press Ctrl-L and select an item from the list. Figure 13.5 shows the list of valid investment goals.

    The `Type` and `Goal` fields do not affect significantly the way Quicken processes information. (The `Type` field does dictate whether share prices are recorded using decimal or fractional numbers.) You can use the `Type` and `Goal` fields to sort and organize information on reports. How to define different investment types and goals will be discussed later in the chapter.

11. After you complete the Set Up Mutual Fund Security screen, press Enter while the cursor is on the `Goal` field. Alternatively, press Ctrl-Enter when the cursor is on one of the other fields. Quicken displays the Select Account to Use screen.

Repeat steps 1 through 7 for each investment and cash account you choose to set up. For each mutual fund account you establish, repeat steps 1 through 10.

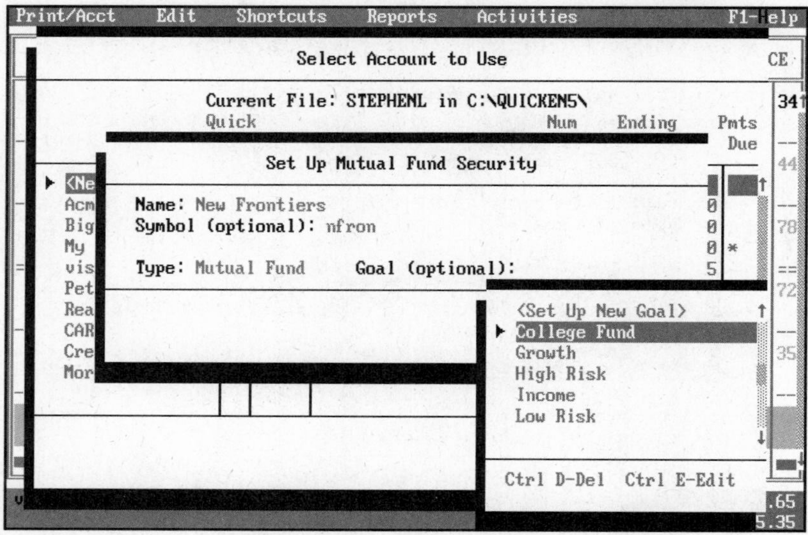

Fig. 13.5. The Investment Goals List screen.

After you have created an investment account, you are ready to use the register to record initial balances, changes in the investment balance due to purchases or sales, and fluctuations in the market value. The next two sections—"Working With Mutual Funds" and "Working with Other Investments"—explain how to use the investment accounts you have created. Because mutual fund accounts are easier to work with than investment and cash accounts, consider starting with the next section—even if most of your investment record keeping pertains to stocks and bonds.

Working with Mutual Funds

Using Quicken to monitor a mutual fund investment consists of recording your starting balance and periodically recording changes in the balance due to the purchase of additional shares or the redemption of shares. To put things in perspective, you record the same information that appears on your mutual fund statements. By recording the information in the Quicken register, however, you can use the information in several calculations that show you how you really are doing with your investments.

The first step in working with a mutual fund is to record the initial purchase. To record the initial purchase of a mutual fund, follow these steps:

1. With the Select Account to Use screen displayed, select the mutual fund investment account for which you want to record an initial balance. Quicken displays the Create Opening Share Balance screen (see fig. 13.6). The easiest way to set up a mutual fund balance is to follow steps 1, 2, 3, and 4. However, if you want reports that accurately summarize the complete history of a mutual fund investment, skip steps 2, 3, and 4, and enter each of the mutual fund transactions you make.

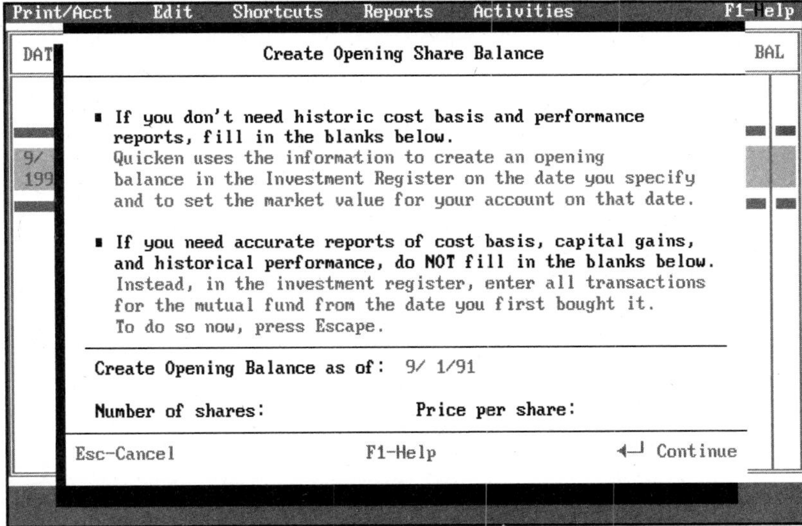

Fig. 13.6. The Create Opening Share Balance screen.

2. Enter the date that you want to begin recording the opening share balance and enter the price per share.

3. Move the cursor to the `Number of shares` field and enter the number of shares that you now own.

4. Move the cursor to the `Price per share` field and enter today's price per share for the mutual fund. You do not need to enter a dollar sign. If the price happens to be a whole number, you do not need to enter a decimal point and two zeros after the price. (You can find price per share information in many local newspapers and in daily financial newspapers such as the Wall Street Journal.)

   By default, stock and bond prices use fractions. For example, a stock price might be 7 1/8 and a bond price might be 97 1/8. Other investment prices, such as mutual funds and certificates of deposit, use decimals. A mutual fund price, for example, might be 14.02. You can use the + and – keys to increase and decrease the price of a security. The + key increases the price 1/8 or .125, and the – key decreases the price 1/8 or .125.

5. When the Create Opening Share Balance screen is complete, press Enter while the cursor is on the `Price per share` field. Alternatively, press Ctrl-Enter or F10 when the cursor is on any of the fields. Quicken displays the register into which you can record investment transactions (see fig. 13.7).

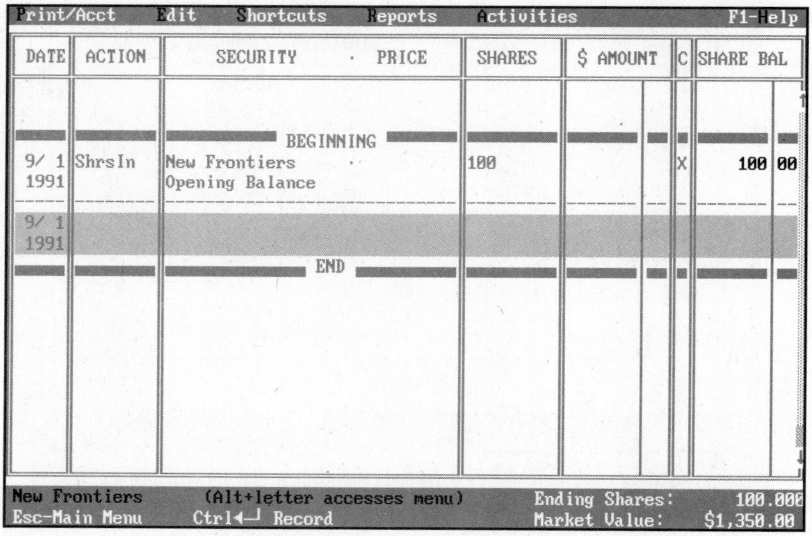

Print/Acct Edit Shortcuts Reports Activities F1-Help

DATE	ACTION	SECURITY · PRICE	SHARES	$ AMOUNT	C	SHARE BAL
		BEGINNING				
9/ 1 1991	ShrsIn	New Frontiers Opening Balance	100		X	100 00
9/ 1 1991						
		END				

New Frontiers (Alt+letter accesses menu) Ending Shares: 100.000
Esc-Main Menu Ctrl◄┘ Record Market Value: $1,350.00

Fig. 13.7. The mutual fund investment register with the opening mutual fund balance.

After you have set up the initial mutual fund investment balance, you are ready to record a wide variety of transactions: purchases, sales, dividends, and so forth. The basic process of recording each type of investment transaction is the same.

To record transactions in the mutual fund register, follow these steps:

1. Enter the date of the transaction in the `Date` field. You can use the + and – keys to change the date one day at a time.

2. Move the cursor to the Action field and choose the type of action that best describes the transaction you're recording.

   To choose from a list of valid investment types, press Ctrl-L when the cursor is on the Action field. Alternatively, select Action List from the Shortcuts menu. The Action List screen shown in figure 13.8 appears. When you choose from the Action List, specific action descriptions appear in pop-up box menus. Table 13.1 summarizes the general actions shown in figure 13.8 and describes the specific actions that fall into the general category.

   After you learn the various mutual fund actions, consider using the auto-completion feature: Type just enough of the action for Quicken to uniquely identify it and then press Enter. Quicken completes the rest of the action for you.

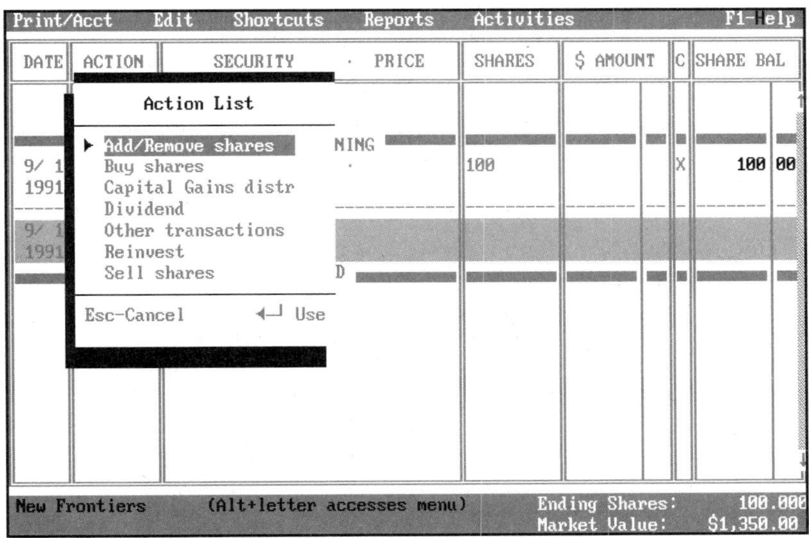

Fig. 13.8. The Action List screen.

Table 13.1
Investment Actions for Mutual Fund Accounts

Action	*Description*
Add/Remove shares	
ShrsIn	Investment shares transferred into the account
ShrsOut	Investment shares transferred out of the account
Buy shares	
BuyX	Purchase investment shares with cash transferred into the account
Capital Gains distr	
CGLongX	Cash received from a long-term capital gain transferred out of the account
CGShortX	Cash received from a short-term capital gain transferred out of the account
Dividend	
DivX	Cash received from a dividend transferred out of the account
Other transactions	
MiscInc	Receive miscellaneous income (Quicken displays a category field if you choose this action, so that you categorize the income.)
Reminder	Reminder note tied to future date (Billminder reminds you about these notes)
StkSplit	Increase or decrease in number of shares because of a stock split
Reinvest	
ReinvDiv	Reinvest cash dividends or interest by purchasing more investment shares
ReinvInt	Reinvest interest by purchasing more investment shares

Action	*Description*
ReinvLg	Reinvest long-term; capital gains distribution by purchasing more investment shares
ReinvSh	Reinvest short-term capital gains distribution by purchasing more investment shares
Sell Shares	
SellX	Sell investment shares, but transfer cash received out of the investment account

You must enter an account for any action that involves transferring money into or out of an account (always indicated with an "X" at the end of the action name). If you do not want to record a transfer account, use ShrsIn or ShrsOut, because these options do not require you to enter an account.

If you have questions about transferring money between accounts, refer to Chapter 4, "Using Quicken's Register." Chapter 4 describes the logic and mechanics of transferring money between bank accounts. The same principles apply to transferring money between an investment account and a bank account.

3. Move the cursor to the `Price` field and enter the price per share of the mutual fund. When entering a price, you can use up to three decimal places (for example, $11.594). In the `Price` field, you can use the + key to increase the price by $.125 and the – key to decrease the price by $.125.
4. Move the cursor to the `Shares` field and enter the number of shares involved in the transaction. You can use up to four decimal places when entering the number of shares. Press Enter or Tab to leave the `Shares` field, and Quicken calculates the `Amount` field. (Quicken calculates the `Amount` field by multiplying the price times the number of shares.)
5. (Optional) Move the cursor to the `Memo` field and enter a further description of the transaction.

6. (Optional) When you enter a purchase or sale transaction (BuyX or SellX), Quicken displays the `Comm/Fee` field. Enter into the `Comm/Fee` field any commission or brokerage fee you paid to execute the transaction. When you press Tab or Enter, Quicken calculates the `XferAmt` field by adding the transaction amount to the commission or fee.

   Quicken adjusts the dollar amount of the transaction to include the commission or fee amount. For a `BuyX` transaction, Quicken adds the commission or fee. For a `SellX` transaction, Quicken subtracts the commission or fee. If you enter the share price, number of shares, and dollar amount of the purchase, Quicken fills in the `Comm/Fee` field itself, if the `Amount` field doesn't equal the `Price` field multiplied by the `Shares` field. In this case, Quicken uses the `Comm/Fee` field to store the difference between what you entered as the dollar amount and the calculated result (price times the number of shares).

7. (Optional) Move the cursor to the `Account` field and record the bank account from which you withdrew the cash to purchase the mutual fund shares or the account in which you deposited cash from the sale of mutual fund shares, receipt of dividends, or receipt of capital gains distributions. Remember that you can display the Select Account to Use screen by pressing Ctrl-C. You also can use Quicken's auto-completion feature: type enough of the account name for Quicken to uniquely identify the account and then press Enter.

8. To record the transaction, press Enter when the cursor is on the `XferAmt` field. Alternatively, press Ctrl-Enter or F10 when the cursor is on any field in the investment register.

Figure 13.9 shows a sample transaction recording the purchase of additional shares of a mutual fund.

Although the preceding eight steps illustrate only one type of investment transaction, the steps for recording other kinds of investment transactions are identical. The key is to choose the correct action description (see table 13.1). The following paragraphs describe when to choose particular actions when executing mutual fund transactions.

The action descriptions of the mutual fund transactions you most often execute are **BuyX** for purchases or **SellX** for sales. If you invest in an income-oriented fund, you probably have monthly dividend or income payments. Record the monthly dividend or income payments as **DivX** if you withdraw the money from the fund. If you reinvest the dividends by buying more fund shares, record the dividend payments as **ReinvDiv**. Or, if you reinvest interest by buying more fund shares, record the interest payments as **ReinvInt**.

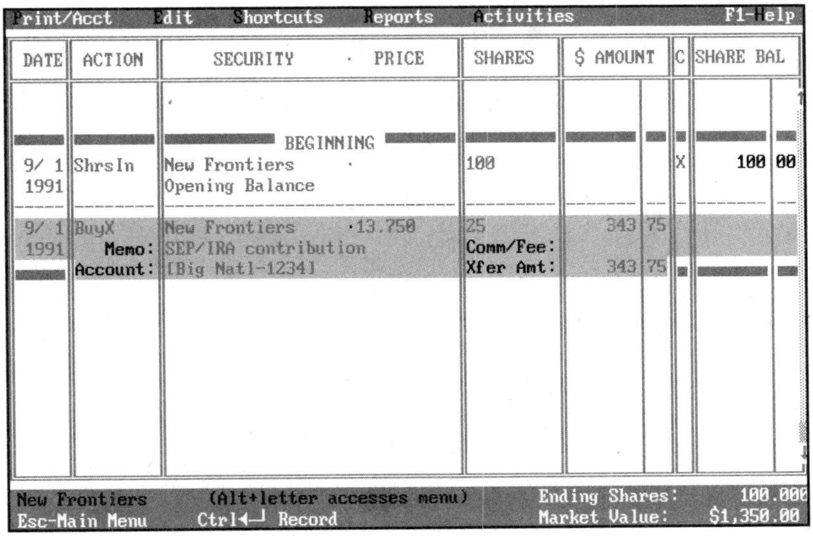

```
Print/Acct   Edit   Shortcuts   Reports   Activities                F1-Help
DATE  ACTION    SECURITY         PRICE   SHARES     $ AMOUNT  C SHARE BAL
                       BEGINNING
9/ 1  ShrsIn    New Frontiers            100                  X   100 00
1991            Opening Balance
9/ 1  BuyX      New Frontiers   13.750   25         343 75
1991     Memo:  SEP/IRA contribution     Comm/Fee:
      Account:  [Big Natl-1234]          Xfer Amt:  343 75
New Frontiers    (Alt+letter accesses menu)   Ending Shares:     100.000
Esc-Main Menu    Ctrl◄┘ Record                Market Value:    $1,350.00
```

Fig. 13.9. A sample transaction recorded in the mutual fund version of the investment register.

At the end of the year, the fund will make a capital gain distribution, which you record as **CGLongX** or **CGShortX** if you withdraw the money and as **ReinvLg** or **ReinvSh** if you reinvest the capital gains by buying more shares. (At this time, the income tax treatment for long- and short-term capital gains is identical; however, this may change.) When the mutual fund reports the capital gain, the statement should indicate whether the gain is long-term or short-term.

Occasionally, you may need to choose the **StkSplit** action, which adjusts the number of shares without changing the dollar amount. A **StkSplit** transaction does not require entries in the `Price`, `Shares`, or `Amount` fields. **StkSplit** records the date on which a certain number of new shares equals a certain number of old shares. The first number equals the number of new shares; the second number equals the number of old shares.

Suppose, for example, that the New Frontiers mutual fund declares a stock split in which each old share is converted into two new shares. Figure 13.10

shows just such a stock split transaction in which you receive two new shares for every old share. You also can use this approach to record nontaxable stock dividends. For example, when you receive a 10 percent stock dividend, record the stock dividend as a 1.1:1 stock split.

Both **Stock Split** and **Reminder** are under **Other Transactions** in the Action list.

```
Print/Acct   Edit   Shortcuts   Reports   Activities                   F1-Help
DATE  ACTION    SECURITY            PRICE    SHARES   $ AMOUNT   C  SHARE BAL
                        BEGINNING
9/ 1  ShrsIn    New Frontiers                100                 X     100 00
1991            Opening Balance
9/ 1  BuyX      New Frontiers       13.750   25         343 75         125 00
1991            SEP/IRA contribution
9/ 2  StkSplit  New Frontiers                                          250 00
1991     Memo:
        Split:  2           for: 1
9/ 1
1991
                           END
New Frontiers      (Alt+letter accesses menu)     Ending Shares:     250.000
Esc-Main Menu      Ctrl←┘ Record                  Market Value:    $3,437.50
```

Fig. 13.10. A stock split transaction.

The last action description that is used with mutual fund transactions is the **Reminder** option. **Reminder** transactions do not have a share or dollar amount—only the `Security` and `Memo` fields are filled. You can use the **Reminder** option in two ways: to make notes in your investment register and to remind yourself about certain transactions through the Quicken Billminder feature. The Billminder feature will display messages that alert you to **Reminder** transactions (just as Billminder will display messages that alert you to unprinted checks and scheduled transaction groups). To turn off a **Reminder** transaction, mark the transaction as cleared by entering an * or *X* in the `C` field.

CPA TIP

If you buy mutual fund shares, you should know the difference between load funds and no load funds. You usually purchase load funds through a broker, who charges a commission that can run from 3 to 10 percent. The commission is compensation for the salesperson who placed the order and helped you select the fund. Even though you may need the help of a broker in selecting a fund and placing an order, you should be aware that you can save yourself the commission (which means you're ahead from the start) by choosing a no-load mutual fund.

Research shows that on the average, load funds perform no better than no-load funds. Therefore, many investors see no reason to choose a load fund over a no-load fund. No-load funds deal directly with their customers, which means the customer pays no commission. To find a no-load mutual fund, flip through the Wall Street Journal and look for mutual fund advertisements that specify "no load." T. Rowe Price, Vanguard, and Scudder are large investment management companies that offer families of no-load mutual funds.

Working with Other Investments

If you have worked with the mutual fund version of the investment register, you quickly can adapt to the investment and cash version. The investment and cash account register tracks the number of shares you hold in the account of each individual security and any extra cash you are holding because you have just sold (or plan to purchase) a security. This process mirrors the way many brokerage accounts work: your account can have a cash component and a component detailing stock, bond, and certificate of deposit investments.

The steps for using the investment and cash account register mirror those for using the mutual fund register. To use the investment and cash account register, follow these steps:

1. With the Select Account to Use screen displayed, select the investment and cash account for which you want to record an initial balance. (You have to define an investment and cash account prior to selecting the account.)

Quicken displays the regular version of the investment register screen with the First Time Setup screen displayed (see fig. 13.11). The First Time Setup screen informs you that you need to add shares by entering a ShrsIn transaction. You will enter a **ShrsIn** transaction later in this process.

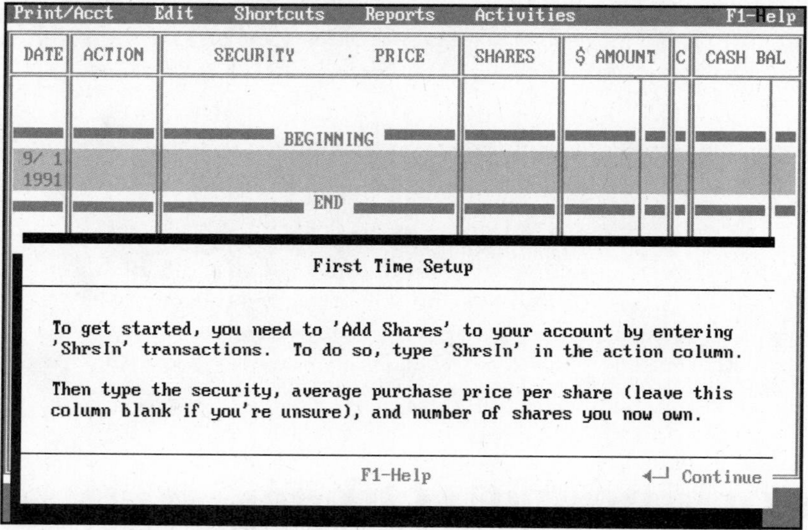

Fig. 13.11. The First Time Setup screen.

2. To continue past the First Time Setup screen, press Enter. Quicken displays the investment and cash account register. Position the cursor on the `Date` field and enter the purchase date of the first security you want to record in the register.

3. Move the cursor to the `Action` field and press Ctrl-L to display the Action List (see fig. 13.8). Alternatively, choose **Action List** from the Shortcuts menu. Choose the action that best describes the transaction you are recording. When Quicken lists the specific actions that fall into the general category, choose the appropriate action.

   Table 13.2 summarizes the general and specific actions for the investment and cash account version of the investment register. In essence, this list is an expanded version of the investment actions available for mutual fund accounts. The list is expanded because you can hold cash in an investment and cash account. When a transaction involves cash, you need to tell Quicken whether you are transferring the cash out of the account or leaving the cash in the account.

Table 13.2
Investment Actions for Investment and Cash Accounts

Action	*Description*
Add/Remove shares	
ShrsIn	Investment shares transferred into the account
ShrsOut	Investment shares transferred out of the account
Buy shares	
Buy	Purchase investment shares with cash in the investment account
BuyX	Purchase investment shares with cash transferred into the account
Capital Gains distr	
CGLong	Cash representing a long-term capital gain received into the account
CGLongX	Cash received from a long-term capital gain transferred out of the account
CGShort	Cash representing a short-term capital gain received into the account
CGShortX	Cash received from a short-term capital gain transferred out of the account
Dividend	
Div	Cash received representing a dividend
DivX	Cash received from a dividend transferred out of the account
Interest	
IntInc	Cash received representing interest income
MargInt	Cash paid on margin loan interest using cash in account
Other transactions	
MiscExp	Pay for expenses, using cash from the account
MiscInc	Receive miscellaneous income

continues

Table 13.2 *(continued)*

Action	*Description*
Reminder	Reminder note tied to future date (Billminder reminds you about these notes)
RtrnCap	Cash received that represents return of initial capital investment
StkSplit	Increase or decrease in number of shares because of a stock split
Reinvest	
ReinvDiv	Reinvest cash dividends or interest by purchasing more investment shares
ReinvInt	Reinvest interest by purchasing more investment shares
ReinvLg	Reinvest long-term capital gains distribution by purchasing more investment shares
ReinvSh	Reinvest short-term capital gains distribution by purchasing more investment shares
Sell Shares	
Sell	Sell investment shares and leave cash received in the investment account
SellX	Sell investment shares, but transfer cash received out of the investment account
Transfer Cash	
XIn	Cash transferred into the investment account
XOut	Cash transferred out of the investment account. (If you do not want to record a transfer account, use ShrsIn or ShrsOut, because these options do not require you to enter an account.)

4. Move the cursor to the `Security` field and enter the name of the security you are recording. If you have not used the security name before (which is the case the first time you record the security),

Quicken displays the Security Not Found screen (see fig. 13.12). The Security Not Found screen lists two options: **Add to Security List** and **Select from Security List**.

After you define a security, you can use Quicken's auto-completion feature. To use the auto-completion feature, type enough of the security name to uniquely identify the security and press Enter. Quicken completes the security name for you.

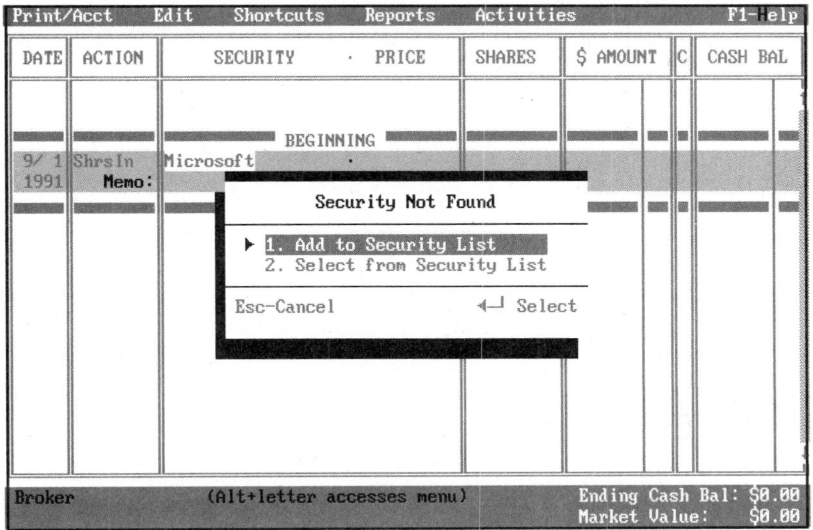

Fig. 13.12. *The Security Not Found screen.*

5. If you entered a new security in step 4, press 1 (or highlight **Add to Security List**) to add the new security. Quicken displays the Set Up Security screen shown in figure 13.13. Entering the security symbol in the `Symbol` field is optional. (You use security symbols for importing price data from a separate ASCII file, a process described later in this chapter.) Define the type of investment by moving the cursor to the `Type` field, pressing Ctrl-L, highlighting the current investment type (see fig. 13.4), and pressing Enter. Define the investment goal by moving the cursor to the `Goal` field, pressing Ctrl-L, highlighting the investment goal (see fig. 13.5), and pressing Enter. (You also can use the auto-completion feature to fill the `Type` and `Goal` fields.) When the Set Up Security screen is complete, press Enter when the cursor is on the `Goal` field.

If the security name you entered in step 4 has been defined, press 2 to choose the **Select from Security List** option. Quicken displays the Security List screen, shown in figure 13.14. The Security List shows the securities you have previously defined. Highlight the security you want and press Enter.

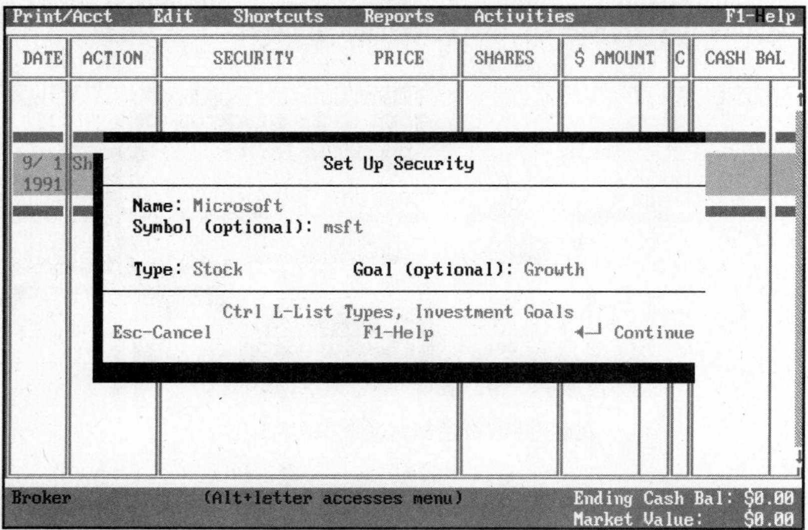

Fig. 13.13. *The Set Up Security screen.*

6. Move the cursor to the `Price` field and enter the per share price of the security.

   For investments without an actual share price, you can enter the `Price` field value as 1 (representing one dollar) and subsequently enter the number of shares as the number of dollars of the investment. For investments that have a share or unit price, enter that figure in the `Price` field.

   By default, stock and bond prices use fractions. A stock price might be 6 7/8. A bond price might be 98 1/8. Other prices, such as mutual funds and certificates of deposit, use decimals. A mutual fund price, for example, might be 13.02. As noted earlier in the chapter, you can use the + and – keys to increase and decrease the price of a security. The + key increases the price 1/8, or .125, and the – key decreases the price 1/8, or .125.

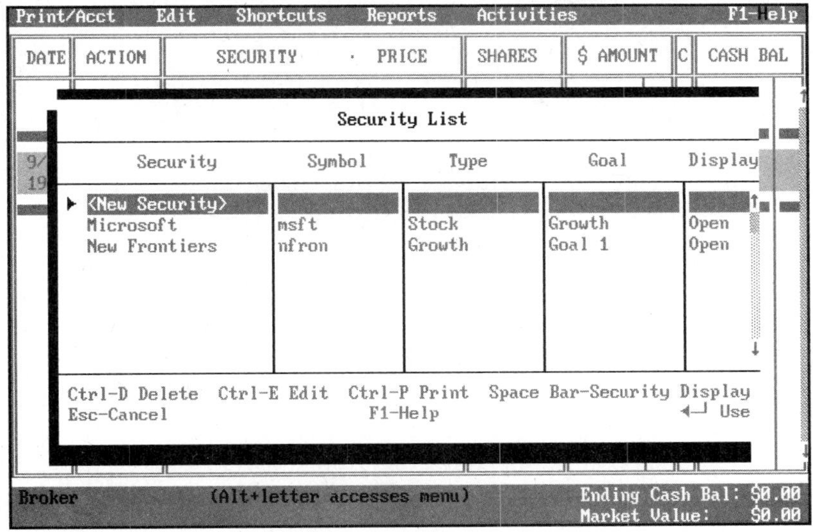

Fig. 13.14. *The Security List screen.*

You easily can find stock share prices in the newspaper. Other securities' prices, however, can be more difficult to determine. Some securities, such as money market funds and nonnegotiable certificates of deposit, do not have a share price. In these cases, enter the price as 1 (representing one dollar). The number of shares will equal the number of dollars' worth of the security you hold.

For other investments, such as bonds and negotiable certificates of deposit, the price shows as a percent. A bond price might be 98 3/8, which indicates the bond is 98 3/8 percent of its face value. (Usually the face value of a bond is $1,000.) A negotiable certificate of deposit price might be 100.971, which indicates that the certificate of deposit is worth 100.971 percent of its face value. (Negotiable certificates of deposit are available in a wide variety of denominations usually less than $100,000.)

As a general rule, enter the security price using whatever form appears in the newspaper or on your brokerage statement. Then enter the number of shares as the value that, when multiplied by the share price, equals the total dollar value of the investment.

7. Move the cursor to the `Shares` field and enter the number of shares or units of the transaction. You can use up to four decimal places when entering the number of shares. When you press Enter or Tab to leave the `Shares` field, Quicken calculates the `Amount` field.

You can enter any two of the three fields—`Price`, `Shares`, and `Amount`—and Quicken will calculate the third field. If you enter all three fields and the price times the number of shares does not equal the amount, Quicken puts the difference in the `Comm/Fee` field.

8. (Optional) Move the cursor to the `Memo` field and enter a further description of the transaction.
9. (Optional) If you enter a purchase and sales transaction, Quicken displays the `Comm/Fee` field. Move the cursor to the `Comm/Fee` field and enter any commission or brokerage fee you paid to execute the transaction. When you press Tab or Enter, Quicken calculates the `XferAmt` field by adding the transaction amount and the commission or fee.
10. If the action isn't **ShrsIn** or **ShrsOut**, move the cursor to the `Account` field and record the bank account you tapped for cash to purchase the investment. Remember that you can display the Select Account to Use screen by pressing Ctrl-C. Alternatively, you can use Quicken's auto-completion feature: type enough of the account name to uniquely identify the account and press Enter. Quicken finishes typing the name for you.
11. Record the transaction by pressing Enter when the cursor is on the `XferAmt` field. Alternatively, press Ctrl-Enter or F10 when the cursor is on any of the fields on the investment register. Quicken displays the standard message box and asks whether you want to record the transaction. Press Enter to record the transaction.

Figure 13.15 shows several sample transactions. The first transaction records the initial purchase of stock shares. The second transaction records the initial deposit of cash into the brokerage account. The third transaction shows the purchase of a bond, the fourth transaction shows the receipt of interest income from the bond, and the fifth transaction shows the sale of a portion of the stock purchased in the first transaction.

To record each transaction, follow the steps listed in the preceding paragraphs. Notice that the investment and cash account version of the register (as compared to the mutual fund version) does not track share balances. However, the investment and cash account version of the register tracks the cash you have available to purchase additional investments.

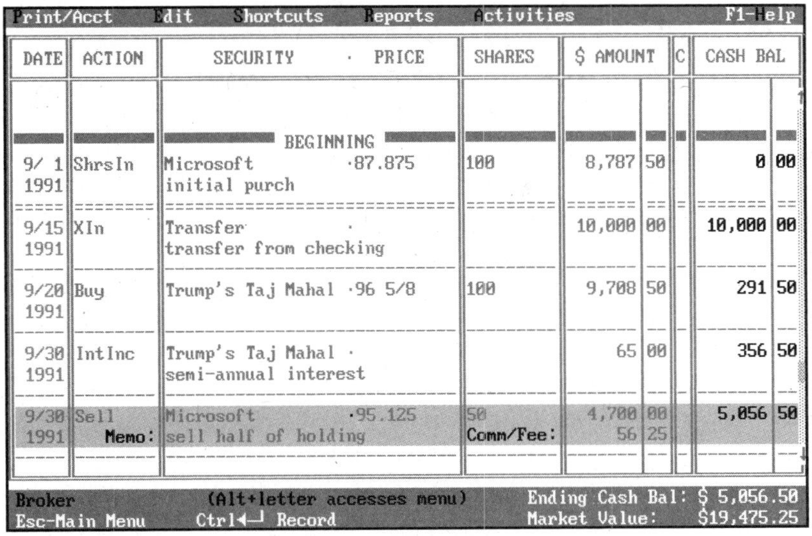

Print/Acct Edit Shortcuts Reports Activities F1-Help

DATE	ACTION	SECURITY · PRICE	SHARES	$ AMOUNT	C	CASH BAL
		BEGINNING				
9/ 1 1991	ShrsIn	Microsoft ·87.875 initial purch	100	8,787 50		0 00
9/15 1991	XIn	Transfer · transfer from checking		10,000 00		10,000 00
9/20 1991	Buy	Trump's Taj Mahal ·96 5/8	100	9,708 50		291 50
9/30 1991	IntInc	Trump's Taj Mahal · semi-annual interest		65 00		356 50
9/30 1991	Sell Memo:	Microsoft ·95.125 sell half of holding	50 Comm/Fee:	4,700 00 56 25		5,056 50

Broker (Alt+letter accesses menu) Ending Cash Bal: $ 5,056.50
Esc-Main Menu Ctrl◄┘ Record Market Value: $19,475.25

Fig. 13.15. *Sample transactions recorded in the investment and cash account version of the register.*

Working with the Investment Register

The preceding sections of this chapter describe the fundamentals of working with the Quicken investment registers. You can set up mutual fund accounts, create investment and cash accounts, and record transactions in the register.

The remaining sections of this chapter describe how to work with the Quicken securities lists. You learn how to define your own investment types and goals; how to update your investment records because of changes in market values; and how to reconcile your investment records with those provided by the mutual fund company, brokerage house, or bank. The last section in the chapter offers tips on investments and investment record keeping that may save you headaches and money.

Working with the Securities Lists

When working with the investment and cash account register, you can add securities to the list that Quicken maintains. Although this approach may be all you ever need, Quicken's **Security List** option enables you to work with the securities list before entering transactions in the register. This option is helpful when, for example, you know that over the coming months you will be purchasing shares of several companies. The **Security List** option saves you time by enabling you to define the securities before you purchase them.

You can access the **Security List** option by pressing Alt-S, and then selecting **Security List** from the Shortcuts menu (see fig. 13.16). Alternatively, you can press Ctrl-Y. Either method produces the Security List screen shown in figure 13.17. From this screen, you can add, edit, delete, and print lists of securities. You also can use the Security List screen to access screens that enable you to add, edit, and delete investment types and goals.

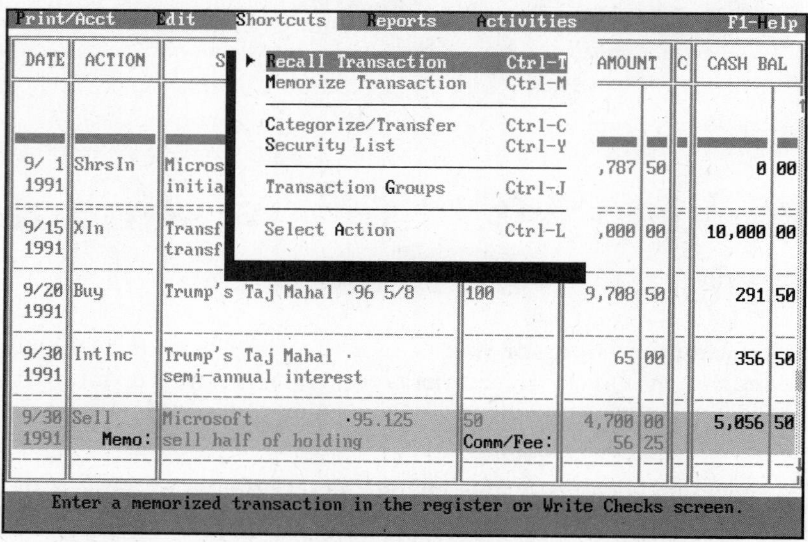

Fig. 13.16. The investment register version of the Shortcuts menu.

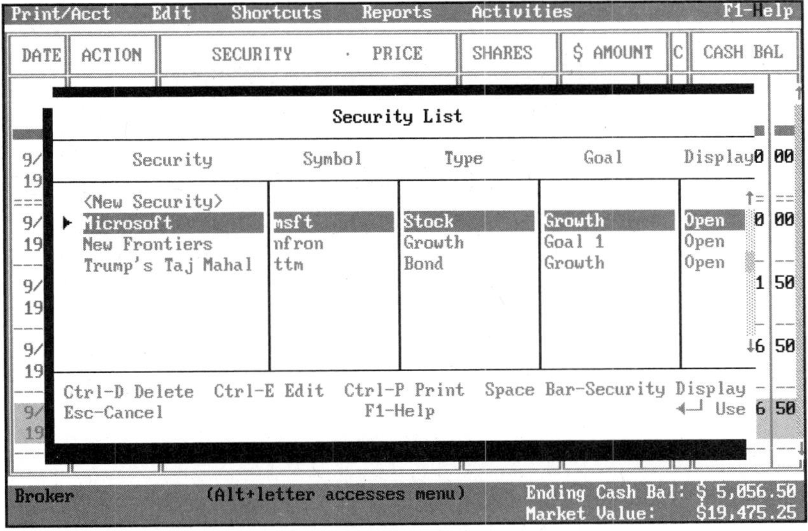

***Fig. 13.17.** The Security List screen.*

To add a security to the securities list, follow these steps:

1. Press Ctrl-Y to display the Securities List screen.

2. Use the up- and down-arrow keys to highlight `New Security`, and then press Enter. Quicken displays the Set Up Security screen shown in figure 13.13.

3. Enter the security name in the `Name` field. You can enter a maximum of 18 characters.

4. (Optional) Enter the security symbol in the `Symbol` field. (You use security symbols for importing price data from a separate ASCII file, a process described later in the chapter.) You can enter a maximum of 12 characters.

5. To define the investment type, move the cursor to the `Type` field, press Ctrl-L, highlight the investment type in the Type List box, and press Enter. You also can use the auto-completion feature to fill the `Type` field.

   Alternatively, if you want to define a new investment type, move the cursor to the `Type` field, press Ctrl-L, and select the **Set Up New Type** option from the Type List box. Quicken displays the Set Up

Security Type screen (see fig. 13.18). To define a new security type, describe the security type in the Type field and indicate whether you want the price calibrated in fractional or decimal units. You can have up to eight types. Only six security types fit in the Type List box at one time, so if you use more than six security types, use PgUp and PgDn to see the first and last parts of the type list. You can have up to 16 security types.

The Type field is optional and has no effect on record keeping, other than determining the form in which a security price is shown. The Type field enables you to enter another piece of information about your investment. Quicken provides several investment types that you may find valuable: Bond, CD, Mutual Funds, and Stock. However, you may have another piece of data that is more important to collect and store. If you are investing money based on the advice of several investment advisors, for example, you can keep track of which advisor suggested which security. Or, if you invest in several different industries, such as utilities, transportation, banking, and computers, you can keep track of the industry of individual issuers.

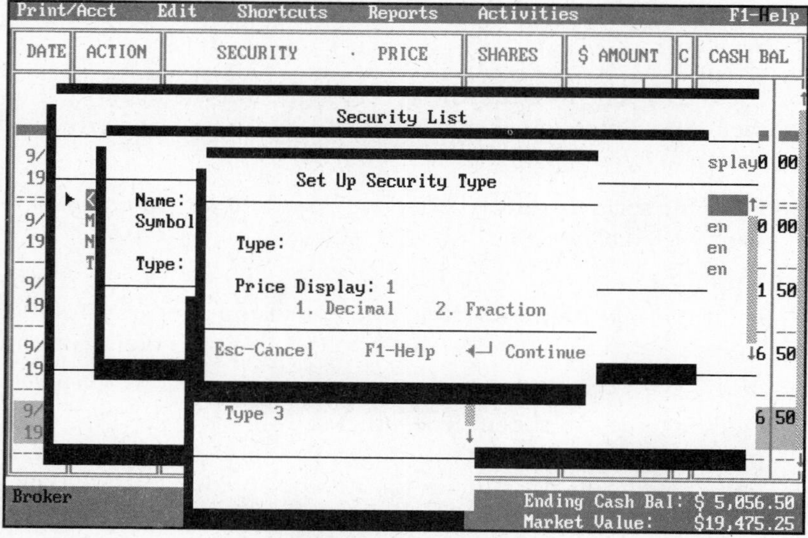

Fig. 13.18. The Set Up Security Type screen.

You also can edit and delete security types. To delete a security type, press Ctrl-D when the security you want to delete is highlighted in the Type List box. Quicken warns you that a security type is about to be deleted and alerts you if the type is in use. If you want to delete the security type, press Enter. Press Esc if you do not want to delete the security type.

To edit a security type, press Ctrl-E when the security you want to edit is highlighted in the Type List box. Quicken displays the Set Up Security Type screen (see fig. 13.18), which you use as described in the preceding paragraph to change the security type name or the price calibration.

6. To define the investment goal, move the cursor to the `Goal` field, press Ctrl-L, highlight the current investment type from the Goal List box, and press Enter. You also can use the auto-completion feature to fill the `Goal` field.

   To define a new investment goal, move the cursor to the `Goal` field, press Ctrl-L, and select the Set Up New Goal option. Quicken displays the Set Up Investment Goal screen (see fig. 13.19). To define a new investment goal, describe the goal in the `Goal` field. You can have up to eight goals. As is the case with the Type List box, only six goals fit on the Goal List screen at one time. Use the PgUp and PgDn keys to view the first and last parts of the goal list. You can have up to 16 investment goals.

   The `Goal` field is optional and has no effect on the way that you track or monitor a particular investment. Like the `Type` field, the Goal field enables you to record another piece of information about your investment. Quicken provides several investment goals that you may find valuable. However, you may have another piece of information that is more important to collect and store. Rather than using the `Goal` field to describe the investment, for example, you can use the `Goal` field to categorize how you want to spend the money you make on the investment. In that case, you can choose other goals, such as Retirement, Vacation, Emergency, and so on.

   You also can edit and delete investment goals. To delete an investment goal, press Ctrl-D when the goal you want to delete is highlighted on the Goal List screen. Quicken warns you that a goal is about to be deleted and alerts you if the goal is in use.

   To edit a goal (to change the goal's name), press Ctrl-E when the goal is highlighted in the Goal List box. Quicken displays the Set Up Investment Goal screen, which you use to edit the name (see fig. 13.19). After you enter the goal, press Enter to return to the Set Up Security screen.

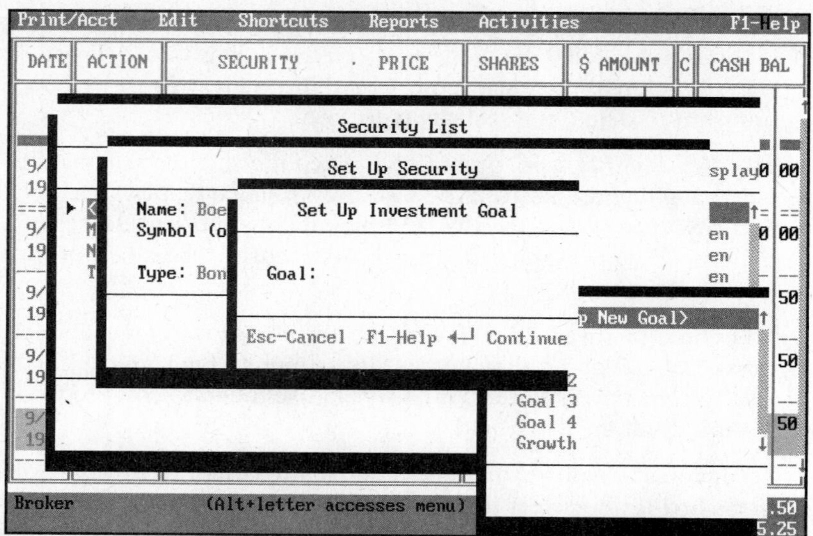

Fig. 13.19. *The Set Up Investment Goal screen.*

7. When the Set Up Security screen is complete, press Enter while the cursor is on the `Goal` field.

Even if you are a long-term investor, you eventually will decide to sell a certain stock or bond and never purchase that security again. Because there is no reason to clutter your securities list, Quicken enables you to delete securities in which you no longer invest.

To delete a security from the Securities List screen, follow these steps:

1. To display the Securities List screen, press Ctrl-Y.

2. Use the up- and down-arrow keys to mark the security you want to delete.

3. With the security you want to remove highlighted, press Ctrl-D. Quicken alerts you the security is about to be deleted permanently. Press Enter to delete the security or press Esc if you do not want to delete the security.

   When a security is in use, Quicken presents a message that the security is in use and cannot be deleted at this time.

As you know, Quicken stores four pieces of information about a security on the Securities List: name, symbol, type, and goal. Over time, one or more of these elements may change. When changes in the name, symbol, type, or goal occur, you can edit the security.

To edit a security on the securities list, follow these steps:

1. Press Ctrl-Y to display the Securities List screen.
2. Use the up- and down-arrow keys to mark the security you want to modify.
3. With the security you want to modify highlighted, press Ctrl-E. Quicken displays the Set Up Security screen. The process for editing a security mirrors the process of adding a new security. If you have questions about how to complete the Set Up Security screen, refer to the steps that describe how to add a new security.

To print a list of the securities on the securities list, follow these steps:

1. Press Ctrl-Y to display the Securities List screen.
2. Press Ctrl-P when the securities list is displayed. Quicken displays the Print Securities List screen, which is similar to the Print Register screen.
3. Complete the Print Securities List screen as you would the Print Register screen: Indicate which printer setting you want to use, and then press Enter.

You also can hide certain securities so that they do not appear on Quicken's investment reports. Suppose that you do not want your children (who print out reports of investments for their college education) to see your retirement savings balance. You can hide the investments that you do not want them to see.

To hide a security, follow these steps:

1. Press Ctrl-Y to display the Securities List screen.
2. Highlight the security you want to hide and press the space bar. Quicken changes the display setting to Never.

Follow the same process to "unhide" the security. The space bar acts as a toggle between three choices: **Open**, **Never**, and **Always**. **Always** causes a security to appear on the Update Prices screen even if you don't own the security. **Open** causes a security to appear as long as you own it. **Never** hides the security.

Updating Your Investment Records for Market Values

One of the most common investment record keeping activities is tracking the market value of your investments. Quicken provides several tools that enable you to update your investment records and determine the overall market value of your investments.

To record manually the market value of an investment, follow these steps:

1. Access the register that records the transactions for an investment. (The register may be a mutual fund account register or an investment and cash account register, depending on the investment.)

2. Press Alt-A to access the Activities menu. Figure 13.20 shows the investment register version of the Activities menu.

3. Select the **Update Prices** option or press Ctrl-U. Quicken displays the Update Prices and Market Value screen shown in figure 13.21.

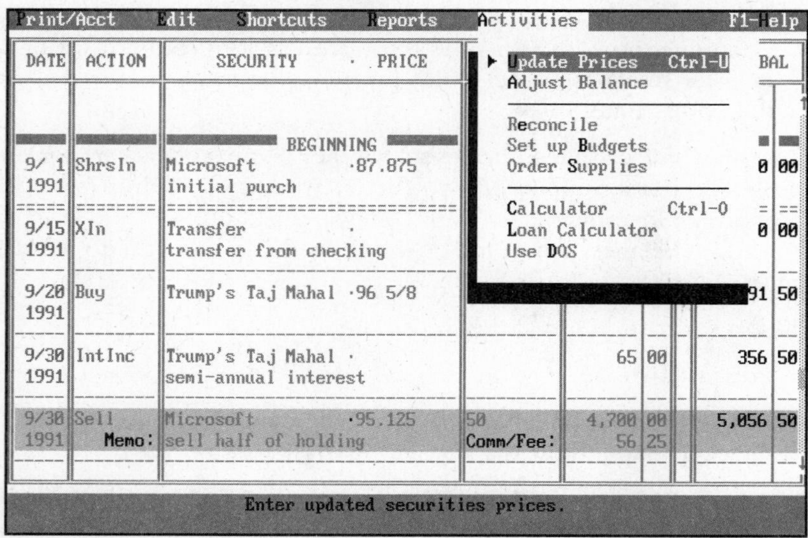

Fig. 13.20. The investment register version of the Activities menu.

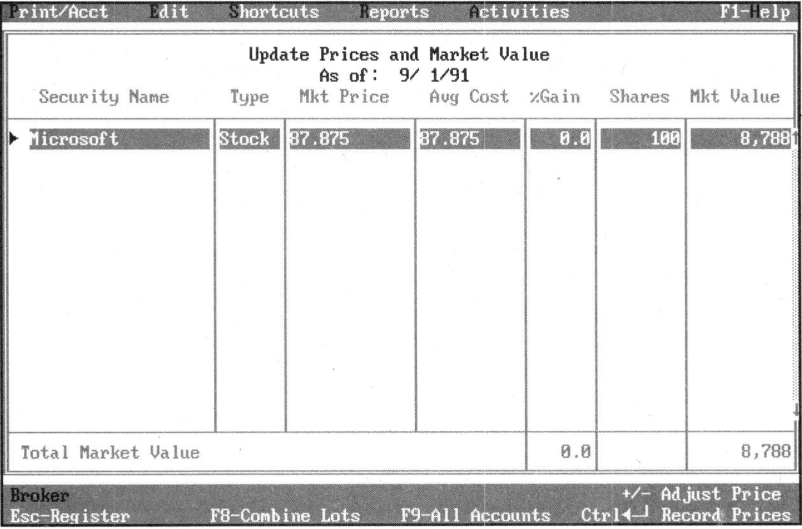

Fig. 13.21. *The Update Prices and Market Value screen.*

4. Use the up- and down-arrow keys to highlight the security whose price you want to update.

5. With the cursor positioned on the `Mkt Price` field, enter the current market price. You also can use the + and – keys to increase or decrease the price by 1/8 or .125.

6. Repeat steps 3 and 4 for each security on the screen. If you want to update investments in your other accounts, press F9 to display a complete list of your securities.

   After you record the change in the market price, Quicken asks you whether it is OK to record the new prices and whether the system date is appropriate. If so, press Enter. To change the date, use the + and – keys to change to the date of record. Otherwise, F9 acts as a toggle between the current investment register and all accounts.

   The Update Prices and Market Value screen shows several pieces of data with which you are familiar: the security name, the type, the market price, the number of shares, and the total market value. However, two additional fields appear: `Avg Cost` and `%Gain`. The `Avg Cost` field shows the average unit cost of all the shares or units of a particular security that you currently hold. The %Gain field shows the percentage difference between the total cost and the total market value of all the shares you currently hold. A negative percentage indicates a loss.

When you record security prices using the Update Prices and Market Values screen, you create a price history for each security. To see the price history for the currently selected security when you are on the Update Prices and Market Value screen, press Alt-S to access the Shortcuts menu. Quicken displays a special version of the menu (see fig. 13.22).

From this special version of the Shortcuts menu, select **Price History** or press Ctrl-H. Quicken displays the Price History screen shown in figure 13.23, which lists each of the price updates you entered for the security. The dates shown in the price history are the system dates on which you recorded new security prices.

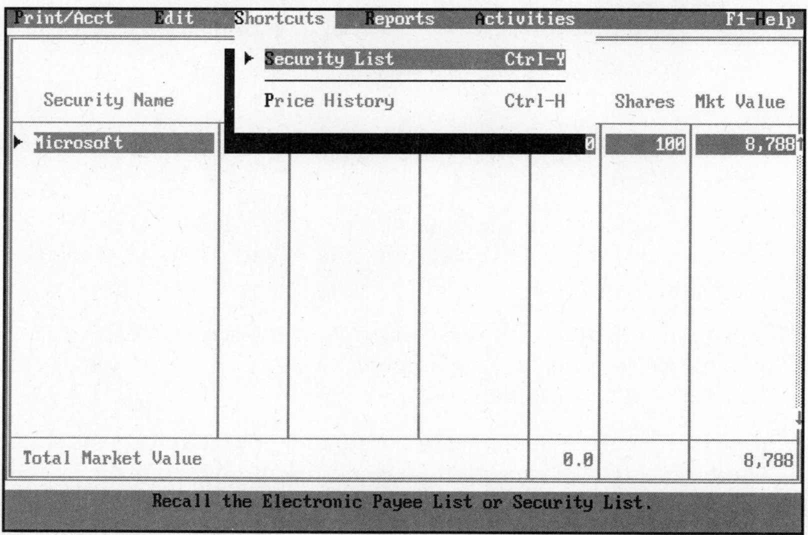

Fig. 13.22. *The Update Prices and Market Value screen's version of the Shortcuts menu.*

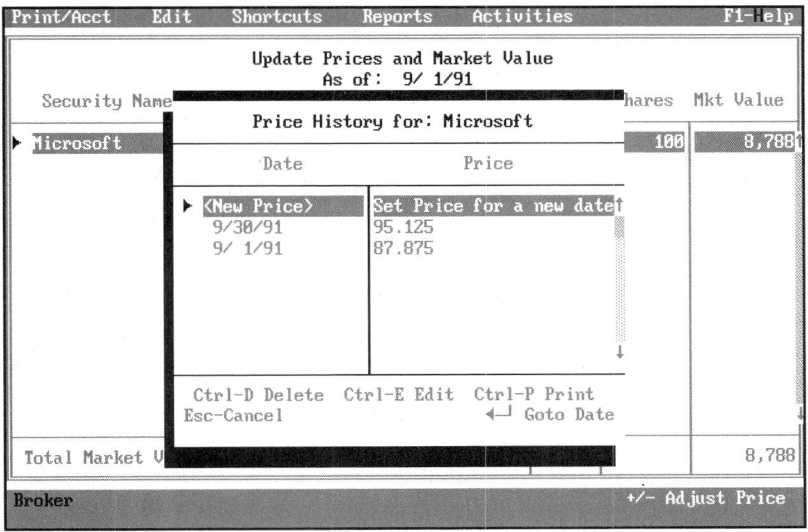

Fig. 13.23. *The Price History screen.*

You can request reports that show the market value of your investments on different dates. (Chapter 14 discusses Quicken's reports in detail.) Quicken uses the security prices from the price history to prepare these reports. If you want to see market values as of June 1, for example, Quicken uses the securities prices from the price history that are on or before June 1. For this reason, you may want to update security prices regularly. However, with the Update Prices and Market Value screen, you add a price to the price history for the current date.

To add to the price history a price for some date other than the current system date, select the **New Price** item from the Price History screen. Quicken displays the New Price screen shown in figure 13.24, with the date filled in as the current system date. Enter the correct date and price. To record the date and price combination, press Enter.

You likewise may edit or delete a price from the price history of a particular investment. Use Quicken's standard key combinations: Ctrl-D to delete and Ctrl-E to edit. The changes you make will be reflected on the Update Prices and Market Value screen after you complete the entry of new or updated information.

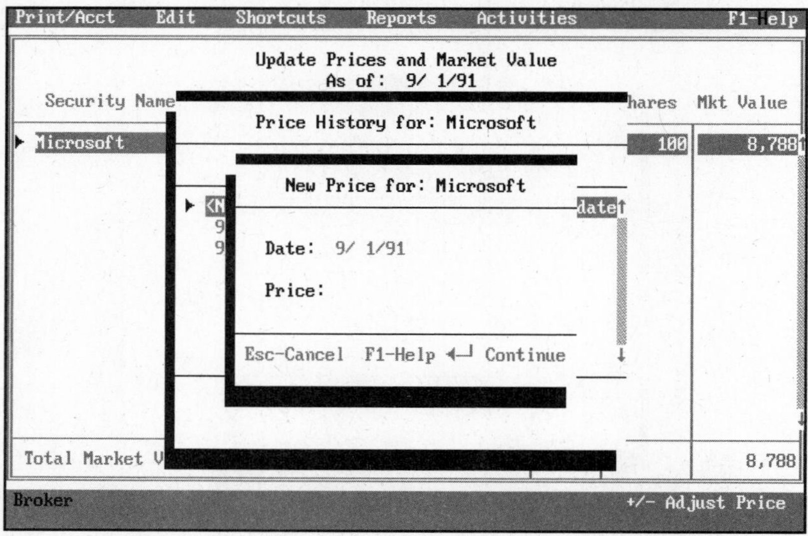

Fig. 13.24. The New Price screen.

You also can import price history data from an ASCII text file. The steps for doing so aren't difficult, as long as the ASCII text file looks the way Quicken expects it to. The file needs to contain at least two pieces of information: the security symbol and the price in decimal form. You also can (optionally) include a third piece of information—the date. The three pieces of information that make up a price must be together on a single line, must be separated by commas, and must not contain any embedded spaces. Quicken can import the data even if one or more of the elements are enclosed in quotation marks. If the price history does not include a date, Quicken uses a default date that you specify as part of the import operation. All of the following, for example, can be imported as price history data:

MSFT,87.125,6/30/91
MSFT,87.125
"MSFT",87.125,"6/30/91"
"MSFT","87.125","6/30/91"

To import price history data, access the Update Prices and Market Values screen and follow these steps:

1. Press Alt-P to display the Update Prices and Market Values version of the Print/Acct menu (see fig. 13.25).

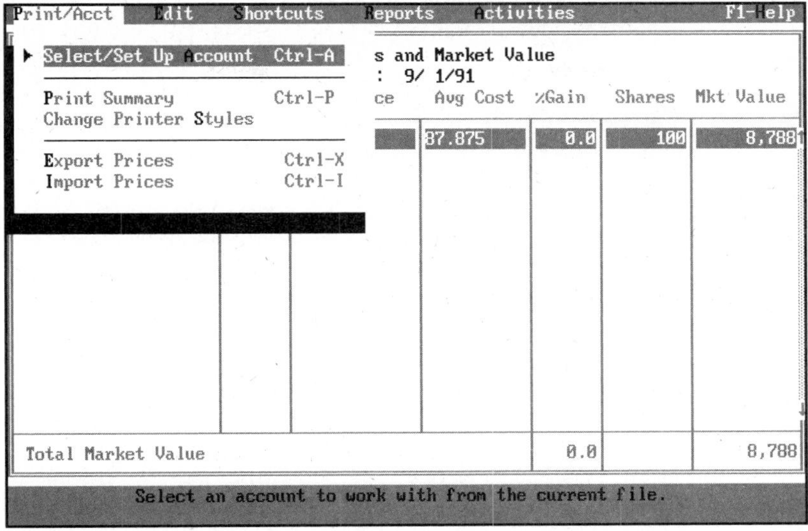

Fig. 13.25. The Update Prices and Market Value screen's version of the Print/Acct menu.

2. Select the **Import Prices** option or press Ctrl-I. Quicken displays the Import Price Data screen (see fig. 13.26).

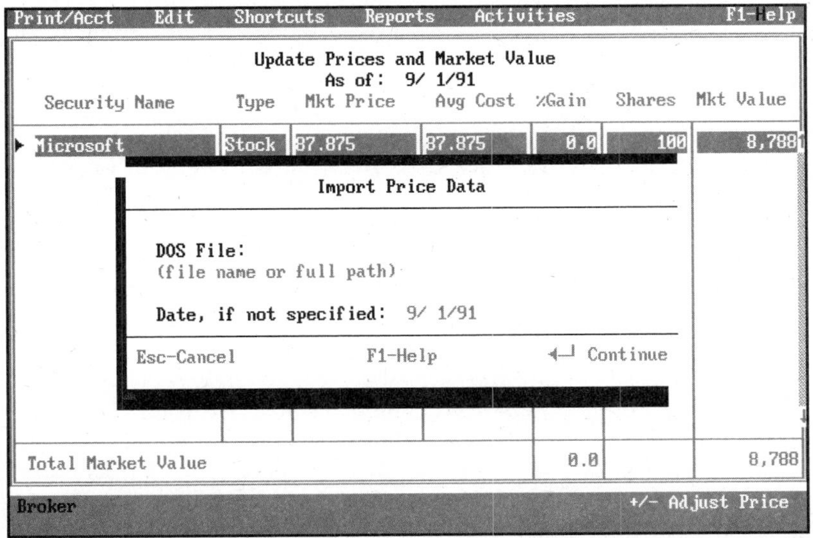

Fig. 13.26. The Import Price Data screen.

3. Enter the file name and extension of the ASCII text file that contains the price history information you want to import. If the ASCII file is not in the current directory, also specify the drive and directory where the ASCII file can be found.

4. Enter the date that should be used as the default price date in case a date is not specified in the ASCII text file.

5. When the Import Price Data screen is complete, press Enter. Quicken imports the price history data contained in the ASCII text file and updates the appropriate security price histories.

Reconciling Your Investment Accounts

Quicken enables you to reconcile mutual fund and investment and cash accounts. For the most part, the steps for reconciling these account types parallel the steps for reconciling other Quicken accounts. There are, however, a few minor differences.

In a mutual fund account, you reconcile the shares in the account—not the dollars. The basic process of reconciling a mutual fund account closely resembles the process described in Chapter 8 for reconciling bank accounts.

To reconcile a mutual fund account, follow these steps:

1. Press Alt-A to access the Activities menu on the investment register and select the **Reconcile** option. The Reconcile Mutual Fund Account screen appears (see fig. 13.27).

2. Enter the starting and ending shares balance from your mutual fund statement.

3. Mark the transactions that appear on the mutual fund statement in your register, using an abbreviated transaction list (see fig. 13.28).

   You can mark transactions individually by using the space bar to toggle the * character in the C field. Alternatively, press F8, and Quicken asks you to indicate cleared transactions between two dates. Pressing F9 toggles you between the **Reconcile** option and the investment register that you are reconciling. Quicken records a balance adjustment in the investment register to balance the account.

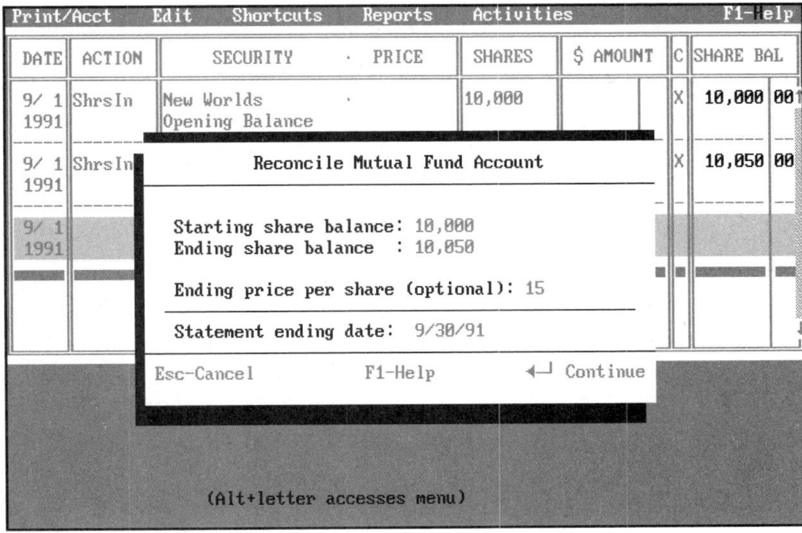

Fig. 13.27. The Reconcile Mutual Fund Account screen.

```
Print/Acct   Edit   Shortcuts   Reports   Activities                F1-Help
DATE  ACTION   SECURITY              · PRICE  SHARES   $ AMOUNT  C SHARE BAL
9/ 1  ShrsIn   New Worlds            ·        10,000             X  10,000 00
1991           Opening Balance
9/ 1  ShrsIn   New Worlds            ·        50                    10,050 00
1991     Memo: Balance Adjustment
9/ 1
1991  ________ ____________ END ___________________________________________

                        RECONCILIATION SUMMARY
   Items You Have Marked Cleared (*)
  ----------------------------------------  Cleared (X,*) Balance     10,000
   0    Decreases                  0        Statement Balance         10,050
   0    Increases                  0          Difference                 -50
Esc-Main Menu      F8-Mark Range       F9-View as List         Ctrl F10-Done
```

Fig. 13.28. The mutual fund account transaction list screen.

4. When the difference equals zero, press Ctrl-F10.

As with the process of reconciling bank accounts, the basic idea is that the difference in shares between your records and the mutual fund's record should stem only from transactions that (for reasons of timing) have not yet appeared on the mutual fund statement.

In an investment and cash account, you reconcile the cash balance. Predictably, this process parallels that for reconciling a bank account. (The cash balance in an investment and cash account also may be a bank account.) To reconcile the cash balance, enter the beginning and ending statement balances on the Reconcile Investment Account screen (see fig. 13.29). Just as for a bank account, mark the transactions that have cleared the cash account, using an abbreviated transaction list (see fig. 13.30). Use the space bar to toggle, and mark transactions that have cleared with an *.

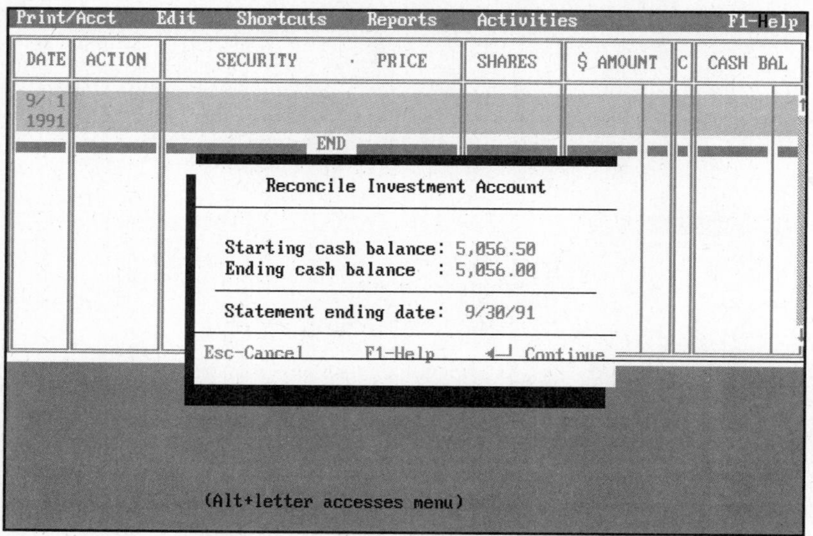

Fig. 13.29. *The Reconcile Investment Account screen.*

If you want to reconcile an account but have questions about the mechanics of the reconciliation process, refer to Chapter 8. The basic principles described there also apply to investment accounts.

If you do not want to reconcile your account, you may want to use the **Adjust Balance** option that appears on the investment register version of the Activities menu. If the investment is an investment and cash account, Quicken displays the Adjust Balance menu (see fig. 13.31), which lists options for adjusting the cash balance or the share balance. Select the balance you want to adjust. Figure 13.32 shows the Adjust Cash Balance screen.

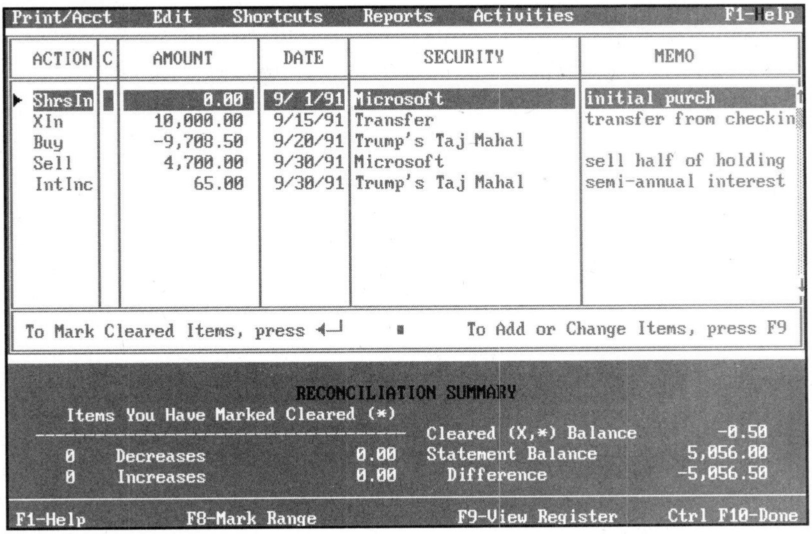

Fig. 13.30. The investment and cash account transaction list screen.

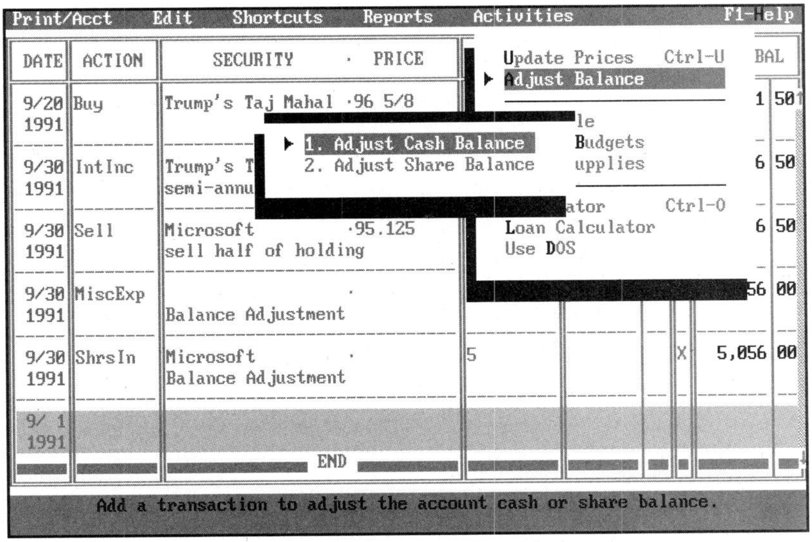

Fig. 13.31. The Adjust Balance menu.

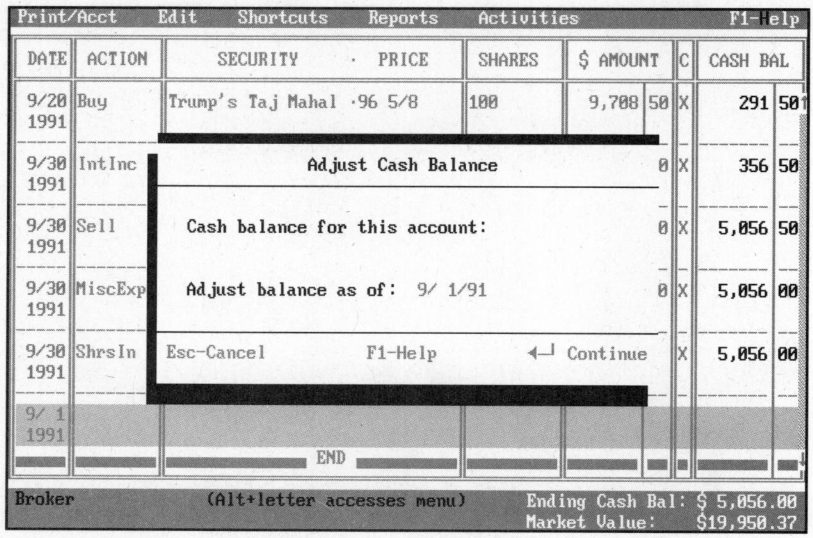

***Fig. 13.32.** The Adjust Cash Balance screen.*

To update the cash balance in the account, follow these steps:

1. Enter the current cash account balance.
2. Move the cursor to the `as of date` field and enter the date for which the cash adjustment transaction should be recorded.
3. When the Adjust Cash Balance screen is complete, press Enter to update the cash balance.

Figure 13.33 shows the Adjust Share Balance screen. To update the share balance for a specific security, follow these steps:

1. Enter the current share balance for a particular security.
2. Move the cursor to the `Security` field and enter the name of the security whose share balance needs to be corrected. You can use the auto-completion feature here. You also can press Ctrl-Y to see the security list.
3. Move the cursor to the `as of date` field and enter the date for which the share adjustment transaction should be recorded.
4. When the Adjust Share Balance screen is complete, press Enter to update the share balance.

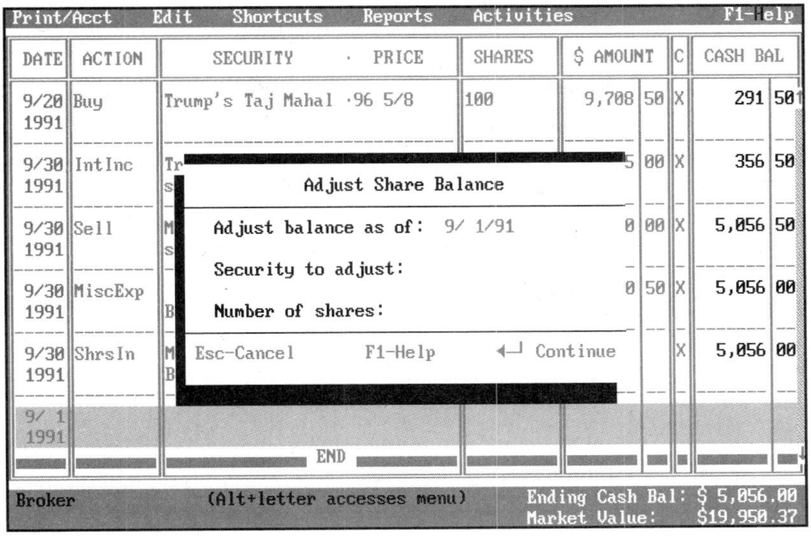

Fig. 13.33. The Adjust Share Balance screen.

If the investment is a mutual fund account, Quicken does not display the Adjust Balance menu. Quicken displays the mutual fund version of the Adjust Share Balance screen (see fig. 13.34).

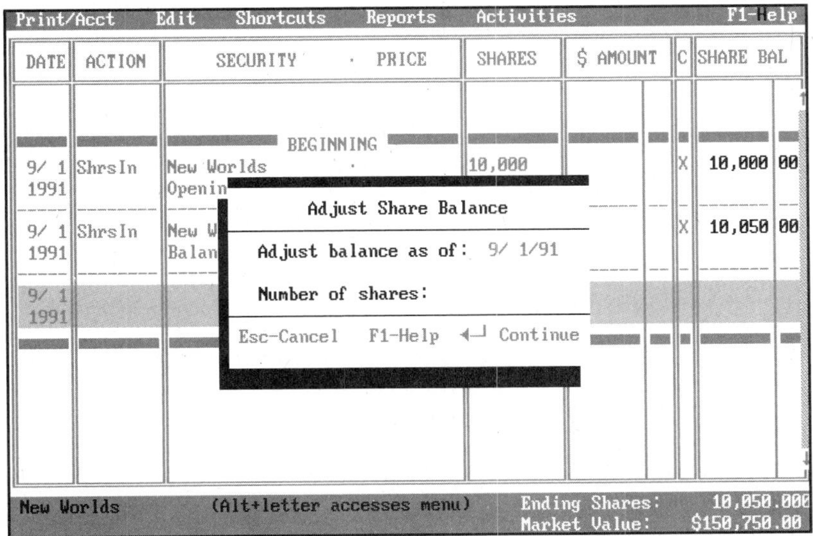

Fig. 13.34. The mutual fund version of the Adjust Share Balance screen.

Mutual funds sometimes reinvest the interest on dividend income. Accordingly, with each interest or dividend payment, you may need to update or adjust the share balance.

To update the share balance for a specific security, follow these steps:

1. Enter the current share balance of the mutual fund.
2. Move the cursor to the `as of date` field and enter the date for which the share adjustment transaction should be recorded.
3. When the Adjust Share Balance screen is complete, press Enter to update the share balance.

Although the **Adjust Balance** option enables you to forgo the work of reconciling an account, **Adjust Balance** has disadvantages. As Chapter 8 points out, the purposes of reconciling include catching errors, recording forgotten transactions, and discovering fraudulent transactions. By not reconciling an account, you miss out on significant benefits.

Tips on Investments and Investment Record Keeping

Earlier sections of this book explained the procedural details of using Quicken; this section covers three additional tips.

First, you should know that Quicken applies the *first-in, first-out* (often called *Fifo*) method of record keeping. This means that when you sell shares of Apple Computer, for example, Quicken assumes that the shares you sell are the first shares that you bought.

The Fifo assumption conforms with Internal Revenue Service regulations. The problem with Fifo is that often the first shares you bought were the least expensive. This means that when you calculate the actual taxable gain by subtracting the original purchase price from the sales price, you end up calculating the largest possible gain and, as a result, the highest income taxes.

You can use another method, called *specific identification*, to record the sales and purchases of investments. Specific identification requires that you record all purchases of a particular stock as different investments, or lots. When you sell shares of Apple Computer, for example, you actually sell the shares from a specific lot. The obvious tax-saving opportunity results from picking the lot with the highest purchase price, because doing so minimizes your gain or maximizes your loss. (See your tax advisor for specific details.)

To keep your tax planning options open, set up each lot as a separate security.

Second, if you record meticulously the transactions that affect an investment, you can use one of Quicken's investment reports (the performance report) to measure the actual rate of return an investment produces. Although most individual investors are not accustomed to measuring the performance of their investments, you will find doing so an invaluable exercise. Too often, individual investors do not get to measure the performance of stocks a broker recommends, of a mutual fund an advertisement touts, or the bonds a financial planner suggests. But with the Quicken performance report, which is described in the next chapter, you have a convenient way to calculate precisely how well or how poorly an investment has performed. Investment performance information can help you make better investment decisions.

Finally, there is more to investing than just record keeping. Despite the fact that Quicken provides an excellent record-keeping tool, understanding how the tool works is not the same as understanding investments. To better understand investments, read *A Random Walk Down Wall Street*, by Burton G. Malkiel, a Princeton economics professor. You should be able to find the most recent edition (1990) in any good bookstore.

Chapter Summary

This chapter described how to monitor your investments using Quicken's new investment versions of the register. The chapter listed the steps for tracking mutual funds with Quicken and the steps for tracking other investments, such as stocks, bonds, and certificates of deposit. The next chapter describes Quicken's investment report capabilities.

14

Tapping the Power of Quicken's Reports

When you collect information about your financial affairs in a Quicken register, you essentially construct a database. With a database, you can arrange, retrieve, and summarize the information that database contains. With a financial database, you can determine your cash flows, profits, tax deductions, and net worth. You do need a way to arrange, retrieve, and summarize the data, however, and within Quicken, this need is met with the Reports menu.

This chapter describes the eight options available on the Reports menu, accessed by selecting **Reports** from the Main Menu or from the Activities menu on the Write Checks and Register screens. Figure 14.1 shows the Reports menu.

The first three options on the Reports menu display menus of additional choices. Figure 14.2 shows the Personal Reports menu. Figure 14.3 shows the Business Reports menu. Figure 14.4 shows the Investment Reports menu.

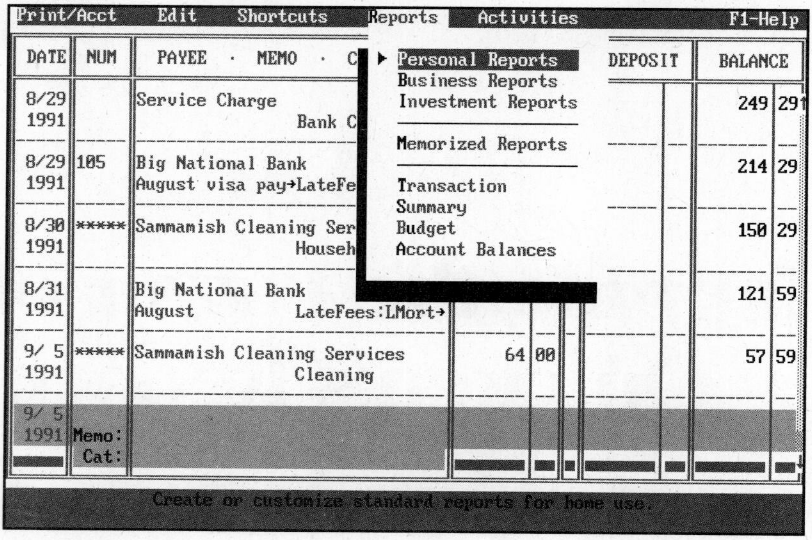

Fig. 14.1. The Reports menu.

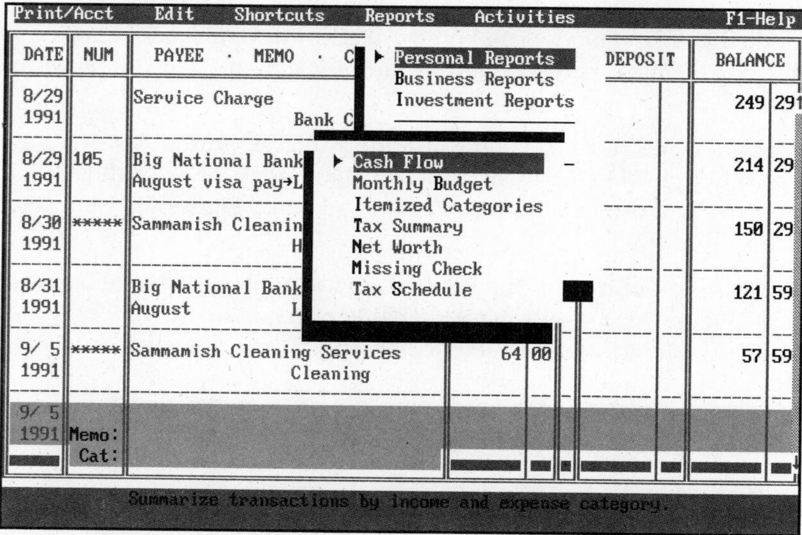

Fig. 14.2. The Personal Reports menu.

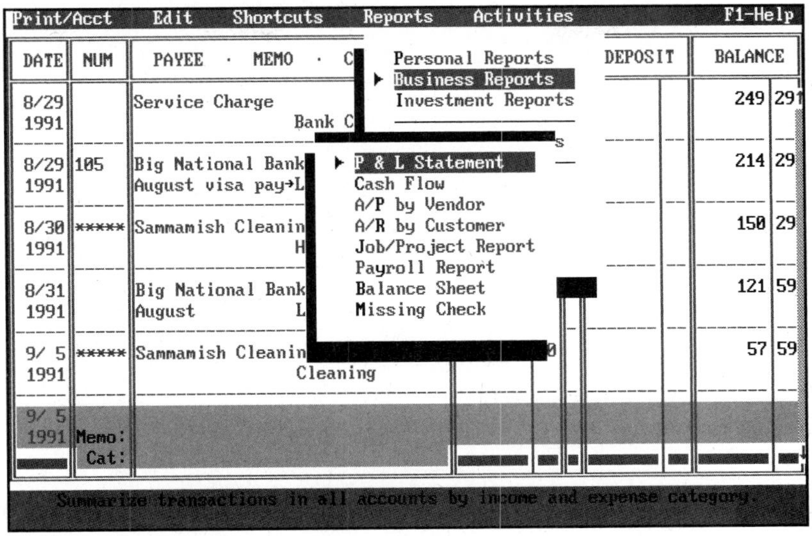

Fig. 14.3. The Business Reports menu.

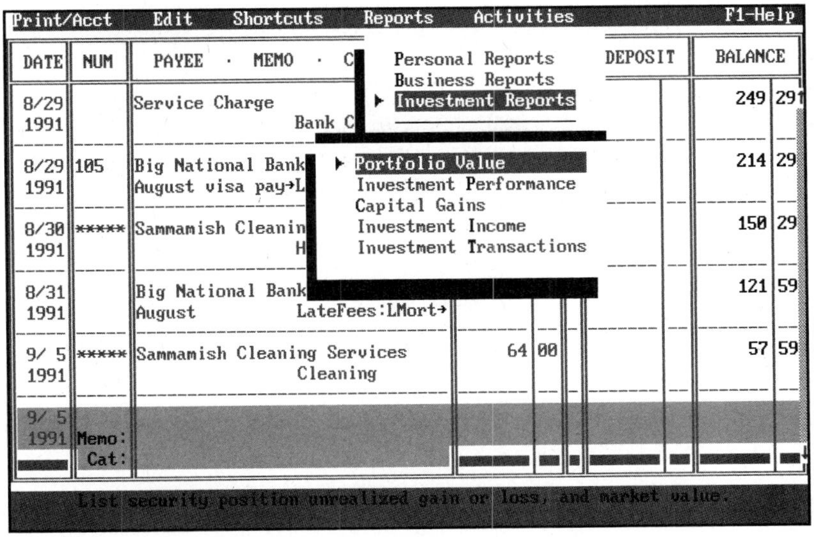

Fig. 14.4. The Investment Reports menu.

The fourth option, **Memorized Reports**, enables you to use report descriptions you have created. The final four options on the Reports menu enable you to create custom reports as discussed later in this chapter.

Reviewing Printing Basics

No matter which Quicken report you want to print, you need to take the same basic steps. To print any report, you complete the following steps:

1. Select the menu option for the report you want to print. If, for example, you want to print a personal cash flow report, select the **Personal Reports** option from the Reports menu, and then select the **Cash Flow** option from the Personal Reports menu.

   Quicken displays the screen you use to create the report. The Cash Flow Report screen is shown in figure 14.5, but this screen closely resembles the screens you use for several of the reports. (The rest of this chapter describes how you complete the individual create report screens.)

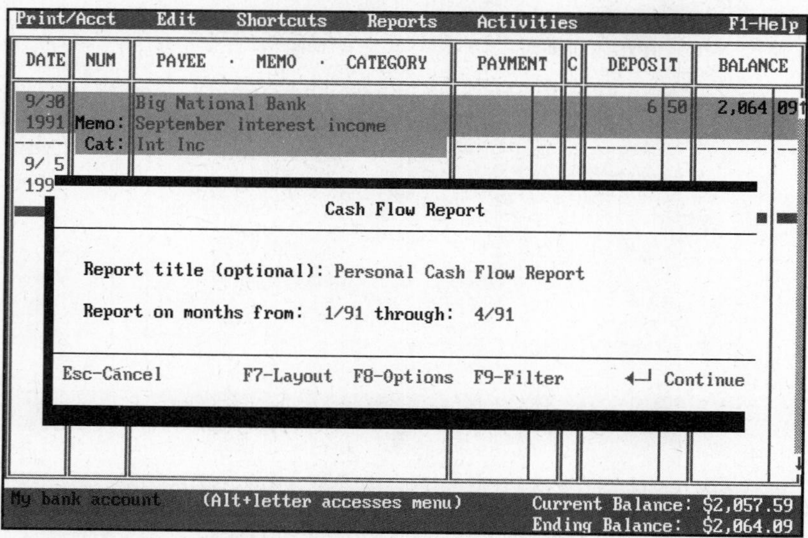

Fig. 14.5. The Cash Flow Report screen.

2. (Optional) Enter a report title.

   If you don't enter a report title, Quicken names the report using the menu option. The report produced by the **Cash Flow** option, for example, is named `Cash Flow Report`. The report produced by the **Monthly Budget** option is named `Monthly Budget Report`.

3. (Optional) Press Enter or Tab to move the cursor to the `Report on months from` and `through` fields. Set up the time frame the report should cover by entering the starting month and year and the ending month and year you want included in the report. If you don't enter these dates, the report covers January of the current year through the current date. (Remember that you can use the special date editing keys described in Chapter 2.)

4. Press Enter when the cursor is on the `Report on months through` field. You also can press F10 or Ctrl-Enter when the cursor is on any of the other fields. Quicken generates and displays the report on-screen.

   You can use the cursor-movement keys to see different portions of the report. You also can use the Home and End keys to see the first and last pages of the report.

5. When you are ready to print the report, press Ctrl-P. Quicken displays the Print Report screen shown in figure 14.6. This screen enables you to specify where you want the report printed to.

6. In the `Print to` field, press 1 for printer 1, 2 for printer 2, and so on.

If you select 4 in the `Print to` field, Quicken prints an ASCII file. *ASCII files* are standardized text files that you can use to import a Quicken report into a word processing program, such as WordPerfect or Microsoft Word. Before creating the ASCII file, Quicken uses the Print To Disk screen to request three pieces of information (see fig. 14.7). Complete the following steps:

1. (Optional) In the `File` field, enter a name for Quicken to use for the ASCII file. To use a data directory other than the Quicken data directory, QUICKEN5, you can specify a path name. (See your DOS user's manual for information on path names.)

2. (Optional) In the `Lines per page` field, set the number of report lines between page breaks. If you are using 11-inch paper, the page length usually is 66 lines.

3. (Optional) In the `Width` field, set the number of characters (including blanks) that Quicken prints on a line. If you are using 8 1/2-inch paper, the characters per line usually is 80. Figure 14.7 shows the completed Print To Disk screen with the file name `printer.txt`.

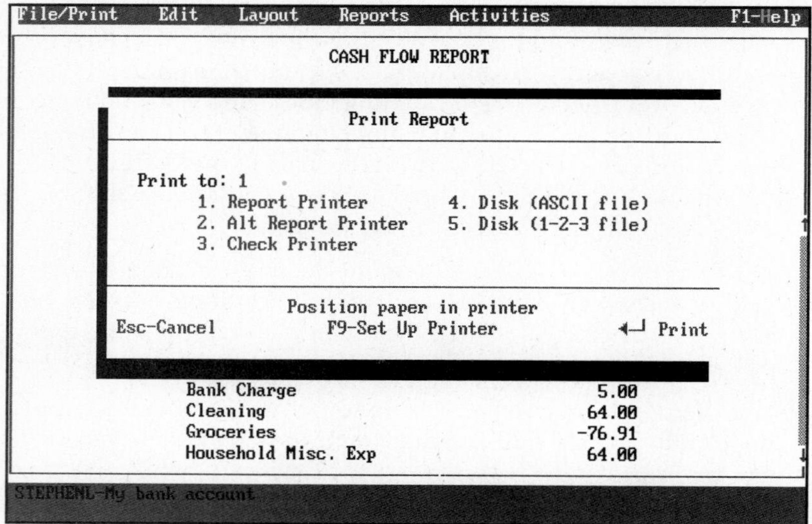

Fig. 14.6. The Print Report screen.

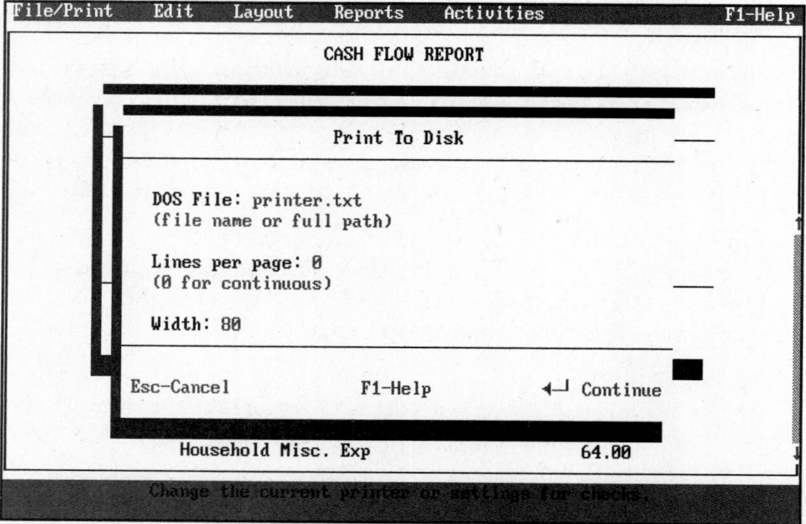

Fig. 14.7. The completed Print To Disk screen.

If you select 5 at the `Print to` field on the Print Report screen, Quicken displays the Print to Lotus File screen (see fig. 14.8). (1-2-3 is a popular spreadsheet program manufactured by Lotus Development Corporation.) You need to complete one more step.

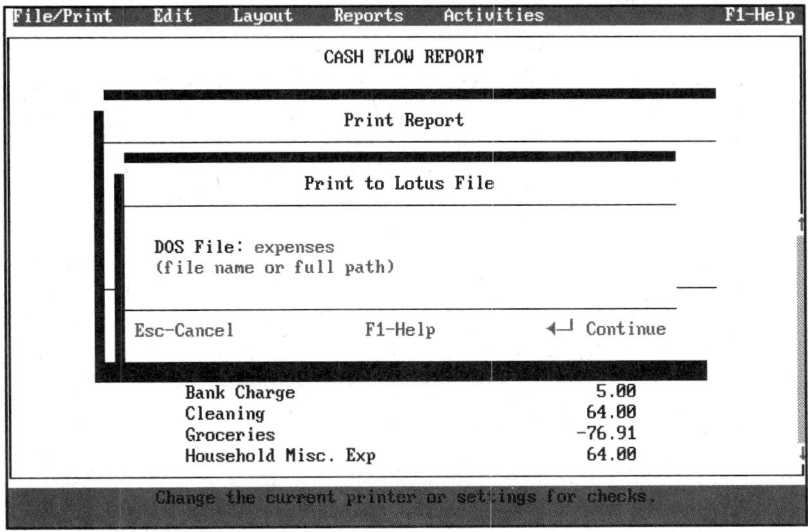

Fig. 14.8. *The Print to Lotus File screen.*

To create a 1-2-3 file, Quicken requests the name of the file you want to create using the Print to Lotus File screen. As with the ASCII file creation option, if you want to use a data directory other than QUICKEN5, you also can specify a path name. Figure 14.8 shows the completed Print to Lotus File screen with the file specified as `expenses`. (You don't have to worry about the correct file extension. Quicken adds the extension for you.)

Tracking Personal Finances with Personal Reports

On the Personal Reports menu, you have seven choices. To create any of the five reports, you need to complete the screen that appears when you select a report from the Personal Reports menu.

Cash Flow

Figure 14.5 shows the Cash Flow Report screen completed so that the report title is `Personal Cash Flow Report` and the report includes transactions between 1/91 and 4/91.

Figure 14.9 shows an example of a personal cash flow report. The cash flow report shows the total money you have received and expended by category. The report also shows transfers. The last two lines of the outflows section of the report show transfers to two investment accounts: Discnt Brkge and New Frontiers. The report includes transactions from all the bank, cash, and credit card accounts in the current account group.

```
                          Personal Cash Flow Report
                          1/ 1/91 Through 4/30/91
Bank,Cash,CC Accounts                                                  Page 1
4/ 2/91
                                                 1/ 1/91-
             Category Description                4/30/91
           ----------------------------- ---------------------
           INFLOWS
             Interest Income                               10.75
             Salary Income                              2,000.00
                                                     -----------
           TOTAL INFLOWS                                2,010.75

           OUTFLOWS
             Automobile Service                            34.91
             Bank Charge                                    5.00
             Entertainment                                 28.94
             Home Repair & Maint.                          24.53
             Housing                                        0.00
             Late fees:
               Late payment fees-credit        11.59
               Late payment fees-mortg.        28.73
                                         -----------
             Total Late fees                               40.32
             Office Expenses                               34.56
             Water, Gas, Electric                          75.39
             Outflows - Other                          16,082.88
             TO Discnt Brkge                           24,708.50
             TO New Frontiers                           1,200.00
                                                     -----------
           TOTAL OUTFLOWS                              42,235.03

                                                     -----------
           OVERALL TOTAL                              -40,224.28
                                                     ===========
```

Fig. 14.9. *The personal cash flow report.*

The cash report can be extremely valuable. The cash report shows the various categories of cash flowing into and out of your personal banking accounts. If you question why you seem to have a bigger bank balance than usual or you always seem to run out of money before the end of the month, for example, this report provides the answers.

Monthly Budget Report

The monthly budget report shows the total money you have received and expended by category and the amounts you budgeted to spend. The report also calculates the difference between what you budgeted and what you actually spent. This report includes transactions from all the bank, cash, and credit card accounts within the account group. Figure 14.10 shows the Monthly Budget Report screen.

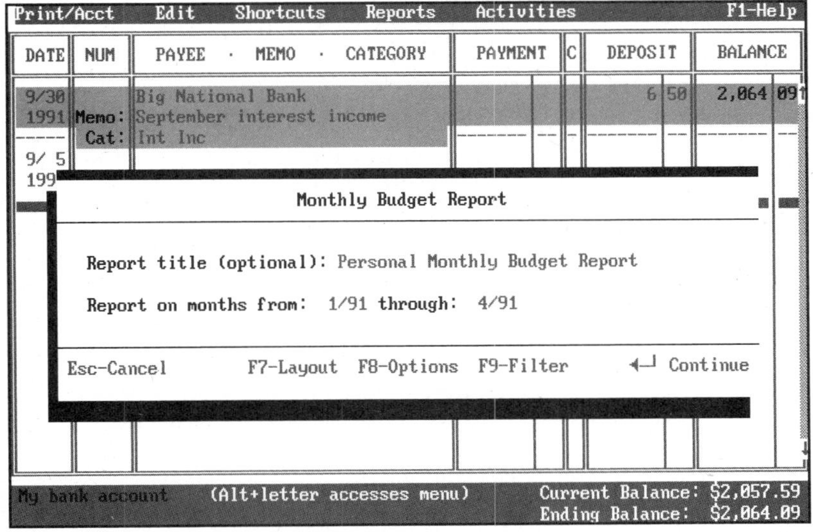

***Fig. 14.10.** The Monthly Budget Report screen.*

To produce a monthly budget report, you need to have first set up your budget. Refer to Chapter 16, "Using Quicken To Budget," if you need information on this.

Itemized Category Report

The itemized category report shows each transaction in an account group sorted and subtotaled by category. This type of report provides a convenient way to see the detailed transactions that add up to a category total. The Itemized Category Report screen, shown in figure 14.11, works like the other report request screens.

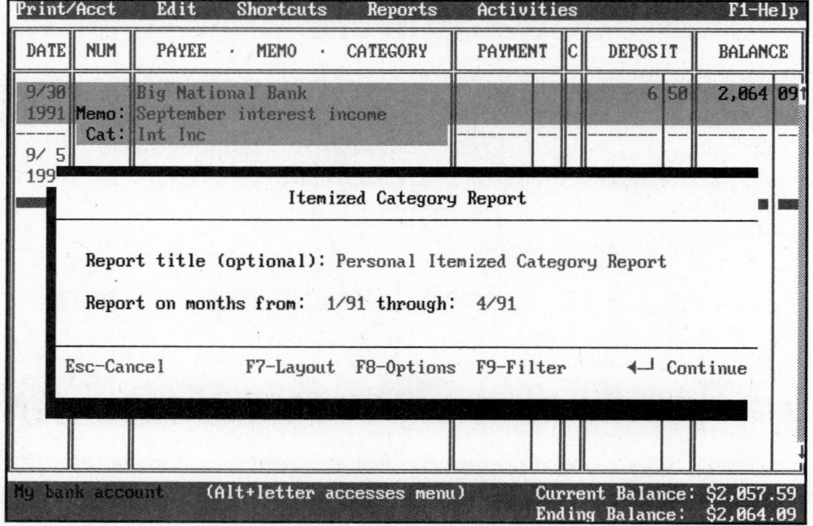

Fig. 14.11. *The Itemized Category Report screen.*

You can replace the default report title, Itemized Category Report, with a more specific title, such as *Personal Itemized Category Report*, by using the optional `Report title` field. You also can specify a range of months to be included on the report. Figure 14.12 shows a page of a sample of the itemized category report. (The defaults have been changed in this figure to customize the report titles.)

The itemized category resembles the cash-flow report in purpose and information, except that the itemized category does not include account transfers. If you want to see your cash inflows and outflows grouped and summarized by category, this is the report you want.

Tax Summary Report

The tax summary report shows all the transactions assigned to categories you marked as tax-related. Transactions are sorted and subtotaled by category. The Tax Summary Report screen, shown in figure 14.13, works like the other request screens, enabling you to give the tax summary report a more specific title or to include only transactions from specified months. Figure 14.14 shows a page from a sample tax summary report.

```
                          Personal Itemized Category Report
                              1/ 1/91 Through 4/30/91
All Accounts
4/ 2/91

Date   Acct     Num    Description       Memo        Category      Clr  Amount
----- -------- ------ ---------------- ----------- -------------- - ----------
                                                                     ----------
        Total Entertainment                                              -28.94

        Home Repair & Maint.
        --------------------
1/ 9 Big Nati      S Big National Ban               Home Rpair            -24.53
                                                                     ----------
        Total Home Repair & Maint.                                        -24.53

        Housing
        -------
1/15 Big Nati      VOID Puget Sound January         Housing        X        0.00
                                                                     ----------
        Total Housing                                                       0.00

        Late fees:
        ----------

          Late payment fees-credit
          ------------------------
1/ 9 Big Nati      S Big National Ban               Latefees:LCred        -11.59
                                                                     ----------
          Total Late payment fees-credit                                  -11.59

          Late payment fees-mortg.
          ------------------------
1/ 9 Big Nati      S Big National Ban               Latefees:LMort        -28.73
                                                                     ----------
          Total Late payment fees-mortg.                                  -28.73
                                                                     ----------
        Total Late fees                                                   -40.32

        Office Expenses
        ---------------
1/ 3 Big Nati 767    Sammamish Cleani               Office         X      -34.56
                                                                     ----------
        Total Office Expenses                                             -34.56

        Water, Gas, Electric
        --------------------
1/ 2 Big Nati 765    Seattle Power Co December      Utilities      X      -75.39
                                                                     ----------
        Total Water, Gas, Electric                                        -75.39

        Expenses - Other
        ----------------
1/ 3 Big Nati 766    National Motors car payment                   X     -200.08
1/23 Big Nati                        money for m                       -8,821.00
2/ 9 Big Nati                        employer co                       -1,200.00
3/ 1 Big Nati                        employer co                       -1,000.00
3/ 8 Big Nati                                                          -2,546.00
3/ 8 Big Nati                                                            -815.79
```

Fig. 14.12. A sample itemized category report.

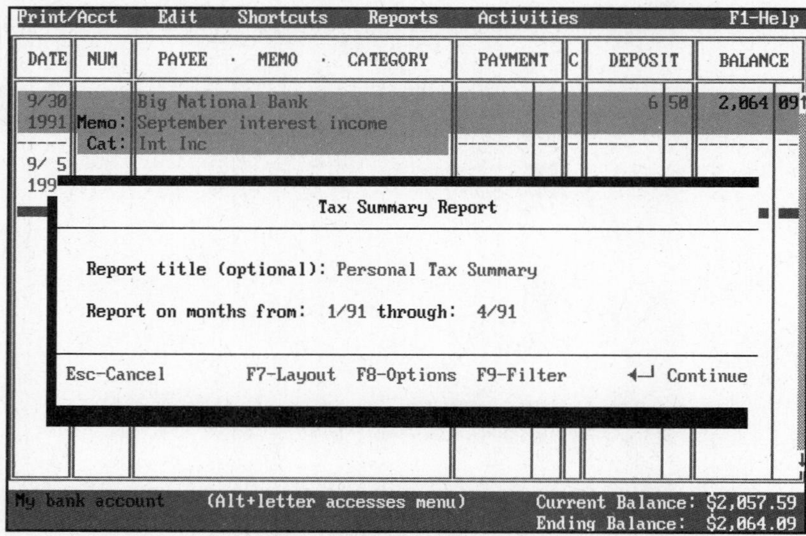

Fig. 14.13. *The Tax Summary Report screen.*

The tax summary report is a handy tax preparation tool to use at the end of the year. This report summarizes the tax deductions you need to report on your federal and state income tax returns. (The report, however, summarizes only tax deductions paid with those bank accounts and cash accounts you choose to track with Quicken. If you have two checking accounts, write tax-deductible checks using both accounts, and track only one of the accounts with Quicken, you are missing half of your deductions.)

Net Worth Reports

A net worth report shows the balance in each of the accounts in a file on a particular date. If the file includes all your assets and liabilities, the resulting report is a balance sheet and provides one estimate of your financial net worth. (Balance sheets are described in Chapter 12, "Tracking Your Net Worth, Other Assets, and Liabilities.") Figure 14.15 shows the Net Worth Report screen.

```
                         Personal Tax Summary Report
                           1/ 1/91 Through 4/30/91
All Accounts                                                              Pa
4/ 2/91

Date  Acct     Num    Description     Memo       Category       Clr Amount
----- -------- ------ --------------- ---------- -------------- - ---------

     Note: Investment transaction amounts represent changes in cash
           and the value of your investments.  See Chapter 20.

      INCOME/EXPENSE
        INCOME
          Interest Income
          ---------------
1/ 2 Big Nati          Interest        October    Int Inc        X      5.75
1/ 6 Big Nati          Interest Earned            Int Inc        X      4.50
1/ 6 Big Nati          Balance Adjustme           Int Inc        X      0.50
                                                                   ---------
          Total Interest Income                                        10.75

          Investment Interest Inc
          -----------------------
2/13 Discnt B IntInc Trump's T        semi annual _IntInc        X     65.00
                                                                   ---------
          Total Investment Interest Inc                                65.00

          Realized Gain/Loss
          ------------------
2/13 Discnt B SellX  50 Microsoft                 _RlzdGain      X    362.50
                                                                   ---------
          Total Realized Gain/Loss                                    362.50

          Salary Income
          -------------
1/24 Big Nati          Washington Manuf payroll che Salary          2,000.00
                                                                   ---------
          Total Salary Income                                       2,000.00
                                                                   ---------
        TOTAL INCOME                                                2,438.25


        EXPENSES
          Late fees:
          ----------

            Late payment fees-credit
            ------------------------
1/ 9 Big Nati       S Big National Ban            Latefees:LCredi     -11.59
                                                                   ---------
            Total Late payment fees-credit                            -11.59

            Late payment fees-mortg.
            ------------------------
1/ 9 Big Nati       S Big National Ban            Latefees:LMortg     -28.73
                                                                   ---------
            Total Late payment fees-mortg.                            -28.73
                                                                   ---------
```

Fig. 14.14. *A sample tax summary report.*

The Net Worth Report screen differs from other personal report screens because you cannot enter a range of dates; you can enter only one date. The net worth report does not report on activity for a period of time but provides a snapshot of certain aspects of your financial condition—the account balances in your file—at a point in time. Figure 14.16 shows a sample net worth report.

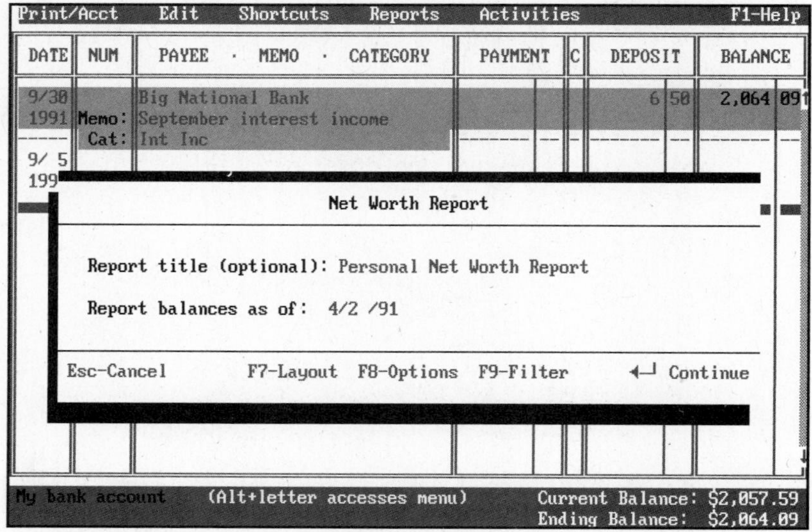

Fig. 14.15. The Net Worth Report screen.

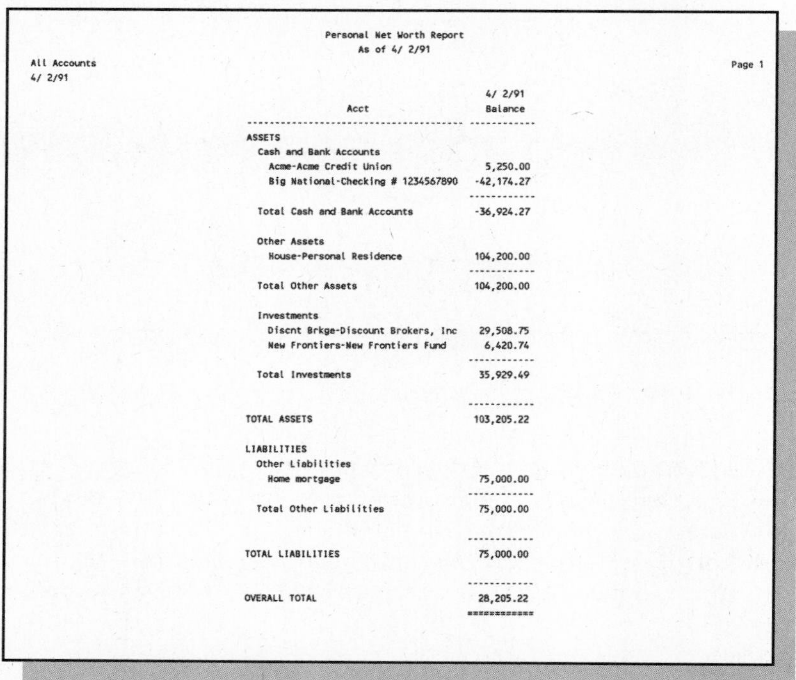

Personal Net Worth Report
As of 4/ 2/91

All Accounts
4/ 2/91 Page 1

Acct	4/ 2/91 Balance
ASSETS	
Cash and Bank Accounts	
Acme-Acme Credit Union	5,250.00
Big National-Checking # 1234567890	-42,174.27
Total Cash and Bank Accounts	-36,924.27
Other Assets	
House-Personal Residence	104,200.00
Total Other Assets	104,200.00
Investments	
Discnt Brkge-Discount Brokers, Inc	29,508.75
New Frontiers-New Frontiers Fund	6,420.74
Total Investments	35,929.49
TOTAL ASSETS	103,205.22
LIABILITIES	
Other Liabilities	
Home mortgage	75,000.00
Total Other Liabilities	75,000.00
TOTAL LIABILITIES	75,000.00
OVERALL TOTAL	28,205.22

Fig. 14.16. A sample net worth report.

Monitoring your financial worth probably is more important than most people realize. Over the years that you work, one of your financial goals may be to increase your net worth. During your retirement years, you probably will look to your net worth to provide income and security. Your net worth, for example, may include investments that produce regular interest or dividend income. Your net worth also may include your personal residence, completely paid for by the time you retire.

Missing Check Report

The Missing Check Report displays a list of all checking account transactions in check number order with any gaps in the check number sequence identified. To request a Missing Check report, you use the Missing Check Report screen shown in figure 14.17. The Missing Check Report screen works just like the other report screens. Figure 14.18 shows a sample Missing Check Report on the screen with a missing check—number 107—identified.

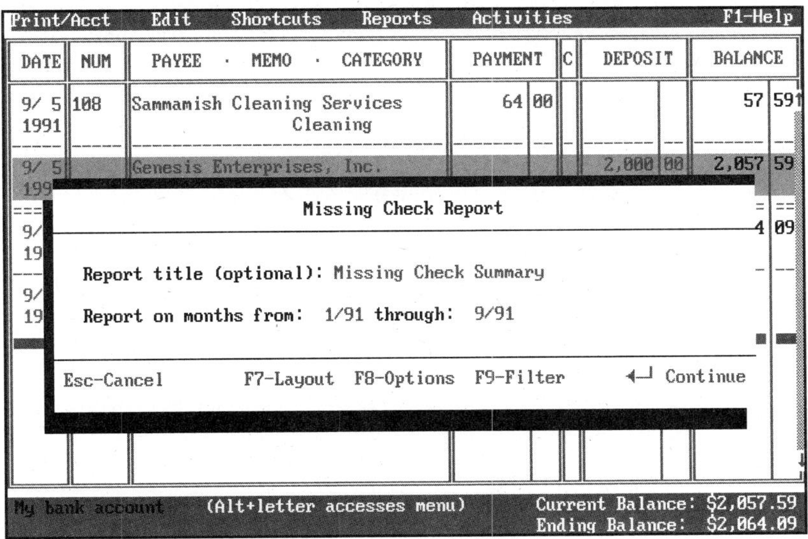

Fig. 14.17. The Missing Check Report screen.

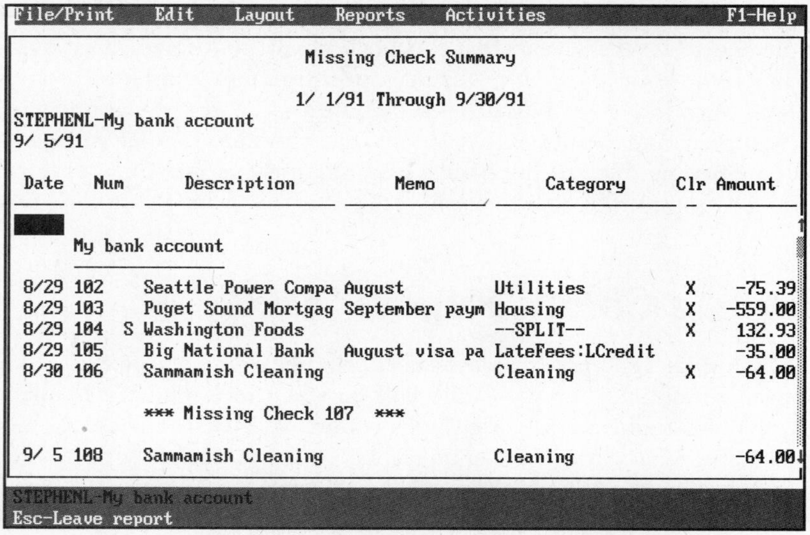

```
File/Print   Edit   Layout   Reports   Activities                    F1-Help
                          Missing Check Summary

                        1/ 1/91 Through 9/30/91
STEPHENL-My bank account
9/ 5/91

 Date  Num      Description          Memo            Category        Clr Amount


      My bank account

 8/29 102    Seattle Power Compa August         Utilities           X    -75.39
 8/29 103    Puget Sound Mortgag September paym Housing             X   -559.00
 8/29 104  S Washington Foods                   --SPLIT--           X    132.93
 8/29 105    Big National Bank   August visa pa LateFees:LCredit         -35.00
 8/30 106    Sammamish Cleaning                 Cleaning            X    -64.00

             *** Missing Check 107  ***

 9/ 5 108    Sammamish Cleaning                 Cleaning                 -64.00
STEPHENL-My bank account
Esc-Leave report
```

Fig. 14.18. *The Missing Check Summary displayed on-screen.*

Tax Schedule Report

The Tax Schedule Report summarizes tax-related categories in a way that makes it easy to prepare every common income tax schedule. Using category information, it adds up the transactions that go onto each line of each tax schedule. To create a tax schedule report, you use the Tax Schedule Report screen shown in figure 14.19. The Tax Schedule Report screen works like the other report screens. Chapter 19, "Using Quicken To Prepare for Income Taxes," describes and illustrates this handy report.

Tracking Your Business Finances with Business Reports

The Business Reports menu, shown in figure 14.3, provides eight reports. To request any of the reports, complete the report request screen with an optional title and the period of time you want the report to cover. (The eighth report is a missing check report which mirrors the personal missing check report already described. Accordingly, it is not discussed here again.)

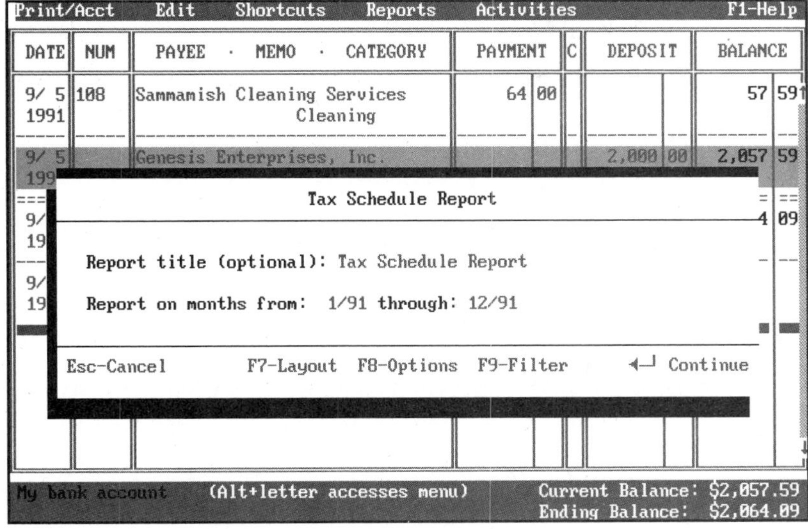

Fig. 14.19. The Tax Schedule Report screen.

Profit and Loss Statement

A profit and loss statement shows the total income and expense transactions by category for all accounts on a monthly basis. Transactions from any of the accounts in the account groups are included, but transfers between accounts are not. Figure 14.20 shows the Profit & Loss Statement screen. Like most of the report request screens, you have two options: to use your own report title or the default title and to specify the months to be included on the report or to use the default (from January of the current year to the current date). Figure 14.21 shows a sample profit and loss statement.

Unless a business makes money, the business cannot keep operating for very long. Accordingly, business owners and managers must monitor profits. The profit and loss statement provides the means to do so.

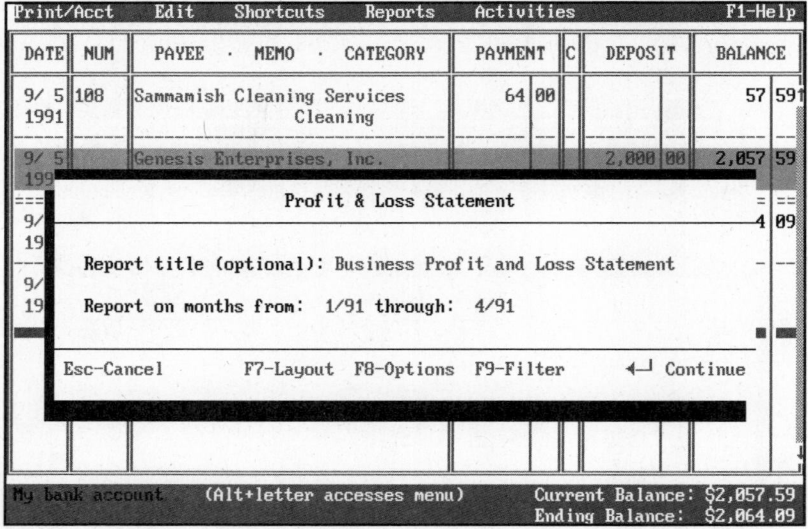

Fig. 14.20. The Profit & Loss Statement screen.

Business Profit & Loss Statement
1/ 1/91 Through 4/30/91

BUSINESS-All Accounts
4/ 2/91

Page 1

Category Description	1/ 1/91- 4/30/91
INCOME/EXPENSE	
INCOME	
Gross Sales	106,000.00
TOTAL INCOME	106,000.00
EXPENSES	
Advertising	135.72
Building Lot	0.00
Building Materials	0.00
Cost of Goods Sold	90,000.00
Late Payment Fees	23.85
Legal & Prof. Fees	75.89
Office Expenses	584.68
Subcontractor labor	0.00
Expenses - Other	400.00
TOTAL EXPENSES	91,220.14
TOTAL INCOME/EXPENSE	14,779.86

Fig. 14.21. A sample profit and loss statement.

Cash Flow Report

A cash flow report resembles a profit and loss statement. This report includes all bank, cash, and credit card accounts and shows the money received (inflows) and the money spent (outflows) by category for each month. The cash flow report also shows transfers between accounts. Figure 14.22 shows the Cash Flow Report screen.

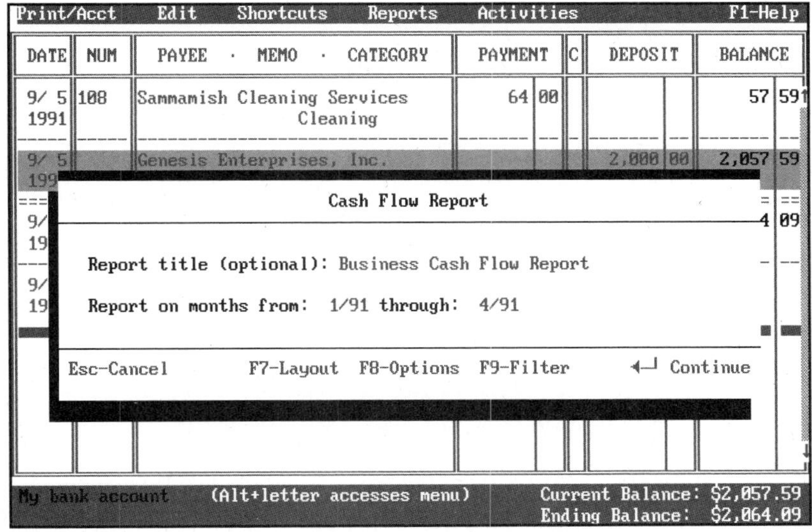

Fig. 14.22. *The Cash Flow Report screen.*

Like the Profit & Loss Statement screen, the Cash Flow Report screen provides fields for you to enter the range of months for which you want the cash flow report prepared. You can enter your own report title for Quicken to print on the cash flow report in place of the default title, `Cash Flow Report`. You also can use the F8-Customize and F9-Filter keys to fine-tune the report produced.

Figure 14.23 shows a sample cash flow report. The major difference between this report and the profit and loss statement is that transfers to other accounts are shown on the cash flow report. The transfer To Inventory is the last outflow listed.

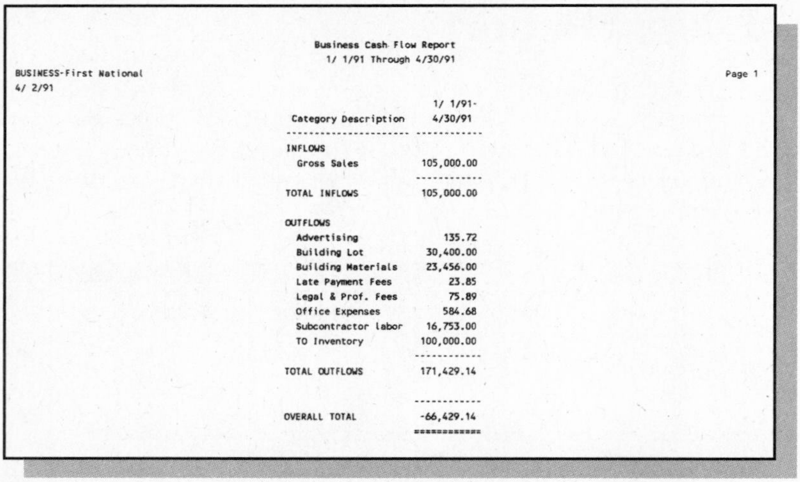

Business Cash Flow Report
1/ 1/91 Through 4/30/91

BUSINESS-First National — Page 1
4/ 2/91

Category Description	1/ 1/91- 4/30/91
INFLOWS	
Gross Sales	105,000.00
TOTAL INFLOWS	105,000.00
OUTFLOWS	
Advertising	135.72
Building Lot	30,400.00
Building Materials	23,456.00
Late Payment Fees	23.85
Legal & Prof. Fees	75.89
Office Expenses	584.68
Subcontractor Labor	16,753.00
TO Inventory	100,000.00
TOTAL OUTFLOWS	171,429.14
OVERALL TOTAL	-66,429.14

Fig. 14.23. *A sample business cash flow report.*

Cash flow is just as important as profits—particularly over shorter time periods. Besides making money, businesses need to have cash to purchase inventory or equipment, to wait for customers to pay their bills, and to pay back loans from banks and vendors. The cash flow report, which summarizes your cash inflows and outflows by category and account, provides a method for monitoring your cash flow—and for pinpointing problems that arise.

A/P by Vendor Report

Because Quicken uses what is called cash-basis accounting, expenses are recorded only when you actually pay the bill. By not paying bills, or even paying bills late, you can improve profits or cash flows. The problem, of course, is that this concept is clearly illogical. Just because you haven't paid a bill by the end of the month doesn't mean the bill shouldn't be considered in assessing the month's financial performance. To partially address this shortcoming, Quicken provides the A/P (unprinted checks) by vendor report, which enables you to see which bills have not been paid.

The A/P by vendor report lists all the unprinted checks, sorted and subtotaled by payee. (A/P is an abbreviation for *accounts payable*, the unpaid bills of a business.) Figure 14.24 shows the A/P (Unprinted Checks) by Vendor screen. You do not enter a date or a range of dates on this screen, but you can enter a substitute report title for Quicken to use instead of the default report title.

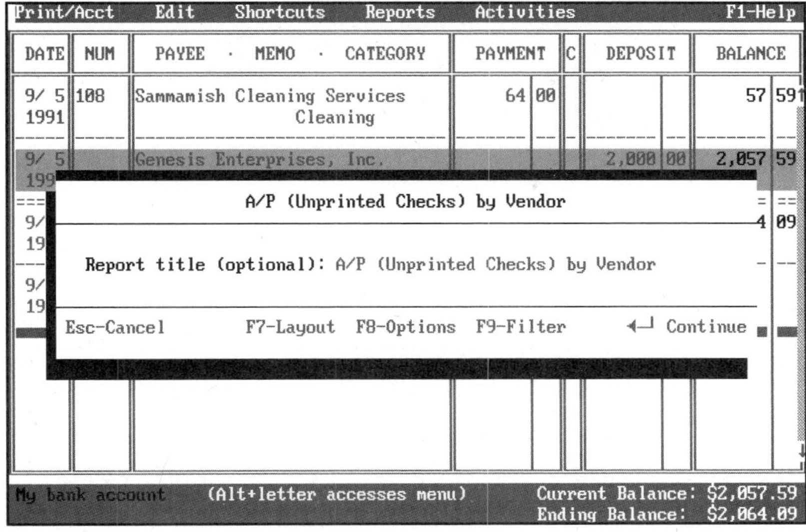

Fig. 14.24. *The A/P (Unprinted Checks) by Vendor screen.*

Figure 14.25 shows a sample A/P by vendor report. Two vendor totals appear: one for Hugh D. James and another for Stouffer's Office Supplies. Quicken subtotals unprinted checks with the exact payee names. If you type the payee name differently for different checks, the payee is not recognized by Quicken as the same payee, and the amounts are not subtotaled. If you plan to use this report (or the A/R by customer report described next), use the memorized transactions feature. When you use this feature, the payee name is identical for each transaction.

A/P Unprinted Checks by Vendor Report
4/ 1/91 Through 4/30/91

BUSINESS-First National Page 1
4/ 2/91

Payee	4/91
Hugh D. James	-820.00
Stouffer's Office Supplies	-944.90
OVERALL TOTAL	-1,764.90

Fig. 14.25. *A sample A/P by vendor report.*

A/R by Customer Report

The A/R by customer report shows the transactions in all of the other asset accounts, sorted and subtotaled by payee. The report, however, does not include transactions marked as cleared—those transactions marked with an asterisk or X in the C field of the register. (A/R is an abbreviation for *accounts receivable*, the amounts a business's customers owe.) Figure 14.26 shows the A/R by Customer screen. You can enter a title to replace the default report title, A/R by Customer Report.

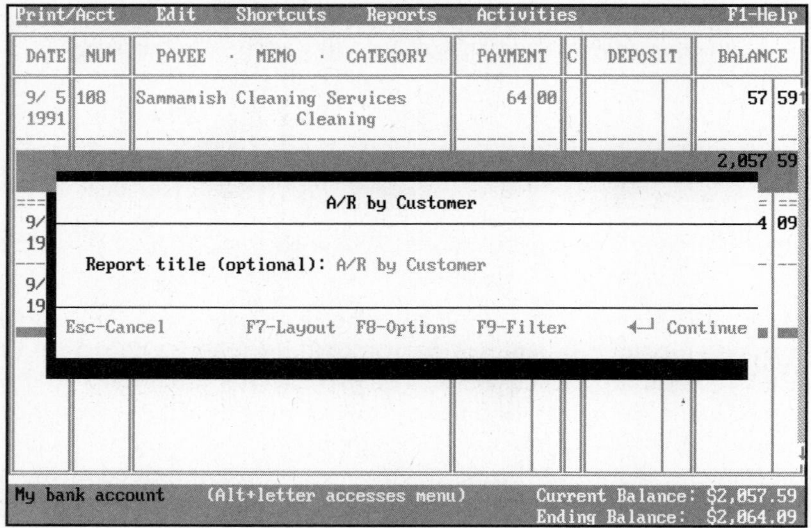

Fig. 14.26. The A/R by Customer screen.

After you complete the request screen, press Enter. Quicken displays the Select Accounts to Include screen (see fig. 14.27).

Quicken initially selects all asset account types for inclusion on the A/R by customer report. If you have other asset accounts besides accounts receivable, exclude these accounts. For example, figure 14.27 shows one account marked for inclusion, `Accts Rec`. To exclude or include accounts, follow these steps:

1. Use the up- and down-arrow keys to move the selection triangle to the left of the account you want to exclude or include.

2. Press the space bar. The space bar acts as a toggle switch, alternately marking the account for inclusion or exclusion.
3. (Optional) To select all the accounts, press F9.

Figure 14.28 shows a sample A/R by customer report.

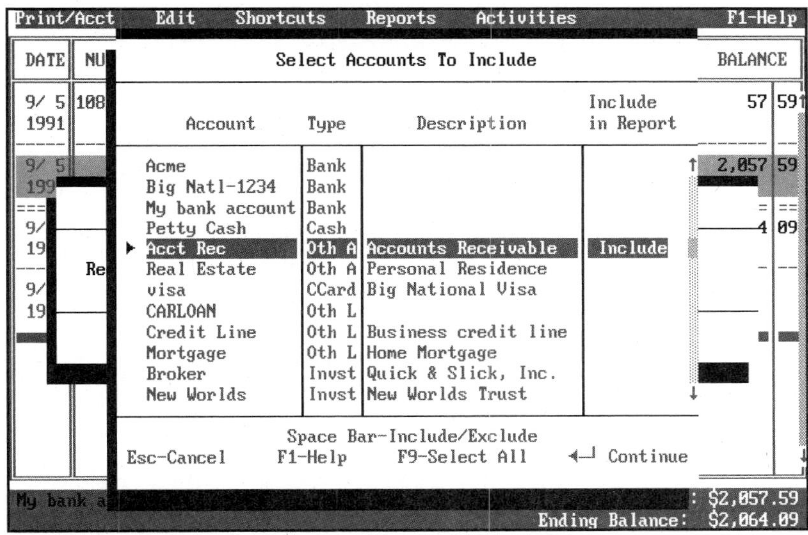

Fig. 14.27. *The Select Accounts to Include screen.*

A/R by Customer Report
4/ 1/91 Through 4/30/91

BUSINESS-Accts Rec
4/ 2/91

Page 1

Payee	4/91
Graham Howard Construction	3,461.45
Raul Castroverde, Inc.	9,949.55
Whipley Nash	3,634.74
OVERALL TOTAL	17,045.74

Fig. 14.28. *A sample A/R by customer report.*

For businesses that extend customer credit—which is what you do anytime you allow a customer to "buy now, pay later"—monitoring the amounts the customers owe is essential to profits and cash flows. Unfortunately, some customers don't pay unless you remind them several times, some customers frequently lose invoices and then forget that they owe you, and sometimes customers never receive your bill. To make sure that these small problems don't become big cash flow problems, you can use the A/R by customer report.

Good collection procedures usually improve cash flows dramatically, so consider using the customer aging report as a collection guide. You may, for example, want to telephone any customer with an invoice 30 days past due, and you may want to stop granting additional credit to any customer with invoices more than 60 days past due, and—in the absence of special circumstances—you may want to initiate collection procedures for any customer with invoices more than 90 days past due.

Job/Project Report

The job/project report shows category totals by month for each month in the specified date range. The report also shows account balances at the end of the last month. (If you are using classes, the report shows category totals by classes in separate columns across the report page.) Figure 14.29 shows the Job/Project Report screen. Figure 14.30 shows a sample job/project report. (Refer to Chapter 18 for more information on job costing.)

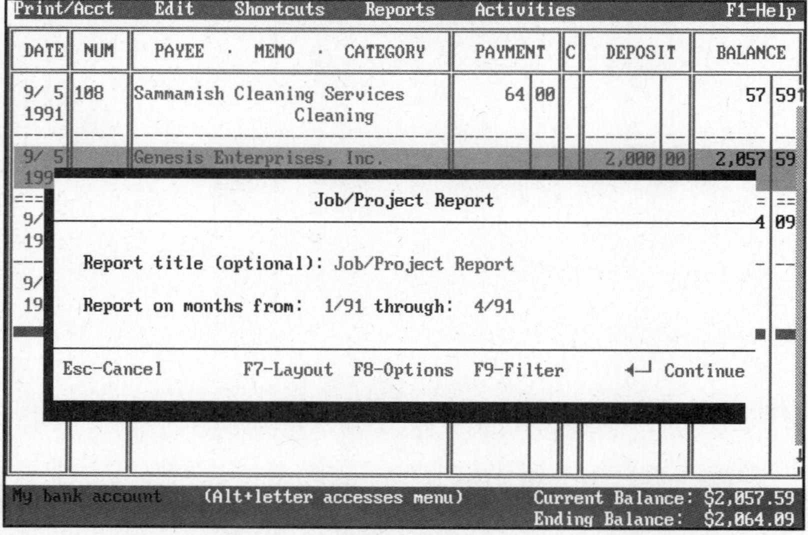

Fig. 14.29. The Job/Project Report screen.

Job/Project Report
1/ 1/91 Through 4/30/91

BUSINESS-All Accounts Page 1
4/ 2/91

Category Description	California	Oregon	Washington	Other	OVERALL TOTAL
INCOME/EXPENSE					
INCOME					
Gross Sales	3,634.74	5,811.00	7,600.00	106,000.00	123,045.74
TOTAL INCOME	3,634.74	5,811.00	7,600.00	106,000.00	123,045.74
EXPENSES					
Advertising	0.00	135.72	0.00	0.00	135.72
Building Lot	0.00	0.00	0.00	0.00	0.00
Building Materials	0.00	0.00	0.00	0.00	0.00
Cost of Goods Sold	0.00	0.00	0.00	90,000.00	90,000.00
Late Payment Fees	0.00	0.00	23.85	0.00	23.85
Legal & Prof. Fees	125.89	120.00	650.00	0.00	895.89
Office Expenses	584.68	0.00	124.76	0.00	709.44
Subcontractor labor	0.00	0.00	0.00	0.00	0.00
Expenses - Other	0.00	0.00	0.00	400.00	400.00
TOTAL EXPENSES	710.57	255.72	798.61	90,400.00	92,164.90
TOTAL INCOME/EXPENSE	2,924.17	5,555.28	6,801.39	15,600.00	30,880.84
TRANSFERS					
TO Inventory	0.00	0.00	0.00	-100,000.00	-100,000.00
FROM First National	0.00	0.00	0.00	100,000.00	100,000.00
TOTAL TRANSFERS	0.00	0.00	0.00	0.00	0.00
BALANCE FORWARD					
Deerfield lot 2	0.00	0.00	0.00	0.00	0.00
Delivery Truck	0.00	0.00	0.00	12,000.00	12,000.00
Fed WH	0.00	0.00	0.00	0.00	0.00
Inventory	0.00	0.00	0.00	30,000.00	30,000.00
Invoice 90-03	0.00	0.00	0.00	3,000.00	3,000.00
Loan	0.00	0.00	0.00	-12,000.00	-12,000.00
TOTAL BALANCE FORWARD	0.00	0.00	0.00	33,000.00	33,000.00
OVERALL TOTAL	2,924.17	5,555.28	6,801.39	48,600.00	63,880.84

Fig. 14.30. *A sample job/project report.*

Payroll Report

The payroll report shows the total amounts paid to individual payees when the transaction category starts with `payroll`. (The search argument used is *payroll*. See the discussions of exact and key-word matches in Chapters 5 and 7 for more information.) This report type includes transactions from all accounts. Figure 14.31 shows the Payroll Report screen.

Figure 14.32 shows a sample payroll report. (Refer to Chapter 18 for more information on preparing payrolls with Quicken. For specific information on using Quicken for processing employee payroll, see Chapter 17.)

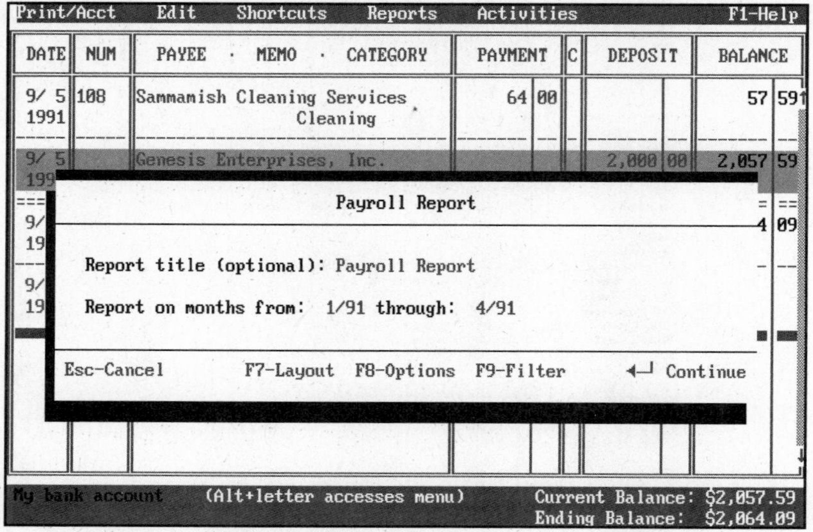

Fig. 14.31. The Payroll Report screen.

Payroll Report
4/ 1/91 Through 4/30/91

BUSINESS-All Accounts
4/ 2/91

Page 1

Payee	INC/EXP EXPENSES Payroll
Christopher Druce	550.00
Jack Colby	1,000.00
Mavis Armstrong	300.00
OVERALL TOTAL	1,850.00

Fig. 14.32. A sample payroll report.

Balance Sheet

The balance sheet report shows the account balances for all the accounts in the file at a specific point in time. If the file includes accounts for all of your assets and liabilities, the resulting report is a balance sheet and shows the net worth of your business. (Chapter 12, "Tracking Your Net Worth, Other Assets, and Liabilities," describes balance sheets in more detail.) Figure 14.33 shows the Balance Sheet screen. Figure 14.34 shows an example of a business balance sheet.

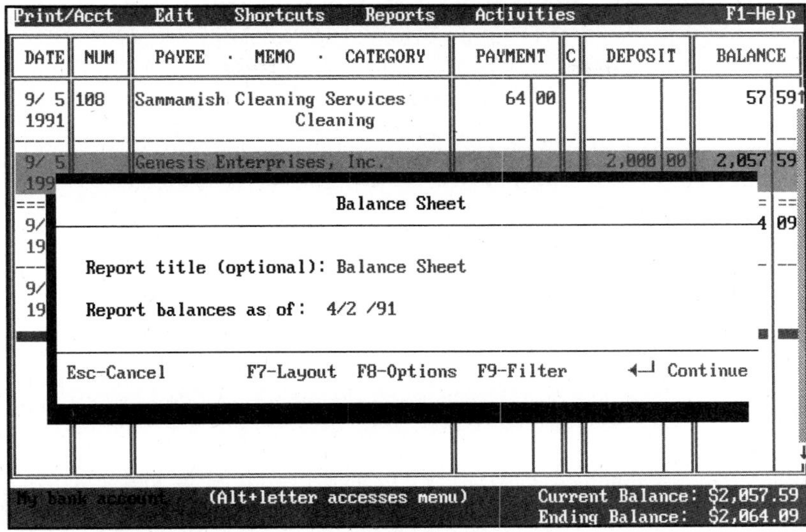

Fig. 14.33. The Balance Sheet screen.

Even for small businesses, balance sheets are important reports. Because a balance sheet shows what a business owns and what it owes, balance sheets give an indication of the financial strength or weakness of a business. For example, the smaller the total liabilities amount in relation to the total assets amount, the stronger the business. Alternatively, the larger the total liabilities in relation to the total assets, the weaker the business. As a result of these and similar financial insights, banks usually require a balance sheet in order to evaluate loan applications from businesses.

Tracking Your Investments with Quicken's Investment Reports

The Investment Reports menu provides five report options (see fig. 14.4). As with personal and business reports, the basic steps for printing an investment report are straightforward. To print any of the five reports, you complete the appropriate report request screen and then print the report.

Balance Sheet
As of 4/ 2/91

BUSINESS-All Accounts
4/ 2/91

Page 1

Acct		4/ 2/91 Balance
ASSETS		
Cash and Bank Accounts		
First National		
Ending Balance	180,776.10	
plus: Checks Payable	1,764.90	
Total First National		182,541.00
Total Cash and Bank Accounts		182,541.00
Other Assets		
Accts Rec-Accounts Receivable		17,045.74
Deerfield lot 2		70,609.00
Delivery Truck		12,000.00
Inventory		40,000.00
Invoice 90-01		1,000.00
Invoice 90-03		3,000.00
Total Other Assets		143,654.74
TOTAL ASSETS		326,195.74
LIABILITIES & EQUITY		
LIABILITIES		
Checks Payable		1,764.90
Other Liabilities		
Fed WH-Federal Withholding		400.00
Loan		12,000.00
Total Other Liabilities		12,400.00
TOTAL LIABILITIES		14,164.90
EQUITY		312,030.84
TOTAL LIABILITIES & EQUITY		326,195.74

***Fig. 14.34.** An example of a business balance sheet.*

If you haven't reviewed the material in Chapter 13, "Monitoring Your Investments," you may need to skim that chapter before trying to print investment reports.

Portfolio Value Reports

A portfolio value report shows the estimated market values of each of the securities in your Quicken investment accounts on a specific date. To estimate the market values, Quicken uses each security's individual price history (a list of prices on certain dates). Quicken determines which price to use by comparing the date in the Report value as of field to the dates that have prices in the price history. Ideally, Quicken uses a price for the same date as the Report value as of field date. When the price history does not contain a price for the same date as the field entry, Quicken uses the price for the date closest to the field entry.

To request a portfolio value report, you use the screen shown in figure 14.35. You can enter a report title, and you need to enter a date in the Report value as of field. You can specify that the information on the report be summarized by account, investment type, and investment goal. You also can specify whether the report should include the current account, all accounts, or only selected accounts, by using a screen that mirrors the one shown in figure 14.27. Figure 14.36 shows an example of the portfolio value report.

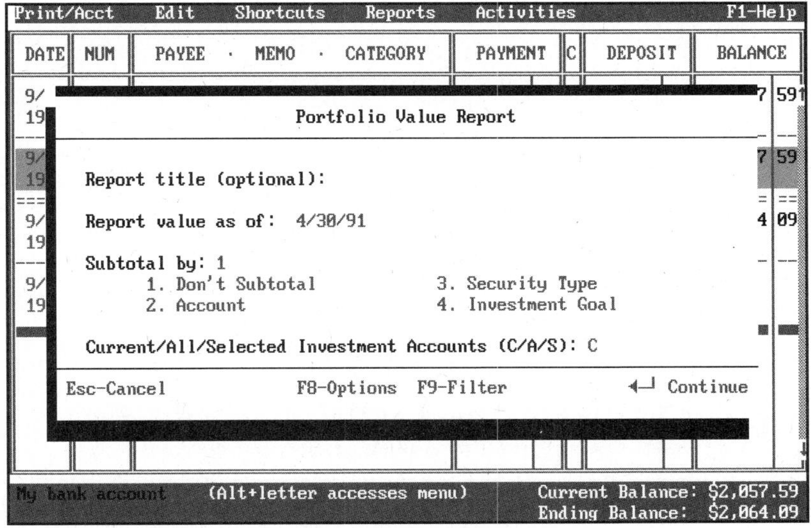

Fig. 14.35. The Portfolio Value Report screen.

Investment Performance Reports

Investment performance reports help you measure how well or how poorly your investments are doing. These reports look at all the transactions for a security and calculate an annual rate of return—in effect, the interest rate—an investment has paid you. To generate an investment performance report, you use the report request screen shown in figure 14.37.

Portfolio Value Report
As of 4/ 2/91

Discnt Brkge — Page 1
4/ 2/91

Security	Shares	Curr Price	Cost Basis	Gain/Loss	Balance
Microsoft Corp	50.00	97 7/8	4,393.75	500.00	4,893.75
Trump's Taj Mahal	100.00	95 1/2	9,708.50	-158.50	9,550.00
-Cash-	15,065.00	1	15,065.00	0.00	15,065.00
Total Investments			29,167.25	341.50	29,508.75

Fig. 14.36. A sample of the portfolio value report.

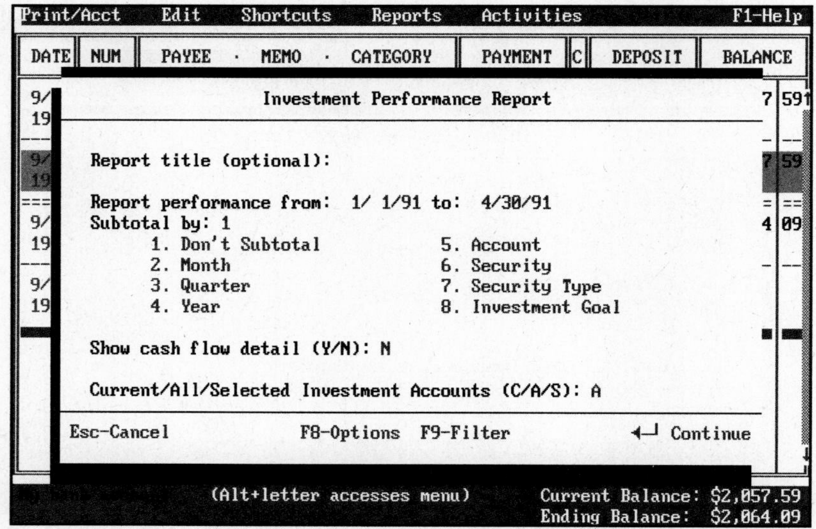

Fig. 14.37. The Investment Performance Report screen.

The report request screen enables you to use a custom title for the report. The screen also requires that you enter dates into the `Report performance from` and `to` fields. These dates tell Quicken for which time frame you want to calculate returns. The report request screen also enables you to subtotal rates of return by different time periods, by account, by security, by investment type, or by investment goals. You also can specify whether you want rates of return calculated for just the current account, for all accounts, or for selected accounts. Quicken notifies you if one or more of the total return calculations cannot be completed and displays the value as NA. Figure 14.38 shows an example of the investment performance report.

Investment Performance Report
1/ 1/91 Through 4/30/91

All Investment Accounts
4/ 2/91
Page 1

Description	Avg. Annual Tot. Return
Total Microsoft Corp	79.5%
Total New Frontiers	-15.2%
Total Trump's Taj Mahal	-4.5%

Fig. 14.38. A sample investment performance report.

Capital Gains (Schedule D) Reports

The capital gains report attempts to print all the information you need to complete the federal income tax form, Schedule D. Taxpayers use Schedule D to report capital gains and losses. To generate a capital gains report, use the Capital Gains (Schedule D) Report screen shown in figure 14.39.

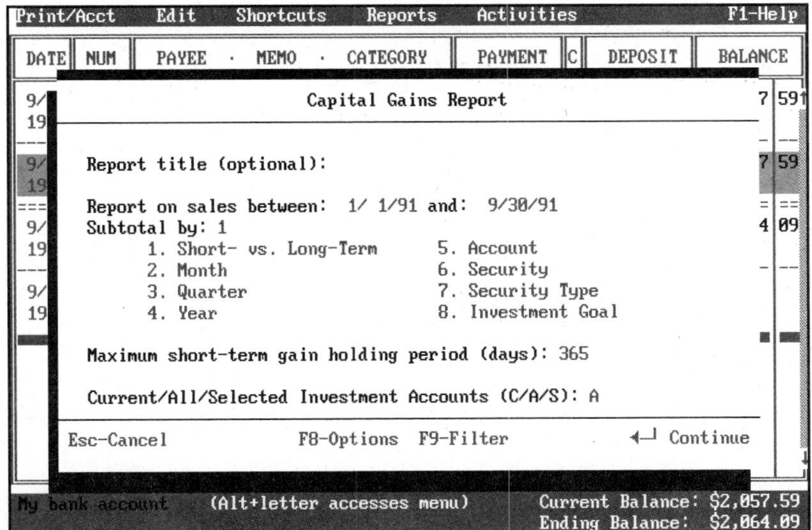

Fig. 14.39. The Capital Gains Report screen.

Most of the fields on the Capital Gains Report screen should be familiar to you, and the fields that also appear on the other investment report screens are not described here. Two fields do deserve mention, however: the `Subtotal by Short- vs Long-Term` and the `Maximum short-term gain holding period (days)` fields. Although income tax laws currently in effect treat short-term capital gains the same as long-term capital gains, Congress may change this treatment. Accordingly, Quicken enables you to subtotal by short-term and long-term gains and losses.

Currently, gains and losses that stem from the sale of capital assets held for more than one year are considered long-term. However, the `Maximum short-term gain holding period` field enables you to change the default number of days Quicken uses to determine whether a gain or loss is long-term. Figure 14.40 shows an example of a capital gains report.

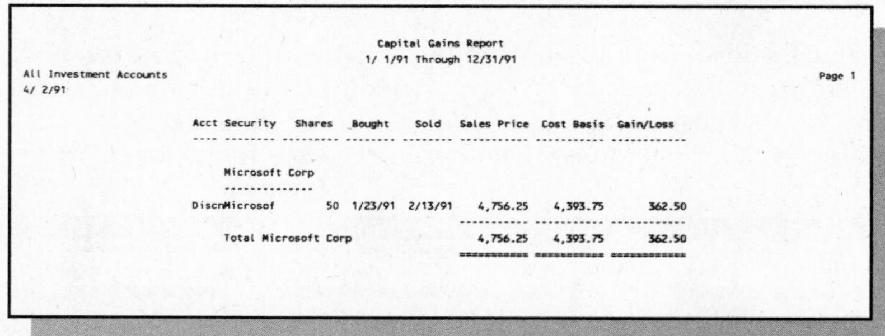

Capital Gains Report
1/ 1/91 Through 12/31/91

All Investment Accounts
4/ 2/91

Page 1

Acct	Security	Shares	Bought	Sold	Sales Price	Cost Basis	Gain/Loss
	Microsoft Corp						
Discr	Microsof	50	1/23/91	2/13/91	4,756.25	4,393.75	362.50
	Total Microsoft Corp				4,756.25	4,393.75	362.50

Fig. 14.40. A sample capital gains report.

Investment Income Reports

The investment income report summarizes all the income transactions you recorded in one or more of the investment accounts. To generate the report, use the report request screen shown in figure 14.41. Figure 14.42 shows an example of the report.

Realized gains and losses are calculated when the investment is actually sold and cash is received, by comparing the cash received with the original cost. Unrealized gains and losses are calculated when the cost of the investment is compared with the market value to determine what the gain or loss would have been if the investment had been sold.

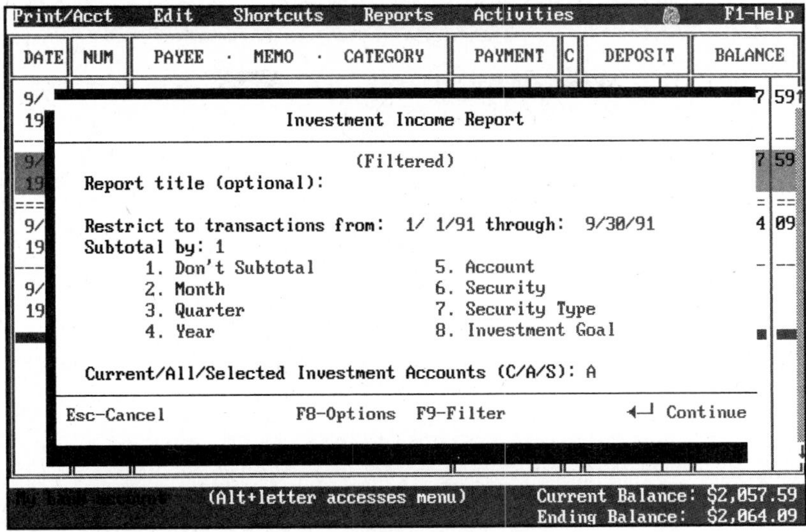

***Fig. 14.41.** The Investment Income Report screen.*

Investment Income Report
1/ 1/91 Through 3/31/91

All Investment Accounts
4/ 2/91

Page 1

Category Description	Microsoft C	New Frontie	Trump's Taj	OVERALL TOTAL
INCOME/EXPENSE				
INCOME				
Investment Interest Inc	0.00	0.00	65.00	65.00
Realized Gain/Loss	362.50	0.00	0.00	362.50
Unrealized Gain/Loss	362.50	2,237.96	-108.50	2,491.96
TOTAL INCOME	725.00	2,237.96	-43.50	2,919.46
EXPENSES				
Expenses - Other	0.00	0.00	0.00	0.00
TOTAL EXPENSES	0.00	0.00	0.00	0.00
TOTAL INCOME/EXPENSE	725.00	2,237.96	-43.50	2,919.46

***Fig. 14.42.** A sample investment income report.*

Investment Transactions Reports

The investment transactions report lists each of the investment transactions in the register. To request the report, use the Investment Transactions Report screen shown in figure 14.43. As with many of the other report request screens, Quicken enables you to enter an optional title, specify the time frame the report should cover, indicate whether you want transactions subtotaled according to some convention, and which accounts you want included on the report. Figure 14.44 shows an example of the investment transactions report.

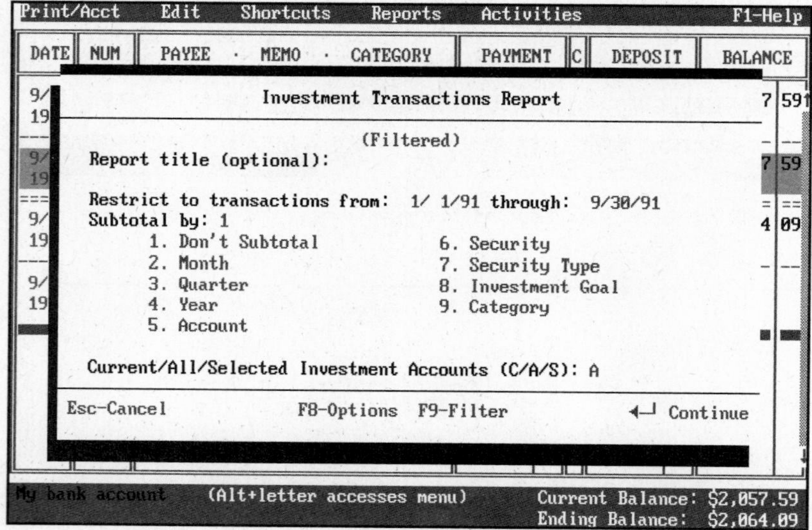

Fig. 14.43. The Investment Transactions Report screen.

Using the Report Screen's Menu Options

While Quicken displays a report on your screen, as figure 14.45 illustrates, it also provides five menus of options: File/Print, Edit, Layout, Reports, and Activities. Two of the five menus provide options you've previously seen.

The Reports menu, for example, provides the same options as the menu shown In figure 14.1. The Activities menu provides three of the options, which are simply a subset of the options that appear on the regular activities menu: **Register**, **Write Checks**, and **Calculator**. The other three menus, however, provide options specifically related to creating and printing reports.

Investment Transactions Report
1/ 1/91 Through 3/31/91

All Investment Accounts
4/ 2/91

Page 1

Date	Acct	Action	Secur	Categ	Price	Shares	Commssn	Cash	Invest. Value	Cash + Invest.
	Microsoft Corp									
1/23	Discnt	ShrsIn	Micros		87 7/8	100		-8,787.50	8,787.50	
				[Discn				8,787.50		8,787.50
2/13	Discnt	SellX	Micros		95 1/8	50		4,393.75	-4,393.75	
				[Discn				-4,756.25		-4,756.25
				Realized Gain/Loss				362.50		362.50
2/13		UnrlzGn	Micros	Unreal	95 1/8				362.50	362.50
	Total Microsoft Corp							0.00	4,756.25	4,756.25
	New Frontiers									
2/ 5	New Fr	ShrsIn	New Fr		11.590	86.281		-1,000.00	1,000.00	
				[New F				1,000.00		1,000.00
2/ 5		UnrlzGn	New Fr	Unreal	11.590				-22.35	-22.35
2/ 9	New Fr	BuyX	New Fr		11.810	101.609		-1,200.00	1,200.00	
				[Big N				1,200.00		1,200.00
2/ 9		UnrlzGn	New Fr	Unreal	11.810				2,260.31	2,260.31
2/28	New Fr	StkSpli	New Fr			2:1				
	Total New Frontiers							0.00	4,437.96	4,437.96
	Trump's Taj Mahal									
2/13	Discnt	BuyX	Trump'		96 5/8	100	46.00	-9,708.50	9,708.50	
				[Big N				9,708.50		9,708.50
2/13	Discnt	IntInc	Trump'	Investment Interest Inc				65.00		65.00
2/13		UnrlzGn	Trump'	Unreal	96 5/8				-46.00	-46.00
3/17		UnrlzGn	Trump'	Unrealized	96				-62.50	-62.50
	Total Trump's Taj Mahal							65.00	9,600.00	9,665.00
	-Cash-									
1/31	Discnt	XIn	-Cash-	[Big N				15,000.00		15,000.00
	Total -Cash-							15,000.00	0.00	15,000.00
	OVERALL TOTAL							15,065.00	18,794.21	33,859.21

Fig. 14.44. A sample investment transactions report.

```
File/Print   Edit   Layout   Reports   Activities                F1-Help

                          CASH FLOW REPORT

                   1/ 1/91 Through 9/30/91
        STEPHENL-Bank,Cash,CC Accounts
        9/ 5/91
                                               1/ 1/91-
           Category Description                9/30/91

        INFLOWS
          Interest Income                            12.25
          Salary Income                           2,000.00

        TOTAL INFLOWS                             2,012.25

        OUTFLOWS
          Automobile Expenses                        -6.23
          Bank Charge                                 5.00
          Cleaning                                  128.00
          Groceries                                 -76.91
          Housing                                   559.00

STEPHENL-My bank account
Esc-Leave report
```

Fig. 14.45. *The personal Cash Flow Report displayed on-screen.*

Using the File/Print Menu

Figure 14.46 shows the File/Print menu and its three options: **Print Report**, **Memorize Report**, and **QuickZoom**. **Print Report** works just like Ctrl-P. When you choose the **Print Report** option, Quicken displays the Print Report screen shown in figure 14.6. You complete the Print Report screen as described earlier in the chapter.

Memorize Report records the information you've entered on the Report screen—such as the report title, the range of dates—and gives the memorized report information a name. Then, if you later want to print a report using the same creation parameters, you just tell Quicken which memorized report information you want to use. I'll postpone describing the steps for memorizing report creation information until the end of the chapter because the subject makes sense once you learn about the other Report screen menu options.

QuickZoom lets you see a list of transactions that go into any amount displayed in a report. Here's how **QuickZoom** works. Suppose you had just displayed the report shown in figure 14.45, but couldn't remember where or why you had earned $12.25 of interest income. The easiest way to answer your questions would be to use **QuickZoom**. To do this, you highlight the amount in question using the arrow keys—$12.25 in this illustration. Then, you select the **QuickZoom** option from the File/Print menu or press Ctrl-Z, the **QuickZoom** short-cut key combination. Quicken displays the Transaction List screen shown in figure 14.47, which shows the individual transactions that make up the $12.25 of interest income. If you want to see the actual transaction in the register, highlight the transaction using the arrow keys and press F9.

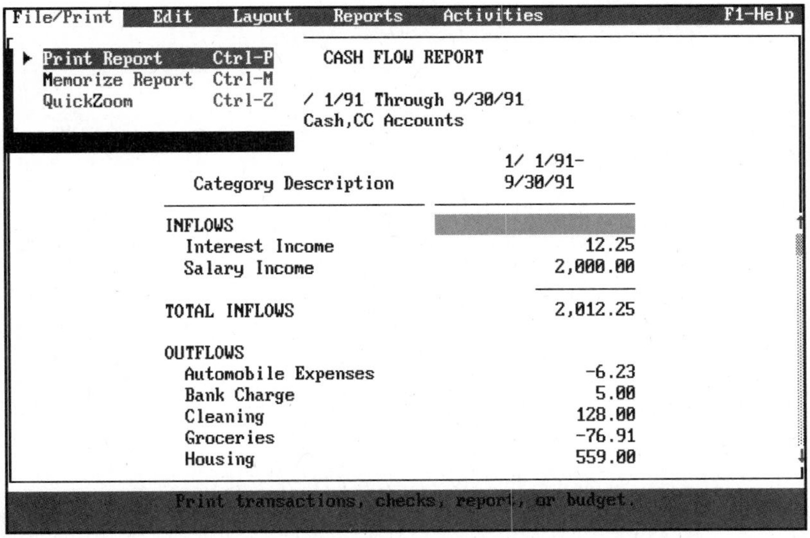

```
File/Print   Edit   Layout   Reports   Activities                    F1-Help

 ▸ Print Report     Ctrl-P    CASH FLOW REPORT
   Memorize Report  Ctrl-M
   QuickZoom        Ctrl-Z   / 1/91 Through 9/30/91
                             Cash,CC Accounts

                                                1/ 1/91-
                 Category Description           9/30/91
             ------------------------------   ------------
             INFLOWS
               Interest Income                       12.25
               Salary Income                      2,000.00
                                                  --------
             TOTAL INFLOWS                        2,012.25

             OUTFLOWS
               Automobile Expenses                   -6.23
               Bank Charge                            5.00
               Cleaning                             128.00
               Groceries                            -76.91
               Housing                              559.00

           Print transactions, checks, report, or budget.
```

Fig. 14.46. The File/Print menu.

Using the Edit Menu

The Edit menu options let you control which information is included in a report. Figure 14.48 shows the Edit menu and its five options. If you've been reading this chapter from its start, you already know the first option. The **Set Title & Date Range** option redisplays the report screen used to create the report. You use this option to change the report date or the range of dates covered by the report.

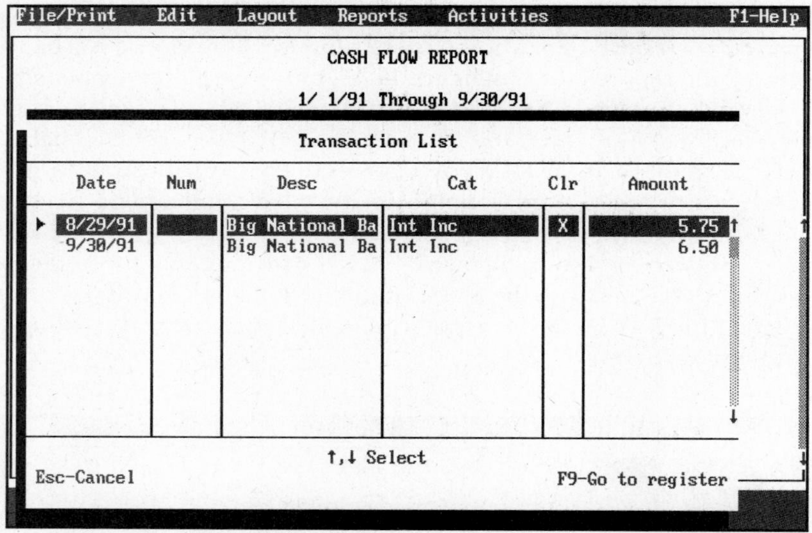

Fig. 14.47. The Transaction List screen.

```
File/Print  Edit   Layout   Reports   Activities                  F1-Help

          ▸ Set Title & Date Range   EPORT
            Filter Transactions
            Accounts                 h 9/30/91
            Categories               nts
            Classes
                                            1/ 1/91-
                                            9/30/91

          INFLOWS
            Interest Income                   12.25
            Salary Income                  2,000.00

          TOTAL INFLOWS                    2,012.25

          OUTFLOWS
            Automobile Expenses               -6.23
            Bank Charge                        5.00
            Cleaning                         128.00
            Groceries                        -76.91
            Housing                          559.00

      Change the title or beginning and ending dates of the report.
```

Fig. 14.48. The Edit menu.

The **Accounts** option enables you to specify which accounts from the selected account group should be included on the report. When you select this option, Quicken displays a submenu which lists three options: **Current**,

All, and **Selected**. Choose Current to display just the current account. Choose **All** to display all the accounts in the file. Choose **Selected** to display only a selected group of accounts.

If you choose only selected accounts, Quicken displays the Select Accounts To Include screen shown in figure 14.27. To include an account, use the up- and down-arrow keys to move the selection triangle to the left of the account you want to include and press the space bar. The space bar acts as a toggle switch, alternately marking the account for inclusion and exclusion. To select all the accounts, press F9.

For the net worth and balance sheet reports, you have three choices that the space bar toggles. You can include an account, exclude an account, and show any class detail. Pressing the space bar alternately displays `Include`, `Detail`, or nothing next to the option.

If you select the **Filter Transactions** option, Quicken displays the Filter Report Transactions screen shown in figure 14.49.

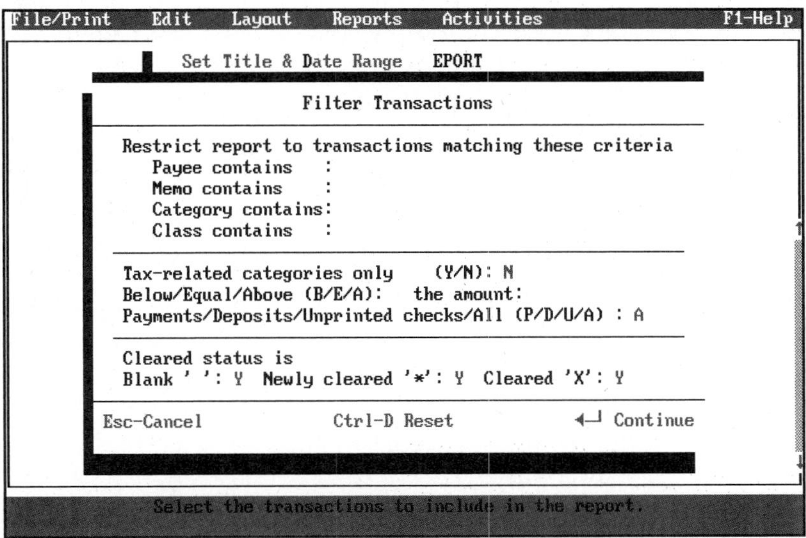

***Fig. 14.49.** The Filter Transactions screen.*

You can use a variety of fields to include or exclude transactions from a report. Complete the following basic steps:

1. From the report screen, press Alt-E and then F to access the Filter Report Transactions screen shown in figure 14.49.

2. Use the Enter or Tab key to move through the various fields on-screen and then enter the appropriate values or figures. These fields are described in the following paragraphs.
3. (Optional) If you start modifying these fields and then want to reset them to the original values, press Ctrl-D.
4. When you complete the screen, press Enter when the cursor is on the last field. You also can press F10 or Ctrl-Enter when the cursor is on any of the fields.

The `Payee contains` field enables you to instruct Quicken to include or exclude a certain payee or transaction description from a transaction report based on exact or key-word matches. (Chapters 5 and 7 describe in detail the mechanics of exact and key-word matches.) If you leave this field blank, you do not affect transactions being included or excluded from the report.

The `Memo contains` field works like the `Payee contains` field, except that Quicken compares the `Memo contains` field entry to the transactions' `Memo` field entries. This field affects the transactions included or excluded on the report, as does the `Payee contains` field. Using this field is optional.

The `Category contains` field enables you to instruct Quicken to include or exclude transactions assigned to certain categories based on exact or key-word matches. If you leave this field blank, the transactions being included or excluded from the report are not affected.

The `Class contains` field works like the `Category contains` field, except that Quicken compares the `Class contains` field entry to entries in the transactions' class. Like the `Category contains` field, this optional field affects the transactions included or excluded on the report.

The `Tax-related categories only` field enables you to include each of the categories you marked as tax-related when initially defining the category. (Chapter 10 describes how you identify a category as tax-related.)

Matching Transaction Amounts

The `Below/Equal/Above` and amount fields enable you to include transactions on a report based on the transaction amount. By using these two fields, you tell Quicken that you want transactions included on your report only when the transaction amount is less than, equal to, or greater than some amount. Type *b* to indicate below, *e* to indicate equal, or *a* to indicate above.

Enter the amount you want transaction amounts compared to in the `amount` field.

The `Payments/Deposits/Unprinted checks/All` field enables you to include only certain types of transactions. To include only payments, enter a *p*; to include only deposits, enter a *d*; to include only unprinted checks, enter a *u*; to include all transactions, enter an *a*.

You can use this report to determine your cash flow requirements. If you have entered all of your bills and want to know the total, press U for unprinted checks. Your report tells you the total cash required for all unpaid bills.

The `Cleared status is blank` field enables you to include transactions on a report based on the contents of the `C field` in the register. The `C field` shows whether or not a transaction has been marked as cleared. Three valid entries exist for the `C` field: `*`, X, and nothing. As the Filter Report Transactions screen shows, you can include transactions on a report by entering a Y for yes next to the `is blank`, `*`, or `X` fields. You also can exclude transactions by entering a N for no next to the same three fields.

The **Categories** option enables you to specify an entire set of categories to be included on a report. If you select this option, Quicken displays a submenu with two options: **Selected** and **All**. If you choose **Selected** from the submenu, Quicken displays the Select Categories to Include screen that you can use to mark the categories you want included on a report (see fig. 14.50).

To include a category, use the up- and down-arrow keys to move the selection triangle to the left of the category and press the space bar. The space bar acts as a toggle switch, alternately marking the category for inclusion or exclusion. To select all the categories, press F9.

The **Classes** option enables you to specify an entire set of classes to be included on a report. If you choose this option, Quicken displays a submenu that lists two choices: **Selected** and **All**. If you choose **Selected**, Quicken displays the Select Classes To Include screen that you can use to mark individual categories you want included on a report (see fig. 14.51).

File/Print Edit Layout Reports Activities F1-Help

Select Categories To Include

Category	Type	Description	Tax	Include in Report
Auto	Expns	Automobile Expenses		Include
▸ Fuel	Sub	Auto Fuel		Include
Loan	Sub	Auto Loan Payment		Include
Service	Sub	Auto Service		Include
Bank Chrg	Expns	Bank Charge		Include
Charity	Expns	Charitable Donations	♦	Include
Childcare	Expns	Childcare Expense		Include
Christmas	Expns	Christmas Expenses		Include
Cleaning	Expns	Cleaning		Include
Clothing	Expns	Clothing		Include
Dining	Expns	Dining Out		Include
Dues	Expns	Dues		Include

Space Bar-Include/Exclude
Esc-Cancel F1-Help F9-Select All ↵ Continue

Fig. 14.50. The Select Categories To Include screen.

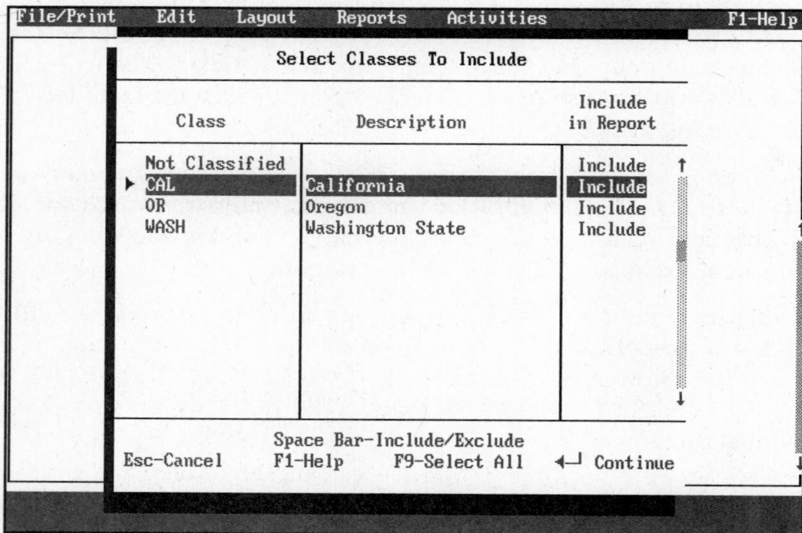

Fig. 14.51. The Select Classes To Include screen.

To include a class, use the up- and down-arrow keys to move the selection triangle to the left of the class and then press the space bar. The space bar acts as a toggle switch, alternately marking the class for inclusion and exclusion. To select all classes, press F9.

Using the Layout Menu

With the Layout menu's 10 options, you control the appearance of a report (see fig. 14.52). Many of the options are self-explanatory, but they are explained here briefly.

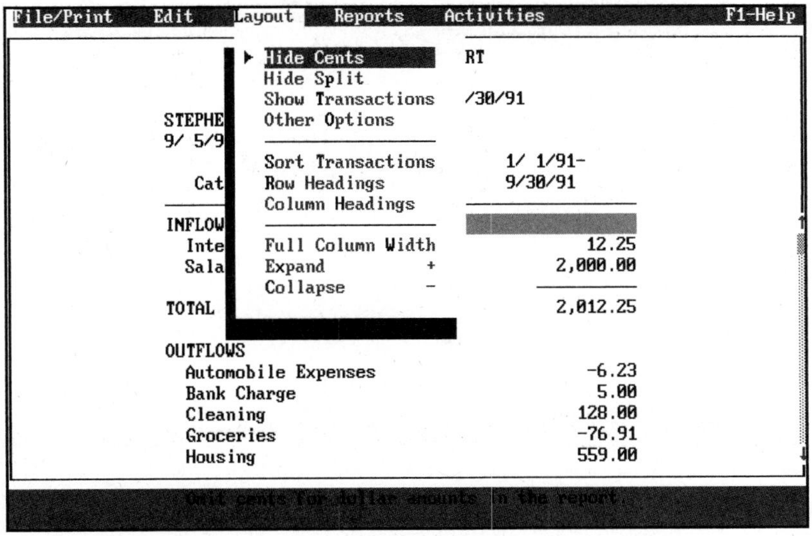

Fig. 14.52. *The Layout menu.*

The **Hide Cents** option causes Quicken to display amounts in dollars rather than in dollars and cents. Once you select the option, the option name changes to **Show Cents**. Predictably, by selecting the **Show Cents** option, Quicken again displays amounts in dollars and cents.

The **Hide Split** option, if selected, causes Quicken to display transactions as they appear in the register—with their splits hidden. After you select this option, the option name changes to **Show Splits**. If you then select the **Show Splits** option, Quicken displays split transaction detail.

The **Hide Transactions** option causes Quicken to remove individual transactions from a report so only subtotals and totals are displayed. Once you select this option, the option name changes to **Show Transactions**. By selecting the **Show Transactions** option, Quicken again displays individual transactions. (The **Hide/Show Split** and **Hide/Show Transaction** options only affect reports that list individual transactions—not those that only summarize transactions.

Select the **Other Options** option and Quicken displays the Report Options screen (see fig. 14.53). The Report Options screen gives you several ways to affect report appearance.

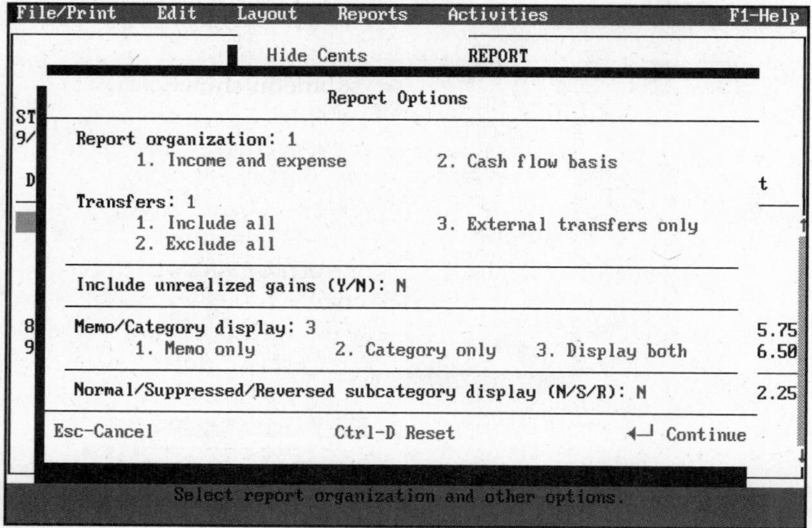

Fig. 14.53. The Report Options screen.

Using the `Report organization` field determines whether the report includes only transactions assigned to categories (income and expense transactions, cash flow, net worth, or balance sheet) or transactions assigned to categories and transactions representing transfers. Using the `Transfers` field determines whether all transfers are included or excluded or whether only transfers including an account outside of the set of selected accounts are included. Using the `Include Unrealized Gain` field determines whether an investment report includes unrealized or paper gains and losses. (Unrealized investment gains and losses are those gains and losses which would occur if you immediately sold an investment.)

Using the `Show memo/category/both` field determines whether just the memo, just the category, or the memo and category entries appear on the report. You also can specify the report to show subcategories and subclasses by setting the `Normal/Suppressed/Reversed Subcategory display` field to N for Normal, can specify the report not show subcategories and classes by setting the field to S for Suppressed, and can specify the report reverse the order of categories and subcategories and classes and subclasses by displaying subcategories and subclasses first by setting the field to R for reversed.

The **Sort Transactions** option displays a submenu which lists the keys you can use to sort or order transactions on a report: Account, Date, Check Number, and Amount. By default, Transactions are sorted by account. To use some other sort order, however, simply select one of the other options on the Sort Transactions submenu.

The **Row Heading** option displays the submenu shown in figure 14.54. Mechanically, the **Row Headings** option enables you to select the order in which transactions are segregated and subtotaled in rows down a report page. To segregate and subtotal transactions based on transaction dates, select one of the time intervals listed: week, two week, half month, month, quarter, six month, or year. To segregate and subtotal transactions by category, class, payee, or account, select one of the menu's last four options. If you don't want to segregate and subtotal transactions, select the first option on the menu, **Don't Subtotal**. By the way, not every row heading option shown in figure 14.54 is available for every report.

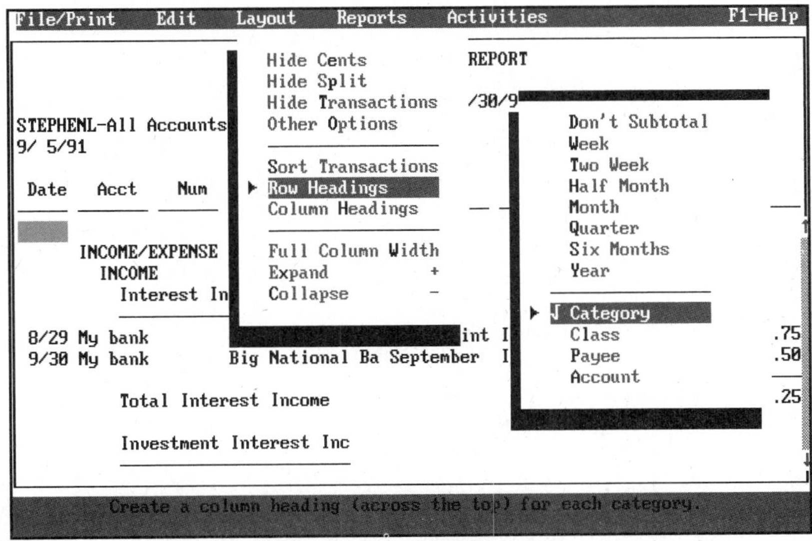

Fig. 14.54. The Row Headings submenu.

The **Column Headings** option displays the submenu shown in figure 14.55. In essence, it works just like the Row Headings submenu with one exception: The **Column Headings** option controls the order in which transactions are segregated and subtotaled in columns across the report page. As is the case with the **Row Headings** option, not every column heading option shown in figure 14.55 is available for every report.

You use the **Row Headings** and **Column Headings** options to organize your financial information just the way you want. If, for example, you're tracking expenses on a monthly basis, you could set the rows to categories and the columns to months. Or, if you were tracking different real estate investments with classes and wanted to see what each property produced in rent over a year, you might set the rows to categories and the columns to classes.

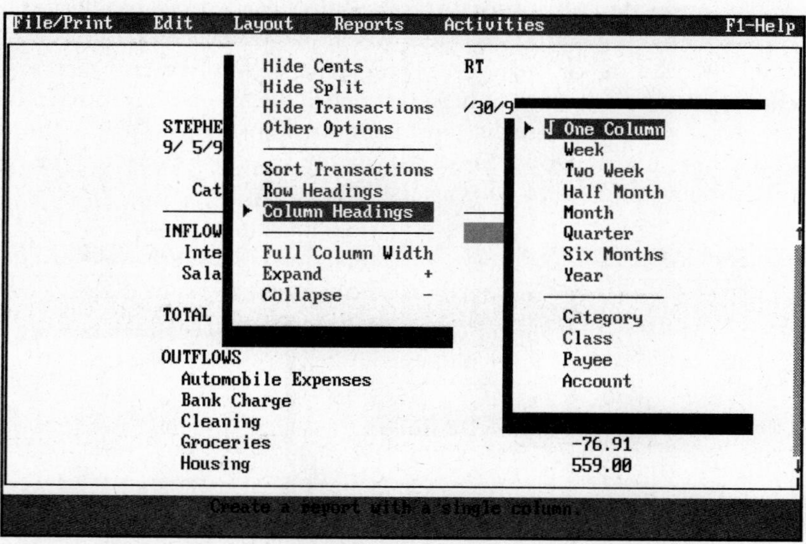

Fig. 14.55. The Column Headings submenu.

The Layout menu's **Full Column Width** option controls whether Quicken uses full-width columns or half-width columns for reports that list transactions. By default, Quicken uses half-width report columns and displays the option name as Full Column Width. If you select the **Full Column Width** option, Quicken uses full-width columns and changes the option name to **Half Column Width**. Selecting the **Half Column Width** option causes Quicken to use half-width columns and to change the option name back to **Full Column Width**. With regard to the **Full/Half Column Width** option, the basic rule is to use columns wide enough to display the information you want to see. If, for example, the descriptions or memos in a report are cropped because the columns are too narrow, use full column widths.

The **Expand** and **Collapse** commands work together. **Collapse** causes Quicken to hide the rows that go together to make up a subtotal row. To use it, first highlight the subtotal row you want to collapse using the arrow keys. Then, select the **Collapse** option from the Layout menu. Or, press the – (minus) key. **Expand**, of course, uncollapses previously collapsed rows. To use it, highlight the collapsed row. Then, select the **Expand** option or press the + (plus) key.

Using Function Keys

At the bottom of many of the report screens, you'll see references to function keys such as F7 (Layout), F8 (Options), and F9 (Filter). In essence, these function keys simply enable you to select combinations of report screen menu options.

Pressing the F7 (Layout) function key, for example, causes Quicken to display a create report screen like that shown in figure 14.56. Essentially, this screen is an expanded version of the report screen you use to create a report. The layout screen, however, provides additional fields for specifying things like subtotaling schemes and for selecting which accounts should be included in a report. (On some screens, you specify the subtotaling scheme by choosing a row heading or report heading.)

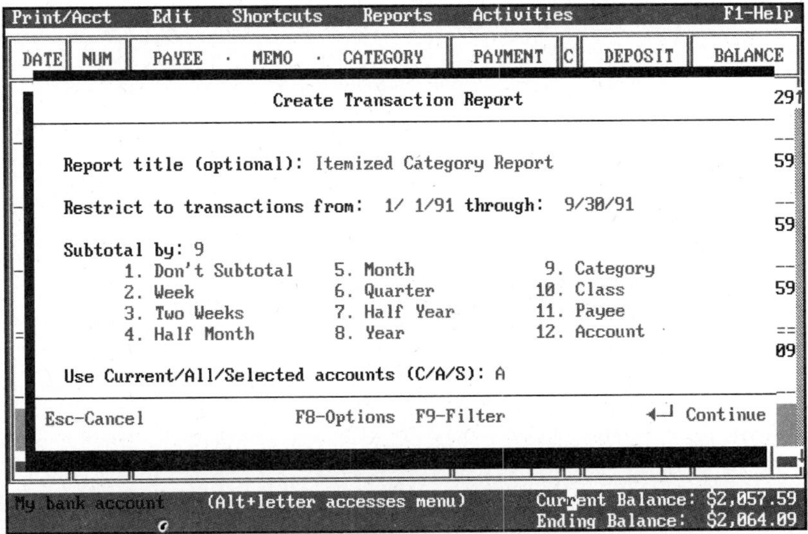

Fig. 14.56. The Create Transaction Report screen.

Pressing the F8 (Options) key causes Quicken to display a report options screen like that works and looks like that shown in figure 14.53. Finally, pressing the F9 (Filter) key causes Quicken to display a report filters screen that looks and works like the screen shown in figure 14.49.

Memorizing Reports

Earlier in the chapter, the **Memorize Report** option on the File/Print menu was briefly discussed. The **Memorize Report** option enables you to record and add a title to a set of report descriptions. These report descriptions include the results of any menu option you execute with the Edit or Layout menus, what you enter on the report request screen, the F7 (Layout) screen, the F8 (Options) screen, and the F9 (Filter) screen. You can use this feature to customize a special report so that you do not have to re-invent the wheel every time you need the report.

To memorize a report, select the **Memorize Report** option or press Ctrl-M after you complete the descriptions of the report you want to print. Quicken displays the Memorizing Report screen shown in figure 14.57. Enter a unique title for the report description and then press Enter. (You can press Ctrl-M anytime after the Create Report screen is displayed.)

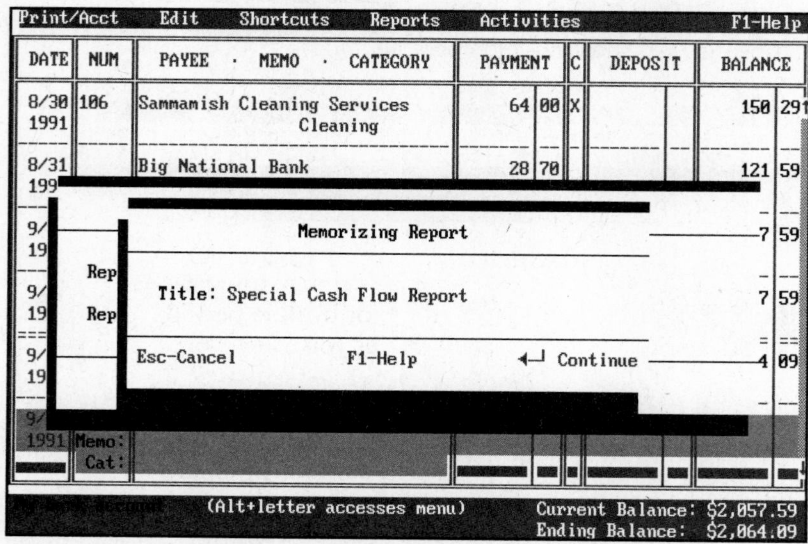

Fig. 14.57. The Memorizing Report screen.

To later use the memorized report description, select the **Memorized Reports** option from the Reports menu and use the arrow keys to mark the memorized report you want to print on the Memorized Reports List and press Enter (see fig. 14.58). Quicken displays the Memorized Report screen (see fig. 14.59). To generate the report, press Enter.

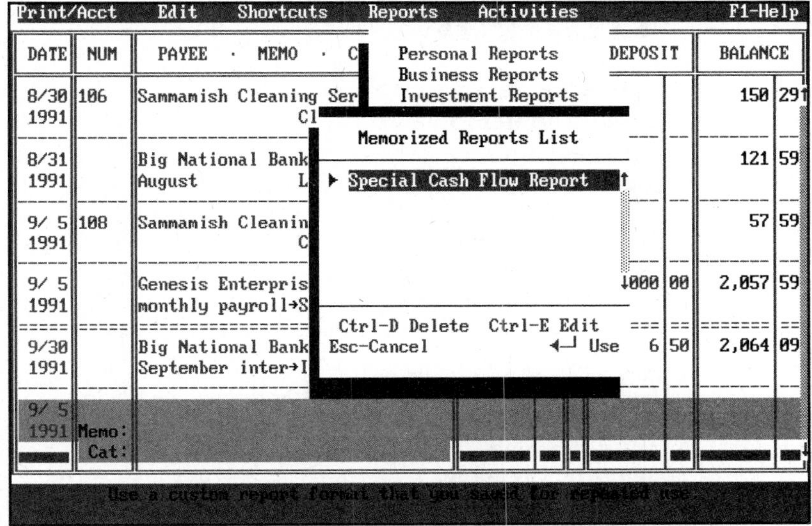

Fig. 14.58. The Memorized Reports List.

Creating a Transaction Report

You may want to view your register transactions in some order other than chronologically by date. For example, you may find value in sorting and summarizing transactions by the payee or by time periods such as a week or month. The transaction report enables you to see your account transactions in any of these ways.

To create a transaction report, follow these steps:

1. Select the **Transaction** option from the Reports menu. Quicken displays the Create Transaction Report screen (see fig. 14.60.)

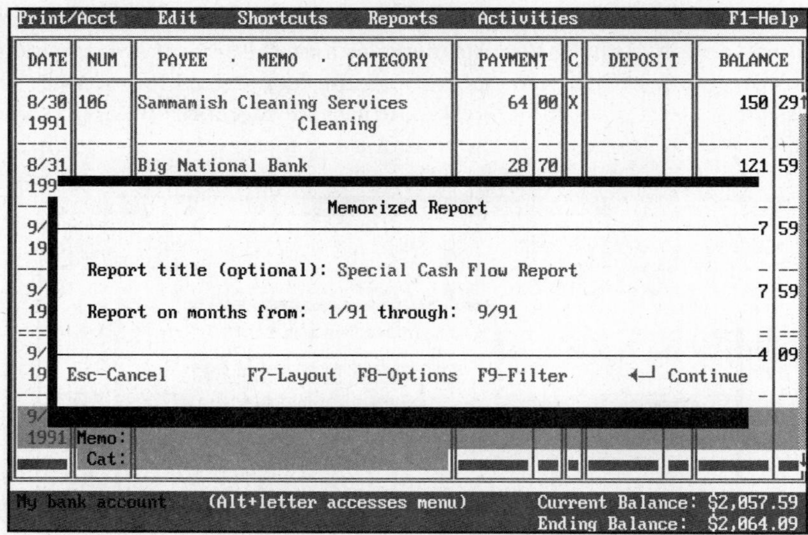

Fig. 14.59. *The Memorized Report screen.*

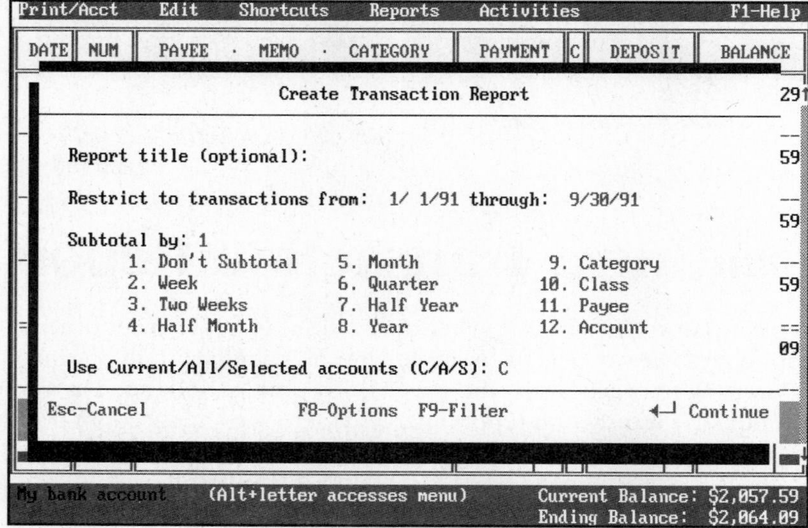

Fig. 14.60. *The Create Transaction Report screen.*

2. (Optional) Enter a report title. If you don't enter a report title, Quicken names the report "Transaction Report."

3. (Optional) Press Enter or Tab to move the cursor to the `Restrict to transactions from` and `through` fields. Enter the time frame the report should cover by entering the starting and the ending dates you want included in the report. If you don't enter these dates, the report covers from January of the current year through the current date.
4. (Optional) Press Enter or Tab to move the cursor to the `Subtotal by` field. Pick one of the 12 subtotal choices by typing the number that appears to the left of the choice.
5. (Optional) Press Enter or Tab to move the cursor to the `Use Current/All/Selected accounts` field. You can use the `Use Current/All/Selected accounts` field to determine whether just the current account's transactions are included, just the selected account's transactions are included, or all the accounts' transactions are included. If you choose just selected accounts, Quicken displays the Select Accounts to Include screen.
6. (Optional) Press F8 (Options) to access the Report Options screen. Complete the Report Options screen as described earlier in the chapter.
7. (Optional) Press F9 (Filter) to access the Filter Report Transactions screen. Complete the Filter Report Transactions screen as described earlier in the chapter.
8. When the Create Transaction Report screen is complete, press Enter when the cursor is on the `Use Current/All/Selected accounts` field. You also can press F10 or Ctrl-Enter when the cursor is on any of the other fields. Quicken generates and displays the report on-screen.

   You can use the arrow keys, PgUp, and PgDn to see different portions of the report. You also can use the Home and End keys to see the first and last pages of the report. On reports too wide to fit comfortably on-screen, you can use F9 to toggle between a full column-width and a half column-width version of the report.
9. When you are ready to print the report, press Ctrl-P. Quicken displays the Print Report screen shown in figure 14.6. This screen enables you to specify to where you want the report printed.
10. Answer the `Print to` field by pressing a 1 for printer 1, 2 for printer 2, and so on.

If you select 4 at the `Print to` field, Quicken prints an ASCII file. To create an ASCII file, Quicken requests three pieces of information, using the Print to Disk screen. Follow these steps:

1. In the Print to Disk screen's `File` field, enter a name for Quicken to use for the ASCII file. To use a data directory other than the Quicken data directory, QUICKEN5, you also can specify a path name. (See your DOS user's manual for information on path names.)

2. In the Print to Disk screen's `Lines per page` field, set the number of report lines between page breaks. If you are using 11-inch paper, the page length usually is 66 lines.

3. In the Print to Disk screen's `Width` field, set the number of characters, including blanks, that Quicken prints on a line. If you are using 8 1/2-inch paper, the characters per line number usually is 80.

If you select 5 at the `Print to` field on the Print Report screen, Quicken displays the Print to Lotus File screen. To create a 1-2-3 file, Quicken requests the name of the file you want to create. As with the ASCII file creation option, to use a data directory other than QUICKEN5, you also can specify a path name.

Creating a Summary Report

Like a transaction report, a summary report extracts information from the financial database you create using Quicken's registers. A summary report, however, gives you totals by category, class, payee, or account, in addition to any of the other subtotals you request. With this type of report, you also can select the accounts to include.

To print a summary report, you follow essentially the same steps as for creating a transaction report, except that you select the **Summary** option from the Custom Reports menu. Quicken then displays the Create Summary Report screen, shown in figure 14.61, which you use to specify how the custom report should appear. The five fields you use to create custom summary report are described earlier in the chapter.

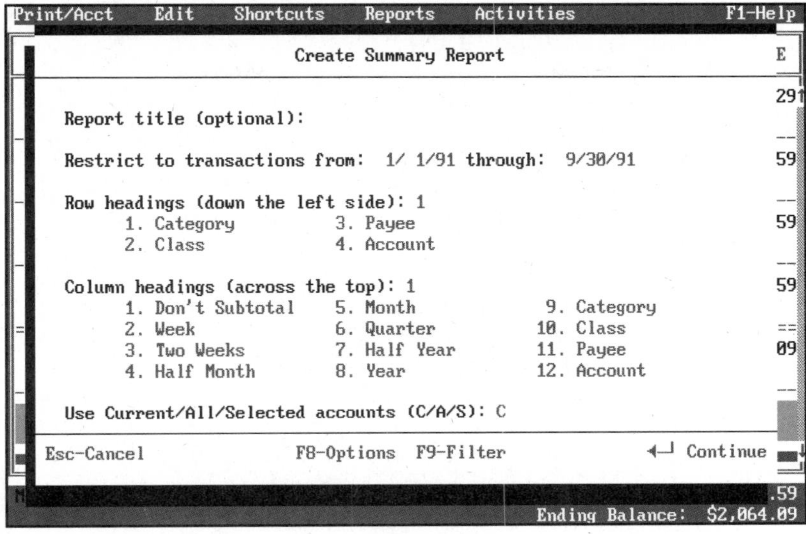

Fig. 14.61. The Create Summary Report screen.

Creating a Budget Report

Chapter 16 describes budgeting as a fundamental tool that businesses and individuals can use to better manage their finances. One of the ongoing steps in using a budget as a tool is to compare the amount you spent with the amount you planned to spend, or budgeted. Quicken's Budget option on the Reports menu enables you to create customized budget reports tailored to your business or personal needs.

To print a budget report, you follow the same steps you use when creating any other custom report. Select the **Budget** option from the Reports menu. Quicken then displays the Create Budget Report screen, shown in figure 14.62, which you use to specify how the custom report should appear. The five fields you use to create a custom summary report are described earlier in the chapter.

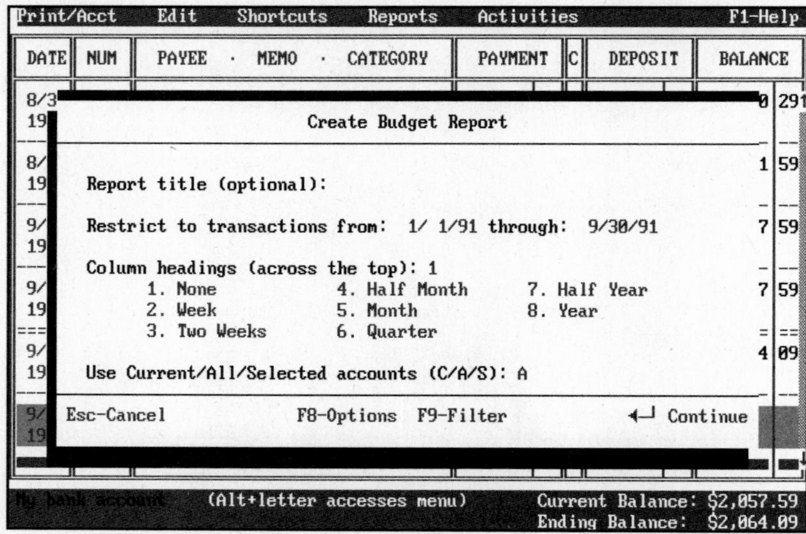

Fig. 14.62. *The Create Budget Report screen.*

Creating an Account Balances Report

You can use the eighth and final option on the Reports menu to create customized account balances reports. If you have extensive investments with several brokers, for example, and you want a report that specifies only those accounts, you can create this report (or a specialized version of this report). Figure 14.63 shows the Create Account Balances Report screen that you use to construct customized account balances reports.

The basic steps you follow for creating an account balances report are the same as for any of the other reports. You select the **Account Balances** option from the Reports menu, and Quicken displays the Create Account Balances Report screen. You complete this screen like the other custom report creation screens. However, some of the fields differ from those you use on other report creation screens.

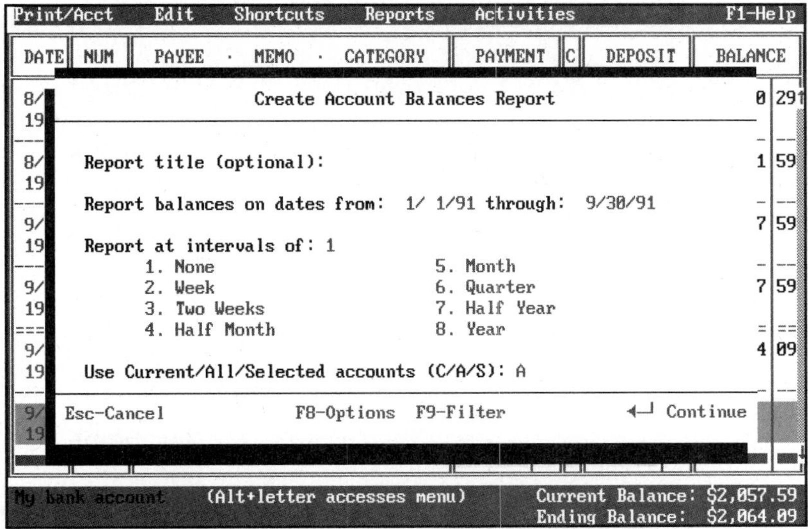

Fig. 14.63. The Create Account Balances Report screen.

Using the Report Title Field

You can use the optional, 34-character `Report title` field to label reports. If you leave this field blank, Quicken supplies the title "Account Balances Report."

Using the Report Balances on Dates from and through Fields

The `Report balances on dates from` and `through` fields are slightly different from the `Restrict to transactions from` and `through` fields on other report creation screens. The account balances report shows the account balances at a specific point in time. This field sets a boundary around the points in time for which an account balances report is generated.

Using the Report at Intervals of Field

The `Report at intervals of` field determines the points in time for which an account balances report is generated. The start of the first interval is the first day of the year. Assuming that the `Report balances on dates from` field is 1/1/91, the first account balances column is for 1/1/91. The next date depends on the interval. If the interval is weekly, the second column is 1/7/91. If the interval is biweekly, the second column is for 1/14/91. If the interval is by half month, the second column is for 1/15/91, and so on. The report shows account balances for each interval between the from and through dates. The last column of the report shows the account balances on the through date.

If the `Report at intervals of` field is set to 1 for None, the only point in time for which the account balances report is generated is the `Report balances on dates through` field.

Using the Use Current/All/Selected Accounts Field

As with the other Quicken reports, the `Use Current/All/Selected accounts` field enables you to determine which account balances are reported on the account balances report. A C designates just the current account; an S designates only the selected accounts; an A designates all accounts. If you choose only selected accounts, Quicken displays the Select Accounts to Include screen shown in figure 14.27.

Chapter Summary

This chapter reviewed the basics of printing any Quicken report and detailed the steps and tricks for printing each of Quicken's personal, business, investment, and custom reports. These reports use the information stored in your account register to provide you with a wealth of financial information that you can use to better manage your personal or business finances.

15

Paying Bills Electronically

With Versions 4.0 and 5.0, Quicken enables you to use CheckFree, an electronic bill payment service, to pay bills. By using Quicken and and a modem, you can send payment instructions to CheckFree Corporation. Your payment instructions include all the information CheckFree needs to actually pay the bill: who you owe the money to, when the bill needs to be paid, how much you owe, and so forth. CheckFree Corporation then either draws a check on or electronically transfers funds from your bank account to whomever you owe the money.

Paying bills electronically isn't for everybody. By getting one more party involved in the bill-paying process, you may just make things more complicated. For those Quicken users who have a modem and who want to stop printing checks, however, electronic payment is appealing. This chapter explains how to set up your system for electronic payment using the CheckFree service, how to identify the people you will pay, and how to actually pay bills.

Setting Up Your System for Electronic Payment

To begin using electronic bill paying, you need to complete three steps. First, you need to complete the paperwork. Second, you need to tell Quicken you want to use CheckFree. Third, you may need to spend a few minutes telling Quicken about your modem. None of the three steps is difficult. Completing your part of the work should take you no more than a few minutes.

Completing the CheckFree Paperwork

Before you begin using the CheckFree service, you need to complete the CheckFree Service Form (see fig. 15.1). The form is not particularly confusing. You need to tell CheckFree Corporation how much memory your computer has, give CheckFree some personal information, including your Social Security number, name, address, and so on, and provide CheckFree with a credit card account number so that CheckFree can charge your credit card account if they—acting on your payment instructions—overdraw your account. (For security reasons, use a security code—similar to what you use for automated teller machines—to gain access to your account.)

After you provide that basic information, you also need to tell CheckFree which phone lines you will be using, specify which account number/security code you will use to gain access to the CheckFree system, and sign an authorization so that CheckFree can deduct funds from your bank account. (If you don't choose an account number/security code, CheckFree creates one for you.)

After you complete the CheckFree Service Form, attach a voided check to the form and then mail the form to Intuit. To mail the form, use the business reply envelope that's specifically included for returning the CheckFree Service Form. Intuit forwards the service form to CheckFree Corporation. In a few days, CheckFree sends you a confirmation letter that confirms or assigns the account number/security code, gives you the telephone number you will use for CheckFree transmissions, and the baud rate, or transmission speed, you will use for sending payment information.

Telling Quicken You Will Use Electronic Bill Paying

After you receive the confirmation letter from CheckFree, you are ready to tell Quicken you are going to use the CheckFree service. Select the **Set Preferences** option from the Main Menu. Quicken then displays the Set Preferences menu shown in figure 15.2. From the Set Preferences menu, select the **Electronic Payment Settings** option. Quicken displays the Electronic Payment menu (see fig. 15.3).

FORMSERVE • (614) 442-8980

CheckFree

CONFIDENTIAL

CHECKFREE SERVICE FORM

(To receive CheckFree service, please complete this form and return the top copy in the enclosed postage paid envelope as soon as possible. As with all CheckFree data, the information on this form is handled with the strictest security. Please print all information.)

IMPORTANT

PLEASE ATTACH A VOIDED CHECK FROM YOUR PAYMENT ACCOUNT TO THE TOP OF THIS FORM.

YOUR EQUIPMENT

How much RAM does your computer have? ___ 384 ___ 512 ___ more than 512

What disk size do you require? ___ 3 1/2 ___ 5 1/4

PERSONAL IDENTIFICATION

Your social security number ___ ___ ___ - ___ ___ - ___ ___ ___ ___

Name ______________________________
Last First Middle

Current Address ______________________________
Street City State Zip

CREDIT CARD INFORMATION

CheckFree requires an account number for at least one credit card, should an overdraft occur. CheckFree reserves the right to charge the account only for the purpose of overdraft protection.

MasterCard or Visa Account Number ____________________ Exp. __________

COMMUNICATIONS INFORMATION

Home Phone (____) ______ - ______ Work Phone (____) ______ - ______

Circle number from which you will be transmitting.

CHECKFREE ACCOUNT NUMBER

Your CheckFree account number/security code is a four digit number which you may choose yourself. You will need to enter this number in your Quicken software and use it as a password to run your software. My number is |__|__|__|__| . If you have no number preference, leave the space provided blank and CheckFree will assign a number for you. You will be given this number at the same time you receive your CheckFree network access telephone number.

Date ____________________ Signature ____________________

Your use of the CheckFree service signifies that you have read and accepted all of the terms and conditions of the CheckFree service contained in the Quicken 3.0 EP package.

CHECKFREE BANK REGISTRATION

I, ______________________________
(Last Name) (First Name) (Middle Initial)

authorize my bank to post my bill payment transactions from CheckFree to my account as indicated below.
I understand that I am in full control of my account. If at any time I decide to discontinue service,
I will simply call or write CheckFree to cancel service.

____
(Bank Name)

____
(Street Address)

____
(City) (State) (Zip)

____
Customer Signature

Return the top copy of this entire form to Intuit in the postage paid envelope provided and retain the bottom copy for your records. Also,

DON'T FORGET TO PROVIDE A VOIDED CHECK WITH THE INFORMATION YOU RETURN TO INTUIT.

X

Return to Intuit in the enclosed postage paid envelope with your order form. Intuit 66 Willow Place, Menlo Park, CA 94025.

CheckFree

Fig. 15.1. The CheckFree Service Form.

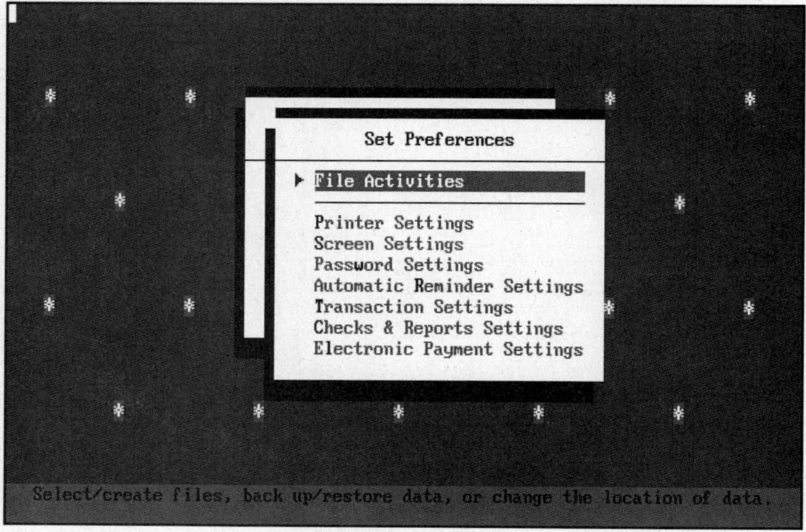

Fig. 15.2. The Set Preferences menu.

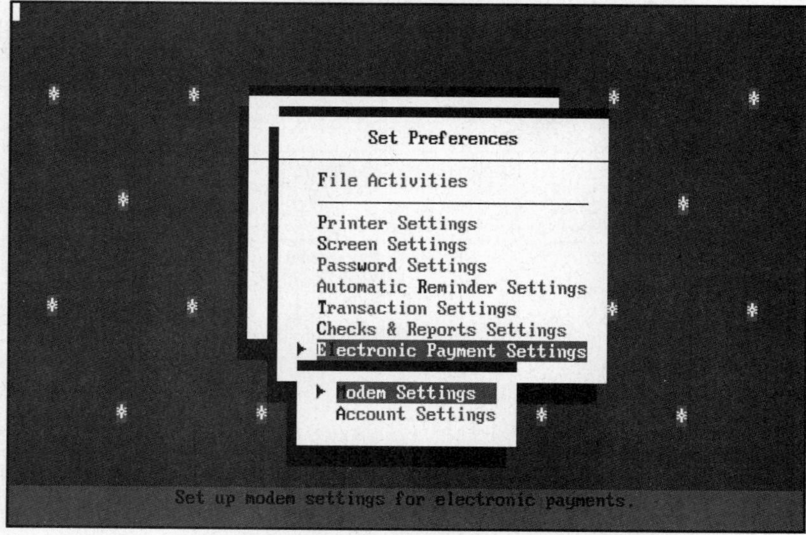

Fig. 15.3. The Electronic Payment Settings menu.

You need to do two things when telling Quicken you will use electronic bill paying. One is to configure your modem. The other is to set up the bank accounts you will use to make the payments.

To configure your modem, complete these steps:

1. Select the **Modem Settings** option from the Electronic Payment Settings menu. Quicken displays the Electronic Payment Settings screen shown in figure 15.4.

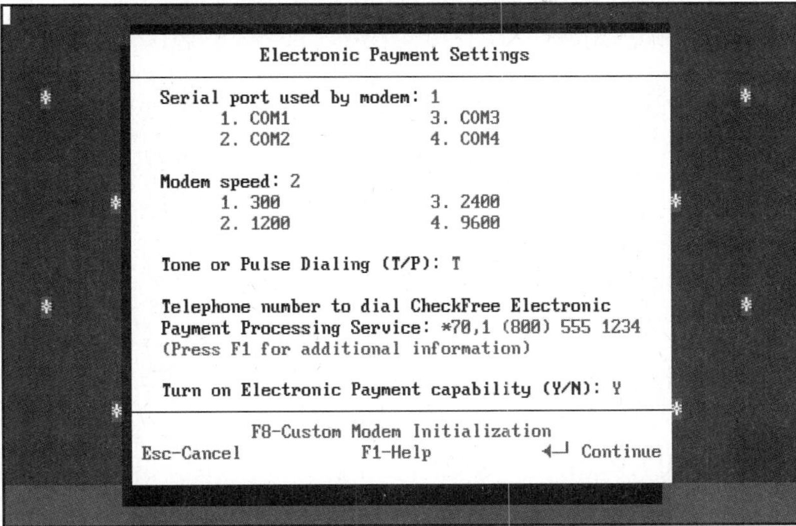

```
Electronic Payment Settings

Serial port used by modem: 1
      1. COM1                 3. COM3
      2. COM2                 4. COM4

Modem speed: 2
      1. 300                  3. 2400
      2. 1200                 4. 9600

Tone or Pulse Dialing (T/P): T

Telephone number to dial CheckFree Electronic
Payment Processing Service: *70,1 (800) 555 1234
(Press F1 for additional information)

Turn on Electronic Payment capability (Y/N): Y

          F8-Custom Modem Initialization
Esc-Cancel            F1-Help           ◄┘ Continue
```

Fig. 15.4. *The Electronic Payment Settings screen.*

2. With the cursor positioned on the `Serial port` field, enter the number of the serial port that your modem uses: 1 for serial communications port 1; 2 for serial communications port 2; and so on. If you don't know which serial communications port your modem uses, follow the cable that connects your modem to your computer and see whether the socket into which the modem cable plugs is labeled. The socket should be labeled with something like "COM1" or "Serial 1."

3. Move the cursor to the `Modem speed` field. Pick the fastest modem speed setting that CheckFree supports and your modem can handle. The CheckFree confirmation letter gives the modem speed settings that CheckFree supports. Your modem user's manual indicates which transmission speeds your modem is capable of running.

4. Move the cursor to the `Tone or Pulse Dialing` field. Press T if your telephone service is tone; press P if your telephone service is pulse. If you aren't sure, refer to your monthly telephone bill or call the telephone company.

5. Move the cursor to the `Telephone number` field. Enter the telephone number given in the confirmation letter you receive from CheckFree. Include any special characters you want to dial. If, for example, you have call waiting, **70* may turn it off. You can start the dialing with **70* so that the beep a call-waiting call makes does not interfere with your data transmission. You can use a comma to pause. Quicken ignores any spaces and parentheses you enter.

6. Move the cursor to the `Turn on Electronic Payment capability` field and press Y for yes. Figure 15.4 shows an example of the completed Electronic Payment Settings screen.

7. (Optional) If your modem is not Hayes-compatible, you need to give Quicken the initialization codes the modem uses to access the telephone line and get a dial tone. The odds are that your modem is Hayes-compatible, so you probably don't have to worry about the codes. If your modem isn't Hayes-compatible, press F8 when the Electronic Payment Settings screen is displayed. Quicken displays the Custom Modem Initialization screen shown in figure 15.5. Enter the initialization code that Quicken should send to the modem to access your telephone line and get a dial tone. The modem user's manual should give the needed initialization code.

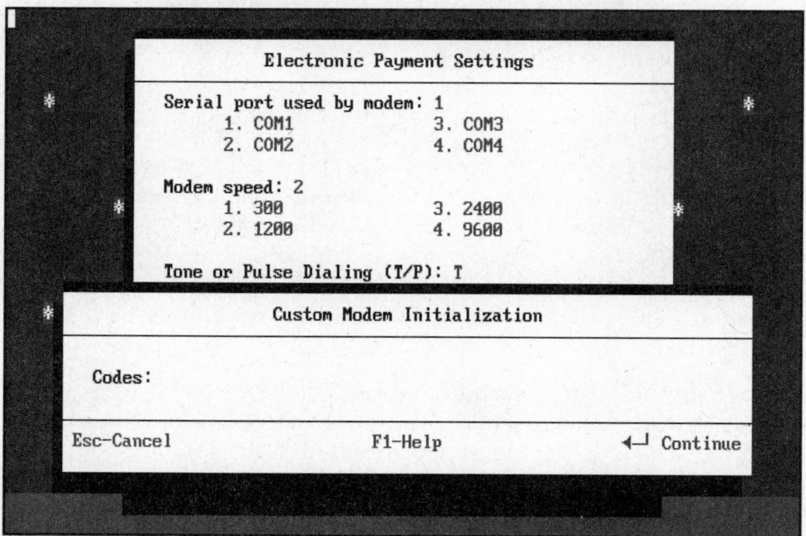

Fig. 15.5. *The Custom Modem Initialization screen.*

Identifying CheckFree Bank Accounts

After you complete the Electronic Payment Settings screen, you are ready to identify the CheckFree bank account or accounts. Essentially, all you do here is identify which bank accounts will be used for electronic payment. You cannot use a credit card, other asset, other liability, or investment account for electronic payment—only bank accounts.

Quicken does not enable you to select an account to use for electronic payment until the modem settings menu has been filled out and the `Turn on Electronic Payment capability` field has been set to Y.

To set up a bank account for electronic payment, follow these steps:

1. Select the **Account Settings** option from the Electronic Payment menu. Quicken next displays the Set Up Account for Electronic Payment screen shown in figure 15.6. Because you can set up only bank accounts for electronic payment, Quicken only lists bank accounts on the screen.

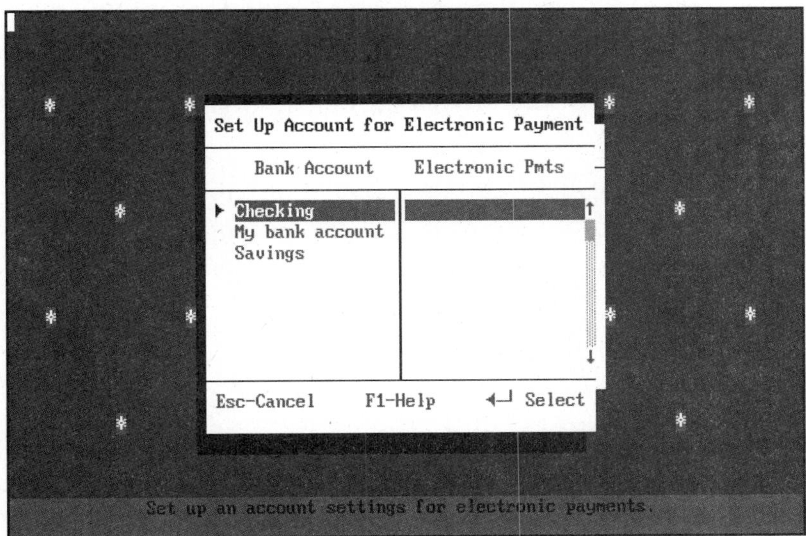

Fig. 15.6. *The Set Up Account for Electronic Payment screen.*

2. To indicate that you may pay bills electronically using the money in an account, use the arrow keys to mark the account you want to pay electronically. Press Enter.

   Quicken next displays a message box that asks whether you want to set up the account for electronic payment (see fig. 15.7).

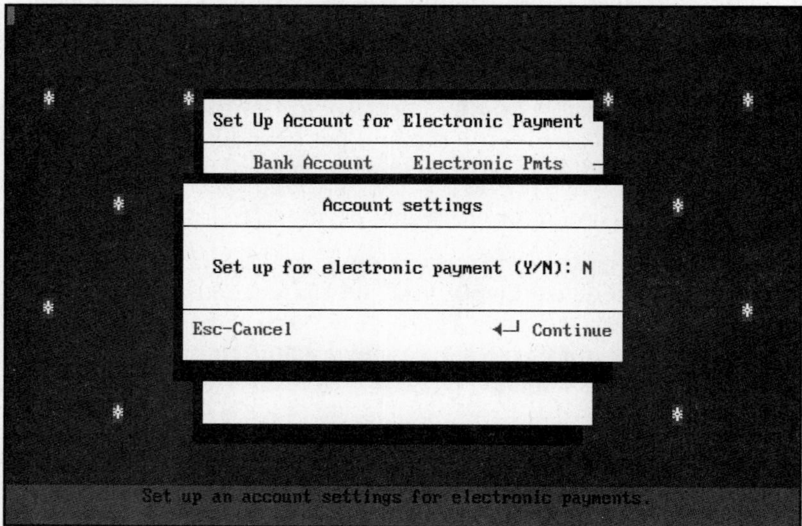

Fig. 15.7. *Quicken asks you to confirm that you want to set up the account for electronic payment.*

3. Press Y for yes and press Enter. Quicken next displays the Electronic Payment Account Settings screen (see fig. 15.8).
4. With the cursor positioned on the `Your First Name` field, enter your first name.
5. Move the cursor to the `MI` field and enter your middle initial.
6. Move the cursor to the `Last` field and enter your last name.
7. Move the cursor to the `Street Address` field and enter the appropriate information.
8. Move the cursor to the `City` field and enter the name of the city or town in which you live.

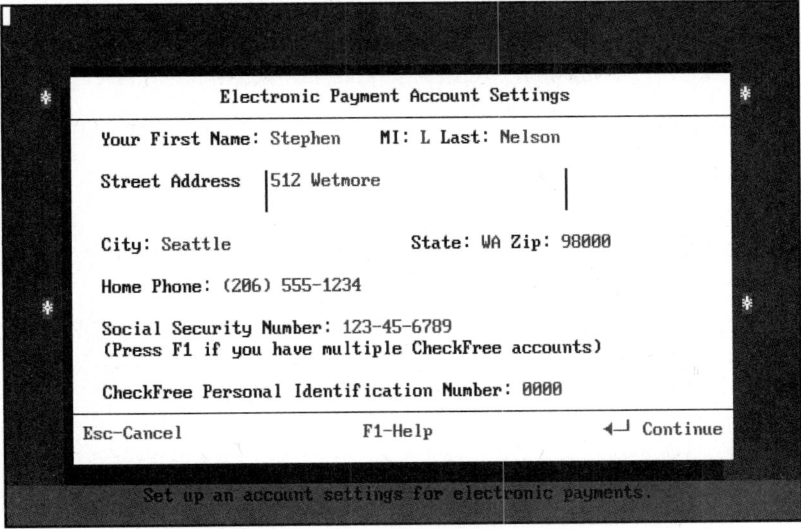

Fig. 15.8. The Electronic Payment Account Settings screen.

9. Move the cursor to the `State` field and enter the two-character abbreviation for your state. If you don't know the two-character abbreviation, enter the first letter of the state name and press Enter. Quicken displays a list of valid state abbreviations from which you choose your state's abbreviation.

10. Move the cursor to the `Zip` field and enter your ZIP code. Quicken validates your entry against a list of valid ZIP codes. If Quicken doesn't recognize what you enter, but you know the code is correct anyway, press Ctrl-Z to force Quicken to accept the ZIP code.

11. Move the cursor to the `Home Phone` field and enter your home phone number, including the area code. You don't have to include the punctuation characters like hyphens and parentheses; Quicken adds these automatically when you press Enter.

12. Move the cursor to the `Social Security Number` field and enter your Social Security number, or the alternative identification number assigned by CheckFree. If you have more than one bank account set up for electronic bill paying—meaning you filled out more than one CheckFree Service Agreement Form—CheckFree gives you identifying numbers based on your Social Security number for each account. That identifying number is what you should enter here.

13. Move the cursor to the `CheckFree Processing Service Account Number` field and enter your account number/security number. Figure 15.8 shows an example of a completed screen.

14. When the Electronic Payment Account Settings screen is complete, press Enter. Quicken redisplays the Set Up Account for Electronic Payment screen. The account you set up now is marked as "enabled" for electronic payment. When the account is the one selected, Quicken adds several additional menu options that you can use for processing electronic payments.

Identifying the People You Will Pay

To pay a bill electronically, you need to collect and store information about each person or company you will pay so that CheckFree Corporation can process payments to the person or business. To collect and store this information, follow these steps:

1. From the Main Menu, select the **Write/Print Checks** option. Quicken displays the electronic payment version of the screen (see fig. 15.9).

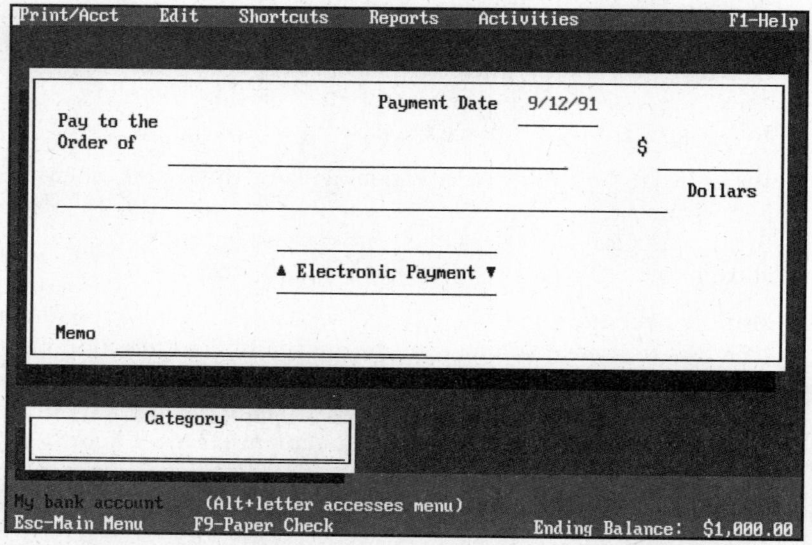

***Fig. 15.9.** The electronic payment version of the Write/Print Checks screen.*

2. Press Ctrl-Y to access the Electronic Payee List. Alternatively, press Alt-S to access the Shortcuts menu and then choose the Electronic **Payee List** option from that menu. Either way, Quicken displays the Electronic Payee List screen shown in figure 15.10.

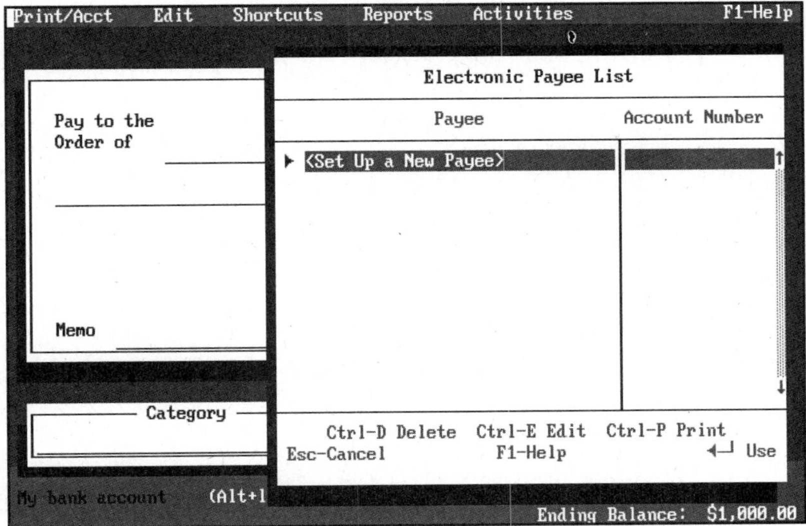

Fig. 15.10. The Electronic Payee List.

3. To set up your first electronic payee, select `Set Up New Payee` on the list. Quicken displays the Set Up Electronic Payee screen (see fig. 15.11).

4. Move the cursor to the `Name` field and enter the complete name of the person or company you want to pay. You have up to 28 characters of space.

5. Move the cursor to the `Street Address` field and enter the mailing address for sending payments to the payee.

6. Move the cursor to the `City` field and enter the name of the payee's city or town.

7. Move the cursor to the `State` field and enter the two-character abbreviation for the payee's state. If you don't know the two-character abbreviation, enter the first letter of the state name and press Enter. Quicken displays a list of valid state abbreviations from which you can pick the correct one.

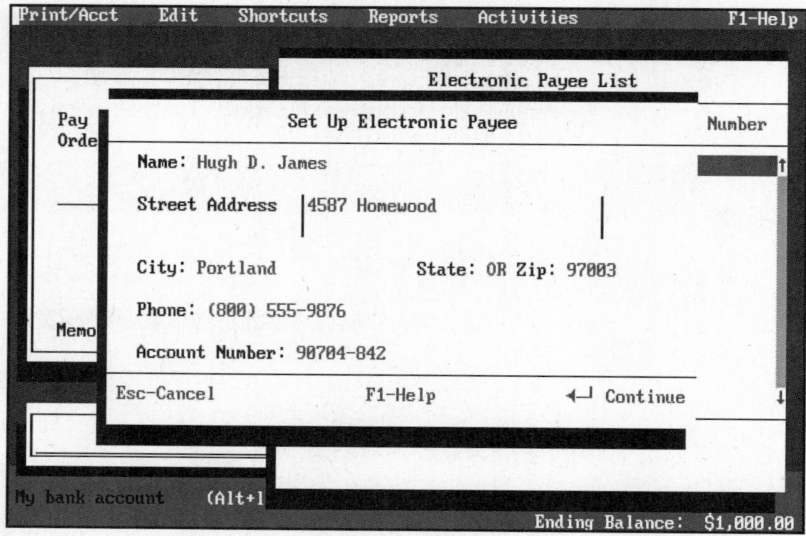

Fig. 15.11. *The Set Up Electronic Payee screen.*

8. Move the cursor to the `Zip` field and enter the payee's ZIP code. Quicken validates your entry against a list of valid ZIP codes. If Quicken doesn't recognize what you enter but you know the code is correct, press Ctrl-Z to force Quicken to accept the ZIP code.

9. Move the cursor to the `Phone` field and enter the person's phone number, including the area code. You don't have to include the punctuation characters like hyphens and parentheses; Quicken adds these automatically when you press Enter.

10. Move the cursor to the `Account Number` field and enter the account number the person or business uses to identify you.

11. When the Set Up Electronic Payee screen is complete, press Enter. Quicken returns you to the Electronic Payee List screen. Figure 15.11 shows an example of a completed Set Up Electronic Payee screen. If you want to define additional electronic payees, repeat steps 3 through 11.

As on other lists in the Quicken system, you can use Ctrl-D to delete a payee from the Electronic Payee List, you can use Ctrl-E to edit a payee on the Electronic Payee List and you can use Ctrl-P to print a list of electronic payees. The only difference in working with electronic payees as compared to accounts, categories, classes, and so on is that you cannot edit or delete an electronic payee if an untransmitted transaction exists for that payee. The next section explains more about untransmitted transactions.

Paying Bills with CheckFree

Paying bills electronically closely resembles the process of writing and printing checks with Quicken. For that reason, this chapter doesn't repeat the discussions of Chapters 6 and 7, which cover how you write and print checks with Quicken. Instead, this section concentrates on those parts of the process that are different. (If you haven't used the Quicken Write/Print Checks feature, you may want to review Chapters 6 and 7 before going further in this chapter.)

After you set up for electronic payment and identify the people you will pay, you are ready to begin paying bills electronically. For each bill you want to pay, follow these steps:

1. From Quicken's Main Menu, select the **Write/Print Checks** option. Quicken displays the electronic payment version of the Write Checks screen (see fig. 15.9).

2. Complete the electronic payment version of the Write Checks screen in the same way you complete the regular version of the screen, except for the following differences.

   Rather than typing in the payee's name, you select the payee from the electronic payee list. To display the electronic payee list, press Ctrl-Y. To use one of the electronic payees shown on the list, use the arrow keys to select the payee and then press Enter. You also can use Quicken's auto-completion feature to enter an electronic payee.

   Rather than track unprinted checks, Quicken shows you the `Checks to Xmit` (transmit) in the lower right corner of the screen.

3. When the Write Checks screen is complete, press Enter when the cursor is on the `Category` field, or you can press Ctrl-Enter or F10 when the cursor is on one of the other fields.

The check containing the electronic payment scrolls off the screen, leaving behind an empty check that you can use to complete another electronic payment. Until the time you transmit the electronic payments, you can edit the electronic payments just like those for a check.

You also can enter and edit electronic payments using the Quicken register. Quicken identifies electronic payment transactions in the Quicken register with >>>>> in the `Num` field.

After you enter the electronic payments, you are ready to transmit the electronic payments to CheckFree Corporation so that they can be paid. To transmit the electronic payments, follow these steps:

1. Turn on your modem.

   Quicken first attempts to initialize the modem and then retries the modem twice before Quicken informs you that it is unable to initialize the modem.

2. Press Ctrl-I to initiate the electronic payment transmission, or press Alt-P to access the Print/Acct menu (see fig. 15.12) and select the **Transmit Payments** option.

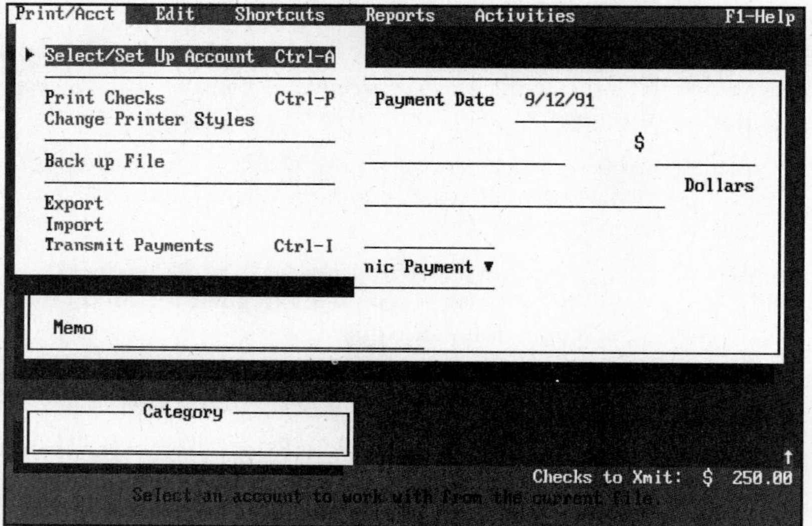

Fig. 15.12. The electronic payment version of the Print/Acct menu.

   Quicken displays the message box shown in figure 15.13, which tells you how many payments you have to transmit.

3. If you are ready to transmit, press Enter. Alternatively, if you want to review the payments that are ready to be transmitted, press F9, and Quicken displays the Preview Transmission to CheckFree screen (see fig. 15.14). The screen lists the payments Quicken will transmit. After you do transmit, CheckFree sends confirmation numbers back to Quicken for each of the transmitted payments. Confirmation numbers are stored in the Memo field.

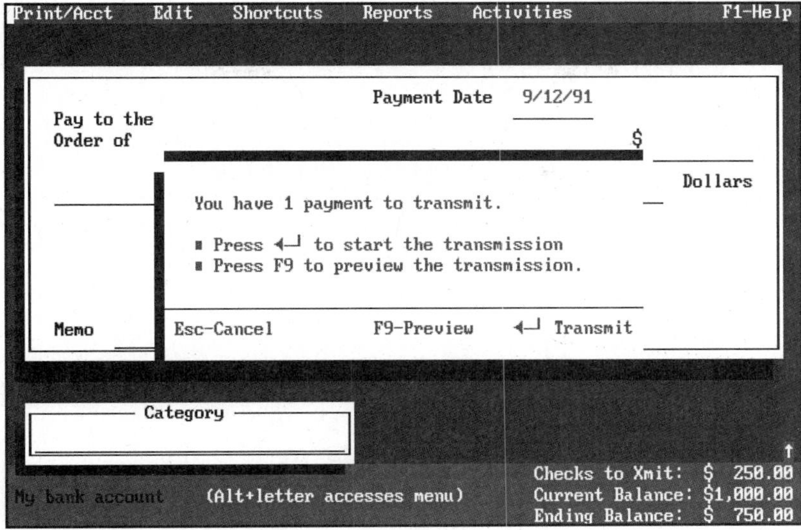

Fig. 15.13. The message box that tells you how many payments you have to transmit.

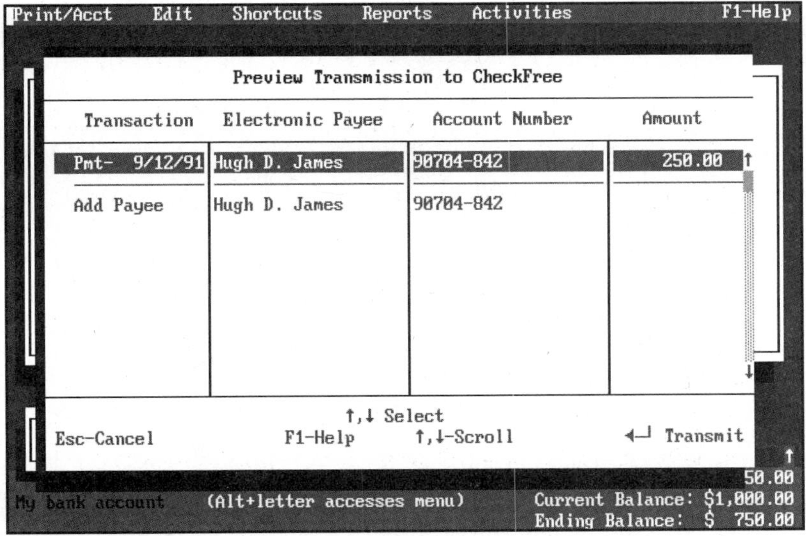

Fig. 15.14. The Preview Transmission to CheckFree screen.

Using the Special CheckFree Functions

Quicken adds a couple of menu options to the Edit menu and one menu option to the Activities menu for processing electronic payments (see figs. 15.15 and 15.16). The Edit menu has a **Transmit Stop Payment Request** feature and an **Electronic Payment Inquiry** feature. The Activities menu has a **Send Electronic Mail** option. If you use the CheckFree service, you have the opportunity to use all three of these features.

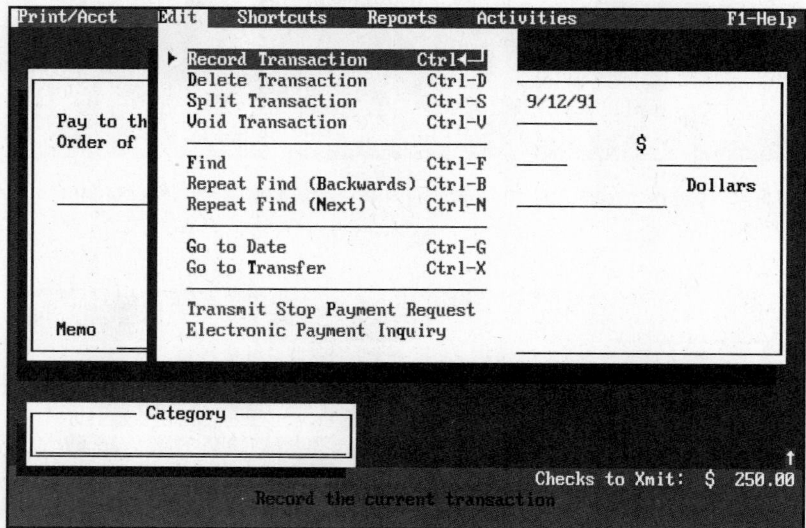

Fig. 15.15. The electronic payment version of the Edit menu.

Issuing a Stop Payment Request

You can use Quicken to issue stop payment requests on electronic payments you transmitted previously. To do so, first turn on your modem. Highlight the payment in the register, press Alt-E to access the Edit menu, and then press P to initiate the stop payment request. Quicken asks you to confirm that you want to stop payment. Press Y for yes. Quicken immediately transmits your request to CheckFree. If the transmission is successful, Quicken marks the transaction as "Void." Obviously, as with stop payment requests issued directly to the bank, you need to make the request before the transaction is processed.

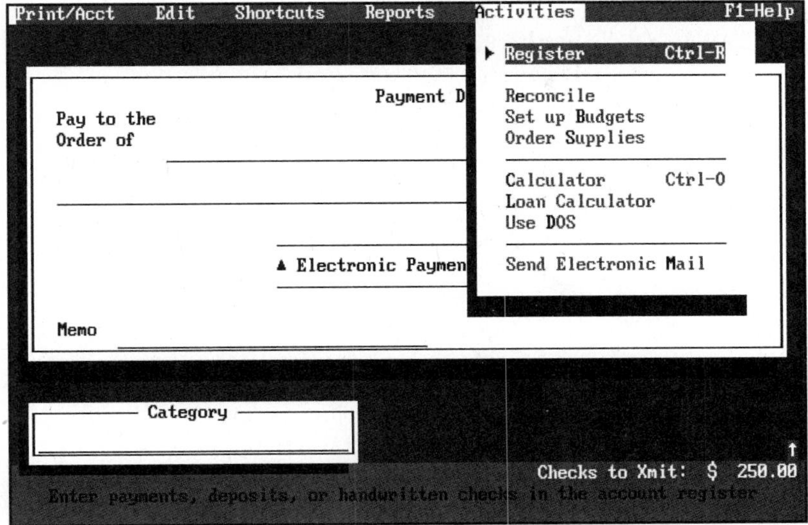

Fig. 15.16. The electronic payment version of the Activities menu.

Making an Electronic Payment Inquiry

You can inquire about a payment you transmitted previously. Say, for example, that you receive a telephone call from someone who wants to know whether you have sent a check yet. First turn on your modem. Highlight the payment in the register, press Alt-E to access the Edit menu, and press Q to initiate the payment inquiry. Quicken displays the Payment Information screen, which gives all the details of the transmitted payment, including the payee, the scheduled payment date, the amount, the account number, and the confirmation number you received from CheckFree. The screen also indicates whether you can stop payment. Finally, Quicken also asks whether you want to send a message to CheckFree regarding the transaction.

Sending Electronic Mail

You also can send an electronic message to CheckFree. To do so, use the **Send Electronic Mail** option on the electronic payment version of the Activities menu. To send a mail message, first turn on your modem. Press

Alt-A to access the Activities menu and select the **Send Electronic Mail** option. Quicken displays the Transmit Inquiry to CheckFree screen (see fig. 15.17). Type the message you want to send and then press Enter. When you press Enter, Quicken sends the message.

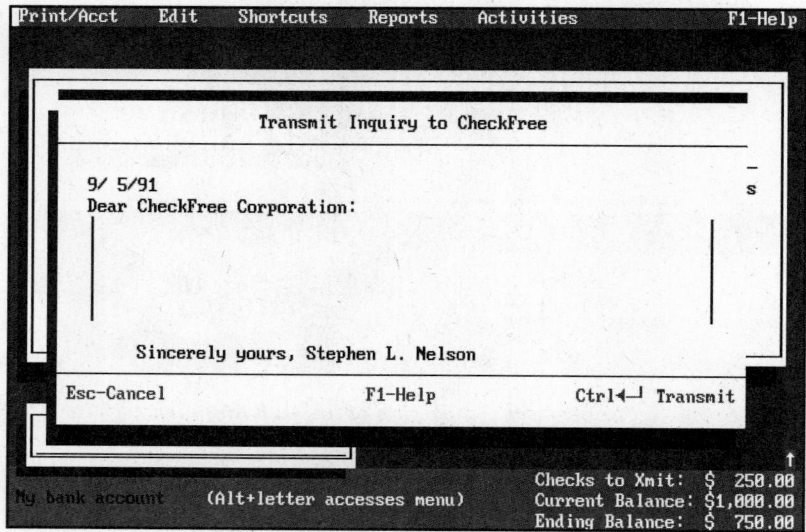

Fig. 15.17. *The Transmit Inquiry to CheckFree screen.*

Chapter Summary

This chapter described Quicken's electronic payment capability. The chapter described what you need to do to set up your system for electronic payment, how to identify the people you will pay electronically, and how to actually transmit payments to those people. The chapter also gave an overview of the three special menu options that Quicken adds for supporting the electronic payment feature: transmitting stop payment requests, making electronic payment inquiries, and sending electronic mail messages to CheckFree Corporation.

Part IV

Putting Quicken To Work

Includes

Using Quicken To Budget

Using Quicken for Home Accounting

Using Quicken in Your Business

Using Quicken To Prepare for Income Taxes

16

Using Quicken To Budget

Budgeting has an undeserved bad reputation. People tend to think of a budget as something like financial handcuffs—an obstacle to enjoyment and a drag on financial freedoms. Actually, nothing could be further from the truth. Budgeting is a simple tool with astonishingly positive benefits for businesses and households. Essentially, budgets represent game plans that calibrate, or specify, what you need to do to succeed in your business or personal financial life.

Because one of Quicken's most significant benefits is that you can monitor your success in achieving a budget, this chapter reviews the three steps of budgeting, describes how Quicken helps, and provides some tips on how to budget successfully.

Defining Budgeting

Budgeting consists of the following three steps:

1. Setting your business or personal financial goals.
2. Using your list of goals as a guide to developing a financial game plan, or budget.
3. Using the budget to monitor your spending to determine how closely you are progressing toward your business or personal goals.

Setting Your Goals

Budgeting begins with identifying your goals in business or life. You are on your own here. When building a list of your goals, however, keep the following two things in mind:

- Keep your goals general.
- Involve other people—particularly those who have to live within the budget—in setting the goals.

By stating your goals in more general terms, you don't start with built-in constraints and conflicts. Suppose that your goal is to live in an opulent fashion where the weather is warm and sunny. With this goal, you have a world of choices and an incredible range of prices. If your goal is to live in a mansion in Beverly Hills, you have limited yourself. Living in a Beverly Hills mansion is one way to live in an opulent fashion where the weather is warm and sunny, but it is not the only way. Keep your options open as you build a list of life goals, and you are more likely to get more of the things you want out of life and to achieve more in your business.

A second point about setting goals is to involve other people. The reason for this rule is that people who work together to build a list of goals later work together to achieve the goals. But working together also produces better goal lists.

The United States Air Force and many businesses play a game called Desert Survival that demonstrates the results of a group working to make a decision. You pretend that a plane on which you are a passenger crashes in the desert. You are 30 miles off course and at least that far from civilization; it's more than 100 degrees in the shade, and you can salvage about 15 or 20 items before the plane bursts into flames. First, you decide by yourself whether you stay with the wreckage or start towards civilization and which of the items you keep. Next, you repeat the analysis in groups of four or five people, and this time the entire group must agree on the plan and which items to keep. The interesting thing about the game and the reason that this whole issue applies to budgeting is that in almost every case, when people make the decisions together, they dramatically increase their chances of survival.

Making the wrong budgeting decision may not cost you your life or your business, but the moral of the desert survival game still applies. Whether you are budgeting your personal or business finances, you build better goal lists when you get more people involved. Your spouse may end up discovering some option you did not consider. A daughter may admit that she is not interested in piano lessons or business school. Your partner may point out a subtle flaw you overlooked.

When you finish setting your goals, write them down. Do not limit yourself to just financial goals. You may have financial goals, such as accumulating the down payment for a new car or taking a special vacation. You also may have nonfinancial goals, such as spending more time with your family or beginning some recreational or charitable activity.

Designing a Game Plan

After you build a list of goals, you are ready to create a game plan for achieving them. As you work through the details, you undoubtedly will modify your goals and make compromises. If you describe your goals in general terms and include everybody's good ideas, you should be able to come up with a detailed list of the costs of pursuing and achieving your business or personal goals.

At this stage, you decide what you are going to spend on entertainment or a vacation, how much you can spend on housing, and other such issues. As a rough yardstick to use to build your own detailed game plan, table 16.1 summarizes what percent of their income most people spend on the average in various spending categories. This list comes from the July 1990 issue of *Survey of Current Business*, which is published by the U.S. Department of Commerce. The survey data is one year old, but because the results show as percentages of total income, the data are still valid for planning and comparison purposes.

If you are budgeting for a business, you can visit your local public library to obtain similar information. Dun and Bradstreet and Robert Morris Associates annually publish financial information on businesses grouped by industry and business size. For business or personal budgeting, however, do not interpret the averages as anything other than general guidelines. Seeing other people's spending provides a useful perspective on your own spending, but your goals should determine the details of your financial game plan.

Table 16.1
Average Spending Based on After-Tax Income

Spending Category	*Percent*
Durable Goods	
Motor vehicles and parts	5.43
Furniture and household equipment	4.50
Other durables	2.29
Nondurable goods	
Food	15.74
Clothing and shoes	5.38
Gasoline and oil	2.13
Other nondurables	6.57
Services	
Housing	14.34
Utilities	5.46
Transportation	3.47
Medical care	12.12
Other Services	14.71
Interest	2.74
Savings	5.12

When budgeting for taxes you should be able to estimate the amount fairly precisely. You can pick up one of the personal income tax guides to give you all the details, but the following general rules apply: Social Security amounts to 7.65 percent of your earnings up to a maximum amount of $53,400 of taxable income for 1991, and Medicare amounts to 1.45 percent of your earnings from $53,400 to $125,000. Federal income taxes depend upon your filing status and your taxable income. Generally, you can calculate your taxable income as follows:

(Total income) – (your deductions) – (your personal exemptions) = your taxable income

Your income includes wages, salaries, interest, dividends, and so on. Deductions include individual retirement accounts, alimony, and your itemized deductions or your standard deduction. Personal exemptions are $2,100 allowances you subtract from your total income for each person in your family. Your filing status relates to whether you are single, married, and have dependents. The standard deductions for the various filing statuses for 1991 are shown in table 16.2. The tax-rate schedules for the various filing statuses that show the taxes you pay on your taxable income are shown in table 16.3. For 1992 and beyond, the dollar amounts for personal exemptions, the standard deduction amounts, and the tax-rate schedules are adjusted for inflation.

Table 16.2
Standard Deductions for 1991

Filing Status	*Standard Deduction*
Married filing joint return and qualifying widow(er)	$5,700*
Head of household	$5,000*
Single	$3,400*
Married filing separately	$2,850*

*To these amounts, you can add the following amounts:

For the elderly or blind—an additional standard deduction of $650 is allowed for a married individual (whether filing jointly or separately) or a qualifying widow(er) who is 65 or older or blind ($1,300 if the individual is 65 or older and blind, $2,600 if both spouses are 65 or older and blind); an additional standard deduction of $850 is allowed for an unmarried individual (single or head of household) who is 65 or older or blind ($1,700 if the individual is 65 or older and blind).

Limited standard deduction for dependents—if you can be claimed as a dependent on another person's return, your standard deduction is the greater of (a) $550 or (b) your earned income, up to the standard deduction amount. To this amount, add any amount for the elderly or blind as discussed in the preceding paragraph.

Deduction for Exemptions

The amount you may deduct for each exemption is increased to $2,150. But your deduction may be reduced or eliminated if your adjusted gross income is more than: (a) $150,000 if your filing status is married filing jointly or qualifying widow(er); (b) $125,000 if your filing status is head of household; (c) $100,000 if your filing status is single; or (d) $75,000 if your filing status is married filing separately. If your adjusted gross income is more than the amount shown for your filing status, get IRS Publication 505, "Tax Withholding and Estimated Tax," to figure the amount, if any, you may deduct on line 4 of the worksheet on page 3 or IRS Form 1040-ES.

Note: If you can be claimed as a dependent on another person's 1991 return, your personal exemption is not allowed, even if that person's deduction for exemptions is reduced or eliminated.

Table 16.3
1991 Tax Rate Schedules*

Single—Schedule X

If line 5 is: Over	But not over	**The tax is:**	of the amount over
$0	$20,350	15%	$0
20,350	49,300	$3,052.50+28%	20,350
49,300	———	11,158.50+31%	49,300

Head of household—Schedule Z

If line 5 is: Over	But not over	**The tax is:**	of the amount over
$0	$27,300	15%	$0
27,300	70,450	$4,095.00+28%	27,300
70,450	———	16,177.00+31%	70,450

Married filing jointly or Qualifying widow(er)—Schedule Y-1

If line 5 is: Over	But not over	**The tax is:**	of the amount over
$0	$34,000	15%	$0
34,000	82,150	$5,100.00+28%	34,000
82,150	———	18,582.00+31%	82,150

Married filing separately—Schedule Y-2

If line 5 is: Over	But not over	**The tax is:**	of the amount over
$0	$17,000	15%	$0
17,000	41,075	$2,550.00+28%	17,000
41,075	———	9,291.00+31%	41,075

***Caution:** *Do not use these Tax Rate Schedules to figure your 1990 taxes. Use only to figure your 1991 estimated taxes.*

When you finish setting your goals, write down your spending game plan. Now that you know how much time and money you can allocate to each of your goals, you often can expand your list of goals to include estimates of costs and time. Table 16.4 lists a set of sample personal goals, and table 16.5 lists a set of sample business goals. Table 16.6 shows an example of an annual personal budget with monthly breakdowns supporting the goals from table 16.4. Table 16.7 shows an example of an annual business budget that supports the goals from table 16.5.

Table 16.4
Sample Personal Budget Goals

Goal	*Cost*	*Timing*
Visit Egypt	$5,000	1995
Start fishing again	$50	ASAP
Prepare for retirement	$100,000	2025
Spend time with family	$0	ASAP

Table 16.5
Sample Business Budget Goals

Goal	*Cost*	*Timing*
Generate 20% more annual sales	$20,000	over year
Pay down credit line	$5,000	year-end
Make profits of $25,000	$25,000	over year
Provide better quality service	$0	ASAP

Table 16.6
Sample Budget To Support Personal Goals

Personal budget	*Annual*	*Monthly*
Income	$25,000	$2,083
Outgo		
Income taxes	$1,750	$146
Social Security	1,878	156

continues

Table 16.6 *(continued)*

Personal budget	*Annual*	*Monthly*
Rent	6,000	500
Other housing	3,000	250
Food	4,800	400
Transportation	2,500	208
Vacation, recreation	1,200	100
Fishing gear	50	4
Clothing	1,250	104
Savings—IRA	500	42
Other	1,200	100
Total Expenses	24,628	2,052
Leftover/Contingency	373	31

Table 16.7
Sample Budget To Support Business Goals

Business budget	*Annual*	*Monthly*
Sales	$125,000	$10,417
Expenses		
Materials	$30,000	$2,500
Labor	30,000	2,500
Rent	12,000	1,000
Transportation	12,500	1,042
Supplies	12,000	1,000
Legal/Accounting	1,200	100
Other	2,100	175
Total expenses	99,800	8,317
Profits	25,200	2,100

Notice a few things about the relationships between the goals and budget. First, some of your goals represent things you can achieve almost immediately, and others may take much longer. Second, some goals on your list do not directly affect your budget. Third, some expenditures do not tie to formal, or stated, goals, but still represent implied goals. You do not, for example, list feeding the children or staying in business as goals, but these goals may be your most important ones.

Monitoring Your Progress

The third and final step in budgeting relates to monitoring your progress in achieving your personal or business goals. On a periodic basis—every month or quarter—compare the amount you budgeted to spend with the amount you actually spent. Sometimes, people view these comparisons as negative, but the idea is that if you are following your budget, you are moving toward your goals. If, for example, you get through the first month of the year and are operating under the budget shown in table 16.6, you can compare what you spent with your budget. If you see that you are having difficulty salting away extra money for the trip to Egypt and into your individual retirement account, you know that your spending or your goals need to change.

Using Quicken To Budget

Quicken provides two related features that enable you to budget more effectively for your personal finances and for small businesses: categories and reporting.

Using Categories

With categories, you can distribute each of the checks you record into a spending category such as housing, contribution, entertainment, or taxes. You also can identify each of the deposits you record as falling into a revenue category such as wages, gross sales, or interest income. The steps and benefits of using categories are discussed in more detail in Chapter 10. By noting the category into which every check and deposit you record belongs, you can produce reports that summarize and total the amounts spent for each category. Figure 16.1 shows an example of a Quicken spending report.

Example Category Report
1/ 1/91 Through 1/31/91

Bank,Cash,CC Accounts Page 1
1/10/91

Category Description		1/ 1/91- 1/31/91
INFLOWS		
Interest Income		10.75
Salary Income		2,000.00
TOTAL INFLOWS		2,010.75
OUTFLOWS		
Automobile Service		34.91
Bank Charge		5.00
Entertainment		28.94
Home Repair & Maint.		24.53
Housing		0.00
Late fees:		
Late payment fees-credit	11.59	
Late payment fees-mortg.	28.73	
Total Late fees		40.32
Office Expenses		34.56
Water, Gas, Electric		75.39
Outflows - Other		200.08
TOTAL OUTFLOWS		443.73
OVERALL TOTAL		1,567.02

Fig. 16.1. *A sample category report.*

If you decide to tap the power of budgeting, reports such as the report shown in figure 16.1 are invaluable. The report shows what you actually spend. What you actually spend can be compared to what you budgeted. When your actual spending matches your budgeted spending, you know you are following your financial game plan. When your spending doesn't match your budget, you know you are not following your game plan.

Creating Budgeting Reports

Quicken also enables you to enter any amount budgeted for a category. With this information, Quicken calculates the difference, called a variance, between the total spent on a category and the budgeted amount for a category. Quicken does the arithmetic related to monitoring how closely you follow your budget and how successfully you are marching toward your life goals. Figure 16.2 shows an example of a Quicken budget report.

Example Budget Report
1/ 1/91 Through 1/31/91

Bank,Cash,CC Accounts
1/10/91

Page 1

Category Description	1/ 1/91 Actual	- Budget	1/31/91 Diff
INFLOWS			
Salary Income	2,000.00	2,000.00	0.00
TOTAL INFLOWS	2,000.00	2,000.00	0.00
OUTFLOWS			
Automobile Service	34.91	50.00	-15.09
Bank Charge	5.00	0.00	5.00
Entertainment	28.94	50.00	-21.06
Home Repair & Maint.	24.53	0.00	24.53
Late Payment Fees	0.00	0.00	0.00
Office Expenses	34.56	25.00	9.56
Water, Gas, Electric	75.39	60.00	15.39
TOTAL OUTFLOWS	203.33	185.00	18.33
OVERALL TOTAL	1,796.67	1,815.00	-18.33

***Fig. 16.2.** A sample budget report.*

Setting Up Budgets

Of course, to print budget reports, you first need to enter the budget amounts that Quicken uses for its actual-to-budget comparisons. Quicken 5 provides a handy new feature to make setting up a budget fast and easy, a spreadsheet screen into which you enter budgeted amounts for each category and subcategory.

To use Quicken's budgeting spreadsheet, you select the **Set Up Budgets** option on the Activities menu. When you select this option, Quicken displays a spreadsheet screen into which you enter monthly budgeted amounts for each of the categories and, optionally, subcategories and account transfers on your category list. Figure 16.3 shows the budget spreadsheet screen.

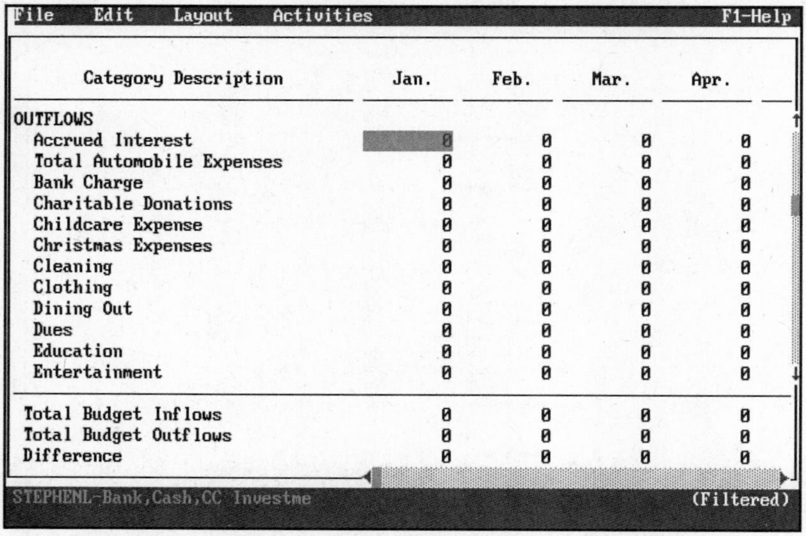

```
File    Edit    Layout    Activities                                F1-Help

     Category Description          Jan.       Feb.       Mar.       Apr.

OUTFLOWS
  Accrued Interest                    0          0          0          0
  Total Automobile Expenses           0          0          0          0
  Bank Charge                         0          0          0          0
  Charitable Donations                0          0          0          0
  Childcare Expense                   0          0          0          0
  Christmas Expenses                  0          0          0          0
  Cleaning                            0          0          0          0
  Clothing                            0          0          0          0
  Dining Out                          0          0          0          0
  Dues                                0          0          0          0
  Education                           0          0          0          0
  Entertainment                       0          0          0          0

 Total Budget Inflows                 0          0          0          0
 Total Budget Outflows                0          0          0          0
 Difference                           0          0          0          0
STEPHENL-Bank,Cash,CC Investme                                 (Filtered)
```

Fig. 16.3. *The budget spreadsheet screen.*

Changing the Spreadsheet Layout

By default, Quicken assumes you want to budget on a monthly basis so the spreadsheet displays a column for each month. However, you can also budget on a quarterly and monthly basis. To do this, press Alt-L to display the Layout menu (see fig. 16.4). Then, select the appropriate option, **Quarter** or **Year**.

Entering and Editing Budget Data

One way to enter budgeted amounts is directly into the spreadsheet. You can enter this information by moving the cursor to the budget amount you want to enter—such as childcare expenses for January—and then typing the new budget figure. A second way to enter budget amounts is to copy amounts into the spreadsheet using one of the Edit menu commands. Figure 16.5 shows the Edit menu that is available on the budget spreadsheet screen.

Select the Edit menu's **AutoCreate** option if you want to set the budgeted amounts for a month or series of months based on previous actual income and expense figures. When you select the **AutoCreate** option, Quicken displays the Automatically Create Budget screen shown in figure 16.6. Enter the date range of the actual monthly figures you want to copy in the `Copy`

From and Through fields. Identify the first budgeting period in which the first copied number should be placed in the Place budget in month field. To indicate how Quicken should round copied values before using them as your new budgeted amounts, move the cursor to the Round values to nearest field and select a rounding option: 1 to round to the nearest penny, 2 to round to the nearest 10 dollars, and 3 to round to the nearest 100 dollars. Finally, if you want Quicken to calculate the average for the copied actual figures and use that as the budgeted figure, move the cursor to the Use average for period field and enter a *Y*.

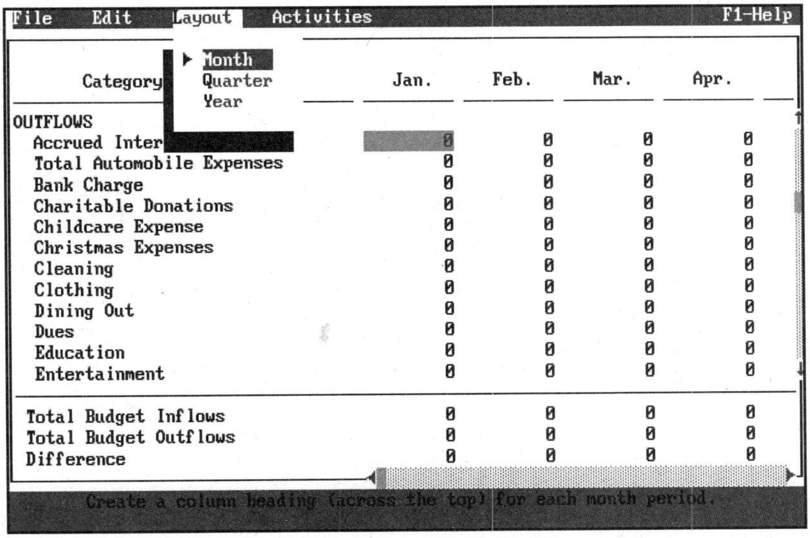

```
File   Edit   Layout   Activities                               F1-Help
                    ▸ Month
     Category       Quarter         Jan.      Feb.      Mar.      Apr.
                    Year
OUTFLOWS
  Accrued Inter                       0         0         0         0
  Total Automobile Expenses           0         0         0         0
  Bank Charge                         0         0         0         0
  Charitable Donations                0         0         0         0
  Childcare Expense                   0         0         0         0
  Christmas Expenses                  0         0         0         0
  Cleaning                            0         0         0         0
  Clothing                            0         0         0         0
  Dining Out                          0         0         0         0
  Dues                                0         0         0         0
  Education                           0         0         0         0
  Entertainment                       0         0         0         0

 Total Budget Inflows                 0         0         0         0
 Total Budget Outflows                0         0         0         0
 Difference                           0         0         0         0

   Create a column heading (across the top) for each month period.
```

Fig. 16.4. *The Layout menu options.*

The Edit menu's **Two Week** option enables you to budget amounts that occur every two weeks, such as salary paid biweekly. To use this handy option, first select the category or subcategory for which you want to budget. Then, select the **Two Week** option from the Edit menu. Quicken displays the Set Up 2 Week Budget screen (see fig. 16.7). Next, enter the income or expense figure which will occur every two weeks in the Enter the amount field. Then, move the cursor to Every 2 weeks starting field and enter the date the income or expense will first occur.

The **Fill Right** option copies the highlighted budget amount right into each of the subsequent months' budget fields. If, for example, you used the arrow keys to highlight the January entertainment expense budget, which is set to $25, and then you select the **Fill Right** option, Quicken copies 25 to the entertainment expense budgets for February, March, April, May, and so on.

```
File   Edit   Layout   Activities                                F1-Help

          ▸ AutoCreate
            Two Week                 Jan.      Feb.      Mar.      Apr.
            Fill Right
OUTFLOW     Fill Columns
  Accru     Budget Subcats              0         0         0         0
  Total     Budget Transfers            0         0         0         0
  Bank                                  0         0         0         0
  Chari                                 0         0         0         0
  Childcare Expense                     0         0         0         0
  Christmas Expenses                    0         0         0         0
  Cleaning                              0         0         0         0
  Clothing                              0         0         0         0
  Dining Out                            0         0         0         0
  Dues                                  0         0         0         0
  Education                             0         0         0         0
  Entertainment                         0         0         0         0

 Total Budget Inflows                   0         0         0         0
 Total Budget Outflows                  0         0         0         0
 Difference                             0         0         0         0

           Derive a budget from your actual transaction data.
```

Fig. 16.5. *The budget spreadsheet Edit menu.*

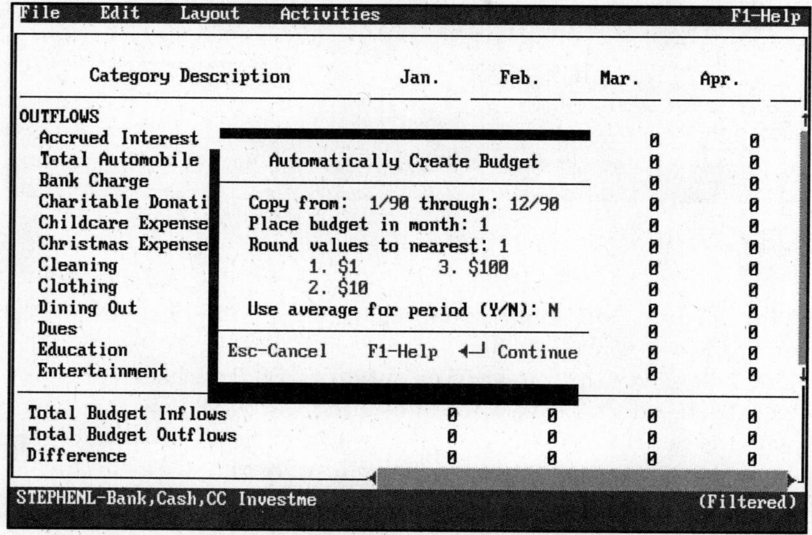

Fig. 16.6. *The Automatically Create Budget screen.*

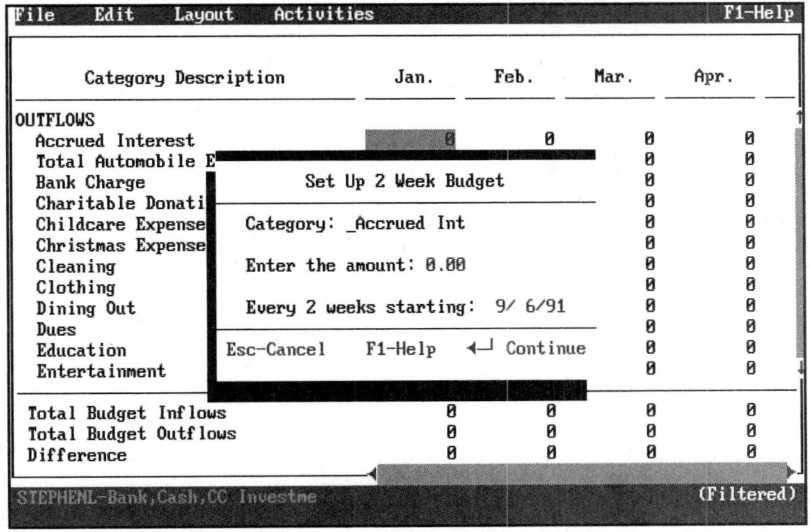

Fig. 16.7. The Set Up 2 Week Budget screen.

The **Fill Column** option works like the **Fill Right** option except that **Fill Column** doesn't copy a single budget amount. **Fill Column** copies a column of budget amounts. If, for example, you used the arrow keys to select one of the budget amounts in the July column and then select the **Fill Column** option, Quicken copies the budgeted figures in the July column to the August, September, October, November, and December budget columns.

The Edit menu's last two options—**Budget Subcats** and **Budget Transfer**— control whether rows for budgeting subcategories and budgeting account transfers appear in the budget spreadsheet. Both the **Budget Subcats** and **Budget Transfers** options are toggle switches that alternately turn on and turn off the display of these extra subcategory and account transfer rows. If, for example, the budget spreadsheet doesn't show subcategories, simply select the **Budget Subcats** option to have them displayed. If you later decide you don't want them displayed, select the **Budget Subcats** option again.

Using the Activities Menu Options

The budget spreadsheet screen's Activities menu provides a subset of the options found on the Register and Write Checks screens' Activities menus. If you press Alt-A to display the Activities menu, you will see three options on the Activities menu: **Register**, **Write Checks**, and **Calculator**. You probably already know how these options work. Select the **Register** option to display the Register screen. Select the **Write Checks** option to display the Write Checks screen. Finally, select the **Calculator** option to display the on-line 10-key calculator that Quicken provides.

Printing, Exporting and Importing Budget Data

The budget spreadsheet's File menu provides three options: **Print Budgets**, **Export Budget**, and **Import Budget** (see fig. 16.8). The first File menu option, **Print Budgets**, prints a copy of the budget spreadsheet. When you select this option, Quicken displays a Print Budget screen that looks like and works like the Print Register screen described in Chapter 4.

The second and third File menu options, **Export Budget** and **Import Budget**, let you move data between Quicken and other application programs. **Export Budget** creates a QIF file that stores the information contained in your budget spreadsheet. **Import Budget** imports a QIF file storing budget information and uses that information to fill out the budget spreadsheet screen. When you select either the **Export Budget** or **Import Budget** option, Quicken displays a screen you use to name the QIF file. Exporting, importing, and QIF files are all discussed in more detail in Chapter 9, so you can refer there if you have questions.

Reviewing Tips for Successful Budgeting

Even if you started out listing your personal or business goals, involved the entire family or company in the process, and created a budget compatible with your stated and implied goals, you can take other precautions to succeed in budgeting. These precautions include paying yourself first, recognizing after-tax shares, providing for unplanned or emergency events, and using zero-based budgeting.

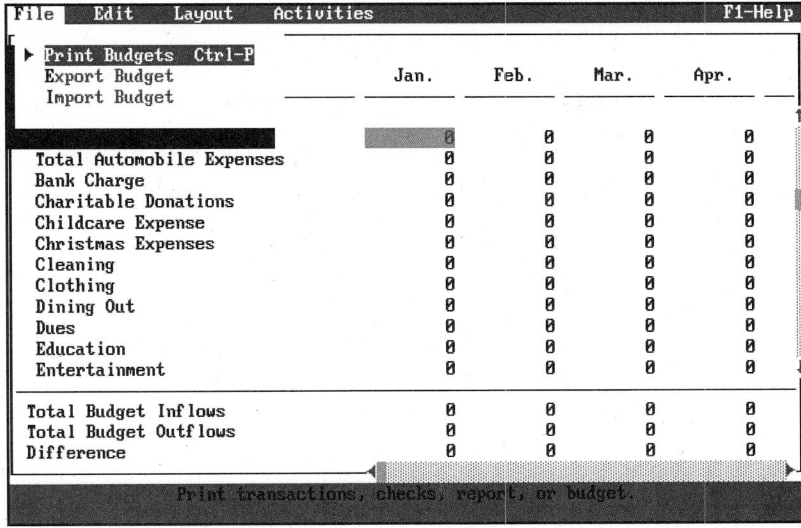

Fig. 16.8. *The File menu.*

Paying Yourself First

Families need savings to provide cushions for financial emergencies, money for major expenditures such as a home or a child's education, and the means for financial support during retirement. Small businesses need savings to provide funds for growing the business, for replacing assets, and for unexpected delays in collecting from customers.

You always have bills to pay, however, and you have to resist a lot of financial temptations. Getting to the end of the month with extra money is difficult—which is why you need to pay yourself first. For many people, paying yourself first is the only way to successfully save money.

Figure 16.9 shows the amount you ultimately accumulate if you put away $25 a month and earn 10 percent interest, assuming various income tax rates. (The logic behind including income taxes is that if you earn $100 in interest and are taxed on the money at, say, the 28 percent tax rate, you need to withdraw $28 of the $100 to pay income taxes.)

Ultimate Savings accumulated at $25 of savings per month assuming 8% annual interest				
Years	Marginal Income Tax Rates			
	0%	15%	28%	31%
5	$1,837	$1,781	$1,734	$1,723
10	4,574	4,280	4,044	3,992
15	8,651	7,788	7,124	6,980
20	14,726	12,711	11,228	10,916
25	23,776	19,622	16,699	16,100
30	37,259	29,323	23,990	22,926
35	57,347	42,938	33,709	31,917

Fig. 16.9. *Saving $25 a month adds up.*

If you save $50 a month, double the amounts shown in the figure. If you save $100, quadruple the amounts shown in the table, and so on.

If you save money for retirement, try to use options like individual retirement accounts (IRA) and 401(k) plans. Figure 16.9 shows that when you save $25 a month for 35 years in one of these investment vehicles where you pay 0 percent income tax, you end up with roughly twice as much as you would if you were paying a 28 or 31 percent income tax on your interest income. (If you are saving for retirement, refer to Appendix C, which discusses how to estimate how much you should save for retirement.)

Eventually, you will pay income taxes on the money you contributed to a 401(k) or IRA if you received a tax deduction for the contribution. You also will pay income taxes on earnings accumulated in the account over the years. You don't need to begin withdrawing monthly, however, until you're 70 1/2 years old. And even if you begin withdrawing at the earliest possible date—age 59 1/2—you have a very good chance of paying at a lower rate.

Recognizing After-Tax Shares of Bonuses and Raises

A second important budgeting consideration in personal and business situations is that you need to recognize that if you receive an extra $1,000 as a bonus, raise, or windfall, you cannot spend the entire $1,000. For 1991, a 7.65 percent Social Security tax and a 15.3 percent self-employment tax are levied on up to $53,400 of earned income. You also have to pay any federal income taxes of 15, 28, or 31 percent, plus any state income taxes. You may even have other expenses that, like income taxes, decrease your take-home share of any bonus or windfall, such as an automatic contribution to a deferred compensation plan or charitable giving to which you have made a commitment. Totaled, you typically need to deduct at least 20 percent and as much as 60 percent from any bonus or windfall to figure out what you have available for spending.

Allowing for Unplanned and Emergency Expenses

Unfortunately, people lose their jobs, cars break down, and children get sick. Over the time period your budget covers, all sorts of unforeseen and unplanned events occur and cost you money. If you can afford to, the best approach is to budget and set aside a little each month to cover these unexpected expenses.

Budget planners use several rules of thumb regarding how much emergency savings is enough. If your primary reason for emergency savings is in case you lose your job—because you are well-insured for medical, disability, and life claims—the following is an approach you should use:

1. Consider the length of time you need to find a new job. (A traditional rule of thumb says that you need a month for every $10,000 of annual salary. If, for example, you make $10,000 a year, figure on one month. If you make $50,000 a year, figure on five months.)

2. Take the salary you would have earned over the period of unemployment and subtract any employment benefits or severance pay you receive.

3. Reduce that remainder by the income taxes you do not pay and any amounts you do not save because you have no income.

To illustrate, suppose that it will take as long as six months to find a job; you currently earn $2,500 a month; you get half a month's severance pay if you lose your job; unemployment amounts to $100 a week; and you pay 7.65 percent social security tax and a 15 percent income tax. You then can calculate your emergency savings as:

((6*$2500)–(26*$100)–$1250)*(1–7.65%–15%)=$8,625

Using Zero-Based Budgeting

Large businesses use zero-based budgeting with success, and individuals and smaller businesses also can use it successfully. Basically, zero-based budgeting says that although you spent money on some category last year, you should not necessarily spend money on the same category this year.

Looking at what you spent last year can provide a valuable perspective, but this year's spending should be determined by this year's goals. Saying, "Well, last year I spent $500 on furniture, and therefore I will spend $500 this year," is dangerous. Your house or apartment may not have room for any more furniture. What about the dues for the athletic club you haven't used for months or years? Or the extra term life insurance you bought when your kids were living at home? Or the advertising money you spent to attract your first customers? Budgeting and spending amounts as you have in the past is easy to do even though your goals, your lifestyle, or your business have meanwhile made the expense unnecessary.

Chapter Summary

This chapter outlined the budgeting process, told why budgeting is important in managing your personal and business finances, described how Quicken helps with the process, and provided some tips on how to budget and manage your finances more successfully. With this information as a background, you should be able to decide whether you want to use the budgeting tools that Quicken provides.

17

Using Quicken for Home Accounting

If you read the first three parts of this book ("Getting Started Using Quicken," "Learning the Basics," and "Supercharging Quicken"), you know the mechanics of using Quicken. Using any software—particularly an accounting program—takes more than understanding how the software works. Like most people, you probably have questions about where Quicken fits in, how Quicken changes the way you keep financial records, and when to use different Quicken options. This chapter answers these kinds of questions.

Where Quicken Fits In

Where Quicken fits into personal financial management or home accounting depends on what you want to get from Quicken. You can use Quicken for home accounting in three ways:

- To track income tax deductions
- To automate record keeping
- To monitor how closely you are following a budget

Tracking Income Tax Deductions

When tracking income tax deductions, you need to make sure that transactions that produce an income tax deduction are entered into one of the Quicken registers. You also need to be sure that you use a category marked as tax-related.

This process is not as difficult as it sounds. First, although you currently may make payments that represent income tax deductions from a variety of accounts, often you can change the way you make payments so that every transaction that produces an income tax deduction is recorded in one or two accounts. If you currently make charitable contributions in cash and with a credit card, rather than set up a cash account and a credit card account, you can change the way you do things and start writing checks on an account you are tracking with Quicken. In this way, if you use Quicken for tracking income tax deductions only, you need to set up only one account—a bank account is probably the easiest method—and use this bank account only for charity contributions.

Second, you probably don't need the power of Quicken to track and tally income tax deductions. The organization to which you make a tax-deductible payment may track and tally the tax deduction for you. Consider the case of a home mortgage. At the end of the year, the bank sends you a statement that identifies how much you have paid over the year in interest, principal, and, if applicable, for items like property taxes and insurance. Similarly, a charity may send a statement that shows all contributions for the year. A bank or brokerage firm also may indicate the total individual retirement account contributions. Although you may need to track and tally certain income tax deductions, you may not want to go to all this work if an organization tracks these deductions.

Automating Record Keeping

As a rule, any financial record keeping you now perform manually is probably a candidate for Quicken. People go to different lengths in their efforts to keep clean, precise accounting records. The obvious candidate is bank accounts—particularly checking accounts. You may be someone, however, who also tracks investments carefully, tracks personal spending in a precise manner, or keeps records of personal assets or liabilities. In all these cases, Quicken probably can make the job easier.

Consider the following three cautions when automating financial record keeping. First, as with income-tax deductions, don't go to a great deal of effort to account for items that someone else already tracks for you. You probably don't need to use Quicken if all your investments appear on the same monthly statements from a broker or a mutual fund manager. You probably don't need to track other items, such as a monthly pension fund or 401(k) contributions, when your employer pays professional accountants to track these finances.

The second caution to consider is that keeping financial records isn't fun. Keeping records is tedious, requires attention to detail, and can take a great deal of time. For these reasons, carefully consider whether you need to keep financial records for a specific asset or liability. You can track the value of a home or car, but is the result worth the effort? Often, tracking these values isn't worth the effort. Whenever you go to the work of keeping a detailed, transaction-by-transaction record of an asset or liability, the resulting information should enable you to better manage your personal finances. If the information doesn't help you manage your finances, the data aren't worth collecting and storing.

The third caution to consider is to remember that in a Quicken register, you record transactions that change the balance of an asset or liability. The values of possessions, such as a home, stocks, or bonds can change without a transaction occurring. Therefore, you cannot point to an event and say, "Well, yes, this event needs to be recorded." Not surprisingly, you usually have difficulty tracking changes in the value of something when you don't have actual transactions to which you can point and then record.

Monitoring a Budget

As suggested in Chapter 16, one of the most powerful home accounting uses for Quicken is to monitor how closely you are following a budget. Although the budgeting tools that Quicken provides are superb, the process of using Quicken to monitor monthly spending can be a challenge. Because you probably spend money in several ways—using checks, credit cards, and cash—the only way to really track your monthly spending is to record all three spending groups in registers. Otherwise, you see only a piece of the picture. Recording all three groups can involve a great deal of work. To simplify monitoring a budget, consider several budgeting ideas: focus on discretionary items, aggregate spending categories, and consider the spending method.

Focusing on Discretionary Items

In Chapter 16, budgeting is described as a three-step process:

1. Setting financial goals
2. Using financial goals as a guide to developing a financial game plan, or budget, that covers how you want to spend your money
3. Using the financial game plan, or budget, to monitor spending to track how closely you are progressing toward your business goals

Quicken helps you with the third step—using the budget to monitor spending. You then need to monitor only discretionary spending—and not spending fixed by contract or by law. Keep this spending difference in mind when you define categories and describe accounts. Some spending may not need to be monitored at all. Consider a mortgage payment or a rent payment: although you certainly want to include these major expenditures in a budget, you probably don't need to monitor whether you are spending money on these payments. The spending is fixed by a mortgage contract or a rental agreement. You cannot, therefore, spend less than the budgeted amount unless you want to be evicted from the home. You also won't spend more than the budgeted amount because you have no reason to do so. Even if you do overpay the amount, the mortgage company or landlord may just return the overpayment.

The Quicken monthly budget report is the principal tool you use to monitor a budget. (Refer to Chapter 14 for more information.)

Other examples of fixed spending are loan or lease payments for a car, income and Social Security taxes, and child care. Which spending categories are fixed in this case depends on the specifics of the situation. But in general, you probably don't need to monitor as closely categories already fixed—or locked in—by a contract, by law, or by the terms of employment. You do need to include fixed spending in the budget because you want to make sure that you have enough money for the item, but this kind of spending doesn't need to be monitored. The rule is that for purposes of monitoring a budget, focus on monitoring discretionary spending.

Aggregating Spending Categories

When you monitor discretionary spending, working with a handful of categories rather than a big clump of specific categories is the easier method. Take the case of spending on entertainment. You can choose to track spending on entertainment by using just one category, which you name *Entertain*. You also can break down the spending into all the various ways you spend entertainment dollars, as shown in the following list:

- Eating at restaurants
- Going to the movies
- Seeing plays at the theater
- Playing golf
- Attending sports events

Tracking exactly how you spend entertainment dollars takes a certain precision and usually takes effort for two reasons. The first reason is that you end up recording more transactions. A credit card bill that contains charges for only the five spending groups listed needs to have one transaction recorded if only one general category is used, but five split transactions must be recorded if all five specific categories are used.

The second reason is that you budget by category, so the more categories you use, the more budgeted amounts you need to enter. If you feel you must have the detail that comes with using many, specific categories, consider using subcategories that at least minimize the work of entering budgeted amounts. You don't budget by subcategory—only by category.

Consider these general rules for aggregating spending categories:

1. Lump together items which are substitutes for each other.
2. Lump together items of similar importance, or priority, to you and the other members of the family.

Both rules stem from the idea that if you overspend in a category, consider reducing further spending in this category. A couple of examples may help you use these rules in budgeting. Suppose that you lump together the five spending groups listed previously into one general category. Suppose that you go golfing with friends over three straight weekends so that you also have no money left for restaurants and the theater—favorite activities of your spouse—or no money left for movies and sporting events—the favorite activities of your two children. In this case, don't not lump all five categories together because not spending money in one category may not be a practical remedy for overspending in another category. A sensible solution is to budget for golf as one category, for the theater and restaurants as a second category, and for the movies and sporting events as a third category. You then can make sure that overspending on golf doesn't occur. If your spouse overspends on the theater, a reasonable response is to minimize or curtail spending on restaurants. If the children insist on seeing two movies, they must forego a trip to the ballpark.

Considering the Spending Method

Researchers have proven with empirical studies that the method people use to spend money—credit cards, checks, or cash—affects how they spend. In general, people spend more when they use a credit card than they do when spending cash or writing a check, and that people often spend less when they use cash than when they write a check. This phenomenon doesn't directly affect how you work with Quicken but in terms of monitoring a budget, consider this information before you decide which accounts you set up to monitor spending.

You can find a budget more manageable if you choose an easily controlled spending method. The accounts you set up to monitor spending should recognize this reality. Remember that Quicken enables you to set up special accounts for bank accounts, credit cards, and cash. For monitoring the spending categories you want to watch, choose a spending method that makes staying within a budget easier.

How To Use Quicken

With the information covered so far, you are in a good position to know when and where to use Quicken for home accounting. This section covers a few tips that elaborate on the preceding discussion and covers bank account reconciliation, tracking credit card spending, and recording tax-deductible cash outlays.

Using Quicken for Bank Accounts

Usually, you can use Quicken for any bank accounts you want to reconcile on a monthly basis. You also can use Quicken for checking accounts for which you want to print checks. Finally, you may want to track certain bank accounts used for income tax deductions or budget monitoring reasons.

You probably don't need to use Quicken—unless you want to—for bank accounts that don't need to be reconciled. You probably don't need to use Quicken for certificates of deposit or for savings accounts with no activity other than monthly interest or fees.

Using Quicken for Credit Cards

You don't need to use Quicken to track credit card spending for credit cards in which you pay off the balance at the end of the month. When you write the monthly check to pay off the credit card company, you can record the spending categories.

For credit cards in which you don't pay off the balance on a monthly basis, but still need to track income tax deductions or monitor spending, you can set up and use Quicken accounts. For credit cards where you want to use the reconcile feature, you also need to set up and use Quicken accounts.

If you set up accounts for credit cards, you need to enter each credit card transaction into the register. Therefore, you need to collect the credit card slips and then periodically enter the amounts into the register.

Using Quicken for Cash

If you spend cash making income tax deductions, you can use Quicken to track these deductions. If you are using Quicken to monitor cash spending so that you can compare actual spending with budgeted spending, you also can use Quicken to track this information. Essentially, every time you withdraw cash from the bank, you increase cash. Every time you spend money, you need to collect a receipt for the expense. You then periodically enter these cash transactions into the register.

One practical problem with tracking cash spending is that you cannot get a receipt for small items, such as candy, a newspaper, or tips to a bellhop. Therefore, you need to keep a record of these small transactions, or you need to adjust the register's cash balance periodically to match the actual cash reserve. You can give this kind of adjustment category a descriptive name, such as *Sundries* or *Misc*.

For credit card and cash transactions, collect in an envelope the credit card and cash receipts you need to enter. On a periodic basis (such as once a week or month), enter the receipt amounts in the appropriate register, mark the receipts as entered, and label the outside of the envelope with a descriptive name, such as "credit card and cash receipts from week beginning 6/1/92." If you have a large number of receipts, number the receipts and then use these numbers as the transaction numbers in the register so that you can specifically tie a transaction in the register to a receipt.

Tracking the Adjusted Basis of Your Home

By law, the gain on the sale of a home is taxable unless you purchase another home of equal or greater value within a certain time frame, or unless you can use the one-time $125,000 exclusion to eliminate the gain. The gain on the sale of a home is calculated roughly as:

(sales price) – (original cost + cost of improvements)

The sales price and the original cost are set and are connected to the purchase and to the sale. One way to reduce the calculated gain—and therefore to minimize the income tax on the gain—is to track the cost of improvements.

Improvements don't include repairs or maintenance, such as fixing a roof, painting the walls, or sealing an asphalt driveway. Over the years, however, you probably will make a series of improvements that, if tracked, may reduce the gain. These improvements may include the landscaping you put in after you buy the house, bookshelves you add to the family room, and the extra bathroom a remodeler puts in upstairs. Figure 17.1 shows an example of a register used to collect this kind of information. (Remember that the account transfer feature means you may never need to go into the register for the asset, `House`, because you can record the cost of the improvement when you write the check to pay for the improvement.)

Print/Acct Edit Shortcuts Reports Activities F1-Help

DATE	REF	PAYEE · MEMO · CATEGORY	DECREASE	C	INCREASE	BALANCE
		BEGINNING				
9/ 1 1986		Opening Balance [Real Estate]			75,000 00	75,000 00
1/31 1989	235	Puget Landscaping back yard [Big Natl-1234]			2,000 00	77,000 00
6/15 1991	472 Memo: Cat:	Tom's Remodeling book shelves for family room [Big Natl-1234]			1,200 00	78,200 00
6/15 1991						
		END				

Real Estate (Alt+letter accesses menu)
Esc-Main Menu Ctrl◄┘ Record Ending Balance: $78,200.00

Fig. 17.1. *A Quicken register provides a convenient format to collect the costs of improvements to a home.*

Tracking the Non-Deductible Portions of an IRA

One of the record-keeping nightmares from the last decade's ever-changing tax laws is the non-deductible individual retirement account (IRA) contribution. Essentially, although you may not qualify for an IRA deduction, you still may have the option of contributing to an IRA. An IRA contribution can be beneficial financially because without the income taxes on the investment earnings, the account grows faster.

Over long periods, You can accumulate a great deal more money—even though the original contribution didn't generate a tax deduction. Figure 16.9 in Chapter 16 shows that by contributing $25 a month over 35 years, you may accumulate $94,916 if you pay no taxes, but $47,231 if you pay the 28 percent federal income tax. In other words, you may accumulate almost twice as much money by not paying income taxes on the earnings. Non-deductible IRA contributions enable you to defer income taxes on money earned until you withdraw the money.

The problem with non-deductible IRA contributions is that the amount you contribute is not taxed when you withdraw the money; you need a way to track the non-deductible contributions. For most people, Quicken is an excellent solution. The basic process is to set up an investment account for non-deductible IRA contributions. Whenever you make a non-deductible contribution, record the payment as a transfer to the account you use to track non-deductible IRA contributions. Over the years, you build a detailed record of all the non-deductible contributions you make. Figure 17.2 shows an example of an investment register that tracks the asset Nondeduct IRA.

```
Print/Acct   Edit   Shortcuts   Reports   Activities                F1-Help

DATE  ACTION   SECURITY          · PRICE   SHARES   $ AMOUNT   C SHARE BAL

                          BEGINNING
4/15  ShrsIn   Nondeduct IRA     ·10       200      2,000 00      200 00
1991           1990 contribution
      ShrsIn   Nondeduct IRA     ·12       150      1,800 00      350 00
               1991 contribution
4/15
1992
                             END

Nondeduct IRA     (Alt+letter accesses menu)    Ending Shares:    350.000
Esc-Main Menu     Ctrl◄┘ Record                 Market Value:   $4,200.00
```

Fig. 17.2. Use Quicken to track non-deductible IRA contributions.

When To Perform Quicken Tasks

One final question that you often have with using Quicken is when to perform the various Quicken tasks. Table 17.1 divides these tasks into three groups: tasks to perform on a daily and weekly basis, tasks to perform on a monthly basis, and tasks to perform on an annual basis. Consider the information in table 17.1 as a rough guideline—as you use Quicken, you learn what works best for you.

Table 17.1
When To Perform Quicken Tasks

Daily and Weekly Tasks

Record transactions in the registers.

Print checks.

Print a temporary copy of the month's register.

Back up the files.

Monthly Tasks

Print monthly reports.

Reconcile accounts.

Print a final copy of the month's register.

Throw away the daily or weekly copies of the register because all this information is contained on the final copy of the month's register.

Back up the files.

File or store the month's bank statement, register, reports, and backup files.

Annual Tasks

Print annual reports.

Print a permanent copy of the transaction report that subtotals by tax deduction category. (This report is your permanent record for income tax purposes.)

Back up files for the year.

Create new year's budget and enter the budget.

Shrink the file.*

* *When you shrink the file, you don't want to lose the transaction detail in accounts that you maintain on a long-term basis for income tax purposes, such as for ultimately calculating the gain on the sale of a home or for determining the total non-deductible IRA contributions. So that you do not lose detail in the shrink file operation, do not mark transactions in these registers as cleared and set the* `Include only cleared transactions` *switch to yes. Chapter 9 describes how to shrink files.*

Chapter Summary

This chapter covered information you ultimately learn on your own through trial and error. This chapter discussed where Quicken fits in home accounting, how to use Quicken for home accounting, and when to use the various Quicken options and features. You now can more easily incorporate Quicken into your personal financial management activities.

18

Using Quicken in Your Business

You may be surprised to learn that more people use Quicken as a business accounting package than as a home accounting package. The reasons for this usage are logical: you do not need to know double-entry bookkeeping (as you do for many other small-business accounting packages), and you use a simple and familiar tool, the check register. Because Quicken isn't a true full-fledged business accounting package, however, this chapter covers some of the special techniques and procedures for using Quicken in business.

The procedures for using Quicken are well documented in this book. For this chapter you are better armed if you know how to enter transactions into a register, set up accounts, define categories, and print reports. If you are not familiar with these features of Quicken, review the material covered in the first three sections of the book, "Getting Started Using Quicken," "Learning the Basics," and "Supercharging Quicken."

This chapter begins by discussing the overall approach for using Quicken in a business. This discussion is followed by short sections that detail these six basic accounting tasks:

- Invoicing customers
- Tracking receivables
- Accounting for fixed assets
- Preparing payroll
- Tracking inventory
- Job costing

When you combine basic bill paying and check writing—described throughout this book's chapters—with the details of the six basic accounting tasks described in this chapter, you should have the information you need to perform business accounting with Quicken.

Understanding the Basics

Using Quicken for business accounting is easier if you understand the following three basic concepts: what Quicken accounts track, what should be recorded in a register, and what categories calculate.

Knowing What Quicken Accounts Track

You can use Quicken accounts to track the values of business assets or liabilities. You need to set up one account for each business asset or liability you want to track.

A business asset is anything you own. Common examples of business assets include the cash in a checking account, the receivable a customer or client owes you, an investment in stock, inventory you resell, a piece of furniture, a piece of equipment, and real estate.

A business liability is everything you owe. Common examples of business liabilities include the loan on a car or delivery truck, payroll taxes you owe the government, the mortgage on the building, and the balance on a bank credit line.

Assets and liabilities have something in common: at any time, you can calculate the value of the asset or liability. Usually, you are not interested in the day-to-day or week-to-week change in a particular asset but rather the value at a specific time.

All the accounts you set up for a business must be included in the same file account group. If you perform accounting for several businesses, each business needs a separate file. If you use Quicken at business and at home, you need to create a file for each (see Chapter 2).

Quicken enables you to define up to 255 accounts with a file.

Defining a Transaction

Transactions are dealings you record in a register to show the change in the value of an asset or liability. No change ever affects only one asset or liability, however, so each time you record the change in the value of some asset or liability, you also need to record how the change affects other accounts, or income or expenses categories. You actually perform double-entry book-keeping without thinking or worrying about debits and credits.

When you transfer money from a checking account to a savings account, for example, you record the decrease in the checking account balance with one transaction and the increase in the savings account balance with another transaction. Similarly, when you write a check to pay for utilities, you record the decrease in the bank account due to the check, and you indicate the expense category the transaction affects—such as Utilities. You always need to categorize a transaction or show the transaction as a transfer.

This discussion of transactions may seem redundant, but you need to verify that all assets and liabilities are true assets and true liabilities. You also need to verify that items you want to record as transactions in a register are true transactions and not assets or liabilities.

Suppose that you want to track receivables and record customer payments on these receivables. You must set up an account each time you create an individual receivable. If you bill Johnson Manufacturing $1,000 for a service, you must set up an account for this asset. The temptation with a group of similar assets, such as receivables, is to group all receivables as one asset by using one account group. Using the grouping approach, however, obscures information on specific accounts. You cannot tell whether Johnson Manufacturing still owes the $1,000 or how the $1,000 original asset value has changed. Changes in the value of this asset—such as when you receive the customer's payment—need to be recorded as transactions in the register.

The key to using Quicken as a small-business accounting system is knowing your assets, liabilities, and transactions. Throughout this chapter, you find many tips and suggestions to assist you in this analysis.

Knowing What Categories Calculate

The term *bottom line* refers to the figure at the bottom of a profit and loss statement that shows whether you made or lost money in business. The reason you use categories within Quicken is to calculate the bottom line to determine whether you are making or losing money. You use two kinds of categories to perform this calculation: Income and Expense. Income categories count business revenues, or *inflows*. Common income categories include sales of products or services, interest and dividends from investments, and even the proceeds from the sale of an asset. Expense categories count business costs, or *outflows*. Examples of expense categories include the cost of advertising, insurance, utilities, and employee wages.

Income and expense categories have something in common: both categories enable you to count business inflows and outflows over a period of time—such as for the week, month, or year. You can use the income and expense category information to tell whether you made or lost money during the last week, month, or year.

When you use Quicken categories to track only cash inflows and outflows—bank and cash accounts—you are using *cash-basis* accounting. Cash-basis accounting means that you record income only when you deposit money, and you record expenses only when you pay money. This system makes sense. When you make the bank deposit or the check payment, you are categorizing the transaction as income or expense.

When you use Quicken categories to track other assets and liabilities, however, you move toward *accrual-* or *modified accrual-basis* accounting. Accrual-basis accounting means that you record income when you earn it, and you record expenses when you use the goods or services from which the expenses stem. If you use Quicken to account for customer receivables, you recognize the transaction as income when you record the receivable. If you use Quicken to account for fixed assets and depreciation, you categorize the expense of using the asset when you record depreciation.

Accrual-basis accounting gives you better estimates of income and expenses to better measure profits. Accrual-basis accounting also results in better record keeping because you keep registers for all assets and liabilities—not just cash. If accurately measuring profits is important to the business, try to use accrual-basis accounting. If you use this method, you have a better idea of whether you're making money.

Invoicing Customers

Although Quicken provides no invoicing feature, you can create a report that works as an invoice. Set up an account to record the new asset you have because a customer or client now owes you money. You probably want to name the account by combining *invoice* with the actual invoice number. Select 4 as the account type, which indicates the account type is `Other Asset`. Set the balance to zero and leave the description blank. Figure 18.1 shows an example of the Set Up New Account screen filled in to define this kind of account.

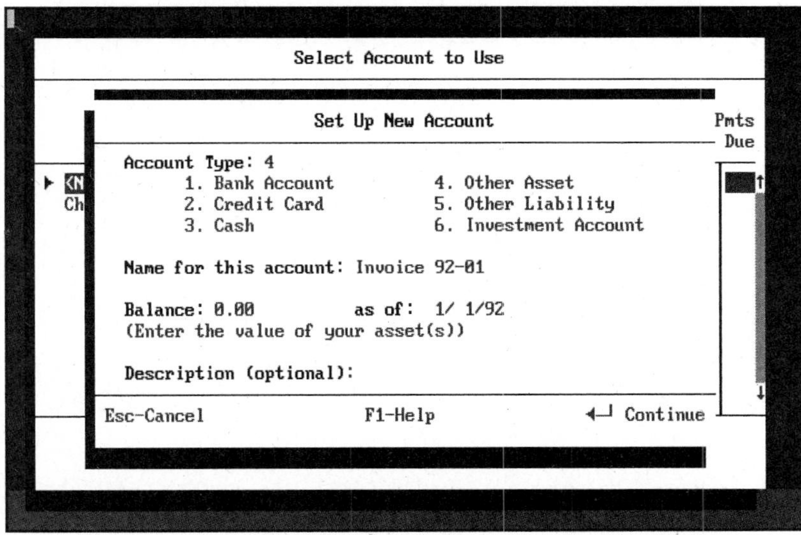

Fig. 18.1. *The Set Up New Account screen filled in to define the receivable that results from creating an invoice.*

Select the account so that you can access the register for the account. To record the invoice, edit the opening balance entry Quicken makes when you set up an account. You enter the customer name in the `Payee` field, the total invoice amount in the `Increase` field, and a customer reference number in the `Memo` field. Select **Split Transaction** from the Edit menu or press the speed key equivalent, Ctrl-S, to provide details on the total invoice amount. Anything that has an amount associated with it must be categorized and described—even if every item has the same category.

Suppose that you are an attorney, and you want to create a $1,000 invoice to send to a client, Johnson Manufacturing, for $300 of work on a real estate lease, $600 of work on a bank loan agreement, and $100 for out-of-pocket expenses. Figure 18.2 shows an example of the completed Register screen and the Split Transaction window to record this invoice. (Remember that you can split a transaction into as many as 30 lines, therefore, you can create an invoice that lists up to 30 charges.)

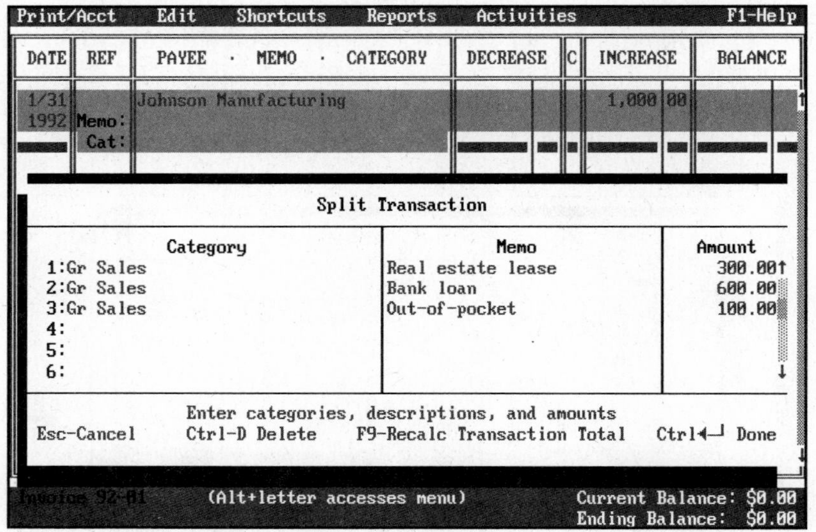

Fig. 18.2. *The Register and Split Transaction screens completed for creating an invoice.*

You are now ready to record and print the invoice. Record the invoice by pressing Ctrl-Enter. To print the invoice, press Alt-R to access the Reports menu and then select the fifth option, **Transaction**. Quicken displays the Create Transaction Report screen. Enter the company name as the *Report Title*, enter the billing period or the billing date in the `Restrict to transactions from` field, and set the `Subtotal by` field to 12 for subtotaling by account (see fig. 18.3). Press F8 to access the Report Options screen, set `Show split transaction detail` to Y for yes and the `Memo/category display` field to 1 for memo only (see fig. 18.4). Leave the other fields set to the default values, as shown in figure 18.4. After you complete the Report Options screen, press Ctrl-Enter to return to the Create Transaction Report screen. To generate an on-screen version of the invoice, press Ctrl-Enter again. To print the invoice, press Ctrl-P, complete the Print Report screen, and press Ctrl-Enter.

If you plan to generate invoices frequently by using the approach described in the preceding paragraph, remember that the **Memorize Report** command gives you a way to permanently record the information you enter on the Create Transaction Report and Report Options screens.

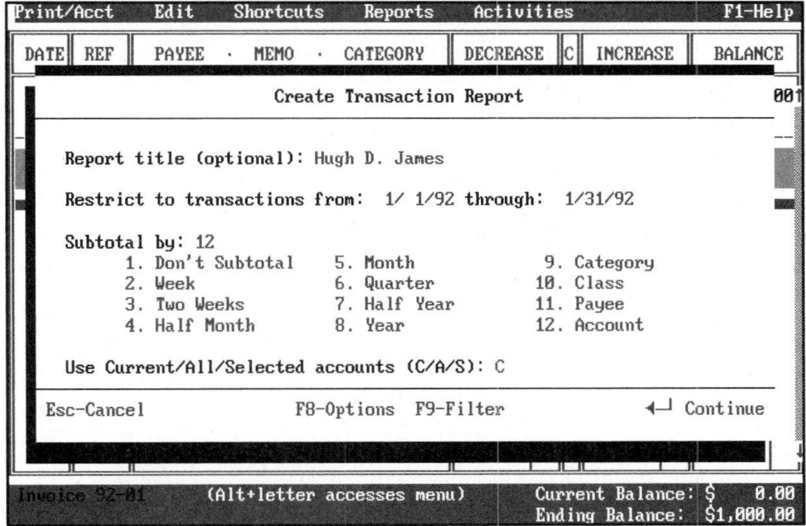

Fig. 18.3. *The Create Transaction Report screen for an invoice.*

Figure 18.5 shows the resulting invoice. The business name, and the billing period or billing date, appears at the top of the invoice. *Business* is the name of the account group for the business. The Payee field shows the customer or client name. The Memo field shows the descriptions and amounts of the various charges that make up the invoice. Finally, the total shows the invoice amount.

The invoice in figure 18.5 is not as sophisticated or custom-tailored as invoices produced by accounting packages designed to generate invoices. Depending on the requirements of the business, however, this invoice can be satisfactory. Remember that you can export the report to an ASCII file you can edit with almost any word processing program.

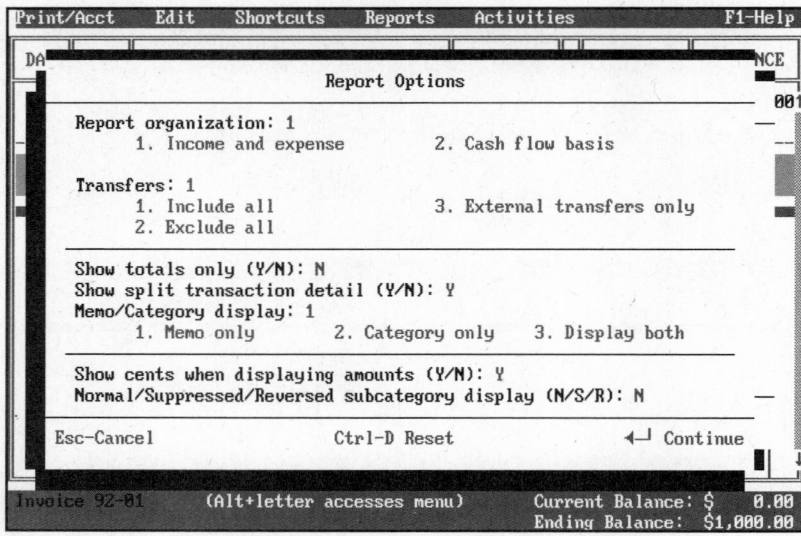

Fig. 18.4. The Report Options screen for an invoice.

Hugh D. James, Attorney
1/ 1/92 Through 1/31/92

BUSINESS-Invoice 92-01
9/ 6/91

Page 1

Date	Num	Description	Memo	Clr	Amount
	Invoice 92-01				
1/31	S	Johnson Manufacturing	Real estate lease		300.00
			Bank loan		600.00
			Out-of-pocket		100.00
	Total Invoice 92-01				1,000.00

Fig. 18.5. An invoice generated with Quicken.

Customers need the due date, your business address, and your business's federal tax identification number to report to the Internal Revenue Service all payments made to you. If you generate invoices solely with Quicken, make sure that the customers already have this information from another source. If you export the invoice as an ASCII text file so that you can edit the invoice, you can add the needed due date, federal tax identification number, and address.

Tracking Customer Payments and Receivables

To track customer payments and receivables, you also need to follow the steps described in the preceding section to record the receivable as an asset. After you record the receivable as an asset, you can record customer payments on the receivable and monitor receivables—topics covered in the following sections.

Recording Customer Payments

To record customer payments, select the bank account you use to deposit the check and record the deposit in the usual way. To categorize the transaction, record the deposit as a transfer from the actual receivable account. If you receive a $500 check from Johnson Manufacturing for partial payment of the $1,000 receivable created by Invoice 92-01, for example, you complete the register for the bank account into which you are depositing the money, as shown in figure 18.6. (Remember that Quicken lists the categories and the accounts when you press Ctrl-C and when you select **Categorize/Transfer** from the Shortcuts menu.)

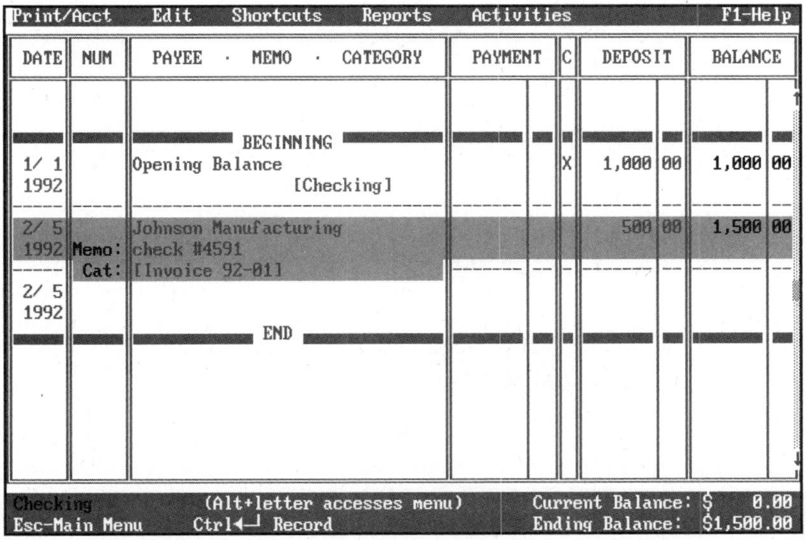

```
Print/Acct   Edit   Shortcuts   Reports   Activities            F1-Help

DATE  NUM    PAYEE  ·  MEMO  ·  CATEGORY    PAYMENT  C   DEPOSIT    BALANCE

                    BEGINNING
1/ 1       Opening Balance                       X   1,000 00   1,000 00
1992                        [Checking]
2/ 5       Johnson Manufacturing                       500 00   1,500 00
1992 Memo: check #4591
      Cat: [Invoice 92-01]
2/ 5
1992
                       END

Checking          (Alt+letter accesses menu)    Current Balance: $    0.00
Esc-Main Menu     Ctrl◄┘ Record                 Ending Balance:  $1,500.00
```

Fig. 18.6. Recording a $500 partial payment on the $1,000 receivable created by the invoice.

Quicken records a $500 reduction in the account you use to track the $1,000 receivable. Figure 18.7 shows the register for the Invoice 92-01 account after you record the $500 partial payment from Johnson Manufacturing as a deposit to the bank account. Quicken records the decrease in the Invoice 92-01 receivable.

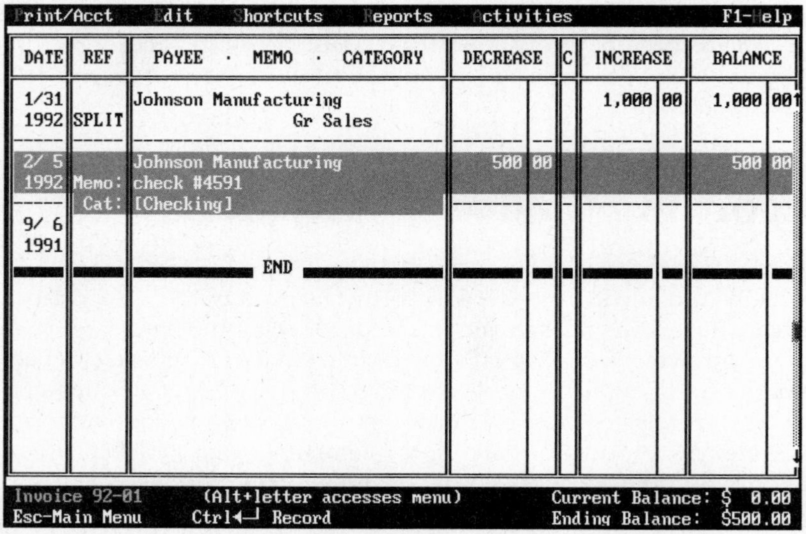

```
Print/Acct   Edit   Shortcuts   Reports   Activities                F1-Help

DATE  REF   PAYEE · MEMO · CATEGORY     DECREASE  C  INCREASE   BALANCE
1/31        Johnson Manufacturing                    1,000 00   1,000 00
1992  SPLIT               Gr Sales
2/ 5        Johnson Manufacturing       500 00                    500 00
1992  Memo: check #4591
      Cat:  [Checking]
9/ 6
1991
                        END

Invoice 92-01    (Alt+letter accesses menu)    Current Balance: $  0.00
Esc-Main Menu    Ctrl←┘ Record                 Ending Balance:  $500.00
```

Fig. 18.7. Quicken records the second half of the transfer transaction.

Tracking Customer Receivables

Another basic receivables accounting task is tracking how much customers owe you and how long customers have owed you. The age of a receivable usually determines the collection efforts you make. You probably don't worry about receivables that aren't yet due. You may call customers with receivables more than 30 days past due. You may even turn over to a collection agency or an attorney receivables more than 60 or 90 days past due. To create a summary report that shows receivables account balances grouped by age, follow these steps:

1. Select the **Summary** option from the Reports menu by pressing Alt-R. Quicken displays the Create Summary Report screen (see fig. 18.8).

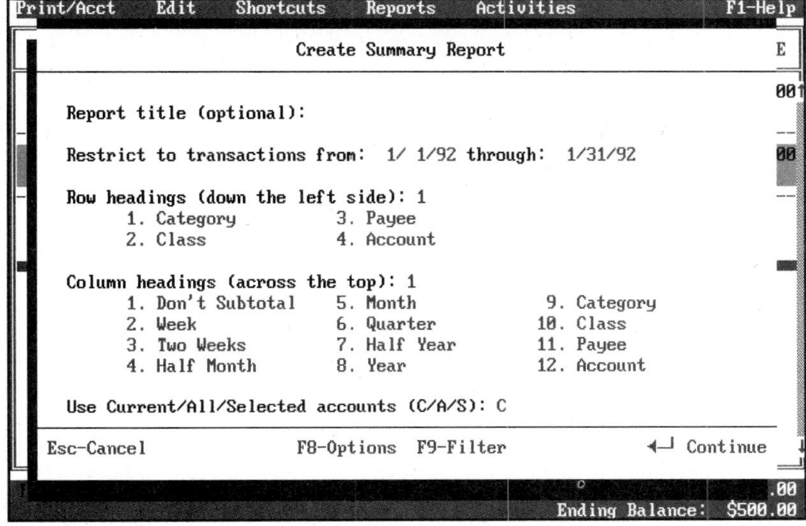

Fig. 18.8. The Create Summary Report screen completed for a receivables aging.

2. To complete the screen to show receivables balances only, enter a report title and a range of dates in the `Restrict to transactions from` and `through` fields that begins with the date of the oldest receivable and ends with the current date.

3. Set the `Row headings` field to 4 for `Account`. Next, set the `Column headings` field to whatever time intervals you want to use to age receivables. (Usually, businesses age receivables on a monthly basis.)

An *aging* refers to segregating receivables into different age groups. Ages are calculated as the difference between the invoice date and the current date.

4. Set the `Current/All/Selected accounts` field to S for selected, and press Enter.

   Quicken next displays the Select Accounts to Include screen (see fig. 18.9). Exclude all accounts that are not receivables.

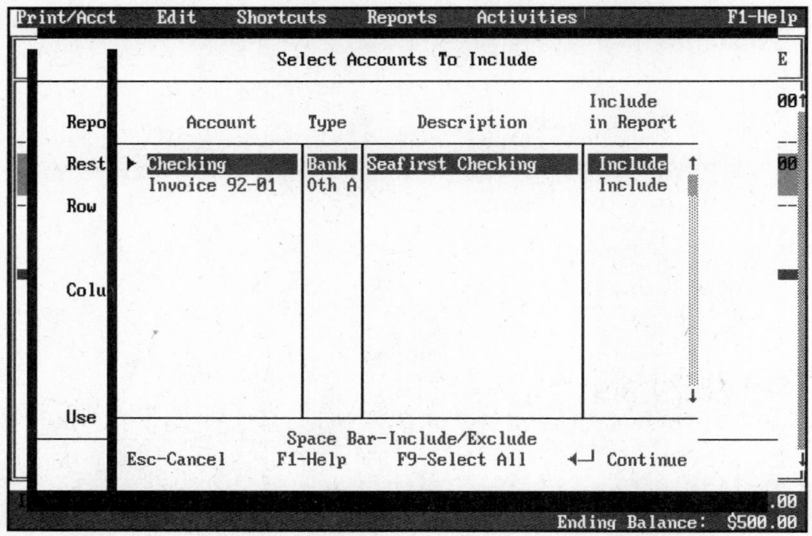

Fig. 18.9. The Select Accounts To Include screen.

5. To exclude these accounts, move the cursor to the account you want to exclude and press the space bar. The space bar acts as a toggle between include and exclude.

6. After you complete the Select Accounts to Include screen, press Enter, and Quicken displays the Accounts Receivable Aging report summary (see fig. 18.10).

The summary report shows how much money each of the receivables customers owe you and also the ages of the receivables. Invoice 90-01, for example, appears as $1,000 in January because the date of this account's first transaction is in January, and as $500 in March because you received a partial payment on the receivable at this time.

One problem with this approach is that the account names do not indicate the customers. If you do not use Quicken to generate invoices, you can lessen this problem by naming accounts with the invoice number and the customer name. You can name the account that tracks invoice 90-01 from Johnson Manufacturing as *I-9001 Johnson*.

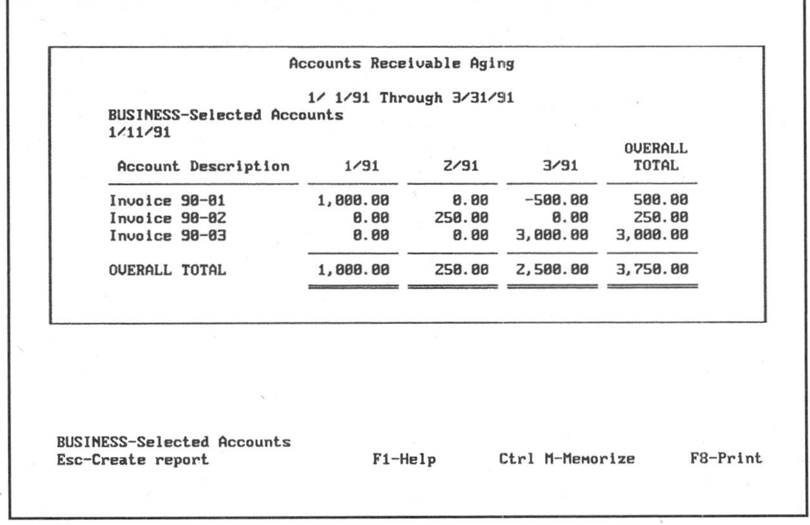

Accounts Receivable Aging

1/ 1/91 Through 3/31/91

BUSINESS-Selected Accounts

1/11/91

Account Description	1/91	2/91	3/91	OVERALL TOTAL
Invoice 90-01	1,000.00	0.00	-500.00	500.00
Invoice 90-02	0.00	250.00	0.00	250.00
Invoice 90-03	0.00	0.00	3,000.00	3,000.00
OVERALL TOTAL	1,000.00	250.00	2,500.00	3,750.00

BUSINESS-Selected Accounts

Esc-Create report F1-Help Ctrl M-Memorize F8-Print

Fig. 18.10. The Accounts Receivable Aging report shown on-screen.

The Quicken user's manual offers another approach for recording receivables and two other approaches for recording payments on the receivables. The manual suggests that you record all receivables, or at least all of a specific customer's receivables, in one account. Regarding recording payments, the manual suggests that you enter the payment as a decrease transaction in a large Receivables register or as a negative transfer amount for a specific receivable transaction by using the Split Transaction window. (If you have more questions about these approaches, refer to the user's manual.) The benefit of the manual's two approaches is that you do not use as many accounts—the limit is 255. These suggestions, however, have the following problems:

- If you record invoices and payment transactions in a large register, you have difficulty determining how much money a customer owes you or has previously paid you on a specific invoice.
- If you use the Split Transaction window to record payments on an invoice, a second problem arises. To apply a payment to five invoices, you must go into the Receivables register and edit five transactions to show the payment. Bank reconciliation also is more difficult because you recorded the payment as five deposits rather than as one payment.
- You cannot generate invoices if you do not set up receivables in separate accounts.

Accounting for Fixed Assets

Accounting for fixed assets represents another activity most businesses need to address. You may own furniture, equipment, and even real estate that needs to be depreciated. Although you can depreciate different assets, the mechanics of recording depreciation are consistent.

If you need to record depletion for natural resources, such as timber, or if you need to record amortization expenses for intangible assets, such as copyrights or patents, the procedures are the same as those described for depreciation.

Understanding Depreciation

Suppose that you purchase a delivery truck for $12,000. You plan to use the truck for five years and then sell the truck for $2,000. The rationale for depreciating the truck is that over the five years, you need to include the expense of the truck when measuring profits. Depreciation is a way of allocating the cost of an asset over two or more years. Several methods are available to make this allocation, but a common method is *straight-line* depreciation. Straight-line depreciation works in the following manner: if you buy the truck for $12,000, intending to sell the truck five years later for $2,000, the overall cost of using the truck over the five years is $10,000. To calculate the yearly cost, divide the $10,000 by five years, and $2,000 is the annual depreciation expense to include in the calculations of profits.

On balance sheets, assets are listed at an amount equal to the original cost, minus the depreciation already taken. Continuing with the delivery truck example, at the end of year one the balance sheet lists the truck at $10,000—calculated as $12,000 original cost minus $2,000 of depreciation. Similarly, at the end of year two, three, four, and five, the balance sheet lists the truck at the original cost minus the depreciation taken to date. After the end of year five, when the truck is listed at $2,000—calculated as $12,000 minus $10,000 of depreciation—you stop depreciating the asset because you do not depreciate the asset below its salvage value.

CPA TIP

Other depreciation methods exist, and the methods the federal tax laws prescribe are often confusing. In essence, however, how you use Quicken to record depreciation works the same way no matter what depreciation method you use. This chapter cannot give you complete information about how to calculate the depreciation on assets, but if you want more information on the tax laws, call the Internal Revenue Service and ask for Internal Revenue Service Publication 534. For more information on how to calculate depreciation according to Generally Accepted Accounting Principles, which is different from depreciation calculated for the tax laws, consult a certified public accountant.

Recording Fixed Assets and Depreciation

To record fixed assets and the depreciation expense related to fixed assets, set up an account for each asset that must be depreciated. Enter a descriptive account name, set the account type to 4 for the `Other assets` fields, and enter the purchase price as the initial balance. Figure 18.11 shows the Set Up New Account screen filled to define a new account for a $12,000 delivery truck.

If you have groups of similar assets with similar life spans, you usually can depreciate these assets as a group. You probably do not need to depreciate individually each piece of furniture you buy during the year; you can aggregate and depreciate all the furniture together, as one asset.

To record depreciation, you can enter a decrease transaction that categorizes $2,000 a year to the Depreciation Expense category. If you did not set up a category for depreciation, Quicken prompts you to add the category. Remember that Quicken does not use a transaction in calculating profit unless the date is within the range you specify on the Create Report screens. Therefore, you can enter all five years of depreciation at one time by using transaction dates in each of the five years. Figure 18.12 shows the Register screen for the delivery truck filled in with the depreciation expense record for 1991, 1992, and 1993.

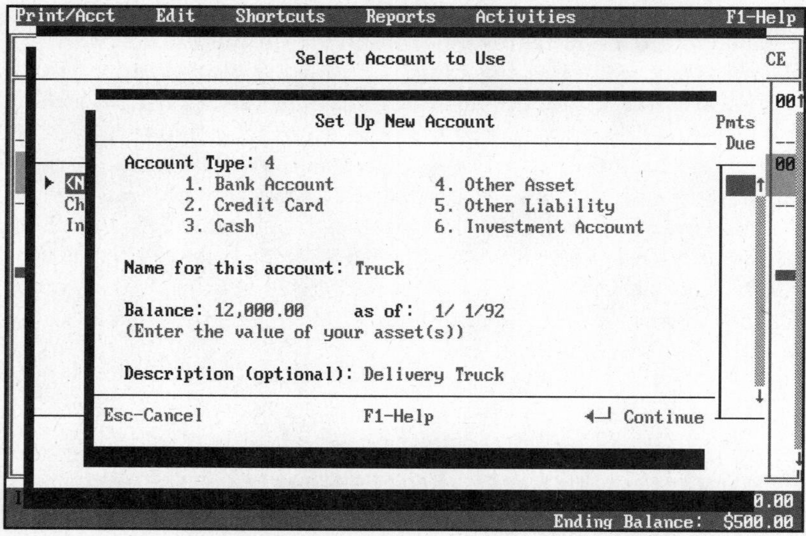

Fig. 18.11. *The Set Up New Account screen filled in to define a new account for a $12,000 delivery truck.*

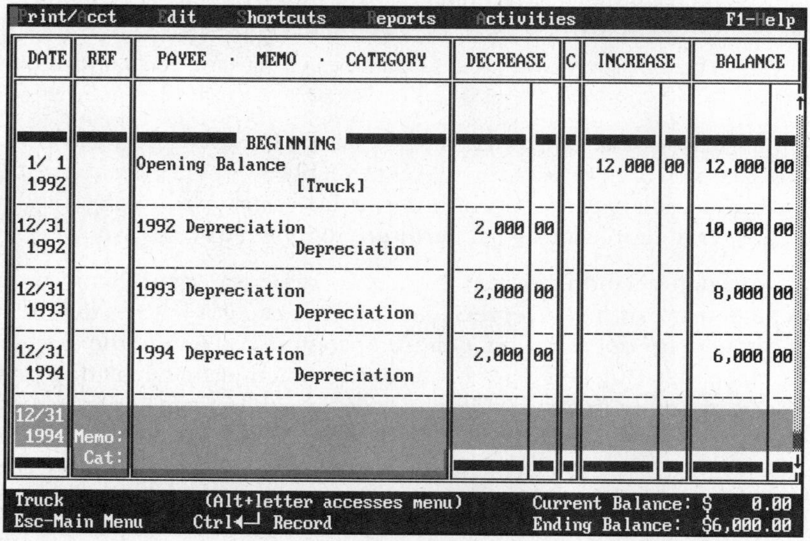

Print/Acct Edit Shortcuts Reports Activities F1-Help

DATE	REF	PAYEE · MEMO · CATEGORY	DECREASE	C	INCREASE	BALANCE
		BEGINNING				
1/ 1 1992		Opening Balance [Truck]			12,000 00	12,000 00
12/31 1992		1992 Depreciation Depreciation	2,000 00			10,000 00
12/31 1993		1993 Depreciation Depreciation	2,000 00			8,000 00
12/31 1994		1994 Depreciation Depreciation	2,000 00			6,000 00
12/31 1994	Memo: Cat:					

Truck (Alt+letter accesses menu) Current Balance: $ 0.00
Esc-Main Menu Ctrl← Record Ending Balance: $6,000.00

Fig. 18.12. *The delivery truck register that shows the asset depreciation schedules.*

Preparing Payroll

One of the more common business applications of Quicken is to prepare employee payroll checks and reports. Suppose that you want to prepare a payroll check for an employee who earns $1,000 a month. The employee's Social Security tax is $62.00, the employee's Medicare tax is $14.50, and the employee's federal income tax withholding amount is $100. You also can assume that the employer's matching share of Social Security is $62.00, the employer's matching share of Medicare is $14.50, and you must pay $10.00 for federal unemployment tax.

Getting Ready for Payroll

To record this payroll transaction, set up a liability account for each of the payroll taxes payable accounts. Enter the account type as 5, for `Other Liability`, and enter the initial amount (the amount you already owe). In this example, the amount includes the federal income tax withholding, the employee's Social Security and Medicare amount, your matching Social Security and Medicare taxes, and the federal unemployment tax. To define each of the payroll tax accounts, use the Set Up New Account screen. Figure 18.13 shows how to set up the account for the federal income tax withholding amount. Use the screen, filled out in similar fashion, to define each of the payroll tax liability accounts.

You also need to define a category for each of the employer's payroll expenses: the employee's wages, the employer's matching share of the Social Security and Medicare tax, and the federal unemployment tax. You do not define categories for the employee's Social Security tax, Medicare tax, or the employee's federal income tax withholding amounts, however, because these amounts are expenses of the employee, not the employer.

Paying Employees

To record the payroll check, enter a transaction (see fig. 18.14). If you write payroll checks using the same bank account you use to write other checks, enter the `Memo` description as payroll, or payroll and the pay date, so that you can use the `Memo` field as the basis for including transactions on reports. Select the **Split Screen** option when you are at the `Category` field. You do not need to fill in the net paycheck amount because Quicken subtracts the taxes withheld and enters the net portion in the register. If you use checks with vouchers—a good idea for payroll—the employee's gross wages and the employee's deductions should appear on the first 16 lines of the Split Transaction screen so that the split transaction appears on the voucher.

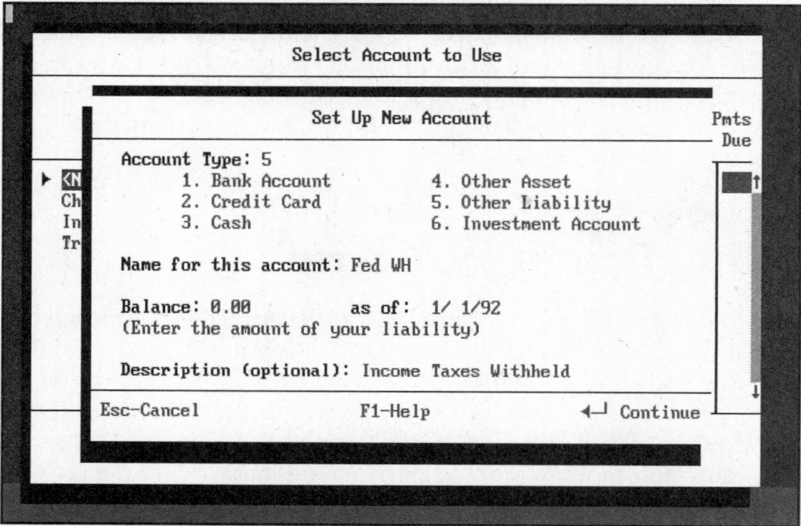

Fig. 18.13. *The Set Up New Account screen filled in to define the federal income tax withholding liability.*

On the Checks and Reports Settings screen, make sure that the `Print categories on voucher checks` switch is set to yes so that the gross wages and deductions information prints on the voucher. (Chapter 11 describes the Checks and Reports Settings screen.)

Enter the other wages expenses (such as the employer's matching share of Social Security, Medicare, and the federal unemployment tax) starting on line 17 of the Split Transaction screen so that the expense does not appear on the payroll check's voucher (see fig. 18.15).

After you complete the Split Transaction screen, press Ctrl-Enter. Figure 18.16 shows the completed check. The net wages amount is $823.50, which is $1,000 in gross wages minus $100 in federal withholding, minus $62.00 in Social Security, and minus $14.50 in Medicare.

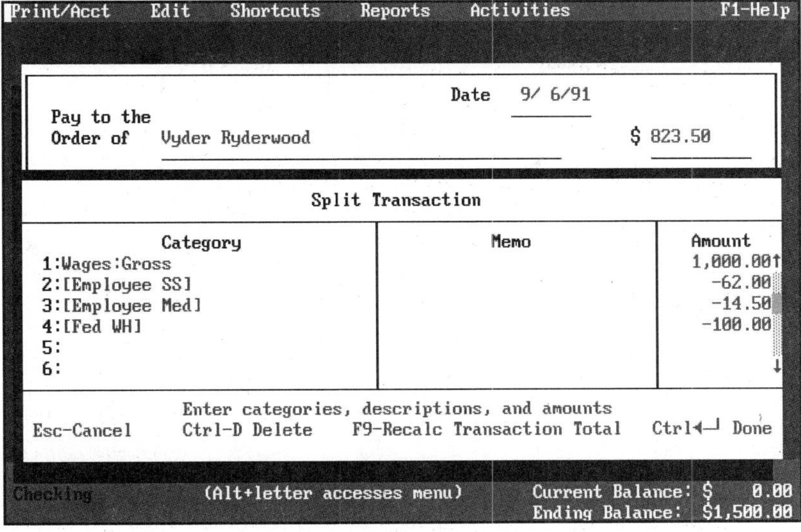

Fig. 18.14. The gross wages and employee deductions should be entered on the first 16 lines of the Split Transaction screen.

Print/Acct Edit Shortcuts Reports Activities F1-Help

Date 9/ 6/91

Pay to the
Order of Vyder Ryderwood $ 823.50

Split Transaction

Category	Memo	Amount
16:		
17:Wages:payroll taxes		86.50
18:[Employer SS]		-62.00
19:[Employer Med]		-14.50
20:[FUTA]		-10.00
21:		

Enter categories, descriptions, and amounts
Esc-Cancel Ctrl-D Delete F9-Recalc Transaction Total Ctrl↵ Done

50

Checking (Alt+letter accesses menu) Current Balance: $-823.50
Ending Balance: $ 676.50

Fig. 18.15. The other wages expenses start on line 17.

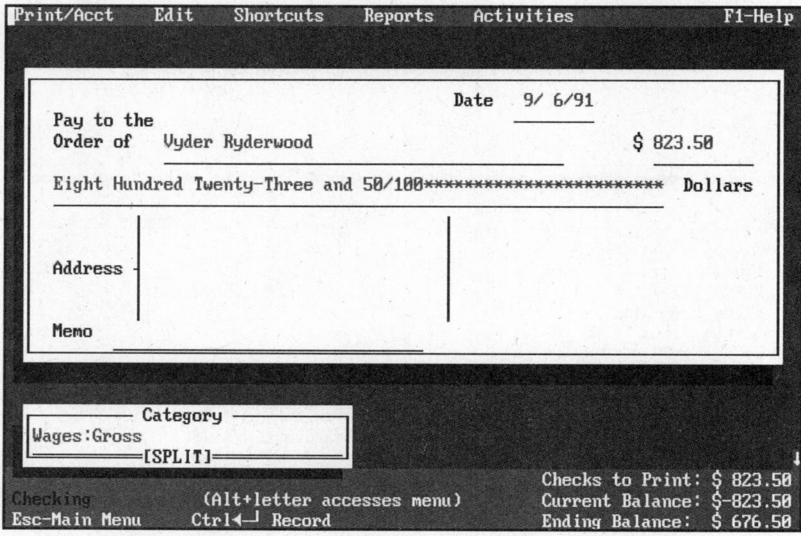

Fig. 18.16. The completed payroll check.

Using the Create Payroll Support Assistant

As you may recall from Chapter 1, the Tutorials and Assistants menu, which you access from Quicken's Main Menu, provides several utilities that make working with Quicken 5.0 easier. One of these utilities, the **Create Payroll Support** option, makes setting up payroll easier. In essence, the **Create Payroll Support** option sets up the categories and accounts you need to prepare payroll in your state. When you select this option, Quicken displays a message screen that gives you this information and tells you the process takes about 20 seconds. To continue, press Enter. Next, Quicken prompts you for the state's two-letter abbreviation, such as CA for California or NY for New York. (If you don't know the state's two-letter abbreviation, press Enter without making an entry. Quicken displays a box that lists state names and abbreviations, and you select one of the states on the list.) After you enter or identify the state's two-letter abbreviation, Quicken creates each of the accounts and categories needed in your state.

The accounts and categories that Quicken sets up differ from the generic accounts and categories used for illustrating payroll. Quicken sets up accounts and categories specific to the state.

You may know that most payroll deductions and taxes are calculated as a percentage of gross wages. Social Security deductions and matching payroll taxes are calculated as 6.2 percent, and up, of the gross wages to a ceiling amount ($53,400 in 1991). Medicare deductions and matching payroll taxes are 1.45 percent of the gross wages amount to a ceiling amount ($125,000 in 1991). With this feature of payroll preparation, you can often have Quicken calculate most of the payroll deductions and payroll taxes by using the new percentage split feature. The previous example of the employee named Vyder Ryderwood, who is receiving $1,000 of gross wages (see figs. 18.14 and 18.15) shows how this feature works. First, enter the gross wages amount ($1,000) as the check amount. Then, for any payroll where this split equals a percentage of the $1,000, enter the percentage, not the amount, in the Split Transaction screen. Using the example categories and accounts from figures 18.4 and 18.5, the *wages:gross* amount is calculated as 100 percent of the $1,000 check amount. The *employee SS* deduction and *employer SS* liability are both calculated as 6.2 percent of the $1,000 check amount. The *employee med* deduction and *employer med* liability are both calculated as 1.45 percent of the $1,000 check amount. The FUTA liability is calculated as 1 percent of the $1,000 check amount, and the *wages:payroll tax* amount is calculated as 8.65 percent of the $1,000 check amount. (this percentage is calculated by adding together the 6.2 percent employer's matching social security, the 1.45 percent employer's matching medicare, and the 1 percent FUTA.) In this example, therefore, the only split transaction amount you enter is the federal income taxes withheld amount, a figure you can look up in the Employer's Circular E.

A minor problem with this approach, however, is that initially the check amount isn't $1,000; the gross wages amount is $1,000. The check amount is $1,000 minus the payroll deductions. This problem isn't difficult to fix. You may recall that, to make the split transaction lines equal the check amount, Quicken adds another split transaction line. With the payroll check shown in Figures 18.4 and 18.5, Quicken adds a line for $186.50 because the check amount is $1,000 and the split transaction lines total $823.50. ($186.50 is the difference between $1,000 and $823.50.) Because the split transactions total of $823.50 also is the check amount, you need to delete only the split transaction line for $186.50 and then press F9 to direct Quicken to recalculate the check amount by using the split transaction lines.

Finally, Quicken enables you to create memorized transactions that use percentages rather than amounts. If you use the previously described approach, you can use this capability to make preparing payroll checks even easier.

Paying Payroll Taxes

When you pay the government, you already have recorded the expense of the taxes and are carrying as a liability the payroll taxes you still owe. When you write the check to the government, the `Category` field needs to show the payroll tax liability account. If you write a check to pay the $10 in federal unemployment taxes, you enter the category as [*FUTA*] because FUTA is the name of the liability account you use to track the amount you owe in federal unemployment tax.

You also use the same approach to record paying all the other payroll tax liabilities you owe. You write a check to the government and categorize the transaction as a transfer from the payroll taxes liability account.

In real life, of course, you may have several more payroll tax expenses and liabilities for items, such as state and local income taxes, state unemployment insurance, and disability insurance. The accounting procedures you follow to record and then pay each of these liabilities, however, are the same as the procedures described in the preceding paragraphs.

You need to segregate the payroll tax liability money. The best approach is to set up a separate bank account to collect and disburse payroll taxes. Do not, for any reason, *borrow* money from the payroll taxes bank account. Although the act may seem innocuous, this money is not yours to spend. This money belongs to an employee or the federal government; you only hold the money in trust.

Completing Quarterly and Annual Tax Reports

The final aspect of preparing payroll relates to the filing of the quarterly and annual payroll forms and reports to the state and local government. A series of federal reporting requirements exists for W-2s, W-3s, 940s, and 941s. Depending on where you live, you also may have several state and local payroll forms and reports to complete. You may be able to retrieve the numbers for these forms by printing a summary report based on the bank account you use to write payroll checks (see fig. 18.17).

Payroll Summary Report
1/ 1/91 Through 3/31/91

BUSINESS-Cash
1/11/91

Page 1

Payee	INC/EXP EXPENSES Wages & Job Cr Gross Wages	INC/EXP EXPENSES Wages & Job Cr Payroll taxes	INC/EXP EXPENSES Wages & Job Cr TOTAL	INC/EXP EXPENSES TOTAL	INC/EXP TOTAL	TRANSFERS FROM Employee FICA	TRANSFERS FROM Employer FICA
Batum Schrag	2,500.00	216.25	2,716.25	2,716.25	-2,716.25	191.25	191.25
Vyder Ryderwood	1,000.00	86.50	1,086.50	1,086.50	-1,086.50	76.50	76.50
OVERALL TOTAL	3,500.00	302.75	3,802.75	3,802.75	-3,802.75	267.75	267.75

Payroll Summary Report
1/ 1/91 Through 3/31/91

BUSINESS-Cash
1/11/91

Page 2

Payee	TRANSFERS FROM FUTA	TRANSFERS FROM Fed WH	TRANSFERS TOTAL	OVERALL TOTAL
Batum Schrag	25.00	300.00	707.50	-2,008.75
Vyder Ryderwood	10.00	100.00	263.00	-823.50
OVERALL TOTAL	35.00	400.00	970.50	-2,832.25

***Fig. 18.17.** A transaction report that subtotals by category.*

To print the summary report, select the **Summary** option from the Reports menu. You may want to subtotal the report by category. If you write the payroll checks on the same account you use to write other checks and include *payroll* in the Memo field, you can use the F9-Filter option to specify that only transactions with *payroll* appear on the summary report.

Completing the W-2 and W-3

You use the gross wages figures ($2,500 for Batum Schrag and $1,000 for Vyder Ryderwood) as the total wages amounts on the employees' W-2s. You use the transfers from withholding figures ($300 for Schrag and $100 for

Ryderwood) as the federal income tax withholding amounts. You use the transfers from employee's FICA ($191.25 for Schrag and $76.50 for Ryderwood) as the Social Security and Medicare taxes withheld amounts.

The W-3 summarizes the W-2 forms you complete. You enter the employer totals for the individual amounts on each employee's W-2. You can use the totals from the summary report for these employer totals.

One difference between the transaction report shown in figure 18.17 and the one you use to prepare the W-2 and W-3 forms is that the range of transaction dates encompasses the entire *calendar* year.

Completing Other Forms and Reports

The federal and the state governments have other tax forms and reports you must complete. You use the 940 form to calculate and report annual federal unemployment tax liability. You also use the 941 form each quarter to calculate and report federal income and Social Security taxes withheld and the employer's share of the Social Security taxes. Again, you may be able to use a summary report similar to the report shown in figure 18.17 to complete the quarterly return.

For the Employer's Annual Unemployment Tax (form 940), the range of transaction dates must encompass the entire year. For the Employer's Quarterly Federal Tax (form 941), the range of transaction dates must cover the quarter.

Typically, the Internal Revenue Service provides a great deal of help and information about federal payroll taxes. You may want to take advantage of the IRS help guides. Specifically, you need the Employer's Tax Guide (also known as Circular E). If you do not already have this document, call the nearest Internal Revenue Service office and request a guide. If you are a sole proprietor, you also may want to request the information packet "Your Business Tax Kit for Sole Proprietor," which provides information about the taxes you pay as a sole proprietor. Some IRS locations provide free small-business tax education seminars. You also may call the state revenue office and request all information they have on the state income and payroll taxes.

Preparing Inventory Accounting

An good inventory accounting system answers two questions: how much inventory do you currently hold and how much inventory did you sell over the year? A perpetual inventory system can answer both questions. Unfortunately, Quicken does not provide the tools to maintain a perpetual system. A perpetual inventory system tracks every change in inventory as the changes occur, in dollars and in units. As a result, you always know exactly how much inventory you hold, in dollars and in units. Because Quicken tracks only dollars, not units, you can answer only the second question: How much inventory did you sell over the year? You can answer this question with a simple periodic inventory system.

Understanding Periodic Inventory Systems

A periodic system works in the following way: at the end of every year, you count the inventory you are holding and add up the cost of the inventory. Calculate the cost of the goods, or inventory, you sold by taking the inventory purchases you made over the year and subtracting the change in inventory.

Suppose that you sell cars and that each car costs $10,000. You held three cars in inventory at the beginning of the year, purchased ten cars over the year, and have four cars in inventory at the end of the year. Using the equation described previously, you can calculate the value of the inventory you sold over the year as follows:

Car purchases: ($10,000 * 10) = $100,000
Change over year:
Ending: ($10,000 * 4 cars) = $40,000
Beginning: ($10,000 * 3 cars) = $30,000
Minus change over year: –$10,000
Cost of inventory sold over year: $90,000

You know that during the year you bought $100,000 of cars and that you are holding $10,000 more inventory than you held at the end of the previous year, which means that you did not sell all the cars you bought.

Implementing a Periodic Inventory System

If you want to enjoy the benefits of a periodic inventory system, you can use Quicken to construct a simple, but crude, inventory system.

The following steps describe how you implement a periodic inventory system using Quicken:

1. Set up an `Other asset` account for the inventory you buy and sell. The name can be Inventory. Select 4 as the account type. The starting balance is the starting inventory balance. (If you are just starting a business, the starting inventory balance can be zero if you have not yet begun to purchase inventory.)
2. When you purchase inventory, do not categorize the purchase as an expense—transfer the total purchase amount to the inventory account.
3. When you are ready to calculate net income, select the inventory account and use the **Update Account Balance** option from the Activities menu to reset the inventory account balance to whatever the physical count shows. Categorize the adjustment transaction as cost of goods sold. You may have to add the category *Cost of goods sold* as an expense category.

Figure 18.18 shows an inventory account register after a month of purchases and the adjustment transaction that calculates the actual cost of goods sold amount.

Reviewing the Problems of a Periodic System

As you know, a periodic inventory system is not without problems. Make sure that you can live with the problems of a periodic inventory system before you spend a great deal of time and energy to implement this kind of system.

Although you have accurate measures of cash flow, you have an accurate measure of profits only through the last adjustment transaction. If you need to measure profits frequently, you must take frequent physical counts of the inventory and make the physical adjustment transaction.

```
Print/Acct    Edit    Shortcuts    Reports    Activities              F1-Help

 DATE | REF |  PAYEE  ·  MEMO  ·  CATEGORY  | DECREASE  |C| INCREASE  |  BALANCE
------+-----+-------------------------------+-----------+-+-----------+-----------
      |     |          BEGINNING            |           | |           |
 1/ 1 |     |Opening Balance                |           | | 30,000 00 | 30,000 00
 1992 |     |               [Inventory]     |           | |           |
 1/31 |101  |Carl's Convertibles            |           | | 30,000 00 | 60,000 00
 1992 |     |3 ragtops        [Checking]    |           | |           |
 4/30 |234  |Raleigh's Hot Rods             |           | | 40,000 00 |100,000 00
 1992 |     |4 roadsters      [Checking]    |           | |           |
 7/31 |361  |Camille's Sports Cars Wholesale|           | | 30,000 00 |130,000 00
 19'2 |     |3 coupes         [Checking]    |           | |           |
12/31 |     |Balance Adjustment             | 90,000 00 | |           | 40,000 00
 1992 |Memo:|                               |           | |           |
      | Cat:|cost goods                     |           | |           |

Inventory          (Alt+letter accesses menu)     Current Balance: $      0.00
Esc-Main Menu      Ctrl◄┘ Record                  Ending Balance:  $40,000.00
```

Fig. 18.18. *An inventory account register with sample transactions.*

You don't know the details or components of the cost of goods sold because you get the cost of goods sold from an adjustment transaction. As a result, you do not know the portion of cost of goods sold that stems from sales to specific customers or the portion that stems from breakage, shoplifting, or spoilage. This loss of information can be especially troublesome if the business has more than one kind of item sold, such as books and tapes and CDs. You may have to set up separate accounts for each kind of item in the inventory and be sure that you segregate all purchases by using the **Split Screen** option.

Except when you make physical counts of inventory, you also never know how much inventory you actually have on hand. You never can use this inventory system, therefore, to see the items you need to reorder or how many units of a specific item are presently in stock.

Job Costing

Job costing refers to tracking the costs of a specific project, or job, and comparing these costs to the amount you planned to spend. Home builders, advertising agencies, and specialty manufacturers are examples of businesses with projects you must monitor for actual and planned costs.

The Quicken user's manual suggests one approach for job costing: categorize each expense into a category and a class. When you print a transaction or summary report, you can choose to subtotal by the classes. Because you used classes to represent jobs, the total for a class is the total for a job. This approach, however, is not strong. The following paragraphs describe alternative approaches that help you avoid two problems you encounter when categorizing expenses into categories and classes. (See Chapter 10 for a detailed discussion of categories and classes.)

The first problem with using classes as the basis for a job costing system is that within Quicken, you budget by classes, not by categories. If you use the class approach, you omit one of the basic job costing tasks: comparing the amount you planned to spend with the actual amount spent. Fortunately, you can solve this problem by setting up a group of categories that you use only for a specific job. You may even include a code or an abbreviation in the category name to indicate the job.

Suppose that you are a home builder constructing a house on lot 23 in Deerfield and that you use three rough categories of expenses on all the homes you build: land, material, and labor. Here, you can create three special categories: *D23 land*, *D23 material*, and *D23 labor*, which you can use exclusively to budget and track the costs of the house under construction. Remember that you cannot budget for subcategories; you can budget only for categories. Figure 18.19 shows the on-screen version of the budgeting report that you can generate to monitor job costs if you follow the approaches described in the preceding paragraph.

A second problem with using classes as the basis for a job-costing system is that you don't always have to categorize as expenses the costs you incur on a job. Often, you need to treat these costs as assets. The costs of building the home on lot 23 in the Deerfield subdivision should be carried as inventory until the home is sold. When the home is sold, the total costs of the home may be categorized as the cost of goods sold.

During the job, if you categorize the costs of building the home as expenses when you pay the costs, you overstate expenses (which understates profits), and you understate assets (which understates net worth). These understatements of profits and net worth can become a real problem if you have investors or lenders looking carefully at your financial performance and condition. To solve this problem, create a transaction in which you move cost dollars out of the job cost categories into an asset account.

BUDGET REPORT

3/ 1/92 Through 3/31/92

BUSINESS-All Accounts

3/31/91

Category Description	3/ 1/92 Actual	- Budget	3/31/92 Diff
INCOME/EXPENSE			
EXPENSES			
Building Lot	30,400.00	30,000.00	400.00
Building Materials	23,456.00	25,000.00	-1,544.00
Subcontractor labor	16,753.00	20,000.00	-3,247.00
TOTAL EXPENSES	70,609.00	75,000.00	-4,391.00
TOTAL INCOME/EXPENSE	-70,609.00	-75,000.00	4,391.00

BUSINESS-All Accounts

Esc-Create report   F1-Help   Ctrl M-Memorize   F8-Print

Fig. 18.19. A budget report for a job.

Chapter Summary

This chapter provided you with a basic approach to accounting for any business asset or liability and gave specific suggestions and tips for performing six basic accounting tasks. You now have the necessary information to use Quicken as the basis of a business accounting system.

19

Using Quicken To Prepare for Income Taxes

A basic accounting requirement for businesses and individuals is to complete the required federal income tax forms at the end of the year to report income and expenses. When using Quicken, you need to use categories that enable you to complete the appropriate income tax forms. The beginning of this chapter explains how to use categories for income tax forms. Some Quicken users also want to know how to export the income tax deduction data inside Quicken to external income tax preparation packages, such as TurboTax. The mechanics of exporting income tax data are covered near the end of this chapter.

Using Categories

The basic rule for completing end-of-the-year income tax forms with Quicken is that you need to use Quicken categories easily reconcilable with the income and expense categories shown on the actual tax forms and that you create categories that identify tax forms and specific line numbers. The most straightforward approach is to create categories for each of the income and expense lines on the income tax form you file and to use these categories to account for income and expense transactions. For more detail than the tax form income and expense lines provide, you can use subcategories that fall under the income and expense categories. Chapter 10 describes how to create and use categories and subcategories.

The following examples may help you to better understand how to use categories and subcategories. Real estate investors complete the Schedule E tax form (see fig. 19.1); farmers complete the Schedule F tax form (see fig. 19.2); sole proprietors complete the Schedule C tax form (see fig. 19.3); partnerships complete the Schedule 1065 tax form (see fig. 19.4); and corporations complete one of the three corporate income tax forms: 1120-A for small corporations (see fig. 19.5), 1120S for S corporations (see fig. 19.6), and 1120 for all other corporations (see fig. 19.7).

S Corporations are corporations that have elected to be treated as partnerships for income tax purposes.

If you live in a state with income taxes, you also may need to complete an equivalent state income tax form. Make sure that you or an accountant can easily prepare the tax return with the information Quicken produces. (The more time the accountant takes, the more money you pay to have the accountant prepare the return.)

You also can work with categories that you need to combine with other categories to calculate a tax form entry. Suppose that you are a sole proprietor and own a restaurant. Although total wages goes on one line of the Schedule C tax form, you may want to track several categories of wages, including waitresses, dishwashers, cooks, bartenders, and so on. Here, you have several wage categories that must be added to calculate the wages amount that goes on the tax form. The Tax Schedule Report can help you accomplish this task.

If you are using Quicken for a sole proprietorship and you hold and resell inventory, you need Part III of the Schedule C form to calculate the cost of goods sold and the inventory balances (see fig. 19.3). You can use the periodic inventory approach described in Chapter 18 to produce the information for Part III of the Schedule C form.

If you are using Quicken for a partnership or a corporation, you must report asset and liability amounts on the tax return (see figs. 19.4 through 19.7). You also want to verify that Quicken provides the raw data necessary to complete these lines of the tax return. The easiest approach probably is to set up accounts to track each asset and liability that appears on the tax return. Another approach is to use accounts that you can combine to calculate the total asset or liability figure that needs to be entered on the tax return.

This book contains copies of the 1990 federal income tax forms for businesses at the end of this chapter. (The 1991 forms were unavailable when this book was written.) You can use these forms to build the lists of required categories and accounts. The forms, however, change almost every year. Unfortunately—and you can thank your congressman for these changes—the forms are not finalized until late in the year. You cannot know with certainty which income and expense categories or which asset and liability accounts to use until the year is nearly over. The practical approach is to use the categories and accounts indicated by the preceding year and make adjustments when the new forms arrive.

Sole proprietors must consider one other thing: you may need to complete more than one Schedule C form. You cannot aggregate a series of dissimilar businesses and report the consolidated results on one Schedule C. If you own a tavern, practice law, and run a small manufacturing business, you must complete three Schedule C forms: one form for the tavern, one form for the law practice, and still another form for the manufacturing firm. Quicken can handle this situation but you need to account for each business that needs a separate Schedule C in a separate account group. (Chapter 3 describes how to set up and select different account groups.)

When you use Quicken's categories, extracting the information you need to complete a form is simple. You just print the report that summarizes the categories that track income tax deductions. For individuals, the Tax Summary Report is valuable; for businesses, the Profit and Loss statement is valuable.

> Although tax forms give most of the general information about the kinds of expenses, the instructions and regulations made by the IRS may require that you gather additional information. One example is that the business usage of a vehicle owned by a business is subject to different limitations, which are not necessarily found in Quicken. Consult a tax advisor when you encounter questionable areas.

Importing Quicken Data into TurboTax

You can import the financial data you collect and store in Quicken directly into several popular income tax preparation packages. TurboTax, for example, imports Quicken data if you follow general steps.

Even if you don't have TurboTax, you still may be able to apply the same general steps to export Quicken data to other tax preparation packages.

To export Quicken data to TurboTax, follow these steps:

1. Display the Reports menu and select the **Personal** option. Quicken displays the Personal Reports menu.
2. Select the **Tax Schedule** option from the Personal Reports menu. Quicken displays the Tax Schedule Report screen.
3. Assign the report a title; indicate the range of dates; and press Enter. Quicken displays an on-screen version of the Tax Schedule Report.
4. Press Ctrl-P to display the Print Report screen.
5. Select the **Tax File Print to** option by pressing 6 and Enter.

Then follow the instructions described in the TurboTax user's manual for importing the data contained in the ASCII disk file you create. (For this information and for other help with TurboTax, you may want to read *Using TurboTax: 1992 Edition*, published by Que Corporation.)

Chapter Summary

This chapter described the basic steps to take to ensure that Quicken produces the raw data necessary to complete federal and state income tax returns. The steps are neither complex nor difficult. You are required from the very beginning, however, to use categories that enable you to summarize income and expense data correctly.

SCHEDULE E
(Form 1040)
Department of the Treasury
Internal Revenue Service (X)

Supplemental Income and Loss
(From rents, royalties, partnerships, estates, trusts, REMICs, etc.)
▶ Attach to Form 1040 or Form 1041.
▶ See Instructions for Schedule E (Form 1040).

OMB No. 1545-0074
1990
Attachment Sequence No. 13

Name(s) shown on return | Your social security number

Part I Income or Loss From Rentals and Royalties **Note:** *Report farm rental income or loss from **Form 4835** on page 2, line 39.*

1 Show the kind and location of each **rental property:**
A
B
C

2 For each rental property listed on line 1, did you or your family use it for personal purposes for more than the greater of 14 days or 10% of the total days rented at fair rental value during the tax year? (See Instructions.)

	Yes	No
A		
B		
C		

Rental and Royalty Income:		Properties A	Properties B	Properties C	D Totals (Add columns A, B, and C)
3 Rents received	3				3
4 Royalties received	4				4
Rental and Royalty Expenses:					
5 Advertising	5				
6 Auto and travel	6				
7 Cleaning and maintenance	7				
8 Commissions	8				
9 Insurance	9				
10 Legal and other professional fees	10				
11 Mortgage interest paid to banks, etc. (see Instructions)	11				11
12 Other interest	12				
13 Repairs	13				
14 Supplies	14				
15 Taxes	15				
16 Utilities	16				
17 Wages and salaries	17				
18 Other (list) ▶	18				
19 Add lines 5 through 18	19				19
20 Depreciation expense or depletion (see Instructions)	20				20
21 Total expenses. Add lines 19 and 20	21				
22 Income or (loss) from rental or royalty properties. Subtract line 21 from line 3 (rents) or line 4 (royalties). If the result is a (loss), see Instructions to find out if you must file **Form 6198**	22				
23 Deductible rental loss. **Caution:** *Your rental loss on line 22 may be limited. See Instructions to find out if you must file **Form 8582***	23	( )	( )	( )	
24 **Income.** Add rental and royalty income from line 22. Enter the total income here					24
25 **Losses.** Add royalty losses from line 22 and rental losses from line 23. Enter the total losses here					25 ( )
26 Total rental and royalty income or (loss). Combine amounts on lines 24 and 25. Enter the result here. If Parts II, III, IV, and line 39 on page 2 do not apply to you, enter the amount from line 26 on Form 1040, line 18. Otherwise, include the amount from line 26 in the total on line 40 on page 2.					26

For Paperwork Reduction Act Notice, see Form 1040 Instructions. **Schedule E (Form 1040) 1990**

113

Fig. 19.1. The Schedule E form indicates the general income and expense categories real estate investors use to report profits and losses.

Schedule E (Form 1040) 1990 — Attachment Sequence No. 13 — Page 2

Name(s) shown on return. (Do not enter name and social security number if shown on other side.) | Your social security number

Note: *If you report amounts from farming or fishing on Schedule E, you must include your gross income from those activities on line 41 below.*

Part II — Income or Loss From Partnerships and S Corporations

If you report a loss from an at-risk activity, you MUST check either column **(e)** or **(f)** of line 27 to describe your investment in the activity. See Instructions. If you check column **(f)**, you must attach **Form 6198.**

27	(a) Name	(b) Enter P for partnership; S for S corporation	(c) Check if foreign partnership	(d) Employer identification number	Investment At Risk? (e) All is at risk	(f) Some is not at risk
A						
B						
C						
D						
E						

	Passive Income and Loss		Nonpassive Income and Loss		
	(g) Passive loss allowed (Attach **Form 8582** if required)	(h) Passive income from **Schedule K-1**	(i) Nonpassive loss from **Schedule K-1**	(j) Section 179 expense deduction from **Form 4562**	(k) Nonpassive income from **Schedule K-1**
A					
B					
C					
D					
E					
28a Totals					
b Totals					

29 Add amounts in columns (h) and (k) of line 28a. Enter the total income here . . . 29

30 Add amounts in columns (g), (i), and (j) of line 28b. Enter the total here . . . 30 ( )

31 Total partnership and S corporation income or (loss). Combine amounts on lines 29 and 30. Enter the result here and include in the total on line 40 below . . . 31

Part III — Income or Loss From Estates and Trusts

32	(a) Name	(b) Employer identification number
A		
B		
C		

	Passive Income and Loss		Nonpassive Income and Loss	
	(c) Passive deduction or loss allowed (Attach **Form 8582** if required)	(d) Passive income from **Schedule K-1**	(e) Deduction or loss from **Schedule K-1**	(f) Other income from **Schedule K-1**
A				
B				
C				
33a Totals				
b Totals				

34 Add amounts in columns (d) and (f) of line 33a. Enter the total income here . . . 34

35 Add amounts in columns (c) and (e) of line 33b. Enter the total here . . . 35 ( )

36 Total estate and trust income or (loss). Combine amounts on lines 34 and 35. Enter the result here and include in the total on line 40 below . . . 36

Part IV — Income or Loss From Real Estate Mortgage Investment Conduits (REMICs)—Residual Holder

37 (a) Name	(b) Employer identification number	(c) Excess inclusion from **Schedules Q**, line 2c (see Instructions)	(d) Taxable income (net loss) from **Schedules Q**, line 1b	(e) Income from **Schedules Q**, line 3b

38 Combine amounts in columns (d) and (e) only. Enter the result here and include in the total on line 40 below . . . 38

Part V — Summary

39 Net farm rental income or (loss) from **Form 4835**. (Also complete line 41 below.) . . . 39

40 TOTAL income or (loss). Combine amounts on lines 26, 31, 36, 38, and 39. Enter the result here and on Form 1040, line 18 . . . ▶ 40

41 **Reconciliation of Farming and Fishing Income:** Enter your **gross** farming and fishing income reported in Parts II and III, and on line 39 (see Instructions) . . . 41

114

Fig. 19.1. Schedule E, Form 1040, continued.

SCHEDULE F (Form 1040)
Department of the Treasury Internal Revenue Service (X)

Farm Income and Expenses
▶ Attach to Form 1040, Form 1041, or Form 1065.
▶ See Instructions for Schedule F (Form 1040).

OMB No. 1545-0074
1990
Attachment Sequence No. 14

Name of proprietor | Social security number (SSN)

A Principal product. (Describe in one or two words your principal crop or activity for the current tax year.)
B Enter principal agricultural activity code (from page 2) ▶

C Accounting method: ☐ Cash ☐ Accrual
D Employer ID number (Not SSN)

E Did you make an election in a prior year to include Commodity Credit Corporation loan proceeds as income in that year? ☐ Yes ☐ No
F Did you "materially participate" in the operation of this business during 1990? (If "No," see Instructions for limitations on losses.) ☐ Yes ☐ No
G Do you elect, or did you previously elect, to currently deduct certain preproductive period expenses? (See Instructions.) ☐ Does not apply ☐ Yes ☐ No

Part I Farm Income—Cash Method—Complete Parts I and II (Accrual method taxpayers complete Parts II and III, and line 11 of Part I.)
Do not include sales of livestock held for draft, breeding, sport, or dairy purposes; report these sales on Form 4797.

1 Sales of livestock and other items you bought for resale . . . 1
2 Cost or other basis of livestock and other items you bought for resale . 2
3 Subtract line 2 from line 1 . . . 3
4 Sales of livestock, produce, grains, and other products you raised . . . 4
5a Total cooperative distributions (Form(s) 1099-PATR) 5a | 5b Taxable amount 5b
6a Agricultural program payments (see Instructions) 6a | 6b Taxable amount 6b
7 Commodity Credit Corporation (CCC) loans:
a CCC loans reported under election (see Instructions) . . . 7a
b CCC loans forfeited or repaid with certificates . 7b | 7c Taxable amount 7c
8 Crop insurance proceeds and certain disaster payments (see Instructions):
a Amount received in 1990 . . . 8a | 8b Taxable amount 8b
c If election to defer to 1991 is attached, check here ▶ ☐ . 8d Amount deferred from 1989 . . 8d
9 Custom hire (machine work) income . . . 9
10 Other income, including Federal and state gasoline or fuel tax credit or refund (see Instructions) . . 10
11 Add amounts in the right column for lines 3 through 10. If accrual method taxpayer, enter the amount from page 2, line 51. This is your **gross income** . . . ▶ 11

Part II Farm Expenses—Cash and Accrual Method (Do not include personal or living expenses such as taxes, insurance, repairs, etc., on your home.)

Line	Expense	Line	Expense
12	Breeding fees	24	Labor hired (less jobs credit)
13	Chemicals	25	Pension and profit-sharing plans
14	Conservation expenses (you must attach **Form 8645**)	26	Rent or lease (see Instructions):
15	Custom hire (machine work)	26a	Vehicles, machinery, and equip.
16	Depreciation and section 179 expense deduction not claimed elsewhere (see Instructions)	26b	Other (land, animals, etc.)
17	Employee benefit programs other than on line 25	27	Repairs and maintenance
18	Feed purchased	28	Seeds and plants purchased
19	Fertilizers and lime	29	Storage and warehousing
20	Freight and trucking	30	Supplies purchased
21	Gasoline, fuel, and oil	31	Taxes
22	Insurance (other than health)	32	Utilities
23	Interest:	33	Veterinary fees and medicine
23a	Mortgage (paid to banks, etc.)	34	Other expenses (specify):
23b	Other	34a	a
		34b	b
		34c	c
		34d	d
		34e	e

35 Add amounts on lines 12 through 34e. These are your **total expenses** . . . ▶ 35
36 **Net farm profit or (loss).** Subtract line 35 from line 11. If a profit, enter on Form 1040, line 19, and on Schedule SE, line 1. If a loss, you MUST go on to line 37. (Fiduciaries and partnerships, see Instructions.) 36
37 If you have a loss, you MUST check the box that describes your investment in this activity (see Instructions). 37a ☐ All investment is at risk. 37b ☐ Some investment is not at risk.
If you checked 37a, enter the loss on Form 1040, line 19, and Schedule SE, line 1.
If you checked 37b, you MUST attach **Form 6198.**

For Paperwork Reduction Act Notice, see Form 1040 Instructions. Schedule F (Form 1040) 1990

115

Fig. 19.2. The Schedule F form indicates the general income and expense categories farmers use to report profits and losses.

Schedule F (Form1040) 1990 Page 2

Part III Farm Income—Accrual Method

Do not include sales of livestock held for draft, breeding, sport, or dairy purposes; report these sales on Form 4797 and do not include this livestock on line 46 below.

38	Sales of livestock, produce, grains, and other products during year	38	
39a	Total cooperative distributions (Form(s) 1099-PATR) 39a — 39b Taxable amount	39b	
40a	Agricultural program payments (see Instructions) 40a — 40b Taxable amount	40b	
41	Commodity Credit Corporation (CCC) loans:		
a	CCC loans reported under election (see Instructions)	41a	
b	CCC loans forfeited or repaid with certificates 41b — 41c Taxable amount	41c	
42	Crop insurance proceeds	42	
43	Custom hire (machine work) income	43	
44	Other income, including Federal and state gasoline or fuel tax credit or refund (see Instructions)	44	
45	Add amounts in the right column for lines 38 through 44	45	
46	Inventory of livestock, produce, grains, and other products at beginning of year — 46		
47	Cost of livestock, produce, grains, and other products purchased during year — 47		
48	Add lines 46 and 47 — 48		
49	Inventory of livestock, produce, grains, and other products at end of year — 49		
50	Cost of livestock, produce, grains, and other products sold. Subtract line 49 from line 48*	50	
51	Subtract line 50 from line 45. Enter the result here and on page 1, line 11. This is your **gross income** ▶	51	

*If you use the unit-livestock-price method or the farm-price method of valuing inventory and the amount on line 49 is larger than the amount on line 48, subtract line 48 from line 49. Enter the result on line 50. Add lines 45 and 50. Enter the total on line 51.

Part IV Principal Agricultural Activity Codes

Select one of the following codes and write the 3-digit number on page 1, line B. (**Note:** *If your principal source of income is from providing agricultural services such as soil preparation, veterinary, farm labor, horticultural, or management for a fee or on a contract basis, you should file* ***Schedule C*** *(Form 1040), Profit or Loss From Business.*)

- 120 **Field crop,** including grains and nongrains such as cotton, peanuts, feed corn, wheat, tobacco, Irish potatoes, etc.
- 160 **Vegetables and melons,** garden-type vegetables and melons, such as sweet corn, tomatoes, squash, etc.
- 170 **Fruit and tree nuts,** including grapes, berries, olives, etc.
- 180 **Ornamental floriculture and nursery products**
- 185 **Food crops grown under cover,** including hydroponic crops
- 211 **Beefcattle feedlots**
- 212 **Beefcattle,** except feedlots
- 215 **Hogs, sheep, and goats**
- 240 **Dairy**
- 250 **Poultry and eggs,** including chickens, ducks, pigeons, quail, etc.
- 260 **General livestock,** not specializing in any one livestock category
- 270 **Animal specialty,** including fur-bearing animals, pets, horses, etc.
- 280 **Animal aquaculture,** including fish, shellfish, mollusks, frogs, etc., produced within confined space
- 290 **Forest products,** including forest nurseries and seed gathering, extraction of pine gum, and gathering of forest products
- 300 **Agricultural production,** not specified

116

Fig. 19.2. Schedule F, Form 1040, continued.

SCHEDULE C (Form 1040)

Department of the Treasury
Internal Revenue Service (X)

Profit or Loss From Business
(Sole Proprietorship)
Partnerships, Joint Ventures, Etc., Must File Form 1065.
▶ Attach to Form 1040 or Form 1041. ▶ See Instructions for Schedule C (Form 1040).

OMB No. 1545-0074
1990
Attachment Sequence No. 09

Name of proprietor | Social security number (SSN)

A Principal business or profession, including product or service (see Instructions) | B Enter principal business code (from page 2) ▶

C Business name and address (include suite or room no.) ▶ | D Employer ID number (Not SSN)

E Accounting method: (1) ☐ Cash (2) ☐ Accrual (3) ☐ Other (specify) ▶

F Method(s) used to value closing inventory: (1) ☐ Cost (2) ☐ Lower of cost or market (3) ☐ Other (attach explanation) (4) ☐ Does not apply (if checked, go to line H) | Yes | No

G Was there any change in determining quantities, costs, or valuations between opening and closing inventory? (If "Yes," attach explanation.)

H Are you deducting expenses for business use of your home? (If "Yes," see Instructions for limitations.)

I Did you "materially participate" in the operation of this business during 1990? (If "No," see Instructions for limitations on losses.)

J If this is the first Schedule C filed for this business, check here ▶ ☐

Part I Income

1 Gross receipts or sales. ***Caution:*** *If this income was reported to you on Form W-2 and the "Statutory employee" box on that form was checked, see the Instructions and check here* ▶ ☐	1	
2 Returns and allowances	2	
3 Subtract line 2 from line 1. Enter the result here	3	
4 Cost of goods sold (from line 38 on page 2)	4	
5 Subtract line 4 from line 3 and enter the **gross profit** here	5	
6 Other income, including Federal and state gasoline or fuel tax credit or refund (see Instructions)	6	
7 Add lines 5 and 6. This is your **gross income** ▶	7	

Part II Expenses

8 Advertising	8		21 Repairs and maintenance	21	
9 Bad debts from sales or services (see Instructions)	9		22 Supplies (not included in Part III)	22	
10 Car and truck expenses (attach **Form 4562**)	10		23 Taxes and licenses	23	
11 Commissions and fees	11		24 Travel, meals, and entertainment:		
12 Depletion	12		a Travel	24a	
13 Depreciation and section 179 expense deduction (not included in Part III) (see Instructions)	13		b Meals and entertainment		
			c Enter 20% of line 24b subject to limitations (see Instructions)		
14 Employee benefit programs (other than on line 19)	14		d Subtract line 24c from line 24b	24d	
15 Insurance (other than health)	15		25 Utilities	25	
16 Interest:			26 Wages (less jobs credit)	26	
a Mortgage (paid to banks, etc.)	16a		27a Other expenses (**list type and amount**):		
b Other	16b				
17 Legal and professional services	17				
18 Office expense	18				
19 Pension and profit-sharing plans	19				
20 Rent or lease (see Instructions):					
a Vehicles, machinery, and equip.	20a				
b Other business property	20b		27b Total other expenses	27b	

28 Add amounts in columns for lines 8 through 27b. These are your **total expenses** ▶	28	
29 **Net profit or (loss).** Subtract line 28 from line 7. If a profit, enter here and on Form 1040, line 12. Also enter the net profit on Schedule SE, line 2 (statutory employees, see Instructions). If a loss, you MUST go on to line 30 (fiduciaries, see Instructions)	29	

30 If you have a loss, you MUST check the box that describes your investment in this activity (see Instructions). If you checked 30a, enter the loss on Form 1040, line 12, and Schedule SE, line 2 (statutory employees, see Instructions). If you checked 30b, you MUST attach **Form 6198.**
30a ☐ All investment is at risk.
30b ☐ Some investment is not at risk.

For Paperwork Reduction Act Notice, see Form 1040 Instructions. **Schedule C (Form 1040) 1990**

107

Fig. 19.3. *The Schedule C form indicates which income and expense categories sole proprietors use to report profits and losses.*

Schedule C (Form 1040) 1990 Page **2**

Part III **Cost of Goods Sold** (See Instructions.)

Line	Description	Box	Amount
31	Inventory at beginning of year. (If different from last year's closing inventory, attach explanation.)	31	
32	Purchases less cost of items withdrawn for personal use	32	
33	Cost of labor. (Do not include salary paid to yourself.)	33	
34	Materials and supplies	34	
35	Other costs	35	
36	Add lines 31 through 35	36	
37	Inventory at end of year	37	
38	**Cost of goods sold.** Subtract line 37 from line 36. Enter the result here and on page 1, line 4	38	

Part IV **Principal Business or Professional Activity Codes**

Locate the major category that best describes your activity. Within the major category, select the activity code that most closely identifies the business or profession that is the principal source of your sales or receipts. **Enter this 4-digit code on page 1, line B.** *For example, a grocery store is under the major category of "Retail Trade," and the code is "3210." (**Note:** If your principal source of income is from farming activities, you should file **Schedule F** (Form 1040), Farm Income and Expenses.)*

Construction

Code

- 0018 Operative builders (for own account)

General contractors

- 0034 Residential building
- 0059 Nonresidential building
- 0075 Highway and street construction
- 3889 Other heavy construction (pipe laying, bridge construction, etc.)

Building trade contractors, including repairs

- 0232 Plumbing, heating, air conditioning
- 0257 Painting and paper hanging
- 0273 Electrical work
- 0299 Masonry, dry wall, stone, tile
- 0414 Carpentering and flooring
- 0430 Roofing, siding, and sheet metal
- 0455 Concrete work
- 0885 Other building trade contractors (excavation, glazing, etc.)

Manufacturing, Including Printing and Publishing

- 0638 Food products and beverages
- 0653 Textile mill products
- 0679 Apparel and other textile products
- 0695 Leather, footware, handbags, etc.
- 0810 Furniture and fixtures
- 0836 Lumber and other wood products
- 0851 Printing and publishing
- 0877 Paper and allied products
- 1032 Stone, clay, and glass products
- 1057 Primary metal industries
- 1073 Fabricated metal products
- 1099 Machinery and machine shops
- 1115 Electric and electronic equipment
- 1883 Other manufacturing industries

Mining and Mineral Extraction

- 1511 Metal mining
- 1537 Coal mining
- 1552 Oil and gas
- 1719 Quarrying and nonmetallic mining

Agricultural Services, Forestry, Fishing

- 1933 Crop services
- 1958 Veterinary services, including pets
- 1974 Livestock breeding
- 1990 Other animal services
- 2113 Farm labor and management services
- 2212 Horticulture and landscaping
- 2238 Forestry, except logging
- 0836 Logging
- 2246 Commercial fishing
- 2469 Hunting and trapping

Wholesale Trade—Selling Goods to Other Businesses, Etc.

Durable goods, including machinery, equipment, wood, metals, etc.

- 2618 Selling for your own account
- 2634 Agent or broker for other firms—more than 50% of gross sales on commission

Nondurable goods, including food, fiber, chemicals, etc.

- 2659 Selling for your own account
- 2675 Agent or broker for other firms—more than 50% of gross sales on commission

Retail Trade—Selling Goods to Individuals and Households

- 3012 Selling door-to-door, by telephone or party plan, or from mobile unit
- 3038 Catalog or mail order
- 3053 Vending machine selling

Selling From Showroom, Store, or Other Fixed Location

Food, beverages, and drugs

- 3079 Eating places (meals or snacks)
- 3086 Catering services
- 3095 Drinking places (alcoholic beverages)
- 3210 Grocery stores (general line)
- 0612 Bakeries selling at retail
- 3236 Other food stores (meat, produce, candy, etc.)
- 3251 Liquor stores
- 3277 Drug stores

Automotive and service stations

- 3319 New car dealers (franchised)
- 3335 Used car dealers
- 3517 Other automotive dealers (motorcycles, recreational vehicles, etc.)
- 3533 Tires, accessories, and parts
- 3558 Gasoline service stations

General merchandise, apparel, and furniture

- 3715 Variety stores
- 3731 Other general merchandise stores
- 3756 Shoe stores
- 3772 Men's and boys' clothing stores
- 3913 Women's ready-to-wear stores
- 3921 Women's accessory and specialty stores and furriers
- 3939 Family clothing stores
- 3954 Other apparel and accessory stores
- 3970 Furniture stores
- 3996 TV, audio, and electronics
- 3988 Computer and software stores
- 4119 Household appliance stores
- 4317 Other home furnishing stores (china, floor coverings, etc.)
- 4333 Music and record stores

Building, hardware, and garden supply

- 4416 Building materials dealers
- 4432 Paint, glass, and wallpaper stores
- 4457 Hardware stores
- 4473 Nurseries and garden supply stores

Other retail stores

- 4614 Used merchandise and antique stores (except motor vehicle parts)
- 4630 Gift, novelty, and souvenir shops
- 4655 Florists
- 4671 Jewelry stores
- 4697 Sporting goods and bicycle shops
- 4812 Boat dealers
- 4838 Hobby, toy, and game shops
- 4853 Camera and photo supply stores
- 4879 Optical goods stores
- 4895 Luggage and leather goods stores
- 5017 Book stores, excluding newsstands
- 5033 Stationery stores
- 5058 Fabric and needlework stores
- 5074 Mobile home dealers
- 5090 Fuel dealers (except gasoline)
- 5884 Other retail stores

Finance, Insurance, Real Estate, and Related Services

- 5520 Real estate agents or brokers
- 5579 Real estate property managers
- 5710 Subdividers and developers, except cemeteries
- 5538 Operators and lessors of buildings, including residential
- 5553 Operators and lessors of other real property
- 5702 Insurance agents or brokers
- 5744 Other insurance services
- 6064 Security brokers and dealers
- 6080 Commodity contracts brokers and dealers, and security and commodity exchanges
- 6130 Investment advisors and services
- 6148 Credit institutions and mortgage bankers
- 6155 Title abstract offices
- 5777 Other finance and real estate

Transportation, Communications, Public Utilities, and Related Services

- 6114 Taxicabs
- 6312 Bus and limousine transportation
- 6361 Other highway passenger transportation
- 6338 Trucking (except trash collection)
- 6395 Courier or package delivery services
- 6510 Trash collection without own dump
- 6536 Public warehousing
- 6551 Water transportation
- 6619 Air transportation
- 6635 Travel agents and tour operators
- 6650 Other transportation services
- 6676 Communication services
- 6692 Utilities, including dumps, snowplowing, road cleaning, etc.

Services (Personal, Professional, and Business Services)

Hotels and other lodging places

- 7096 Hotels, motels, and tourist homes
- 7211 Rooming and boarding houses
- 7237 Camps and camping parks

Laundry and cleaning services

- 7419 Coin-operated laundries and dry cleaning
- 7435 Other laundry, dry cleaning, and garment services
- 7450 Carpet and upholstery cleaning
- 7476 Janitorial and related services (building, house, and window cleaning)

Business and/or personal services

- 7617 Legal services (or lawyer)
- 7633 Income tax preparation
- 7658 Accounting and bookkeeping
- 7518 Engineering services
- 7682 Architectural services
- 7708 Surveying services
- 7245 Management services
- 7260 Public relations
- 7286 Consulting services
- 7716 Advertising, except direct mail
- 7732 Employment agencies and personnel supply
- 7799 Consumer credit reporting and collection services
- 7856 Mailing, reproduction, commercial art and photography, and stenographic services
- 7872 Computer programming, processing, data preparation, and related services
- 7922 Computer repair, maintenance, and leasing
- 7773 Equipment rental and leasing (except computer or automotive)
- 7914 Investigative and protective services
- 7880 Other business services

Personal services

- 8110 Beauty shops (or beautician)
- 8318 Barber shop (or barber)
- 8334 Photographic portrait studios
- 8532 Funeral services and crematories
- 8714 Child day care
- 8730 Teaching or tutoring
- 8755 Counseling (except health practitioners)
- 8771 Ministers and chaplains
- 6882 Other personal services

Automotive services

- 8813 Automotive rental or leasing, without driver
- 8839 Parking, except valet
- 8953 Automotive repairs, general and specialized
- 8896 Other automotive services (wash, towing, etc.)

Miscellaneous repair, except computers

- 9019 TV and audio equipment repair
- 9035 Other electrical equipment repair
- 9050 Reupholstery and furniture repair
- 2881 Other equipment repair

Medical and health services

- 9217 Offices and clinics of medical doctors (MDs)
- 9233 Offices and clinics of dentists
- 9258 Osteopathic physicians and surgeons
- 9241 Podiatrists
- 9274 Chiropractors
- 9290 Optometrists
- 9415 Registered and practical nurses
- 9431 Other health practitioners
- 9456 Medical and dental laboratories
- 9472 Nursing and personal care facilities
- 9886 Other health services

Amusement and recreational services

- 8557 Physical fitness facilities
- 9597 Motion picture and video production
- 9688 Motion picture and tape distribution and allied services
- 9613 Videotape rental
- 9639 Motion picture theaters
- 9670 Bowling centers
- 9696 Professional sports and racing, including promoters and managers
- 9811 Theatrical performers, musicians, agents, producers, and related services
- 9837 Other amusement and recreational services

- 8888 Unable to classify

108

Fig. 19.3. Schedule C, Form 1040, continued.

Form **1065** Department of the Treasury Internal Revenue Service

U.S. Partnership Return of Income

For calendar year 1990, or tax year beginning ________________, 1990, and ending ______________, 19___.

▶ See separate instructions.

OMB No. 1545-0099

1990

	Use IRS label. Otherwise, please print or type.	
A Principal business activity	Name	D Employer identification number
B Principal product or service	Number, street, and room or suite no. (If a P.O. box, see page 9 of the instructions.)	E Date business started
C Business code number	City or town, state, and ZIP code	F Total assets (see Specific Instructions) $

G Check applicable boxes: (1) ☐ Initial return (2) ☐ Final return (3) ☐ Change in address (4) ☐ Amended return

H Check accounting method: (1) ☐ Cash (2) ☐ Accrual (3) ☐ Other (specify) ▶ ____________

	Yes	No
I Number of partners in this partnership ▶ ____________		
J Is this partnership a limited partnership?		
K Are any partners in this partnership also partnerships?		
L Is this partnership a partner in another partnership?		
M Is this partnership subject to the consolidated audit procedures of sections 6221 through 6233? If "Yes," see "Designation of Tax Matters Partner" on page 2		
N Does this partnership meet **all** the requirements shown in the instructions for **Question N**?		
O Does this partnership have any foreign partners?		
P Is this partnership a publicly traded partnership as defined in section 469(k)(2)?		

	Yes	No
Q Has this partnership filed, or is it required to file, **Form 8264,** Application for Registration of a Tax Shelter?		
R Was there a distribution of property or a transfer (for example, by sale or death) of a partnership interest during the tax year? If "Yes," see the instructions concerning an election to adjust the basis of the partnership's assets under section 754		
S At any time during the tax year, did the partnership have an interest in or a signature or other authority over a financial account in a foreign country (such as a bank account, securities account, or other financial account)? (See the instructions for exceptions and filing requirements for form TD F 90-22.1.) If "Yes," enter the name of the foreign country. ▶ ____________		
T Was the partnership the grantor of, or transferor to, a foreign trust which existed during the current tax year, whether or not the partnership or any partner has any beneficial interest in it? If "Yes," you may have to file Forms 3520, 3520-A, or 926		

Caution: *Include **only** trade or business income and expenses on lines 1a through 21 below. See the instructions for more information.*

Income

1a	Gross receipts or sales	1a	
b	Less returns and allowances	1b	1c
2	Cost of goods sold (Schedule A, line 7)		2
3	Gross profit—Subtract line 2 from line 1c		3
4	Ordinary income (loss) from other partnerships and fiduciaries *(attach schedule)*		4
5	Net farm profit (loss) *(attach Schedule F (Form 1040))*		5
6	Net gain (loss) from Form 4797, Part II, line 18		6
7	Other income (loss) (see instructions) *(attach schedule)*		7
8	**Total** income (loss)—Combine lines 3 through 7		8

Deductions (see instructions for limitations)

9a	Salaries and wages (other than to partners)	9a	
b	Less jobs credit	9b	9c
10	Guaranteed payments to partners		10
11	Rent		11
12	Interest		12
13	Taxes		13
14	Bad debts		14
15	Repairs		15
16a	Depreciation (see instructions)	16a	
b	Less depreciation reported on Schedule A and elsewhere on return	16b	16c
17	Depletion **(Do not deduct oil and gas depletion.)**		17
18a	Retirement plans, etc.		18a
b	Employee benefit programs		18b
19	Other deductions *(attach schedule)*		19
20	**Total** deductions—Add lines 9c through 19		20
21	Ordinary income (loss) from trade or business activities—Subtract line 20 from line 8		21

Please Sign Here

Under penalties of perjury, I declare that I have examined this return, including accompanying schedules and statements, and to the best of my knowledge and belief, it is true, correct, and complete. Declaration of preparer (other than general partner) is based on all information of which preparer has any knowledge.

▶ Signature of general partner ▶ Date

Paid Preparer's Use Only

Preparer's signature ▶ Date Check if self-employed ▶ ☐ Preparer's social security no.

Firm's name (or yours if self-employed) and address ▶ E.I. No. ▶ ZIP code ▶

For Paperwork Reduction Act Notice, see page 1 of separate instructions. Form **1065** (1990)

Fig. 19.4. *The 1065 form indicates which income and expense categories partnerships use to report profits and losses.*

Form 1065 (1990) Page 2

Schedule A Cost of Goods Sold

1	Inventory at beginning of year	1	
2	Purchases less cost of items withdrawn for personal use	2	
3	Cost of labor	3	
4a	Additional section 263A costs (see instructions) *(attach schedule)*	4a	
b	Other costs *(attach schedule)*	4b	
5	Total—Add lines 1 through 4b	5	
6	Inventory at end of year	6	
7	Cost of goods sold—Subtract line 6 from line 5. Enter here and on page 1, line 2	7	

8a Check all methods used for valuing closing inventory:

(i) ☐ Cost (ii) ☐ Lower of cost or market as described in Regulations section 1.471-4

(iii) ☐ Writedown of "subnormal" goods as described in Regulations section 1.471-2(c)

(iv) ☐ Other (specify method used and attach explanation) ►

b Check this box if the LIFO inventory method was adopted this tax year for any goods *(if checked, attach Form 970)* ► ☐

c Do the rules of section 263A (with respect to property produced or acquired for resale) apply to the partnership? ☐ Yes ☐ No

d Was there any change in determining quantities, cost, or valuations between opening and closing inventory? ☐ Yes ☐ No
If "Yes," attach explanation.

Schedule L Balance Sheets

Caution: *Read the instructions for **Question N** on page 9 of the instructions before completing Schedules L and M.*

Assets	Beginning of tax year (a)	(b)	End of tax year (c)	(d)
1 Cash				
2a Trade notes and accounts receivable				
b Less allowance for bad debts				
3 Inventories				
4 U.S. government obligations				
5 Tax-exempt securities				
6 Other current assets *(attach schedule)*				
7 Mortgage and real estate loans				
8 Other investments *(attach schedule)*				
9a Buildings and other depreciable assets				
b Less accumulated depreciation				
10a Depletable assets				
b Less accumulated depletion				
11 Land (net of any amortization)				
12a Intangible assets (amortizable only)				
b Less accumulated amortization				
13 Other assets *(attach schedule)*				
14 **Total** assets				
Liabilities and Capital				
15 Accounts payable				
16 Mortgages, notes, bonds payable in less than 1 year				
17 Other current liabilities *(attach schedule)*				
18 All nonrecourse loans				
19 Mortgages, notes, bonds payable in 1 year or more				
20 Other liabilities *(attach schedule)*				
21 Partners' capital accounts				
22 **Total** liabilities and capital				

Schedule M Reconciliation of Partners' Capital Accounts
(Show reconciliation of each partner's capital account on Schedule K-1 (Form 1065), Item K.)

(a) Partners' capital accounts at beginning of year	(b) Capital contributed during year	(c) Income (loss) from lines 1, 2, 3c, and 4 of Schedule K	(d) Income not included in column (c), plus nontaxable income	(e) Losses not included in column (c), plus unallowable deductions	(f) Withdrawals and distributions	(g) Partners' capital accounts at end of year (combine columns (a) through (f))
				( )	( )	

Designation of Tax Matters Partner (See instructions.)

Enter below the general partner designated as the tax matters partner (TMP) for the tax year of this return:

Name of designated TMP ► Identifying number of TMP ►

Address of designated TMP ►

Fig. 19.4. Form 1065, continued.

Form 1065 (1990) Page 3

Schedule K Partners' Shares of Income, Credits, Deductions, Etc.

	(a) Distributive share items		(b) Total amount
Income (Loss)	1 Ordinary income (loss) from trade or business activities (page 1, line 21)	1	
	2 Net income (loss) from rental real estate activities *(attach Form 8825)*	2	
	3a Gross income from other rental activities — 3a		
	b Less expenses *(attach schedule)* — 3b		
	c Net income (loss) from other rental activities	3c	
	4 Portfolio income (loss) (see instructions):		
	a Interest income	4a	
	b Dividend income	4b	
	c Royalty income	4c	
	d Net short-term capital gain (loss) *(attach Schedule D (Form 1065))*	4d	
	e Net long-term capital gain (loss) *(attach Schedule D (Form 1065))*	4e	
	f Other portfolio income (loss) *(attach schedule)*	4f	
	5 Guaranteed payments to partners	5	
	6 Net gain (loss) under section 1231 (other than due to casualty or theft) *(attach Form 4797)*	6	
	7 Other income (loss) *(attach schedule)*	7	
Deductions	8 Charitable contributions (see instructions) *(attach list)*	8	
	9 Section 179 expense deduction *(attach Form 4562)*	9	
	10 Deductions related to portfolio income (see instructions) (itemize)	10	
	11 Other deductions *(attach schedule)*	11	
Investment Interest	12a Interest expense on investment debts	12a	
	b (1) Investment income included on lines 4a through 4f above	12b(1)	
	(2) Investment expenses included on line 10 above	12b(2)	
Credits	13a Credit for income tax withheld	13a	
	b Low-income housing credit (see instructions):		
	(1) From partnerships to which section 42(j)(5) applies for property placed in service before 1990	13b(1)	
	(2) Other than on line 13b(1) for property placed in service before 1990	13b(2)	
	(3) From partnerships to which section 42(j)(5) applies for property placed in service after 1989	13b(3)	
	(4) Other than on line 13b(3) for property placed in service after 1989	13b(4)	
	c Qualified rehabilitation expenditures related to rental real estate activities *(attach Form 3468)*	13c	
	d Credits (other than credits shown on lines 13b and 13c) related to rental real estate activities (see instructions)	13d	
	e Credits related to other rental activities (see instructions)	13e	
	14 Other credits (see instructions)	14	
Self-Employment	15a Net earnings (loss) from self-employment	15a	
	b Gross farming or fishing income	15b	
	c Gross nonfarm income	15c	
Adjustments and Tax Preference Items	16a Accelerated depreciation of real property placed in service before 1987	16a	
	b Accelerated depreciation of leased personal property placed in service before 1987	16b	
	c Depreciation adjustment on property placed in service after 1986	16c	
	d Depletion (other than oil and gas)	16d	
	e (1) Gross income from oil, gas, and geothermal properties	16e(1)	
	(2) Deductions allocable to oil, gas, and geothermal properties	16e(2)	
	f Other adjustments and tax preference items *(attach schedule)*	16f	
Foreign Taxes	17a Type of income ▶		
	b Foreign country or U.S. possession ▶		
	c Total gross income from sources outside the U.S. *(attach schedule)*	17c	
	d Total applicable deductions and losses *(attach schedule)*	17d	
	e Total foreign taxes (check one): ▶ ☐ Paid ☐ Accrued	17e	
	f Reduction in taxes available for credit *(attach schedule)*	17f	
	g Other foreign tax information *(attach schedule)*	17g	
Other	18a Total expenditures to which a section 59(e) election may apply	18a	
	b Type of expenditures ▶		
	19 Other items and amounts required to be reported separately to partners (see instructions) *(attach schedule)*		
Analysis	20a Total distributive income/payment items—Combine lines 1 through 7 above	20a	

20b Analysis by type of partner:	(a) Corporate	(b) Individual i. Active	(b) Individual ii. Passive	(c) Partnership	(d) Exempt organization	(e) Nominee/Other
(1) General partners						
(2) Limited partners						

Fig. 19.4. Form 1065, continued.

Form **1120-A** Department of the Treasury Internal Revenue Service

U.S. Corporation Short-Form Income Tax Return

Instructions are separate. See them to make sure you qualify to file Form 1120-A.

For calendar year 1990 or tax year beginning ...., 1990, ending ...., 19 ....

OMB No. 1545-0890

1990

A Check this box if corp. is a personal service corp. (as defined in Temp. Regs. sec. 1.441-4T—see Instructions) ▶ ☐

Use IRS label. Other-wise, please print or type.

Name

Number, street, and room or suite no. (If a P.O. box, see page 2 of Instructions.)

City or town, state, and ZIP code

B Employer identification number

C Date incorporated

D Total assets (see Specific Instructions)

$

E Check applicable boxes: (1) ☐ Initial return (2) ☐ Change in address

F Check method of accounting: (1) ☐ Cash (2) ☐ Accrual (3) ☐ Other (specify) ▶

Income

1a	Gross receipts or sales ...... b Less returns and allowances ...... c Balance ▶	1c
2	Cost of goods sold (see Instructions)	2
3	Gross profit (line 1c less line 2)	3
4	Domestic corporation dividends subject to the 70% deduction	4
5	Interest	5
6	Gross rents	6
7	Gross royalties	7
8	Capital gain net income (attach Schedule D (Form 1120))	8
9	Net gain or (loss) from Form 4797, Part II, line 18 (attach Form 4797)	9
10	Other income (see Instructions)	10
11	**Total income**—Add lines 3 through 10 ▶	11

Deductions (See Instructions for limitations on deductions.)

12	Compensation of officers (see Instructions)	12
13a	Salaries and wages ...... b Less jobs credit ...... c Balance ▶	13c
14	Repairs	14
15	Bad debts	15
16	Rents	16
17	Taxes	17
18	Interest	18
19	Contributions **(see Instructions for 10% limitation)**	19
20	Depreciation (attach Form 4562) 20	
21	Less depreciation claimed elsewhere on return 21a	21b
22	Other deductions (attach schedule)	22
23	**Total deductions**—Add lines 12 through 22 ▶	23
24	Taxable income before net operating loss deduction and special deductions (line 11 less line 23)	24
25	**Less: a** Net operating loss deduction (see Instructions) 25a	
	b Special deductions (see Instructions) 25b	25c

Tax and Payments

26	**Taxable income**—Line 24 less line 25c	26
27	**Total tax** (Part I, line 7)	27
28	**Payments:**	
a	1989 overpayment credited to 1990 ...... 28a	
b	1990 estimated tax payments 28b	
c	Less 1990 refund applied for on Form 4466 ...... 28c ( ) Bal ▶ 28d	
e	Tax deposited with Form 7004 ...... 28e	
f	Credit from regulated investment companies (attach Form 2439) 28f	
g	Credit for Federal tax on fuels (attach Form 4136). See Instructions 28g	
h	**Total payments**—Add lines 28d through 28g	28h
29	Enter any **penalty** for underpayment of estimated tax—Check ▶ ☐ if Form 2220 is attached	29
30	**Tax due**—If the total of lines 27 and 29 is larger than line 28h, enter amount owed	30
31	**Overpayment**—If line 28h is larger than the total of lines 27 and 29, enter amount overpaid	31
32	Enter amount of line 31 you want: **Credited to 1991 estimated tax** ▶ ...... **Refunded** ▶	32

Please Sign Here

Under penalties of perjury, I declare that I have examined this return, including accompanying schedules and statements, and to the best of my knowledge and belief, it is true, correct, and complete. Declaration of preparer (other than taxpayer) is based on all information of which preparer has any knowledge.

▶ Signature of officer — Date ▶ Title

Paid Preparer's Use Only

Preparer's signature ▶ — Date — Check if self-employed ▶ ☐ — Preparer's social security number

Firm's name (or yours if self-employed) and address ▶ — E.I. No. ▶ — ZIP code ▶

For Paperwork Reduction Act Notice, see page 1 of the Instructions. Form **1120-A** (1990)

***Fig. 19.5.** The 1120-A form indicates which income and expense categories small corporations should use to report profits and losses.*

Form 1120-A (1990) Page 2

Part I Tax Computation

1	Income tax (see Instructions to figure the tax). Check this box if the corp. is a qualified personal service corp. (see Instructions). ▶ ☐	1	
2a	General business credit. Check if from: ☐ Form 3800 ☐ Form 3468 ☐ Form 5884 ☐ Form 6478 ☐ Form 6765 ☐ Form 8586	2a	
b	Credit for prior year minimum tax (attach Form 8801)	2b	
3	**Total credits**—Add lines 2a and 2b	3	
4	Line 1 less line 3	4	
5	Recapture taxes. Check if from: ☐ Form 4255 ☐ Form 8611	5	
6	Alternative minimum tax (attach Form 4626). See Instructions	6	
7	**Total tax**—Add lines 4 through 6. Enter here and on line 27, page 1	7	

Additional Information (See General Instruction F.)

G Refer to the list in the Instructions and state the principal:

(1) Business activity code no. ▶ ....

(2) Business activity ▶ ....

(3) Product or service ▶ ....

H Did any individual, partnership, estate, or trust at the end of the tax year own, directly or indirectly, 50% or more of the corporation's voting stock? (For rules of attribution, see section 267(c).) Yes ☐ No ☐

If "Yes," attach schedule showing name, address, and identifying number.

I Enter the amount of tax-exempt interest received or accrued during the tax year . . . ▶ $

J (1) If an amount for cost of goods sold is entered on line 2, page 1, complete (a) through (c):

(a) Purchases (see Instructions)

(b) Additional sec. 263A costs (see Instructions —attach schedule)

(c) Other costs (attach schedule)

(2) Do the rules of section 263A (with respect to property produced or acquired for resale) apply to the corporation? . . . Yes ☐ No ☐

K At any time during the tax year, did you have an interest in or a signature or other authority over a financial account in a foreign country (such as a bank account, securities account, or other financial account)? (See General Instruction F for filing requirements for form TD F 90-22.1.) . . . Yes ☐ No ☐

If "Yes," enter the name of the foreign country ▶ ....

L Enter amount of cash distributions and the book value of property (other than cash) distributions made in this tax year ▶ $

Part II Balance Sheets

			(a) Beginning of tax year	(b) End of tax year
Assets	1	Cash		
	2a	Trade notes and accounts receivable		
	b	Less allowance for bad debts	( )	( )
	3	Inventories		
	4	U.S. government obligations		
	5	Tax-exempt securities (see Instructions)		
	6	Other current assets (attach schedule)		
	7	Loans to stockholders		
	8	Mortgage and real estate loans		
	9a	Depreciable, depletable, and intangible assets		
	b	Less accumulated depreciation, depletion, and amortization	( )	( )
	10	Land (net of any amortization)		
	11	Other assets (attach schedule)		
	12	Total assets		
Liabilities and Stockholders' Equity	13	Accounts payable		
	14	Other current liabilities (attach schedule)		
	15	Loans from stockholders		
	16	Mortgages, notes, bonds payable		
	17	Other liabilities (attach schedule)		
	18	Capital stock (preferred and common stock)		
	19	Paid-in or capital surplus		
	20	Retained earnings		
	21	Less cost of treasury stock	( )	( )
	22	Total liabilities and stockholders' equity		

Part III Reconciliation of Income per Books With Income per Return (Must be completed by all filers.)

1 Net income per books

2 Federal income tax

3 Excess of capital losses over capital gains

4 Income subject to tax not recorded on books this year (itemize) ....

5 Expenses recorded on books this year not deducted on this return (itemize)

6 Income recorded on books this year not included on this return (itemize) ....

7 Deductions on this return not charged against book income this year (itemize) ....

8 Income (line 24, page 1). Enter the sum of lines 1 through 5 less the sum of lines 6 and 7

☆U.S.GPO: 1990-265-254 E.I.43-1410168

Fig. 19.5. Form 1120-A, continued.

Form **1120S** Department of the Treasury Internal Revenue Service

U.S. Income Tax Return for an S Corporation

For calendar year 1990, or tax year beginning ______, 1990, and ending ______, 19__

▶ See separate instructions.

OMB No. 1545-0130

1990

A Date of election as an S corporation	Use IRS label. Otherwise, please print or type.	Name	C Employer identification number
		Number, street, and room or suite no. (If a P.O. box, see page 7 of the instructions.)	D Date incorporated
B Business code no. (see Specific Instructions)		City or town, state, and ZIP code	E Total assets (see Specific Instructions) $

F Check applicable boxes: (1) ☐ Initial return (2) ☐ Final return (3) ☐ Change in address (4) ☐ Amended return

G Check this box if this is an S corporation subject to the consolidated audit procedures of sections 6241 through 6245 (see instructions before checking this box) ▶ ☐

H Enter number of shareholders in the corporation at end of the tax year ▶

Caution: *Include **only** trade or business income and expenses on lines 1a through 21. See the instructions for more information.*

Income	1a	Gross receipts or sales ___ b Less returns and allowances ___ c Bal ▶		1c
	2	Cost of goods sold (Schedule A, line 7)		2
	3	Gross profit (subtract line 2 from line 1c)		3
	4	Net gain (loss) from Form 4797, Part II, line 18		4
	5	Other income (see instructions) *(attach schedule)*		5
	6	**Total** income (loss)—Combine lines 3 through 5 ▶		6
Deductions (See instructions for limitations.)	7	Compensation of officers		7
	8a	Salaries and wages ___ b Less jobs credit ___ c Bal ▶		8c
	9	Repairs		9
	10	Bad debts		10
	11	Rents		11
	12	Taxes		12
	13	Interest		13
	14a	Depreciation (see instructions)	14a	
	b	Depreciation reported on Schedule A and elsewhere on return	14b	
	c	Subtract line 14b from line 14a		14c
	15	Depletion (**Do not deduct oil and gas depletion.** See instructions.)		15
	16	Advertising		16
	17	Pension, profit-sharing, etc., plans		17
	18	Employee benefit programs		18
	19	Other deductions *(attach schedule)*		19
	20	**Total** deductions—Add lines 7 through 19 ▶		20
	21	Ordinary income (loss) from trade or business activities—Subtract line 20 from line 6		21
Tax and Payments	22	**Tax:**		
	a	Excess net passive income tax *(attach schedule)*	22a	
	b	Tax from Schedule D (Form 1120S)	22b	
	c	Add lines 22a and 22b (see instructions for additional taxes)		22c
	23	**Payments:**		
	a	1990 estimated tax payments	23a	
	b	Tax deposited with Form 7004	23b	
	c	Credit for Federal tax on fuels *(attach Form 4136)*	23c	
	d	Add lines 23a through 23c		23d
	24	Enter any **penalty** for underpayment of estimated tax—Check ▶ ☐ if Form 2220 is attached		24
	25	**Tax due**—If the total of lines 22c and 24 is larger than line 23d, enter amount owed. See instructions for depositary method of payment ▶		25
	26	**Overpayment**—If line 23d is larger than the total of lines 22c and 24, enter amount overpaid ▶		26
	27	Enter amount of line 26 you want: **Credited to 1991 estimated tax** ▶ **Refunded** ▶		27

Please Sign Here

Under penalties of perjury, I declare that I have examined this return, including accompanying schedules and statements, and to the best of my knowledge and belief, it is true, correct, and complete. Declaration of preparer (other than taxpayer) is based on all information of which preparer has any knowledge.

▶ Signature of officer Date ▶ Title

Paid Preparer's Use Only

Preparer's signature ▶	Date	Check if self-employed ▶ ☐	Preparer's social security number
Firm's name (or yours if self-employed) and address ▶		E.I. No. ▶	
		ZIP code ▶	

For Paperwork Reduction Act Notice, see page 1 of separate instructions. Form **1120S** (1990)

Fig. 19.6. *The 1120S form indicates which income and expense categories S corporations should use to report profits and losses.*

Form 1120S (1990) Page 2

Schedule A Cost of Goods Sold (See instructions.)

1	Inventory at beginning of year	1	
2	Purchases	2	
3	Cost of labor	3	
4a	Additional section 263A costs (see instructions) *(attach schedule)*	4a	
b	Other costs *(attach schedule)*	4b	
5	Total—Add lines 1 through 4b	5	
6	Inventory at end of year	6	
7	Cost of goods sold—Subtract line 6 from line 5. Enter here and on line 2, page 1	7	

8a Check all methods used for valuing closing inventory:
(i) ☐ Cost
(ii) ☐ Lower of cost or market as described in Regulations section 1.471-4
(iii) ☐ Writedown of "subnormal" goods as described in Regulations section 1.471-2(c)
(iv) ☐ Other (specify method used and attach explanation) ▶

b Check this box if the LIFO inventory method was adopted this tax year for any goods *(if checked, attach Form 970)* ▶☐

c If the LIFO inventory method was used for this tax year, enter percentage (or amounts) of closing inventory computed under LIFO . . . 8c

d Do the rules of section 263A (with respect to property produced or acquired for resale) apply to the corporation? ☐ Yes ☐ No

e Was there any change in determining quantities, cost, or valuations between opening and closing inventory? ☐ Yes ☐ No
If "Yes," attach explanation.

Additional Information Required (continued from page 1)

		Yes	No
I	Did you at the end of the tax year own, directly or indirectly, 50% or more of the voting stock of a domestic corporation? For rules of attribution, see section 267(c). If "Yes," attach a schedule showing: **(1)** name, address, and employer identification number; and **(2)** percentage owned.		
J	Refer to the list in the instructions and state your principal: **(1)** Business activity ▶ .... **(2)** Product or service ▶		
K	Were you a member of a controlled group subject to the provisions of section 1561?		
L	At any time during the tax year, did you have an interest in or a signature or other authority over a financial account in a foreign country (such as a bank account, securities account, or other financial account)? (See instructions for exceptions and filing requirements for form TD F 90-22.1.) If "Yes," enter the name of the foreign country ▶		
M	Were you the grantor of, or transferor to, a foreign trust that existed during the current tax year, whether or not you have any beneficial interest in it? If "Yes," you may have to file Forms 3520, 3520-A, or 926		
N	During this tax year did you maintain any part of your accounting/tax records on a computerized system?		
O	Check method of accounting: **(1)** ☐ Cash **(2)** ☐ Accrual **(3)** ☐ Other (specify) ▶		
P	Check this box if the S corporation has filed or is required to file **Form 8264,** Application for Registration of a Tax Shelter ▶☐		
Q	Check this box if the corporation issued publicly offered debt instruments with original issue discount ▶☐ If so, the corporation may have to file **Form 8281,** Information Return for Publicly Offered Original Issue Discount Instruments.		
R	If the corporation: **(1)** filed its election to be an S corporation after 1986, **(2)** was a C corporation before it elected to be an S corporation **or** the corporation acquired an asset with a basis determined by reference to its basis (or the basis of any other property) in the hands of a C corporation, and **(3)** has net unrealized built-in gain (defined in section 1374(d)(1)) in excess of the net recognized built-in gain from prior years, enter the net unrealized built-in gain reduced by net recognized built-in gain from prior years (see instructions) ▶ $		
S	Check this box if the corporation had subchapter C earnings and profits at the close of the tax year (see instructions) ▶☐		

Designation of Tax Matters Person (See instructions.)

Enter below the shareholder designated as the tax matters person (TMP) for the tax year of this return:

Name of designated TMP ▶ Identifying number of TMP ▶

Address of designated TMP ▶

Fig. 19.6. *Form 1120S, continued.*

Form 1120S (1990) Page 3

Schedule K Shareholders' Shares of Income, Credits, Deductions, Etc.

		(a) Pro rata share items		(b) Total amount
Income (Loss)	1	Ordinary income (loss) from trade or business activities (page 1, line 21)	1	
	2	Net income (loss) from rental real estate activities *(attach Form 8825)*	2	
	3a	Gross income from other rental activities . . . 3a		
	b	Less expenses *(attach schedule)* . . . 3b		
	c	Net income (loss) from other rental activities	3c	
	4	Portfolio income (loss):		
	a	Interest income	4a	
	b	Dividend income	4b	
	c	Royalty income	4c	
	d	Net short-term capital gain (loss) *(attach Schedule D (Form 1120S))*	4d	
	e	Net long-term capital gain (loss) *(attach Schedule D (Form 1120S))*	4e	
	f	Other portfolio income (loss) *(attach schedule)*	4f	
	5	Net gain (loss) under section 1231 (other than due to casualty or theft) *(attach Form 4797)*	5	
	6	Other income (loss) *(attach schedule)*	6	
Deductions	7	Charitable contributions (see instructions) *(attach list)*	7	
	8	Section 179 expense deduction *(attach Form 4562)*	8	
	9	Deductions related to portfolio income (loss) (see instructions) (itemize)	9	
	10	Other deductions *(attach schedule)*	10	
Investment Interest	11a	Interest expense on investment debts	11a	
	b	(1) Investment income included on lines 4a through 4f above	11b(1)	
		(2) Investment expenses included on line 9 above	11b(2)	
Credits	12a	Credit for alcohol used as a fuel *(attach Form 6478)*	12a	
	b	Low-income housing credit (see instructions):		
		(1) From partnerships to which section 42(j)(5) applies for property placed in service before 1990	12b(1)	
		(2) Other than on line 12b(1) for property placed in service before 1990	12b(2)	
		(3) From partnerships to which section 42(j)(5) applies for property placed in service after 1989	12b(3)	
		(4) Other than on line 12b(3) for property placed in service after 1989	12b(4)	
	c	Qualified rehabilitation expenditures related to rental real estate activities *(attach Form 3468)*	12c	
	d	Credits (other than credits shown on lines 12b and 12c) related to rental real estate activities (see instructions)	12d	
	e	Credits related to other rental activities (see instructions)	12e	
	13	Other credits (see instructions)	13	
Adjustments and Tax Preference Items	14a	Accelerated depreciation of real property placed in service before 1987	14a	
	b	Accelerated depreciation of leased personal property placed in service before 1987	14b	
	c	Depreciation adjustment on property placed in service after 1986	14c	
	d	Depletion (other than oil and gas)	14d	
	e	(1) Gross income from oil, gas, or geothermal properties	14e(1)	
		(2) Deductions allocable to oil, gas, or geothermal properties	14e(2)	
	f	Other adjustments and tax preference items *(attach schedule)*	14f	
Foreign Taxes	15a	Type of income ▶		
	b	Name of foreign country or U.S. possession ▶		
	c	Total gross income from sources outside the U.S. *(attach schedule)*	15c	
	d	Total applicable deductions and losses *(attach schedule)*	15d	
	e	Total foreign taxes (check one): ▶ ☐ Paid ☐ Accrued	15e	
	f	Reduction in taxes available for credit *(attach schedule)*	15f	
	g	Other foreign tax information *(attach schedule)*	15g	
Other Items	16a	Total expenditures to which a section 59(e) election may apply	16a	
	b	Type of expenditures ▶		
	17	Total property distributions (including cash) other than dividends reported on line 19 below	17	
	18	Other items and amounts required to be reported separately to shareholders (see instructions) *(attach schedule)*		
	19	Total dividend distributions paid from accumulated earnings and profits	19	
	20	Income (loss) (Required only if Schedule M-1 must be completed.)—Combine lines 1 through 6 in column (b). From the result subtract the sum of lines 7 through 11a, 15e, and 16a	20	

***Fig. 19.6.** Form 1120S, continued.*

Form 1120S (1990) Page 4

Schedule L Balance Sheets

Assets	Beginning of tax year (a)	(b)	End of tax year (c)	(d)
1 Cash				
2a Trade notes and accounts receivable				
b Less allowance for bad debts				
3 Inventories				
4 U.S. government obligations				
5 Tax-exempt securities				
6 Other current assets *(attach schedule)*				
7 Loans to shareholders				
8 Mortgage and real estate loans				
9 Other investments *(attach schedule)*				
10a Buildings and other depreciable assets				
b Less accumulated depreciation				
11a Depletable assets				
b Less accumulated depletion				
12 Land (net of any amortization)				
13a Intangible assets (amortizable only)				
b Less accumulated amortization				
14 Other assets *(attach schedule)*				
15 Total assets				
Liabilities and Shareholders' Equity				
16 Accounts payable				
17 Mortgages, notes, bonds payable in less than 1 year				
18 Other current liabilities *(attach schedule)*				
19 Loans from shareholders				
20 Mortgages, notes, bonds payable in 1 year or more				
21 Other liabilities *(attach schedule)*				
22 Capital stock				
23 Paid-in or capital surplus				
24 Retained earnings				
25 Less cost of treasury stock		( )		( )
26 Total liabilities and shareholders' equity				

Schedule M-1 Reconciliation of Income per Books With Income per Return (You are not required to complete this schedule if the total assets on line 15, column (d), of Schedule L are less than $25,000.)

1 Net income per books		5 Income recorded on books this year not included on Schedule K, lines 1 through 6 (itemize): a Tax-exempt interest $	
2 Income included on Schedule K, lines 1 through 6, not recorded on books this year (itemize):			
3 Expenses recorded on books this year not included on Schedule K, lines 1 through 11a, 15e, and 16a (itemize): a Depreciation $ b Travel and entertainment $		6 Deductions included on Schedule K, lines 1 through 11a, 15e, and 16a, not charged against book income this year (itemize): a Depreciation $	
		7 Total of lines 5 and 6	
4 Total of lines 1 through 3		8 Income (loss) (Schedule K, line 20)—Line 4 less line 7	

Schedule M-2 Analysis of Accumulated Adjustments Account, Other Adjustments Account, and Shareholders' Undistributed Taxable Income Previously Taxed (See instructions.)

	(a) Accumulated adjustments account	(b) Other adjustments account	(c) Shareholders' undistributed taxable income previously taxed
1 Balance at beginning of tax year			
2 Ordinary income from page 1, line 21			
3 Other additions			
4 Loss from page 1, line 21	( )		
5 Other reductions	( )	( )	
6 Combine lines 1 through 5			
7 Distributions other than dividend distributions			
8 Balance at end of tax year—subtract line 7 from line 6			

☆U.S. GOVERNMENT PRINTING OFFICE: 1990—265-280

Fig. 19.6. Form 1120S, continued.

Form **1120** Department of the Treasury Internal Revenue Service

U.S. Corporation Income Tax Return

For calendar year 1990 or tax year beginning ______________, 1990, ending ______________, 19 ____

► Instructions are separate. See page 1 for Paperwork Reduction Act Notice.

OMB No. 1545-0123 **1990**

Check if a—
A Consolidated return ☐
B Personal holding co. ☐
C Personal service corp.(as defined in Temp. Regs. sec. 1.441-4T—see Instructions) ☐

Use IRS label. Otherwise, please print or type.
Name
Number, street, and room or suite no. (If a P.O. box, see page 2 of Instructions.)
City or town, state, and ZIP code

D Employer identification number
E Date incorporated
F Total assets (see Specific Instructions) $

G Check applicable boxes: (1) ☐ Initial return (2) ☐ Final return (3) ☐ Change in address

Income

1a	Gross receipts or sales ____ b Less returns and allowances ____ c Bal ►	1c
2	Cost of goods sold (Schedule A, line 7)	2
3	Gross profit (line 1c less line 2)	3
4	Dividends (Schedule C, line 19)	4
5	Interest	5
6	Gross rents	6
7	Gross royalties	7
8	Capital gain net income (attach Schedule D (Form 1120))	8
9	Net gain or (loss) from Form 4797, Part II, line 18 (attach Form 4797)	9
10	Other income (see Instructions—attach schedule)	10
11	**Total income**—Add lines 3 through 10 ►	11

Deductions (See instructions for limitations on deductions.)

12	Compensation of officers (Schedule E, line 4)	12
13a	Salaries and wages ____ b Less jobs credit ____ c Balance ►	13c
14	Repairs	14
15	Bad debts	15
16	Rents	16
17	Taxes	17
18	Interest	18
19	Contributions (**see Instructions for 10% limitation**)	19
20	Depreciation (attach Form 4562) — 20	
21	Less depreciation claimed on Schedule A and elsewhere on return — 21a	21b
22	Depletion	22
23	Advertising	23
24	Pension, profit-sharing, etc., plans	24
25	Employee benefit programs	25
26	Other deductions (attach schedule)	26
27	**Total deductions**—Add lines 12 through 26 ►	27
28	Taxable income before net operating loss deduction and special deductions (line 11 less line 27)	28
29	**Less: a** Net operating loss deduction (see Instructions) — 29a	
	b Special deductions (Schedule C, line 20) — 29b	29c

Tax and Payments

30	**Taxable income**—Line 28 less line 29c	30
31	**Total tax** (Schedule J, line 10)	31
32	**Payments: a** 1989 overpayment credited to 1990 — 32a	
b	1990 estimated tax payments — 32b	
c	Less 1990 refund applied for on Form 4466 — 32c ( ) d Bal ► 32d	
e	Tax deposited with Form 7004 — 32e	
f	Credit from regulated investment companies (attach Form 2439) — 32f	
g	Credit for Federal tax on fuels (attach Form 4136). See Instructions — 32g	32h
33	Enter any **penalty** for underpayment of estimated tax—Check ► ☐ if Form 2220 is attached	33
34	**Tax due**—If the total of lines 31 and 33 is larger than line 32h, enter amount owed	34
35	**Overpayment**—If line 32h is larger than the total of lines 31 and 33, enter amount overpaid	35
36	Enter amount of line 35 you want: **Credited to 1991 estimated tax** ► **Refunded** ►	36

Please Sign Here

Under penalties of perjury, I declare that I have examined this return, including accompanying schedules and statements, and to the best of my knowledge and belief, it is true, correct, and complete. Declaration of preparer (other than taxpayer) is based on all information of which preparer has any knowledge.

► Signature of officer — Date — ► Title

Paid Preparer's Use Only

Preparer's signature ► — Date — Check if self-employed ☐ — Preparer's social security number

Firm's name (or yours if self-employed) and address ► — E.I. No. ► — ZIP code ►

Fig. 19.7. The 1120 form indicates which income and expense categories some corporations should use to report profits and losses.

Form 1120 (1990) Page 2

Schedule A Cost of Goods Sold (See Instructions for line 2, page 1.)

1 Inventory at beginning of year	1	
2 Purchases	2	
3 Cost of labor	3	
4a Additional section 263A costs (see Instructions—attach schedule)	4a	
b Other costs (attach schedule)	4b	
5 **Total**—Add lines 1 through 4b	5	
6 Inventory at end of year	6	
7 **Cost of goods sold**—Line 5 less line 6. Enter here and on line 2, page 1	7	

8a Check all methods used for valuing closing inventory:
(i) ☐ Cost (ii) ☐ Lower of cost or market as described in Regulations section 1.471-4 (see Instructions)
(iii) ☐ Writedown of "subnormal" goods as described in Regulations section 1.471-2(c) (see Instructions)
(iv) ☐ Other (Specify method used and attach explanation.) ▶
b Check if the LIFO inventory method was adopted this tax year for any goods (if checked, attach Form 970) ☐
c If the LIFO inventory method was used for this tax year, enter percentage (or amounts) of closing inventory computed under LIFO 8c
d Do the rules of section 263A (with respect to property produced or acquired for resale) apply to the corporation? ☐ Yes ☐ No
e Was there any change in determining quantities, cost, or valuations between opening and closing inventory? If "Yes," attach explanation ☐ Yes ☐ No

Schedule C Dividends and Special Deductions (See Instructions.)	(a) Dividends received	(b) %	(c) Special deductions: (a) × (b)
1 Dividends from less-than-20%-owned domestic corporations that are subject to the 70% deduction (other than debt-financed stock)		70	
2 Dividends from 20%-or-more-owned domestic corporations that are subject to the 80% deduction (other than debt-financed stock)		80	
3 Dividends on debt-financed stock of domestic and foreign corporations (section 246A)		see Instructions	
4 Dividends on certain preferred stock of less-than-20%-owned public utilities		41.176	
5 Dividends on certain preferred stock of 20%-or-more-owned public utilities		47.059	
6 Dividends from less-than-20%-owned foreign corporations and certain FSCs that are subject to the 70% deduction		70	
7 Dividends from 20%-or-more-owned foreign corporations and certain FSCs that are subject to the 80% deduction		80	
8 Dividends from wholly owned foreign subsidiaries subject to the 100% deduction (section 245(b))		100	
9 **Total**—Add lines 1 through 8. See Instructions for limitation			
10 Dividends from domestic corporations received by a small business investment company operating under the Small Business Investment Act of 1958		100	
11 Dividends from certain FSCs that are subject to the 100% deduction (section 245(c)(1))		100	
12 Dividends from affiliated group members subject to the 100% deduction (section 243(a)(3))		100	
13 Other dividends from foreign corporations not included on lines 3, 6, 7, 8, or 11			
14 Income from controlled foreign corporations under subpart F (attach Forms 5471)			
15 Foreign dividend gross-up (section 78)			
16 IC-DISC and former DISC dividends not included on lines 1, 2, or 3 (section 246(d))			
17 Other dividends			
18 Deduction for dividends paid on certain preferred stock of public utilities (see Instructions)			
19 **Total dividends**—Add lines 1 through 17. Enter here and on line 4, page 1. ▶			
20 **Total deductions**—Add lines 9, 10, 11, 12, and 18. Enter here and on line 29b, page 1 ▶			

Schedule E Compensation of Officers (See Instructions for line 12, page 1.)
Complete Schedule E only if total receipts (line 1a, plus lines 4 through 10, of page 1, Form 1120) are $500,000 or more.

(a) Name of officer	(b) Social security number	(c) Percent of time devoted to business	Percent of corporation stock owned (d) Common	(e) Preferred	(f) Amount of compensation
1		%	%	%	
		%	%	%	
		%	%	%	
		%	%	%	
		%	%	%	

2 Total compensation of officers	
3 **Less:** Compensation of officers claimed on Schedule A and elsewhere on return	( )
4 Compensation of officers deducted on line 12, page 1	

Fig. 19.7. Form 1120, continued.

Form 1120 (1990) Page 3

Schedule J **Tax Computation**

1 Check if you are a member of a controlled group (see sections 1561 and 1563) . . . . . . ▶ ☐
2 If the box on line 1 is checked:
a Enter your share of the $50,000 and $25,000 taxable income bracket amounts (in that order):
(i) $ (ii) $
b Enter your share of the additional 5% tax (not to exceed $11,750) ▶ $
3 Income tax (see Instructions to figure the tax). Check this box if the corporation is a qualified personal service corporation (see Instructions on page 12). ▶ ☐ 3
4a Foreign tax credit (attach Form 1118) 4a
b Possessions tax credit (attach Form 5735) 4b
c Orphan drug credit (attach Form 6765) 4c
d Credit for fuel produced from a nonconventional source (see Instructions) 4d
e General business credit. Enter here and check which forms are attached:
☐ Form 3800 ☐ Form 3468 ☐ Form 5884
☐ Form 6478 ☐ Form 6765 ☐ Form 8586 . . . . . 4e
f Credit for prior year minimum tax (attach Form 8801) 4f
5 **Total**—Add lines 4a through 4f 5
6 Line 3 less line 5 6
7 Personal holding company tax (attach Schedule PH (Form 1120)) 7
8 Recapture taxes. Check if from: ☐ Form 4255 ☐ Form 8611 8
9a Alternative minimum tax (attach Form 4626). See Instructions 9a
b Environmental tax (attach Form 4626) 9b
10 **Total tax**—Add lines 6 through 9b. Enter here and on line 31, page 1 10

Additional Information (See General Instruction F.) Yes No

H Refer to the list in the Instructions and state the principal:
(1) Business activity code no. ▶
(2) Business activity ▶
(3) Product or service ▶

I (1) Did the corporation at the end of the tax year own, directly or indirectly, 50% or more of the voting stock of a domestic corporation? (For rules of attribution, see section 267(c).) . .
If "Yes," attach a schedule showing: (a) name, address, and identifying number; (b) percentage owned; and (c) taxable income or (loss) before NOL and special deductions of such corporation for the tax year ending with or within your tax year.
(2) Did any individual, partnership, corporation, estate, or trust at the end of the tax year own, directly or indirectly, 50% or more of the corporation's voting stock? (For rules of attribution, see section 267(c).) If "Yes," complete (a) through (c) . . . .
(a) Attach a schedule showing name, address, and identifying number.
(b) Enter percentage owned ▶
(c) Was the owner of such voting stock a foreign person? (See Instructions.) **Note:** *If "Yes," the corporation may have to file Form 5472* . . . . .
If "Yes," enter owner's country ▶

J Was the corporation a U.S. shareholder of any controlled foreign corporation? (See sections 951 and 957.) . . . . .
If "Yes," attach Form 5471 for each such corporation.

Yes No

K At any time during the tax year, did the corporation have an interest in or a signature or other authority over a financial account in a foreign country (such as a bank account, securities account, or other financial account)? . . . . .
(See General Instruction F and filing requirements for form TD F 90-22.1.)
If "Yes," enter name of foreign country ▶

L Was the corporation the grantor of, or transferor to, a foreign trust that existed during the current tax year, whether or not the corporation has any beneficial interest in it? . . . . .
If "Yes," the corporation may have to file Forms 3520, 3520-A, or 926.

M During this tax year, did the corporation pay dividends (other than stock dividends and distributions in exchange for stock) in excess of the corporation's current and accumulated earnings and profits? (See sections 301 and 316.) . . . . .
If "Yes," file Form 5452. If this is a consolidated return, answer here for parent corporation and on **Form 851**, Affiliations Schedule, for each subsidiary.

N During this tax year, did the corporation maintain any part of its accounting/tax records on a computerized system? . . . . .

O Check method of accounting:
(1) ☐ Cash
(2) ☐ Accrual
(3) ☐ Other (specify) ▶

P Check this box if the corporation issued publicly offered debt instruments with original issue discount . . . . . ☐
If so, the corporation may have to file Form 8281.

Q Enter the amount of tax-exempt interest received or accrued during the tax year ▶ $

R Enter the number of shareholders at the end of the tax year if there were 35 or fewer shareholders ▶

Fig. 19.7. Form 1120, continued.

Form 1120 (1990) Page 4

Schedule L Balance Sheets

Assets	Beginning of tax year (a)	(b)	End of tax year (c)	(d)
1 Cash				
2a Trade notes and accounts receivable				
b Less allowance for bad debts	( )		( )	
3 Inventories				
4 U.S. government obligations				
5 Tax-exempt securities (see Instructions)				
6 Other current assets (attach schedule)				
7 Loans to stockholders				
8 Mortgage and real estate loans				
9 Other investments (attach schedule)				
10a Buildings and other depreciable assets				
b Less accumulated depreciation	( )		( )	
11a Depletable assets				
b Less accumulated depletion	( )		( )	
12 Land (net of any amortization)				
13a Intangible assets (amortizable only)				
b Less accumulated amortization	( )		( )	
14 Other assets (attach schedule)				
15 Total assets				
Liabilities and Stockholders' Equity				
16 Accounts payable				
17 Mortgages, notes, bonds payable in less than 1 year				
18 Other current liabilities (attach schedule)				
19 Loans from stockholders				
20 Mortgages, notes, bonds payable in 1 year or more				
21 Other liabilities (attach schedule)				
22 Capital stock: a Preferred stock				
b Common stock				
23 Paid-in or capital surplus				
24 Retained earnings—Appropriated (attach schedule)				
25 Retained earnings—Unappropriated				
26 Less cost of treasury stock		( )		( )
27 Total liabilities and stockholders' equity				

Schedule M-1 Reconciliation of Income per Books With Income per Return (This schedule does not have to be completed if the total assets on line 15, column (d), of Schedule L are less than $25,000.)

1 Net income per books		7 Income recorded on books this year not included on this return (itemize):	
2 Federal income tax		a Tax-exempt interest $	
3 Excess of capital losses over capital gains			
4 Income subject to tax not recorded on books this year (itemize):		8 Deductions on this return not charged against book income this year (itemize):	
5 Expenses recorded on books this year not deducted on this return (itemize):		a Depreciation $	
a Depreciation $		b Contributions carryover $	
b Contributions carryover $			
c Travel and entertainment $			
		9 Total of lines 7 and 8	
6 Total of lines 1 through 5		10 Income (line 28, page 1)—line 6 less line 9	

Schedule M-2 Analysis of Unappropriated Retained Earnings per Books (line 25, Schedule L) (This schedule does not have to be completed if the total assets on line 15, column (d), of Schedule L are less than $25,000.)

1 Balance at beginning of year		5 Distributions: a Cash	
2 Net income per books		b Stock	
3 Other increases (itemize):		c Property	
		6 Other decreases (itemize):	
		7 Total of lines 5 and 6	
4 Total of lines 1, 2, and 3		8 Balance at end of year (line 4 less line 7)	

*U.S. Government Printing Office: 1990 — 265-253

Fig. 19.7. Form 1120, continued.

Part V

Protecting Yourself from Embezzlement, Forgery, and Other Disasters

Includes

20

Preventing Forgery and Embezzlement

By this point, you have installed the Quicken software on the computer, set up the accounts, fine-tuned the system settings, and defined all the categories you want to use. Now you need to protect the system and your money.

First, you learn how Quicken can help you protect you from forgery and embezzlement. This issue is important, particularly for a small business. The U.S. Department of Commerce estimates that employee theft costs American business about $40 billion annually.

Second, you learn about internal controls—ways in which you can minimize intentional and unintentional human errors within the Quicken system. Internal controls protect the accuracy and the reliability of the Quicken data files and the cash you have in bank accounts.

Defining Forgery and Embezzlement

Forgery is fraudulently marking or altering any writing that changes the legal liability of another person. When someone signs your name to your check or endorses a check made payable to you, this person has committed forgery. Forgery also occurs when somebody alters a check that you wrote.

Embezzlement is fraudulently appropriating property or money owned by someone else. In a home or small business accounting system, an embezzler usually is an insider—employee, partner, friend, or family member—who intercepts incoming deposits or makes unauthorized withdrawals from a bank account. The steps you can take to prevent either crime are not difficult. Providing the computer system with protection is not an accusation of guilt. Making embezzlement and forgery more difficult or almost impossible is a wise investment of money and time.

Preventing Forgery

Typically, a professional forger finds out when the bank mails monthly statements. The forger then intercepts one of your monthly bank statements, which provides samples of your signature, information about your average balances, and when you make deposits and withdrawals. The forger is now ready to take action by ordering preprinted checks from a printer—just as you do—or by stealing blank check forms from you. If the forger follows the latter course, the forms usually are taken from the back of the checkbook or from an unused set of blank checks so that you do not immediately notice the disappearance. Unfortunately, you may not discover the forged checks until they clear the account or until you reconcile the bank account.

You need to know a few things about forgery. First, the bank is responsible for paying only on checks with genuine signatures. To judge the authenticity of the signature on the checks, the bank is supposed to use the signature card that you signed when you opened the account. The bank, therefore, cannot deduct from your account amounts stemming from forged checks. If the bank initially deducts money based on forged checks, these amounts must be added back to your account later. In certain cases, however, you are responsible for the money involved with forged checks.

You can make mistakes that cause you to bear the cost of a forgery. One mistake is to be careless and sloppy, or negligent, in managing a checking account. Your business may use a check-signing machine easily available to anyone within the company, including a check forger. Another example of negligence is to routinely leave the checkbook on the dashboard of your red convertible. The courts are responsible for determining whether such behavior represents negligence; if the court determines that your conduct falls short of the care a reasonable person may exercise, the bank may not have to pay for the forger's unauthorized transactions.

Another mistake that may leave you liable for forgery losses is failure to review monthly statements and canceled checks. Always examine these items closely for any forged signature, and report the forgeries promptly. If you do not—generally, you have one year—the bank is not obligated to add back to your account the amount stolen by the check forger.

If you do not examine the monthly statements and canceled checks within 14 days of receiving them, you lose the right to force the bank to add back to the account additional amounts stolen by the same check forger. If a forger writes ten checks for $50 on your account, and you look at the bank statement a month later, the bank must add back only the first forged $50 check but is not liable for the nine other checks that followed.

Never allow someone to occasionally sign checks for you. If you are out of town, do not allow an employee or neighbor to use your checkbook to pay urgent bills. If this person signs your check and you do not report the signature as a forgery to the bank within 14 days, and if this person later forges checks without your knowledge, the bank may not be responsible for payment on these forgeries.

At the least, check forgery wastes your time and the bank's time. If you are careless, forgery can cost you all the money you have. To avoid this catastrophe, you may want to take some of the following useful precautions:

1. Treat blank checks as you treat cash. Do not leave check forms in places easily accessible to others. Better yet, lock up checks or at least put away the forms in a desk drawer or cabinet to make them more difficult to find. (This rule also applies to the box of Quicken computer checks.)

2. Use Quicken to keep the check register up-to-date. This precaution enables you to notify the bank immediately to stop payment on checks not yet recorded in the check register but missing from the pad or box of blank checks.

3. Watch for the monthly bank statement and canceled checks. If these items do not arrive at the usual time of the month, call the bank to find out whether the statements are late that month. You want to make sure that the statement was not intercepted by a forger who then can use the canceled checks to practice your signature.

4. Review all canceled checks you receive with the bank statement and verify that you, or one of the other signers on the checking account, wrote the checks. Also verify that none of the canceled checks were altered.

5. Reconcile the balance shown in the check register with the balance shown on the monthly bank statement as soon as possible. The reconciling process does not take long. For more information on reconciling an account, see Chapter 8.

6. Be sure to write *VOID* in large bold letters across the face of checks you do not use. If you have old blank check forms you no longer need—if your name or address has changed or if you have closed the account—destroy these old check forms.

7. Fill in all the blanks, particularly the payee and amount fields on a check form, to prevent a forger from altering a check you wrote and signed. If you have the alignment set correctly on the printer, Quicken completely fills out each of the required check form fields. For checks you write manually, however, do not leave space on the payee line for a forger to include a second payee, and do not leave space on one of the amount fields so that $5.00 can be changed to $500.00 (see figs. 20.1 and 20.2). The first figure is a perfect example of a check so poorly filled out that it almost invites forgery. The second figure shows how a forger may modify a check written like the one shown in figure 20.1.

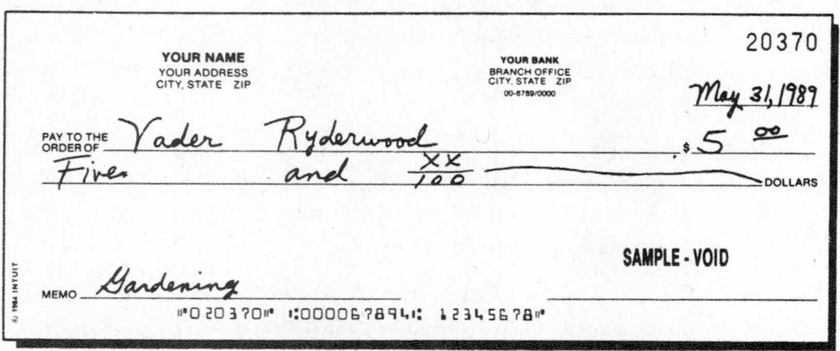

Fig. 20.1. A good example of a bad way to write a check.

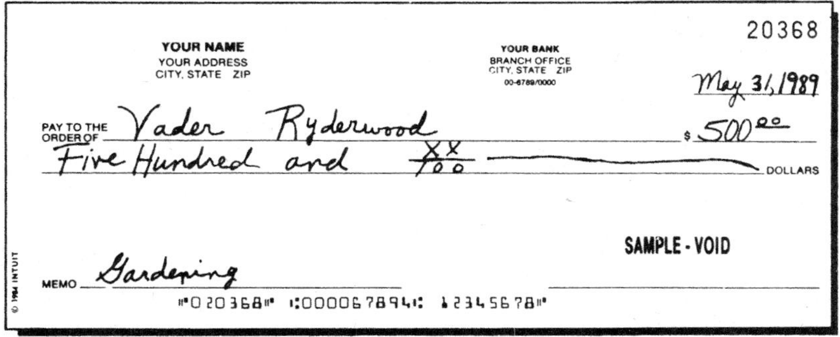

Fig. 20.2. How your check can be altered by a forger.

Preventing Embezzlement

Embezzlement is more of an issue for business users of Quicken than for home users. Accordingly, the following sections focus on the business aspects of the embezzlement problem.

Generally, embezzlement is a risk whenever you have others working with business assets, such as cash, inventory, or equipment, or with a business's financial records. Because embezzlement takes so many different forms, the process cannot be generalized. Take precautions against embezzlement even if you have no suspicions that this crime may be a risk to you. When you fail to erect barriers to embezzlement, you become an appealing target. Often, the embezzler is the least likely person you may suspect of this crime.

Keeping Complete Financial Records

In many small-business embezzlement cases, messy or incomplete financial records are involved. If the accounting records are a mess, locating certain transactions usually is difficult or impossible—especially fraudulent transactions.

By using Quicken, you keep complete financial records for most parts of a business. If other areas exist in which you are not using Quicken, however, such as in billing and collecting from customers, be especially diligent and careful.

Segregating Duties

Try to separate physical custody of an asset, such as cash or accounts receivable, from the records for the asset. If one employee uses Quicken to keep the company checking account records, a second employee should sign all the checks and collect all the cash. If one employee keeps track of the amounts customers owe and how much they pay on bills, someone else should count and deposit the incoming cash. In these examples, the person who keeps the records indirectly double-checks the work of the person with physical custody of the asset, and the person with physical custody of the asset indirectly checks the work of the person keeping the records.

Checking Employee Backgrounds

Before hiring any employee, check both background and references carefully. Be sure that you check carefully the background of persons on which you rely for important parts of the business, such as counting cash and accounting. Embezzlement tends to be a habit with some people. Often, you find that an embezzler has stolen from a previous employer.

Requiring Vacations

Even if you follow the three precautions described previously, a clever embezzler still can steal from you, but embezzling becomes difficult. Usually these schemes require a lot of ongoing effort and maintenance on the part of the embezzler. You can, however, take steps to uncover these efforts. Require your employees to take vacations. By following this precaution, you can take over or reassign a person's duties, and the embezzlement scheme crumbles or becomes obvious to others if an embezzler skims a portion of the incoming cash deposits. If an embezzler writes checks for more than the actual amount and pockets the difference, you may notice that cash expenses decrease during the embezzler's vacation.

Using Internal Controls

Internal controls are rules and procedures that protect business assets—including cash—and the accuracy and reliability of financial records. You can use internal controls to prevent forgery and embezzlement and to make recovering from forgery and embezzlement easier, if you are unlucky enough to become a victim. Within Quicken, you can use the following internal controls to further protect the system:

- Leave a paper audit trail
- Retain your documents
- Use the Quicken password feature

Creating Paper Trails

One of the most important internal control procedures you can use is to create paper evidence that accurately describes and documents each transaction. The capability of producing this paper trail is one of Quicken's greatest strengths—a strength you should take advantage of as much as possible.

Obviously, you record every check you write and every deposit you make in the check register. You also can record individual cash withdrawals from automated teller machines, bank service fees, and monthly interest expenses. Entering these transactions provides you with solid descriptions of each transaction that affects cash flow.

The extensive reports that Quicken offers provide you with another important piece of the paper trail for transactions. As an audit trail, the check register links the individual checking account transactions to the summary reports. Suppose that you notice a balance in an expense category that seems much larger than you expected. By using the Reports feature, you can look through the check register for the specific transactions that affected the expense category.

Computer-based accounting systems, including Quicken, probably use and generate more paper than any manual system. From an internal control perspective, this fact is comforting. The clean, easy-to-read, and well-organized information produced by Quicken makes reviewing transactions, checking account balances, and researching suspicious income or expense conditions much easier. As a result, you are more likely to find all errors of omission—and even fraudulent transactions—in the checking account records.

Retaining Documents

After looking at all the paper a computer-based accounting system can generate (check forms, registers, and other special reports), you may wonder how long you need to keep this paperwork.

Table 20.1 provides guidelines on the length of time to keep canceled checks, check registers, and any of the other special reports generated by Quicken. These guidelines are based on statutory and regulatory requirements and statutes of limitations. If you have more questions about other personal or business financial records and documents, talk to a tax advisor.

Table 20.1
Document Storage Guidelines

Reports and Forms	*1 year*	*3 years*	*7 years*	*Permanent*
Check register				X
Backup files	X			
Canceled checks				X
Category lists				X
Monthly personal income/expense statements		X		
Yearly personal income/expense statements			X	
Other personal reports	X			
Monthly business income/expense statements		X		
Yearly business income/expense statements			X	
Other businesses report	X			

Using Passwords

Passwords represent a third internal control mechanism. With Quicken, you can use passwords to limit access to the account groups you use to store financial records. To set a password, select the **Password Settings** option from the Set Preferences menu (see fig. 20.3). Quicken then displays the Password Settings menu shown in figure 20.4.

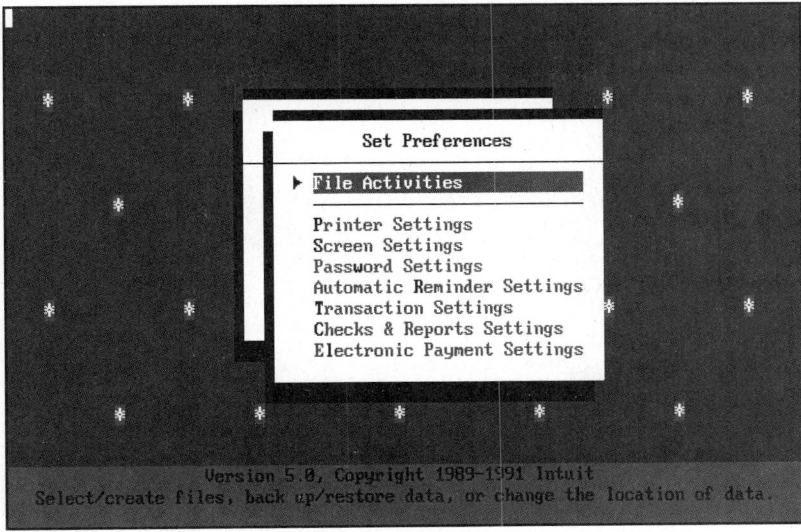

Fig. 20.3. *The Set Preferences menu.*

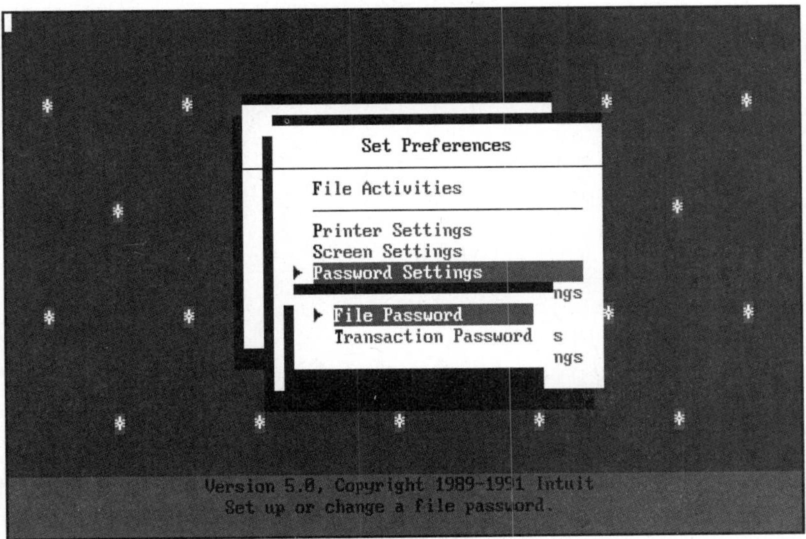

Fig. 20.4. *The Password Settings menu.*

You can use two types of passwords in Quicken: file and transaction passwords. The file password provides access to a file. If you want each file to have a password, you need to set up a password for each. If you select the **File Password** option, Quicken displays the Set Up Password screen shown in figure 20.5.

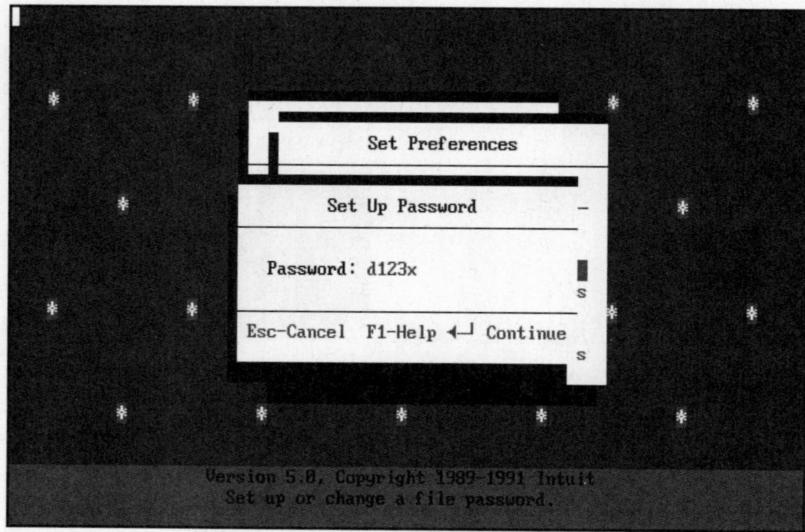

Fig. 20.5. *The Set Up Password screen.*

To define a file password, type the combination of letters and numbers you want to use as a password. You can use up to 16 characters.

Quicken does not distinguish between the use of upper- and lower-case letters in establishing or using passwords.

After you press Enter, Quicken asks you to retype the password to confirm that you know exactly what you entered. After setting the password, Quicken asks you for the password before allowing you to view or modify transactions in any of the accounts with the group. Figure 20.5 shows the main password set to d123x. The next time you try to access the Write Checks, Register, or Reports screen for the account group with the password *d123x*, Quicken requires that you enter this password. Figure 20.6 shows the screen on which you type the password. As an additional precaution, Quicken does not display the password as you type.

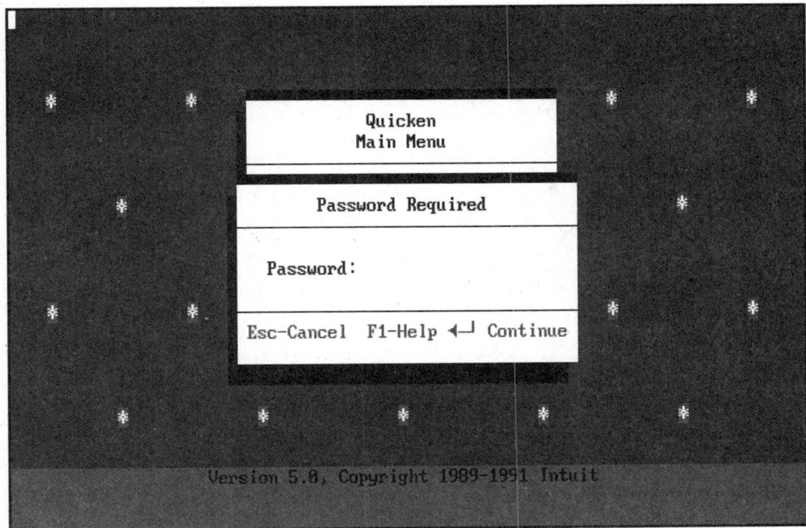

Fig. 20.6. *Entering the main password.*

To change or remove the password, reselect the **File Password** option. Quicken displays the Change Password screen shown in figure 20.7. Type the old and new passwords and press Enter. You now can use the new password. If you no longer want to use passwords, leave the `New Password` field blank.

You can require transaction date passwords to make changes to the account before a certain date. These passwords are useful to restrict or limit transactions recorded or modified for prior months. To define a transaction password, select the **Transaction Password** option. The screen shown in figure 20.8 appears.

On this screen, you enter the password and the date through which the transaction password is required. Figure 20.8 shows the password, `f12g4`, required for entering or modifying transactions dated through 12/31/91. If you want to record a transaction dated 12/31/91 or earlier, Quicken requires that you enter the transaction password on the screen shown in figure 20.9. As with main passwords, Quicken does not display the transaction password as you type.

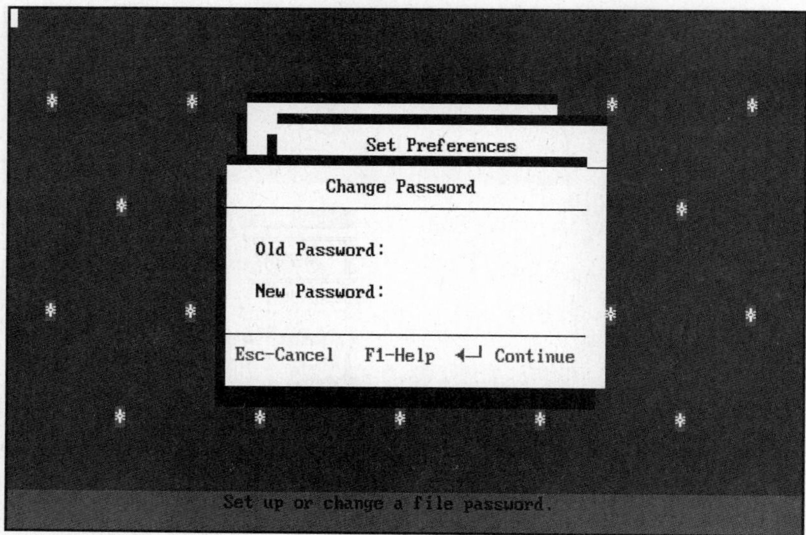

Fig. 20.7. The Change Password screen.

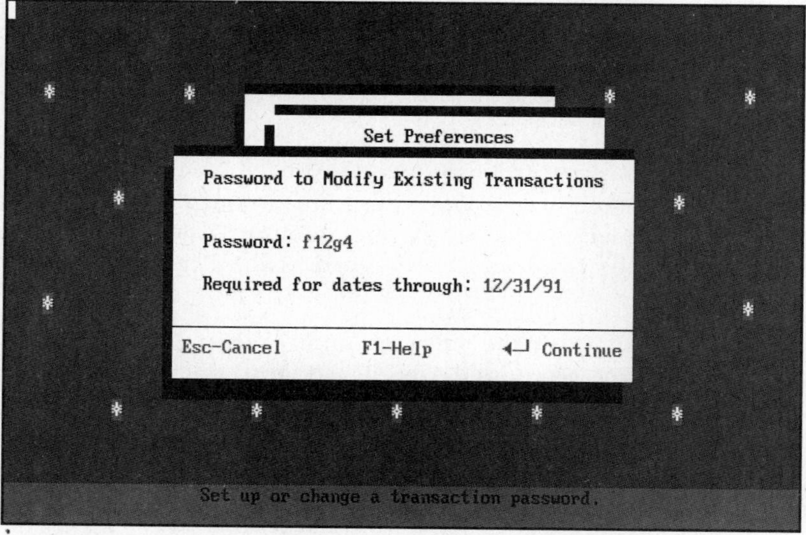

Fig. 20.8. The Password to Modify Existing Transactions screen.

Quicken enables you to enter all the information, and when you are ready to record the transaction, Quicken requests the password. You cannot record the transaction without the password.

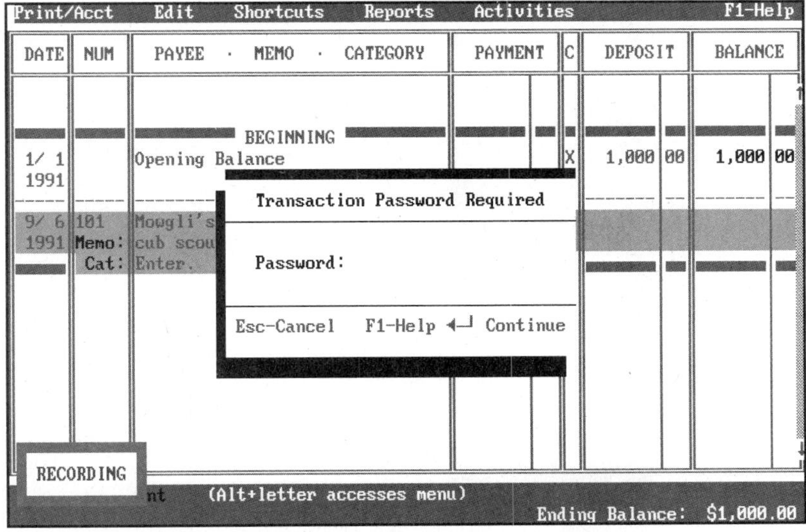

Fig. 20.9. Entering the transaction password.

To change a transaction password, reselect the **Transaction Password** option and the old and new passwords. You also can specify the old and new passwords (see fig. 20.10).

When using passwords, consider the following conventions:

- Make sure that you do not lose or forget the password. If you lose the password, you lose your data. Record the password in a safe place.
- If you are worried about someone accessing Quicken and then writing computer checks, initiating electronic payments, or modifying the account group information, use nonsensical passwords of at least six characters. The passwords you create with this procedure are extremely difficult to guess.

- Be sure that you don't use a seemingly clever password scheme, such as month names or colors, as passwords. If you set the transaction password to *blue*, the curious user may not take long to figure out the main password—even if the password is *chartreuse* to *mauve*.

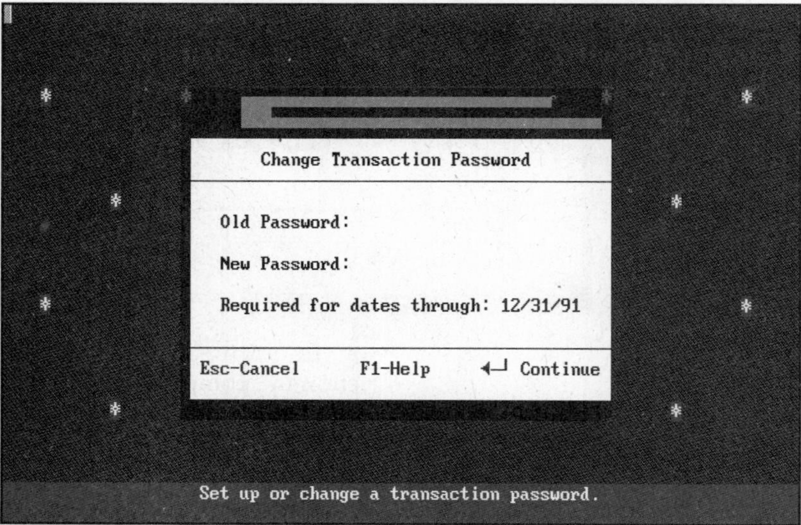

Fig. 20.10. *The Change Transaction Password screen.*

Chapter Summary

This chapter described actions you can take to prevent forgery and embezzlement. Admittedly, these topics are unpleasant. By thinking about this subject and taking a few precautions, however, you can minimize the chances of even more unpleasant subject—being a victim of forgery or embezzlement.

21

Preventing System Disasters

System disasters affect more than the Quicken program and data files. System disasters may, in fact, affect every program and all the data on your computer. For many users, however, the creation of financial records with Quicken is the most important function the computer performs. The data that Quicken collects and stores are, for many businesses, essential to stay in business. For many individuals, the data Quicken collects and stores are critical to tax preparation and investment management. It is important, therefore, for Quicken users to understand the reasons for and some of the precautions against some of the more common and the more dangerous system errors.

The information in this chapter doesn't apply just to Quicken program and data files. Although the information covered here is in the interest of protecting financial records, the information also applies to all other software and data.

Defining a Few Basic Terms

One of the most appealing features of Quicken is that you don't have to be a computer wizard to make good use of the program. In fact, you really don't need to know much at all about computers, how they work, and how they are put together. You may want to keep it that way—you may have no desire or inclination to increase your computer knowledge. If you want to look into the ways you can prevent system disasters, however, you should learn a few computer terms before getting into specifics.

Files

Files are the basic storage tools of computers. For example, if you look in the QUICKEN5 directory, you see a list of files. You can try this by typing *dir c:\quicken5* at the C> prompt (see fig. 21.1). Generally, two kinds of files exist: program files and data files.

```
 Directory of  C:\QUICKEN5

.            <DIR>      08-24-91  11:20a
..           <DIR>      08-24-91  11:20a
PRINTER2 DAT     43694 08-29-91   7:02a
BUSINESS QIF       701 08-29-91   7:02a
HOME     QIF      1853 08-29-91   7:02a
BILLMIND EXE     10286 08-29-91   7:02a
ASSIST   SRC     11121 08-29-91   7:02a
Q        HLP    243118 08-29-91   7:02a
Q        EXE    822272 08-29-91   7:03a
TAX      SCD      6615 08-29-91   7:03a
QCHECKS  DOC      6672 08-29-91   7:03a
Q        PIF       545 08-29-91   7:03a
Q        ICO       766 08-29-91   7:03a
INSTALL  CFG        29 08-29-91   7:03a
Q        CFG      1615 09-05-91   5:55p
Q3       DIR        85 09-05-91   4:57p
STEPHENL QDT      6656 09-05-91   5:15p
STEPHENL QMT      4014 09-05-91   5:15p
STEPHENL QDI       436 09-01-91   3:30p
STEPHENL QNX      2566 09-05-91   5:15p
       20 File(s)   74084352 bytes free

17:58 C:\QUICKEN5>
```

Fig. 21.1. A list of the files in the QUICKEN5 directory.

Program files store the instructions, or software, that tell a computer what to do. You usually can tell program files by the extensions because program files are named with EXE, COM, or BAT file extensions.

Data files store information. The checking account information you enter into the Quicken register, for example, is stored in data files.

If you are interested in which Quicken files are program files and which are data files, refer to Chapter 9.

Software

The *software* represents actual instructions that tell the computer what to do. People often segregate software into system software, which generally controls the physical components of a computer system, and application software, which uses the operating software to create and process data. DOS, an acronym for *disk operating system*, is an example of system software. Quicken is an example of application software.

Hardware

Hardware refers to the physical components of a computer, such as the monitor, keyboard, printer, disk drives, memory, microprocessor chips, and so on.

Preventing Hardware Disasters

Computers, like people, don't always operate perfectly. Although worrying about a personal computer breaking down is probably a needless waste of energy, you still need to be prepared for a breakdown. Better yet, you can take steps to prevent a breakdown.

Dealing with Dirty Power

The electric power you use to run the computer and everything else in the home or office may pose a danger to the hardware and the data you store on and with the computer. This danger comes from dirty electrical power that surges and sags in strength. Usually, these fluctuations cause no problem, but if the surge is severe enough, the surge may cause the computer to reset. In effect, the power surge causes the computer to temporarily turn itself off, which means that—at the least—you lose all the transactions you entered during the current session of Quicken. Unfortunately, this situation can become worse: if a power surge causes the computer to reset at the same time the computer is writing data to or reading data from a hard disk or a floppy disk, the data on the disk can become damaged.

To prevent this particular disaster, you can use a simple device known as a *surge protector* or *surge suppressor*. You plug the surge protector into the wall socket and then plug the computer into the surge protector. The surge protector removes power surges and—because the electricity that powers the computer comes from the surge protector—the computer may never receive power surges. Talk to a local computer supplier to see which kind of surge protector is best for the system. You probably can buy a good surge protector for less than $50.

Handling Hard Disk Failures

Hard disks are remarkably reliable when you consider that while the computer runs, the hard disk is spinning constantly. Sooner or later, however, the hard disk may fail, so always back up data files to a floppy disk regularly to minimize the time and work you may lose by having to reenter transactions. (Chapter 9 describes the process for backing up files.)

Consider two preventive measures against hard disk failure. First, don't turn on and off the computer several times a day. Instead, just leave the machine running. A computer doesn't use much electrical power—probably about the same as a desk lamp. By leaving the computer running all day—even while you are out running errands, going to lunch, or working with customers—you minimize the most wearing and stressful operation the computer goes through: starting the system.

A second preventive measure relates to the fact that too much heat isn't good for a computer. Keep the room where the computer is located at a comfortable temperature. For the same reason, don't stack books, a computer manual, or check forms on top of the computer in such a way that these items may block the ventilation holes. Some circuitry, such as the microprocessor, needs to stay below a certain temperature to work correctly. You may have heard horror stories about the personal computer circuit boards—the laminated cardboard boards into which the electronic circuitry is plugged—delaminating when temperatures become extreme.

Handling Floppy Disk Problems

You undoubtedly will use floppy disks to store Quicken data files—even if you have a hard disk on the computer. You should know a little about preventing floppy disk failures.

Floppy disks are amazingly durable. Floppy disks store data on a thin plastic disk coated with a material that can store magnetic charges. Magnetic charges on the disk's surface represent the binary digits, or *bits*, that are the basic building blocks of program and data files. As long as you treat floppy disks with a reasonable degree of care, you really shouldn't have problems. You should consider a few things, however, when handling floppy disks.

First, because the actual disk is plastic, you don't want the disk to become very cold or very hot. A very cold floppy disk—one whose temperature drops below freezing—becomes brittle and may change shape. A very hot disk—one whose temperature rises above 140 degrees—may warp or even melt. In either case, because the actual plastic disk becomes damaged, you can lose the data on the disk. You shouldn't, therefore, leave floppy disks in a car if the car is parked outside and the temperature is below freezing. You also shouldn't leave disks on the dashboard of a car on a hot, sunny day. And you shouldn't set a steaming mug of hot coffee on top of the disk.

A second set of problems relates to the fact that the information on the disk is stored as a series of magnetic charges on the disk's surface. Because of this, you don't want to do things that change or foul the charges. Don't, for example, store disks next to a magnet, even if the magnet is only a small one for holding paper clips. And don't store disks next to appliances that generate magnetic fields, such as refrigerators, televisions, and telephones. You also don't want to touch the actual disk surface (which you can see through the opening on the plastic sleeve of the disk), spill things on the disk, or write on the disk with a sharp object.

Reviewing and Preventing Software Disasters

Software poses as many potential dangers to a computer and to the use of Quicken and the Quicken files as does the hardware. Potential problems include the possibility of accidentally deleting files, of somehow *catching* a computer virus, and the myriad difficulties that can come from working with *beta* (prerelease) software, freeware, and shareware. All these things can damage a computer, the Quicken data files, and your ability to use Quicken.

Recovering Deleted Files

You can use a variety of ways to delete files: with DOS commands such as DEL or ERASE, with Quicken, and with other application programs, such as Lotus 1-2-3 and Microsoft Word. You can accidentally delete files in many different ways—much as you can accidentally throw out an important financial document. You should know, however, that if you do accidentally delete a file, you can recover the file as long as you understand what happens when you delete a file. You also need to know which tools you can use to recover, or *undelete*, previously deleted files.

Do not change or add to the files on the hard disk or floppy disk that contains the deleted files. When DOS marks a file as erased in the list of files and file locations, DOS assumes that the portion of the disk containing the deleted file can be used to store other program and data files. If you create any new data files, increase the size of existing data files, or install new program files—such as the software to recover the deleted files—you may overwrite the files you want to recover. For this reason, if you accidentally delete and then decide to recover these files, do so immediately.

When DOS deletes a file, it doesn't actually remove the file from the hard disk or floppy disk. Instead, DOS erases the first letter of the file's name on its list of files and file locations. At this point, the file and the file name—minus its first letter—are still there. But DOS considers the deleted file gone. You can still recover the file—although you cannot use DOS to do so. Several relatively inexpensive programs that provide an undelete file feature are available. These programs include PC Tools Deluxe, Norton Utilities, Lotus Magellan, and Mace Utilities.

If you need to recover a deleted file, you can go to the local software store, purchase one of these utilities—such as PC Tools Deluxe—and use the program to undelete the deleted files. Whichever program you choose, the process works the same way. PC Tools Deluxe looks at the DOS list of files and file locations and displays on-screen a list of the files that have the first letters of the file name erased. Quicken data files that are not erased usually resemble the following list:

STEPHENL.QDT

STEPHENL.QNX

STEPHENL.QMT

STEPHENL.QDI

Using an undelete program, the files appear on a list in the following way:

?TEPHENL.QDT

?TEPHENL.QNX

?TEPHENL.QMT

?TEPHENL.QDI

You follow the program's directions for undeleting the files, which means you tell the software that replaces these files the first letter of the file names that were deleted—in this example, the letter *S*.

The newest version of DOS, DOS 5.0, also provides an undelete file command.

Protecting Against Viruses

Viruses have been around for some time—probably for almost 20 years. Some say the existence and, therefore, the danger of viruses is exaggerated. Other experts counter this view by pointing to the widely reported examples of viruses that you may have read about in the local newspaper. Whatever the truth, you should understand—and know how to protect a computer from—viruses.

Defining Viruses

Viruses are small programs that often do rather innocuous things, such as displaying on-screen political or supposedly humorous messages, either at random or on specific dates. (April 1 is a popular choice for this kind of virus.) Often, viruses operate more nefariously. A virus may secretly and slowly destroy program and data files bit by bit. Because the corruption of the data files is so slow, you may not notice the virus's effect until too late, when the virus has infected even the backup copies of the data files. Another virus may incrementally use more of a computer's power so that the computer operates more and more slowly. In each of these cases, however, you don't want the computer to become infected. Usually, the steps you can take to ensure that the computer isn't infected or to disinfect a computer aren't difficult—if you understand where viruses come from and how you can detect and rid viruses from a computer.

Determining Where Viruses Originate

Because a virus is actually a program, the virus program file somehow must be copied to the computer to infect the system. Usually, the virus program file is copied to the computer from an infected floppy disk. You also can infect a computer by *downloading* a virus (using a modem to copy an infected file from a computer bulletin board). For this reason, the basic rule is not to copy program files blindly.

You probably don't need to worry about copying program files as part of installing a program from a major software company. Software companies usually thoroughly test all the parts of a program long before you install the program. Do, however—and this preventative step is highly recommended—be leery about copying program files on a floppy disk that came from a friend, or from a friend of a friend. Aside from the legal and moral issues (don't copy pirated software), and even if the original software is fine, the floppy disk from which you copy the program files may be infected.

Although not everyone agrees, you probably should not use the free software that people pass around for the same reasons mentioned in the preceding paragraph. Ensuring that the program files aren't infected is just too difficult. If you insist on using these programs, you may want to contact the original writer to confirm that the program files you are copying are, in fact, the same programs. You also may want to confirm that the file date and file size, which appear when you list the program files by using the DOS DIR command shown in figure 21.1, are identical to the original program files.

Detecting Viruses

If in the past you indiscriminately copied program files to the hard disk, the machine already may be infected. Predictably, the steps you must take to cure the machine depend on the virus. Different viruses behave differently, but be on the watch for several signs of infection.

First, keep a sharp eye out for program files that you don't understand or that don't seem related to the programs you use. If you find a suspicious-looking file, refer to the appropriate software user's manual to confirm that the file is indeed a valid program file. (As noted previously, program files use the file extensions COM, EXE, or BAT.) If you find a program file you know you don't use, remove the file from the disk.

Second, watch for increases in the file size of program files. Some viruses don't actually appear as a separate program file, but rather append themselves to existing program files. If you see program files increasing in size for no apparent reason, consider the possibility that the existing program file is contaminated by a virus. You can check with the software manufacturer if you have questions about this possibility. Obviously, all software manufacturers are extremely interested when a virus is specifically infecting one of their programs.

A third sign to watch for are hidden files. You may have two or three hidden files on a disk. PC DOS uses the two hidden files IBMIO.COM and IBMDOS.COM. MS-DOS uses the two hidden files IO.SYS and MSDOS.SYS. If you use volume labels on the hard disk or on floppy disks, a third hidden file for the label may exist. These disks should have no other hidden files. If other hidden files are present, either you or someone else hid these files. This someone else may be the creator of the virus.

To check for the presence of hidden files, use the DOS CHKDSK command. To use the CHKDSK command, type *chkdsk*, followed by a space, the drive letter, and a colon. To look for hidden files on drive C (usually the name of the hard disk), type *chkdsk c:*. DOS then displays on-screen information about the disk, including the number of hidden files (see fig. 21.2). For an example of other information that the CHKDSK command can display on-screen, refer to the DOS user's manual that came with the computer.

```
C:\>chkdsk c:

 31344640 bytes total disk space
    55296 bytes in 3 hidden files
   133120 bytes in 59 directories
 22822912 bytes in 1317 user files
  8333312 bytes available on disk

   655360 bytes total memory
   519376 bytes free

C:\>
```

Fig. 21.2. *Use the DOS CHKDSK command to look for hidden files.*

Some software packages search disks specifically for viruses. If you are someone who is rather careless about what you copy to disks, you may want to purchase one of these programs. Ask a local software dealer for help.

Working with Beta Software

Beta software is the prerelease software that software manufacturers distribute to small groups of users—usually experienced and sophisticated users—to test before the program is released to the software-buying public. In some people's minds, working with beta copies of software carries a certain prestige—particularly beta copies of popular programs. You may not want to work with a beta on any machine that stores important personal or business financial records. Beta copies may have programming *bugs*, or errors, that cause the program to exit to DOS unexpectedly, lock up the keyboard, or damage—and even destroy—data files.

A related point is that, for the same reasons stated in the preceding paragraph, you may not want to use a beta copy of the software in place of a released-to-the-public version.

Chapter Summary

This chapter covered a topic that most people don't regularly think about: preventing system disasters. If you use a computer as a tool for managing something as important as money, you should understand how to prevent hardware and software disasters.

Tips for Specific Business Situations

This appendix gives you some tips for using Quicken in specific business situations. Before starting this appendix, read the previous sections of the book because this appendix does not focus on the mechanics of menu options or the way in which you complete screens.

Tips for Lawyers, Consultants, and Other Professionals

A professional service business probably is the simplest kind of business for which you can perform accounting. You may be able to run accounting records out of a checkbook. If you record an income category when you make deposits and record an expense category when you write checks or withdraw money, you can produce helpful financial reports that enable you to gauge the business's performance.

If you sell services, think about how billing is handled. Billing produces another major asset besides cash—receivables—in addition to determining cash inflow.

If the volumes of invoices and clients are low, you probably can perform billing and collecting by using a combination of manual techniques and Quicken. You may be able to track the hours you spend with various clients in an appointment calendar.

If the volumes of invoices and clients are high, you need a fast way to accumulate the amounts clients owe you, to aggregate these amounts, and to produce an invoice. You also need an easy way to track outstanding invoices. If you are unhappy with the way the current billing and receivables tracking works, consider acquiring a stand-alone billing package. One popular package is Timeslips III, which provides a convenient way to record the hours you spend on a client's behalf, accounts for the out-of-pocket expenses you incur, and generates invoices at the end of the month.

Tips for Restaurants

You can use Quicken for restaurant accounting. As part of closing out the cash register, you can record the daily cash and credit-card sales as a deposit transaction into the register. You also can record expenses directly into Quicken as they occur by categorizing any checks you write.

Although you may be tempted to carry the inventory in an account because inventory is an asset, this method is probably not worth the effort. Food inventories are too short-lived. What you record on Monday as food inventory, you probably use up or throw out by the following Monday. Categorize food purchases in an expense category instead of setting up a food inventory account that you must adjust every time you calculate profits. You need to calculate an inventory balance for income tax returns but only one time each year.

Tips for Retailers

Retail businesses—especially businesses that do not have to prepare invoices or statements—also can use Quicken with good results. You need a point-of-sale system (such as a cash register) to ring up sales and make change. At the end of the day, you can enter the total sales for the day as a deposit transaction into the check register.

For a retail business that holds extensive inventory, Quicken has one weakness—you do not have a good way to track the units and dollars of inventory you hold. You may want to implement a manual inventory tracking system and use a common tool for setting priorities, such as ABC analysis and classification.

ABC analysis and classification is a commonsense approach to breaking down an inventory into classes—A, B, or C—to show each class's relative value to you. Items in the A class are the most valuable, and items in the C class are the least valuable. After categorizing items in the three classes, you decide which control and management procedures are appropriate and cost-effective for each class.

Usually, class A items constitute about 20 percent of the total number of items in the inventory and make up 80 percent of an inventory's dollar value. You may want (or be required by law) to count class A items on a weekly or daily basis and maintain precise manual records of balances and changes in the balances.

Class B items are at the next level of importance and value. These items usually constitute 40 to 50 percent of the total number of items in inventory, but they may account for less than 15 percent of the dollar value of the inventory. Accordingly, you may want to use a periodic inventory approach for class B items and take a physical count of the inventory once per quarter or month.

For some retailers and manufacturers, class C items can constitute up to 40 percent of the total number of items in inventory, although class C may account for less than 5 percent of the inventory's value. Naturally, the effort expended on controlling this inventory is considerably less than the effort connected with classes A and B. For example, you may decide to count class C items annually.

ABC analysis and classification is a straightforward approach to setting priorities in the control and management of inventory. Although all items in your inventory may be important, do not succumb to the temptation to classify all items as class A. Categorize the inventory holdings into meaningful and manageable groups.

Tips for Churches, Synagogues, and Nonprofit Organizations

Most churches, synagogues and nonprofit organizations have simple accounting needs, and tracking of donations and disbursements fits easily into the checkbook register structure. A couple of common accounting requirements exist, however, for nonprofit businesses.

Tracking Pledges

Some nonprofit organizations, as part of the budgeting process, solicit pledges from the donors who support the organization. Often, the organization tracks actual donations and compares these donations to the pledged amounts—just as a for-profit business tracks actual income and compares that amount to budgeted income.

To make these kinds of comparisons, set up income categories for each person who pledges donations and enter a budgeted amount as the pledged amount. When you record donations, categorize donations as coming from a specific donor. If you have pledges from Vyder Ryderwood and Batum Schrag, for example, you have income categories for both donors. That way, at any time, you can generate a budget report that compares the budgeted, or pledged, donation income category amounts with the actual donation income category amounts.

Tracking Fund Designations

Some nonprofit businesses accept designated donations. A contributor may designate that he wants his donation to go into the new building fund or for the children's breakfast program. The easiest way to track such designations is to set up separate bank accounts for each designation. When someone designates a donation for a specific purpose, you can deposit the money into the separate fund.

Outgrowing Quicken

Quicken's simplicity and friendliness make the program a popular package. However, you may outgrow the product. You may become more sophisticated in financial management, or the business may grow too large or complex for Quicken. This appendix concludes with some pointers on where you go when you need to move to something new.

Becoming More Sophisticated

Even if you are not an accountant, you may want to become more sophisticated in financial management. The more sophisticated you become, the harder getting what you want from Quicken becomes. You may want to create elaborate invoices or monthly customer statements, generate recurring invoices or purchase orders, use a perpetual inventory system, use double-entry bookkeeping, and account for multiple companies that you later want to consolidate. Occasionally, you can accomplish these tasks with Quicken but the solution may prove awkward and incomplete compared to what is available from a more advanced accounting package.

You may consider taking two or three community college or university accounting classes. Often, colleges offer two introductory accounting courses and a managerial accounting course. An introductory course on business financial management also may be helpful. If you want to become more sophisticated in financial management, the place to start is often your knowledge base.

Becoming Too Large for Quicken

Increased business volumes can cause you to outgrow Quicken. You may find that you are spending a great deal of time printing checks, entering transactions into Quicken registers, and generating reports. You may not have time to become a full-time accountant or bookkeeper. To be candid, if you apply all the tricks and techniques described in Chapter 18, you are probably expecting too much from Quicken.

If this situation sounds familiar, look at similar batches of transactions that seem to take an inordinate amount of time and consider moving these transactions to an outside service bureau or processing the transactions with a more convenient tool. If you are spending too much time preparing payroll, for example, outside service bureaus, such as ADP and PayChex, can prepare payroll checks and payroll tax forms. If you are spending a great deal of time recording invoices and customer payments, consider using one of the stand-alone billing packages, such as Timeslips III, which enables you to generate invoices and record payments much faster than Quicken.

You can continue to use Quicken as a master accounting system, but groups of similar transactions can be processed elsewhere. All you need to do is enter at the end of the month single transactions that summarize the individual transactions that you recorded elsewhere. If Quicken seems to come up short in several areas, you may need a full-fledged accounting system, such as DacEasy or Pacioli 2000.

B

Using This Book with Version 4.0

Although this book is written for Version 5.0, if you are working with Version 4.0 of Quicken, *Using Quicken 5* still can be helpful to you. To use this book for Quicken Version 4.0, you first must learn the operational differences between these two versions. You also need to be aware of the features that exist only in Version 5.0 so that you can ignore the parts of this book that deal exclusively with Version 5.0.

Operational Differences

Several operational differences exist between Version 5.0 and Version 4.0. One major difference is that in Version 5.0, one of the ways you select menu options is by pressing the keyboard equivalent of the highlighted letter in the option name. On Quicken's Main Menu, the letter **X** in the **Exit** option is highlighted so you can press X to select the **Exit** option. This option selection technique, however, isn't available in Version 4.0. In Version 4.0, to select a menu option by typing a key, you press the option number or letter. So, to select the first option on a menu, you press the number 1. To select the second option on a menu, you press the number 2. You don't have to count down a menu's options or remember menu option numbers, however; Quicken displays on-screen the menu option numbers and letters in front of the option names.

A related operational difference in Quicken Version 4.0 is that to display the menus on the Write Checks and Register screens, you don't press the Alt key and then the menu letter. Rather, you press the menu's function key. Again, however, you don't have to remember which function key goes with a particular menu because Quicken Version 4.0 identifies the function key that you use to access a menu on the menu bar.

Some other differences exist in menu structure and names between the two versions. Usually, you can easily figure out the differences. In Version 4.0, for example, a Main Menu option named **Register** is available; in Version 5.0, the same menu option is named **Use Register**. This kind of discrepancy should cause you no problems. In one area, however, Quicken 5.0 provides entirely new menus that don't even exist in Version 4.0: the report screens menus. These menus, which appear when you display a report on-screen in Version 5.0, aren't available in Version 4.0.

Some menus in Quicken Version 4.0 are slightly reorganized in Version 5.0. These changes should cause you no trouble. If you encounter a problem, you can figure out where a topic is covered in this book by thumbing through the index.

Finally, if you're a Quicken 4.0 user, a series of minor operational changes also exist that you should know about as you use this book. Version 4.0—unlike 5.0—doesn't support a mouse. Version 4.0 provides only two date editing keys, the + and – keys. Finally, the Version 4.0 Help facility is slightly less sophisticated.

New Version 5.0 Features

Not surprisingly, Version 5.0 also adds a series of new features. However, these features don't cause a problem if you are a Version 4.0 user who is trying to use this book. All you need to do is ignore the sections of this book that deal with these new features. The loan calculator, described in Chapter 12, isn't available in Version 4.0. The Tax Schedule report, described in Chapters 14 and 19, isn't available in Version 4.0. The Budgeting Spreadsheet, described in Chapter 16, isn't available in Version 4.0. (In Version 4.0, you set up budget amounts when you produce the monthly budget report.) Finally, the Tutorials and Assistants menu, and this menu's options, aren't available in Version 4.0.

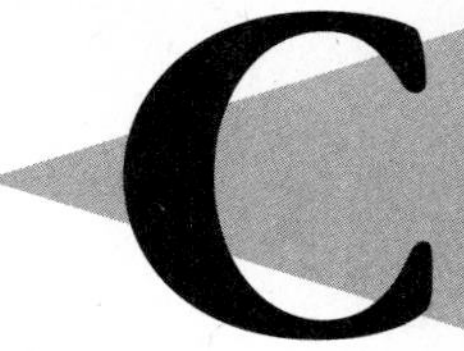

Planning for Your Retirement

Most people aspire to quit working someday, and most people support themselves with a paycheck. How do you plan to pay for living expenses after the paycheck stops? You may believe this topic to interest only readers who are retiring soon, but this is not the case. The irony is that the easiest time to prepare for retirement is when the time you stop working is still a long way off, and the hardest time to prepare for retirement is when retirement is right around the bend.

This problem resembles the dilemma of the swimmer who chooses a river that goes over a waterfall some distance downstream. Because the waterfall is still a long way off—perhaps the swimmer can hear only faintly the roar of the falls—swimming to shore still is easy. As the sound of the waterfall grows louder, however, the current also becomes stronger. The swimmer must work harder and harder to reach the shore safely. If the swimmer doesn't try to escape from the river until the waterfall is approaching, the current becomes too strong, the roar of the waterfall is deafening, and the danger obvious. At this point, the swimmer is at the mercy of the river's increasing strength.

The opening paragraphs of this book suggest that the reasons for using Quicken probably stem from a desire to make better financial decisions, to increase your sense of well-being, and to make life more enjoyable. The chapter on budgeting, Chapter 16, talks about the benefits of creating and using a financial game plan. This appendix walks you through the steps you can take to increase the chance that your retirement years also are golden years. You learn how to estimate living expenses, how to figure what you may receive in pension and Social Security benefits, and how to make up any shortfall between income and expenses. Although this whole topic may seem like something only 50-year-olds should read, younger readers who peruse the following paragraphs may find this information beneficial. Contrary to what you may think, preparing for retirement at age 30 is much easier than at age 50 or 60.

Preparing a Living Expenses Budget

The first step in planning for retirement is to estimate living expenses. Obviously, the further away your retirement, the less precise are the estimates. Even if retirement is 20 years away, however, your current spending can provide a useful benchmark for estimating future expenses. The general rule of thumb is that retirement expenses are roughly 80 percent of current living expenses. Generally, three reasons account for this calculation:

- Housing expenses may go down, either because you owned a home and paid off your mortgage or you moved to a smaller house or apartment.
- Children grow up and—usually— cease to be financial responsibilities.
- Work expenses, such as special clothing, transportation, tools, dues, and so on, stop because you stop working.

Be careful, however, that you don't drastically reduce your planned living expenses. Remember that certain expenses also may increase because you age or retire. Medical expenses—such as the insurance an employer paid previously—may increase. Entertainment and vacation expenses may increase because you have more free time on your hands. Consider also that retirement may mean new hobbies or activities with attendant costs.

In any event, the reports that Quicken provides should prove immensely helpful. In particular, Quicken's Itemized Category Report should be useful because the report shows the ways you currently are spending money. (Refer to Chapter 14 if you have questions about how to print a particular report.) Figure C.1 provides a worksheet you can use to estimate the living expenses you may have during retirement. You can fill in the first column, the one that records your current expenses, using the Itemized Category Report. (Refer to Chapter 14.) Using this information and the ideas already touched on, you can fill in the second column to come up with an estimate of retirement expenses. Remember that Quicken's calculator provides a convenient way to compute the total expenses for retirement. Figure C.2 provides a sample completed worksheet.

Estimated Living Expenses Worksheet		
Expense	Current	Retirement
Housing		
Mortgage or rent		
Property taxes		
Property insurance		
Maintenance		
Food		
Transportation		
Work		
Hobby		
Vacation		
Recreation		
Healthcare/Insurance		
Clothing		
Other		
Total Expenses		

Fig. C.1. *A worksheet you can use to estimate living expenses.*

Keep in mind two more things about estimating retirement living expenses. First, don't adjust the expense estimates for the inflation that probably will occur between now and the time you retire, because you address the ravages of inflation elsewhere. Second, although the worksheet in figure C.1 doesn't provide space to budget taxes, you cover this important topic in a following section.

Estimated Living Expenses Worksheet		
Expense	Current	Retirement
Housing		
Mortgage or rent	8,000	0
Property taxes	1,000	1,000
Property insurance	500	500
Maintenance	500	500
Food	3,000	500
Transportation	3,000	3,000
Work	1,500	0
Hobby	0	1,500
Vacation	1500	1,500
Recreation	500	500
Healthcare/Insurance	0	3,000
Clothing	1,000	1,000
Other	1,000	1,000
Total Expenses	21,500	14,000

Fig. C.2. *A sample completed worksheet.*

Estimating Tentative Retirement Income

Estimating tentative retirement income is the second step in planning a retirement income. In general, a person's retirement income essentially consists of three components: Social Security, investment income, and pension income. To tally these three sources, you need to do the following:

1. Contact the local Social Security office and ask for the form called "Request for Earnings and Benefit Estimate Statement." Figure C.3 shows a sample of the form.

SOCIAL SECURITY ADMINISTRATION

Request for Earnings and Benefit Estimate Statement

To receive a free statement of your earnings covered by Social Security and your estimated future benefits, all you need to do is fill out this form. Please print or type your answers. When you have completed the form, fold it and mail it to us.

1. Name shown on your Social Security card:

   First　Middle Initial　Last

2. Your Social Security number as shown on your card:

   ☐☐☐-☐☐-☐☐☐☐

3. Your date of birth: Month　Day　Year

4. Other Social Security numbers you have used:

   ☐☐☐-☐☐-☐☐☐☐

   ☐☐☐-☐☐-☐☐☐☐

5. Your Sex: ☐ Male ☐ Female

6. Other names you have used (including a maiden name):

7. Show your actual earnings for last year and your estimated earnings for this year. Include only wages and/or net self-employment income covered by Social Security.

   A. Last year's actual earnings:

   $☐☐☐,☐☐☐.00
   Dollars only

   B. This year's estimated earnings:

   $☐☐☐,☐☐☐.00
   Dollars only

8. Show the age at which you plan to retire: ☐☐
   (Show only one age)

9. Below, show the average yearly amount that you think you will earn between now and when you plan to retire. Your estimate of future earnings will be added to those earnings already on our records to give you the best possible estimate.

   Enter a yearly average, not your total future lifetime earnings. Only show earnings covered by Social Security. Do not add cost-of-living, performance or scheduled pay increases or bonuses. The reason for this is that we estimate retirement benefits in today's dollars, but adjust them to account for average wage growth in the national economy.

   However, if you expect to earn significantly more or less in the future due to promotions, job changes, part-time work, or an absence from the work force, enter the amount in today's dollars that most closely reflects your future average yearly earnings.

   Most people should enter the same amount that they are earning now (the amount shown in 7B).

   Your future average yearly earnings:

   $☐☐☐,☐☐☐.00
   Dollars only

10. Address where you want us to send the statement:

    Name

    Street Address (Include Apt. No., P.O. Box, or Rural Route)

    City　State　Zip Code

I am asking for information about my own Social Security record or the record of a person I am authorized to represent. I understand that if I deliberately request information under false pretenses I may be guilty of a federal crime and could be fined and/or imprisoned. I authorize you to send the statement of earnings and benefit estimates to the person named in item 10 through a contractor.

Please sign your name (Do not print)

Date　(Area Code) Daytime Telephone No.

ABOUT THE PRIVACY ACT

Social Security is allowed to collect the facts on this form under Section 205 of the Social Security Act. We need them to quickly identify your record and prepare the earnings statement you asked us for. Giving us these facts is voluntary. However, without them we may not be able to give you an earnings and benefit estimate statement. Neither the Social Security Administration nor its contractor will use the information for any other purpose.

Form SSA-7004-PC-OP1 (9-89) Destroy Prior Edition

Fig. C.3. *The Social Security Administration's "Request for Earnings and Benefit Estimate Statement."*

2. Complete the "Request for Earnings and Benefit Estimate Statement" by following the directions on the form. You need to enter your Social Security number, information about your earnings, and indicate when you plan to retire. After you complete the form, send it to the address given. In a few weeks, you will receive an estimate of what you may receive in Social Security benefits when you retire. Enter the Social Security benefits estimate on Line 1 of the Estimated Retirement Income Worksheet shown in figure C.4.

3. If you qualify for an employer's pension, contact the pension fund administrator or trustee and ask for whatever information you need to estimate your future retirement benefits. The administrator should be more than happy to give this information to you. In fact, the pension fund trustee is required to give you the information. (If you feel uncomfortable asking, tell the trustee or administrator

that you need the information for a personal financial plan currently being prepared.) Enter any pension fund benefits estimate on Line 2 of the Estimated Retirement Income Worksheet shown in figure C.4.

Estimated Retirement Income Worksheet

Line 1 - Social security benefits

Line 2 - Pension benefits

Line 3 - Current savings

Line 4 - Future value factor

Line 5 - Future value of savings
(Note: multiply line 4 by line 3.)

Line 6 - Annual interest rate

Line 7 - Interest Income Savings
(Note: multiply line 7 by line 6)

Line 8 - Total Retirement Income
(Note: Add lines 1, 2 and 7)

Line 9 - Estimated Income Taxes

Line 10 - Spendable Income
(Note: Subtract line 9 from line 8.)

***Fig. C.4.** The Estimated Retirement Income Worksheet.*

4. Enter current retirement savings on Line 3 of the Estimated Retirement Income Worksheet. If you use Quicken to track the investments and savings you have made for retirement, you may be able to obtain this information from the Portfolio Value Report. (Refer to Chapter 14 if you have questions about how to print a report.)

5. Enter the appropriate future value factor as shown in the Future Value Factors table in figure C.5. Find the number in the Years of Interest column that matches the number of years until you begin drawing on the money. For example, if you won't retire for another 20 years, locate the number 20. Next, choose the factor that corresponds to the interest rate. If you will retire in 20 years and expect an annual return of 5 percent, for example, you use the factor 2.6533.

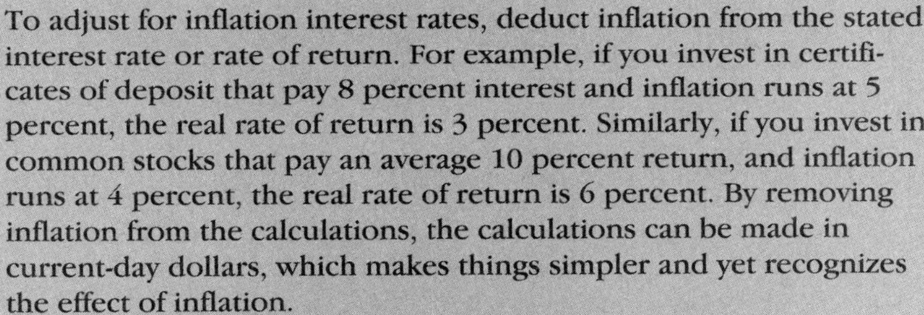
To adjust for inflation interest rates, deduct inflation from the stated interest rate or rate of return. For example, if you invest in certificates of deposit that pay 8 percent interest and inflation runs at 5 percent, the real rate of return is 3 percent. Similarly, if you invest in common stocks that pay an average 10 percent return, and inflation runs at 4 percent, the real rate of return is 6 percent. By removing inflation from the calculations, the calculations can be made in current-day dollars, which makes things simpler and yet recognizes the effect of inflation.

As a frame of reference in picking appropriate real rates of return, you may find several pieces of data helpful. Over the last 60 years or so, inflation has averaged a little more than 3 percent, common stocks have averaged 10 percent, long-term bonds have averaged around 5 percent, and short-term treasury bills have averaged roughly 3.5 percent. Therefore, when you subtract inflation, stocks produced real returns of 7 percent, long-term bonds produced real returns of about 2 percent, and treasury bills essentially broke even. Accordingly, if half of the retirement savings is invested in long-term bonds yielding 2 percent and the other half invested in common stocks yielding 7 percent, you may want to guess the return as somewhere between 4 and 5 percent.

Future Value Factors				
Years of Interest	Annual Interest Rates			
	3%	4%	5%	6%
1	1.0300	1.0400	1.0500	1.0600
2	1.0609	1.0816	1.1025	1.1236
3	1.0927	1.1249	1.1576	1.1910
4	1.1255	1.1699	1.2155	1.2625
5	1.1593	1.2167	1.2763	1.3382
6	1.1941	1.2653	1.3401	1.4185
7	1.2299	1.3159	1.4071	1.5036
8	1.2668	1.3686	1.4775	1.5938
9	1.3048	1.4233	1.5513	1.6895
10	1.3439	1.4802	1.6289	1.7908
11	1.3842	1.5395	1.7103	1.8983
12	1.4258	1.6010	1.7959	2.0122
13	1.4685	1.6651	1.8856	2.1329
14	1.5126	1.7317	1.9799	2.2609
15	1.5580	1.8009	2.0789	2.3966
16	1.6047	1.8730	2.1829	2.5404
17	1.6528	1.9479	2.2920	2.6928
18	1.7024	2.0258	2.4066	2.8543
19	1.7535	2.1068	2.5270	3.0256
20	1.8061	2.1911	2.6533	3.2071
21	1.8603	2.2788	2.7860	3.3996
22	1.9161	2.3699	2.9253	3.6035
23	1.9736	2.4647	3.0715	3.8197
24	2.0328	2.5633	3.2251	4.0489
25	2.0938	2.6658	3.3864	4.2919
26	2.1566	2.7725	3.5557	4.5494
27	2.2213	2.8834	3.7335	4.8223
28	2.2879	2.9987	3.9201	5.1117
29	2.3566	3.1187	4.1161	5.4184
30	2.4273	3.2434	4.3219	5.7435
31	2.5001	3.3731	4.5380	6.0881
32	2.5751	3.5081	4.7649	6.4534
33	2.6523	3.6484	5.0032	6.8406
34	2.7319	3.7943	5.2533	7.2510
35	2.8139	3.9461	5.5160	7.6861

Fig. C.5. *The Future Value Factors table.*

6. On Line 5, calculate the future value of your current retirement savings by multiplying the savings amount on Line 3 by the future value factor on Line 4. If the appropriate factor is 2.6533 and the current savings amounts to $10,000, the future value of the savings amounts to $26,533.

7. On Line 6, enter the annual real interest rate you expect to earn on the retirement savings. (Refer to the preceding CPA Tip for help with this figure.)

8. On Line 7, calculate the annual investment or interest income you may earn on the retirement savings by multiplying the figure on Line 5 by the figure on Line 6.

9. On Line 8, calculate the total retirement income by adding the figures on Lines 1, 2, and 7.

10. On Line 9, estimate the income taxes you will owe on the total retirement income figure shown on Line 8.

    Of course, you don't know what the tax law and tax rates will be next year, let alone by the time you retire. The best approach, however, is to apply the current income tax laws. You calculate the income taxes, based on the current laws—and assume that this figure is close to the amount you actually pay when you retire.

For help on calculating income taxes, refer to Chapter 16, "Using Quicken to Budget," which describes the steps for estimating the income and Social Security taxes you will owe, based on the current income tax laws and rates.

11. On Line 10, calculate the actual money you will have to spend on living expenses by subtracting estimated income taxes expense on Line 9 from the total retirement income figure on Line 8. Figure C.6 shows a sample completed Estimated Retirement Income Worksheet.

If the total spendable income shown on Line 10 of the Retirement Income Worksheet equals or exceeds the total living expenses figure you developed on the Living Expenses Worksheet, congratulations! Assuming that all goes well, you are in good shape financially for retirement. If, however, the estimate of total spendable income in retirement is less than the estimate of retirement living expenses, you need to save additional money for retirement, which is described in the following section.

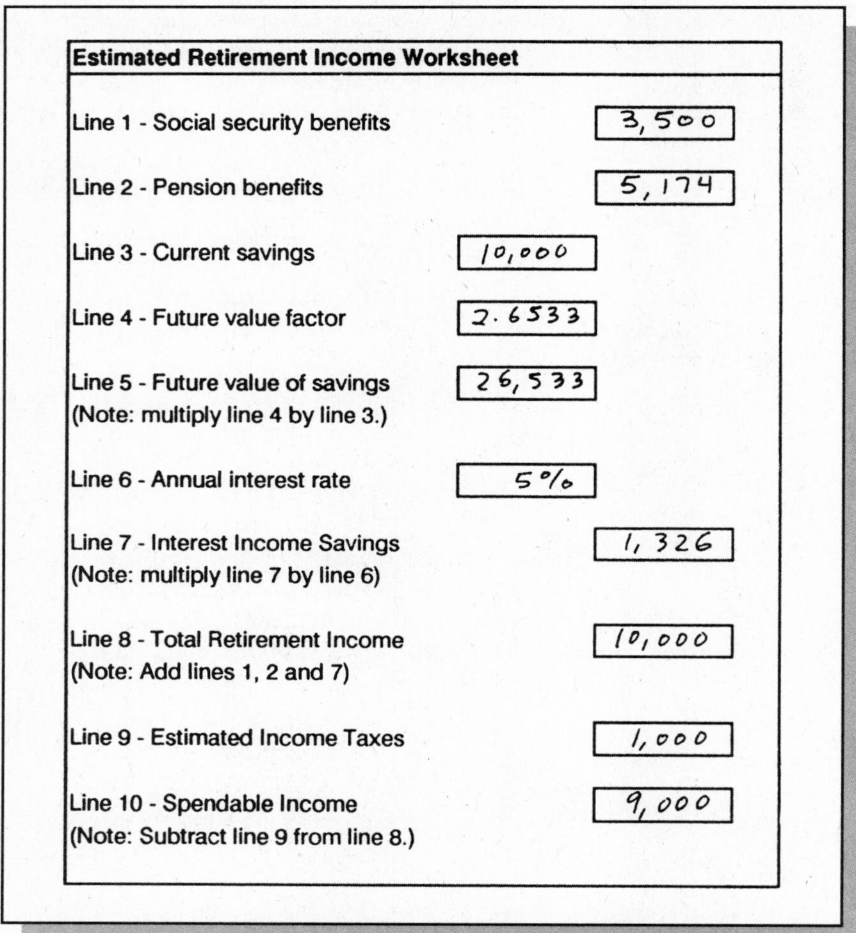

Estimated Retirement Income Worksheet

Line 1 - Social security benefits		3,500
Line 2 - Pension benefits		5,174
Line 3 - Current savings	10,000	
Line 4 - Future value factor	2.6533	
Line 5 - Future value of savings (Note: multiply line 4 by line 3.)	26,533	
Line 6 - Annual interest rate	5%	
Line 7 - Interest Income Savings (Note: multiply line 7 by line 6)		1,326
Line 8 - Total Retirement Income (Note: Add lines 1, 2 and 7)		10,000
Line 9 - Estimated Income Taxes		1,000
Line 10 - Spendable Income (Note: Subtract line 9 from line 8.)		9,000

Fig. C.6. A sample completed Estimated Retirement Income Worksheet.

Estimating Needed Retirement Savings

Don't be discouraged if you worked through the steps described in the preceding two sections only to conclude that you cannot retire the way you may want. Recognizing the problem means you are in better shape than most people who don't even realize they have a problem just over the horizon. You can do something about the potential shortfall—you can save additional money.

To figure out what you need to save over the years, follow these steps by using the Retirement Savings Worksheet (see fig. C.7):

Retirement Savings Worksheet	
Line 1 - Extra Income Needed	
Line 2 - Annual real interest rate	
Line 3 - Extra Savings Needed (note: divide line 1 by line 2.)	
Line 4 - Monthly Savings Factor	
Line 5 - Monthly Savings Required (note: multiply line 3 by line 4.)	

Fig. C.7. The Retirement Savings Worksheet.

1. On Line 1, enter the extra retirement income you need. This amount should be the difference between what the Estimated Living Expenses Worksheet shows and what the Estimated Retirement Income Worksheet shows.
2. On Line 2, enter the annual real interest rate you think you will earn, based on the investments you plan to make with the money you save.
3. On Line 3, calculate the extra savings you need to accumulate by dividing the extra retirement income figure (Line 1) by the annual real interest rate (Line 2). For example, if the extra retirement income needed is $5,000 and the annual real interest rate is 5 percent, you need an extra $100,000 of savings, calculated as ($5,000 / 5 percent).

4. On Line 4, enter the appropriate monthly savings factor from the Monthly Savings Factors table (see fig. C.8). To locate the appropriate monthly savings factor, look down the Years of Savings column until you come to the number that equals the same number of years you plan to save. Pick the factor in the same column as the annual real rate of return you assume that you will earn on investments. If you want to save a certain amount on a monthly basis over the coming 20 years and you think you can earn a 4 percent real rate of return, enter *.002726*.

The Monthly Savings Factor table assumes that you save for retirement by using investment options in which you don't have to pay taxes on the interest earned, such as individual retirement accounts, employer-provided 401(k) plans, tax-deferred annuities, and so on.

5. On Line 5, calculate the approximate required monthly savings by multiplying Line 4 by Line 3. If Line 3 shows $100,000 as the extra savings you need to accumulate, and Line 4 shows a factor of .002726, you need to save $272.60 each month to accumulate $100,000 in today's dollars—not inflated dollars—by the end of the 20-year period. Figure C.9 shows an example of a completed Retirement Savings Worksheet.

More Tips on Retirement Planning

Planning for retirement can be frustrating and difficult. Before you decide you never can quit working, however, consider the following suggestions and observations.

First, invest retirement money in tax-deferred investments, such as individual retirement accounts, 401(k)s, annuities, and so on. Consider these kinds of investments even if you don't receive an immediate tax deduction because paying income taxes on the interest or investment income you earn greatly reduces the real interest rate you enjoy.

Suppose that you choose to invest in a mutual fund you expect will return around 7.5 percent annually. If you don't have to pay income taxes on the interest, you may be left with a real interest rate of around 4.5 percent (calculated as the 7.5 percent minus the 3 percent historical inflation rate).

Monthly Savings Factors				
Years of Savings	Annual interest rates			
	3%	4%	5%	6%
1	0.082194	0.081817	0.081441	0.081066
2	0.040481	0.040092	0.039705	0.039321
3	0.026581	0.026191	0.025804	0.025422
4	0.019634	0.019246	0.018863	0.018485
5	0.015469	0.015083	0.014705	0.014333
6	0.012694	0.012312	0.011938	0.011573
7	0.010713	0.010335	0.009967	0.009609
8	0.009230	0.008856	0.008493	0.008141
9	0.008077	0.007708	0.007351	0.007006
10	0.007156	0.006791	0.006440	0.006102
11	0.006404	0.006043	0.005698	0.005367
12	0.005778	0.005422	0.005082	0.004759
13	0.005249	0.004898	0.004564	0.004247
14	0.004797	0.004450	0.004122	0.003812
15	0.004406	0.004064	0.003741	0.003439
16	0.004064	0.003727	0.003410	0.003114
17	0.003764	0.003431	0.003120	0.002831
18	0.003497	0.003169	0.002864	0.002582
19	0.003259	0.002935	0.002636	0.002361
20	0.003046	0.002726	0.002433	0.002164
21	0.002853	0.002538	0.002251	0.001989
22	0.002679	0.002368	0.002086	0.001831
23	0.002520	0.002214	0.001937	0.001688
24	0.002375	0.002074	0.001802	0.001560
25	0.002242	0.001945	0.001679	0.001443
26	0.002120	0.001827	0.001567	0.001337
27	0.002007	0.001719	0.001464	0.001240
28	0.001903	0.001619	0.001369	0.001151
29	0.001806	0.001526	0.001282	0.001070
30	0.001716	0.001441	0.001202	0.000996
31	0.001632	0.001361	0.001127	0.000927
32	0.001554	0.001288	0.001058	0.000864
33	0.001481	0.001219	0.000995	0.000806
34	0.001413	0.001154	0.000935	0.000752
35	0.001349	0.001094	0.000880	0.000702

Fig. C.8. The Monthly Savings Factors table.

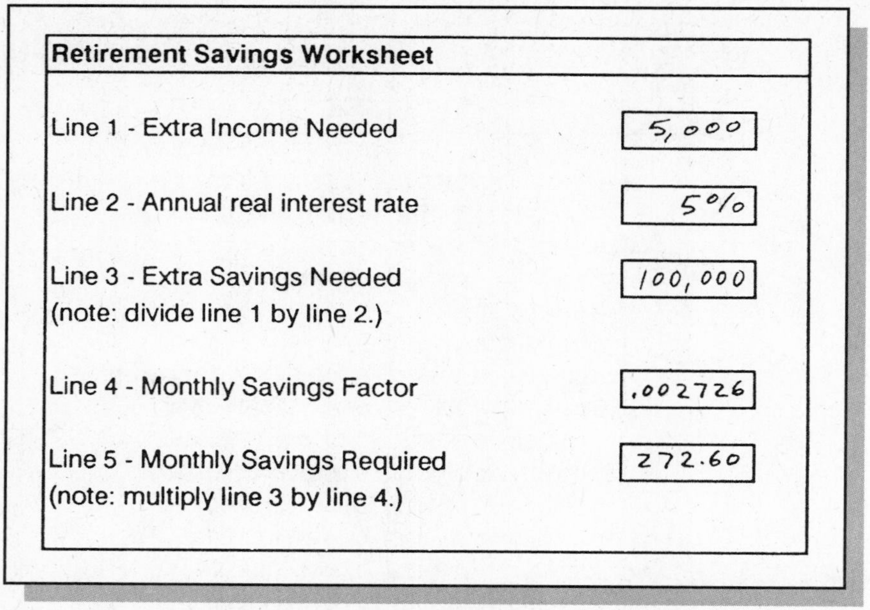

Retirement Savings Worksheet

Line 1 - Extra Income Needed	5,000
Line 2 - Annual real interest rate	5%
Line 3 - Extra Savings Needed (note: divide line 1 by line 2.)	100,000
Line 4 - Monthly Savings Factor	.002726
Line 5 - Monthly Savings Required (note: multiply line 3 by line 4.)	272.60

Fig. C.9. A sample completed Retirement Savings Worksheet.

If you have to pay income taxes, however, the story is different. Suppose that your highest dollars of income are taxed at the 33 percent tax rate. To subtract the income taxes you pay, multiply the 7.5 percent by (1 - 33 percent). This means that the real *adjusted-for-income-taxes* interest rate is 5 percent. When you calculate the real interest rate by taking this 5 percent interest rate and subtracting the 3 percent inflation rate, the annual real interest rate amounts to a measly 2 percent—less than half the amount you receive if you use an investment option that allows you to defer income taxes.

Here, using investment options in which you can defer the taxes more than doubles the return, which makes a huge difference in the amounts you accumulate over the years you save.

A second consideration is that the longer you postpone retirement, the more retirement income you typically enjoy when you do retire. This tactic isn't much of a revelation, of course, because it makes intuitive sense. However, the difference postponed retirement makes may surprise you. If you postpone retirement, you have several things working in your favor.

Social Security benefits may increase because you begin drawing benefits later or because the average earnings are higher. Any retirement savings you accumulate have a few more years to earn interest, and you probably can save more money. Finally, pension plans usually pay benefits based on years of service, so working a little longer can increase this source of retirement income. You can rework the numbers by using the planning worksheets given in this appendix to see the specific numbers for your case.

A third and final point to consider relates to a fundamental assumption of the worksheets. The worksheets assume that you live off only the annual investment income, Social Security, and pensions. This means that you never actually spend the money you save—only the interest those savings earn. If you have $100,000 in savings that earns $5,000 in annual interest, for example, you spend only the $5,000, and you leave the $100,000 intact. As a practical matter, however, you probably can spend some of the $100,000. The trick is to make sure that the $100,000 doesn't run out before you do.

Using the QuickPay Payroll Utility

If you're a business user of Quicken and the payroll tricks and tips described in Chapter 18 don't give you the payroll horsepower you need, don't despair. Still another option is available that works seamlessly with Quicken: the QuickPay payroll utility.

QuickPay is a payroll program that works with Quicken. In essence, the QuickPay program calculates the amounts you usually have to calculate outside the Quicken program—including the gross wages and the federal, state, and local taxes—and uses these amounts to prepare and record payroll checks.

The following paragraphs briefly describe how to use the QuickPay utility. Quicken users considering the QuickPay utility and new QuickPay users may find the ensuing discussion useful in deciding whether to acquire QuickPay and in getting started with the program.

The QuickPay utility isn't described here in great detail. This kind of discussion could easily require several chapters—perhaps even an entire book—to cover all the material necessary for every QuickPay user to prepare payroll in his or her state.

Installing and Starting QuickPay

Installing QuickPay is very easy. You need just two other items: an installed copy of Quicken 3.0, 4.0, or 5.0 and at least 82K of memory more than the minimum amount Quicken requires. Assuming you meet these two requirements, you simply insert the QuickPay disk into your A drive, make the A drive active by typing *a:*, and then type *install* at the DOS prompt.

QuickPay's installation program next displays a screen telling you where it found Quicken—probably in the QUICKEN5 directory—and asks you to confirm its discovery. If the identified directory is the correct Quicken program directory, press Enter.

If the identified directory isn't the correct one, enter the correct pathname and then press Enter. QuickPay's installation program next copies the QuickPay program files to the Quicken program directory. When it finishes, it returns you to the DOS prompt.

To start Quicken and the QuickPay program, type *qp* at the DOS prompt. The Quicken program starts and its Main Menu appears. The QuickPay program is always available, however, by pressing F7, which is the payroll function key.

Setting Up QuickPay Payroll Processing

Just two steps are necessary for setting up QuickPay payroll processing: describing the employer and describing the employees.

The first step is to describe the employer. When you press F7 the first time to access the QuickPay utility, QuickPay displays a set up screen that you use to describe the employer. Predictably, to describe the employer, you enter all the employer information that you might use to prepare an employee's payroll check or that you might use to prepare any employer payroll tax returns. For example, you enter such information as your company name and address, your federal and state tax identification numbers, and your state unemployment tax rate.

Menus and screens work the same way in QuickPay as they do in Quicken, so you shouldn't have any trouble learning how to move around in the QuickPay program.

describing employees whom you will pay. In describing an employee, QuickPay simply collects the information necessary to prepare a payroll check and to calculate an employee's gross wages, any deductions, and any payroll taxes. This information includes such items as the employee's name and address, his salary or hourly pay rate, and his Social Security number.

Processing Payroll by Using QuickPay

After you describe the employer and the employees, you're ready to begin preparing payroll checks. To do this, you just press F7 to access the payroll utility. If you have already described the employer and at least one employee, QuickPay displays its main menu, which simply lists the employees you've already described.

To prepare a check for a listed employee, select the employee from the list. QuickPay next displays a screen on which you enter any information specific to the payroll check being prepared—usually just the hours worked because QuickPay already knows the standard hourly pay rate. When you finish, you press Ctrl-Enter. QuickPay displays the Quicken Write Checks screen, fills it as necessary for the employee's payroll check, displays the Split Transaction screen, and fills it as necessary to record the payroll expenses and deductions.

Tips and Suggestions for Using QuickPay

If QuickPay sounds like something you would benefit from using, let me offer two suggestions for making your use of this tool as easy as possible.

First, use the Create Payroll Support assistant, described in Chapter 18, to create the categories and accounts you will need.

The reason for doing this is that QuickPay requires that certain categories and accounts exist. If they don't exist, QuickPay doesn't work correctly. The Create Payroll Support assistant is the easiest way to be certain that your payroll categories and accounts have the right names.

Second, recognize that QuickPay isn't the same thing as a payroll accountant or tax attorney. For example, you cannot expect the QuickPay program or the QuickPay documentation to provide payroll tax knowledge or to answer your questions about how state unemployment taxes get calculated.

Like every other payroll program, the QuickPay program only automates payroll processing. The bottom line is that if you need to prepare payroll but don't understand how the basic process works, you first need to acquire an understanding of payroll processing.

What do you do if you first need to acquire payroll processing knowledge? Several options are available. The Internal Revenue Service and many state taxing authorities offer tax workshops that explain how to calculate federal and state payroll taxes.

The Internal Revenue Service also provides, free to small businesses, several well-written books and booklets that explain about all kinds of accounting requirements, including those related to payroll processing. Finally, in a pinch, you can always use outside service bureaus, such as ADP or PayChex, until you feel confident about tackling payroll on your own.

Index

Symbols

A

B

C

E

F

G

H

N

Q

R

T

U

V

W-Z

Free Catalog!

Mail us this registration form today, and we'll send you a free catalog featuring Que's complete line of best-selling books.

Name of Book ____________________

Name ____________________

Title ____________________

Phone ( ) ____________________

Company ____________________

Address ____________________

City ____________________

State ____________ ZIP ____________

Please check the appropriate answers:

1. Where did you buy your Que book?
   - ☐ Bookstore (name: ________)
   - ☐ Computer store (name: ______)
   - ☐ Catalog (name: __________)
   - ☐ Direct from Que
   - ☐ Other: __________

2. How many computer books do you buy a year?
   - ☐ 1 or less
   - ☐ 2-5
   - ☐ 6-10
   - ☐ More than 10

3. How many Que books do you own?
   - ☐ 1
   - ☐ 2-5
   - ☐ 6-10
   - ☐ More than 10

4. How long have you been using this software?
   - ☐ Less than 6 months
   - ☐ 6 months to 1 year
   - ☐ 1-3 years
   - ☐ More than 3 years

5. What influenced your purchase of this Que book?
   - ☐ Personal recommendation
   - ☐ Advertisement
   - ☐ In-store display
   - ☐ Price
   - ☐ Que catalog
   - ☐ Que mailing
   - ☐ Que's reputation
   - ☐ Other: __________

6. How would you rate the overall content of the book?
   - ☐ Very good
   - ☐ Good
   - ☐ Satisfactory
   - ☐ Poor

7. What do you like *best* about this Que book?

   ____

   ____

8. What do you like *least* about this Que book?

   ____

   ____

9. Did you buy this book with your personal funds?

   ☐ Yes ☐ No

10. Please feel free to list any other comments you may have about this Que book.

    ____

    ____

    ____

QUE

Order Your Que Books Today!

Name ____________________

Title ____________________

Company ____________________

City ____________________

State ____________ ZIP ____________

Phone No. ( ) ____________________

Method of Payment:

Check ☐ (Please enclose in envelope.)

Charge My: VISA ☐ MasterCard ☐

American Express ☐

Charge # ____________________

Expiration Date ____________________

Order No.	Title	Qty.	Price	Total

You can **FAX** your order to **1-317-573-2583.** Or call **1-800-428-5331, ext. ORDR** to order direct.
Please add $2.50 per title for shipping and handling.

Subtotal	
Shipping & Handling	
Total	

QUE

NO POSTAGE
NECESSARY
IF MAILED
IN THE
UNITED STATES

BUSINESS REPLY MAIL

First Class Permit No. 9918 Indianapolis, IN

Postage will be paid by addressee

11711 N. College
Carmel, IN 46032

NO POSTAGE
NECESSARY
IF MAILED
IN THE
UNITED STATES

BUSINESS REPLY MAIL

First Class Permit No. 9918 Indianapolis, IN

Postage will be paid by addressee

11711 N. College
Carmel, IN 46032